W9-AOP-889

2012—2013

TOWNSEND**PRESS** SUNDAY SCHOOL

COMMENTARY

92ND EDITION

KING JAMES
VERSION

NEW
INTERNATIONAL
VERSION

Based on the International Lessons Series

Sunday School Publishing Board
National Baptist Convention, USA, Inc.
Dr. Kelly M. Smith Jr.,
Executive Director

Copyright © 2012

Townsend Press, Nashville, Tennessee. A division of the Sunday School Publishing Board, NBC, USA, Inc. All rights reserved. No part of this book may be reproduced or transmitted in any form by any means, electronic or mechanical, including photocopying, recording, or by any information storage or retrieval system without expressed permission in writing from the Sunday School Publishing Board, 330 Charlotte Avenue, Nashville, Tennessee 37201-1188. E-mail: customercare@sspbnbc.com.

The *Commentary* lesson expositions have been developed from the International Sunday School Lessons Series, 2010-2016 Cycle, copyright © 2008 by the Committee on the Uniform Series of the National Council of Churches USA. The Home Daily Bible Readings are prepared by the Committee on the Uniform Series, copyright © 2008. Used by permission.

Bible passages are taken from the *King James Version* unless otherwise noted.

Unmarked contemporary translation of Scripture or passages marked NRSV are from the *New Revised Standard Version* of the Bible, copyright by the National Council of the Churches of Christ in the USA, and are used by permission.

Scripture quotations marked NIV are taken from the Holy Bible, *New International Version.* Copyright © 1973, 1978, 1984 by the International Bible Society. Used by permission of Zondervan. All rights reserved.

Scripture quotations marked NKJV are taken from the *New King James Version.* Copyright © 1982 by Thomas Nelson, Inc. Used by permission. All rights reserved.

Scripture quotations marked NCV are taken from the *New Century Version.* Copyright © 1987, 1988, 1991 by Thomas Nelson, Inc. Used by permission. All rights reserved.

Scripture quotations marked NASB are taken from the *New American Standard Bible.* Copyright © 1960, 1962, 1963, 1968, 1971, 1972, 1973, 1975, 1977, 1995 by The Lockman Foundation. Used by permission.

Scripture quotations marked NLT taken from the *New Living Translation,* copyright © 1996, are used by permission of Tyndale House Publishers, Inc., Wheaton, Illinois 60189. All rights reserved.

Scripture quotations marked AMP are taken from the *Amplified® Bible.* Copyright © 1954, 1958, 1962, 1964, 1965, 1987 by The Lockman Foundation. Used by permission. (www.Lockman.org)

*Some Scripture passages may represent the writer's paraphrase.

Dr. Julius R. Scruggs, *Convention President;* Dr. Kelly M. Smith Jr., *Executive Director;* Mrs. Kathlyn Pillow, *Associate Director;* Rev. Debra Berry, *Director of Publishing Administration.*
Writers: Dr. Geoffrey V. Guns; Dr. Forrest E. Harris Sr.; Dr. William Franklin Buchanan; *Editor:* Rev. Wellington A. Johnson Sr.; *Copy Editors:* Yalemzewd Worku, Tanae C. McKnight Murdic, Lucinda Anderson; *Layout Designer:* Royetta Davis.

ISBN: 1-932972-28-5

CONTENTS

Fall Quarter, 2012—A Living Faith

Winter Quarter, 2012-2013—Jesus Is Lord

Spring Quarter, 2013—Beyond the Present Time

March: UNIT I—*The Kingdom of God*

UNIT II—*Resurrection Hope*

April

May: UNIT III—A Call to Holy Living

Summer Quarter, 2013—God's People Worship

June: UNIT I—*The Prophet and Praise*

UNIT II—*Worshipping in Jerusalem Again (Ezra)*

July

August: UNIT III—*Worshipping in Jerusalem Again (Nehemiah)*

2010–2016 SCOPE AND SEQUENCE—CYCLE SPREAD

Arrangement of Quarters According to the Church School Year,
September through August

FALL 2010 GOD **The Inescapable God** Exodus; Psalms 8, 19, 46, 47, 63, 66, 90, 91, 139	*WINTER 2010–2011* HOPE **Assuring Hope** Isaiah; Matthew; Mark	*SPRING 2011* WORSHIP **We Worship God** Matthew; Mark; 1 & 2 Timothy; Philippians; Jude; Revelation	*SUMMER 2011* COMMUNITY **God Instructs the** **People of God** Joshua; Judges; Ruth
FALL 2011 TRADITION **Tradition and Wisdom** Proverbs; Psalms 16, 25, 111, 119; Ecclesiastes; Song of Solomon; Esther	*WINTER 2011–2012* FAITH **God Establishes a** **Faithful People** Genesis; Exodus; Luke; Galatians	*SPRING 2012* CREATION **God's Creative Word** John	*SUMMER 2012* JUSTICE **God Calls for Justice** Exodus; Leviticus; Deuteronomy; 1 & 2 Samuel; 1 & 2 Kings; 2 Chronicles; Psalm 146; Isaiah; Jeremiah; Ezekiel
FALL 2012 FAITH **A Living Faith** Psalm 46; 1 Corinthians 13:1-13; Hebrews; Acts	*WINTER 2012–2013* GOD: JESUS CHRIST **Jesus Is Lord** Ephesians; Philippians; Colossians	*SPRING 2013* HOPE **Beyond the Present Time** Daniel; Luke; Acts; 1 & 2 Peter; 1 & 2 Thessalonians	*SUMMER 2013* WORSHIP **God's People Worship** Isaiah; Ezra; Nehemiah
FALL 2013 CREATION **First Things** Genesis; Exodus; Psalm 104	*WINTER 2013–2014* JUSTICE **Jesus and the Just** **Reign of God** Luke; James	*SPRING 2014* TRADITION **Jesus' Fulfillment of** **Scripture** Zechariah; Malachi; Deuteronomy; Matthew	*SUMMER 2014* COMMUNITY **The People of God Set** **Priorities** Haggai; 1 & 2 Corinthians
FALL 2014 HOPE **Sustaining Hope** Jeremiah; Habakkuk; Job; Ezekiel; Isaiah 52	*WINTER 2014–2015* WORSHIP **Acts of Worship** Psalm 95:1-7; Daniel; Matthew; Mark; Luke; John; Ephesians; Hebrews; James	*SPRING 2015* GOD: THE HOLY SPIRIT **Work of the Spirit** Mark; John; Acts; 1 Corinthians 12–14; 1 John; 2 John; 3 John	*SUMMER 2015* JUSTICE **God's Prophets Demand** **Justice** Amos; Micah; Isaiah; Jeremiah; Ezekiel; Zechariah; Malachi
FALL 2015 COMMUNITY **The Community of Believers** **Comes Alive** Matthew; John; 1 John	*WINTER 2015–2016* TRADITION **Traditions of Israel** Leviticus; Numbers; Deuteronomy	*SPRING 2016* FAITH **The Gift of Faith** Mark; Luke	*SUMMER 2016* CREATION **Toward a New Creation** Genesis; Psalms; Zephaniah; Romans

LIST OF PRINTED TEXTS

The Printed Scriptural Texts used in the *2012-2013 Townsend Press Sunday School Commentary* are arranged here in the order in which they appear in the Bible. Opposite each reference is the page number on which Scriptures appear in this edition of the *Commentary*.

PREFACE

The *Townsend Press Sunday School Commentary*, based on the International Lessons Series, is a production of the Sunday School Publishing Board, National Baptist Convention, USA, Incorporated. These lessons were developed consistent with the curriculum guidelines of the Committee on the Uniform Series, Education Leadership Ministries Commission, National Council of the Churches of Christ in the United States of America. Selected Christian scholars and theologians—who themselves embrace the precepts, doctrines, and positions on biblical interpretation that we have come to believe—are contributors to this publication. By participating in Scripture selection and the development of the matrices for the Guidelines for Lesson Development with the Committee on the Uniform Series, this presentation reflects the historic faith that we share within a rich heritage of worship and witness.

The format of the *Townsend Press Sunday School Commentary* lessons consists of the following: the Unit Title, the general subject with age-level topics, Printed Text from the *King James Version* and the *New International Version* of the Bible, Objectives of the Lesson, Unifying Lesson Principles, Points to Be Emphasized, Topical Outline of the Lesson—with the Biblical Background of the Lesson, Exposition and Application of the Scripture, and Concluding Reflection (designed to focus on the salient points of the lesson), Word Power, and the Home Daily Bible Readings. Each lesson concludes with a prayer.

The *Townsend Press Sunday School Commentary* is designed as an instructional aid for persons involved in the ministry of Christian education. While the autonomy of the individual soul before God is affirmed, we believe that biblical truths find their highest expression within the community of believers whose corporate experiences serve as monitors to preserve the integrity of the Christian faith. As such, the Word of God must not only be understood, but it must also be embodied in the concrete realities of daily life. This serves to allow the Word of God to intersect in a meaningful way with those realities of life.

The presentation of the lessons anticipates the fact that some concepts and Scripture references do not lend themselves to meaningful comprehension by children. Hence, when this occurs, alternative passages of Scripture are used, along with appropriate content emphases, that are designed to assist children in their spiritual growth. There will, however, remain a consistent connection between the children, youth, and adult lessons through the Unifying Principle developed for each session.

We stand firm in our commitment to Christian growth, to the end that lives will be transformed through personal and group interaction with the Word of God. The challenge issued by the apostle Paul continues to find relevance for our faith journey: "Do your best to present yourself to God as one approved by him, a worker who has no need to be ashamed, rightly explaining the word of truth" (2 Timothy 2:15, NRSV). May we all commit ourselves to the affirmation expressed by the psalmist, "Your word is a lamp to my feet and a light for my path" (Psalm 119:105, NIV).

ACKNOWLEDGMENTS

The *Townsend Press Sunday School Commentary* is recognized as the centerpiece of a family of church-school literature designed especially to assist teachers in their presentation of the lessons as well as to broaden the knowledge base of students from the biblical perspective. Our mission has been and will always be to provide religious educational experiences and spiritual resources for our constituency throughout this nation, as well as many foreign countries. To achieve this end, the collaborative efforts of many people provide the needed expertise in the various areas of the production process. Although under the employ of the Sunday School Publishing Board, personnel too numerous to list approach their respective tasks with the dedication and devotion of those who serve God by serving His people. This *Commentary* is presented with gratitude to God for all those who desire a more comprehensive treatment of the selected Scriptures than is provided in the church-school quarterlies, and it is intended to be a complementary resource to the quarterlies.

We acknowledge the Executive Director of the Sunday School Publishing Board in the person of Dr. Kelly M. Smith Jr., who has given a charge to the publishing family to focus on QTC—Quality, Timeliness, and Customer Care—in our interaction with our constituency. Special appreciation is appropriately accorded to Dr. Smith for his continued insightful and inspiring leadership and motivation. Through Dr. Smith's tenure at the Sunday School Publishing Board, the SSPB continues to prosper. It continues as the publisher and printer for the National Baptist Convention, USA, Inc. and its constituent components. There is a greater emphasis on addressing issues germane to the local, national, and international communities, utilizing the latest technologies to promote and distribute our materials—and doing all this based on Christian principles for the advancement of the kingdom of Jesus Christ.

The Sunday School Publishing Board consists of employees with expertise in their assigned areas whose self-understanding is that of "workers together with God" and partners with those who labor in the vineyard of teaching the Word of God in order to make disciples and nurture others toward a mature faith.

Our gratitude is expressed to Dr. Geoffrey V. Guns, expositor for the Fall and Winter Quarters, to Dr. Forrest E. Harris, expositor for the Spring Quarter, and to Dr. William F. Buchanan, expositor for the Summer Quarter, for their devotion to the development of the respective lessons. These three writers bring diversity and a broad spectrum of ministerial and educational experience to bear on the exposition and application of the Scripture.

We acknowledge and express our appreciation to Dr. Bruce Alick, pastor of the Mt. Zion Baptist Church of Germantown, Pennsylvania, for his theological review of the *2012-2013 Commentary*.

Appreciation is also expressed to Dr. Kelly M. Smith Jr., Executive Director, Mrs. Kathy Pillow, Associate Director, and Rev. Debra Berry, Director of Publishing Administration, for their ongoing leadership. It is a credit to their leadership that the employees have embraced the mission of the Sunday School Publishing Board with a self-perspective that enhances their personal commitment to the cause of Christ as they interact with one another and intersect with the greater community of faith.

The task in which we are all involved would be meaningless and fruitless were it not for the many readers for whom this publication has been so diligently prepared. The faithfulness of our constituency has been enduring for over a century, and we consider ourselves blessed to be their servants in the ministry of the printed Word exalting the living Word, our Lord and Savior Jesus Christ. We pray that God's grace will complement our efforts so that lives will be transformed within and beyond the confines of classroom interaction as the Spirit of God manifests Himself through the intersection of teaching and learning.

Wellington A. Johnson Sr.
Associate Director of Curriculum Publishing

KNOW YOUR WRITERS

Reverend Dr. Geoffrey V. Guns ▼
Fall and Winter Quarters

Dr. Geoffrey V. Guns is a native of Newport, Rhode Island. He is the son of a retired Baptist pastor and co-pastor. Dr. Guns received his elementary and secondary education in the Norfolk public school system. He earned his B.S. degree in Business Administration from Norfolk State University in 1972.

In 1981, he earned his Master of Divinity degree from the School of Theology, Virginia Union University, graduating *summa cum laude*. He earned his Doctor of Ministry degree from the School of Religion, Howard University in Washington, D.C., in 1985.

Dr. Guns is the senior pastor of Second Calvary Baptist Church in Norfolk, Virginia, where he has served for over twenty-five years. He is active in his denomination, the National Baptist Convention, USA, Inc. Dr. Guns served as the president of the Virginia Baptist State Convention (VBSC) from 1997 to 2001 and is currently the moderator for the Tidewater Peninsula Baptist Association.

He has written articles for the *Christian Education Informer* of the Division of Christian Education of the Sunday School Publishing Board. Dr. Guns also serves as vice chairman of the Council of Christian Education for the Division of Christian Education of the Sunday School Publishing Board of the NBC. He works with the Home Mission Board of the NBC and serves as the regional representative for the Southeast region.

Dr. Guns is the author of two books: *Church Financial Management* (1997), which is published by Providence House Publishers; and *Spiritual Leadership: A Practical Guide to Developing Spiritual Leaders in the Church* (2000), published by Orman Press, Inc.

He is married to the former Rosetta Harding of Richmond, Virginia. Mrs. Guns is a licensed social worker and works as a school social worker.

Reverend Dr. Forrest E. Harris Sr. ▼
Spring Quarter

Forrest Harris was born August 24, 1949, in Memphis, Tennessee, to Wilbur T. and Sallie Mae Harris. Harris's siblings include a twin brother and seven other sisters and brothers.

Harris matriculated at Knoxville College in Knoxville, Tennessee, where he completed a Bachelor's degree in Psychology and Sociology in 1971.

From 1971 to 1979, he was a Federal Compliance Officer with the Energy and Research Development Administration in Oak Ridge, Tennessee. During his tenure as an employee with the federal government, Harris responded to a call to professional Christian ministry. In 1979, he completed a Th.B. (Bachelor of Theology) at American Baptist College in Nashville, Tennessee. He earned a M.Div. (Master of Divinity) and D.Min. (Doctor of Ministry) from Vanderbilt University Divinity School in 1983 and 1989, respectively. At Vanderbilt, Harris was a Benjamin E. Mays Fellow and a recipient of the Florence Conwell prize for preaching.

Harris was ordained in 1975 at Oak Valley Baptist Church in Oak Ridge, Tennessee. While a seminary student at Vanderbilt, he served as the pastor of this church. During this pastorate, Harris brought together several community organizations and founded the Oak Valley Development Corporation. He also served a three-year term as president of the Oak Ridge Branch of the NAACP. From 1985 to 1987, he taught at Roane State Community College, where he initiated a black studies curriculum and coordinated social outreach programs and special events.

Since 1988, Harris has served on the Vanderbilt Divinity School faculty. He is the Director of the Kelly Miller Smith Institute on Black Church Studies, Assistant Dean for Black Church Studies, and Assistant Professor for the Practice of Ministry.

His teaching responsibilities include courses in the theology of ministry in the black church tradition. Under Harris's leadership, the endowment of the Kelly Miller Smith Institute on Black Church Studies has grown to be in excess of one million dollars.

In 1999, Harris was appointed President of American Baptist College in Nashville. During his presidency, the College's endowment has increased by 65 percent.

In addition to his presidential duties, Harris is a husband and father. He is married to Jacqueline Borom Harris, a research nurse at Vanderbilt University Medical Center. They have four children: Kara, Elliot Jr., Morgan, and Alexis.

Reverend Dr. William F. Buchanan ▼
Summer Quarter

William F. Buchanan was born in Broxton, Georgia—the third of four children born to the late Millinease and John L. Buchanan. He spent his formative years in Georgia, but later the family moved to Florida, where he graduated from high school. In 1976, he received a Bachelor of Science degree from Bethune-Cookman College. He later matriculated at the University of Florida's business school in Gainesville. In 1983, he received a Master of Divinity degree in Pastoral Counseling from the Morehouse School of Religion–Interdenominational Theological Center. Subsequently, he was a Proctor-Booth Fellow at United Theological Seminary, where he earned the Doctor of Ministry degree in 1995.

Dr. Buchanan was ordained into the ministry in 1985, and from 1985 to 1988 served as youth minister at Greenforest Baptist Church in Decatur, Georgia, and as a chaplain intern at Emory University Hospital in Atlanta. He was called to be the senior pastor of First Baptist Church in Huntington, West Virginia, in 1988. In 1994, he was called to the pastorate of the historic Fifteenth Avenue Baptist Church in Nashville, Tennessee.

Since coming to Fifteenth Avenue, Dr. Buchanan has transformed this church into a beacon of light for all persons in the community. The church continues to grow spiritually and numerically, and to serve as a model for twenty-first-century ministry.

Dr. Buchanan has received many awards and honors. He was most recently honored with being named the recipient of the Lily Foundation's Clergy General Grant, which allowed him to take a brief sabbatical to study at Harvard University's School of Divinity. He is a board member of the Nashville Housing Fund, Oasis, Saint Thomas Pastoral Care Advisory Board (chairman), Vanderbilt Divinity School Board of Visitors, and Operation Andrew Group (former board chairman). Dr. Buchanan is an adjunct professor at American Baptist College in Nashville, and a Field Education supervisor at Vanderbilt University's School of Divinity. Additionally, he is in great demand as a preacher, lecturer, and facilitator at churches throughout the nation.

In addition to his busy schedule as a pastor and teacher, Dr. Buchanan is the loving husband of Audrey Cave Buchanan. They are the parents of four children—Kwame, Shani, Dashan, and Aubrey Buchanan—and have six grandchildren.

A Living Faith

GENERAL INTRODUCTION

This quarter has three units. The first unit uses selected texts from the book of Hebrews to move the participants toward a definition of faith. The second and third units continue the study of faith through the lens of the early church. Both units draw on selected texts from the Acts of the Apostles.

Unit I, *What Is Faith?* is a five-lesson study of the closing chapters of the book of Hebrews (10–13). These lessons engage the learners in responsive obedience to God's love, revealed in Jesus. This response is an act of faith. Lesson 1 is a description of the perseverance of faith. Lesson 2 encourages us to find the assurance that comes with faith. In lesson 3, we consider those who have gone before us as witnesses and models for our faith. Lesson 4 serves as a reminder that faith is a gift for which we can give thanks, and lesson 5 looks at the relationship of love to faith.

Unit II, *Who Understands Faith?* has four lessons. The first two lessons focus on Stephen's message and martyrdom. The third lesson explores the repercussions that come upon those who treat faith as a commodity. The fourth lesson looks at the faith that guided Philip the evangelist and the Ethiopian seeker to examine the Scriptures together.

Unit III, *Where Does Faith Take Us?* is a four-lesson study of Paul's faith and ministry. The first lesson is an examination of Paul's speech before King Agrippa. The second lesson goes with Paul aboard the ship to Rome. The final two lessons focus on Paul's ongoing ministry—even though he was a prisoner.

LESSON 1   September 2, 2012

FAITH CALLS FOR PERSEVERANCE

FAITH PATHWAY/FAITH JOURNEY TOPIC: **Steadfast Determination**

DEVOTIONAL READING: **Romans 5:1-5**
PRINT PASSAGE: **Hebrews 10:19-31**

BACKGROUND SCRIPTURE: **Hebrews 10:19-31**
KEY VERSE: **Hebrews 10:23**

Hebrews 10:19-31—KJV

19 Having therefore, brethren, boldness to enter into the holiest by the blood of Jesus,

20 By a new and living way, which he hath consecrated for us, through the veil, that is to say, his flesh;

21 And having an high priest over the house of God;

22 Let us draw near with a true heart in full assurance of faith, having our hearts sprinkled from an evil conscience, and our bodies washed with pure water.

23 Let us hold fast the profession of our faith without wavering; (for he is faithful that promised;)

24 And let us consider one another to provoke unto love and to good works:

25 Not forsaking the assembling of ourselves together, as the manner of some is; but exhorting one another: and so much the more, as ye see the day approaching.

26 For if we sin wilfully after that we have received the knowledge of the truth, there remaineth no more sacrifice for sins,

27 But a certain fearful looking for of judgment and fiery indignation, which shall devour the adversaries.

28 He that despised Moses' law died without mercy under two or three witnesses:

29 Of how much sorer punishment, suppose ye, shall he be thought worthy, who hath trodden under foot the Son of God, and hath counted the blood of the covenant, wherewith he was sanctified, an unholy thing, and hath done despite unto the Spirit of grace?

30 For we know him that hath said, Vengeance belongeth unto me, I will recompense, saith the Lord. And again, The Lord shall judge his people.

31 It is a fearful thing to fall into the hands of the living God.

Hebrews 10:19-31—NIV

19 Therefore, brothers, since we have confidence to enter the Most Holy Place by the blood of Jesus,

20 by a new and living way opened for us through the curtain, that is, his body,

21 and since we have a great priest over the house of God,

22 let us draw near to God with a sincere heart in full assurance of faith, having our hearts sprinkled to cleanse us from a guilty conscience and having our bodies washed with pure water.

23 Let us hold unswervingly to the hope we profess, for he who promised is faithful.

24 And let us consider how we may spur one another on toward love and good deeds.

25 Let us not give up meeting together, as some are in the habit of doing, but let us encourage one another—and all the more as you see the Day approaching.

26 If we deliberately keep on sinning after we have received the knowledge of the truth, no sacrifice for sins is left,

27 but only a fearful expectation of judgment and of raging fire that will consume the enemies of God.

28 Anyone who rejected the law of Moses died without mercy on the testimony of two or three witnesses.

29 How much more severely do you think a man deserves to be punished who has trampled the Son of God under foot, who has treated as an unholy thing the blood of the covenant that sanctified him, and who has insulted the Spirit of grace?

30 For we know him who said, "It is mine to avenge; I will repay," and again, "The Lord will judge his people."

31 It is a dreadful thing to fall into the hands of the living God.

UNIFYING LESSON PRINCIPLE

People wonder about, may even envy, others who feel secure about their spiritual lives. What security is available? The writer of the book of Hebrews told us that our sins can be forgiven because of the blood of Jesus, and that we can experience the presence of God in a new and life-giving way through faith—and Jesus tells of how the centurion's strong faith resulted in the healing of his servant.

TOPICAL OUTLINE OF THE LESSON

I. Introduction
  A. Holding On in Trying Circumstances
  B. Biblical Background

II. Exposition and Application of the Scripture
  A. We Have Access to God (Hebrews 10:19-21)
  B. Persevering in Our Faith (Hebrews 10:22-25)
  C. The Consequences of a Sinful Life (Hebrews 10:26-31)

III. Concluding Reflection

LESSON OBJECTIVES

Upon the completion of the lesson, the students will be able to do the following:

1. Gain knowledge about the power of faith in Jesus Christ;
2. Reflect on their security in Jesus Christ; and,
3. Increase their confidence in sharing Jesus Christ with others.

POINTS TO BE EMPHASIZED

ADULT/YOUTH

Adult Topic: Steadfast Determination
Youth Topic: Got Faith?
Adult Key Verse: Hebrews 10:23
Youth Key Verse: Hebrews 10:22
Print Passage: Hebrews 10:19-31

—The book of Hebrews addresses a Jewish Christian audience, reassuring them of the validity of their faith in Jesus.
—Once a year, only the Jewish high priest could enter through the curtain to the entrance of the Holy of Holies in order to be in the presence of God.
—Now that we have access to God, we need to approach God with true hearts of faith and unwavering hope.
—The writer of the book of Hebrews encouraged Christians to fellowship regularly, to be loving toward one another, and to do good deeds.
—Those who reject God's mercy will face God's judgment.

CHILDREN

Children Topic: Great Faith
Key Verse: Matthew 8:13
Print Passage: Matthew 8:5-13

—The centurion's faith in Jesus gave him the strength to overcome the many obstacles between Jesus and himself (pride, doubt, power, ethnicity, culture, language).
—This Gentile's faith put to shame the piety of some Jewish leaders.
—All the faithful people of God will be gathered to feast at God's table in the kingdom of heaven.
—No one enters God's kingdom because of heritage or connections.
—Entrance into God's kingdom depends on each person's faith in the message of Jesus.

I. INTRODUCTION

A. Holding On in Trying Circumstances

During the weekend of April 1-3, 2011, Southwest Airlines was forced to cancel more than six hundred flights. Flight 812, bound for Sacramento, California, left Phoenix Sky Harbor International Airport as scheduled. At 36,000 feet, there was a loud sound in the cabin that sent shock waves through the hearts of many of the passengers. The pilot was forced to declare a mid-flight emergency due to a tear which occurred—producing a gaping hole at the top of the fuselage of the airplane. The oxygen masks came down as the plane suddenly lost cabin pressure and was forced to make an emergency landing in Yuma, Arizona. As the news of the mishap began to circulate, the management of Southwest Airlines immediately began to reassure their customers that there was no need to lose confidence in the airline. However, no doubt there were many people who did lose confidence, not just in Southwest Airlines, but in flying altogether. Security is one of the most important aspects of flying today.

Today's lesson is the first of five from the book of Hebrews. The lesson teaches us the importance of holding on to our faith during the most trying circumstances of life. Believers can gain strength from their faith in Jesus Christ as we take comfort in knowing that our sins have been forgiven because of the blood of Jesus Christ. As we grow stronger spiritually, we are able to experience the presence of God in greater ways—the result of a deepening of our faith in Jesus Christ. It is our faith in Jesus Christ that empowers us to become more secure and confident in sharing the Good News of the Gospel.

B. Biblical Background

The epistle to the Hebrews was written to a largely Jewish congregation, sometime prior to the destruction of the City of Jerusalem and the Temple by the Romans in AD 70. There have been divided opinions as to the identity of the author of the epistle. The heading found in the *King James Version* of the Bible indicates that it is the work of the apostle Paul. However, there is no internal evidence to suggest that Paul wrote the letter. Internal evidence refers to whether or not the style of writing, language, words, and phrases are similar to those found in Paul's other writings. General consensus among scholars holds that we are not sure who wrote the book of Hebrews; however, that does not lessen its importance.

The epistle speaks to a group of believers who have knowledge of Jewish practices, beliefs, and the Torah. Throughout the early chapters of the epistle, the writer pointed out the superiority of Jesus Christ as the sacrifice for the sins of the world. Jesus is our great high priest who cleanses us permanently from the stench and guilt of sin. Believers are able to hold fast or hold out because of the hope that is laid up for us in Jesus Christ. In the lesson, the writer reminded the readers that he did not speak as one who stood over and against them—he was one with them. He assured them that they could and should have faith in the Lord Jesus Christ.

II. EXPOSITION AND APPLICATION OF THE SCRIPTURE

A. We Have Access to God
(Hebrews 10:19-21)

Having therefore, brethren, boldness to enter into the holiest by the blood of Jesus, By a new and living way, which he hath consecrated for us, through the veil, that is to say, his flesh; And having an high priest over the house of God.

In verse 19, the word *therefore* links what follows to all that has been previously stated. Throughout the epistle, the writer of the book of Hebrews had laid the groundwork for what it means for believers to have Jesus Christ as our great high priest (see Hebrews 4:14-16). It is through Him that we gain this new confidence or boldness to come before the presence of the heavenly Father for ourselves (see Ephesians 3:12). Here, the reference is not to the earthly Temple but to the heavenly temple, where we find the throne room of God. The Most Holy Place was the Holy of Holies, which was entered into only once a year by the high priest, and that was on the Day of Atonement (see Hebrews 9:7-8; compare with Leviticus 16:1-28). It was not through the blood of goats, but through the shed blood of Jesus Christ that we gain forgiveness and peace with God. The blood of Jesus has removed forever every obstacle to believers' having a right relationship with God.

Verse 20 points out that the death of Jesus upon the cross was a once-and-for-all-time act of redemption and sacrifice for the sins of the world (see Romans 6:10; 1 Peter 3:18). It was new because this sacrifice had never been available nor had it been done before. It was living because it involved the Lord Jesus Christ Himself, who became the way to eternal life (see John 3:14-17; 10:7, 9; 14:6). The word *curtain* refers to the veil of the Temple which was torn from top to bottom on the Day of the Crucifixion (see Mark 15:38). Jesus removed the barrier between God and humanity through His death. His death made/makes it possible for all people to be reconciled to God and to each other.

According to verse 21, the descendants of Aaron and the descendants of the long line of Levitical priests were responsible for the service of the tabernacle and later the Temple. They performed the ritual services and offered the sacrifices. They kept watch over the tabernacle and Temple. But now, in Jesus Christ, there is no longer a need for them to stand guard over the Most Holy Place. We have One who has entered once for all for us; that One now stands over the house of God. His death has opened up a new way into the sanctuary of God's presence—and consequently, we can all draw near to Him.

B. Persevering in Our Faith
(Hebrews 10:22-25)

Let us draw near with a true heart in full assurance of faith, having our hearts sprinkled from an evil conscience, and our bodies washed with pure water. Let us hold fast the profession of our faith without wavering; (for he is faithful that promised;) And let us consider one another to provoke unto love and to good works: Not forsaking the assembling of ourselves together, as the manner of some is; but exhorting one another: and so much the more, as ye see the day approaching.

Throughout the entire tenth chapter of the book of Hebrews, the writer pointed out how the sacrifice of Jesus for our sins was a much better sacrifice than those offered by the priests under the Levitical laws. Beginning with verse 22, he pointed to three of the most significant exhortations found in the New Testament. Verse 25 is not viewed as one of those exhortations; rather, it is seen as a continuation of the third exhortation (found in verse 24). Each exhortation begins with the words "let us." The writer did not leave himself out; rather, he, too, must come before the presence of the Lord in the same manner as those to whom he preached and taught.

Verse 22 begins the first of the three exhortations that detail the response of the believer to the sacrifice of Jesus Christ. Here is the supreme duty and privilege of worship which is accorded the believer because of Jesus Christ. How are believers to draw near to God? First, with sincere hearts. The word *sincere* (Greek: *aletinos*) means "the opposite of fiction or counterfeit." The heart of the true worshipper must be open to the full truth of the Gospel. God is neither interested in nor pleased with lofty platitudes and cozy words that are not reflected in the lifestyle of the worshipper. Second, we draw near in full assurance of faith. This means that when we go to God, there can be neither doubts nor hesitation. Third, we draw near with sprinkled hearts that are cleansed from a guilty conscience. The conscience is the moral barometer that governs our decisions and actions. It distinguishes between right and wrong. The sacrifice of Jesus Christ gives us peace with God, which overcomes the guilt and mental oppression of the guilty conscience (see Romans 5:1; 8:1-3). Fourth, we come with our bodies washed. This could be a reference to the ritual of baptism or the ritual washing which was required to be done prior to entering the Temple precincts. The writer was not referring to an external washing, but an internal washing of the heart and spirit (see Psalm 24:1-4).

Verse 23 is the second exhortation which encourages believers to hold on to their hope in God without failure or collapse. The words *hold fast* (Greek: *katecho*) mean "to keep from going away or keep secure." What is a more powerful witness than believers' continuing in their faith in the face of searing persecution? The faithful believer holds on without wavering or swerving to the right or left.

In verses 24-25, the final exhortation speaks to how believers are to encourage one another to love others and serve the least of the earth. Verse 25 is not to be taken as a separate exhortation. The people of God are to live in ways that give mutual support and encouragement to each other. This unconditional love for each other and the determination to provoke to do good deeds drives each believer to do the work of ministry and mission (see Hebrews 6:10; 13:1; compare with Matthew 25:31-46; Ephesians 2:8-10).

Verse 25 sets forth the reason why they must continue to provoke and encourage. Some of the believers had been beset by fear and intimidation because of the persecution of the church. They began to forsake the weekly gatherings of the believers. Or they had become discouraged that Jesus Christ had not returned to claim the church as His bride. Believers live each day in glorious anticipation of the blessed hope of the return of Christ and therefore must always be ready (see Matthew 25:1-13; 1 Thessalonians 4:13-18).

C. The Consequences of a Sinful Life (Hebrews 10:26-31)

For if we sin wilfully after that we have received the knowledge of the truth, there remaineth no more sacrifice for sins, But a certain fearful looking for of judgment and fiery indignation, which shall devour the adversaries. He that despised Moses' law died without mercy under two or three witnesses: Of how much sorer punishment, suppose ye, shall he be thought worthy, who hath trodden under foot the Son of God, and hath counted the blood of the covenant, wherewith he was sanctified, an unholy thing, and hath done despite unto the Spirit of grace? For we know him that hath said, Vengeance belongeth unto me, I will recompense, saith the Lord. And again, The Lord shall judge his people. It is a fearful thing to fall into the hands of the living God.

How is the church to handle people who verbally assert change, but live in a way that shows something entirely different? What problem was the writer of the book of Hebrews seeking to address in the verses above? We are not sure; however, we are certain that there were differences between their professions of faith and their day-to-day living.

In verse 26, "if" introduces a hypothetical condition in which there may have been believers who deliberately continued to live in sin (see Hebrews 6:4; compare with Romans 6). *Knowledge* (Greek: *epignosis*) is knowledge that is "precise and correct." It is knowledge that is derived from having received the truth of the sacrifice of Jesus Christ for our sins. The word *Epignosis* is more than the accumulation of facts and figures; rather, it is spiritual wisdom and spiritual understanding of the truth—regarding the death of Jesus Christ—that leads to salvation (see Colossians 1:9-11). To have come to the knowledge of the truth and then turn away is to reach a point of no return. Jesus Christ is the only sacrifice there is for sins.

There is no other! It would have been better to have never been saved than to do so and then reject the Christ. Those who reject the gift of salvation in Jesus Christ will receive the harshest of punishments. There is no alternative.

In verses 28 and 29, the writer of the book of Hebrews built his argument from the lesser to the greater.[1] The Law of Moses was the lesser, and trampling the Son of God underfoot was the greater. During the days of Moses, the Law prescribed strict guidelines for the meting out of punishment for sin. Willfully breaking the Law and worshipping other gods were grounds for death without mercy or appeal (see Deuteronomy 13:6-11; 17:6; 19:15-21).[2] The writer of the book of Hebrews raised a rhetorical question, using three metaphors to justify the severity of the punishment for those who reject Christ.[3] First, they trample the Son of God under foot. Second, they treat as unholy the blood of the covenant that sanctified them. Third, they insult the Spirit of grace.

Verse 30 is like a quote from Deuteronomy 32:35-36, which is the Song of Moses delivered to the Israelites just prior to his death. The writer of the book of Hebrews reinforced the truth that God is the one to whom all men and women must ultimately answer. He is the One before whom we will all stand on the Day of Judgment. He concluded by stating how serious a matter it is to ignore, reject, and renounce the gift of God's salvation. Who can save anyone who falls into the hands of the living God? Just as God has mercy on us, even so His judgment can be even more dreadful (see 2 Samuel 24:14).

III. CONCLUDING REFLECTION

The one thing that each believer must never forget to do in troubled times is to worship. Worship is the source of our hope and strength. It is in worship that we experience the joy of the Lord. Many people forget to worship, praise God, and celebrate their way through their long night of pain. The lesson reminds us not to always think about what we are going through, how dark our situations are, nor how tedious and tasteless our days may be—but to try to encourage others. Paul often reminded those in his congregations that he was praying for them (see Philippians 1:3-4). How much stronger our congregations would be if we were more encouraging and filled with less condemnation!

PRAYER

Lord God, we beseech You for the courage to face every challenge of life. Grant that we will never waver when we are called upon to be witnesses to the grace of our Lord Jesus Christ. In Jesus' name we pray. Amen.

WORD POWER

Confidence (Greek: *parrhesia* [par-rhay-see'ah])—one's having the characteristics of fearlessness and boldness to do things that he or she would not have done otherwise.
Sanctified (Greek: *hagiazo* [hag-ee-ad'-zo])—to separate from profane things and to be used exclusively in the service of God.

HOME DAILY BIBLE READINGS
(August 27–September 2, 2012)

Faith Calls for Perseverance
> MONDAY, August 27: "A Great Faith" (Matthew 8:5-13)
> TUESDAY, August 28: "A Saving Faith" (Romans 10:8-17)
> WEDNESDAY, August 29: "A Justifying Faith" (Galatians 2:15-21)
> THURSDAY, August 30: "An Examined Faith" (2 Corinthians 13:5-10)
> FRIDAY, August 31: "An Enduring Faith" (Romans 5:1-5)
> SATURDAY, September 1: "An Exemplary Faith" (1 Thessalonians 1:2-10)
> SUNDAY, September 2: "The Full Assurance of Faith" (Hebrews 10:19-31)

End Notes

---

[1] McKnight, Edgar V. and Christopher Church, *Hebrews–James: Smyth & Helwys Bible Commentary,* (Macon: Smyth & Helwys Publishing, Inc., 2004), p. 246.
[2] Ibid.
[3] Ibid.

FAITH IS ASSURANCE

Faith Pathway/Faith Journey Topic: Steadfast Confidence

DEVOTIONAL READING: Psalm 27:1-6
PRINT PASSAGE: Hebrews 11:1-3, 6;
Psalm 46:1-3, 8-11

BACKGROUND SCRIPTURE: Hebrews 11:1-7;
Psalm 46:1-11
KEY VERSE: Hebrews 11:1

Hebrews 11:1-3, 6; Psalm 46:1-3, 8-11 —KJV

NOW FAITH is the substance of things hoped for, the evidence of things not seen.

2 For by it the elders obtained a good report.

3 Through faith we understand that the worlds were framed by the word of God, so that things which are seen were not made of things which do appear.

.....

6 But without faith it is impossible to please him: for he that cometh to God must believe that he is, and that he is a rewarder of them that diligently seek him.

.....

GOD IS our refuge and strength, a very present help in trouble.

2 Therefore will not we fear, though the earth be removed, and though the mountains be carried into the midst of the sea;

3 Though the waters thereof roar and be troubled, though the mountains shake with the swelling thereof.

.....

8 Come, behold the works of the LORD, what desolations he hath made in the earth.

9 He maketh wars to cease unto the end of the earth; he breaketh the bow, and cutteth the spear in sunder; he burneth the chariot in the fire.

10 Be still, and know that I am God: I will be exalted among the heathen, I will be exalted in the earth.

11 The LORD of hosts is with us; the God of Jacob is our refuge.

Hebrews 11:1-3, 6; Psalm 46:1-3, 8-11 —NIV

NOW FAITH is being sure of what we hope for and certain of what we do not see.

2 This is what the ancients were commended for.

3 By faith we understand that the universe was formed at God's command, so that what is seen was not made out of what was visible.

.....

6 And without faith it is impossible to please God, because anyone who comes to him must believe that he exists and that he rewards those who earnestly seek him.

.....

GOD IS our refuge and strength, an ever-present help in trouble.

2 Therefore we will not fear, though the earth give way and the mountains fall into the heart of the sea,

3 though its waters roar and foam and the mountains quake with their surging.

.....

8 Come and see the works of the LORD, the desolations he has brought on the earth.

9 He makes wars cease to the ends of the earth; he breaks the bow and shatters the spear, he burns the shields with fire.

10 "Be still, and know that I am God; I will be exalted among the nations, I will be exalted in the earth."

11 The LORD Almighty is with us; the God of Jacob is our fortress.

UNIFYING LESSON PRINCIPLE

Because of all the conflicts in the world, people may lose hope for positive change. What prompts people to hope for positive change? By believing in God's strength, said the writers of the books of Psalms and Hebrews, we can be rescued and change can take place because God is with us; Jesus assures us that God will be with us—if we trust as children do.

TOPICAL OUTLINE OF THE LESSON

I. Introduction
A. The Personal Dimension of Faith
B. Biblical Background

II. Exposition and Application of the Scripture
A. The Importance of Faith (Hebrews 11:1-3, 6)
B. Our Refuge and Strength (Psalm 46:1-3)
C. A Glorious Invitation (Psalm 46:8-11)

III. Concluding Reflection

LESSON OBJECTIVES

Upon completion of the lesson, the students will be able to do the following:

1. Explore the meaning of faith and its implications for our lives;
2. Appreciate and grow from the faith of others; and,
3. Develop a practice of relying on God for positive change.

POINTS TO BE EMPHASIZED

ADULT/YOUTH

Adult Topic: Steadfast Confidence
Youth Topic: What Is Faith?
Adult/Youth Key Verse: Hebrews 11:1
Print Passage: Hebrews 11:1-3, 6; Psalm 46:1-3, 8-11

—Hebrews 11:1 is a description of what faith does, not a definition.
—In Hebrews 11:6, faith is mandatory for those who approach God.
—Psalm 46 is a psalm of trust that rejoices in divine deliverance in battle or siege.
—"Our refuge and strength" refers to God as an impenetrable and impregnable defense.
—The writer of the book of Hebrews offered a definitive understanding of faith in a changing world.
—Our ancestors responded to God by faith and God responded with approval.
—Psalm 46 is a hymn of praise to God for providing refuge in times of calamity.
—We can depend on God to be our present help, regardless of the type of trouble.

CHILDREN

Children Topic: Childlike Faith
Key Verse: Mark 10:15
Print Passage: Psalm 23; Mark 10:13-16

—Jesus spent quality time with children.

—The loving look and gentle touch of Jesus assured the children that He cared for them.

—When Jesus' disciples criticized Him for including children, Jesus said that unless we trust God with a childlike faith, we shall not enter God's kingdom.

—God's love, protection, and provision will be with believers forever.

I. INTRODUCTION

A. The Personal Dimension of Faith

The eleventh chapter of the book of Hebrews is the high-water mark in the epistle to the Hebrews. There is no other chapter in the Bible that discusses faith with the loftiness and majesty of this chapter. The writer began with a description of faith and moved to the spiritual resumés of some of the Bible's most faithful personalities (see Hebrews 11:4-40). From their lives we learn that faith is one of the greatest virtues that any believer can cultivate. Someone has said that "Faith is the hinge that holds the believer to a personal relationship with God." He reminded us of the faith of Abel and how Abel obtained a righteous testimony before God (see verse 4). He told us about Enoch and how he walked with God and how God took him (see verse 5). Noah was warned by God to prepare for rain by building an ark (see verse 7). Abraham was called to go out from his family and look for a city whose architect and builder was God (see verse 8). All believers have some measure of faith (see Romans 12:3; 2 Corinthians 10:13). However, what makes the difference in men and women who achieve extraordinary results in their lives is not always talent, but belief that they can do the impossible with God's help (see Philippians 4:13).

B. Biblical Background

Hebrews 11:1 is not a definition of faith; rather, it is a theological description of faith. It depicts what it means to have confidence in God. The writer declared that faith treats "things hoped for" as reality and as proven conviction. In Hebrews 11:6, we are reminded that faith is the mandatory prerequisite for approaching God—for whoever comes to God must believe that He exists. The remainder of the lesson comes from Psalm 46, which is one of the most cherished psalms in the Bible. There is no historical information within the psalm or its heading that gives us the historical or social context out of which the psalm grew. One suggestion for the historical context could be the time when Israel was faced with the threat of invasion by the Assyrian army (see 2 Kings 18–19).

Psalm 46 is for the "director of music" (NIV) and is attributed to the "Sons of Korah" (NIV). Whatever the situation, the writer expressed confidence that God would deliver His people from the overwhelming forces of their enemies. The writer reminded the hearers that God is the one who can be trusted in all situations. He is both refuge and strength and can be relied upon in the midst of life's most turbulent moments. This psalm has been a stalwart of hope. Martin Luther was so inspired by the words of Psalm 46 that he wrote that great Reformation hymn, "A Mighty Fortress Is Our God."

II. EXPOSITION AND APPLICATION OF THE SCRIPTURE

A. The Importance of Faith
(Hebrews 11:1-3, 6)

NOW FAITH is the substance of things hoped for, the evidence of things not seen. For by it the elders obtained a good report. Through faith we understand that the worlds were framed by the word of God, so that things which are seen were not made of things which do appear. ...But without faith it is impossible to please him: for he that cometh to God must believe that he is, and that he is a rewarder of them that diligently seek him.

Verse 1 contains a definition of faith—from a theological perspective. Faith is that confident, steadfast, assured trust in God. Faith allows us to absolutely believe that God will honor His every word. It is the absolute belief that no matter how challenging the circumstances, how dark the night, or how hopeless the moments look, God is able (see Ephesians 3:19; Jude 24-25). Faith is the unquenchable fire that burns in the hearts of people who will not quit. Having faith means moving ahead in the cloud, not because we see the bridge, but because we know that it is there (see 2 Corinthians 4:7-10, 16; 5:7).

Faith is an important discipline for each believer to cultivate. It is one of the three chief Christian virtues—along with love and hope (see 1 Corinthians 13:13). It is the lack of faith that limits our progress in the work of mission and ministry (see Matthew 13:58; 17:20; Mark 6:6). How does the believer increase his or her faith? In Romans 10:17, the apostle Paul wrote, "So then faith cometh by hearing, and hearing by the word of God." What is faith? Having faith means being sure; it is the confidence or the realization that what we cannot see is still visible in the plan and purpose of God. The writer of the book of Hebrews stated that underneath faith in God there is a strong support system that is based upon concrete evidence.

Verse 2 reminds us that it was the faith of ancients—who trusted God in spite of what they could not see—that they received the commendation of God. As we trust God more, it increases our witness of who God is and what God can do. As we trust God more, we are driven to live in such a way that God is pleased. Thus, it was by and through the exercise of their faith that the men and women listed in this chapter gained commendation from God. The word *commendation* comes from a word that means "witness." Men and women of faith are living witnesses that God can be trusted.

Have you not found God to be faithful in your own life? It is through your faith in the living God that you come to gain God's favor.

In verse 6, the writer pointed out that faith is the ground upon which believers are able to please God (see John 8:29; Romans 8:8; Colossians 1:9-10; 1 Thessalonians 4:1; 2 Timothy 2:4). God is pleased, very pleased, when we believe Him and trust His promises. God is also pleased as we live in obedience to His Word and commands. This is the point of the verse about pleasing God. The ancients, great men and women of God who lived in the past—who believed and followed—were those who believed that God existed. They turned away from the world, possessions, and pleasures of life and followed God. They believed that God had much more to offer—that His promises of an eternal land and of eternal life were true.

Life today can be characterized by a greater thirst by humans for the things of this world. Men and women are more driven by what they can see, touch, taste, and smell than by the unseen reality of God. For believers, the question of faith is always central to our building commitment to Him. Has God not been faithful in your life? Then you must trust Him even when the foundations of life are crumbling.

B. Our Refuge and Strength (Psalm 46:1-3)

GOD IS our refuge and strength, a very present help in trouble. Therefore will not we fear, though the earth be removed, and though the mountains be carried into the midst of the sea; Though the waters thereof roar and be troubled, though the mountains shake with the swelling thereof.

The psalm begins with the declaration of God's existence: "God is…" These words are a sterling statement of trust and confidence in God's ability to provide protection in times of turmoil and trouble. "Refuge" (Hebrew: *machaceh*) denotes a shelter from all of the extreme elements of the weather: rain, storms, and all other dangers. It is frequently used in the Scriptures to speak of God's protection from hostile forces that seek to destroy His people (see Psalms 62:7-8; 142:5; Proverbs 14:26). The psalmist declared that God is a place we can flee to for safety. He is a safe harbor in the midst of the raging storms of life. We can put our trust and confidence in this word of assurance, knowing that God will never fail us, never forsake us, nor ever leave us (see Joshua 1:5)

The psalmist noted that God has the power to protect His people from whatever and whoever comes against them. God is not just powerful, He has *all* power (omnipotence)—and there is no power in the universe greater (see Psalms 62:11; 63:2; compare these verses with Nahum 1:7). Israel was reminded in the Song of Moses to have no fear of their enemies when they went into the land of Canaan. The God who had defeated the Egyptians before them would do the same in every case (see Deuteronomy 3:24; 4:34; 7:19). Not only is God the strength of His people, but He also shares that might with us through the indwelling presence of the Holy Spirit, who empowers us to live free from condemnation and intimidation (see Acts 1:8; Romans 8:1; 2 Corinthians 10:1-3).

God is the one who is ever-present in the day of trouble. In 2 Chronicles 15:4, God is depicted as the one who can be found in the hour of trouble. The word *trouble* describes people in tight places, like those who are in a corner and unable to get out. When that occurs, the admonition is, "Don't be afraid!"[1]

In verse 2, use of the word *therefore* affirms that the people of God need never stand in awe or fear of trouble, or of those who rise against them. The reason has just been previously stated: "God is…." Even though the very foundations of creation give way to chaos and destruction, the believer has no grounds to live in fear. The image of roaring waters and mountains quaking presents two possible interpretations (see verse 3). The first is the *great Flood* of Genesis 6–9, and the second is *mountains quaking*, referring to earthquakes that did occur in that part of the world (see 1 Kings 19:11; Amos 1:1; Zechariah 14:5;

compare with Matthew 27:54). In each case, the people of God, those who lived in righteousness and obedience, would find in Him a source of protection and comfort.

C. A Glorious Invitation
(Psalm 46:8-11)

Come, behold the works of the LORD, what desolations he hath made in the earth. He maketh wars to cease unto the end of the earth; he breaketh the bow, and cutteth the spear in sunder; he burneth the chariot in the fire. Be still, and know that I am God: I will be exalted among the heathen, I will be exalted in the earth. The LORD of hosts is with us; the God of Jacob is our refuge.

In verse 8, the psalmist gave a grand and glorious invitation for all to come and view firsthand the awesome works of the Lord. The command to "come and see" (NIV) is the first of two imperative commands; the second is in verse 10: "Be still..."[2] The first imperative command is a summons to come and behold the works of the Lord. What are the works of the Lord? Creation and all that is within it (see Psalms 24:1; 66:5; 92:4-6; 111:2-3). There is nothing within the universe that God has not made (see Genesis 1:1-2:7; Isaiah 40:25-26). When Philip accepted the call to follow Jesus, he gave a similar invitation to Nathaniel in John 1:46.[3] After Nathaniel heard Jesus and saw the works He had done, Nathaniel, too, hailed Jesus as King of Israel.[4]

The word *Desolations* (Hebrew: *shammah*) literally means "waste." The reader is summoned to call to mind the picture of a broad battlefield upon which lie the corpses of men and animals killed in fierce battle. It also calls to mind the desolation wreaked upon the Egyptians both at the Red Sea and on the night that the death angel visited the home of the first born of the Egyptians (see Exodus 10:7; 12:30;

14:30; Joshua 11:20; 2 Chronicles 20:23; Isaiah 24:1; 34:2). This image of desolation is not the product of men's doing, but it is the doing of the Lord. He gave Himself the victory.

Verse 9 is a description of what God had done to cause the desolation. He brought an end to the wars or crushed the armies of those who sought to oppress His people. He broke the bow, shattered the spear, and burnt the shield with fire (see Isaiah 2:4; 11:9; 60:18; Micah 4:3-4). These three acts speak of the total destruction of the capability of an opposing army to wage war against God's people (see 2 Kings 19:35-36; compare these verses with Psalm 76:3; Ezekiel 39:3, 9-10; Joshua 11:6, 9; Micah 5:10).

Verse 10 begins with the second imperative command in the passage. These are not the words of the psalmist, but the Lord. "Be still" is not a command to sit and quietly reflect on the goodness of God, as some might think. Rather, it is the command to cease fighting—lay down their weapons. Israel was called to trust God for the outcome of their conflicts and not their armies. Within the command, the Lord made three statements: first, "I am God"; second, "I will be exalted" among the nations or heathen; third, God said that He would not only be exalted among the nations, but also, all of the earth would recognize His sovereignty over the earth.

The psalm concludes with a declaration of assurance and faith. The Lord almighty is with us, and because He is with us, we need not fear (see Exodus 14:13-14). The psalmist declared that the God who was with them at that very moment was the same God who stood with Jacob. Jacob faced one trying situation after another, yet it was the Lord God of his fathers who had preserved him.

III. CONCLUDING REFLECTION

The words of Psalm 46 contain some of the most inspirational words found anywhere. They are words that are capable of lifting dispirited and disheartened men and women from the crater of certain defeat by instilling within them the added courage to face the challenges that confront them. Whenever men and women from across the centuries have needed a word of strength and fresh hope, they have found them in these words: "God is our refuge and strength, a very present help in trouble." God has granted to them that dynamic zeal to press on in spite of the obstacles that were in the way. Christians have found in the life and teachings of Jesus Christ the model of one who trusted God in spite of the situation. We, too, are invited to put all of our confidence and hope in Him. Why? Because God continues to be our refuge and strength.

PRAYER

Lord God, grant Your servants the spirit of courage, so that we may face and endure whatever trials may come our way. Increase our faith so that we can live as boldly in the world as the great heroes of the Bible. In Jesus' name we pray. Amen.

WORD POWER

Strength (Hebrew: *oze*)—**literally means "might or power." It denotes having the capacity to prevail against every foe or challenge.**

Selah (Hebrew: *celah*)—**a technical musical term that denotes a pause or interruption to what is being played or sung.**

HOME DAILY BIBLE READINGS
(September 3-9, 2012)

Faith Is Assurance

MONDAY, September 3: "The Trusting Child" (Mark 10:13-16)
TUESDAY, September 4: "The Trust of the Weak" (2 Chronicles 14:2-12)
WEDNESDAY, September 5: "The Prayer of Trust" (Psalm 3)
THURSDAY, September 6: "The Security of Trust" (Psalm 4)
FRIDAY, September 7: "The Confidence of Trust" (Psalm 27:1-6)
SATURDAY, September 8: "The Patience of Trust" (Psalm 27:7-14)
SUNDAY, September 9: "The Certain Refuge" (Hebrews 11:1-3, 6; Psalm 46:1-3, 8-11)

End Notes

[1] *Bible Exposition Commentary* (BE Series) Old Testament: Wisdom and Poetry.
[2] McCann, J. Clinton Jr., *Psalms New Interpreters Bible: A Commentary in Twelve Volumes, Volume IV* (Nashville: Abingdon Press, 1996), p. 886.
[3] Ibid.
[4] Ibid.

LESSON 3   September 16, 2012

FAITH IS ENDURANCE

Faith Pathway/Faith Journey Topic: Steadfast Fortitude

DEVOTIONAL READING: James 5:7-11
PRINT PASSAGE: Hebrews 12:1-11

BACKGROUND SCRIPTURE: Hebrews 12:1-11
KEY VERSES: Hebrews 12:1-2

Hebrews 12:1-11—KJV

WHEREFORE SEEING we also are compassed about with so great a cloud of witnesses, let us lay aside every weight, and the sin which doth so easily beset us, and let us run with patience the race that is set before us,

2 Looking unto Jesus the author and finisher of our faith; who for the joy that was set before him endured the cross, despising the shame, and is set down at the right hand of the throne of God.

3 For consider him that endured such contradiction of sinners against himself, lest ye be wearied and faint in your minds.

4 Ye have not yet resisted unto blood, striving against sin.

5 And ye have forgotten the exhortation which speaketh unto you as unto children, My son, despise not thou the chastening of the Lord, nor faint when thou art rebuked of him:

6 For whom the Lord loveth he chasteneth, and scourgeth every son whom he receiveth.

7 If ye endure chastening, God dealeth with you as with sons; for what son is he whom the father chasteneth not?

8 But if ye be without chastisement, whereof all are partakers, then are ye bastards, and not sons.

9 Furthermore we have had fathers of our flesh which corrected us, and we gave them reverence: shall we not much rather be in subjection unto the Father of spirits, and live?

10 For they verily for a few days chastened us after their own pleasure; but he for our profit, that we might be partakers of his holiness.

11 Now no chastening for the present seemeth to be joyous, but grievous: nevertheless afterward it yieldeth the peaceable fruit of righteousness unto them which are exercised thereby.

Hebrews 12:1-11—NIV

THEREFORE, SINCE we are surrounded by such a great cloud of witnesses, let us throw off everything that hinders and the sin that so easily entangles, and let us run with perseverance the race marked out for us.

2 Let us fix our eyes on Jesus, the author and perfecter of our faith, who for the joy set before him endured the cross, scorning its shame, and sat down at the right hand of the throne of God.

3 Consider him who endured such opposition from sinful men, so that you will not grow weary and lose heart.

4 In your struggle against sin, you have not yet resisted to the point of shedding your blood.

5 And you have forgotten that word of encouragement that addresses you as sons: "My son, do not make light of the Lord's discipline, and do not lose heart when he rebukes you,

6 because the Lord disciplines those he loves, and he punishes everyone he accepts as a son."

7 Endure hardship as discipline; God is treating you as sons. For what son is not disciplined by his father?

8 If you are not disciplined (and everyone undergoes discipline), then you are illegitimate children and not true sons.

9 Moreover, we have all had human fathers who disciplined us and we respected them for it. How much more should we submit to the Father of our spirits and live!

10 Our fathers disciplined us for a little while as they thought best; but God disciplines us for our good, that we may share in his holiness.

11 No discipline seems pleasant at the time, but painful. Later on, however, it produces a harvest of righteousness and peace for those who have been trained by it.

UNIFYING LESSON PRINCIPLE

People know that to win a race we sometimes have to suffer some pain—but we must keep our eyes on the goal. What help is available? The writer of the book of Hebrews told us that there is a huge crowd of witnesses to the faith who have trained well, have kept their eyes on God and Jesus, and have grown in grace and character.

TOPICAL OUTLINE OF THE LESSON

I. **Introduction**
   A. Spiritual Endurance
   B. Biblical Background

II. **Exposition and Application of the Scripture**
   A. Run the Race with Perseverance (Hebrews 12:1)
   B. Jesus: The Author and Perfecter of Faith (Hebrews 12:2-3)
   C. The Purpose of the Lord's Discipline (Hebrews 12:4-11)

III. **Concluding Reflection**

LESSON OBJECTIVES

Upon completion of the lesson, the students will be able to do the following:

1. Understand that following Jesus in faith leads to persevering through any suffering we encounter, and disciplining ourselves in Christian living;
2. Declare what it means to them to follow Jesus' example in their lives; and,
3. Utilize their faith in Jesus Christ in order to determine and reach spiritual goals.

POINTS TO BE EMPHASIZED

ADULT/YOUTH

Adult Topic: Steadfast Fortitude
Youth Topic: Endurance to Run the Race
Adult/Youth Key Verses: Hebrews 12:1-2
Print Passage: Hebrews 12:1-11

—The faithfulness of the "great cloud of witnesses" is an encouragement to those who are in the race.
—The Christian life of hard work and suffering requires us to run patiently in the Spirit as we struggle against sin.
—After affirming the support of a "cloud of witnesses," the writer encouraged Christians to join the race of faith bearers.
—To join the faith bearers, the readers must lay aside all the weight of sin which is hindering them from running.
—Each faith bearer "must run with endurance," remembering what Jesus, the perfecter of faith, endured in His suffering.
—We may face obstacles such as trials and difficulties, but with the Lord's loving discipline, we can endure them and not be discouraged by them.

CHILDREN

Children Topic: Following Jesus' Example
Key Verses: Hebrews 12:1b-2a
Print Passage: Hebrews 12:1-11

—The Bible provides examples of people whose faith encourages us to persevere.
—To live the Christian life, we must follow Jesus Christ as our example.
—The Christian life involves hard work and discipline.
—Suffering for Christ's sake develops patience and serves as the training ground for Christian maturity.
—God's discipline is a sign of His deep love for us.
—The appropriate response to God's discipline is grateful acceptance.

I. INTRODUCTION

A. Spiritual Endurance

In 2008, a Jamaican-born sprinter by the name of Usain Bolt established himself as the world's fastest human being. During the 2008 Beijing Olympics, Usain Bolt set world records in the three premier sprinting events: the 100 meters, 200 meters, and the 4x100-meter relay. The last time anyone achieved this unparalleled feat was during the 1984 Olympic Games, when Carl Lewis became the world record holder. Usain Bolt was not finished, because during the 2009 World Championships in Berlin he set new world records in the same events. These stunning achievements have established Usain Bolt as one of the greatest sprinters in history. What does it take to achieve such consistently remarkable results? How much physical endurance, strength, and stamina are required to run with such speed? How much mental and emotional stamina does it take to compete at that level? It requires a consistent commitment to physical training and mental development. In the lesson today, we learn that the same type of determination and drive is necessary in our walk of faith. People know that to win a race we sometimes have to suffer some pain, but we must keep our eyes on the goal.

B. Biblical Background

The book of Hebrews was written for a largely Jewish Christian community (see lesson 1). As we have already learned, we are not sure of the extent or intensity of the trials that this Christian community faced. Whatever the challenge, they needed to be encouraged and reminded that God was ever faithful. Chapter 12 of the book of Hebrews is a series of exhortations encouraging believers to persevere through the hardships and trials brought on by their faith in Jesus Christ. Throughout the epistle, the writer exhorted the saints to remain confident because of the greatness of the sacrifice of Jesus Christ. Beginning at Hebrews 10:39, he issued a clarion call to remain faithful to God by reminding them that they were not alone. Nothing had befallen them that had not been the lot of other men and women who trusted God. Across the centuries, there have been countless believers who have faced the searing fires of tribulation and trials, yet did not give in or give up. In the eleventh chapter, he called the roll of some of the greatest saints in the Bible. All of them overcame their trials by holding to their faith in God, who had been at the center of their faith for centuries. The key to remaining steadfast and immovable is perseverance and discipline. One of the most important lessons of the passage is that believers develop character and fortitude through adversity, all while recognizing that God's discipline is sometimes experienced through trials.

II. EXPOSITION AND APPLICATION OF THE SCRIPTURE

A. Run the Race with Perseverance (Hebrews 12:1)

WHEREFORE SEEING we also are compassed about with so great a cloud of witnesses, let us lay aside every weight, and the sin which doth so easily beset us, and let us run with patience the race that is set before us.

Verse 1 marks the point of transition between the examples of the heroes of the faith and those who were currently involved in what is termed as "the race." The writer of the book of Hebrews used inclusive language ("we")—suggesting that they were all involved in the race. He stated that they were surrounded (compassed)(Greek: *perikeimai*—literally means "lying around us") by a great cloud of witnesses. The metaphor of a great cloud was used in ancient writings to denote a massive throng of people. Who were these witnesses and in what sense were they witnesses to those who were running the race? Those in this cloud of witnesses were not spectators gazing across the balcony of eternity, encouraging the saints to persevere. Rather, as F. F. Bruce has noted, it is through their example of faithfulness and endurance that they bear witness to the possibility of remaining faithful to God under extreme situations.[1] "It is not so much they look at us as we look to them—for encouragement."[2]

The writer called upon them to throw off everything that hindered a successful completion. He called upon the saints to do two things: first, they must shed the excess baggage that got in the way of remaining faithful.

What are the sorts of things that hinder the full development of faith today? Disobedience, unfaithfulness, lack of commitment to ministry, and persisting in our sins are among the chief causes of stunted spiritual growth.

Lastly, he called upon the saints to *persevere* (Greek: *hupomone*—literally means "patience or endurance"). It is used in the New Testament to denote the character of a man or woman who is so determined to remain faithful that not even the most severe trials can quench his or her faith.

B. Jesus: The Author and Perfecter of Faith (Hebrews 12:2-3)

Looking unto Jesus the author and finisher of our faith; who for the joy that was set before him endured the cross, despising the shame, and is set down at the right hand of the throne of God. For consider him that endured such contradiction of sinners against himself, lest ye be wearied and faint in your minds.

For the second time, the writer of the book of Hebrews made a statement of inclusion: "Let us fix our eyes on Jesus." The writer called on the saints to look away from the lures and enticements of the world—the struggles caused by their personal trials—and look to Jesus. The language of the passage was written in such a way as to express continuous action when it comes to fixing our eyes on Jesus. This is not a one-time event or action, but it denotes constantly looking to Jesus. Remember that the intention of the writer was to urge the saints on toward rock-solid faith or confidence in God. Who best embodied this? Jesus of Nazareth did. Why were they encouraged to fix their eyes on Jesus? He is the *author* (Greek: *archegos*—literally, "chief leader"). The Greek word implies that Jesus is the one who takes the lead in matters of faith. He is the pioneer who is the genesis of all faith in God.

One of the more serious challenges that the Christian faith faces in the twenty-first century is the loss of contact and connection to the purpose of the Lord Jesus Christ. Christianity has become an institutionalized religion; it does not have as much of a commitment to a relationship with Jesus. Neither individuals nor congregations can expect to endure the challenge of witnessing in a post-modern, post-Christian culture without a serious commitment to faith in the Lord Jesus Christ.

The second part of verse 2 is better understood by phrasing it this way: "Who saw the great joy that lay before Him, was not overcome by the shame and humiliation that came from suffering crucifixion." Jesus did not give in to the Cross; rather, He faced it as a conquering king and endured it. "It was sheer faith in God, unsupported by any visible or tangible evidence, that carried Him through the taunting, the scourging, the crucifying, and the more bitter agony of rejection, desertion, and dereliction."[3] Jesus did not die, get buried, and remain locked in the bowels of the earth as a victim. Rather, He was the Victor. Therefore, God has highly exalted Him and Jesus sat down at the right hand of the throne of God.

Verse 3 points to another challenge endured by Jesus: the opposition and criticisms of people who were described as "sinners"; those who were committed to a life of disobedience and defiance of God. We see what happens when a believer looks away from Jesus and becomes preoccupied with his or her own stressful situation; he or she can lose heart—literally his or her capacity to hold on is dissolved in despair. How does a man or woman under pressure hold up and hold on to his or her faith? It begins with the intensity

and commitment of our relationship to the Lord Jesus Christ. It is about having a deep desire to be formed in the very image of the Lord Jesus Christ. Spend time looking away from your problems and asking God to reveal how to be a witness to those who labor under the same burden as you.

C. The Purpose of the Lord's Discipline (Hebrews 12:4-11)

Ye have not yet resisted unto blood, striving against sin. And ye have forgotten the exhortation which speaketh unto you as unto children, My son, despise not thou the chastening of the Lord, nor faint when thou art rebuked of him: For whom the Lord loveth he chasteneth, and scourgeth every son whom he receiveth. If ye endure chastening, God dealeth with you as with sons; for what son is he whom the father chasteneth not? But if ye be without chastisement, whereof all are partakers, then are ye bastards, and not sons. Furthermore we have had fathers of our flesh which corrected us, and we gave them reverence: shall we not much rather be in subjection unto the Father of spirits, and live? For they verily for a few days chastened us after their own pleasure; but he for our profit, that we might be partakers of his holiness. Now no chastening for the present seemeth to be joyous, but grievous: nevertheless afterward it yieldeth the peaceable fruit of righteousness unto them which are exercised thereby.

Beginning with verse 4, the writer took up a very important theme of why believers may be called upon to suffer. Jesus once stated that some suffering and persecution are the results of our commitment to righteousness and because of our faith in Him (see Matthew 5:10-12; compare with Acts 5:41; 1 Timothy 4:10; 1 Peter 3:14, 17; 4:15-16). Here, the language picks up the imagery of a wrestler or boxer who is engaged in hand-to-hand combat, only in this instance the fight is not against another human being, but against the prevailing presence of sin which seeks to undermine the work of grace in the life of the believer (see Romans 6:1-23; compare with Galatians 5:16-21). In all that they faced and endured, the believers who first received this message had not been called upon to seal their faith through the shedding of their own blood.[4]

Sin is taken so lightly today that it is almost dismissed as a normal way of living. Even among believers today, the repulsiveness of sin is overshadowed by their willingness to wink at ungodly conduct and see it as humanity's failed attempt to live holy. What are the secret sins of your life? How do you approach sin? What are the greatest struggles that you face in living godly? Paul reminded us that we should examine ourselves to determine whether we are in the faith (see 2 Corinthians 10:12; 13:5).

In verse 5, the writer called upon believers to remember the Word of God, which had been spoken to them or that they had read. That word of exhortation addressed them as sons, not as strangers who were afar off without any rights of citizenship (see Ephesians 2:1-4). They were sons and daughters of God (see John 1:12-13). Here, the writer established that discipline was to be the perspective from which they were to view and understand their trials. He found support for this position in Proverbs 3:11-12, most likely the Septuagint (Greek translation of the Hebrew Scriptures). He reminded them that they were not to see discipline as rejection or punishment but as a means to an end. Rather than lose heart, they must embrace discipline as a sign that God loved them and treated them as sons (see verse 6). How else could believers be trained for the rigors and hardships of missions and ministry?

The runner cannot win without discipline. The fighter cannot overcome his opponent without discipline. The believer cannot overcome trials except he or she be disciplined. What son, who has a loving father, does not face discipline? Without discipline from the father, one may as well be considered to be an illegitimate child and not a true son (see verse 8).

Verse 9 is an argument from the lesser to the greater. If our earthly fathers disciplined us and we became more obedient, how much more obedient should we be when our heavenly Father disciplines us? Our fathers disciplined us for the purpose of correcting some behavioral defect in our character or to teach us an important lesson about life. Similarly, God disciplines us so that we might share in His holiness and have our characters shaped into the image of the Lord Jesus Christ. Even though discipline is an unpleasant experience at the time it happens, yet the outcome is a harvest of righteousness and peace for those who have been trained by it.

How often have we viewed hardship as a sign that God has taken His hand of blessing from us or that He may have even rejected us? How much more rich would be the lives of believers who embraced discipline as the means for building us up so that we might face the trials of life with steadfast courage?

III. CONCLUDING REFLECTION

The late Dutch theologian Henri Nouwen once said, "The spiritual life is a life in which we are set free by the Spirit of God to enjoy life in all its fullness."[5] How does one find freedom in the midst of a world of broken lives, sin, and hostility toward the Savior of men and women? How does a believer face up to the trials of life and remain steadfast and immovable? It all begins and ends with having the right perspective from which to view and comprehend life. When viewing life purely from the perspective of the material world, it is easy to become disillusioned when material things are taken away or destroyed (see Philippians 3:6-14). However, it is in Jesus Christ that we live, move, and have our very being.

PRAYER

Lord God, we bless You for the fact that in Jesus Christ we find the perfect example of how to face the challenges of life without giving in to despair and discouragement. Grant that Your servants may walk upright before You in peace and courage. In Jesus' name we pray. Amen.

WORD POWER

Sin (Greek: *hamartia* [ham-ar-tee-ah])—This word is mentioned more than 480 times in the Bible. It literally means "to miss the mark." Sin does not refer to single acts of disobedience or defiance against the Word of God. Rather, it denotes an attitude of one who disregards God's Word and seeks to live life on his or her own terms (see Genesis 3:1-15; John 8:34; Romans 3:20; 6:1-23).

HOME DAILY BIBLE READINGS
(September 10-16, 2012)

Faith Is Endurance

MONDAY, September 10: "The Discipline of the Lord" (Job 5:8-18)
TUESDAY, September 11: "The Death of Sin" (Romans 6:1-11)
WEDNESDAY, September 12: "The Race for the Prize" (1 Corinthians 9:24-27)
THURSDAY, September 13: "The Training for Godliness" (1 Timothy 4:6-10)
FRIDAY, September 14: "The Endurance of the Faithful" (James 5:7-11)
SATURDAY, September 15: "The Example of Faithfulness" (1 Peter 2:18-25)
SUNDAY, September 16: "The Pioneer of Faith" (Hebrews 12:1-11)

End Notes

[1] F. F. Bruce, *The Epistle to the Hebrews: NICNT* (Grand Rapids: William B. Eerdmans's Publishing Co., 1964), p. 346.
[2] Ibid.
[3] Ibid., p. 352.
[4] Ibid., p. 357.
[5] Henri Nouwen, *Spiritual Formation*, with Michael J. Christiansen and Rebecca J. Laird (New York: HarperCollins, 2010), p. xxix.

LESSON 4   **September 23, 2012**

FAITH INSPIRES GRATITUDE

FAITH PATHWAY/FAITH JOURNEY TOPIC: Steadfast Thanks

DEVOTIONAL READING: 2 Thessalonians 1:1-7
PRINT PASSAGE: Hebrews 12:18-29

BACKGROUND SCRIPTURE: Hebrews 12:14-29
KEY VERSE: Hebrews 12:28

Hebrews 12:18-29—KJV

18 For ye are not come unto the mount that might be touched, and that burned with fire, nor unto blackness, and darkness, and tempest,

19 And the sound of a trumpet, and the voice of words; which voice they that heard intreated that the word should not be spoken to them any more:

20 (For they could not endure that which was commanded, And if so much as a beast touch the mountain, it shall be stoned, or thrust through with a dart:

21 And so terrible was the sight, that Moses said, I exceedingly fear and quake:)

22 But ye are come unto mount Sion, and unto the city of the living God, the heavenly Jerusalem, and to an innumerable company of angels,

23 To the general assembly and church of the firstborn, which are written in heaven, and to God the Judge of all, and to the spirits of just men made perfect,

24 And to Jesus the mediator of the new covenant, and to the blood of sprinkling, that speaketh better things than that of Abel.

25 See that ye refuse not him that speaketh. For if they escaped not who refused him that spake on earth, much more shall not we escape, if we turn away from him that speaketh from heaven:

26 Whose voice then shook the earth: but now he hath promised, saying, Yet once more I shake not the earth only, but also heaven.

27 And this word, Yet once more, signifieth the removing of those things that are shaken, as of things that are made, that those things which cannot be shaken may remain.

Hebrews 12:18-29—NIV

18 You have not come to a mountain that can be touched and that is burning with fire; to darkness, gloom and storm;

19 to a trumpet blast or to such a voice speaking words that those who heard it begged that no further word be spoken to them,

20 because they could not bear what was commanded: "If even an animal touches the mountain, it must be stoned."

21 The sight was so terrifying that Moses said, "I am trembling with fear."

22 But you have come to Mount Zion, to the heavenly Jerusalem, the city of the living God. You have come to thousands upon thousands of angels in joyful assembly,

23 to the church of the firstborn, whose names are written in heaven. You have come to God, the judge of all men, to the spirits of righteous men made perfect,

24 to Jesus the mediator of a new covenant, and to the sprinkled blood that speaks a better word than the blood of Abel.

25 See to it that you do not refuse him who speaks. If they did not escape when they refused him who warned them on earth, how much less will we, if we turn away from him who warns us from heaven?

26 At that time his voice shook the earth, but now he has promised, "Once more I will shake not only the earth but also the heavens."

27 The words "once more" indicate the removing of what can be shaken—that is, created things—so that what cannot be shaken may remain.

UNIFYING LESSON PRINCIPLE

People fear many things, especially judgment and death. What is it we can believe in that will relieve our fears? The writer of the book of Hebrews said that God in Christ Jesus brought us forgiveness and promise of eternal life. In telling the story of the good Samaritan, Jesus assures us that by putting our fears aside and caring for our neighbors, we will find faith.

28 Wherefore we receiving a kingdom which cannot be moved, let us have grace, whereby we may serve God acceptably with reverence and godly fear:

29 For our God is a consuming fire.

28 Therefore, since we are receiving a kingdom that cannot be shaken, let us be thankful, and so worship God acceptably with reverence and awe,

29 for our "God is a consuming fire."

TOPICAL OUTLINE OF THE LESSON

I. **Introduction**
   A. Showing Gratitude
   B. Biblical Background

II. **Exposition and Application of the Scripture**
   A. The Mount of the Old Covenant (Hebrews 12:18-21)
   B. The Mount of the New Covenant (Hebrews 12:22-24)
   C. The Dangers of Rejecting God (Hebrews 12:25-29)

III. **Concluding Reflection**

LESSON OBJECTIVES

Upon completion of the lesson, the students will be able to do the following:

1. Explore the meaning of God's forgiveness and promise of eternal life;
2. Explore their fears about death and assurances of God's grace to relieve their fears; and,
3. Repent for the ways in which we reject God's grace and to worship God with reverence and awe.

POINTS TO BE EMPHASIZED

ADULT/YOUTH

Adult Topic: **Steadfast Thanks**

Youth Topic: **Fearful or Thankful Faith?**

Adult/Youth Key Verse: **Hebrews 12:28**

Print Passage: **Hebrews 12:18-29**

—In these verses, the writer was contrasting Christian experience with Israel's experience at Mount Sinai (see Exodus 20ff).

—The writer described Christian experience lived out in the presence of angels and the righteous dead.

—The Israelites experienced fear and trembling when receiving the first covenant.

—The Israelites refused to listen to Moses, who was the mediator between God and themselves.

—Jesus is the mediator of the new covenant between God and the people of God.

CHILDREN

Children Topic: **Living Our Faith**

Key Verse: **Luke 10:27**

Print Passage: **Luke 10:25-37**

—Jesus' parable illustrated the great commandment for believers to love and care for their neighbors.

—Even though one's traditions may justify ignoring a neighbor's needs, such action is never right.

—Our neighbor is anyone of any ethnic group, creed, or social background who is in need.

—Love includes acting to meet the needs of others.

I. INTRODUCTION

A. Showing Gratitude

Dutch theologian Henri Nouwen was one of the leading voices in the twentieth century on matters relating to spiritual formation. He taught psychology and pastoral theology at Notre Dame, Yale, and Harvard universities. Later in life, he took a position as senior pastor of L'Arche Daybreak in Toronto, Canada. Prior to his death in 1996, he authored numerous books on the subject of spiritual formation. In one of his works, he wrote about the importance of Christians living with hearts that are deeply grateful for God's love and grace. He stated that gratitude is the opposite of resentment and anger, which can crop up when believers are unappreciative of God's work of grace in the lives of others.[1] He wrote, "Gratitude is the attitude that enables us to let go of anger, receive the hidden gifts of those we want to serve, and make these gifts visible to the community as a source of celebration."[2] What can be more destructive of the unity and fellowship of a body of believers than a spirit of resentment? What can show disdain for God's loving-kindness more than a spirit that rejects God's love and grace? As believers, we are exhorted to always show gratitude for God's gracious gift of salvation and eternal life. A vital part of showing gratitude is learning to live with each other in mutually supportive and loving communities. The writer of the book of Hebrews reminded us that the Christian life calls for us to live up to the measure of God's holiness.

B. Biblical Background

In the previous lesson, we learned that believers are called to persevere under the raging fires of persecution and scorn. God has not left us without witnesses to His saving grace and mercy. Their examples of faithfulness encourage us to stand firm during times of trial. In today's lesson, we are reminded that in addition to letting go of the "sin that so easily entangles" us, we are to relentlessly pursue lives of peace and holiness. In these verses, the writer drew a contrast between the Christian experience of grace and Israel's experience at Mount Sinai (see Exodus 20:1ff). He described Christian experience lived out in the presence of myriads of angels and the righteous dead. This passage draws a clear line of distinction between the enduring nature of God's kingdom and the temporary nature of things on the earth. Peace and holiness are so vital in the believer's life that they must be pursued with great urgency.

The writer reminded believers that unless they lived holy lives they would never see God. Ancient Israel was commanded to live holy, because the Lord had called them out to be a holy nation (see Exodus 19:6; Leviticus 20:6; 1 Peter 1:15). Peace and harmony are very delicate and precious gifts in a congregation. They can be easily disrupted by the smallest of disagreements. The book of Hebrews is filled with several warnings against rejecting God's grace and the gift of salvation (see Hebrews 2:3; 6:4-6; 10:26-27). The passage closed by encouraging believers to respond with gratitude and awe as they consider the majesty of God's eternal kingdom.

II. EXPOSITION AND APPLICATION OF THE SCRIPTURE

A. The Mount of the Old Covenant (Hebrews 12:18-21)

For ye are not come unto the mount that might be touched, and that burned with fire, nor unto blackness, and darkness, and tempest, And the sound of a trumpet, and the voice of words; which voice they that heard intreated that the word should not be spoken to them any more: (For they could not endure that which was commanded, And if so much as a beast touch the mountain, it shall be stoned, or thrust through with a dart: And so terrible was the sight, that Moses said, I exceedingly fear and quake:)

The writer assumed that the readers or hearers had some understanding of the Old Testament era and the giving of the Law to Israel. There is no mention of the name of Sinai, but clearly the reference "unto the mount" speaks of Mount Sinai—where God entered into covenant with Israel (see Exodus 19:1-6, 12-22 and 20:18-21). Three months after being liberated from slavery in Egypt, the Israelites arrived at Sinai (see Exodus 19:1). It was here that God ratified the covenant between Himself and His chosen people. The covenant was expressed in the words of the Ten Commandments (see Exodus 20:1-17).

The writer of the book of Hebrews drew a distinction between the experiences of ancient Israel and the experiences of Christians who did not come to faith in God in the same way as the Israelites. The experience of the ancient Israelites was one that was visual and filled with loud sounds. They could see the mountain covered in smoke and fire, but could not come near (see Exodus 19). The imagery of fire and smoke are all descriptions of the presence of God. As God approached the mountain, His voice was that of the sound of a mighty trumpet that grew louder and louder. When God answered Moses, He answered so loudly that His voice was as thunder. The mountain was so mysterious and sacred that no one was allowed to go near to or set foot on it without paying with his or her life. Awe, reverence, and dread describe this experience (see Deuteronomy 5:23-27). If an animal were to touch the mountain and had to be stoned, what could a human being expect who touched the mountain? Even Moses was terrified by the sights and sounds (see Deuteronomy 9:9).

B. The Mount of the New Covenant (Hebrews 12:22-24)

But ye are come unto mount Sion, and unto the city of the living God, the heavenly Jerusalem, and to an innumerable company of angels, To the general assembly and church of the firstborn, which are written in heaven, and to God the Judge of all, and to the spirits of just men made perfect, And to Jesus the mediator of the new covenant, and to the blood of sprinkling, that speaketh better things than that of Abel.

In contrast to the experience of ancient Israel, Christians have come to a different mountain with a far different experience of God. It was not a mountain that could be touched, but a spiritual mountain, called Mount Zion. This is the place where God commanded the blessing and set His name forever (see 2 Chronicles 7:16). The writer of the book of Hebrews said that this was the heavenly Jerusalem, the city of the living God (see Psalms 48:2; 87:3). On this mountain, there is the picture of inclusion where thousands of angels gather with the saints to worship God in joyfulness (see Deuteronomy 33:3).

Who are those in the church of the firstborn? In ancient Israel, there could only be one firstborn, who received all of the rights and privileges of that status (see Genesis 25:31-34; also Exodus 4:22). However, in Jesus Christ, every born-again believer is treated as an heir of the promises of God (see Ephesians 1:11; Romans 8:17; compare with Galatians 3:19-27; 4:21-31). As sons and daughters of God, our names have been recorded in the Lamb's Book of Life. It is the blood of Jesus that makes the believer righteous before God. One day, all people will stand before the judgment seat of God, yet those who have been saved will need not fear—because through the shed blood of Jesus, we are saved (see 2 Corinthians 5:10). Even those who died before Jesus Christ (yet believed God) will be declared righteous (see Romans 4:6; Galatians 3:6).

In Jesus Christ, the promise of a new covenant reached its fulfillment. He died for sin once—for all time. Through His shed blood all men and women experience God's gracious forgiveness (see Ephesians 1:7; Hebrews 9:12; 10:10).

C. The Dangers of Rejecting God (Hebrews 12:25-29)

See that ye refuse not him that speaketh. For if they escaped not who refused him that spake on earth, much more shall not we escape, if we turn away from him that speaketh from heaven: Whose voice then shook the earth: but now he hath promised, saying, Yet once more I shake not the earth only, but also heaven. And this word, Yet once more, signifieth the removing of those things that are shaken, as of things that are made, that those things which cannot be shaken may remain. Wherefore we receiving a kingdom which cannot be moved, let us have grace, whereby we may serve God acceptably with reverence and godly fear: For our God is a consuming fire.

The final verses begin with an imperative command: "See that" they did not disobey or reject God. When God appeared on the earth, Israel entered into covenant relationship with God and received the Law of God. Although they saw God's presence on the earth, some still rejected Him and did not escape His judgment. How can we then escape, if we reject the very One whose sacrifice at Calvary opened the door for our salvation? Jesus Christ now sits at the right hand of God (see Hebrews 1:1-3). Verse 26 draws distinction between the giving of the first covenant and the giving of the new covenant in Jesus Christ. At Sinai, God shook the earth, but one day heaven and earth will shake, which will be the beginning of the final judgment (see Haggai 2:6). Believers need not stand in dread nor fear this moment, because we are part of the kingdom and have a foundation which cannot be shaken. Our eternal security in Christ is one of the compelling reasons to give God our highest worship and praise (see John 10:28-29; Revelation 4:5-11). Worship is not something we plan in committees and then perform on Sunday; rather, it is the lifeblood of the believer. God is worthy to be worshipped, because He is not just the God of Israel—He is our God.

III. CONCLUDING REFLECTION

Erik Routley wrote in his study of the book of Psalms that, "The most precious achievement and duty of the Hebrew people was the worship of God."[3] It was through their worship that Israel remembered the experiences of their past. They remembered how God had brought them out of slavery in Egypt and drowned the army of the mighty Egyptian Pharaoh in the Red Sea. In worship, they remembered how He had met their physical and spiritual needs, and finally brought them into a land flowing with milk and honey. The writer of the book of Hebrews reminded us that Christians have an even more glorious reason to worship—our salvation that has been wrought through the personal sacrifice of Jesus Christ for our sins. The next time you attend a worship service, let the overwhelming sense of what God in Christ has done for you be the motivating factor.

PRAYER

Heavenly Father, grant that we may love not only in word, but also in deed. You have given to us an example of how to love even the most unlovable persons. Empower us through the Holy Spirit to live in a manner that is well pleasing to You. In Jesus' name we pray. Amen.

WORD POWER

Bitterness (Greek: *pikria*)—an extreme form of wickedness and resentment caused by unresolved differences between people or the failure to forgive others and move on. Nothing can be more disruptive and destructive in a congregation than believers who are bitter about past experiences. Their emotional hang-ups can reverberate in a congregation and cause lingering problems that last for years.

HOME DAILY BIBLE READINGS
(September 17-23, 2012)

Faith Inspires Gratitude

MONDAY, September 17: "Listening to the Voice of Warning" (Ezekiel 33:1-9)

TUESDAY, September 18: "Listening to the Spirit" (Revelation 3:1-13)

WEDNESDAY, September 19: "Anticipating a Better Covenant" (Hebrews 8:1-7)

THURSDAY, September 20: "Giving Thanks for the Faithful" (2 Thessalonians 1:1-7)

FRIDAY, September 21: "Loving with God's Kind of Love" (Matthew 5:43-48)

SATURDAY, September 22: "Pursuing Peace and Holiness" (Hebrews 12:12-17)

SUNDAY, September 23: "Offering Acceptable Worship" (Hebrews 12:18-29)

End Notes

[1]Henri Nouwen, *Spiritual Formation: Following the Movements of the Spirit*, with Michael J. Christensen and Rebecca J. Laird (New York: Harper Collins Publishers, 2010), pp. 57-61.

[2]Ibid, p. 63.

[3]Erik Routley, *Exploring the Psalms,* (Philadelphia: Westminster Press, 1975), p. 17.

FAITH REQUIRES MUTUAL LOVE

FAITH PATHWAY/FAITH JOURNEY TOPIC: Steadfast Love

DEVOTIONAL READING: **John 13:31-35**
PRINT PASSAGE: **Hebrews 13:1-3;**
1 Corinthians 13:1-13

BACKGROUND SCRIPTURE: **Hebrews 13:1-6;**
1 Corinthians 13
KEY VERSE: **1 Corinthians 13:13**

Hebrews 13:1-3; 1 Corinthians 13:1-13 —KJV

LET BROTHERLY love continue.

2 Be not forgetful to entertain strangers: for thereby some have entertained angels unawares.

3 Remember them that are in bonds, as bound with them; and them which suffer adversity, as being yourselves also in the body.

.....

THOUGH I speak with the tongues of men and of angels, and have not charity, I am become as sounding brass, or a tinkling cymbal.

2 And though I have the gift of prophecy, and understand all mysteries, and all knowledge; and though I have all faith, so that I could remove mountains, and have not charity, I am nothing.

3 And though I bestow all my goods to feed the poor, and though I give my body to be burned, and have not charity, it profiteth me nothing.

4 Charity suffereth long, and is kind; charity envieth not; charity vaunteth not itself, is not puffed up,

5 Doth not behave itself unseemly, seeketh not her own, is not easily provoked, thinketh no evil;

6 Rejoiceth not in iniquity, but rejoiceth in the truth;

7 Beareth all things, believeth all things, hopeth all things, endureth all things.

8 Charity never faileth: but whether there be prophecies, they shall fail; whether there be tongues, they shall cease; whether there be knowledge, it shall vanish away.

9 For we know in part, and we prophesy in part.

10 But when that which is perfect is come, then that

Hebrews 13:1-3; 1 Corinthians 13:1-13 —NIV

KEEP ON loving each other as brothers.

2 Do not forget to entertain strangers, for by so doing some people have entertained angels without knowing it.

3 Remember those in prison as if you were their fellow prisoners, and those who are mistreated as if you yourselves were suffering.

.....

IF I speak in the tongues of men and of angels, but have not love, I am only a resounding gong or a clanging cymbal.

2 If I have the gift of prophecy and can fathom all mysteries and all knowledge, and if I have a faith that can move mountains, but have not love, I am nothing.

3 If I give all I possess to the poor and surrender my body to the flames, but have not love, I gain nothing.

4 Love is patient, love is kind. It does not envy, it does not boast, it is not proud.

5 It is not rude, it is not self-seeking, it is not easily angered, it keeps no record of wrongs.

6 Love does not delight in evil but rejoices with the truth.

7 It always protects, always trusts, always hopes, always perseveres.

8 Love never fails. But where there are prophecies, they will cease; where there are tongues, they will be stilled; where there is knowledge, it will pass away.

9 For we know in part and we prophesy in part,

10 but when perfection comes, the imperfect disappears.

UNIFYING LESSON PRINCIPLE

People search for a workable and reliable definition of love. Is there one? The writers of the books of 1 Corinthians and Hebrews defined *love* and told us that love is greater than faith and hope.

which is in part shall be done away.

11 When I was a child, I spake as a child, I understood as a child, I thought as a child: but when I became a man, I put away childish things.

12 For now we see through a glass, darkly; but then face to face: now I know in part; but then shall I know even as also I am known.

13 And now abideth faith, hope, charity, these three; but the greatest of these is charity.

11 When I was a child, I talked like a child, I thought like a child, I reasoned like a child. When I became a man, I put childish ways behind me.

12 Now we see but a poor reflection as in a mirror; then we shall see face to face. Now I know in part; then I shall know fully, even as I am fully known.

13 And now these three remain: faith, hope and love. But the greatest of these is love.

TOPICAL OUTLINE OF THE LESSON

I. **Introduction**
   A. Love: The Strength of Relationships
   B. Biblical Background

II. **Exposition and Application of the Scripture**
   A. Practical Guidelines for Showing Love (Hebrews 13:1-3)
   B. Love Is the Primary Thing (1 Corinthians 13:1-3)
   C. What Love Is and Is Not (1 Corinthians 13:4-7)
   D. Love Never Fails (1 Corinthians 13:8-13)

III. **Concluding Reflection**

LESSON OBJECTIVES

Upon completion of the lesson, the students will be able to do the following:

1. Explain the main points of Hebrews 13 and 1 Corinthians 13;
2. Identify ways that they experience Christian love in their lives; and,
3. List two ways to improve the relationships in their lives through Christian love.

POINTS TO BE EMPHASIZED

ADULT/YOUTH

Adult Topic: Steadfast Love
Youth Topic: Show Some Love
Adult/Youth Key Verse: 1 Corinthians 13:13
Print Passage: Hebrews 13:1-3; 1 Corinthians 13:1-13

—In Greek, there are four words used for "love": *eros, storge, philia,* and *agape*—but only *philia* and *agape* are used in the Christian Scriptures.
—In 1 Corinthians 13:13, the word for "love" is *agape*; in Hebrews 13:1, the word is *philia*.
—Our limited understanding of eternal things will be made clear when Christ comes.

CHILDREN

Children Topic: A Loving Faith
Key Verse: 1 Corinthians 13:13
Print Passage: 1 Corinthians 13; Hebrews 13:1-3

—Real love for others is revealed through tangible actions.

—Hospitality means making people feel welcome and comfortable.

—Christians represent Christ as they visit prisoners and help the sick and needy.

—The common gift of love is more important than all the spiritual gifts.

—Love is the greatest attribute of God and the greatest human quality.

I. INTRODUCTION

A. Love: The Strength of Relationships

One of the deepest longings of human beings is for close, intimate relationships with other human beings. God has created us in such a way that we find our greatest joy in healthy social environments. The loneliest setting that we can live in is one in which communication has broken down and relationships have become strained and filled with stress. Marriage is among the most complicated of all human relationships—and it becomes stressed and dysfunctional when couples cease to love and care for each other.

Love is one of the most difficult words to define. People search for a workable and reliable definition of love. Is there one? The writers of the books of Hebrews and 1 Corinthians defined love and told us that love is greater than faith and hope. One of the important truths of today's lesson is that love strengthens our relationships with other believers.

B. Biblical Background

Today's lesson comes from two different passages of Scripture, both of which express the theme of love for other believers. The first is Hebrews 13:1-3, which forms part of the conclusion to the book of Hebrews. The writer listed a series of practical things that believers can do that show their love for one another. In Hebrews 6:10, believers were encouraged to continue serving, because God would never forget their ministries and labors of love among each other. He reminded them not to forget to entertain strangers, because strangers (angels) could be heavenly beings.

The second passage comes from 1 Corinthians 13, which is one of Paul's most prolific writings on the subject of love. First Corinthians 13 is one of the twin peaks of all that the Bible says about love—the other: John 3:16. First Corinthians 13 is the point from which one can go no higher, in describing what love is and what love is not.

Indeed, in the entire Bible, there is no single chapter that discusses love the way this chapter does. Yet, as Warren Weirsbe has said, "Few chapters in the Bible have suffered more misinterpretation and misapplication than 1 Corinthians 13."[1] It is important to see 1 Corinthians 13 in its proper historical and biblical context. When we take this provocative and powerful statement of love out of its biblical context, we end up with a wonderfully sentimental hymn about love that has no real relevance for the relational life in the local church.

II. EXPOSITION AND APPLICATION OF THE SCRIPTURE

A. Practical Guidelines for Showing Love (Hebrews 13:1-3)

LET BROTHERLY love continue. Be not forgetful to entertain strangers: for thereby some have entertained angels unawares. Remember them that are in bonds, as bound with them; and them which suffer adversity, as being yourselves also in the body.

The writer of the book of Hebrews began the chapter with three imperative commands—each with a qualifier. First, they were to keep on loving each other, as brothers. The word translated "love" in this case is *philia*, which refers to the love between brothers and sisters. He appealed to them to continue loving each other, which suggests that they had already demonstrated this matchless virtue.

Second, they must remember to be hospitable, because they never knew if an emissary from God would show up at their door (see Genesis 18:2-10; 19:1-3; Judges 13:15). In the first century, missionaries, evangelists, and even the apostles depended upon fellow believers' extending invitations to reside with them for short periods of time (see Matthew 25:35, 43; Romans 12:13). Hospitality was one of the traits sought in church leaders (see 1 Timothy 3:2).

Third, they were to remember people who were incarcerated by putting themselves in their places. They were to also consider those who were suffering adversity or from some other calamity. Christians who are arrested, convicted of crimes, and put into prison are often forgotten and neglected. One reason for this is our discomfort with being identified with people who have committed crimes. Yet, we are reminded to see ourselves in their places. This passage highlights the importance of prison ministry and the need of congregations to take seriously the words of Jesus in Matthew 25:31-46.

B. Love Is the Primary Thing (1 Corinthians 13:1-3)

THOUGH I speak with the tongues of men and of angels, and have not charity, I am become as sounding brass, or a tinkling cymbal. And though I have the gift of prophecy, and understand all mysteries, and all knowledge; and though I have all faith, so that I could remove mountains, and have not charity, I am nothing. And though I bestow all my goods to feed the poor, and though I give my body to be burned, and have not charity, it profiteth me nothing.

Paul began by using a literary technique called *hyperbole*, or highly exaggerated speech; an example of this is a statement such as "He is as strong as an ox," or, "she is as stubborn as a mule." The person is not really an ox or a mule. The language is exaggerated to make a point. There are several key words in the verse. The word "resounding" (NIV) comes from the Greek word *echeo*, which gives us our English word *echo*. The word *literally* refers to "loud sounds, noises, or roaring such as produced by the sea." These clanging cymbals that are referred to were instruments that were used in the fertility cults and mystery religions of the Corinthian cities.

Paul expressed his thoughts about love in a series of conditional statements that were hypothetical situations—each beginning with "if." In verse 2, Paul lifted three of the most important gifts of the Holy Spirit, or those whom the Corinthians admired the most: the gifts of prophecy, knowledge, and faith. Prophecy referred not so much to being able to predict the future, but to the declaration of the Word of God. New Testament church prophets were preachers who sought to build up the church through inspired preaching. Their messages were fresh revelations from God.

Knowledge, in this case, referred to intellectual knowledge. Paul said that if he had all knowledge—that is, if he knew everything—yet did not have love, then it meant nothing. One may be able to impress people with what he or she knows, but without love this would not mean anything. It is knowledge that puffs up rather than edifies. The Corinthians prided themselves on having intellectual and spiritual knowledge.

One may understand all mysteries. Mystery (in this instance) has to do with something that can only be known by a special revelation from God. There are some things about God that we do not know, cannot know, and never will know in this life. These are what the Bible calls *mysteries*. For instance, the Bible never says where God came from or how He came to be. It is a mystery which can only be revealed to us by God Himself.

Paul said that even if he gave all of his possessions away, it would mean nothing without love. And here the emphasis is not just in giving them away, but giving them in order to feed the poor. There is nothing greater than lifting the poor and helping to meet their many needs. *If I give all of my money and possessions to feed the poor and have not love, then it means nothing.*

Even if he made a martyr out of himself by giving his body to be burned yet had no love, it would mean nothing. Paul said that even if he was offered as a sacrifice or if he voluntarily offered himself as a sacrifice, as did Joan of Arc or Bishop Polycarp—even if he made the ultimate sacrifice: gave not only his possessions, but also his very life—it would still mean nothing without love.

You can give of your resources, give your time, give your energy, or give even your very life to some noble cause, but if you do not have love then the sacrifice means nothing.

C. What Love Is and Is Not (1 Corinthians 13:4-7)

Charity suffereth long, and is kind; charity envieth not; charity vaunteth not itself, is not puffed up, Doth not behave itself unseemly, seeketh not her own, is not easily provoked, thinketh no evil; Rejoiceth not in iniquity, but rejoiceth in the truth; Beareth all things, believeth all things, hopeth all things, endureth all things.

In the next four verses (verses 4-7), Paul pointed out fifteen different ways to describe love in action—because love is not just a passive emotion, but an active response to other human beings. He began by describing the positive traits of love. Love is patient and kind. He listed the things that love is not. Love is not envious. Envy is resentment toward others for their good fortune or blessings. Love is not boastful or arrogant. Love is not proud, or filled with unfounded self-confidence. Love is not ill-mannered, or blatantly disrespectful for the customs and practices of other people. Love is not selfish, nor does love display an attitude of "me first" at all costs—at all times. Love is not easily provoked to anger, which is the picture of a person who is able to keep his or her emotions under control. Love does not think evil by keeping a record of wrongs. Love does not delight in evil—which, conversely, is the picture of a man or woman who relishes the failure of others. The contrast to delighting in another's downfall is to rejoice with him or her when he or she has sought to live right.

Believers who love deeply and genuinely will always do what is best in protecting others. In other words, the word *protecting* has in it the idea of not needlessly exposing the faults and failures of others. Trusting always refers to being open and not suspicious of everything and everyone. Hoping always is having an attitude of optimism about the outcome of every situation that believers face, even when they fail in their personal lives. Perseverance and learning to put up with the negative attitudes of others are much-needed traits among believers.

These verses provide a descriptive analysis of what love is and what love is not. They provide for us a profile of the kind of behavior that love produces in the heart and life of every true believer.

D. Love Never Fails
(1 Corinthians 13:8-13)

Charity never faileth: but whether there be prophecies, they shall fail; whether there be tongues, they shall cease; whether there be knowledge, it shall vanish away. For we know in part, and we prophesy in part. But when that which is perfect is come, then that which is in part shall be done away. When I was a child, I spake as a child, I understood as a child, I thought as a child: but when I became a man, I put away childish things. For now we see through a glass, darkly; but then face to face: now I know in part; but then shall I know even as also I am known. And now abideth faith, hope, charity, these three; but the greatest of these is charity.

In verse 8, *love* is the supreme Christian virtue because it mirrors the very heart of God. The phrase "Love never fails" (NIV) literally means that love "never falls." Unlike God's love—which will never fail—the things that the Corinthians coveted the most were transitory. Prophecies, speaking in tongues, and knowledge were all gifts given by the Holy Spirit that would one day pass away.

In verses 9-12, we are told that at our very best, prophecy and any knowledge that we have is very limited. Although he did not explicitly state it, perfection refers to Jesus Christ, who will one day come in glorious majesty. At that time, the gifts that believers have depended upon will no longer be needed. Paul explained what he meant with two illustrations. First, he pointed out that when he was a child, he talked, reasoned, and thought as a child—but as an adult, he no longer behaved in that manner. The second illustration is of a person looking into a mirror. The Corinthians were very well known for their mirrors and hence this example would have been easily understood. Even their best mirrors only provided a visual image of the real person. Only when one comes face-to-face with the living Christ will he or she know fully the joys of God's eternal presence.

Paul concluded his discussion about love by reminding the Corinthians that when all of the other gifts have been done away with, faith, hope, and love would remain. *Faith* refers to the trust that leads to salvation (see Ephesians 2:8-10; compare with Hebrews 11:1-7; 1 John 4:7-18). *Hope* is the expectation of eternal salvation and life with God in heaven (see Romans 8:24-25; 1 Peter 1:3-5). *Love* (Greek: *agape*) is the greatest of these virtues because it is the first in the list of the fruit of the Spirit (see Galatians 5:22). It is best portrayed in the love that the Father has for the Son and the Son for the Father (see John 15:10; 17:26).

III. CONCLUDING REFLECTION

Life in the Spirit reaches its zenith when believers genuinely and authentically love each other—regardless of their mistakes, the wrongs inflicted against them, or the attitudes we may have toward them. It is much easier to talk about this virtue than to live it out. Yet, we can never be fully and truly who we say we are while looking for excuses to dismiss our responsibility to love others. Try to make love a priority in your church and ministry with those whom you find to be the most unlovable.

PRAYER

Lord God, grant that our love will go beyond mere words. Teach us to love those who hate us, despitefully use us, and persecute us. Grant us the peace of mind to never be moved by their acts of disdain toward us. In Jesus' name we pray. Amen.

WORD POWER

Love (Greek: *agape* [agapao])—one of the most important theological terms in the New Testament. It is used 143 times as a verb and 116 times as a noun. The New Testament's love has its origin in the Old Testament commandments for one to love God and neighbor as him- or herself (see Deuteronomy 6:5; Leviticus 19:18). At its heart, it expresses the kind of love that seeks to give without the need to experience reciprocity. Love was the scriptural framework upon which hung the ethical teachings of Jesus regarding love of God and love of neighbor (see Matthew 5:44; 22:36-38; John 13:34-35; Romans 5:8). Love was the foundational cornerstone of the social life of the early Christian communities (see Galatians 5:6, 13-14, 22; Ephesians 4:2; 5:2, 25, 28; Philippians 2:2; 1 Thessalonians 3:12).

HOME DAILY BIBLE READINGS
(September 24-30, 2012)

Faith Requires Mutual Love

MONDAY, September 24: "I Love You, O Lord" (Psalm 18:1-6)

TUESDAY, September 25: "Faithful Love" (Deuteronomy 7:7-11)

WEDNESDAY, September 26: "Obedient Love" (Deuteronomy 5:6-10)

THURSDAY, September 27: "Taught to Love" (Deuteronomy 6:1-9)

FRIDAY, September 28: "Love One Another" (John 13:31-35)

SATURDAY, September 29: "Love Your Enemies" (Luke 6:27-36)

SUNDAY, September 30: "Faith, Hope, and Love" (Hebrews 13:1-3; 1 Corinthians 13)

End Note

[1] Warren Weirsbe, *Be Wise: 1 Corinthians,* (Wheaton, Ill.: Victor Books, 1983), p. 130.

LESSON 6   October 7, 2012

STEPHEN'S ARREST AND SPEECH

FAITH PATHWAY/FAITH JOURNEY TOPIC: **Courage to Speak**

DEVOTIONAL READING: **Proverbs 8:1-11**   BACKGROUND SCRIPTURE: **Acts 6:8–7:53**
PRINT PASSAGE: **Acts 6:8-15; 7:1-2a**   KEY VERSE: **Acts 6:8**

Acts 6:8-15; 7:1-2a—KJV

8 And Stephen, full of faith and power, did great wonders and miracles among the people.

9 Then there arose certain of the synagogue, which is called the synagogue of the Libertines, and Cyrenians, and Alexandrians, and of them of Cilicia and of Asia, disputing with Stephen.

10 And they were not able to resist the wisdom and the spirit by which he spake.

11 Then they suborned men, which said, We have heard him speak blasphemous words against Moses, and against God.

12 And they stirred up the people, and the elders, and the scribes, and came upon him, and caught him, and brought him to the council,

13 And set up false witnesses, which said, This man ceaseth not to speak blasphemous words against this holy place, and the law:

14 For we have heard him say, that this Jesus of Nazareth shall destroy this place, and shall change the customs which Moses delivered us.

15 And all that sat in the council, looking stedfastly on him, saw his face as it had been the face of an angel.

.....

THEN SAID the high priest, Are these things so?

2 And he said, Men, brethren, and fathers, hearken.

Acts 6:8-15; 7:1-2a—NIV

8 Now Stephen, a man full of God's grace and power, did great wonders and miraculous signs among the people.

9 Opposition arose, however, from members of the Synagogue of the Freedmen (as it was called)—Jews of Cyrene and Alexandria as well as the provinces of Cilicia and Asia. These men began to argue with Stephen,

10 but they could not stand up against his wisdom or the Spirit by whom he spoke.

11 Then they secretly persuaded some men to say, "We have heard Stephen speak words of blasphemy against Moses and against God."

12 So they stirred up the people and the elders and the teachers of the law. They seized Stephen and brought him before the Sanhedrin.

13 They produced false witnesses, who testified, "This fellow never stops speaking against this holy place and against the law.

14 For we have heard him say that this Jesus of Nazareth will destroy this place and change the customs Moses handed down to us."

15 All who were sitting in the Sanhedrin looked intently at Stephen, and they saw that his face was like the face of an angel.

.....

THEN THE high priest asked him, "Are these charges true?"

2 To this he replied: "Brothers and fathers, listen to me!"

UNIFYING LESSON PRINCIPLE

People need a bold and perceptive leader to articulate truth in times of uncertainty. How can we find courage to speak the truth? Stephen, in the face of opposition, demonstrated the power and wisdom of the Spirit to speak the truth of Christ.

TOPICAL OUTLINE OF THE LESSON

I. Introduction
   A. Courage to Speak the Truth
   B. Biblical Background

II. Exposition and Application of the Scripture
   A. The Power of Stephen's Ministry (Acts 6:8)
   B. The Opposition against Stephen (Acts 6:9-11)
   C. The Charges Brought against Stephen (Acts 6:12-15)
   D. Stephen Responds to the Charges (Acts 7:1-2a)

III. Concluding Reflection

LESSON OBJECTIVES

Upon completion of the lesson, the students will be able to do the following:

1. Identify the risks of leadership that became known in Stephen's witness;
2. Confront the principalities and powers of our day; and,
3. Seek the power and the wisdom of the Spirit in their efforts to speak truth.

POINTS TO BE EMPHASIZED

ADULT/YOUTH

Adult Topic: **Courage to Speak**
Youth Topic: **Speak Up!**
Adult Key Verse: **Acts 6:8**
Youth Key Verse: **Acts 6:10**
Print Passage: **Acts 6:8-15; 7:1-2a**

—Stephen distinguished himself by his faith.
—After the apostles laid hands on Stephen, he was empowered by the Spirit to perform miracles and boldly proclaim the Gospel (see Acts 6:5-6).
—To the religious leadership, Stephen's statements sounded blasphemous, so he was brought before the Sanhedrin, the Jewish high council made up of Pharisees and Sadducees.
—In his speech (see Acts 7:2-53), Stephen summarized the history of the Jews' relationship with God. He discussed Abraham, Moses, Joshua, David, and Solomon.
—Stephen was undeterred by the opposition he faced from those in the synagogue.

CHILDREN

Children Topic: **Speaking of Faith**
Key Verse: **Acts 6:10**
Print Passage: **Acts 6:8-15**

—Stephen, a faithful follower of Jesus Christ, performed many miracles among the people.
—Among those who heard Stephen speak were persons who were intent on arguing with him.
—Those who argued with Stephen were not able to stand up to the wisdom and power with which he spoke.
—Stephen's enemies instigated others to accuse him of wrongdoing and eventually brought him before the religious council on a false charge.
—As Stephen stood before the council, he had an angelic appearance.

I. INTRODUCTION

A. Courage to Speak the Truth

Standing up to powerful people can be extremely intimidating. Throughout history, there have been men and women who cast aside concerns for their personal safety and welfare for the sake of a larger good. Rosa Parks was such a woman; consequently, she has been called the "Mother of the Civil Rights Movement." On December 1, 1955, she took a courageous stand against the Montgomery City Code that supported unjust segregation laws against African Americans. Eventually, her courage and determination not to yield her dignity led to the Montgomery Bus Boycott—which lasted for a year and a half and all but crippled the Montgomery Bus Company. Eventually, the Jim Crow laws were declared to be unconstitutional and new laws were enacted that ended racial discrimination and segregation on public transportation in Alabama. The Montgomery Bus Boycott was one of the most effective strategies of the Civil Rights Movement and was the catalyst that gave rise to the role of Dr. Martin Luther King Jr. as a leader in the movement to end racial discrimination and injustice in America.

In the lesson today, we see an example of a Christian leader who was courageous under pressure. Christians want and need leaders who are bold, perceptive, and able to articulate truth in times of uncertainty. How can we find the courage to speak the truth? Stephen, in the face of opposition, demonstrated the power and wisdom of the Spirit to speak the truth of Christ, even at the risk of his own life.

B. Biblical Background

The Word of God is rich with examples of men and women who stood as pillars of righteousness and justice. In the early church, there were men and women who sought and received the help of the Holy Spirit to preach and teach the Word of God with boldness (see Acts 4:29; 13:36; 18:26; Ephesians 6:19; Philippians 1:4; 1 Thessalonians 2:2). Today's lesson introduces us to Stephen, one of the early church's pillars of righteousness and faithfulness. Stephen was one of the seven Hellenistic (foreign-born) Jews described as being chosen (in Acts 6:5) to oversee the food distribution to the widows of the Christian community in Jerusalem. He is first introduced, along with the other six, as a man "full of faith and of the Holy Spirit" (Acts 6:5, NIV). Stephen's ministry was accompanied by enormous successes, which soon aroused jealousy and suspicion from the members of the Synagogue of Freedmen. This group of conspirators persuaded some men to lie against Stephen, saying that they heard him speak words of blasphemy against Moses and against God. He was hauled before the Sanhedrin and tried on charges of blasphemy. Eventually, he was stoned to death (see Acts 7:54-59). One of the principles taught in this lesson is that when church leaders are filled with the Holy Spirit, they live and lead in such a way that God can use them in mighty and powerful ways.

II. EXPOSITION AND APPLICATION OF THE SCRIPTURE

A. The Power of Stephen's Ministry
(Acts 6:8)

And Stephen, full of faith and power, did great wonders and miracles among the people.

The name *Stephen* means "crowned." His was the first name listed in verse 5 when the disciples chose seven men to look after the widows and administer the daily distribution of food. In this verse, we learn two important facts about the life of Stephen. First, we see something of his personal character. Second, we see him working miracles and signs among the people. One of the reasons why he was chosen to serve the church was because he was full of the Holy Spirit and faith. Additional information is provided about his character in this verse. He was full of grace and power. The Greek word used in both verses is *pleres,* which means "to be complete" or "filled to the brim." As a Spirit-filled man, this meant that his life was completely submitted to the Lord Jesus Christ. Grace is translated from *charis* and denotes God's favorable presence in his life. "Power" is translated from *dunamis* and denotes the divinely given ability to see a matter or situation through to its completion. Stephen was described as performing great wonders and miraculous signs. We are not told what they were, but they caught the attention of the Jewish leaders.

Church leaders must have impeccable personal character and a determined commitment to carry out the biblical mission and ministry of the church (see Matthew 25:31-46; 28:19-20).

B. The Opposition against Stephen
(Acts 6:9-11)

Then there arose certain of the synagogue, which is called the synagogue of the Libertines, and Cyrenians, and Alexandrians, and of them of Cilicia and of Asia, disputing with Stephen. And they were not able to resist the wisdom and the spirit by which he spake. Then they suborned men, which said, We have heard him speak blasphemous words against Moses, and against God.

The ministry of Stephen did not go unnoticed by the religious leaders in Jerusalem, particularly among those who frequented the Synagogue of the Freedmen. These were Jewish men who had come from several major cities in North Africa and the Mediterranean basin (see Acts 2:9-10; 11:20; compare also Acts 16:9; 18:24; 27:7). The effectiveness and breadth of Stephen's success fueled a rising tide of resentment against him. The word *opposition* is translated from the Greek word *anistemi,* and with it comes the idea of giving birth to something. Freedman comes from the Greek word *libertine.* "Libertine denotes Jews (according to Philo) who had been made captives of the Romans under Pompey, but were afterwards set free; and who, although they had fixed their abode in Rome, had built at their own expense a synagogue at Jerusalem which they frequented when in that city. The name Libertines adhered to distinguish them from free-born Jews who had subsequently taken up their residence at Rome."[1] It is possible that Saul may have been a member of this particular synagogue—since he was of the province of Cilicia (see Acts 21:39).

Stephen was steeped in the Word of God. He successfully fended off every attack leveled against the Gospel and the name of the Lord Jesus Christ (see verse 10). He is described as being gifted with wisdom (Greek: *sophia*), a combination of intelligence and prudence that enabled him to speak with persuasion and power. At every turn and with each new challenge, the Holy Spirit gave him the word for that moment (see John 14:26; compare also Matthew 10:17-20; Luke 21:13-15). We never have to search for the right words—the Holy Spirit will always give us the words that will speak to that very moment. Not only is He the inspiration behind the written Word, but also the spoken Word as well (see Acts 4:8, 31).

Not to be outdone nor publicly humiliated by Stephen, the Freedmen devised a secret plan to have Stephen arrested and tried on trumped-up charges (verse 11). The word *persuaded* is translated from *hupballo* and is a very strong word. It means "to instigate, bribe, or even suggest what is to be said." This word also gives us the English word *hyperbole*, which means "exaggerated speech." The Freedmen persuaded some men to make claims that were not true . They lied, saying that they heard with their own ears Stephen speaking against Moses and God (see John 9:29; compare with John 5:45-47). They accused Stephen of attacking the very heart of Judaism. These charges, if true, would be serious and would warrant the penalty of death by stoning.

Why would they suggest the name of Moses? Primarily because the Sadducees, the men who ran the Temple, only believed that the first five books of the Old Testament were authoritative for the Jews. And since Moses was the author of the Law, it would be an attack at the very heart of what they held to be dear—to say nothing of invoking the name of God as being the object of blasphemous speech.

How often does this happen in churches where groups of people become incensed about change or other innovative ministry initiatives? Those who seek to maintain the status quo and keep things the same often find it difficult to support new movements by God. Thus, they will orchestrate resistance and even raise false or weak allegations to bring against a leader.

C. The Charges Brought against Stephen (Acts 6:12-15)

And they stirred up the people, and the elders, and the scribes, and came upon him, and caught him, and brought him to the council, And set up false witnesses, which said, This man ceaseth not to speak blasphemous words against this holy place, and the law: For we have heard him say, that this Jesus of Nazareth shall destroy this place, and shall change the customs which Moses delivered us. And all that sat in the council, looking stedfastly on him, saw his face as it had been the face of an angel.

The plan of the Freedmen was to arouse the passions and anger of all of the major stakeholders in the Temple religion. They aroused the people—those who attended the daily prayer services at the Temple and offered the sacrifices. The second group was the elders, who were the Sadducees. These were the men who ran the Temple religion, oversaw the day-to-day operation, and stood to lose the most if the sacrifices ceased and the Temple religion collapsed. The third group was the teachers of the law, who were the Pharisees. They seized Stephen, which suggests that the Freedmen went looking for Stephen for the express purpose of bringing him before the Sanhedrin, which was the Jewish high court.

In order to make their case credible, they produced false witnesses, whose identities remain a mystery. The Freedmen were guilty of the very law that they accused Stephen of violating (see Exodus 20:16; compare with Psalms 27:11; 35:11; 56:5). Stephen was accused of constantly speaking against the Temple and the Law. This would be a clear threat to the dominance and control of the Temple by the Sadducees and Pharisees.

Throughout their conspiracy, the Freedmen made it clear that not only had their false witnesses heard these false allegations, but they themselves had also been witnesses to the words of Stephen.

The Freedmen took the time to plan and hatch a carefully developed plot to discredit the work of the Holy Spirit in their midst. One of the most difficult challenges facing many congregations today is the inability to change and break free of traditional customs and practices that hinder and restrict growth. In almost every congregation, there are men and women who are so deeply entangled in their traditions and customs that change is not an option. How often have we allowed our traditions to get in the way of what God wants to do in the midst of people? How does a congregation break free of the restricting presence of traditionalism? First, by recognizing that God is not restricted to a certain time period and that He is free to do as He pleases in every generation; second, by simply being open to new ways of doing ministry in this generation. In the lesson, the Freedmen saw only one way to function, and anyone who advocated a different approach to reaching people and sharing the Word of God was a threat.

Stephen never allowed the accusations and false charges to change his demeanor. The members of the Council looked for a reaction. Would he be fearful? Would Stephen admit some wrongdoing and look for mercy? Would he lash out against them? He held no bitterness nor was there anger in his eyes. He had the look of an angel. The Holy Spirit gave him a spirit of peace and a calmness that comes only from walking with Him.

D. Stephen Responds to the Charges (Acts 7:1-2a)

THEN SAID the high priest, Are these things so? And he said, Men, brethren, and fathers, hearken.

Chapter 7 contains the speech that Stephen gave before the Sanhedrin and that ultimately led to his being stoned to death. It is one of the few speeches in the New Testament that is given by a non-apostle. The high priest at the time was Caiaphas, the same man who was high priest during the arrest and trial of Jesus and the apostles (see John 18:24; Acts 4:6-7; 5:26-28). After looking at Stephen and sensing no reaction that indicated a spirit of fear, the high priest asked him to defend himself. Were the charges true? Stephen addressed the council, not as antagonists, but as brothers and fathers. He did not see them as his enemies, but as family.

What happens when we are accused falsely? How will we respond to those whose intentions are to destroy us or discredit our names? Stephen's example shows us how men and women filled with the Holy Spirit respond in a spirit of love toward those who are against them.

III. CONCLUDING REFLECTION

Believers who seek to be faithful to their calling, who are filled with the Holy Spirit, and who are empowered to witness know that their lives will not always be easy. As followers of the Lord Jesus Christ, we will be held accountable for how we have defended the Gospel message in the face of opposition and criticism. You may find yourself facing a battery of false accusations and slander, but remember that the Holy Spirit is the one who keeps our hearts and minds in the presence of danger. Take your stand today for righteousness and the message of the Gospel.

PRAYER

Lord God, grant that Your servants will be filled with the spirit of courage when we are called to face the opponents of Your kingdom. Grant us the wisdom to be able to answer those who would seek to discredit the work of the church. In Jesus' name we pray. Amen.

WORD POWER

Sadducees—members of the wealthy class. They were the chief holders of the office of the high priest. They were the rulers of the party and many were members of the influential families of Jerusalem. There has been much disagreement among scholars over the exact origin of the party. The Sadducees traced their heritage back to the time of King Solomon, to the priestly family of Zadok, who was installed as high priest during the dedication of the Temple (see 1 Kings 2:35). One of the most notable priests of this family tradition was Caiaphas, who traced his family back to Zadok. The Sadducees are mentioned only in the Synoptic Gospels and the Acts of the Apostles (see Matthew 3:7; 16:1-12; 22:23-34; Mark 12:18-27; Luke 20:27-40; Acts 4:1; 5:17; 23:6-8).

HOME DAILY BIBLE READINGS
(October 1-7, 2012)

Stephen's Arrest and Speech
MONDAY, October 1: "Barriers between You and Your God" (Isaiah 59:1-8)
TUESDAY, October 2: "Falsehood, Deceit, and Deception" (Jeremiah 8:22–9:9)
WEDNESDAY, October 3: "These Things You Shall Do" (Zechariah 8:14-19)
THURSDAY, October 4: "My Mouth Will Utter Truth" (Proverbs 8:1-11)
FRIDAY, October 5: "Guided into All the Truth" (John 16:12-15)
SATURDAY, October 6: "Full of Faith and the Spirit" (Acts 6:1-7)
SUNDAY, October 7: "Full of Grace and Power" (Acts 6:8–7:2a)

End Note

[1]*Bibleworks7* (Norfolk, VA: Bibleworks, LLC, 1992–2005).

STEPHEN'S MARTYRDOM

FAITH PATHWAY/FAITH JOURNEY TOPIC: Paying the Price

DEVOTIONAL READING: **Ephesians 6:13-20**
PRINT PASSAGE: **Acts 7:51-60; 8:1a**

BACKGROUND SCRIPTURE: **Acts 7:1–8:1a**
KEY VERSE: **Acts 7:59**

Acts 7:51-60; 8:1a—KJV

51 Ye stiffnecked and uncircumcised in heart and ears, ye do always resist the Holy Ghost: as your fathers did, so do ye.

52 Which of the prophets have not your fathers persecuted? and they have slain them which shewed before of the coming of the Just One; of whom ye have been now the betrayers and murderers:

53 Who have received the law by the disposition of angels, and have not kept it.

54 When they heard these things, they were cut to the heart, and they gnashed on him with their teeth.

55 But he, being full of the Holy Ghost, looked up stedfastly into heaven, and saw the glory of God, and Jesus standing on the right hand of God,

56 And said, Behold, I see the heavens opened, and the Son of man standing on the right hand of God.

57 Then they cried out with a loud voice, and stopped their ears, and ran upon him with one accord,

58 And cast him out of the city, and stoned him: and the witnesses laid down their clothes at a young man's feet, whose name was Saul.

59 And they stoned Stephen, calling upon God, and saying, Lord Jesus, receive my spirit.

60 And he kneeled down, and cried with a loud voice, Lord, lay not this sin to their charge. And when he had said this, he fell asleep.

.....

AND SAUL was consenting unto his death.

Acts 7:51-60; 8:1a—NIV

51 "You stiff-necked people, with uncircumcised hearts and ears! You are just like your fathers: You always resist the Holy Spirit!

52 Was there ever a prophet your fathers did not persecute? They even killed those who predicted the coming of the Righteous One. And now you have betrayed and murdered him—

53 you who have received the law that was put into effect through angels but have not obeyed it."

54 When they heard this, they were furious and gnashed their teeth at him.

55 But Stephen, full of the Holy Spirit, looked up to heaven and saw the glory of God, and Jesus standing at the right hand of God.

56 "Look," he said, "I see heaven open and the Son of Man standing at the right hand of God."

57 At this they covered their ears and, yelling at the top of their voices, they all rushed at him,

58 dragged him out of the city and began to stone him. Meanwhile, the witnesses laid their clothes at the feet of a young man named Saul.

59 While they were stoning him, Stephen prayed, "Lord Jesus, receive my spirit."

60 Then he fell on his knees and cried out, "Lord, do not hold this sin against them." When he had said this, he fell asleep.

.....

AND SAUL was there, giving approval to his death.

UNIFYING LESSON PRINCIPLE

When strong leaders confront traditional ideas, their words may incite anger and violence. What causes such violent reactions? Stephen's criticism of the religious establishment and his exaltation of Christ enraged the religious leaders, and they stoned him to death.

TOPICAL OUTLINE OF THE LESSON

I. Introduction
    A. The Challenge of Change
    B. Biblical Background

II. Exposition and Application of the Scripture
    A. The Charges of Stephen (Acts 7:51-53)
    B. Reactions to the Charges of Stephen (Acts 7:54-58)
    C. Stephen Is Stoned to Death (Acts 7:59-60; 8:1a)

III. Concluding Reflection

LESSON OBJECTIVES

Upon completion of the lesson, the students will be able to do the following:

1. List the reasons for Stephen's martyrdom;
2. Explain how they feel when their beliefs are attacked; and,
3. Give their personal testimonies about their reasons for serving the Lord Jesus Christ.

POINTS TO BE EMPHASIZED

ADULT/YOUTH

Adult Topic: Paying the Price
Youth Topic: Take a Stand
Adult Key Verse: Acts 7:59
Youth Key Verse: Acts 7:56
Print Passage: Acts 7:51-60; 8:1a

—The Sanhedrin's charge against Stephen was blasphemy (see Acts 6:11).
—Instead of pleading with the council to let him go, Stephen took the opportunity to clarify his message. His speech was the longest in the book of Acts, and it caused him to be the first Christian martyr.
—The spread of Christianity after Stephen's death meant that more people were joining the movement, including Gentiles who heard the Gospel as it spread farther.
—The religious leaders had a long history of opposing and persecuting God's prophets.
—The penalty for blasphemy was death by stoning (see Leviticus 24:14).
—When Stephen saw Jesus standing at the right hand of God, it validated his message to the leaders.
—In the midst of being stoned, Stephen asked God to forgive his enemies.

CHILDREN

Children Topic: Stephen Faces Death
Key Verse: Acts 7:59

Print Passage: Acts 7:51-60

—Stephen rebuked his listeners for their hard-heartedness and failure to obey God.

—Stephen charged that the prophets previously sent by God were persecuted and slain by his listeners' ancestors.

—Stephen's charges against them made his hearers angry.

—Stephen remained calm and filled with the Spirit during this confrontation.

—God gave Stephen a vision of heaven's grandeur.

—Stephen's speech prompted the people to stone him.

I. INTRODUCTION

A. The Challenge of Change

A very poor holy man lived in a remote part of China. Every day before his time of meditation, in order to show his devotion, he would put a dish of butter up on the window sill as an offering to God, since food was so scarce. One day, his cat came in and ate the butter. To remedy this, he began tying the cat to the bedpost each day before the quiet time. This man was so revered for his piety that others joined him as disciples and worshipped as he did. Generations later, long after the holy man was dead, his followers placed an offering of butter on the window sill during their time of prayer and meditation. Furthermore, each one bought a cat and tied it to the bedpost.[1]

How often have congregations become wedded to religious practices that are historically rooted, but have no contemporary relevance? Attempts to make the practices more relevant are often met with stiff resistance in many traditional denominational churches. Congregational change is one of the major challenges facing the Christian church in the twenty-first century. Many congregations have been torn asunder by failed attempts to lead the people to embrace a new vision for the future. Old traditions die very hard in the church, and often congregations find themselves doing things that may make no sense at all. Congregations that seek to change have to be clear about the differences between Christian traditions that are mandated and supported by Scripture and those that are developed and designed by humans. When strong leaders confront traditional ideas, their words may incite anger and violence. What causes such violent reactions? Stephen's criticism of the religious establishment and his exaltation of Christ enraged the religious leaders—hence, they stoned him to death.

B. Biblical Background

In the previous lesson, Stephen had been forcefully seized by the members of the Synagogue of the Freedmen. Beginning in Acts 7:2-50, he began a lengthy defense of his ministry and message, answering all of the charges leveled against him. At that time, he was accused of committing blasphemy and wanting to destroy the traditions that Moses had handed down to them (see Acts 6:11, 14). Stephen believed that the Jews had falsely accused and mistreated many of the prophets and had killed the most important of all of the prophets—Jesus the Messiah. When Stephen raised this accusation against the religious system, he insinuated that the Jewish people had been unfaithful to God and a hindrance to God's mission. Then instead of pleading with the Council to let him go, Stephen took the opportunity to clarify his message. His speech is the longest in the book of Acts and it led to his being the first Christian martyr.

Within a few days of Stephen's stoning, Christians came under severe and unrelenting persecution by the Jews. However, there was one unanticipated consequence of the persecution: the Christian faith began to spread and make huge inroads into Gentile communities. As Christians moved away from Jerusalem and Israel, they carried the message of the Gospel with them, ensuring that Christianity would no longer be a small Jewish sect, based in Jerusalem. In Acts 8:1-3, we meet Saul of Tarsus for the first time, as we are shown Luke's role in the early days of the church's persecution.

II. EXPOSITION AND APPLICATION OF THE SCRIPTURE

A. The Charges of Stephen
(Acts 7:51-53)

Ye stiffnecked and uncircumcised in heart and ears, ye do always resist the Holy Ghost: as your fathers did, so do ye. Which of the prophets have not your fathers persecuted? and they have slain them which shewed before of the coming of the Just One; of whom ye have been now the betrayers and murderers: Who have received the law by the disposition of angels, and have not kept it.

Stephen said that the Jewish religious leaders were no different from their fathers—a reference to those whom God brought out of the land of Egypt. Stephen leveled three very serious charges against the Jewish religious leaders. First, he called them a "stiff-necked people." This is the very same charge that God leveled against the ancient Israelites when He brought them out of Egypt (see 32:9). Being stiff-necked is also a metaphor that describes Israel's rebellion and resistance to living according to the Torah (Law). Their rebellion was one of the reasons why they lived in the wilderness for forty years.

Second, their hearts and ears were uncircumcised. Circumcision was a sign of the covenant and was symbolic of their being true descendants of Abraham (see Genesis 17:1-14). Here, it is used as a metaphor to describe the callousness of their hearts and their failure to hear and obey God's Word.

Third, they resisted the presence and power of the Holy Spirit. The Holy Spirit is the third person in the Godhead, the One from whom we seek guidance and comfort (see John 14:16, 26; 15:26; 16:7). The Jewish religious leaders revealed that their faith was more naturally derived than guided by the Holy Spirit (see 1 Corinthians 2:12-14).

The description of Stephen's charge points out how religion can become more of a show and outward expression than a matter of the heart (see Matthew 23:13-33; Luke 18:9-14). In thousands of churches across America, people gather to perform their duties without affirming their relationship to Jesus Christ.

Verse 52 begins with a rhetorical question followed by an implied answer: "Yes, our fathers did persecute the prophets." The prophets were often ostracized and persecuted for their preaching, and some were even killed (see 1 Kings 19:10; 2 Chronicles 24:19-22; Jeremiah 2:30; 20:2; 26:23). The prophets were persecuted because of their pronouncements against Israel's worship of idols and especially the Canaanite god, Baal. Not only did they persecute the prophets, but Stephen said they were guilty of killing the very ones who foretold of the coming Messiah. And future generations had betrayed the very Messiah whom God sent as Savior—and even killed Him. The irony of Israel's history lay in her being privileged to receive the very Word of God, but not obeying it.

B. Reactions to the Charges of Stephen (Acts 7:54-58)

When they heard these things, they were cut to the heart, and they gnashed on him with their teeth. But he, being full of the Holy Ghost, looked up stedfastly into heaven, and saw the glory of God, and Jesus standing on the right hand of God, And said, Behold, I see the heavens opened, and the Son of man standing on the right hand of God. Then they cried out with a loud voice, and stopped their ears, and ran upon him with one accord, And cast him out of the city, and stoned him: and the witnesses laid down their clothes at a young man's feet, whose name was Saul.

The Jewish religious leaders were seething with rage as they listened to Stephen's speech. He had told them their history (beginning with their chief patriarch, Abraham), saying that they were no more than a band of murderers. The more he spoke, the angrier they grew. *Furious* is not a word which can completely capture the thought of the Greek (*dieprionto*

tais kardiais), which conveys an image of someone cutting a man's heart into two pieces. Their anger was manifested through gnashing their teeth. "Gnashing of teeth" is "an expression of strong and often violent anger, rage, or fury that can boil over into an all-out attack, usually physical, at any moment."[2]

In contrast to the Jewish religious leaders, Stephen was filled with the Holy Spirit (see Acts 2:4; 4:8; 13:9). Stephen was about to become the first Christian martyr and a witness to the resurrected Christ. He looked up to heaven and saw the Shekinah of God, with Jesus standing at the right hand of God (see Psalms 109:31; 110:1; Romans 8:34; Hebrews 1:3; 8:1; 10:12; 12:2). Was this real or imagined? Stephen's seeing the glory of God was not unlike Isaiah's vision of God's presence in the year of Uzziah's death (see Isaiah 6:1-3; Ezekiel 1:1; compare Revelation 4:1ff.). Not only did Isaiah see the glory of God, but more importantly, he also saw the Lord Jesus Christ standing on the right hand of God. When Jesus stood, it was a sign of two things. First, Stephen did not need to fear what was about to happen to him, because Jesus Himself had faced a similar, more horrifying fate and had been raised from the dead. Second, the opening of heaven was a sign of God's approval of Stephen's faithfulness. Stephen was sure to die, but he had reached the pinnacle of faithfulness to God. In Stephen's martyrdom, we have an example of how to remain steadfast and immovable in the face of entrenched opposition.

Verse 56 gives the details of what became the final words that pushed the Jewish religious leaders over the edge and turned a group of religious holy men into an angry mob. When Stephen revealed that he saw the Son of Man—

a clear reference to Jesus of Nazareth and words with which they were all too familiar—this was all that was needed to confirm their charge that He had committed blasphemy. How could Stephen expect to gain a favorable hearing by mixing the name of God with the name of a man whom they had crucified between two criminals (see Luke 23:33)? With Stephen's stoning, we see the close correlation between the arrest, trial, and crucifixion of Jesus and the arrest, trial, and martyrdom of Stephen.

Finally, they had heard enough. Covering their ears and yelling at the top of their voices, they rushed Stephen (see verse 57). Who? The people, the elders, and the teachers of the Law (see Acts 6:12). He was not allowed to walk; they dragged him out of the city, which testified to their anger. According to the Law, all executions had to take place outside of the city walls (see Numbers 15:35; Leviticus 24:11-14; 1 Kings 21:13). John Polhill noted that, "In formal stoning, victims were stripped and pushed over a cliff ten-to twelve-feet high. They were then rolled over on their chests, and the first witness pushed a boulder (as large a stone as he could manage) from the cliff above."[3] This process continued until the victim was dead. In Stephen's case, there was no order to the leaders' violence.

The executioners took off their clothes (more than likely their outer garments and cloaks) so that they might freely hurl stones at Stephen. Luke recorded that a young man by the name of Saul was present, and that it was at his feet that they laid their garments. Saul was his Hebrew name, and Paul was his Greek name (see Acts 13:9). This same Saul would later become the champion of the very same faith that he sought to extinguish. Later in his own ministry, Paul would admit to having committed the greatest of sins, which was persecuting the church (see Philippians 3:6).

C. Stephen Is Stoned to Death
(Acts 7:59-60; 8:1a)

And they stoned Stephen, calling upon God, and saying, Lord Jesus, receive my spirit. And he kneeled down, and cried with a loud voice, Lord, lay not this sin to their charge. And when he had said this, he fell asleep. ...AND SAUL was consenting unto his death.

Stephen did not die in fear, pleading for his life. He did not curse his attackers and ask God to send down fire or legions of angels. Quite the contrary—Stephen prayed, even as they were stoning him. Stephen died like his Lord, with courage and steadfast faith. Jesus prayed to the Father; later, Stephen prayed to the Lord Jesus Christ to receive his spirit (see Luke 23:46). With his dying breath, he fell to his knees and cried out, asking for forgiveness of those who were his executioners (see Luke 23:34).

We are not told whether or not the men who stoned Stephen heard his cries for their forgiveness. It is more than likely that they did hear Stephen's last words. Luke stated that Saul was not only watching their coats, but also, he was there giving approval to what was being done. Is it possible that Stephen's death and the staunch manner in which he faced his final moments became indelibly etched into Saul's mind? Many years later, Paul would remember this very incident when he stood before the same tribunal to account for his own preaching of the Gospel (see Acts 22:20).

III. CONCLUDING REFLECTION

One of the challenges of American Christianity is the difficulty of relating to people and places where the Gospel is not welcome. In America, there are no vigilante squads roaming about the cities to snatch anyone who names Jesus Christ as Lord. Quite the contrary—the church has at times become a comfortable co-conspirator with the powers that seek to deny the lordship of Jesus Christ. The voice of protest against the rampant injustices perpetrated by the wealthy and powerful has all but vanished from American pulpits. Stephen taught that there may come a time and point in our lives when we are forced to choose whom we will stand for and what we willingly sacrifice our lives for. The key to living such a courageous life is recognizing that the persons we are as Christians is deeply rooted in being filled with the Holy Spirit. We will never be able to do what Stephen did until/unless we are willing to become who Stephen sought to be and how he sought to live his life—as a disciple of the Lord Jesus Christ.

PRAYER

Lord God Almighty, teach us to trust You in all matters of faith and life. May what we believe translate into actions that reveal that we have been with You. In Jesus' name we pray. Amen.

WORD POWER

Son of Man—a title that is rich in use, both in the canonical Scriptures and the non-canonical writings. In Hebrew and Aramaic, it is an idiom for "man" in all of his humanness. There is a richness about the term that is found throughout the Old Testament, especially in the book of Daniel—where it has eschatological overtones and refers to the coming Messiah (see Daniel 7:13). It appears 249 times in the New Testament and is used by Jesus to specifically refer to Himself. At its root, the title refers to Jesus as the one who came, did the Father's will, and now serves as the advocate for His church in heaven.

HOME DAILY BIBLE READINGS
(October 8-14, 2012)

Stephen's Martyrdom
MONDAY, October 8: "Equipped to Speak Boldly" (Ephesians 6:13-20)
TUESDAY, October 9: "The Promised Fulfillment Draws Near" (Acts 7:17-22)
WEDNESDAY, October 10: "I Have Come to Rescue Them" (Acts 7:30-34)
THURSDAY, October 11: "The Rejection of Moses" (Acts 7:35-39)
FRIDAY, October 12: "The Rejection of God" (Acts 7:39-43)
SATURDAY, October 13: "The Inadequacy of the Temple" (Acts 7:44-50)
SUNDAY, October 14: "You Are the Ones" (Acts 7:51–8:1a)

End Notes

[1] Source Unknown, taken from www.HigherPraise.com, 10,000 Illustrations. (Copyright 1999).
[2] *Dictionary of Biblical Imagery,* (1998), s.v. "Teeth."
[3] John B. Polhill, *Acts: The New American Commentary* (Nashville: Broadman Press, 1992), p. 209.

SIMON WANTS TO BUY POWER

FAITH PATHWAY/FAITH JOURNEY TOPIC: **Power Brokers**

DEVOTIONAL READING: **1 Corinthians 1:18-25**
PRINT PASSAGE: ACTS **8:9-24**

BACKGROUND SCRIPTURE: **Acts 8:4-24**
KEY VERSE: **Acts 8:18**

Acts 8:9-24—KJV

9 But there was a certain man, called Simon, which beforetime in the same city used sorcery, and bewitched the people of Samaria, giving out that himself was some great one:

10 To whom they all gave heed, from the least to the greatest, saying, This man is the great power of God.

11 And to him they had regard, because that of long time he had bewitched them with sorceries.

12 But when they believed Philip preaching the things concerning the kingdom of God, and the name of Jesus Christ, they were baptized, both men and women.

13 Then Simon himself believed also: and when he was baptized, he continued with Philip, and wondered, beholding the miracles and signs which were done.

14 Now when the apostles which were at Jerusalem heard that Samaria had received the word of God, they sent unto them Peter and John:

15 Who, when they were come down, prayed for them, that they might receive the Holy Ghost:

16 (For as yet he was fallen upon none of them: only they were baptized in the name of the Lord Jesus.)

17 Then laid they their hands on them, and they received the Holy Ghost.

18 And when Simon saw that through laying on of the apostles' hands the Holy Ghost was given, he offered them money,

19 Saying, Give me also this power, that on whomsoever I lay hands, he may receive the Holy Ghost.

20 But Peter said unto him, Thy money perish with thee, because thou hast thought that the gift of God may be purchased with money.

Acts 8:9-24—NIV

9 Now for some time a man named Simon had practiced sorcery in the city and amazed all the people of Samaria. He boasted that he was someone great,

10 and all the people, both high and low, gave him their attention and exclaimed, "This man is the divine power known as the Great Power."

11 They followed him because he had amazed them for a long time with his magic.

12 But when they believed Philip as he preached the good news of the kingdom of God and the name of Jesus Christ, they were baptized, both men and women.

13 Simon himself believed and was baptized. And he followed Philip everywhere, astonished by the great signs and miracles he saw.

14 When the apostles in Jerusalem heard that Samaria had accepted the word of God, they sent Peter and John to them.

15 When they arrived, they prayed for them that they might receive the Holy Spirit,

16 because the Holy Spirit had not yet come upon any of them; they had simply been baptized into the name of the Lord Jesus.

17 Then Peter and John placed their hands on them, and they received the Holy Spirit.

18 When Simon saw that the Spirit was given at the laying on of the apostles' hands, he offered them money

19 and said, "Give me also this ability so that everyone on whom I lay my hands may receive the Holy Spirit."

20 Peter answered: "May your money perish with you, because you thought you could buy the gift of God with money!

Some people try to buy power. What are the consequences of inappropriately seeking power? When Simon the magician tried to buy the power of the Holy Spirit, Peter plainly laid out the fatal consequences for those who thought that the Spirit can be bought or sold.

---

21 Thou hast neither part nor lot in this matter: for thy heart is not right in the sight of God.

22 Repent therefore of this thy wickedness, and pray God, if perhaps the thought of thine heart may be forgiven thee.

23 For I perceive that thou art in the gall of bitterness, and in the bond of iniquity.

24 Then answered Simon, and said, Pray ye to the Lord for me, that none of these things which ye have spoken come upon me.

21 You have no part or share in this ministry, because your heart is not right before God.

22 Repent of this wickedness and pray to the Lord. Perhaps he will forgive you for having such a thought in your heart.

23 For I see that you are full of bitterness and captive to sin."

24 Then Simon answered, "Pray to the Lord for me so that nothing you have said may happen to me."

TOPICAL OUTLINE OF THE LESSON

I. Introduction
  A. Where Does Real Power Lie?
  B. Biblical Background

II. Exposition and Application of the Scripture
  A. Simon the Sorcerer (Acts 8:9-11)
  B. Philip's Preaching Bears Fruit (Acts 8:12-13)
  C. The Apostles Investigate the Revival in Samaria (Acts 8:14-17)
  D. Simon Tries to Buy the Holy Spirit (Acts 8:18-24)

III. Concluding Reflection

LESSON OBJECTIVES

Upon completion of the lesson, the students will be able to do the following:

1. Name the main reason for Simon's motivation to receive the Holy Spirit;
2. Explain what it means to seek God's power for selfish reasons; and,
3. Discuss the reason why every believer should desire to be authentically used by the Holy Spirit.

POINTS TO BE EMPHASIZED

ADULT/YOUTH

Adult Topic: **Power Brokers**

Youth Topic: **Not for Sale!**

Adult Key Verse: **Acts 8:18**

Youth Key Verse: **Acts 8:22**

Print Passage: **Acts 8:9-24**

—The Samaritans eagerly listened to and followed first Simon and then Philip, because of their unusual displays of power (see Acts 8:10-12). The Samaritans, including Simon, "believed Philip," who proclaimed "the good news about the kingdom of God and the name of Jesus Christ" (Acts 8:12, NIV).

—The Samaritans' belief preceded their baptisms (verse 12) and their receiving of the Holy Spirit (see verse 17). Although they had been "baptized in the name of the Lord Jesus" (verse 16), they did not, at that time, receive the Holy Spirit.

—Philip served as the first evangelist to preach the Gospel outside of Jerusalem (see 6:5).

—Simon performed healings, exorcisms, and other wonders under the influence of Satan.

—The only way to receive God's power is to repent, seek forgiveness, and be filled with the Holy Spirit.

—It is significant that while Peter rebuked Simon for his greed (Acts 8:20-23), he also extended to Simon the possibility of forgiveness and restoration.

—Simon acknowledged his wrongdoing and asked for prayer.

CHILDREN
Children Topic: Not for Sale!

Key Verse: Acts 8:20
Print Passage: Acts 8:9-24

—Simon practiced magic and, in Samaria, had a large following of people who attributed his magic to the power of God.

—Philip's preaching led many, including Simon, to believe in Jesus Christ.

—Peter and John came to Samaria and prayed that the new believers would receive the Holy Spirit.

—When Simon saw the power of the Holy Spirit in action, he offered money to the apostles so that he could receive that power.

—Peter chastised Simon and demanded that Simon repent.

—Simon asked for prayer.

I. INTRODUCTION
A. Where Does Real Power Lie?

Who are the real power brokers in America? Are they politicians who wield enormous clout at all levels of government—local, state, and federal? Others would say that the real power belongs/lies in the hands of the citizens who can elect or throw politicians out of office. In many respects, the real power does not lie with the elected leader or in the hands of the voting public. The real power in America lies in the hands of the wealthy individuals and corporations that buy political influence and favor at all levels of government.

In 1975, the U. S. Congress passed a law that created the Federal Election Commission (FEC). This regulatory agency is responsible for ensuring that federal regulations regarding contributions to presidential and congressional campaigns are followed. The agency is charged with ensuring that candidates properly report all financial contributions to their election or re-election campaigns. Contributions to all federal candidates can be viewed at the FEC's Web site. The high cost of running a political campaign has given rise to another form of "influence peddling and buying" called the Political Action Committee, or PAC. There are limits placed on how much PACs can raise or contribute to candidates. There are more than 4,600 in America, which seek to buy political power and influence in Washington.

Not only are there people in our larger society who seek to buy influence and power, but we also see this practice in many congregations. What are the consequences of inappropriately seeking power? When Simon the magician tried to buy the power of the Holy Spirit, Peter plainly laid out the fatal consequences for those who thought that the Spirit could be bought or sold.

B. Biblical Background

In today's lesson, we are introduced to a man named Simon—who was a magician living in Samaria, a region in northern Israel that originally included the tribal lands of Ephraim and western Manasseh. The origin of the Samaritan people dates back to the time of the Assyrian invasion and conquest of the Northern Kingdom in AD 722 and can be found in 2 Kings 17. According to 2 Kings 17:24, the king of Assyria brought people from several countries who eventually intermingled and intermarried with the remaining Israelites, who were not deported to Assyria. The people later came to be called Samaritans. Ancient Jewish historian Josephus wrote extensively of the origins of the Samaritans in his work, *Antiquities of the Jews 9.277–91.*

Shortly after the stoning of Stephen, a period of severe persecution broke out against the church in Jerusalem. Many of the believers were scattered and traveled to places where they believed that they would be safe (see Acts 8:1-4). Philip, who was one of the original seven deacons, went to Samaria and began an active ministry that produced great successes. This is one of the first recorded instances of the Christian faith's expanding outside of Jerusalem and the Jewish community. Traditional first-century Jews viewed Samaritans as impure and treated them as outcasts. Luke's account of Philip's mission to the Samaritan reinforces the character of God, whose worship cannot be limited to a particular place and whose redemptive plan extends to all people everywhere (see Acts 1:8).

Simon was the big man in Samaria. The people eagerly listened to and followed Simon in Samaria. When Philip arrived, people began to listen to and follow him because of his unusual displays of power (see Acts 8:1-12). Philip's preaching of the Gospel of the kingdom of God and message about Jesus Christ led to many of the people believing. They believed that they were baptized in the name of the Lord Jesus Christ, but they did not receive the gift of the Holy Spirit at that time. When news of the revival in Samaria reached Jerusalem, two of the most trusted apostles were sent to verify the news and report back to the apostles in Jerusalem. There is no explanation given by Luke as to why they did not receive the Holy Spirit at conversion; however, when Peter and John laid hands on them, they received the Holy Spirit at that time. Simon was so intrigued by this development that he offered to buy from the apostles the ability to lay hands on people.

II. EXPOSITION AND APPLICATION OF THE SCRIPTURE

A. Simon the Sorcerer
(Acts 8:9-11)

But there was a certain man, called Simon, which beforetime in the same city used sorcery, and bewitched the people of Samaria, giving out that himself was some great one: To whom they all gave heed, from the least to the greatest, saying, This man is the great power of God. And to him they had regard, because that of long time he had bewitched them with sorceries.

Verse 9 is a break in the account of Philip's ministry in Samaria for the purpose of introducing a man named Simon (see Acts 8:5-8). In the latter years of the first century and into the second century, there was a legend that Simon was the father of Gnosticism. Scholars have found no substantial biblical or non-biblical evidence to support such an assertion. We are not told which city of Samaria Simon lived in or any personal details of his life. Simon is described as a man who was able to captivate the imagination of the people with his sorcery. He had built a large following of people from all social classes in the city. Simon used this power for personal gain and personal glory. This led to his boasting about himself and passing himself off as the "Great Power," a reference to his being a god.

The practice of sorcery or magic was not new in the Bible. We first hear of magic and sorcery during the times of the Exodus (see Exodus 7:11, 22; 8:18-19). Within the Law, there were strict prohibitions against going to or having sorcerers or magicians in the tribal communities (see Leviticus 20:6; Deuteronomy 18:10-12). Magic or sorcery was not to be viewed the same way as magical shows today. The sorcery that was performed in biblical days was considered to have its origin in the demonic.

B. Philip's Preaching Bears Fruit
(Acts 8:12-13)

But when they believed Philip preaching the things concerning the kingdom of God, and the name of Jesus Christ, they were baptized, both men and women. Then Simon himself believed also: and when he was baptized, he continued with Philip, and wondered, beholding the miracles and signs which were done.

Verse 12 begins with a contrast between the power of Simon and the power of Philip. Philip's message was convincing because the people believed (Greek: *pisteuo*—"to have confidence in the message") what he preached. What was that message? It was Good News from God (Greek: *euaggelizo*—"announcement of glad tidings"). The kingdom of God is translated from *basileia* and it literally refers to "the rule and reign of God in the earth." The term *kingdom* is not to be understood geographically. The Good News of the kingdom, then, is the message that in Jesus Christ, God has brought about the salvation and redemption of all men and women who believe. Jesus came and reconciled the world back to God through His death and resurrection (see John 3:16-17; Acts 2:22-36; 4:12; Romans 5:8-10; 1 Corinthians 15:1-11; Ephesians 2:8-10; 1 Peter 3:18; 4:6).

The differences between Philip and Simon can be seen further in how the people responded to both men. Simon amazed the people with his bag of tricks and his use of the occult. Philip, on the other hand, met the needs of people who were hurting and in need of hope and healing. Further, Philip's preaching was backed up with miracles and signs from heaven and was accompanied by feelings of joy and gladness. His ministry was credible. When preaching is done in sincerity and under the convicting power of the Holy Spirit, God will always validate the Word by the miraculous. It is God who gives credibility to our work when our lives are filled with the Holy Spirit.

Why did the preaching of Philip have such a powerful impact? The Samaritans were very much open to his message. The reason for their openness stemmed from their belief that they were descendants of Abraham and Moses. They kept many of the traditional practices of the Jews, including circumcision and the reading of the Torah. The Samaritans more than likely had a messianic hope and were looking for a messiah to come. Yet, ethnic Jews did not associate with Samaritans nor permit intermarriage with them (see John 4:9ff.).

The preaching of Philip had an immediate impact in Samaria. We are not told how many people believed and were baptized—just that the numbers consisted of both men and women. Simon, who had been the big chief in town, was also moved to believe and was baptized. Luke's text makes it clear that there was a key difference between Simon's magic and Philip's manifestation of the power of the Holy Spirit.

The preaching was so powerful and convincing that even Simon believed and was baptized. Was he truly converted to following the teaching of Jesus Christ? The answer would come in a few days. Simon followed Philip wherever he went, fascinated and amazed by the mighty demonstrations of the power of God working through Philip.

C. The Apostles Investigate the Revival in Samaria (Acts 8:14-17)

Now when the apostles which were at Jerusalem heard that Samaria had received the word of God, they sent unto them Peter and John: Who, when they were come down, prayed for them, that they might receive the Holy Ghost: (For as yet he was fallen upon none of them: only they were baptized in the name of the Lord Jesus.) Then laid they their hands on them, and they received the Holy Ghost.

News of the preaching and success of Philip reached the apostles in Jerusalem. In order to verify the reports, the apostles sent Peter and John, two of the most respected leaders in the church of Jerusalem. We are not told how the word about the Samaritan revival came to the apostles. Peter and John went and found that the preaching and healing ministry of Philip had produced a great harvest of souls for the kingdom of God. They prayed for the believers that they might receive the Holy Spirit, because up to that moment they had not received the gift of the Holy Spirit. The believers had simply been baptized in the name of the Lord Jesus. It was through the laying on of hands that the Holy Spirit was imparted to the saints in Samaria.

These verses have caused much debate and a great deal of disagreement about the way to properly interpret the events described in the passage. How does one explain the delay between baptism and the reception of the Holy Spirit in the lives of the Samaritans? Roman Catholics connect the impartation of the Holy Spirit by the laying on of hands as supporting their teachings regarding the sacrament of confirmation. They believe confirmation to be an act separate from baptism, whereby an individual receives the Holy Spirit and is fully incorporated into the church. In the Pentecostal tradition, this passage supports the belief that even after a person is saved there is a greater second work of grace that must occur. They refer to this as the baptism of the Holy Spirit, which is then accompanied by speaking in unknown tongues.

The best explanation is to see this event within the scope of the larger design of God. Historically, Jews and Samaritans had no dealings with each other; at this point, however, they were coming to salvation through the preaching of the Gospel, which was confirmation of the words of Jesus in Acts 1:8. Who would believe that God had poured out His Spirit upon them as He had done on the Day of Pentecost? Most New Testament scholars believe that God delayed the impartation of the Holy Spirit so that the apostles might come and dramatically confirm their experience of God's grace and the work of Philip. The laying on of hands by Peter and John would give instant credibility, incorporate them into the fellowship of the church, and connect them to the church in Jerusalem. It would also place them under the apostolic authority of the Jerusalem church. There would be two other instances in the apostolic era when the Holy Spirit would come upon the life of a believer after he confessed his sins and was baptized (see Acts 10:47-48; 19:5-6). This was the first time that the Gospel had been preached to a non-Jewish people, and this made it a special occasion in the growth of the Christian faith. The barriers between Jew and Gentile were finally being broken (see Ephesians 1:11-14; 2:11-17).

D. Simon Tries to Buy the Holy Spirit
   (Acts 8:18-24)

And when Simon saw that through laying on of the apostles' hands the Holy Ghost was given, he offered them money, Saying, Give me also this power, that on whomsoever I lay hands, he may receive the Holy Ghost. But Peter said unto him, Thy money perish with thee, because thou hast thought that the gift of God may be purchased with money. Thou hast neither part nor lot in this matter: for thy heart is not right in the sight of God. Repent therefore of this thy wickedness, and pray God, if perhaps the thought of thine heart may be forgiven thee. For I perceive that thou art in the gall of bitterness, and in the bond of iniquity. Then answered Simon, and said, Pray ye to the Lord for me, that none of these things which ye have spoken come upon me.

Simon knew a good thing when he saw it. When he saw that the apostles could lay hands on people and that the power of the Holy Spirit would come upon them, he knew that he needed this power. He offered to buy the gift from the apostles so that those on whom he laid his hands would receive the Holy Spirit as well. By making this request, Simon revealed that he had not really changed at all. He was fascinated by the things that he saw and the respect accorded to the apostles by the people. Why not get this kind of power and authority?

Peter strongly and openly rebuked Simon and told him that he and his money would perish together. In this act, Simon revealed that his heart was not right toward God. He had believed, but had not been truly changed (see 2 Corinthians 5:17). He was excluded from the newly founded church in Samaria. Peter called Simon's request wicked, because at the very core of it lay selfishness and greed. Peter also saw the spirit of bitterness within him and that Simon had not really changed at all. Simon was like so many people who make claims of having been changed, but whose lifestyles and actions reveal something entirely different. Jesus had warned His disciples that they would be able to recognize false prophets by the fruit that they bore (see Matthew 7:15-20; Acts 20:28-30).

III. CONCLUDING REFLECTION

One of the most important truths revealed in this lesson is the power of preaching the simple message of the Gospel of our Lord Jesus Christ. Philip did not use gimmicks, promises of prosperity, or declarations filled with false hopes. He merely offered the gift of salvation and the forgiveness of sins through faith in the finished work of Jesus Christ at Calvary.

Similarly, if the church of this generation wants to make a bigger impact in the world, she must preach—without fear—the uncompromising truth of the Gospel.

A second truth that comes from the lesson is the principle that God can never be reduced to working in just one way. On Pentecost, the Holy Spirit came upon the believers in Jerusalem in a very dramatic fashion. In Samaria, they received the Holy Spirit in a different manner, but it was just as dramatic. We must never restrict God's actions to our narrow ways of thinking and believing. God is sovereign; hence, He is free to act in ways that best accomplish His will.

PRAYER

Lord God, grant that we may never be unduly influenced in compromising our faith in You for worldly possessions of power. May we find in You all that we need to be fully satisfied. Grant that we may never lose heart in our work of ministry. In Jesus' name we pray. Amen.

WORD POWER

Laying on of hands (Greek: *epitithemi tas cheira*)—this was first mentioned in the Old Testament in connection with conferring authority, making sacrifices, bestowing blessings, and consecrating priests to their office (see Exodus 29:9-19; Leviticus 3:2, 8, 13; 24:14; Numbers 27:18, 23). The practice was seen in the ministry of Jesus when He blessed the children (see Matthew 19:15; Mark 10:16). Within the early Christian practices and traditions, the apostles prayed for and laid their hands on people _____ the church (see Acts 6:6; 13:3). We also see t_____ Samaritans who then received the gift of the _____ 4:14; 2 Timothy 1:6). Last, the laying on of h_____ people who were sick (see Mark 5:23; Luke 4:_____

HOME DAILY BIBLE READINGS
(October 15-21, 2012)

Simon Wants to Buy Po_____

MONDAY, October 15: "W_____
TUESDAY, October 16: "Us_____
WEDNESDAY, October 17: _____3-25)
THURSDAY, October 18: "F_____:26–2:5)
FRIDAY, October 19: "The V_____
SATURDAY, October 20: "The Fruit of the Spirit" (Galatians 5:22-26)
SUNDAY, October 21: "What Money Cannot Buy" (Acts 8:9-24)

UNIT II: Who Understands Faith?   CHILDREN'S UNIT: Who Understands Faith?   FALL QUARTER

LESSON 9   October 28, 2012

PHILIP AND THE ETHIOPIAN EUNUCH

FAITH PATHWAY/FAITH JOURNEY TOPIC: **Erasing the Boundary Lines**

DEVOTIONAL READING: **Isaiah 56:1-8**   BACKGROUND SCRIPTURE: **Acts 8:26-39**
PRINT PASSAGE: **Acts 8:26-39**   KEY VERSE: **Acts 8:36**

Acts 8:26-39—KJV

26 And the angel of the Lord spake unto Philip, saying, Arise, and go toward the south unto the way that goeth down from Jerusalem unto Gaza, which is desert.

27 And he arose and went: and, behold, a man of Ethiopia, an eunuch of great authority under Candace queen of the Ethiopians, who had the charge of all her treasure, and had come to Jerusalem for to worship,

28 Was returning, and sitting in his chariot read Esaias the prophet.

29 Then the Spirit said unto Philip, Go near, and join thyself to this chariot.

30 And Philip ran thither to him, and heard him read the prophet Esaias, and said, Understandest thou what thou readest?

31 And he said, How can I, except some man should guide me? And he desired Philip that he would come up and sit with him.

32 The place of the scripture which he read was this, He was led as a sheep to the slaughter; and like a lamb dumb before his shearer, so opened he not his mouth:

33 In his humiliation his judgment was taken away: and who shall declare his generation? for his life is taken from the earth.

34 And the eunuch answered Philip, and said, I pray thee, of whom speaketh the prophet this? of himself, or of some other man?

35 Then Philip opened his mouth, and began at the same scripture, and preached unto him Jesus.

36 And as they went on their way, they came unto a certain water: and the eunuch said, See, here is water; what doth hinder me to be baptized?

Acts 8:26-39—NIV

26 Now an angel of the Lord said to Philip, "Go south to the road—the desert road—that goes down from Jerusalem to Gaza."

27 So he started out, and on his way he met an Ethiopian eunuch, an important official in charge of all the treasury of Candace, queen of the Ethiopians. This man had gone to Jerusalem to worship,

28 and on his way home was sitting in his chariot reading the book of Isaiah the prophet.

29 The Spirit told Philip, "Go to that chariot and stay near it."

30 Then Philip ran up to the chariot and heard the man reading Isaiah the prophet. "Do you understand what you are reading?" Philip asked.

31 "How can I," he said, "unless someone explains it to me?" So he invited Philip to come up and sit with him.

32 The eunuch was reading this passage of Scripture: "He was led like a sheep to the slaughter, and as a lamb before the shearer is silent, so he did not open his mouth.

33 In his humiliation he was deprived of justice. Who can speak of his descendants? For his life was taken from the earth."

34 The eunuch asked Philip, "Tell me, please, who is the prophet talking about, himself or someone else?"

35 Then Philip began with that very passage of Scripture and told him the good news about Jesus.

36 As they traveled along the road, they came to some water and the eunuch said, "Look, here is water. Why shouldn't I be baptized?"

UNIFYING LESSON PRINCIPLE

Some people want to say who is in and who is out when it comes to membership in certain groups. Why are the boundaries of membership sometimes limited to specific people? Philip's sharing of the Good News about Jesus and the baptism of the Ethiopian official demonstrate the universal availability of the Gospel message.

37 And Philip said, If thou believest with all thine heart, thou mayest. And he answered and said, I believe that Jesus Christ is the Son of God.
38 And he commanded the chariot to stand still: and they went down both into the water, both Philip and the eunuch; and he baptized him.
39 And when they were come up out of the water, the Spirit of the Lord caught away Philip, that the eunuch saw him no more: and he went on his way rejoicing.

37 Philip said, "If you believe with all your heart, you may." The eunuch answered, "I believe that Jesus Christ is the Son of God."
38 And he gave orders to stop the chariot. Then both Philip and the eunuch went down into the water and Philip baptized him.
39 When they came up out of the water, the Spirit of the Lord suddenly took Philip away, and the eunuch did not see him again, but went on his way rejoicing.

TOPICAL OUTLINE OF THE LESSON

I. Introduction
   A. Divine Diversity
   B. Biblical Background

II. Exposition and Application of the Scripture
   A. Philip's New Assignment (Acts 8:26)
   B. The Ethiopian Eunuch (Acts 8:27-28)
   C. An Explanation and Proclamation of the Gospel (Acts 8:29-35)
   D. Baptism in the Desert (Acts 8:36-39)

III. Concluding Reflection

LESSON OBJECTIVES

Upon the completion of the lesson, the students will be able to do the following:

1. Make a connection between Peter's baptism of the Ethiopian eunuch and the universal availability of the Gospel message;
2. Examine any feelings they may have of being excluded, and their motivations for excluding others; and,
3. Develop a strategy for ways to make their church more open and inclusive.

POINTS TO BE EMPHASIZED
ADULT/YOUTH

Adult Topic: Erasing the Boundary Lines
Youth Topic: I Can Belong
Adult Key Verse: Acts 8:36
Youth Key Verse: Acts 8:31
Print Passage: Acts 8:26-39

—The Ethiopian eunuch was God-fearing and was worshipping in Jerusalem, outside his native land.

—Guided by the Spirit, Philip went to the eunuch and helped him understand the Scriptures, starting with the book of Isaiah.

—The Scriptures (8:32-34) that were being read by the eunuch were from Isaiah 53:7-8 and were prophecies about Jesus Christ.

—The eunuch understood the Scriptures after Philip explained them, and then he wanted to be baptized.

—After accepting Jesus as his Lord and Savior, the eunuch went on his way—rejoicing and spreading the Good News.

—God's Spirit was undeniably present and active with the Ethiopian eunuch and Philip—thus affirming the universality of the Gospel.

CHILDREN
Children Topic: **Sharing the Faith**
Key Verse: **Acts 8:35**

Print Passage: Acts 8:26-39

—An angel gave Philip instructions for going to Gaza.

—The Ethiopian official requested the assistance of Philip in order to understand what the Scriptures were saying.

—Philip used the request of the Ethiopian to present to him the message about Jesus Christ.

—As a result of believing the message about Jesus, the Ethiopian requested baptism.

—Philip then baptized the Ethiopian after he confessed Jesus Christ as Savior.

I. INTRODUCTION
A. Divine Diversity

Diversity is one the major strategies used to bridge the cultural divide in the twenty-first century. Diversity is the acknowledgment that people are different and that these differences are not a problem but are a part of how God created the world (see Revelation 7:9). Diversity includes a range of topics from gender to race, geographical regions, age, education, and socio-economic backgrounds.

One man who was very instrumental in the early evangelization of non-Jews was a layman named Philip. Philip's preaching and teaching of the Gospel about Jesus Christ and his baptism of the Ethiopian official demonstrate the universal availability of the Gospel message. It is pointed out in the passage that God is not a respecter of persons when it comes to redemption. Believers are reminded through the example of Philip that one of the greatest opportunities facing the church of the twenty-first century is being able to redraw the boundary lines so that they are free to reach people from different ethnic groups.

B. Biblical Background

In today's lesson, we see the message of God's great act of redemption spreading to Africa through Philip's witness to an Ethiopian eunuch. The Ethiopian was an outcast from mainstream Israel and was denied full participation in the covenant community. We are not told why the man was in Jerusalem. It may have been official business or to observe one of the annual Jewish feast days. If this was so, then the eunuch traveled a great distance to worship the Lord God at the Temple in Jerusalem. These actions were a living testimony of his loyalty and devotion to the worship of God. Yet, as he traveled home, the Ethiopian came to the realization that there was still something missing in his life. Even the lofty political and financial status he held in his homeland were not enough to fill the spiritual emptiness/void present in his life. The man may have identified with the "humiliation" of the servant in the passage he read from the prophetic book of Isaiah. No doubt, his pilgrimage to Jerusalem to worship the God he sought to know more fully left him wondering about his place and future in the household of Israel.

There are several lessons that we will learn about today. The first is the importance of following the lead of the Holy Spirit. The assignment that Philip was given was completely out of the norm, given the direction in which he was asked to travel. Second, Philip's witness to the Ethiopian eunuch conveys the overall plan of God to save the world, not just a few people. As a Jew, Philip had been prepared for witnessing cross-culturally when he traveled north to Samaria. Third, there was the implied lesson of being able to rightly interpret the Word of God. Philip was asked to give an explanation to the Ethiopian about what he was reading. Because Philip listened and obeyed the voice of the Holy Spirit, a man was saved and baptized.

II. EXPOSITION AND APPLICATION OF THE SCRIPTURE

A. Philip's New Assignment
(Acts 8:26)

And the angel of the Lord spake unto Philip, saying, Arise, and go toward the south unto the way that goeth down from Jerusalem unto Gaza, which is desert.

The story of Philip's ministry picks up from Acts 8:13, where it is told that he preached and performed miraculous signs in Samaria. Philip was commanded by the angel of the Lord to head south on a new assignment. There is no mention of the angel's name; hence, it may have been one of the *myriads of angels* who performed various assignments. Some interpreters believe that this may have been the Spirit of God (see Acts 23:9). Angels were often used to convey messages from God (see 2 Kings 1:3, 15; compare Acts 27:22-23). Philip had no idea what to expect on this journey south nor was he told his final destination. We are not told whether he was leaving from Samaria or Jerusalem—only that he was to head south on the desert road that went to Gaza. If he left from Samaria, then he would still have to travel south through Jerusalem to take the route where he eventually met the Ethiopian eunuch.

There are occasions in our lives when God sends us on assignments which seem baffling and totally illogical. The word *south* has a double meaning. On the one hand, it refers to the direction—and on the other hand, it refers to the time of day. God commanded Philip to head south during the hottest time of the day, a time when people would rarely consider traveling in this part of the world.

B. The Ethiopian Eunuch
(Acts 8:27-28)

And he arose and went: and, behold, a man of Ethiopia, an eunuch of great authority under Candace queen of the Ethiopians, who had the charge of all her treasure, and had come to Jerusalem for to worship, Was returning, and sitting in his chariot read Esaias the prophet.

Philip did not debate the assignment nor question its logic. Most people would question the rationality of leaving a place where one had tremendous success to head toward a place where barely anyone lived. He had learned from experience that wherever God sent him, the Holy Spirit would produce a great harvest. As he traveled, he came upon the chariot of an Ethiopian eunuch. The Bible does not tell us where he encountered the Ethiopian on the road.

There are several things that we must be clear about regarding the Ethiopian eunuch. First, the Ethiopia that is mentioned is not to be equated with modern-day Ethiopia—which in biblical days would have been Sheba (see 1 Kings 10:1-13). Biblical Ethiopia is the land of Cush and refers to the kingdom that flourished between the first and sixth cataracts of the Nile, which was south of Egypt and covers the same territory as the Sudan.[1] Second, the term *eunuch* can refer to a man who was physically castrated, as was the case with many slaves who were castrated as young boys to prepare them for service in the king's harem or to work in the treasury. The Ethiopian eunuch was an important official who was responsible for the entire treasury of Candace, which was most likely not the personal name of the queen but an official title for the queen mother, much like the title "Pharaoh" of Egypt. Third, as a eunuch, he had no physical access to the Temple (see Deuteronomy 23:1). He could enter the environs of the Temple, but he was denied access to the place where worship and sacrifice took place. This fact alone heightened the man's deep sincerity and love of God, seeing that he would travel hundreds of miles only to be denied access to the place of sacrifice and worship. As he made his way back to Ethiopia, the man was reading the book of Isaiah the prophet. There is nothing in the text to suggest that the Ethiopian was a proselyte, but that, more than likely, he was a God-fearer, someone who was interested in the Jewish faith but had not converted fully to Judaism.

One of the more important truths from the life of Philip was the absolute necessity that believers practice obedience even when the assignment did not seem to make sense.

C. An Explanation and Proclamation of the Gospel (Acts 8:29-35)

Then the Spirit said unto Philip, Go near, and join thyself to this chariot. And Philip ran thither to him, and heard him read the prophet Esaias, and said, Understandest thou what thou readest? And he said, How can I, except some man should guide me? And he desired Philip that he would come up and sit with him. The place of the scripture which he read was this, He was led as a sheep to the slaughter; and like a lamb dumb before his shearer, so opened he not his mouth: In his humiliation his judgment was taken away: and who shall declare his generation? for his life is taken from the earth. And the eunuch answered Philip, and said, I pray thee, of whom speaketh the prophet this? of himself, or of some other man? Then Philip opened his mouth, and began at the same scripture, and preached unto him Jesus.

In verse 29, the Spirit of the Lord commanded Philip a second time to do something completely out of the ordinary. He was commanded to go stay near the chariot that he saw making its way down the road. Philip ran up to the chariot and he overheard the man reading from the book of Isaiah. This was a very tricky thing to do, because, given the man's status as a high government official and Philip's being a Jew, it is quite possible that his overtures could have been completely misunderstood. However, the Lord had opened the door and hearing the words of Isaiah 53:7-8, Philip knew right away how to approach the man. Philip asked a very pointed question: "Do you understand what you are reading?" This was a very appropriate question, in that the Old Testament often presents many interpretive challenges for people who are not familiar with its teachings.

The Ethiopian replied that he had no idea what he was reading and needed someone to explain the words to him. Philip was invited to come alongside the man and explain to him the message of the prophet (see verse 31). What better place to begin the message of God's redemptive plan of salvation than with the prophecies concerning the coming of the suffering servant? (See verses 32-33.) The man wondered who Isaiah was talking about. It was the Christian church which interpreted these words as having been fulfilled in the life and ministry of Jesus Christ (see Luke 24:44; John 5:39; Acts 2:14-39). The Holy Spirit had prepared the heart and mind of the Ethiopian to receive the message about Jesus Christ. At the right moment, Philip opened his mouth and began to preach the message that was at the heart of Isaiah 53:7-8.

Philip's encounter points out that the Lord often provides numerous opportunities for us to share our faith in the risen Christ. We should be ready at all times to witness to God's grace. Not only should we be ready, but more importantly we should be sufficiently knowledgeable of the Word of God so that we can explain and expound on the simple truths of God's redemptive plan of salvation to those who seek a fresh start in life. Philip's experience helps us to appreciate the importance of knowing where to begin our witness and how to effectively lead someone to faith in Jesus Christ. He began where the man was and led him to faith in the risen Christ.

D. Baptism in the Desert
(Acts 8:36-39)

And as they went on their way, they came unto a certain water: and the eunuch said, See, here is water; what doth hinder me to be baptized? And Philip said, If thou believest with all thine heart, thou mayest. And he answered and said, I believe that Jesus Christ is the Son of God. And he commanded the chariot to stand still: and they went down both into the water, both Philip and the eunuch; and he baptized him. And when they were come up out of the water, the Spirit of the Lord caught away Philip, that the eunuch saw him no more: and he went on his way rejoicing.

As they were traveling they came upon a body of water, quite possibly an oasis in the desert. The eunuch wanted to know if there was any reason why he could not be baptized at that moment. The text implies that Philip must have mentioned baptism as one of the signs of conversion (see John 3:5, 23; Acts 2:38, 41; 8:12-13; Titus 3:5).

Verse 37 is not found in any of the oldest manuscripts of the Acts of the Apostles, and is omitted from the text of the NIV because the textual evidence does not give support for its inclusion. It appears as a footnote in the NIV and as a parenthetical inclusion in the *New American Standard Bible* (NASB). One likely explanation is that a scribe who copied the manuscript from another copy of the book of Acts felt the need to include what must have been an early Christian confession of faith.

The Ethiopian commanded that the chariot be stopped; he and Philip went down in the water—where he was baptized. When they emerged from the water, the Spirit caught Philip up and took him away. This is not to be viewed as some mysterious vanishing; rather, the Holy Spirit led him in a different direction (see 1 Kings 18:12; 2 Kings 2:16; Ezekiel 3:12-14; 8:3; 11:24). His assignment had been accomplished and the Gospel would now spread to the very end of the earth through the witness and conversion of this unnamed African. The eunuch and Philip parted ways, with the man rejoicing that he had received the gift of eternal life and the power of the Holy Spirit.

III. CONCLUDING REFLECTION

In today's lesson, Philip was directed by the Holy Spirit to go to a desert. It is made clear in Scripture (and even in our personal lives) that sometimes God opens a door of opportunity to His followers in unlikely places. We should always be prepared to minister effectively to those with whom we come into contact when we travel. We should also be willing to minister in the name of our Lord to persons of different ethnicities and cultures. We should also be willing to be guided by the Holy Spirit at all times. He will lead us into all truths and give us the words to say in various situations in which we are called upon to minister.

PRAYER

Gracious heavenly Father, may we learn to hear Your voice clearly, and then may we learn to walk in complete obedience to Your command. Grant that doors of opportunity will open for Your servants to witness to others of Your grace and love. In Jesus' name we pray. Amen.

WORD POWER

Baptized (Greek: *baptizo*)—The Christian rite of baptism has its roots in the early Hebrew tradition or ritual cleansing, which was to be done whenever a person came into contact with something or someone who was considered unclean (see Numbers 19:1-13; Leviticus 13; 14:8-9; 15:13; 22:4-6; Deuteronomy 23:11). The rite consisted of a complete immersion in water as a means of ritual cleansing and purification. Within early Christian traditions, baptism was performed in obedience to the command of Jesus (see Matthew 28:19-20). It was viewed as a prerequisite for inclusion within the Christian church and viewed as the first step to receiving the Holy Spirit (see Acts 2:38, 41).

HOME DAILY BIBLE READINGS
(October 22-28, 2012)

Philip and the Ethiopian Eunuch
MONDAY, October 22: "Blemishes that Exclude" (Leviticus 21:16-24)
TUESDAY, October 23: "Lifting Up the Downtrodden" (Psalm 147:1-6)
WEDNESDAY, October 24: "Gathering the Outcasts" (Isaiah 56:1-8)
THURSDAY, October 25: "Changing Shame into Praise" (Zephaniah 3:14-20)
FRIDAY, October 26: "A Ruler Who Seeks Justice" (Isaiah 16:1-5)
SATURDAY, October 27: "A Champion for the Needy" (Job 29:2-16)
SUNDAY, October 28: "The Good News about Jesus" (Acts 8:26-39)

End Note

[1]Katherine Doob Sakenfeld, General Editor, *New Interpreters Dictionary of the Bible,* D–H, Vol. 2, "Ethiopia," (Nashville: Abingdon Press, 2007), p. 348.

LESSON 10   November 4, 2012

PAUL BEFORE KING AGRIPPA

FAITH PATHWAY/FAITH JOURNEY TOPIC: **Taking a Stand**

DEVOTIONAL READING: **Acts 23:1-11**
PRINT PASSAGE: **Acts 26:19-32**

BACKGROUND SCRIPTURE: **Acts 25:23–26:32**
KEY VERSE: **Acts 26:25**

Acts 26:19-32—KJV

19 Whereupon, O king Agrippa, I was not disobedient unto the heavenly vision:

20 But shewed first unto them of Damascus, and at Jerusalem, and throughout all the coasts of Judaea, and then to the Gentiles, that they should repent and turn to God, and do works meet for repentance.

21 For these causes the Jews caught me in the temple, and went about to kill me.

22 Having therefore obtained help of God, I continue unto this day, witnessing both to small and great, saying none other things than those which the prophets and Moses did say should come:

23 That Christ should suffer, and that he should be the first that should rise from the dead, and should shew light unto the people, and to the Gentiles.

24 And as he thus spake for himself, Festus said with a loud voice, Paul, thou art beside thyself; much learning doth make thee mad.

25 But he said, I am not mad, most noble Festus; but speak forth the words of truth and soberness.

26 For the king knoweth of these things, before whom also I speak freely: for I am persuaded that none of these things are hidden from him; for this thing was not done in a corner.

27 King Agrippa, believest thou the prophets? I know that thou believest.

28 Then Agrippa said unto Paul, Almost thou persuadest me to be a Christian.

29 And Paul said, I would to God, that not only thou, but also all that hear me this day, were both almost, and altogether such as I am, except these bonds.

30 And when he had thus spoken, the king rose up, and the governor, and Bernice, and they that sat with them:

Acts 26:19-32—NIV

19 "So then, King Agrippa, I was not disobedient to the vision from heaven.

20 First to those in Damascus, then to those in Jerusalem and in all Judea, and to the Gentiles also, I preached that they should repent and turn to God and prove their repentance by their deeds.

21 That is why the Jews seized me in the temple courts and tried to kill me.

22 But I have had God's help to this very day, and so I stand here and testify to small and great alike. I am saying nothing beyond what the prophets and Moses said would happen—

23 that the Christ would suffer and, as the first to rise from the dead, would proclaim light to his own people and to the Gentiles."

24 At this point Festus interrupted Paul's defense. "You are out of your mind, Paul!" he shouted. "Your great learning is driving you insane."

25 "I am not insane, most excellent Festus," Paul replied. "What I am saying is true and reasonable.

26 The king is familiar with these things, and I can speak freely to him. I am convinced that none of this has escaped his notice, because it was not done in a corner.

27 King Agrippa, do you believe the prophets? I know you do."

28 Then Agrippa said to Paul, "Do you think that in such a short time you can persuade me to be a Christian?"

29 Paul replied, "Short time or long—I pray God that not only you but all who are listening to me today may become what I am, except for these chains."

30 The king rose, and with him the governor and Bernice and those sitting with them.

UNIFYING LESSON PRINCIPLE

It is difficult to stand by our convictions when other people think we are crazy. Where do we find the strength to stand our ground? Confident that he spoke the truth, Paul did not back down from sharing the story of his faith in Christ.

31 And when they were gone aside, they talked between themselves, saying, This man doeth nothing worthy of death or of bonds.
32 Then said Agrippa unto Festus, This man might have been set at liberty, if he had not appealed unto Caesar.

31 They left the room, and while talking with one another, they said, "This man is not doing anything that deserves death or imprisonment."
32 Agrippa said to Festus, "This man could have been set free if he had not appealed to Caesar."

TOPICAL OUTLINE OF THE LESSON

I. Introduction
A. One's Standing for His or Her Convictions
B. Biblical Background

II. Exposition and Application of the Scripture
A. Paul's Obedience to the Heavenly Vision (Acts 26:19-21)
B. Paul's Testimony of the Resurrection (Acts 26:22-23)
C. Paul's Testimony to Festus (Acts 26:24-26)
D. Paul's Testimony to Agrippa (Acts 26:27-32)

III. Concluding Reflection

LESSON OBJECTIVES

Upon the completion of the lesson, the students will be able to do the following:

1. Give examples of other Christians who took a stand for their faith in Jesus Christ;
2. List the key points of Paul's defense before Festus and Agrippa; and,
3. Identify the three common elements of apostolic preaching.

POINTS TO BE EMPHASIZED

ADULT/YOUTH
Adult Topic: Taking a Stand
Youth Topic: Standing by My Convictions
Adult Key Verse: Acts 26:25
Youth Key Verse: Acts 26:22
Print Passage: Acts 26:19-32

—King Agrippa, who was the brother of Felix's wife Drusilla (see Acts 24:24), had been designated as the ruler of the northern part of Judea, but had no power in the region governed by Festus; however, because of his expertise in Jewish affairs, he gave advice to Festus regarding Paul's case.

—Festus took Paul's case before King Agrippa so that he could get something in writing to substantiate Paul's case before Paul brought it to Caesar.

—Paul's presenting and defending himself before King Agrippa fulfilled the prophecy in Acts 9:15.

—Paul delivered his defense with conviction as he told of his conversion and call to preach.

—In spite of being rejected by King Agrippa, Paul appealed to all of his listeners there to believe in Jesus.

—They could find nothing against Paul that called for death or imprisonment.

CHILDREN

Children Topic: Paul Stands before the King

Key Verse: Acts 26:25

Print Passage: Acts 26:19-32

—King Agrippa was married to a Jew and therefore was familiar with Jewish laws and customs, as well as with the new "sect" of Christians whom Paul represented.

—King Agrippa understood that Paul's argument was aimed at persuading him to believe in Jesus.

—King Agrippa did not find Paul guilty, but he was prevented from releasing Paul because Paul, a Roman citizen by birth, had asked to take his case before Caesar.

I. INTRODUCTION

A. One's Standing for His or Her Convictions

Polycarp was one of early Christianity's greatest leaders. He lived between AD 70–155 and was bishop of the church in Smyrna. Tradition holds that he was one of the pupils of the apostle John and therefore was the bridge between the age of the apostles and that of the church fathers. This was the generation of Christian apologists and leaders who were in the generation immediately following the apostolic age. Perhaps Polycarp's greatest contribution to the Christian church was his martyrdom in Smyrna for his refusal to denounce the lordship of Jesus Christ. During the second century, there arose a period of tremendous persecution against Christians who refused to acknowledge that Caesar was lord. Polycarp was arrested for being a Christian—and at his trial before the Roman proconsul, he was asked to denounce Jesus Christ and declare that Caesar was lord. His response to the Roman proconsul was, "Eighty-six years I have served Christ, and He never did me any wrong. How can I blaspheme my King who saved me?" Eventually, he was led out and tied to a stake and burned to death for his stand. His death became a rallying cry for many Christians, who found strength in the courage of Polycarp.

It is difficult to stand by our convictions when other people think we are crazy. It is difficult to be true to who you are when those around you are giving up and giving in to the popular culture of the day. Persecution, imprisonment, and even martyrdom are experiences to which most American Christians cannot relate. In our lesson today, Paul stood trial for his convictions and for preaching the message of the Resurrection. Paul did not back down from his faith and witness of Jesus Christ as he stood before King Agrippa and Festus. In his example, we will find the courage to stand by our convictions.

B. Biblical Background

Today's lesson is the first of four lessons on the faith and ministry of Paul. His missionary days were nearing an end and he was standing trial in Caesarea before the authorities. In this lesson, we will examine the speech that Paul delivered before King Agrippa II. At the time that King Agrippa met Paul, he had already been in custody for two years. A new governor by the name of Porcius Festus was appointed to the office (see Acts 24:27). Felix was replaced by the Roman emperor because he had incited hostilities between the Jews and Greeks in Caesarea.

Usually, it was customary that at the changing of governors, prisoners would be released. Felix left Paul in prison because he wanted to gain the favor of the Jews. Festus was in office only three days before he went to Jerusalem to meet with the leaders of the Jewish nation. The country was in turmoil largely because of the activities of Felix in dealing with the situation between the Jews and the Greeks. The Jews were more interested in having Paul put away for good. They wanted Paul brought to Jerusalem for trial, but Festus refused. He would try Paul in Caesarea, and they were invited to join him there. Again, at the trial the Jews produced no solid evidence of any crime committed by Paul. Paul defended himself by telling Festus that he was not guilty under either Jewish or Roman law. When asked if he would go to Jerusalem, Paul responded by saying that he would appeal his case to Caesar in Rome. After conferring with his advisors, Festus concluded that Paul's right as a citizen of Rome entitled him to appeal to Caesar.

During the time that the trial of Paul was taking place, Herod Agrippa II (AD 27-100), along with his sister Bernice (correctly spelled "Berenice"), arrived in Caesarea. He was in Caesarea to pay his respects to the new governor, Festus. The charges against Paul were set before Agrippa. This issue would not go away, and no one seemed able to settle it. The charges were again brought up by the Jews, but again no witnesses were presented and no evidence was presented that merited the sentence of death. When he appeared before Festus and Agrippa, Paul gave a more detailed defense. His argument was so forceful that Festus declared that Paul must have been mad. Having heard the charges and Paul's defense, Agrippa told his wife, Bernice, that Paul was innocent—and if he had not appealed to Caesar, he would have been released.

II. EXPOSITION AND APPLICATION OF THE SCRIPTURE

A. Paul's Obedience to the Heavenly Vision (Acts 26:19-21)

Whereupon, O king Agrippa, I was not disobedient unto the heavenly vision: But shewed first unto them of Damascus, and at Jerusalem, and throughout all the coasts of Judaea, and then to the Gentiles, that they should repent and turn to God, and do works meet for repentance. For these causes the Jews caught me in the temple, and went about to kill me.

The experience that Paul had on the road to Damascus was the driving motivation in his commitment to fearlessly preach the Gospel of Jesus Christ. There was never any doubt in his mind that he had met the risen Christ and that his life had been permanently changed (see Romans 1:16-17; 1 Corinthians 15:19-20; 2 Corinthians 5:17). After reciting the vision and the dramatic events of that day on the Damascus Road, Paul told King Agrippa that he had not been disobedient to the heavenly vision (see Acts 9:1-9). He stated that he began his preaching ministry in Damascus and eventually made his way back to Jerusalem, where he tried to connect to the disciples (see Acts 9:20-25, 28). Paul said that he preached throughout Judea and also to the Gentiles.

Paul preached that men and women should repent of their sins, turn to God, and do the works that testify of a changed life. It was his preaching of the Resurrection that aroused the most anger and resentment among the Sadducean Jews, and led to his being arrested in the first place (see Acts 21:27-36; 22:22; 23:12-15; 25:3). Had the Roman soldiers not been present at the Temple on that day, the Jews could very well have killed Paul.

B. Paul's Testimony of the Resurrection (Acts 26:22-23)

Having therefore obtained help of God, I continue unto this day, witnessing both to small and great, saying none other things than those which the prophets and Moses did say should come: That Christ should suffer, and that he should be the first that should rise from the dead, and should shew light unto the people, and to the Gentiles.

The Jews had tried on more than one occasion to kill Paul—in order to put an end to the preaching of the message about the Resurrection—but God had been his strength. Paul had not limited his preaching and teaching to one social or economic class; rather, he preached to kings and common people alike. Further, Paul did not withhold anything that was needful from his hearers—he preached the whole counsel of God's Word (see Acts 20:20). He reminded King Agrippa that what he was preaching was not anything new. That Christ would come had been prophesied hundreds of years before Jesus began preaching.

As Paul stood before King Agrippa, he revealed what were among the common elements of apostolic preaching and teaching: first, Christ would suffer (see Mark 8:31-32; 9:31; 10:32); second, Jesus was buried according to the Scriptures (see 1 Corinthians 15:3-4); and third, Christ rose from the dead on the third day (see Acts 2:35-39; 9:20; 10:34-43; 16:26-33; compare with the book of Isaiah).

C. Paul's Testimony to Festus (Acts 26:24-26)

And as he thus spake for himself, Festus said with a loud voice, Paul, thou art beside thyself; much learning doth make thee mad. But he said, I am not mad, most noble Festus; but speak forth the words of truth and soberness. For the king knoweth of these things, before whom also I speak freely: for I am persuaded that none of these things are hidden from him; for this thing was not done in a corner.

Festus reached a point where he had heard enough. Just prior to the arrival of King Agrippa and Bernice, he had previously heard this discussion about Jesus rising from the dead and had already concluded that it was a ridiculous thought (see Acts 25:19f; 1 Corinthians 1:18-23). He may have stood and raised his voice and shouted at Paul that it was evident to him that he was completely out of his mind. He did not totally dismiss Paul as a learned fanatic; rather, the tone of the Greek text suggests that he paid a hint of respect to the aged missionary and preacher. The governor felt that maybe Paul had been studying too much or had come to these conclusions based purely upon the abundance of scrolls that he had been reading.

In verse 26, Paul responded, respectfully to Festus, and told him that he was not out of his mind. He stated that what he was saying was truth—it was fact based upon eyewitness accounts (see Matthew 28:1-8; Mark 16:1-9; Luke 24:1-48; John 20:1-31). Earlier in their conversation, Paul mentioned how he had heard the voice of the Lord Jesus Christ speaking to him, commissioning him to preach the Gospel (compare with his testimony in 1 Corinthians 15:1-9; Galatians 2:1-9). Turning from Festus, Paul spoke directly to King Agrippa, saying that he was quite familiar with these things. How Paul came to that conclusion is not stated in the text. He more than likely reached that conclusion based upon Agrippa's interest in Jewish religious beliefs and practices, although he was neither a Jew nor a Gentile. Paul was convinced that King Agrippa was very much aware of the things that had been said about Jesus and knew firsthand of the impact that He continued to have in Israel.

D. Paul's Testimony to Agrippa
   (Acts 26:27-32)

King Agrippa, believest thou the prophets? I know that thou believest. Then Agrippa said unto Paul, Almost thou persuadest me to be a Christian. And Paul said, I would to God, that not only thou, but also all that hear me this day, were both almost, and altogether such as I am, except these bonds. And when he had thus spoken, the king rose up, and the governor, and Bernice, and they that sat with them: And when they were gone aside, they talked between themselves, saying, This man doeth nothing worthy of death or of bonds. Then said Agrippa unto Festus, This man might have been set at liberty, if he had not appealed unto Caesar.

In verse 27, Paul asked King Agrippa a direct question: "King Agrippa, do you believe the prophets?" And before he could answer, Paul answered for him, "I know that you do." Surely, if King Agrippa knew of the prophecies concerning the Messiah, then it stood to reason that he must believe that Jesus was the Promised Messiah. Whether or not King Agrippa saw Jesus in the same light as Christians is not known. King Agrippa evaded Paul's question by suggesting that Paul could not possibly have assumed that he could be converted in such a short amount of time. In response to the king, Paul indicated that it was his goal not only to convert the king, but also for all men and women to come to the knowledge of the truth in Christ and become as he was.

In verse 30, the king rose from his chair, deciding that he had heard enough to make a fairly clear judgment about Paul's guilt or innocence. As they all left the room, they talked about the events that had just transpired. They all agreed that whatever charges the Jews had brought against Paul were totally without merit or not sufficient to warrant further action. Paul had done nothing that warranted imprisonment or death. Festus had originally been seeking advice on how to handle the situation with Paul. At that point, he had all of the information that he needed to prepare the statement that he would need to send along with Paul to Rome. Agrippa turned to Festus and told him that had Paul not appealed to Caesar—which was every Roman citizen's right—then he would have been released to continue his ministry.

III. CONCLUDING REFLECTION

It is clear from the lesson that Paul was a man of deep convictions. He was not afraid to stand and tell others, even the governor and king, who Jesus Christ was and what He had done in Paul's life.

There are occasions when all of us are put

in positions to testify about the goodness of God. Our witness becomes more powerful, provocative, and convincing as we share with others the depths from which God has lifted us, and that He has given us power over sin and death. When was the last time you held a conversation with someone—not about your church, but about your relationship with the Lord Jesus Christ? A second lesson of equal importance is seen in Paul's obedience to the heavenly vision. God gave Paul a vision of reaching the Gentiles with the Gospel of Jesus Christ. He never wavered from it.

PRAYER

Blessed Lord, teach us to be bold witnesses for the cause of reaching the multitudes in Your name. Lord, grant that we will never back down when we can share our faith. In Jesus' name we pray. Amen.

WORD POWER

Festus Porcius—**Roman procurator of Judea from 59–62 BCE.[1] He was also the governor who sent Paul to stand trial before Caesar (see Acts 25:11). Much of what is known about his tenure as procurator comes from the work of Josephus and the Acts of the Apostles.[2] Festus replaced Felix, who proved to be an ineffective governor, whose tenure was marred by much social unrest and religious upheaval. Additionally, under Felix, the country experienced much violence and robbery. Felix was replaced as governor by Caesar, who appointed Festus sometime during 59 BC.**

HOME DAILY BIBLE READINGS
(October 29–November 4, 2012)

Paul before King Agrippa

MONDAY, October 29: "Appeasing Those Zealous for the Law" (Acts 21:17-26)

TUESDAY, October 30: "A Stirred-up Mob" (Acts 21:27-36)

WEDNESDAY, October 31: "Taken into Custody" (Acts 22:17-24)

THURSDAY, November 1: "You Must Bear Witness in Rome" (Acts 22:30–23:11)

FRIDAY, November 2: "Paul's Background as a Pharisee" (Acts 26:1-8)

SATURDAY, November 3: "Paul's Encounter with Christ" (Acts 26:9-18)

SUNDAY, November 4: "Paul's Testimony before Roman Authorities" (Acts 26:19-32)

End Notes

[1]"Festus, Porcius" *The New Interpreters Dictionary of the Bible, Volume 2*, (Nashville: Abingdon Press), p. 446.
[2]Ibid.

PAUL SAILS FOR ROME

FAITH PATHWAY/FAITH JOURNEY TOPIC: **Weathering the Storm**

DEVOTIONAL READING: **Romans 1:13-17**   BACKGROUND SCRIPTURE: **Acts 27**
PRINT PASSAGE: **Acts 27:1-2, 33-44**   KEY VERSE: **Acts 27:44**

Acts 27:1-2, 33-44—KJV

AND WHEN it was determined that we should sail into Italy, they delivered Paul and certain other prisoners unto one named Julius, a centurion of Augustus' band.

2 And entering into a ship of Adramyttium, we launched, meaning to sail by the coasts of Asia; one Aristarchus, a Macedonian of Thessalonica, being with us.

.....

33 And while the day was coming on, Paul besought them all to take meat, saying, This day is the four-teenth day that ye have tarried and continued fast-ing, having taken nothing.

34 Wherefore I pray you to take some meat: for this is for your health: for there shall not an hair fall from the head of any of you.

35 And when he had thus spoken, he took bread, and gave thanks to God in presence of them all: and when he had broken it, he began to eat.

36 Then were they all of good cheer, and they also took some meat.

37 And we were in all in the ship two hundred three-score and sixteen souls.

38 And when they had eaten enough, they lightened the ship, and cast out the wheat into the sea.

39 And when it was day, they knew not the land: but they discovered a certain creek with a shore, into the which they were minded, if it were possible, to thrust in the ship.

40 And when they had taken up the anchors, they committed themselves unto the sea, and loosed the rudder bands, and hoisted up the mainsail to the wind, and made toward shore.

41 And falling into a place where two seas met, they ran the ship aground; and the forepart stuck fast, and remained unmoveable, but the hinder part was broken with the violence of the waves.

Acts 27:1-2, 33-44—NIV

WHEN IT was decided that we would sail for Italy, Paul and some other prisoners were handed over to a centurion named Julius, who belonged to the Imperial Regiment.

2 We boarded a ship from Adramyttium about to sail for ports along the coast of the province of Asia, and we put out to sea. Aristarchus, a Macedonian from Thessalonica, was with us.

.....

33 Just before dawn Paul urged them all to eat. "For the last fourteen days," he said, "you have been in constant suspense and have gone without food—you haven't eaten anything.

34 Now I urge you to take some food. You need it to survive. Not one of you will lose a single hair from his head."

35 After he said this, he took some bread and gave thanks to God in front of them all. Then he broke it and began to eat.

36 They were all encouraged and ate some food themselves.

37 Altogether there were 276 of us on board.

38 When they had eaten as much as they wanted, they lightened the ship by throwing the grain into the sea.

39 When daylight came, they did not recognize the land, but they saw a bay with a sandy beach, where they decided to run the ship aground if they could.

40 Cutting loose the anchors, they left them in the sea and at the same time untied the ropes that held the rudders. Then they hoisted the foresail to the wind and made for the beach.

41 But the ship struck a sandbar and ran aground. The bow stuck fast and would not move, and the stern was broken to pieces by the pounding of the surf.

UNIFYING LESSON PRINCIPLE

In times of crises, our panic can lead us to behave irrationally. What helps us avoid panic and act with a level head? Paul's confidence in God's faithfulness enabled him to act calmly and assure all the ship's passengers that they would survive the storm.

42 And the soldiers' counsel was to kill the prisoners, lest any of them should swim out, and escape.

43 But the centurion, willing to save Paul, kept them from their purpose; and commanded that they which could swim should cast themselves first into the sea, and get to land:

44 And the rest, some on boards, and some on broken pieces of the ship. And so it came to pass, that they escaped all safe to land.

42 The soldiers planned to kill the prisoners to prevent any of them from swimming away and escaping.

43 But the centurion wanted to spare Paul's life and kept them from carrying out their plan. He ordered those who could swim to jump overboard first and get to land.

44 The rest were to get there on planks or on pieces of the ship. In this way everyone reached land in safety.

TOPICAL OUTLINE OF THE LESSON

I. **Introduction**
   A. Confidence in Crisis
   B. Biblical Background

II. **Exposition and Application of the Scripture**
   A. The Departure for Rome (Acts 27:1-2)
   B. Paul's Declaration of Encouragement (Acts 27:33-38)
   C. The Destruction of the Ship (Acts 27:39-44)

III. **Concluding Reflection**

LESSON OBJECTIVES

Upon completion of the lesson, the students will be able to do the following:

1. Connect Paul's faith in God with his ability to remain calm in the midst of a storm;

2. Recognize and appreciate how their relationship with God helps them cope with crisis; and,

3. Witness to others about how their relationship with God makes a difference in their ability to deal with crises.

POINTS TO BE EMPHASIZED

ADULT/YOUTH

Adult Topic: **Weathering the Storm**

Youth Topic: **A Stressful Journey**

Adult Key Verse: **Acts 27:44**

Youth Key Verse: **Acts 27:34**

Print Passage: **Acts 27:1-2, 33-44**

—This story is not only about Paul's being saved from a violent storm on the sea, but also about greater opportunities to communicate the Gospel in the future.

—This chapter begins with a centurion receiving orders to take Paul and some other prisoners to Rome.

—Paul became concerned about the people, because they had not eaten in two weeks.

—Paul delivered a message of hope and deliverance to the men that God would spare them all.

—In accordance with the angelic message that had been given to Paul, everyone on the ship arrived safely on land.

CHILDREN

Children Topic: **Keeping Calm in the Storm**

Key Verse: **Acts 27:44b**

Print Passage: Acts 27:33-44

—Paul attempted to halt the trip earlier due to poor weather conditions.

—The men on the ship had not eaten, either because of concern and nervousness or because of religious fasting—in hopes of gaining divine intervention.

—Paul encouraged everyone to eat and prepare for the inevitable wreck by casting items overboard.

—Some people on the ship still were not eager to follow Paul's advice.

—Paul's confidence in God's faithfulness enabled him to act calmly and assure all on the ship that they would survive the storm.

I. INTRODUCTION

A. Confidence in Crisis

In times of crises, our panic can lead us to behave irrationally and out of character. What do you do when you face difficulty? Paul's confidence in God was a stabilizing presence during the severe storm that he and the other men faced. The lesson today reminds us that people of faith can make a huge difference during times of grave danger and difficulty.

B. Biblical Background

In the previous lesson, Paul stood trial before King Agrippa, who decided that Paul's request to be tried before Caesar would be allowed to proceed. The danger that Paul faced at this point would shift from a purely political and religious one to facing the dangers associated with maritime travel in the first century. During their journey, the small ship they were on encountered a major storm in the Mediterranean Sea, called a "noreaster." For fourteen days, they were driven, tossed to and fro, and literally pounded by the waves and the winds. The storm was so severe that the captain was unable to steer the ship and simply gave way to the wind's driving it in whatever direction it wished. We are told that after a while, the 276 people on board the ship gave up hope that they would be saved or would reach land safely. They were all looking for and expecting the worst to happen. Everyone on the ship gave up hope, except Paul (see Acts 27:21-25). After receiving the word of encouragement from the angel of God, Paul encouraged those on the ship to eat and take comfort in what had been revealed to him. Although the ship would be lost there would not be one soul lost among the 276 persons on board the ship.

II. EXPOSITION AND APPLICATION OF THE SCRIPTURE

A. The Departure for Rome
   (Acts 27:1-2)

AND WHEN it was determined that we should sail into Italy, they delivered Paul and certain other prisoners unto one named Julius, a centurion of Augustus' band. And entering into a ship of Adramyttium, we launched, meaning to sail by the coasts of Asia; one Aristarchus, a Macedonian of Thessalonica, being with us.

After the trial before King Agrippa and Festus, Paul was handed over to a centurion named Julius who was to escort him along with several other prisoners to Rome. Luke did not mention who they were or their particular crimes of which they had been convicted. What is of keen interest in the passage is Luke's use of the personal pronoun "we." This suggests that Luke had rejoined Paul for the trip to Rome (see Acts 21:18). There is no mention of his whereabouts during the interim period—and anything that is stated regarding those whereabouts is more speculation than fact. Julius served in the Imperial Regiment. "The term 'imperial' was generally used for auxiliary forces drawn largely from the local population, and it is known that an auxiliary cohort was stationed in Caesarea during the time of Agrippa II."[2] Julius may also have been a special envoy on assignment from Rome who was given the task of escorting prisoners back to Rome.

Luke did not indicate the exact location of their departure; more than likely it was Caesarea, since that is where Paul was being held. They boarded a ship whose homeport was Adramyttium, which was a seaport town in the Asian Province Mysia (just southeast of Troas). They would travel as far as that ship would travel and then take a larger vessel to Rome. Smaller ships would travel along the coast so as to avoid the dangers of the open waters.

Accompanying Paul and Luke was a man named Aristarchus, a Christian convert from Macedonia of Thessalonica (see Philemon 4; Colossians 4:10). Luke did not say how he ended up with the group or how long he had been with them. Paul was not alone for what was one of the most important journeys of his life. We all know that the Lord has promised never to leave us alone, but there are occasions in life when the presence of friends who love us and support us is vital.

B. Paul's Declaration of Encouragement (Acts 27:33-38)

And while the day was coming on, Paul besought them all to take meat, saying, This day is the fourteenth day that ye have tarried and continued fasting, having taken nothing. Wherefore I pray you to take some meat: for this is for your health: for there shall not an hair fall from the head of any of you. And when he had thus spoken, he took bread, and gave thanks to God in presence of them all: and when he had broken it, he began to eat. Then were they all of good cheer, and they also took some meat. And we were in all in the ship two hundred threescore and sixteen souls. And when they had eaten enough, they lightened the ship, and cast out the wheat into the sea.

The past fourteen days had been a harrowing experience for the voyagers (see Acts 27:13-32). They had no idea whether they would live or die. Paul had already encouraged them that the angel of the God whom he served had given him the assurance that none of them would be lost (see Acts 27:21-26). Another night had gone by and early in the morning Paul urged the men to eat. For fourteen days, many of them had been either too sick to eat or just too frightened to even think of eating.

In verse 34, Paul urged the beleaguered travelers to eat some food. They would need all of the strength that they could muster in the days to come. Paul's words would later prove to be true. He reminded them that not a single man would be lost—not even a single strand of hair on their heads. Hearing these words must have filled the hearts of the voyagers with renewed hope that perhaps all would be well. Paul did not just encourage the men to eat, but he showed them that it was going to be okay by taking food himself. He took some bread and gave thanks, broke it, and began to eat.

The sight of Paul eating and hearing again his words of encouragement did a lot to spur renewed hope. Paul provided a powerful witness to the men, many of whom were pagan worshippers. He drew a clear distinction between the God whom he served—who had reassured him that all would be well—and the gods of the sailors, which had provided no assurances. Sometimes when people are in the midst of a serious crisis, they must be reminded repeatedly to keep their spirits up and hope for the best. They all ate and they were all encouraged (see Joshua 1:5; Psalm 27:1-6; 46:1). The tone and climate changed on the ship, just as the sun was rising on a new day. Luke mentioned that there were 276 people on board the ship, which was intended to stress the magnitude of the miracle that none would be lost. After they had eaten as much as they wanted, the crew and soldiers began to throw the excess grain overboard. The reason was to keep the ship light in the water as it ran aground so that when it began to break up it would be closer to the shore.

C. The Destruction of the Ship
(Acts 27:39-44)

And when it was day, they knew not the land: but they discovered a certain creek with a shore, into the which they were minded, if it were possible, to thrust in the ship. And when they had taken up the anchors, they committed themselves unto the sea, and loosed the rudder bands, and hoisted up the mainsail to the wind, and made toward shore. And falling into a place where two seas met, they ran the ship aground; and the forepart stuck fast, and remained unmoveable, but the hinder part was broken with the violence of the waves. And the soldiers' counsel was to kill the prisoners, lest any of them should swim out, and escape. But the centurion, willing to save Paul, kept them from their purpose; and commanded that they which could swim should cast themselves first into the sea, and get to land: And the rest, some on boards, and some on broken pieces of the ship. And so it came to pass, that they escaped all safe to land.

Finally, there was the possibility of reaching the shore. As the sun arose, the men spotted land but had no idea where they were. Off in the distance they saw a bay with a sandy beach and it is here that they decided to run the ship aground. What the voyagers did not know was that they had arrived at the island of Malta. The site where the shipwreck occurred is known today as St. Paul's Bay. This is an area that would not have been known to the sailors. Seasoned sailors who traveled this route from Rome to Africa would have recognized the traditional harbor which is located further to the west of the site of the shipwreck on another part of the island.

In verse 40, Luke provided details about the steps that the sailors took to make sure that the ship ran aground. First, they cut loose the four anchors that had held the ship steady. At the same time, they untied the ropes that held the rudders so that they would be able to steer the ship toward the coast. Last, they hoisted the small sail that was at the front of the ship so that they would have some control and power with which to run the ship aground.

At first, it looked like their plan would work. However, being unfamiliar with the area, they were not aware that just below them was a sandbar. Once they struck the sandbar, the ship became completely immobilized and the stern began to break into pieces. This presented a new set of problems for the Roman soldiers. What were they to do with the prisoners? Their first thought was to kill all of the prisoners so as to prevent them from escaping. Julius, however, did not want his troops to make a mistake and kill Paul along with the others. He ordered that none of the prisoners be killed and that any who could swim were to make their way to shore. The rest who could not swim were told to hold on to the broken pieces of the ship and use them as life rafts. Just as Paul had told them, everyone made it safely to the shore and not a single man was lost.

III. CONCLUDING REFLECTION

This is a story about how one man's faith gave hope and inspiration to 275 others who had just about given up hope of surviving the storm—to say nothing of the ship's being broken up as it approached the coastline. People of faith can bring people who are living with fear and panic the calm assurance that God will be their strength in their moments of crisis.

Paul made a huge difference by his very presence on the ship. We should never underestimate the ministry of presence. There are times when God will strategically place us in situations so that we may be witnesses to men and women who do not know Him. Paul's presence on the journey was one of the primary reasons why the Roman soldiers did not kill the other prisoners. His presence encouraged the fainthearted and prevented a slaughter by the Romans.

PRAYER

Lord, teach us how to be pillars of strength for those around us who are weak. May we learn to continually trust in You during our moments of crisis. In Jesus' name we pray. Amen.

WORD POWER

Sailing in the first century—this was one of the primary means of transportation and a principal means of moving commercial goods across the Roman Empire. The Romans built an elaborate road network that was used to move soldiers and materials from one outpost to the next. It is clear from the Acts of the Apostles that Paul spent some portion of each of his three missionary journeys sailing the Mediterranean Sea (see 13:4-5, 13; 14:26; 16:11; 17:14; 18:18, 21-22; 20:2-6, 13-16, 38; 21:1-3; 27–28).

HOME DAILY BIBLE READINGS
(November 5-11, 2012)

Paul Sails for Rome
MONDAY, November 5: "Called to Be an Apostle" (Romans 1:1-7)

TUESDAY, November 6: "Encouraged by Each Other's Faith" (Romans 1:8-12)

WEDNESDAY, November 7: "Eager to Proclaim the Gospel" (Romans 1:13-17)

THURSDAY, November 8: "Paul's Journey to Rome Begins" (Acts 27:3-12)

FRIDAY, November 9: "A Fierce Storm Dashes Hope" (Acts 27:13-20)

SATURDAY, November 10: "Keep Up Your Courage" (Acts 27:21-32)

SUNDAY, November 11: "Brought Safely to Land" (Acts 27:1-2, 33-44)

End Notes

[1]John B. Polhill, *The New American Commentary: Acts*, (Nashville: Broadman Press, 1992), p. 515.
[2]Polhill, p. 529.

LESSON 12   November 18, 2012

PAUL MINISTERS IN MALTA

FAITH PATHWAY/FAITH JOURNEY TOPIC: **Helping One Another**

DEVOTIONAL READING: **Ezekiel 34:11-16**   BACKGROUND SCRIPTURE: **Acts 28:1-10**
PRINT PASSAGE: **Acts 28:1-10**   KEY VERSE: **Acts 28:8**

Acts 28:1-10—KJV

AND WHEN they were escaped, then they knew that the island was called Melita.

2 And the barbarous people shewed us no little kindness: for they kindled a fire, and received us every one, because of the present rain, and because of the cold.

3 And when Paul had gathered a bundle of sticks, and laid them on the fire, there came a viper out of the heat, and fastened on his hand.

4 And when the barbarians saw the venomous beast hang on his hand, they said among themselves, No doubt this man is a murderer, whom, though he hath escaped the sea, yet vengeance suffereth not to live.

5 And he shook off the beast into the fire, and felt no harm.

6 Howbeit they looked when he should have swollen, or fallen down dead suddenly: but after they had looked a great while, and saw no harm come to him, they changed their minds, and said that he was a god.

7 In the same quarters were possessions of the chief man of the island, whose name was Publius; who received us, and lodged us three days courteously.

8 And it came to pass, that the father of Publius lay sick of a fever and of a bloody flux: to whom Paul entered in, and prayed, and laid his hands on him, and healed him.

9 So when this was done, others also, which had diseases in the island, came, and were healed:

10 Who also honoured us with many honours; and when we departed, they laded us with such things as were necessary.

Acts 28:1-10—NIV

ONCE SAFELY on shore, we found out that the island was called Malta.

2 The islanders showed us unusual kindness. They built a fire and welcomed us all because it was raining and cold.

3 Paul gathered a pile of brushwood and, as he put it on the fire, a viper, driven out by the heat, fastened itself on his hand.

4 When the islanders saw the snake hanging from his hand, they said to each other, "This man must be a murderer; for though he escaped from the sea, Justice has not allowed him to live."

5 But Paul shook the snake off into the fire and suffered no ill effects.

6 The people expected him to swell up or suddenly fall dead, but after waiting a long time and seeing nothing unusual happen to him, they changed their minds and said he was a god.

7 There was an estate nearby that belonged to Publius, the chief official of the island. He welcomed us to his home and for three days entertained us hospitably.

8 His father was sick in bed, suffering from fever and dysentery. Paul went in to see him and, after prayer, placed his hands on him and healed him.

9 When this had happened, the rest of the sick on the island came and were cured.

10 They honored us in many ways and when we were ready to sail, they furnished us with the supplies we needed.

UNIFYING LESSON PRINCIPLE

Often we can tell something about the character of people by observing how they respond in difficult situations. What conclusions might others draw from observing our actions? The people of Malta recognized something extraordinary about Paul—because through his faith in Christ a man was healed.

TOPICAL OUTLINE OF THE LESSON

I. Introduction
   A. The Ministry of Hospitality
   B. Biblical Background

II. Exposition and Application of the Scripture
   A. The Reception and Hospitality of the People of Malta
      (Acts 28:1-2)
   B. Paul Protected from the Bite of the Viper
      (Acts 28:3-6)
   C. Paul's Ministry of Healing
      (Acts 28:7-10)

III. Concluding Reflection

LESSON OBJECTIVES

Upon completion of the lesson, the students will be able to do the following:

1. Connect Paul's ministry and the subsequent hospitality he received in Malta;

2. Express awe over God's extraordinary action in their lives; and,

3. Demonstrate their faith by ministering to the needs of others.

POINTS TO BE EMPHASIZED

ADULT/YOUTH

Adult Topic: **Helping One Another**
Youth Topic: **Somebody Is Watching You**
Adult Key Verse: **Acts 28:8**
Youth Key Verse: **Acts 28:6**
Print Passage: **Acts 28:1-10**

—The ship's passengers ended up on the island of Malta, south of Sicily, where they were welcomed.

—Because the people of Malta, who were not already Christians, showed Paul and his band extraordinary kindness, God may have been working through them already.

—Paul was able to shake off the snake and live (see Luke 10:19; Acts 28:3).

—As the natives observed Paul's fate in this difficult situation with the viper, they tried to determine his character.

—When the natives' previously held beliefs were proven false—because Paul survived the viper's bite—they called him a god.

—Through praying and the laying on of hands, Paul was able to heal the sick.

—Publius and the natives were so grateful to Paul that they not only honored the whole crew but also made sure that they were well accommodated when they set sail again.

CHILDREN

Children Topic: **Paul Heals Others**
Key Verse: **Acts 28:9**
Print Passage: **Acts 28:1-10**

—These events occurred on Paul's journey to Rome for his trial before Caesar.

—After surviving the storm, Paul and the others arrived at Malta and were greeted warmly by the natives.

—Paul, having escaped calamity, was attacked by a snake, which indicated to the islanders that Paul must be a very evil sinner.

—Paul's favor with God was shown in both his survival of the snakebite and his successful prayer of healing for others on the island.

—Those whom Paul helped also assisted Paul and the others to continue their journey.

I. INTRODUCTION

A. The Ministry of Hospitality

The ministry of hospitality is one of the most critical ministries within the local church. Its roots extend deep into the biblical traditions of the Old and New Testaments, going back as far as the days of Abraham. Being hospitable meant not only providing for the human guests, but also their animals as well (see Genesis 18:1-8). In all of the ancient cultures, hospitality was viewed as a key element of what it meant to be a civilized community. Within Roman society, the entertainment of guests was considered to be a sacred duty.[1] A common trait of biblical culture was the obligation to extend hospitality to strangers and travelers who may have been passing through one's area.[2] One of the reasons hospitality was considered important was due to the absence of inns and places where travelers could freely stay during long journeys.

In today's lesson, the apostle Paul and his fellow travelers were shipwrecked on the island of Malta. The natives of Malta were very gracious and kind to Paul and the other voyagers. The people of Malta treated the visitors as family and gave them everything that they needed to make their stay pleasant (see James 2:15). Paul in turn was given an opportunity by the Holy Spirit to share the Gospel of the Lord Jesus Christ and to heal many of their diseases. While this is not explicitly stated in the text, we know from previous studies that Paul never missed a chance to preach and teach the Gospel. In this lesson, we learn very valuable principles about how to minister to people during times of their greatest need. Just as the people ministered to the physical needs of Paul and others, likewise he ministered to their spiritual needs (see Hebrews 6:10).

B. Biblical Background

Paul and his fellow voyagers washed up on the shores of the island of Malta (*Melita* in the KJV). They had just survived a sailor's worst nightmare, a noreaster that seemed to have no end. Finally, they were all safe; we are not told whether any of the voyagers were injured during the shipwreck. It was early morning and they were all wet, cold, and hungry. The people of Malta treated the visitors with a gracious and extraordinary kindness that is mentioned in verse 2. Paul's journey to Rome had not been cut short by the storm and shipwreck. The providential hand of God was still with him and he was now on fertile soil, a place where he had never preached, which was one of his driving motivations (see Romans 15:20-28). The Gospel had never penetrated as far as Malta. This was a first for Paul and the Gospel.

The people of Malta had many of the superstitions that people of the ancient world believed, especially when Paul was bitten by a viper. Like many in the ancient world, the people of Malta automatically correlated bad events to sin and they believed that the gods would mete out just punishment for wrongdoing. When Paul survived the bite of the viper, the people thought that he was a god, which was not the first time that this had happened (see Acts 14:11-13). This act of deliverance opened the hearts and the minds of the people to receive the Gospel. It was yet another sign of God's favor and calling upon the life of Paul. The Lord Jesus Christ used Paul in a mighty way to heal the sick and to bring the Gospel to people who had never heard the message of salvation.

Although Paul found himself in a very difficult situation, he would not allow it to dictate the course of his ministry. Often, we can tell something about the character of people by observing how they respond in difficult situations.

II. EXPOSITION AND APPLICATION OF THE SCRIPTURE

A. The Reception and Hospitality of the People of Malta
(Acts 28:1-2)

AND WHEN they were escaped, then they knew that the island was called Melita. And the barbarous people shewed us no little kindness: for they kindled a fire, and received us every one, because of the present rain, and because of the cold.

When all of the survivors reached the shoreline, they realized that they were on the island of Malta. We are not told how they came to this conclusion; most likely an experienced sailor and well-travelled Roman soldier would recognize the place. Malta is located about 60 miles south of the island of Sicily in the Mediterranean Sea and is about 18 miles long and 8 miles wide.[3] The island was colonized by the Phoenicians about 1000 BC and at the time of Paul's shipwreck was a Roman colony. Malta was used primarily as one of the main stops in the shipping lanes between Rome and its colonies in the Mediterranean basin, and was one of the main stopover points for grain ships traveling from Egypt.

The ordeal of those who had been shipwrecked was not over. Once on the dry land they faced the situation of surviving in a strange place. They were all wet and this was compounded by cold and rain. This would have caused them to be miserable. However, the people of Malta graciously received the stranded travelers. In recording this event, Luke made two statements about the people of Malta. First, he called them *barbaroi*; we get the word *barbaric* from this word. There are two primary explanations that interpreters have given for what the word probably meant. One explanation is that the word *barbaroi* was used to describe non-Greek-speaking people. However, this explanation does not carry much weight; given that Malta was a strategic stopping point on the main shipping lines, the native people would most surely be able to speak some Greek and Latin. The best explanation seems to be that the word most likely refers to people who held superstitious beliefs about God; particularly since later they would think that Paul was a god because he did not die from the viper's bite.[4]

Second, Luke said that the people of Malta were very kind. The people of Malta showed an unusual kindness to Paul and the others, the sort of hospitality and reception that deeply impressed Luke. He had traveled throughout the empire and was very much aware of the ways that people expressed hospitality. They built a fire and welcomed the shipwrecked crew and soldiers.

There is much to be learned about receiving strangers and graciously welcoming them into our homes and churches. We tend to be suspicious of new arrivals, but in this case the people saw their condition and need and sought to do whatever they could do to help.

B. Paul Protected from the Bite of the Viper (Acts 28:3-6)

And when Paul had gathered a bundle of sticks, and laid them on the fire, there came a viper out of the heat, and fastened on his hand. And when the barbarians saw the venomous beast hang on his hand, they said among themselves, No doubt this man is a murderer, whom, though he hath escaped the sea, yet vengeance suffereth not to live. And he shook off the beast into the fire, and felt no harm. Howbeit they looked when he should have swollen, or fallen down dead suddenly: but after they had looked a great while, and saw no harm come to him, they changed their minds, and said that he was a god.

Paul was not a lazy man, nor was he one to accept hospitality without working for it (see Acts 20:34; 1 Corinthians 4:12; 1 Thessalonians 4:11; 2 Thessalonians 3:8, 10). He joined in the gathering of the firewood—and as he stooped down to add more wood to the fire, a viper jumped out and bit him on his hand. Witnessing the turn of events, the islanders began to express their beliefs that surely this man must be a murderer. How they came to this conclusion has to do with their ancient beliefs and superstitions about justice and divine retribution. They reasoned that he had escaped the long arm of fate when he survived the shipwreck, but justice had finally caught up with him. "Justice" in verse 4 is not a reference to the philosophical notion of fair play but refers to the ancient mythological beliefs in a god of justice that dispenses punishment to those whose deeds merit it.[5] The islanders reasoned that evidently Paul had committed a crime and he was about to receive his just dues. This belief was also common among the Jews, who believed that a man or woman who became ill or who met some untimely fate must have committed a sin against God (see Luke 13:2, 4; 9:1).

In verse 5, Paul showed no signs of any ill effects as he shook off the snake and it fell into the fire (see Luke 10:19). If he were going to experience the effects of the bite it would have begun shortly after he was bitten. The people expected to see something happen to Paul. He would either drop dead or at least begin to swell up. We are not told how long the people waited, but evidently it was long enough for something to have happened to Paul. When nothing happened, the people began to change their minds about who Paul was and reasoned that he must be a god. This had happened once before (see Acts 14:11-13). There is no mention that the islanders fell to the ground and wanted to worship Paul—and we cannot assume that they did.

The islanders had witnessed two mighty acts of divine deliverance in the course of a single day. First, Paul and his fellow voyagers had survived a horrific storm and shipwreck. Second, one of the passengers survived being bitten by a poisonous snake. What they were not privy to was the promise that God had made to Paul that he would surely stand before Caesar and would reach Rome (see Acts 27:21-26).

C. Paul's Ministry of Healing
(Acts 28:7-10)

In the same quarters were possessions of the chief man of the island, whose name was Publius; who received us, and lodged us three days courteously. And it came to pass, that the father of Publius lay sick of a fever and of a bloody flux: to whom Paul entered in, and prayed, and laid his hands on him, and healed him. So when this was done, others also, which had diseases in the island, came, and were healed: Who also honoured us with many honours; and when we departed, they laded us with such things as were necessary.

News about what had happened to Paul around the fire spread throughout the villages on the island. The leading civic official lived nearby to the place where Paul and his fellow voyagers were being entertained. Luke recorded that the man's name was Publius and that he welcomed them into his home for three days. The question is, "To whom did Luke make reference to when he said *us?*" Was he referring to all of the passengers on the ship or to only some of the passengers? Luke never said who he was talking about, except that he was included in the group. Publius showed Paul and those whom he entertained a gracious kindness that he was surely under no obligation to do.

In verse 8, we are told that Publius's father was sick with fever and dysentery, both of which could be fatal, if left untreated. Paul went in to the man and prayed with him and laid his hands on him, and the sick man recovered. Again, the news about Paul made its way around the island. People came from all over the island to be prayed for and healed of their diseases (see verse 9). One can only imagine the joy that enveloped the island of Malta. We are not told how long this healing ministry lasted—possibly for the entire time that Paul was on the island, which was three months.

In verse 10, we see that the day finally came when the weather and winds were favorable for continuing their journey to Rome. We are not told where the people lodged, but it is obvious that they were treated with the highest favor and kindness, and that the people were also thankful to Paul and the others. When Paul and his companions finally were able to catch another ship going to Rome, the citizens of Malta gave them everything that they needed.

III. CONCLUDING REFLECTION

One of the most important truths that emerge from this period in Paul's life is the reality of God's promise of protection and provision. God's will was going to be accomplished in Paul's life, and although they had run into a period of extreme conditions, they were not the terminus of the apostle's life—just a short detour on the journey. Believers can always be encouraged and take heart in knowing that God's plan for our lives will come to pass. We can do all things through Him who strengthens us and empowers us to overcome the most challenging circumstances (see Philippians 4:13). Finally, there are times in life when we will find the most unusual blessings in the most unlikely places. Who would have ever thought that Paul would experience such warmth and hospitality in the latter days of his life after enduring such a life-threatening time at sea?

Throughout his many years of service to the Lord Jesus Christ, Paul experienced numerous trials and hardships (see 2 Corinthians 11:23-28). On Paul's final journey, God granted him a respite from the struggles of the past. Rather than Paul enduring harsh treatment on his journey, God opened the hearts and doors of people to treat him with kindness. It is true that we reap what we sow—in this life and in the life to come.

PRAYER

Heavenly Father, help us to so love others that we will always be moved to practice the ministry of hospitality and kindness. Grant that Your servants will never grow weary of doing good to others. In Jesus' name we pray. Amen.

WORD POWER

Kindness (Greek: *philanthropia)*—describes someone who has a deep love for humanity. This expression of human love or brotherly love is found throughout the Scriptures and is a fundamental biblical principle regarding the treatment of neighbors and strangers. In the New Testament, the word *chrestotes* is another word that is translated to mean "kindness," and it has in it the idea of moral goodness and integrity (see Ephesians 2:7).

HOME DAILY BIBLE READINGS
(November 12-18, 2012)

Paul Ministers in Malta
MONDAY, November 12: "The Failure to Minister" (Ezekiel 34:1-6)
TUESDAY, November 13: "God's Ministry to the Flock" (Ezekiel 34:11-16)
WEDNESDAY, November 14: "God's Judgment of the Privileged" (Ezekiel 34:17-22)
THURSDAY, November 15: "Extend Hospitality to Strangers" (Romans 12:9-13)
FRIDAY, November 16: "Ready for Every Good Work" (2 Timothy 2:20-26)
SATURDAY, November 17: "Do Good to All" (1 Thessalonians 5:12-22)
SUNDAY, November 18: "Ministering to the Sick" (Acts 28:1-10)

End Notes

[1] *Dictionary of Biblical Imagery, (1998), s.v., "Hospitality."*
[2] Ibid.
[3] Ben Witherington, *The Acts of the Apostles: A Socio-Rhetorical Commentary,* (Grand Rapids: William B. Eerdmans Publishing Co., 1998), p. 775.
[4] *New Interpreters Bible: Acts,* Vol. X (Nashville: Abingdon Press, 2002), p. 355.
[5] Ibid, 356.

UNIT III: Where Does Faith Take Us?   CHILDREN'S UNIT: What Does Faith Cost?   FALL QUARTER

LESSON 13   November 25, 2012

PAUL EVANGELIZES IN ROME

FAITH PATHWAY/FAITH JOURNEY TOPIC: **Spread the News**

DEVOTIONAL READING: **Deuteronomy 4:32-40**   BACKGROUND SCRIPTURE: **Acts 28:16-31**
PRINT PASSAGE: **Acts 28:23-31**   KEY VERSE: **Acts 28:28**

Acts 28:23-31—KJV

23 And when they had appointed him a day, there came many to him into his lodging; to whom he expounded and testified the kingdom of God, persuading them concerning Jesus, both out of the law of Moses, and out of the prophets, from morning till evening.

24 And some believed the things which were spoken, and some believed not.

25 And when they agreed not among themselves, they departed, after that Paul had spoken one word, Well spake the Holy Ghost by Esaias the prophet unto our fathers,

26 Saying, Go unto this people, and say, Hearing ye shall hear, and shall not understand; and seeing ye shall see, and not perceive:

27 For the heart of this people is waxed gross, and their ears are dull of hearing, and their eyes have they closed; lest they should see with their eyes, and hear with their ears, and understand with their heart, and should be converted, and I should heal them.

28 Be it known therefore unto you, that the salvation of God is sent unto the Gentiles, and that they will hear it.

29 And when he had said these words, the Jews departed, and had great reasoning among themselves.

30 And Paul dwelt two whole years in his own hired house, and received all that came in unto him,

31 Preaching the kingdom of God, and teaching those things which concern the Lord Jesus Christ, with all confidence, no man forbidding him.

Acts 28:23-31—NIV

23 They arranged to meet Paul on a certain day, and came in even larger numbers to the place where he was staying. From morning till evening he explained and declared to them the kingdom of God and tried to convince them about Jesus from the Law of Moses and from the Prophets.

24 Some were convinced by what he said, but others would not believe.

25 They disagreed among themselves and began to leave after Paul had made this final statement: "The Holy Spirit spoke the truth to your forefathers when he said through Isaiah the prophet:

26 'Go to this people and say, "You will be ever hearing but never understanding; you will be ever seeing but never perceiving."

27 For this people's heart has become calloused; they hardly hear with their ears, and they have closed their eyes. Otherwise they might see with their eyes, hear with their ears, understand with their hearts and turn, and I would heal them.'

28 Therefore I want you to know that God's salvation has been sent to the Gentiles, and they will listen!"

29 After he said this, the Jews left, arguing vigorously among themselves.

30 For two whole years Paul stayed there in his own rented house and welcomed all who came to see him.

31 Boldly and without hindrance he preached the kingdom of God and taught about the Lord Jesus Christ.

UNIFYING LESSON PRINCIPLE

It is a paradox of human nature that even when we have good news to share, some will ignore or reject it. What will we do when people refuse to listen? Paul persevered in faith, preaching the Gospel and bringing salvation to those who would listen, even though there were many who refused to believe in the Lord Jesus Christ.

TOPICAL OUTLINE OF THE LESSON

I. Introduction
A. A Lasting Testimony
B. Biblical Background

II. Exposition and Application of the Scripture
A. Paul Meets the Jewish Leaders (Acts 28:23)
B. The Jewish Leaders React to Paul's Message (Acts 28:24-29)
C. Paul Continued to Preach and Teach with Boldness (Acts 28:30-31)

III. Concluding Reflection

LESSON OBJECTIVES

Upon completion of the lesson, the students will be able to do the following:

1. Understand Paul's tenacity in making an evangelistic witness;
2. Reflect on times when they could affirm their belief in Christ and times when they had doubts; and,
3. Continue to express their faith in Christ even when some refuse to listen.

POINTS TO BE EMPHASIZED

ADULT/YOUTH

Adult Topic: Spread the News
Youth Topic: I Am Going to Tell It
Adult/Youth Key Verse: Acts 28:28
Print Passage: Acts 28:23-31

—Paul lived in Rome under house arrest, with limited freedom to witness for Christ.
—Paul considered his ministry in Rome to be an important goal for fulfilling his calling.
—The Jewish leaders wanted to hear an explanation from Paul on what was going on with him, for they had not received anything.
—Paul became a tenacious evangelistic witness.
—Paul delivered his evangelical message from morning to evening, while persevering in faith.
—Paul was disappointed that the Jews rejected his message—so he decided to proclaim the Gospel to the Gentiles.
—Paul lived in Rome for two years, gladly proclaiming the kingdom of God and the Gospel of Jesus.

CHILDREN

Children Topic: Paul Preaches in Rome
Key Verses: Acts 28:30-31
Print Passage: Acts 28:23-31

—Upon his arrival in Rome, Paul discovered that no information had been forwarded regarding his trials.
—The local Jewish leaders who met Paul wanted him to defend his beliefs.
—Many of the people came to hear the Gospel and believed; others were not persuaded.

—Many of those who turned from Paul did so because Paul said the Gospel was also for the Gentiles.

—Paul stayed in prison for at least two years, during which time he was allowed to preach without hindrance.

I. INTRODUCTION

A. A Lasting Testimony

In the *Christian Reader,* Ramon Williams writes that on April 28, 1996, a gunman walked into a crowded café in Port Arthur, Australia, and started shooting. Tony Kistan, a Salvation Army soldier from Sydney, and his wife Sarah were in the restaurant when the bullets began to fly. Courageously, Tony stepped in front of his wife to shield her from the gunfire, and he was one of the first to fall. Thirty-four victims eventually died in the incident, including Tony Kistan. As he lay dying in his wife's arms, he spoke his last words: "I'm going to be with the Lord."

Those final words of faith were quoted by the Australian media and carried to the world. "At a press conference," writes Williams, "Tony's son Nesan, 24, explained why his father held this assurance and described his father's dedication to the Gospel. Hardened journalists and photographers were seen wiping tears from their eyes. In life, Tony had been a man who witnessed for his Lord to strangers and friends alike, and now in death, he witnessed to others through his simple last statement."[1]

In the lesson today, Paul was in the final days of his life. He reached Rome, the imperial capital of the Roman Empire. He preached across the Roman Empire, founding numerous churches and leading thousands to faith in the Lord Jesus Christ. Paul persevered in faith, preaching the Gospel and bringing salvation to those who would listen, even though there were many who refused to believe in the Lord Jesus Christ.

B. Biblical Background

Three months after they were shipwrecked on Malta, Paul and the other voyagers set sail for Rome, which was their final destination. Luke provided great details about the journey from Malta to Rome. All along the way, Paul was met and warmly received by brothers who had heard of his arrival (see Acts 28:11-16). When he arrived in Rome, Paul was granted some liberty to live alone, with a soldier to guard him. Three days after his arrival in Rome, Paul set up a meeting with the leaders of the Jews so that he could explain how he ended up in Rome and in custody of the Roman authorities.

Paul considered his ministry in Rome to be an important goal for fulfilling his calling (see Romans 15:23-29). At this initial meeting with the Jewish leaders, they informed Paul that they had not received any bad news about him. However, they had heard about the infant Christian church and how Jews all over were talking about it.

At the second meeting with the Jewish leaders, the reaction was much different. The reaction of the Jewish leaders to Paul's preaching was consistent with the reaction he received from many of the Jews throughout the empire. During his meeting with the Jewish leaders, Paul reasoned with them convincingly from the Scriptures that Jesus is the Messiah sent from God. Paul did not trust the salvation of others to his word only. For two years, Paul remained in Rome, preaching and teaching the Word of God with boldness. It was obvious that some accepted his message, but there were many who did not believe in Jesus Christ as the Messiah.

II. EXPOSITION AND APPLICATION OF THE SCRIPTURE

A. Paul Meets the Jewish Leaders (Acts 28:23)

And when they had appointed him a day, there came many to him into his lodging; to whom he expounded and testified the kingdom of God, persuading them concerning Jesus, both out of the law of Moses, and out of the prophets, from morning till evening.

After the initial meeting, a second meeting date was set so that the Jewish leaders could meet with Paul to hear what he had to say. The second time they came with a much larger number of people. We are not told how many people were present or anything about their standing within the community. What is important is that the numbers were greater and more than likely included many of the key synagogue leaders in Rome. It is possible that their curiosity had been piqued by the first meeting. The meeting with Jewish leaders was in line with Paul's general approach whenever he entered a new city (see Acts 17:2-3; 18:4, 28; 19:8; 26:22-23). He would first reach out to the members of the local synagogue to establish a base for the mission. Only when they rejected his teachings and message would he turn to the Gentiles in the city.

The group gathered at Paul's residence. The Bible does not tell us any specifics about Paul's dwelling. Luke reported that the meeting lasted from morning and until the evening—i.e., well past 6:00 p.m. (see Acts 20:9-11). During the exchange, Paul explained (Greek: *ektithemi*), that is, he took the time to systematically and chronologically lay out the case that Jesus was the fulfillment of every word spoken about the coming of the Messiah. He began with Moses and continued through to the prophets. Paul not only reasoned from the Scriptures, but he also spoke with fervent passion, which is expressed in the word *declared*.

There were two central themes discussed by Paul with the leaders—Jesus as Messiah and the kingdom of God. Luke did not tell us whether there was "give and take" between Paul and the leaders. We can assume that this was not a one-way conversation and that the leaders did engage Paul in dialogue about his theology (see Romans 1:16-18; 1 Corinthians 1:1-23; 15:1-6).

B. The Jewish Leaders React to Paul's Message (Acts 28:24-29)

And some believed the things which were spoken, and some believed not. And when they agreed not among themselves, they departed, after that Paul had spoken one word, Well spake the Holy Ghost by Esaias the prophet unto our fathers, Saying, Go unto this people, and say, Hearing ye shall hear, and shall not understand; and

seeing ye shall see, and not perceive: For the heart of this people is waxed gross, and their ears are dull of hearing, and their eyes have they closed; lest they should see with their eyes, and hear with their ears, and understand with their heart, and should be converted, and I should heal them. Be it known therefore unto you, that the salvation of God is sent unto the Gentiles, and that they will hear it. And when he had said these words, the Jews departed, and had great reasoning among themselves.

It is not stated at what point some of the Jewish leaders became convinced of Paul's argument, but at some point during the day or evening, they did. As in all of his preaching and teaching missions, some were convinced of the reality of God's redemptive work through Jesus Christ—and others were not. The preaching of the Cross was for many Jews a huge stumbling block to faith (see 1 Corinthians 1:18). Luke emphatically stated that they "would not believe." There was nothing that Paul could say to change their minds. There was even debate among the Jewish leaders regarding whether or not what they had heard could be believed.

As they were preparing to leave, Paul made one last statement that changed the tone of the gathering even more. When Paul began to quote from the writings of Isaiah, the debate became even more contentious. This time when they left, the Jewish leaders had no intention of ever coming back. The question was this: Were the Jewish leaders divided among themselves because of the doctrine that Paul espoused, or was it his quoting of Isaiah 6:9-10 that provoked the anger? Essentially, it came down to whether or not the Jews would continue to reject their own Messiah, even though He did not appear in the manner that they had anticipated (see Isaiah 53).

Throughout his ministry, Paul had repeatedly and without much success offered the Gospel to the Jews first, but in many instances they rejected the message and often the messenger. F. F. Bruce noted that the book of Acts records and chronicles the spread of Christianity among the Gentiles, while at the same time it records the rejection of the same message by the Jews.[3] This was the final instance in the New Testament where the message is rejected.[4]

Exactly what is the meaning of the passage that was quoted? First, it is an exact reproduction of the Septuagint (the Greek translation of the Hebrew Scriptures).[5] In the Greek translation, the Holy Spirit spoke through the prophet against the stubbornness and hardheartedness of the people of God. They saw what God was doing, but they had no spiritual insight. They heard the Word spoken through the prophets, but did not receive it. And their hearts had become calloused, or swollen. If they had perceived what God was doing through Jesus Christ, then they would have all turned from their wicked ways and repented and then would have been healed. Consequently, because many of the Jews failed to listen and be converted, Paul announced that God was sending salvation to the Gentiles (see Galatians 2:8).

Many people may glean from this passage that Paul had given up on the Jewish people and that Paul had decided to abandon that part of his mission. We know that there were some Jews of Rome who believed, just as there were in all of the cities and synagogues that Paul visited. In the letter that he wrote to the Romans prior to his arrival, Paul held out hope and faith that God would one day save the Jews and that they would come to full faith in His Son, Jesus Christ (see Romans 9-11). While the book of Acts does not tell the whole story, it is certain that Paul obviously never gave up hope that the Jews might come to salvation. (In the oldest manuscripts, verse 29 does not appear, although it is found in the *King James Version*, which is based on the Western and the Byzantine text of the New Testament).

One of the most remarkable traits of Paul's faith in Jesus Christ was his ability to reason for hours from the Scriptures concerning the redemptive plan of God for the world. He would never relent nor back away from what he knew to be the essence of the truth, even when confronted by men who were just as learned as himself.

C. Paul Continued to Preach and Teach with Boldness (Acts 28:30-31)

And Paul dwelt two whole years in his own hired house, and received all that came in unto him, Preaching the kingdom of God, and teaching those things which concern the Lord Jesus Christ, with all confidence, no man forbidding him.

The book of Acts ends without revealing the final outcome of Paul's appeal before Caesar. One is left to wonder whether he was released after two years or was finally sentenced to death and executed. What is certain is that Paul continued to live in his own rented house in Rome. It is clear that his presence was felt and that there were men and women who came to hear his words. The final image we have of Paul in the Acts of the Apostles is of a man who had not ceased to do what God had apprehended him for on the Damascus Road. He preached with boldness and without any hindrances. He received no interference from the Romans or the Jews. There are several questions that interpreters have raised regarding these final days of Paul's life. First, who supported him during those final days? During this period, Paul wrote what are known as the Prison Epistles: Ephesians, Philippians, Colossians, and the Pastoral Letters of 1 and 2 Timothy, Titus, and Philemon. Quite possibly, the church in Philippi sent Paul support on several occasions and they sent leaders from the church to see how he was doing (see Philippians 1:1; 4:10, 18).

Some believed that Paul was released from prison for a short period and that he eventually made his way to Spain and preached there. Those who hold this position find support in the writings of Clement Bishop of Rome (80–140 BC), who wrote in his letter to the Corinthians that Paul was released from prison and that he was later arrested, tried, and executed. In the letter, he stated that Paul reached the west with the Gospel. Some interpreters have taken this to mean that Paul undertook a fourth missionary journey and reached Spain. There is no credible evidence that has surfaced that would give support to this tradition. Clement could have very well meant that Paul had reached Rome, which he most certainly did.

III. CONCLUDING REFLECTION

One of the most interesting aspects of the life of Paul is how he found his place within the will of God. For many people, this is an elusive concept that is often viewed through the eyes of some abstract idea that can only be discovered through hard work, intense prayer, and laboriously seeking after it. As far as being in the will of God, Paul's life reveals that it is necessary for one to be open to going where God wants him or her to go, and then doing what God wants him or her to do. Paul never set out to become a missionary after his conversion. In fact, he never set out to be a preacher. He went back home to Tarsus and it was Barnabas who brought him to Antioch to help teach the disciples. In that laboratory of instruction, God honed the mind and rhetorical skills of Paul—which would later serve God's will in ways that no one ever imagined. Do you want to find God's will for your life? Just begin to fervently pursue the things that Jesus said to do in mission (see Matthew 28:19-20) and ministry (see Matthew 25:31-46).

PRAYER

Lord, may we live in such a way that we will never be in doubt about Your will in our lives. Grant that all of our days will be lived in the light of Your purpose. In Jesus' name we pray. Amen.

WORD POWER

Kingdom of God (Greek: *basileia*)—this is a term that refers to the rule and reign of God and not to a geographical kingdom. The concept of the kingdom is mentioned throughout the Bible and has its genesis in the Old Testament concept of God as Israel's King (see Psalm 24:7-8; Isaiah 6:1-8; 40:15-27; compare also 2 Samuel 8:7). Jesus often preached about the kingdom of God and the kingdom of heaven. The terms are used interchangeably and do not refer to two different realities.

HOME DAILY BIBLE READINGS
(November 19-25, 2012)

Paul Evangelizes in Rome
MONDAY, November 19: "Will They Listen to Me?" (Exodus 6:6-13)
TUESDAY, November 20: "I Told You So!" (Deuteronomy 1:41-45)
WEDNESDAY, November 21: "Charged to Teach" (Deuteronomy 4:5-14)
THURSDAY, November 22: 'The Voice of Discipline" (Deuteronomy 4:32-40)
FRIDAY, November 23: "The Word Is Very Near" (Deuteronomy 30:6-14)
SATURDAY, November 24: "We Would Like to Hear" (Acts 28:16-22)
SUNDAY, November 25: "Teaching Boldly and without Hindrance" (Acts 28:23-31)

End Notes

[1]Brian Craig Larson and *Leadership Journal, 750 Engaging Illustrations for Preachers, Teachers, and Writers* (Grand Rapids: Baker Books, 2002), p. 609-10.
[2]F. F. Bruce, *The New International Commentary of the New Testament: The Book of Acts* (Grand Rapids: William B. Eerdmans Publishing Co., 1981), p. 533.
[3]Ibid.
[4]Polhill, p. 543.

Jesus Is Lord

GENERAL INTRODUCTION

This quarter has three units that detail the early church's teaching about Christ. These lessons from the books of Ephesians, Philippians, and Colossians draw us to a deeper understanding of who Christ is and what it might mean for us to imitate Christ in our lives.

Unit I, *Victory in Jesus,* is a five-lesson study of the book of Ephesians. The emphasis in these lessons is on the exaltation of Christ over all principalities and powers—from the beginning of time to the end of time. The first two lessons proclaim the power of God as revealed in and through Christ. The third lesson considers the image of the church as the body over which Christ is Head. In keeping with the theme of the Christmas season, lesson 4 focuses on Christ as the Light of the world. Lesson 5 looks at another metaphor for Christ's relationship with the church—that is, as a bridegroom who cares for his bride.

Unit II, *Exalting Christ,* is a four-lesson study of the book of Philippians. The letter to the Philippians encourages believers to follow the pattern laid out for us in Christ and to oppose those who are enemies of Christ's cross. The letter is rich in wisdom, for those who desire to live in a manner worthy of the Gospel of Christ.

Unit III, *Imitating Jesus,* is a four-lesson study of the book of Colossians. These lessons have much to say about the importance of the person and work of Christ—as Lord of all creation and the author of our peace with God.

LESSON 1   December 2, 2012

SPIRITUAL BLESSINGS IN JESUS CHRIST

FAITH PATHWAY/FAITH JOURNEY TOPIC: **Chosen and Claimed**

DEVOTIONAL READING: **Psalm 33:8-12**   BACKGROUND SCRIPTURE: **Ephesians 1**
PRINT PASSAGE: **Ephesians 1:3-14**   KEY VERSES: **Ephesians 1:5-6**

Ephesians 1:3-14—KJV

3 Blessed be the God and Father of our Lord Jesus Christ, who hath blessed us with all spiritual blessings in heavenly places in Christ:

4 According as he hath chosen us in him before the foundation of the world, that we should be holy and without blame before him in love:

5 Having predestinated us unto the adoption of children by Jesus Christ to himself, according to the good pleasure of his will,

6 To the praise of the glory of his grace, wherein he hath made us accepted in the beloved.

7 In whom we have redemption through his blood, the forgiveness of sins, according to the riches of his grace;

8 Wherein he hath abounded toward us in all wisdom and prudence;

9 Having made known unto us the mystery of his will, according to his good pleasure which he hath purposed in himself:

10 That in the dispensation of the fulness of times he might gather together in one all things in Christ, both which are in heaven, and which are on earth; even in him:

11 In whom also we have obtained an inheritance, being predestinated according to the purpose of him who worketh all things after the counsel of his own will:

12 That we should be to the praise of his glory, who first trusted in Christ.

13 In whom ye also trusted, after that ye heard the word of truth, the gospel of your salvation: in whom also after that ye believed, ye were sealed with that holy Spirit of promise,

14 Which is the earnest of our inheritance until the redemption of the purchased possession, unto the praise of his glory.

Ephesians 1:3-14—NIV

3 Praise be to the God and Father of our Lord Jesus Christ, who has blessed us in the heavenly realms with every spiritual blessing in Christ.

4 For he chose us in him before the creation of the world to be holy and blameless in his sight. In love

5 he predestined us to be adopted as his sons through Jesus Christ, in accordance with his pleasure and will—

6 to the praise of his glorious grace, which he has freely given us in the One he loves.

7 In him we have redemption through his blood, the forgiveness of sins, in accordance with the riches of God's grace

8 that he lavished on us with all wisdom and understanding.

9 And he made known to us the mystery of his will according to his good pleasure, which he purposed in Christ,

10 to be put into effect when the times will have reached their fulfillment—to bring all things in heaven and on earth together under one head, even Christ.

11 In him we were also chosen, having been predestined according to the plan of him who works out everything in conformity with the purpose of his will,

12 in order that we, who were the first to hope in Christ, might be for the praise of his glory.

13 And you also were included in Christ when you heard the word of truth, the gospel of your salvation. Having believed, you were marked in him with a seal, the promised Holy Spirit,

14 who is a deposit guaranteeing our inheritance until the redemption of those who are God's possession—to the praise of his glory.

UNIFYING LESSON PRINCIPLE

All people want to feel valued and worthy. Where can we turn to receive affirmation? The writer of the book of Ephesians declared that through Jesus Christ we gain an inheritance as God's own people—to become recipients of forgiveness and salvation's redemption power.

TOPICAL OUTLINE OF THE LESSON

I. Introduction
  A. No Difference
  B. Biblical Background

II. Exposition and Application of the Scripture
  A. Believers Were Chosen by the Father
      (Ephesians 1:3-6)
  B. Believers Have Been Redeemed by the Son
      (Ephesians 1:7-10)
  C. Believers Are Sealed by the Spirit
      (Ephesians 1:11-14)

III. Concluding Reflection

LESSON OBJECTIVES

Upon the completion of the lesson, the students will be able to do the following:

1. Understand Paul's explanation of being adopted by God through Jesus Christ;
2. Express humility at God's affirmation of our worthiness; and,
3. Create a service of praise to God for the remarkable gift of God's adoption of us through Jesus Christ.

POINTS TO BE EMPHASIZED

ADULT/YOUTH

Adult Topic: **Chosen and Claimed**
Youth Topic: **Too Blessed to Be Stressed**
Adult Key Verses: **Ephesians 1:5-6**
Youth Key Verse: **Ephesians 1:3**
Print Passage: **Ephesians 1:3-14**

—Paul urged the believers to give thanks to God for divine blessings.
—Before creation, God had developed a plan to renew human fellowship with Him that would result in human blamelessness before God.
—God decided to make human beings His children through Jesus Christ.
—God should be praised for the gift of Jesus Christ.
—Jesus' death justifies us before God and provides the foundation for human forgiveness from sin.
—In the fullness of time, God will complete His plan and restore the unity of heaven and earth through Jesus Christ.

CHILDREN

Children Topic: **Adopted into the Family**
Key Verse: **Ephesians 1:4**
Print Passage: **Ephesians 1:3-14**

—God gives us many blessings in Jesus Christ, though we do not deserve them.
—God loved us before we were born.
—Through Christ, God forgives us and adopts us into His family.
—Through Christ, who is the fulfillment of God's will, believers are united as one family.
—Praises are given to God for the wonderful blessings He continues to give.
—Affirmation and forgiveness come from God.

I. INTRODUCTION

A. No Difference

In *Reader's Digest*, a contributor told of an Aunt Ruby and Uncle Arnie who adopted a baby boy after five years of trying (unsuccessfully) to conceive. To their surprise, a short time after the adoption, Aunt Ruby discovered that she was pregnant—and she later gave birth to a boy.

One day when the two boys were eight and nine years old, the teller of the story was visiting Aunt Ruby, and a woman in the neighborhood came to visit. Observing the children play, the woman asked, "Which boy is yours, Ruby?"

"Both of them," Aunt Ruby replied. The caller persisted. "But I mean, which one is adopted?" Aunt Ruby did not hesitate. In her finest hour, she looked straight at her guest and replied, "I've forgotten."[1] Aunt Ruby saw no difference between her two sons; in her eyes, they were both equal. The central theme of our lesson today reminds us that through Jesus Christ, God has redeemed us from sin and claimed us for Himself. All people want to feel valued and worthy. In Jesus Christ, we receive affirmation and the assurance of the forgiveness of our sins. The writer of the book of Ephesians declared that through Jesus Christ, we gain an inheritance as God's own people to become recipients of forgiveness and the redemption power of salvation.

B. Biblical Background

Today's lesson begins a five-part study of the book of Ephesians; there is no question that it is one of the most important New Testament writings—both for its peerless doctrine (see chapters 1–3) and its very practical teachings on living out the Christian faith (see chapters 4–6). The emphasis in these five lessons is on the exaltation of Jesus Christ over all principalities and powers, from the beginning of time to the end of time. It is because Christ is exalted above all principalities and powers that God the Father is worthy of the highest praise and honor.

The verses that comprise the lesson are among the most precious in the New Testament and among the most difficult to interpret because of the structure of the passage. The passage describes God's divine choice of us, without regard to how we have lived. God's grace is not based upon anything that we have done; it is freely given without merit (see Ephesians 2:8-10). We were adopted into the family of God through the precious shed blood of Jesus Christ, who died for our sins (see 1 Corinthians 15:1-3). Through the Cross, God intends to unite all disparate and hostile forces of creation into one people for Himself. The mystery of how all of this takes place is found in the Lord Jesus Christ.

II. EXPOSITION AND APPLICATION OF THE SCRIPTURE

A. Believers Were Chosen by the Father
(Ephesians 1:3-6)

Blessed be the God and Father of our Lord Jesus Christ, who hath blessed us with all spiritual blessings in heavenly places in Christ: According as he hath chosen us in him before the foundation of the world, that we should be holy and without blame before him in love: Having predestinated us unto the adoption of children by Jesus Christ to himself, according to the good pleasure of his will, To the praise of the glory of his grace, wherein he hath made us accepted in the beloved.

The apostle began this section of Scripture with a declaration of "Praise to God, who is the Father of our Lord Jesus Christ." The words *praise, blessed,* and *spiritual blessing* are translated from a single Greek word, *eulogia,* which gives us the English word *eulogy.* This word is only used in reference to God. It literally means "to praise, celebrate, and/or acknowledge through words of adoration the One who is worthy to be praised." God deserves our highest praise and adoration because of what He has done for us through Christ. The "heavenly realms" has reference to Christ's being seated at the right hand of the Father (see Ephesians 1:20).

The spiritual blessings are those benefits of grace bestowed upon us freely by God. These are the gifts of grace that cannot be acquired by human intelligence or power. They are freely given to us by God (see Isaiah 55:1). Spiritual blessings are those benefits of God which are not earthly and material; rather, they stand in contrast to the material possessions of life that God also gives (see Deuteronomy 28:1-14; Malachi 3:10; compare with Matthew 4:3-4; Luke 12:13-21). Simply stated, there are some things that money cannot buy: joy; peace; hope; rest; comfort in the midnight hour; love; patience; endurance; and faith. None of these gifts can be purchased—because they are freely given by the Holy Spirit. The greatest of these gifts is the gift of eternal life, through Jesus Christ (see John 3:16).

The apostle made it clear that everything that the believer receives comes through Jesus Christ and from being "in Christ." Christ, then, is both the source of our blessings and the cause of our common life together.

One of the great spiritual blessings that believers have received is being chosen by God to be His unique and special people (see 1 Peter 1:2; 2:9). God chooses people based upon His criteria and sovereign purpose (see 1 Samuel 16:7). God chose us to be holy and blameless before the world began. The word *holy* comes from the Greek word *hagios;* it refers to being separated for a distinct purpose. *Blameless* is from the word *amomos* and it literally means "to be without faults or defects." God has chosen us in Jesus Christ to be different people who make a difference in the world. Before the world was even formed, God chose us to be His people. It is the precious shed blood of Jesus Christ that will enable us to stand before the throne of judgment without defect or blemish.

Because of God's grace, we have been adopted into the family of God and made to be sons and daughters. God was pleased to make us His own through Christ. Verse 6 states that the believer joins the chorus of those who praise God—because of His glorious grace.

B. Believers Have Been Redeemed by the Son
(Ephesians 1:7-10)

In whom we have redemption through his blood, the

forgiveness of sins, according to the riches of his grace; Wherein he hath abounded toward us in all wisdom and prudence; Having made known unto us the mystery of his will, according to his good pleasure which he hath purposed in himself: That in the dispensation of the fulness of times he might gather together in one all things in Christ, both which are in heaven, and which are on earth; even in him.

In verses 7-8, we see three of the greatest spiritual blessings that believers receive through Jesus Christ. The first is *redemption* (Greek: *apolutrosis*), and it literally means "to release or rescue." This redemption that we receive is the result of the shed blood of Jesus Christ (see Matthew 20:28; 26:28; Acts 20:28; Romans 3:24; and Colossians 1:14; compare to Leviticus 16, which describes the annual ritual of the Atonement). God in Christ has set us free from the damning and destructive power of sin and Satan. Paul wrote this statement in such a way that it expresses what God is currently doing for us right now. Sometimes we are prone to see everything as a past event, without any present-day reality. Redemption is something we are experiencing right now. Forgiveness is a present reality as well.

The result of the act of redemption is the forgiveness of sins, which is the second of these spiritual blessings mentioned in this section of Scripture. *Forgiveness* (Greek: *aphesis*) literally means "release from bondage or imprisonment" (see Exodus 34:7; Psalms 32:1; 86:5; 130:4; Isaiah 55:6; Micah 7:18; Acts 13:38; Colossians 2:13). Just think for a moment of the many things of which you have been personally forgiven by God. Who among human beings does not deserve the just punishment for their sins?

The word *sins* (Greek: *paraptoma*) has in it the idea of amassing a large quantity of sins,

failures, faults, or acts of rebellion. In Him— that is, in Christ—all of these sins are forgiven, which further shows us what it means to be holy and without blemish. Through the blood of Jesus Christ, our sinful nature is changed and we are also forgiven of the individual acts of sin that we have committed. We are forgiven through faith in the sacrificial death of Jesus Christ, not because of anything that we have done or said (see Ephesians 2:8-10).

The third blessing described in these verses is that of *wisdom* and *understanding*. The Lord has lavished these gifts on us in accordance with the riches of His grace. The word *lavished* (Greek: *perisseuo*) has in it the idea of "pouring until there is nothing but overflowing abundance." God showers us with an endless monsoon of grace. He gives us *wisdom* (Greek: *sophia*). Having wisdom is having a broad range of knowledge and intelligence. *Understanding* (Greek: *phronesis*) is one's capacity to perceive matters with such keen insight that he or she can make the right decisions.

Wisdom and understanding are given in abundance so that we might know with certainty the will of God and understand the mystery of salvation. *Mystery* (Greek: *musterion*) means something which was hidden or kept secret (verse 9). What is this mystery? It is the revelation that God intends to bring harmony to His creation in the uniting of all people, with Jews and Gentiles together through Christ (see Ephesians 2, where this thought is expounded in detail). Often we think of the will of God as some deep dark secret which we must set out to find. God's will for our lives unfolds daily as we live out what it means to be called and saved. In this light, His will is progressively revealed over time.

Paul made it clear that the will of God has to do with our redemption and forgiveness, and He has made that mysterious secret known in Christ. All of these things will come to pass when the *times* (Greek: *kairos*) arrive. The word *times* refers to "that definitive moment when God will bring an end to this present world." When will this be? No one knows the day or the time (see Matthew 24:42-44; Acts 1:5). In that final day, all things will be united under the lordship of Jesus Christ, who is the Head of the church (see Ephesians 1:18-23; Colossians 1:18).

C. Believers Are Sealed by the Spirit (Ephesians 1:11-14)

In whom also we have obtained an inheritance, being predestinated according to the purpose of him who worketh all things after the counsel of his own will: That we should be to the praise of his glory, who first trusted in Christ. In whom ye also trusted, after that ye heard the word of truth, the gospel of your salvation: in whom also after that ye believed, ye were sealed with that holy Spirit of promise, Which is the earnest of our inheritance until the redemption of the purchased possession, unto the praise of his glory.

In these verses, Paul built upon the position he took regarding the plan of God to include both Jews and Gentiles within the body of Christ, which is the church. According to this plan, Israel was predestined to obtain the inheritance of God. In verse 11a, he used the first-person plural pronoun "we," referring specifically to Jewish believers, who were the first to receive the promise of salvation through Christ (see Romans 1:16-17). Through the seed of Abraham, God brought forth the Messiah—and in Him all nations of the world were/are blessed (see Genesis 12:1-3; 1 Samuel 7:12-14; Isaiah 9:2; 60:1; Matthew

4:16; Luke 1:78; 2:32). It was God's will that Israel would be saved and those Jews who confessed Jesus Christ as Lord were/are saved. God had not abandoned His chosen people, and Paul worked through those thoughts in Romans 9–11.

In verse 12, the purpose of God's will and plan was that His glory might be first seen in the salvation of His chosen people, Israel. The use of the second-person pronoun "you" was a clear reference to Gentile believers who had come to faith in Jesus Christ through the preaching of the Gospel, which is described as the "Word of Truth" (see Romans 6:17; 10:14-17; Ephesians 4:21; Colossians 1:4, 23; 1 Thessalonians 2:13). Since they had come to faith in Christ, they, too, had received the gift of the Holy Spirit, who is the seal of God affirming that they were His people. The Holy Spirit is given to all believers and He is the "deposit guarantee," which is a picture of a person making a partial payment to hold a piece of property or item until he can make the full payment. When will the final redemption of the church take place? Only God knows; however, on that day, those who belong to God will gather in a great throng and give praise and glory to His name forever and ever (see Revelation 7:9-17).

III. CONCLUDING REFLECTION

What does it mean to say that you have been blessed? What does it mean to be a blessing to someone else? What does it mean when the members of a local church proclaim that God has blessed their congregation? How do you measure the benevolent love and mercy of God? Can you objectively quantify what God has done in your life? Usually, when we talk about the blessings of God, we think in terms of the material. There is indeed a place for the material blessings of God (which are so highly regarded in our lives); but what is most important are the things that money can never buy. When we talk of being blessed, we think and talk about our jobs, houses, cars, money, portfolios, land, clothes, promotions, successes, and all of the things that we can see, touch, feel, and use. We count our earthly treasures, often to the exclusion of our heavenly treasures. Spend a few moments each day this week thinking of the blessings that you have in Jesus Christ that cannot be measured by money or possessions.

PRAYER

Lord God, teach us how to love the things that are freely given to us by You: peace, joy, and hope. Grant us the understanding to see You at work in our lives. In Jesus' name we pray. Amen.

WORD POWER

Predestined—a theological term that expresses the intentions of God to include both Jews and Gentiles in the plan of human redemption. The ultimate goal of salvation has always found fulfillment in Jesus Christ.

HOME DAILY BIBLE READINGS
(November 26–December 2, 2012)

Spiritual Blessings in Jesus Christ

MONDAY, November 26: "Blessed by God's Forgiveness" (Psalm 32:1-7)

TUESDAY, November 27: "Blessed by Being Chosen" (Psalm 33:8-12)

WEDNESDAY, November 28: "Blessed by God's Gift of Grace" (1 Corinthians 1:4-9)

THURSDAY, November 29: "Blessed by God's Revelation" (Daniel 2:17-23)

FRIDAY, November 30: "Blessed by the Word of Truth" (Colossians 1:3-8)

SATURDAY, December 1: "Blessed by God's Redemption" (Luke 1:67-79)

SUNDAY, December 2: "God Has Blessed Us" (Ephesians 1:3-14)

End Note

[1]Craig Brian Larson and *Leadership Journal,* 750 Engaging Illustrations for Preachers, Teachers, and Writers (Grand Rapids: Baker Books, 20070), p. 13.

LESSON 2   December 9, 2012

ONE IN JESUS CHRIST

FAITH PATHWAY/FAITH JOURNEY TOPIC: **Unity, Not Uniformity**

DEVOTIONAL READING: **Ephesians 3:14-21**
PRINT PASSAGE: **Ephesians 2:11-22**

BACKGROUND SCRIPTURE: **Ephesians 2–3**
KEY VERSE: **Ephesians 2:21**

Ephesians 2:11-22—KJV

11 Wherefore remember, that ye being in time past Gentiles in the flesh, who are called Uncircumcision by that which is called the Circumcision in the flesh made by hands;

12 That at that time ye were without Christ, being aliens from the commonwealth of Israel, and strangers from the covenants of promise, having no hope, and without God in the world:

13 But now in Christ Jesus ye who sometimes were far off are made nigh by the blood of Christ.

14 For he is our peace, who hath made both one, and hath broken down the middle wall of partition between us;

15 Having abolished in his flesh the enmity, even the law of commandments contained in ordinances; for to make in himself of twain one new man, so making peace;

16 And that he might reconcile both unto God in one body by the cross, having slain the enmity thereby:

17 And came and preached peace to you which were afar off, and to them that were nigh.

18 For through him we both have access by one Spirit unto the Father.

19 Now therefore ye are no more strangers and foreigners, but fellowcitizens with the saints, and of the household of God;

20 And are built upon the foundation of the apostles and prophets, Jesus Christ himself being the chief corner stone;

21 In whom all the building fitly framed together groweth unto an holy temple in the Lord:

22 In whom ye also are builded together for an habitation of God through the Spirit.

Ephesians 2:11-22—NIV

11 Therefore, remember that formerly you who are Gentiles by birth and called "uncircumcised" by those who call themselves "the circumcision" (that done in the body by the hands of men)—

12 remember that at that time you were separate from Christ, excluded from citizenship in Israel and foreigners to the covenants of the promise, without hope and without God in the world.

13 But now in Christ Jesus you who once were far away have been brought near through the blood of Christ.

14 For he himself is our peace, who has made the two one and has destroyed the barrier, the dividing wall of hostility,

15 by abolishing in his flesh the law with its commandments and regulations. His purpose was to create in himself one new man out of the two, thus making peace,

16 and in this one body to reconcile both of them to God through the cross, by which he put to death their hostility.

17 He came and preached peace to you who were far away and peace to those who were near.

18 For through him we both have access to the Father by one Spirit.

19 Consequently, you are no longer foreigners and aliens, but fellow citizens with God's people and members of God's household,

20 built on the foundation of the apostles and prophets, with Christ Jesus himself as the chief cornerstone.

21 In him the whole building is joined together and rises to become a holy temple in the Lord.

22 And in him you too are being built together to become a dwelling in which God lives by his Spirit.

UNIFYING LESSON PRINCIPLE

Adversaries sometimes search for ways to come together, and yearn to do so. What or who can bring the two sides together? The writer of the book of Ephesians proclaimed that it is in Christ that we, who are dead through our trespasses, are brought alive in Christ and that Jesus Christ is the one who breaks down all dividing walls and brings us together as one.

TOPICAL OUTLINE OF THE LESSON

I. Introduction
   A. The Quest for Peace
   B. Biblical Background

II. Exposition and Application of the Scripture
   A. Jews and Gentiles United through the Blood of Christ (Ephesians 2:11-13)
   B. Jews and Gentiles United in Access to the Father (Ephesians 2:14-18)
   C. Jews and Gentiles United as Dwellings for the Holy Spirit (Ephesians 2:19-22)

III. Concluding Reflection

LESSON OBJECTIVES

Upon the completion of the lesson, the students will be able to do the following:

1. Understand Paul's explanation of Jews and Gentiles becoming one in Christ;

2. Express pain and sorrow at the divisions within Christ's church and joy when divisions are broken down; and,

3. Become acquainted with church-uniting and church-dividing issues and name strategies for addressing these issues.

POINTS TO BE EMPHASIZED

ADULT/YOUTH

Adult Topic: Unity, Not Uniformity

Youth Topic: Unity in the Community

Adult/Youth Key Verse: Ephesians 2:21

Print Passage: Ephesians 2:11-22

—Paul reminded the believers that at one time they were apart from Christ.

—Through the blood of Christ, we are brought near to God and near to one another.

—Through Christ, hostility has been replaced by peace for all who have turned to God.

—Humanity was once estranged from God, but through Christ, believers are now citizens and members of the family of God.

—The apostles and the prophets are the foundation of the family of faith, with Jesus as the cornerstone.

—The family of faith is joined and held together by Jesus Christ.

CHILDREN

Children Topic: Love Brings Us Joy

Key Verse: Ephesians 2:4-5

Print Passage: Ephesians 2:1-10

—Sin separates us from God, but in Christ, God reconciles us to Himself, which makes us alive again.

—God has great love for us.

—Our good works do not save us; we are saved to perform good works.

—By God's grace, through our faith, we have been saved.

I. INTRODUCTION

A. The Quest for Peace

There are two groups of people in Israel today who live on the same land—Israelis and Palestinians. Both are descendants of Abraham; both have legitimate claims to the precious, priceless, and picturesque land. Out of a population of over six million people, more than three million are Palestinians, but they are residents without citizenship. They cannot vote or hold political office, and they must carry Israeli-issued pass cards. They cannot move from one part of their country to the next and are generally restricted to living in the poorest regions of the country. Since 1948, there have been numerous failed attempts by American presidents to broker a lasting peace in the land of the Bible. Unfortunately, however, no one has been able to lead Israelis and Palestinians to create a lasting peace.

At the heart of their issue is the quest for lasting peace. It is true that adversaries sometimes search or long for ways to come together. What or who can bring the two sides together? The apostle Paul proclaimed that it is in Christ that we, who are dead through our trespasses, are brought alive in Christ and that Jesus Christ is the one who breaks down all dividing walls and brings us together as one. While the situation looks impossible from a human perspective, we know that in Christ all things are possible.

B. Biblical Background

In today's lesson, the apostle Paul described the historical and racial division between the Jews and the Gentiles. Historically, the open and overt hostilities that existed between the Jews and the Gentiles went back to the time of the Jewish return from Babylon (see Ezra 4:1-6, 8-24). When the Holy Spirit gave birth to the Christian church on Pentecost, the faith grew from a largely Jewish religious movement to become a largely Gentile religious movement. As more and more Gentiles were brought into the church, it naturally fueled tensions between Jews and Gentiles. This was evident in both the Galatian and Ephesian Christian communities.

The church in Ephesus was primarily Gentile. Was there an ethnic or racial problem in Ephesus? We can assume that there were major differences between the Jewish and Gentile members of the church. It is evident that Paul did not make light of the problem of including Gentiles in the church and the consequences for the church. Paul knew that if this problem were not resolved, then the church would never be able to fulfill her mission in the world.

He reminded both groups that the work of creating a unified community of believers is a work of God's grace. Only as insiders can the Gentiles see that they had been outsiders to the covenant. Through Christ, the Gentiles have been brought near to God and the covenant of promise. The law had been the dividing wall between Jew and Gentile, but in Christ it had been broken down. The church, made up of Gentiles and Jews, has become the temple of the Holy Spirit.

II. EXPOSITION AND APPLICATION OF THE SCRIPTURE

A. Jews and Gentiles United through the Blood of Christ
(Ephesians 2:11-13)

Wherefore remember, that ye being in time past Gentiles in the flesh, who are called Uncircumcision by that which is called the Circumcision in the flesh made by hands; That at that time ye were without Christ, being aliens from the commonwealth of Israel, and strangers from the covenants of promise, having no hope, and without God in the world: But now in Christ Jesus ye who sometimes were far off are made nigh by the blood of Christ.

The word *therefore* looks back to everything that previously has been stated; specifically, how the Gentiles came to be included in the covenant community (see Ephesians 2:1-10). Paul invited the Gentiles to remember where they had come from and how they had been incorporated into the new community of faith. They had been separated and alienated from the covenant of grace, but in Christ they were made partakers of the divine community. To remember a place or time is to keep in mind all that had happened in that place or time. Israel was encouraged to remember where God had brought them from so that they would never become too proud (see Deuteronomy 5:15; 8:2; 9:7; 15:15; 16:12; Ezekiel 16:12; 20:43). Whenever Christians gather for the celebration of the Lord's Supper, they are reminded to remember the suffering of the Lord Jesus Christ (see Luke 22:19).

The Gentiles had been excluded by birth and referred to as those who were the *uncircumcision*. This was a word that was often spoken to ridicule non-Jews (see 1 Samuel 17:26, 36; compare Jeremiah 9:25-26). The Gentiles were the people who were not privileged to be partakers of the mercy and grace

of God. In the Jewish community, the sign of the covenant between God and Abraham was circumcision (see Genesis 17:9-14). Every male child born into the family of Abraham had to be circumcised on the eighth day. Jews thought of those who were uncircumcised as unclean and disconnected from the covenant of grace. His circumcision on the eighth day was one of the things that Paul held up as a former source of his spiritual pride (see Philippians 3:3-5). Over time, the Jews viewed circumcision as a sign of religious exclusivity and pride. They looked upon it as a badge of religious superiority. They became proud of their act of circumcision and saw it as a sign that they were holier than other people.

In verse 12, Paul called upon the Gentile believers to remember. He described the spiritual condition of all Gentiles before the coming of Jesus Christ into the world. Paul stated that from a historical perspective, they (Gentiles) were not included in the covenants of promise made by God to Abraham. They were strangers and aliens to the commonwealth of Israel. It was not their fault that they had been born outside of the covenant. Paul described the condition of the Gentiles using several words. They were *separated* from God. Further, they were *excluded* from citizenship and they were *foreigners*, without hope and without God in the world.

Verse 13 introduced the contrasting state of the Ephesians since their conversion. But now, in Christ Jesus, everyone who believes by faith in the finished work of Christ on the Cross has a new citizenship and status. As a result of the work of Christ at Calvary, all of the richness of the heritage of Israel and its unique relationship to God was theirs as well.

B. Jews and Gentiles United in Access to the Father (Ephesians 2:14-18)

For he is our peace, who hath made both one, and hath broken down the middle wall of partition between us; Having abolished in his flesh the enmity, even the law of commandments contained in ordinances; for to make in himself of twain one new man, so making peace; And that he might reconcile both unto God in one body by the cross, having slain the enmity thereby: And came and preached peace to you which were afar off, and to them that were nigh. For through him we both have access by one Spirit unto the Father.

The personal pronoun *he* is emphatic in the Greek text, which means that the emphasis in the verse is exclusively on Jesus Christ. Not only did Jesus bring peace, but He *is* our peace. Thus, when men and women come to know God's salvation, they not only find peace with God (see Romans 5:1), but also peace with one another. The word *peace* denotes a new relationship between Jew and Gentile. Paul may have been making allusions to the words of the prophets of Israel, who proclaimed that the messianic age would be a time of great peace on earth (see Isaiah 9:6-7; 11:1-10; 53:5; Micah 5:4-5; Haggai 2:9; Zechariah 9:9-10).

The phrase "who hath made both one" (verse 14) points to the work of Christ in the sphere of human relationships. He had destroyed the barrier that was dividing the Jews and the Gentiles. It was Christ who united all races, creeds, nations, religions, and peoples through His death and resurrection. In Christ, God has made Jew and Gentile one, whereby divisions and distinctions no longer exist (see John 10:16; 17:11; 1 Corinthians 10:17; 12:13).

What did Jesus Christ do to bring about peace between the races? Paul stated that He has "destroyed the barrier, the dividing wall of hostility" (Ephesians 2:14).

There had existed for centuries a barrier between Jews and Gentiles religiously, racially, and ritually. They were separated on religious and sociological grounds. From a religious standpoint, it was the Law of Moses that commanded a separation, and later it was reenacted by the priest Ezra (see Ezra 9:1-15, especially verse 12). Historically, the Jews considered themselves superior to all other races, because of their covenant relationship with God. And nowhere was this religious superiority more evident than in the practice of the Temple religious ceremonies. Gentiles were forbidden from entering the court area that was exclusively reserved for Jewish males.

In verses 15-18, Paul gave a fivefold description of what the work of Jesus Christ meant for both Jews and Gentiles. First, Christ abolished the Law (verse 15b). The Law of Moses was the very symbol of the separation between Jew and Gentile—and for the Jew, it was the keeping of the Law in every detail that constituted righteousness (see Galatians 3:10; Philippians 3:6; Colossians 1:22; 2:14, 20; compare with Hebrews 10:22). Second, Christ created one new man by uniting Jews and Gentiles (verse 15c). Third, the world was reconciled to God through Jesus Christ (see Romans 5:10; 2 Corinthians 5:18-21; Colossians 1:21-23). It was the cross upon which Jesus died that became the means of our reconciliation (verse 16a). Fourth, it was the preaching of the Cross that brought the healing of the breach between Jew and Gentile. The reference to "He came and preached peace" cannot mean that Jesus physically preached. Rather, it denotes the preaching of the message of reconciliation through those sent by the Holy Spirit (verse 17). The phrase, "Those who were near" is an allusion to the Jews and "those afar off" are the Gentiles. Finally, through Jesus Christ we have this: access to God is made available for all (verse 18).

C. Jews and Gentiles United as Dwellings for the Holy Spirit
(Ephesians 2:19-22)

Now therefore ye are no more strangers and foreigners, but fellowcitizens with the saints, and of the household of God; And are built upon the foundation of the apostles and prophets, Jesus Christ himself being the chief corner stone; In whom all the building fitly framed together groweth unto an holy temple in the Lord: In whom ye also are builded together for an habitation of God through the Spirit.

In verse 19, Paul told the Ephesians, "Now therefore ye are no more strangers and foreigners, but fellowcitizens with the saints, and of the household of God." Paul used the Greek word *xenos* for "foreigner." A *foreigner* was a person from another nation or area. Foreigners were viewed with suspicion; they were never quite accepted into the community. The other Greek word that he used was *paroikos*, which means "sojourners." This is an interesting word because it is made up of two words that mean "to live beside." The sojourner lived in the community and paid taxes, but was never accorded the rights of full and complete citizenship. The foreigner and the sojourner were residents, but they could never quite fit in.

The point of the statement is that we are no longer on the fringes, but a part of the fellowship of the saints. The word *fellowship*, which translates from the Greek word *koinonia*, is a key word in the New Testament. It describes the unique life of the community of believers, who derive their source of life and power from God through the Holy Spirit. The word *Koinonia* describes the relational life of the church. It is that common bond that grows out of our common faith, common goals, and common worship experiences. We have but one Lord, one Savior, one church, and one common bond. We are a fellowship of believers who draw strength from each other as we face the varied circumstances of life.

In verse 20, Paul said that the church was built upon the foundation of the apostles and prophets—with Jesus Christ as the Chief Cornerstone. The foundation that he was referring to was the foundation of the teaching and preaching of the Word. The first Christian churches were marked by a spirit of learning and study. You will recall that when Paul first went to Ephesus (see Acts 19:1ff, verse 10), he spent two years there—teaching and preaching.

Paul's discussion of the church as a building "fitly framed together groweth unto a holy temple in the Lord" can be seen in verse 21. Here, he was making reference to the unbreakable bond of unity and togetherness among believers. Unity is the one indispensable quality of a church. We can do without elaborate buildings, finely tuned programs, large budgets, multilayer staffs, and all of the other trappings of a well-oiled organization. But the church cannot survive without unity. Where there is unity, there is strength and power. Congregations can do more together in harmony with each other than they can when working separately. In John 17, Jesus prayed to the Father that we would all be one, as He and the Father were one. Today, we see standing behind, underneath, and overshadowing the church our unconquerable hero and Lord.

III. CONCLUDING REFLECTION

One of the implied questions raised by this lesson is the following: What constitutes a great church? Are great churches the mega-churches with their huge buildings, multiple worship services, and thousands of people? The one thing the apostle Paul taught us in this lesson is that the greatness of the church is found in the willingness of the people to capitalize on their common spiritual birthright. Jesus Christ, working through the Holy Spirit, gives the church, regardless of its size, the power and presence to make a difference in the world. Great churches realize that their diversity and size are not handicaps, but gifts from God.

The greater the commitment to Jesus Christ, the more resources are available. When more talent, more money, and more minds are available, there is a greater division of labor; more ministries can be started and successfully carried on; more people can be involved, which leads to a greater likelihood of success. Two hundred people who are absolutely committed to the cause of Christ are just as great a congregation as one with a thousand members (which only has 10 percent of them engaged in the work).

PRAYER

Father, grant us the courage of spirit to reach out to those who may not be a part of our ethnicity or culture. Help us to show love and hospitality to all persons, regardless of their backgrounds. In Jesus' name we pray. Amen.

WORD POWER

Xenos [Foreigners/Strangers] (Greek: plural *[xenoi])*—a word used in the Greek language that has a wide range of meanings, signifying such divergent concepts as "enemy stranger" as well as "ritual friend."

HOME DAILY BIBLE READINGS
(December 3-9, 2012)

One in Jesus Christ

MONDAY, December 3: "Reviving the Humble and Contrite" (Isaiah 57:14-19)

TUESDAY, December 4: "Building on the True Foundation" (1 Corinthians 3:10-16)

WEDNESDAY, December 5: "Sharing in the Promise" (Ephesians 3:1-6)

THURSDAY, December 6: "Making Known the Wisdom of God" (Ephesians 3:7-13)

FRIDAY, December 7: "Praying for Spiritual Power" (Ephesians 3:14-21)

SATURDAY, December 8: "Discovering the Gift of Salvation" (Ephesians 2:1-10)

SUNDAY, December 9: "Discovering Our Oneness in Christ" (Ephesians 2:11-22)

LESSON 3 December 16, 2012

UNITY IN THE BODY OF CHRIST

FAITH PATHWAY/FAITH JOURNEY TOPIC: **Living Together**

DEVOTIONAL READING: **Romans 12:3-8**
PRINT PASSAGE: **Ephesians 4:1-16**

BACKGROUND SCRIPTURE: **Ephesians 4:1-16**
KEY VERSES: **Ephesians 4:4-5**

Ephesians 4:1-16—KJV

I THEREFORE, the prisoner of the Lord, beseech you that ye walk worthy of the vocation wherewith ye are called,

2 With all lowliness and meekness, with longsuffering, forbearing one another in love;

3 Endeavouring to keep the unity of the Spirit in the bond of peace.

4 There is one body, and one Spirit, even as ye are called in one hope of your calling;

5 One Lord, one faith, one baptism,

6 One God and Father of all, who is above all, and through all, and in you all.

7 But unto every one of us is given grace according to the measure of the gift of Christ.

8 Wherefore he saith, When he ascended up on high, he led captivity captive, and gave gifts unto men.

9 (Now that he ascended, what is it but that he also descended first into the lower parts of the earth?

10 He that descended is the same also that ascended up far above all heavens, that he might fill all things.)

11 And he gave some, apostles; and some, prophets; and some, evangelists; and some, pastors and teachers;

12 For the perfecting of the saints, for the work of the ministry, for the edifying of the body of Christ:

13 Till we all come in the unity of the faith, and of the knowledge of the Son of God, unto a perfect man, unto the measure of the stature of the fulness of Christ:

14 That we henceforth be no more children, tossed to and fro, and carried about with every wind of doctrine, by the sleight of men, and cunning craftiness, whereby they lie in wait to deceive;

Ephesians 4:1-16—NIV

AS A prisoner for the Lord, then, I urge you to live a life worthy of the calling you have received.

2 Be completely humble and gentle; be patient, bearing with one another in love.

3 Make every effort to keep the unity of the Spirit through the bond of peace.

4 There is one body and one Spirit—just as you were called to one hope when you were called—

5 one Lord, one faith, one baptism;

6 one God and Father of all, who is over all and through all and in all.

7 But to each one of us grace has been given as Christ apportioned it.

8 This is why it says: "When he ascended on high, he led captives in his train and gave gifts to men."

9 (What does "he ascended" mean except that he also descended to the lower, earthly regions?

10 He who descended is the very one who ascended higher than all the heavens, in order to fill the whole universe.)

11 It was he who gave some to be apostles, some to be prophets, some to be evangelists, and some to be pastors and teachers,

12 to prepare God's people for works of service, so that the body of Christ may be built up

13 until we all reach unity in the faith and in the knowledge of the Son of God and become mature, attaining to the whole measure of the fullness of Christ.

14 Then we will no longer be infants, tossed back and forth by the waves, and blown here and there by every wind of teaching and by the cunning and craftiness of men in their deceitful scheming.

UNIFYING LESSON PRINCIPLE

We all feel positive about life when everything goes well after we have worked together on a project. What brings about this feeling of unity? The writer of the book of Ephesians said that although each of us brings different gifts, we find true unity as we grow into Christ, who is the Head of the whole body.

15 But speaking the truth in love, may grow up into him in all things, which is the head, even Christ:
16 From whom the whole body fitly joined together and compacted by that which every joint supplieth, according to the effectual working in the measure of every part, maketh increase of the body unto the edifying of itself in love.

15 Instead, speaking the truth in love, we will in all things grow up into him who is the Head, that is, Christ.
16 From him the whole body, joined and held together by every supporting ligament, grows and builds itself up in love, as each part does its work.

TOPICAL OUTLINE OF THE LESSON

I. **Introduction**
   A. True Unity
   B. Biblical Background

II. **Exposition and Application of the Scripture**
   A. The Unity of the Faith—Part 1 (Ephesians 4:1-6)
   B. The Unity of the Faith—Part 2 (Ephesians 4:7-13)
   C. The Unity of the Body (Ephesians 4:14-16)

III. **Concluding Reflection**

LESSON OBJECTIVES

Upon the completion of the lesson, the students will be able to do the following:

1. Explore characteristics of a life worthy of Christ's calling in building up the body of Christ;
2. Celebrate their gifts that help build up the body of Christ; and,

3. Give an interpretation of having "one faith, one baptism, one God of all"—as it relates to the building up of the body of Christ.

POINTS TO BE EMPHASIZED

ADULT/YOUTH
Adult Topic: **Living Together**
Youth Topic: **We Are One**
Adult Key Verses: **Ephesians 4:4-5**
Youth Key Verse: **Ephesians 4:4**
Print Passage: **Ephesians 4:1-16**
—Christians should live according to the call of Christ.
—God gives spiritual gifts to believers in order to equip them to work together and to carry out the calling that He has given them.
—God's gifts to believers are diverse and are given for the purpose of ministry.
—God wants Christians to grow into mature believers.
—Believers have been given the gift of grace through Christ Jesus.
—Christians are exhorted to help others and speak the truth with an attitude of love.

CHILDREN
Children Topic: **Working Together**
Key Verse: **Ephesians 4:15**
Print Passage: **Ephesians 4:1-16**

—Different spiritual gifts have been given in order to build up the church.

—Unity is possible in the body of Christ when we use our spiritual gifts to work together.

—Maturity in the body of Christ occurs as mature disciples use their spirituals gifts to equip other members for service.

—Christ's Spirit draws us together as one body.

I. INTRODUCTION

A. True Unity

Three times a year, I lead or I am a member of a short-term mission team serving in Kenya. Our work is with the churches and leaders of the Baptist Convention of Kenya, which has 2,583 congregations—with each of the forty-two tribal groups represented. The tribal groups are all different culturally, socially, and politically, and each has its own individual language (which may include several different dialects). The success of our mission teams depends entirely upon the ability of the group to work together and understand the purpose for which we have traveled such a great distance. There has only been one occasion, among the nearly thirty trips taken, when the group was fragmented by strife and internal conflict. The team was able to achieve its purpose—but it was not without its challenges. Just as our short-term mission teams must have unity, the same is true of the local church. We all feel positive about life when everything goes well after we have worked together on a project. What about this feeling of unity? The apostle Paul said that, although each of us brings different gifts, we find true unity as we grow into Christ, who is the Head of the whole body.

B. Biblical Background

Ephesians 4:1-16 is one of the most important, practical groups of teachings in the New Testament, regarding the structure and work of the local church. In these verses, the apostle Paul outlined the various gifts that God had placed in the local church and in the larger body for the purpose of doing ministry. The verses that comprise the lesson today are the beginning of the application of Paul's doctrinal teachings about the church that he laid out in chapters 1–3. In those chapters, he described how God had called the church into existence before the foundation of the world (see Ephesians 1:4); how God redeemed the church through the blood of Jesus (see Ephesians 1:7); and that the church is the physical demonstration of God's intention to unify Jews and Gentiles into one body (see 2:11-18). The church is truly fulfilling the purposes of God when it lives in unity and harmony. Paul affirmed that the Holy Spirit is the source of unity in the body.

The work of unity, however, is the work of every believer in the church. It is the work of the ministry to bring the whole church to spiritual maturity, which leads to further growth (see Ephesians 4:11-16). Without unity, the church fails to live up to and walk in the grace of our Lord Jesus Christ. Verses 2-3 describe what each believer must do to build up unity in the body.

II. EXPOSITION AND APPLICATION OF THE SCRIPTURE

A. The Unity of the Faith—Part 1
(Ephesians 4:1-6)

I THEREFORE, the prisoner of the Lord, beseech you that ye walk worthy of the vocation wherewith ye are called, With all lowliness and meekness, with longsuffering, forbearing one another in love; Endeavouring to keep the unity of the Spirit in the bond of peace. There is one body, and one Spirit, even as ye are called in one hope of your calling; One Lord, one faith, one baptism, One God and Father of all, who is above all, and through all, and in you all.

Verse 1 is the key to unlocking the remaining three chapters in Paul's letter to the Ephesians. As previously noted, chapters 1–3 are doctrinal. The remaining three chapters describe what it means to be the church in a practical way. Paul urged them to live in such a way as to be worthy of the calling they had received from the Lord Jesus Christ. In the KJV, the word *walk* is used instead of the word *live*. The word *walk* is the key word in the second half of the Ephesians' letter. It is used in the New Testament to describe the direction of one's life. In the New Testament, it signified the way and activities that characterize the Christian's lifestyle: walk in the newness of life (see Romans 6:4); walk after the Spirit (see Romans 6:8); walk in honesty (see Romans 13:13); walk by faith (see 2 Corinthians 5:7); walk in good works (see Ephesians 2:10); and walk in love (see Ephesians 5:2). In the second half of the book of Ephesians, the word *walk* appears in 4:1, 17; 5:2, 8, 15.

Paul outlined several practical steps that the believers of Ephesus could take to ensure that unity within the body was maintained. First, they were to be completely humble. Second, they should practice being gentle. Third, he urged them to be patient. Fourth, they were to bear with one another in love. The fifth exhortation called upon them to make every effort to keep the unity of the Spirit, by living in peace with one another. Unity is not something that happens automatically, but must be worked at diligently among believers—hence the exhortation to "make every effort."

In verses 4-6, there is presented the reason why there must be unity within the body. The Christian church is one. The unity of the Spirit of the church is not only related to the character of the individual, but, more importantly, it is bound up with the very character of God. God is One. There is God the Father, God the Son, and God the Holy Spirit (Holy Trinity). Our unity is bound up with the very character and nature of God. God is three persons in one. As a spiritual reality, unity is present within the church; it must continue.

B. The Unity of the Faith—Part 2
(Ephesians 4:7-13)

But unto every one of us is given grace according to the measure of the gift of Christ. Wherefore he saith, When he ascended up on high, he led captivity captive, and gave gifts unto men. (Now that he ascended, what is it but that he also descended first into the lower parts of the earth? He that descended is the same also that ascended up far above all heavens, that he might fill all things.) And he gave some, apostles; and some, prophets; and some, evangelists; and some, pastors and teachers; For the perfecting of the saints, for the work of the ministry, for the edifying of the body of Christ: Till we all come in the unity of the faith, and of the knowledge of the Son of God, unto a perfect man, unto the measure of the stature of the fulness of Christ:

The word *But* (verse 7) introduces a change in the direction of Paul's thought. The unity of the body is maintained as believers live in the bond of peace. *Grace* is from the word *charis,* which means "gift" in this context. Jesus Christ has given to each member of the body a gift of grace, to be used in the work of the church's ministry (see Romans 12:3, 8-11; 1 Corinthians 12:8-11, 28-30; 1 Peter 4:10). These gifts were/are given according to the will and purpose of God. Jesus Christ distributes or apportions the gifts in ways that benefit local congregations. Every congregation has been given gifts which empower that congregation to achieve the mission and ministry of the Lord Jesus Christ.

Verse 8 contains the description of the mighty conqueror—who goes into battle, wins, and leads those who have been held captive to freedom. Jesus Christ is the one who ascended and gave gifts to humanity. Verses 9-10 are the explanation of verse 8; the interpretation has not been without disagreement. In essence, the One who ascended is Jesus Christ, who came from heaven to die on the Cross for the sins of the world. The "lower earthly regions" has been understood by some interpreters to mean that when Jesus Christ died on the Cross, during the interim period between the death and the Resurrection, He went into hell and preached to the spirits there. There is no evidence in the teachings of Jesus that His purpose was to descend into hell. The correct interpretation is to see "the lowerly earthly parts," referring to the earth.

In verse 11, Paul described what are commonly called the "fivefold gifts of leadership." There is a great deal of discussion as to whether some of these gifts are present in the church today, particularly the office of apostle. The Greek word for "apostle," *apostolos,* literally means "one who is sent forth." The word is used in the Gospels to describe the original twelve disciples of Jesus (see Matthew 10:5; Luke 6:13; 9:10).

The Greek word *prophetes* refers to "one who speaks the word of God." Biblically, the prophet was one upon whom the Spirit of God rested (see Numbers 11:17-29) and one through whom God speaks (see Numbers 12:2; Amos 3:7-8). There were numerous prophets in the early church (see Acts 13:1; 15:32; 21:10). Some were considered to be false prophets (pseudo-prophet) (see 1 John 4:1; Matthew 7:15; 24:11; Acts 13:6). The prophets were not just foretellers of the future, but proclaimers of the will of God and declarers of the consequences of disobedience to that will.

The Greek word *evangelistes* refers to one who is "a proclaimer of good news." Like the prophets, the evangelists were wanderers—but with a distinct difference: They were called to preach the Gospel in areas where churches had not been established. They were the rank and file missionaries (see Acts 8:6-40; also 21:8; 2 Timothy 4:5).

The use of the article before these offices describes one person with a dual function. The Greek words used are *poimen* (shepherd/pastor) and *didaskalos* (teacher). The word *pastor* means "one who is the shepherd of the flock." As the shepherd of the flock, the pastor is the church's chief teacher and leader. This does not mean that others in the congregation do not have the gift of teaching; it merely denotes the office of the chief leader, who is responsible for what is taught in the church. The definition further describes the role of pastor as the congregational leader.

The pastor/teacher was the settled leader of a local congregation, whose work was largely confined to his congregation. His job was to lead the flock and feed it the spiritual food necessary to live for Christ and to protect the church from error.

Paul laid out for the Ephesians the goal of the church's ministry, which is growth in Jesus Christ. What is the overall objective of the leadership gifts given to the church? In verse 12, it is specifically stated: to prepare the people for the work of service so that the body of Christ may be built up. Ministry or service is one of the critical components of the overall purpose of the church (see Matthew 25:31-46). It is important to remember that numerical growth of a congregation is not the ultimate goal. The goal is spiritual growth. Numerical growth is a natural byproduct of our spiritual growth. The word *till* or *until* is a conjunction that shows a relationship between verses 12 and 13. *Till* indicates how long the work of building up is to go on. It will go on until we all come to full maturity. Hence, there is no time limit placed on the process.

C. The Unity of the Body
(Ephesians 4:14-16)

That we henceforth be no more children, tossed to and fro, and carried about with every wind of doctrine, by the sleight of men, and cunning craftiness, whereby they lie in wait to deceive; But speaking the truth in love, may grow up into him in all things, which is the head, even Christ: From whom the whole body fitly joined together and compacted by that which every joint supplieth, according to the effectual working in the measure of every part, maketh increase of the body unto the edifying of itself in love.

The word *then* in verse 14 (NIV) implies that the ultimate goal of the unity of the body and the building of the body lead to spiritual and doctrinal maturity. This maturity is measured by several traits. First, believers are no longer infants, helpless as babies. Second, they are no longer subject to being tossed back and forth, driven, and influenced by false teachings and doctrines. The word *wind* gives the impression of something that comes and goes without direction. Teachers of false and distorted doctrines are cunning and shrewd; they are highly deceptive when it comes to their craft.

The image of instability is reversed by the presence of real spiritual maturity. Instead of disunity and disharmony, believers are able to speak to each other in the spirit of love and with truthfulness. In Christ, the body of believers is fitly framed and held together. In verse 16, the image is of a human body which is healthy and growing. Each member of the body is contributing to the overall growth—helping the body to thrive. Within a healthy congregation, each part, each member, and each ministry does its part. This in turn empowers the church to do ministry and mission.

III. CONCLUDING REFLECTION

Whenever there is a discussion of Christian unity, the debate usually degenerates into an argument about the issues that divide Christians. The following issues are highlighted: whether or not one must speak in tongues to receive the Holy Spirit; baptism by immersion versus sprinkling; the confession of one's sins to a priest or to God; whether or not the church is the Holy Ghost headquarters (and all others live in Death Valley); seminary-trained pastors versus untrained pastors; and shouting or not shouting as acceptable in the worship of God. In addition to these issues, there is this misguided, misunderstood idea that unless we are all members of one denomination, there is no true Christian unity.

PRAYER

Lord God, grant that Your people learn to live in unity, striving together for the cause of Your kingdom. In Jesus' name we pray. Amen.

WORD POWER

Gentleness—has the same idea as the word *meekness*. It means having power under control. Aristotle referred to the meek person as the person who lived between excessive anger and complete passivity.

Humility—it is the servant spirit that puts God first, others second, and ourselves last. In the ancient world in which Paul lived, humility was to be avoided. The Greeks considered it a cringing, servile, ignoble, and despised quality to have. But Jesus exalted humility to the highest level (see Matthew 18:4; 23:12).

Love *(agape)*—the kind of love that means we will always seek only the highest good of others. It is a selfless, self-giving, self-sacrificing love. The best commentary on the word *love* as used here is found in Matthew 5:43-48; John 13:34-35; 1 Corinthians 13.

Patience—the quality of self-restraint that the believer displays in the face of provocation, without retaliation. The word literally means "long-tempered." The person who displays this trait has the patience to put up with unlovable and unbearable people, regardless of how these people may treat them.

Peace—as used here, it means having harmonious relationships among individuals, particularly among believers.

HOME DAILY BIBLE READINGS
(December 10-16, 2012)

Unity in the Body of Christ

MONDAY, December 10: "One Lord" (Zechariah 14:6-11)

TUESDAY, December 11: "One Faith" (Philippians 1:27-30)

WEDNESDAY, December 12: "One in Christ Jesus" (Galatians 3:23-29)

THURSDAY, December 13: "One God" (Exodus 20:1-7)

FRIDAY, December 14: "One Spirit" (1 Corinthians 12:4-13)

SATURDAY, December 15: "One Body" (Romans 12:3-8)

SUNDAY, December 16: "Building Up the Body Together" (Ephesians 4:1-16)

LESSON 4   **December 23, 2012**

LIVE IN THE LIGHT

FAITH PATHWAY/FAITH JOURNEY TOPIC: **Living by Example**

DEVOTIONAL READING: **Psalm 97**
PRINT PASSAGE: **John 1:1-5;**
Ephesians 5:1-2, 6-14

BACKGROUND SCRIPTURE: **John 1:1-14;**
Ephesians 4:17–5:20
KEY VERSE: **Ephesians 5:1**

John 1:1-5; Ephesians 5:1-2, 6-14—KJV

IN THE beginning was the Word, and the Word was with God, and the Word was God.

2 The same was in the beginning with God.

3 All things were made by him; and without him was not any thing made that was made.

4 In him was life; and the life was the light of men.

5 And the light shineth in darkness; and the darkness comprehended it not.

…..

BE YE therefore followers of God, as dear children;

2 And walk in love, as Christ also hath loved us, and hath given himself for us an offering and a sacrifice to God for a sweetsmelling savour.

…..

6 Let no man deceive you with vain words: for because of these things cometh the wrath of God upon the children of disobedience.

7 Be not ye therefore partakers with them.

8 For ye were sometimes darkness, but now are ye light in the Lord: walk as children of light:

9 (For the fruit of the Spirit is in all goodness and righteousness and truth;)

10 Proving what is acceptable unto the Lord.

11 And have no fellowship with the unfruitful works of darkness, but rather reprove them.

12 For it is a shame even to speak of those things which are done of them in secret.

13 But all things that are reproved are made manifest by the light: for whatsoever doth make manifest is light.

14 Wherefore he saith, Awake thou that sleepest, and arise from the dead, and Christ shall give thee light.

John 1:1-5; Ephesians 5:1-2, 6-14—NIV

IN THE beginning was the Word, and the Word was with God, and the Word was God.

2 He was with God in the beginning.

3 Through him all things were made; without him nothing was made that has been made.

4 In him was life, and that life was the light of men.

5 The light shines in the darkness, but the darkness has not understood it.

…..

BE IMITATORS of God, therefore, as dearly loved children

2 and live a life of love, just as Christ loved us and gave himself up for us as a fragrant offering and sacrifice to God.

…..

6 Let no one deceive you with empty words, for because of such things God's wrath comes on those who are disobedient.

7 Therefore do not be partners with them.

8 For you were once darkness, but now you are light in the Lord. Live as children of light

9 (for the fruit of the light consists in all goodness, righteousness and truth)

10 and find out what pleases the Lord.

11 Have nothing to do with the fruitless deeds of darkness, but rather expose them.

12 For it is shameful even to mention what the disobedient do in secret.

13 But everything exposed by the light becomes visible,

14 for it is light that makes everything visible. This is why it is said: "Wake up, O sleeper, rise from the dead, and Christ will shine on you."

UNIFYING LESSON PRINCIPLE

People sometimes think that their thoughts, fears, and actions are hidden—or are kept se-cret—from others. What happens when these secrets are exposed to the light? The writer of the book of Ephesians wrote that as Christians we must always live in Christ's light (which overcomes all kinds of darkness), and that the wise men received a light into their lives when they found the baby Jesus and were overwhelmed with joy.

TOPICAL OUTLINE OF THE LESSON

I. **Introduction**
   A. Doing Good Works
   B. Biblical Background

II. **Exposition and Application of the Scripture**
   A. The Divine Life in Essence (John 1:1-5)
   B. Living Examples (Ephesians 5:1-2)
   C. Living in the Light (Ephesians 5:6-14)

III. **Concluding Reflection**

LESSON OBJECTIVES

Upon the completion of the lesson, the students will be able to do the following:

1. Explore images of Jesus as light overcoming darkness (as used in the books of John and Ephesians);
2. Imagine living in constant light, where there are no secrets; and,
3. Commit to discovering how to live lives of the fruit of light.

POINTS TO BE EMPHASIZED

ADULT/YOUTH

Adult Topic: Living by Example
Youth Topic: Go Light!
Adult Key Verse: Ephesians 5:1
Youth Key Verse: Ephesians 5:8
Print Passage: John 1:1-5; Ephesians 5:1-2, 6-14

—The opening verses of the gospel of John are thought to be an early Christian hymn.
—God preceded all things.
—God's Word was with Him in pre-history.
—God's Word is the agent of creation.
—God's Word was full of life, and this life provided life to humanity.
—Christians are urged to imitate the life that Jesus lived.
—Christians are called to be lights and to reject the works of evil and darkness.

CHILDREN

Children Topic: The Best Gift of All
Key Verse: Matthew 2:11
Print Passage: Matthew 2:1-11

—The Magi had traveled from the East to Jerusalem to see the young child Jesus.
—The star from the East guided the Magi to where Jesus and His mother, Mary, lived.
—Herod wanted the Magi to find Jesus in Bethlehem and to tell Herod where Jesus lived.
—Herod stated that he wanted to worship the "King of the Jews," but he actually wanted to kill Him.
—The Magi worshipped Jesus and presented Him with gifts of gold, frankincense, and myrrh.

I. INTRODUCTION

A. Doing Good Works

Twelve United States soldiers were flying home from Iraq on a two-week leave in July of 2004. Before one of the soldiers boarded the plane, a passenger traded his first-class ticket for the soldier's coach ticket. As the plane was being boarded, other passengers asked to trade their first-class seats for the coach seats occupied by the remaining soldiers.

Sevilla Evans, a flight attendant on the American Airlines flight from Atlanta to Chicago, said, "I was so privileged to be flying with these two groups of people. Here you have these kids who are putting their lives on the line, protecting our freedom, and here are these people who gave you these seats that are usually fought over. You really have to have a large heart to do something like that."[1]

This incident is repeated thousands of times each day in America as people are moved by the examples of others to do good works. In the previous lesson, we learned that the goal of the ministry of the church is to bring believers to full spiritual maturity. As believers grow in grace and in the knowledge of the Lord Jesus Christ, they reflect more of the light and life of the Lord Jesus Christ. Examples such as the one in the story above will be commonplace among believers as they live out what it means to be Christians in a world dominated by postmodern philosophies and practices. The greatest compliment that can be given to any Christian is that his or her life is a reflection of the Lord Jesus Christ. As you study this lesson today, think of ways that you can begin to be a greater influence for Jesus Christ in your family, church, and community.

B. Biblical Background

There are two passages that comprise today's lesson. The first is from the opening verses of the gospel of John, often referred to as the Prologue (verses 1-18). These verses are believed to have been one of the earliest Christian hymns celebrating the life of Jesus as light and life. The opening verses of the book of John reveal the foundational theme of the entire Gospel—the life of Jesus of Nazareth. God was uniquely present in Jesus' life, and those who were witnesses to His life and ministry were eyewitnesses of the glory and power of God on the earth. In Jesus Christ, the very Word of God had appeared on the earth as a living present reality.

Our second passage is a continuation of the study of the epistle to the Ephesians. In the lesson today, we will learn practical lessons that empower the believer to live the life of faith in the Lord Jesus Christ. One of the overarching themes in Paul's letter to the Ephesians is the dualism between *light* and *darkness*—with light reflecting the life of Christ, and darkness the presence of sin and evil. The apostle called upon the saints in Ephesus to imitate the life of Jesus. The life that pleases God is sometimes viewed in the Scriptures as a fragrant offering that ascends to God and is pleasing to Him (see Exodus 29:18). One of the primary purposes of the lesson is to exhort believers to live in obedience to Christ.

II. EXPOSITION AND APPLICATION OF THE SCRIPTURE

A. The Divine Life in Essence
(John 1:1-5)

IN THE beginning was the Word, and the Word was with God, and the Word was God. The same was in the beginning with God. All things were made by him; and without him was not any thing made that was made. In him was life; and the life was the light of men. And the light shineth in darkness; and the darkness comprehended it not.

Verses 1-5 are the opening verses of the prologue to the gospel of John. The entire gospel of John gives us a look at Christ that is loftier and more sublime than any of the other gospels. Jesus is God in finite human flesh; He is, at the same time, both God and man. The section begins with a backward glance at the Genesis account of the creation and establishes a canonical connection between the Hebrew Scriptures and John.[2] In the Genesis account, the Word is what God spoke, and the Creation came into existence (see Genesis 1:3, 6, 9, 14, 20, 24). Here in the book of John, the Word is with God from the very beginning, which establishes the eternality of the Word (Greek: *logos*). In the book of John, the Word has reference to Jesus Christ and is therefore a Christological designation for the Son of God. The Word was not just in the beginning—the Word existed with God and the Word *was* in fact God.

Verse 2 establishes the pre-existence of Jesus with the Father. He was with God before there was a creation or before the worlds were ever formed. Everything that exists in creation was made through Him. There is nothing in the whole of creation which He has not had a part in creating. He is the very essence of life. He is not only the One who calls life into existence, but also, He is the *means* by which life

is sustained. Jesus is the source of the believer's spiritual life, as well as his or her physical life. He is the light that illuminates the world and gives order and direction to humanity. *Darkness* in verse 5 refers to "spiritual darkness." Just as God overcame the darkness of chaos in creation, so the presence of Jesus Christ in the world overcomes the spiritual darkness that seeks to engulf the universe. Darkness could not and did not overcome Him.

B. Living Examples
(Ephesians 5:1-2)

BE YE therefore followers of God, as dear children; And walk in love, as Christ also hath loved us, and hath given himself for us an offering and a sacrifice to God for a sweetsmelling savour.

Verse 1 is a continuation of the exhortations at the end of Ephesians 4:32—to be forgiving of others just as God in Christ has forgiven us. Believers are able to live out this ethic of mutual forgiveness when they seek to mimic the very character of God. The apostle Paul exhorted the Ephesians to become imitators of God. The Greek word that is translated by the English word "imitate" is *mimetes*, which literally means "imitator." From this word we get our English word, *mimic*. A mimic is "someone who copies another person in behavior and speech." Thus, the word *followers* really means "imitators." In the New Testament, the word *mimetes* can be expressed by the word *followers*, *examples*, or *imitate*. In 1 Corinthians 11:1, the apostle Paul wrote, "Be ye followers of me, even as I also am of Christ." The apostle told the Corinthians that if they needed a model of Christian behavior and conduct, they could use him, because he was following Christ. Every believer should ask himself or herself what kind of example he or she is setting for others, especially new believers and those who have not reached spiritual maturity.

Therefore, it is all the more amazing that Paul told the Ephesians to become or to be imitators of God. One might ask, *how can I imitate God?* God is eternal, omnipotent, omnipresent, and omniscient. God is immutable. God is a Spirit. One could argue that it is impossible to mimic or even imitate God. That is basically true, for there are many things about God which we cannot imitate or mimic.

The point is this: We imitate God when we treat each other as God treats us. God is merciful, caring, compassionate, and forgiving. He does not hold on to the past. He does not bless nor reward us according to what we have done or have not done in the past. It does not cost a lot to be kind to each other, to be tenderhearted, and to recognize that we are all prone to weakness and should forgive one another.

Verse 2 says that we should walk in love, as Christ also hath loved us, and hath given Himself for us an offering and a sacrifice to God for a "sweetsmelling savour." To *walk in love* means that the whole of our conduct and conversations is the result of hearts full of love. The one thing that makes the difference in anyone's life is for him or her to know that he or she is loved. We all have a need to be loved and appreciated. If we are loved for who we are, then we can face just about any problem that comes along.

Love is the one great distinctive mark of the Christian church. In Matthew 5:44, Jesus said to "Love your enemies, bless them that curse you, do good to them that hate you, and pray for them who despitefully use you, and persecute you." In John 13:34-35, He remarked, "A new commandment I give unto you, That ye love one another; as I have loved you, that ye also love one another. By this shall all men know that ye are my disciples, if ye have love one to another"—and not just a sentimental love or an emotional feeling, but a tough love that would love purely for the sake of loving without any pre-conditions (see 1 Corinthians 13). First Peter 1:22 says that we should love the brethren with fervently pure hearts. That means that there ought not to be anything in one's heart that prevents him or her from loving unconditionally. First John 4:7-8 reads, "Beloved, let us love one another: for love is of God; and every one that loveth is born of God, and knoweth God. He that loveth not knoweth not God; for God is love."

C. Living in the Light (Ephesians 5:6-14)

Let no man deceive you with vain words: for because of these things cometh the wrath of God upon the children of disobedience. Be not ye therefore partakers with them. For ye were sometimes darkness, but now are ye light in the Lord: walk as children of light: (For the fruit of the Spirit is in all goodness and righteousness and truth;) Proving what is acceptable unto the Lord. And have no fellowship with the unfruitful works of darkness, but rather reprove them. For it is a shame even to speak of those things which are done of them in secret. But all things that are reproved are made manifest by the light: for whatsoever doth make manifest is light. Wherefore he saith, Awake thou that sleepest, and arise from the dead, and Christ shall give thee light.

The central point in this section of the lesson has to do with being who we say we are in Jesus Christ, both in word and deed. Paul continued to explain what it meant to live the

Christian life. One aspect of the new life in Jesus Christ is separation from the things of the world and those who seek to live in spiritual darkness. Those who continue to live in disobedience will face the wrath of God. Paul challenged the Ephesians to live above and beyond the reach of the world (see the book of 1 John). He began by making a strong statement, warning them about the presence of deceivers. This is an obvious reference to chapter 4, verse 14, where it is explained that those who are untutored in the faith are subject to being tossed and driven by every wind of doctrine that came along. Were there false teachers and prophets in that day? Obviously this was a real problem with the church, which had to contend with men and women who proclaimed a message that was not grounded in the Old Testament Scriptures nor the teachings of Jesus Christ (see Jeremiah 29:8-9, 31; Ezekiel 13:10f.; Micah 3:5; Matthew 24:4, 24; Galatians 6:7; compare with Acts 20:28-31).

Verse 7 was an appeal for the Ephesians not to associate themselves with the disobedient. Paul appealed to the saints not to be partners with them (see 2 Corinthians 6:14). The reason is stated in verse 8; they were once men and women who lived in sin or darkness, but through the shed blood of Jesus Christ they had experienced God's forgiveness and had become light. And because they had become light, they were to live as light.

Verse 9 is a parenthetical statement that describes the spiritual character of those who live in the light (see Galatians 5:22-23; compare also Psalm 16:2-3). Believers must come to know what pleases God, for only in pleasing God can they live lives that are fruitful and productive (see Colossians 1:10-12).

In verse 11, the interpretation could easily be mistaken to mean that believers are to live in totally separate worlds and never have contact with unbelievers. However, the exhortation is for a believer not to pattern his or her life after them nor their deeds or actions, which are referred to as fruitless deeds of darkness. Exposing them has reference to revealing to those who practice such things the error of their ways. In fact, Paul cautioned against having discussions about the shameful acts of the disobedient. Their acts were so despicable that they should not be mentioned either publicly or privately (see 1 Corinthians 5:1). When the light of the life of Jesus Christ is present within the life of the believer, it produces light. When a light is turned on in a dark room, it dispels the darkness. The believer is to be light—and whenever the believer shows up there should be light and not darkness (see verse 14a). The last portion of verse 14 is not an actual quote from Scripture. It has been understood that it may be a historical hymn of the first-century Christian movement. It is based upon Isaiah 26:19; 51:17; 5:1. The preaching of Jesus was a call for Israel to rise out of its religious stupor of spiritual death and allow the light of Jesus Christ to shine upon them.

III. CONCLUDING REFLECTION

It has been said that "imitation is the best form of flattery." How true that is of our contemporary society. We are, in many ways, a society of imitators. When someone discovers a winning formula, it is usually duplicated by others. Some of us today may be wearing clothing, jewelry, perfume, or cologne that is an imitation of some other brand. After church, we will probably have a meal that will contain some imitation coloring or flavoring. We are surrounded by imitators and imitations.

When we think of imitations, we think of them in negative terms. We do not want to be accused of wearing or possessing an imitation of something, when in point of fact the reason we bought the imitation was because it was so close to the real thing that one could hardly tell the difference.

PRAYER

Lord God Almighty, heavenly Father, Creator of the ends of the earth, may we learn to walk in obedience to Your Word, living to please You in all things. In Jesus' name we pray. Amen.

WORD POWER

Wrath (Greek: *orge* [or-gay])—a word that is used in the Bible to refer to both the wrath of men and the wrath of God. In the current lesson, it speaks directly of the wrath or anger of God against unrighteousness and sin. Wrath is the natural disposition of God toward rebellion and disobedience. The wrath or anger of God can be seen most prominently in the Old Testament, where Israel refused to walk in obedience to God and honor their covenant relationship. Therefore, the nation brought judgment and wrath upon themselves for their disobedience and unfaithfulness (see Deuteronomy 6:15; Joshua 23:16; Judges 2:12; Jeremiah 42:18; Joel 2:13; Colossians 3:6).

HOME DAILY BIBLE READINGS
(December 17-23, 2012)

Live in the Light

MONDAY, December 17: "Light Dawns for the Righteous" (Psalm 97)

TUESDAY, December 18: "The Way of Darkness" (Ephesians 4:17-24)

WEDNESDAY, December 19: "Putting Away the Old Ways" (Ephesians 4:25-32)

THURSDAY, December 20: "Be Careful How You Live" (Ephesians 5:15-20)

FRIDAY, December 21: "We Have Seen His Star" (Matthew 2:1-11)

SATURDAY, December 22: "We Have Seen His Glory" (John 1:6-14)

SUNDAY, December 23: "Light Shines in the Darkness" (John 1:1-5; Ephesians 5:1-2, 6-14)

End Notes

[1]Craig Brian Larson and Phyllis Ten Elshof, General Editors, *1001 Illustrations that Connect: Compelling Stories, Stats, and New Items for Preaching, Teaching, and Writing* (Grand Rapids: Zondervan Publishing Co., 2008), p. 489.
[2]G. K. Beale and D. A. Carson, Editors, *Commentary on the New Testament Use of the Old Testament* (Grand Rapids: Baker Academic, 2007), p. 421.

LESSON 5   December 30, 2012

CHRIST'S LOVE FOR THE CHURCH

FAITH PATHWAY/FAITH JOURNEY TOPIC: **Family Matters**

DEVOTIONAL READING: **John 3:16-21**
PRINT PASSAGE: **Ephesians 5:21-33; 6:1-4**

BACKGROUND SCRIPTURE: **Ephesians 5:21–6:4**
KEY VERSE: **Ephesians 5:21**

Ephesians 5:21-33; 6:1-4—KJV

21 Submitting yourselves one to another in the fear of God.

22 Wives, submit yourselves unto your own husbands, as unto the Lord.

23 For the husband is the head of the wife, even as Christ is the head of the church: and he is the saviour of the body.

24 Therefore as the church is subject unto Christ, so let the wives be to their own husbands in every thing.

25 Husbands, love your wives, even as Christ also loved the church, and gave himself for it;

26 That he might sanctify and cleanse it with the washing of water by the word,

27 That he might present it to himself a glorious church, not having spot, or wrinkle, or any such thing; but that it should be holy and without blemish.

28 So ought men to love their wives as their own bodies. He that loveth his wife loveth himself.

29 For no man ever yet hated his own flesh; but nourisheth and cherisheth it, even as the Lord the church:

30 For we are members of his body, of his flesh, and of his bones.

31 For this cause shall a man leave his father and mother, and shall be joined unto his wife, and they two shall be one flesh.

32 This is a great mystery: but I speak concerning Christ and the church.

33 Nevertheless let every one of you in particular so love his wife even as himself; and the wife see that she reverence her husband.

…..

CHILDREN, OBEY your parents in the Lord: for this is right.

Ephesians 5:21-33; 6:1-4—NIV

21 Submit to one another out of reverence for Christ.

22 Wives, submit to your husbands as to the Lord.

23 For the husband is the head of the wife as Christ is the head of the church, his body, of which he is the Savior.

24 Now as the church submits to Christ, so also wives should submit to their husbands in everything.

25 Husbands, love your wives, just as Christ loved the church and gave himself up for her

26 to make her holy, cleansing her by the washing with water through the word,

27 and to present her to himself as a radiant church, without stain or wrinkle or any other blemish, but holy and blameless.

28 In this same way, husbands ought to love their wives as their own bodies. He who loves his wife loves himself.

29 After all, no one ever hated his own body, but he feeds and cares for it, just as Christ does the church—

30 for we are members of his body.

31 "For this reason a man will leave his father and mother and be united to his wife, and the two will become one flesh."

32 This is a profound mystery—but I am talking about Christ and the church.

33 However, each one of you also must love his wife as he loves himself, and the wife must respect her husband.

…..

CHILDREN, OBEY your parents in the Lord, for this is right.

UNIFYING LESSON PRINCIPLE

People struggle to balance the demands of their daily lives with their need to show love for one another. Where can people find the secret to living a healthy life together? The writer of the book of Ephesians stated that family members should love and care for one another just as Christ loves and cares for the church; the writer of the book of 1 John said that we must put our love in action and make the act of loving our way of life.

2 Honour thy father and mother; which is the first commandment with promise;	2 "Honor your father and mother"—which is the first commandment with a promise—
3 That it may be well with thee, and thou mayest live long on the earth.	3 "that it may go well with you and that you may enjoy long life on the earth."
4 And, ye fathers, provoke not your children to wrath: but bring them up in the nurture and admonition of the Lord.	4 Fathers, do not exasperate your children; instead, bring them up in the training and instruction of the Lord.

TOPICAL OUTLINE OF THE LESSON

I. **Introduction**
   A. It Is about Family
   B. Biblical Background

II. **Exposition and Application of the Scripture**
   A. Submit to One Another (Ephesians 5:21-24)
   B. Guidelines for Husbands and Wives (Ephesians 5:25-33)
   C. Guidelines for Children (Ephesians 6:1-4)

III. **Concluding Reflection**

LESSON OBJECTIVES

Upon the completion of the lesson, the students will be able to do the following:

1. Compare Christ's love for the church with the relationships among family members;

2. Appreciate Christ's sacrifice to show love and care for the church; and,

3. Accept responsibility for showing love in the family, as Christ demonstrated love for the church.

POINTS TO BE EMPHASIZED

ADULT/YOUTH
Adult Topic: Family Matters
Youth Topic: It's Not about You!
Adult/Youth Key Verse: Ephesians 5:21
Print Passage: Ephesians 5:21-33; 6:1-4
—Christ's love for the church is the model for relationships within marriage and within the church.
—Christians are to submit themselves to one another.
—Wives are to submit themselves to their husbands.
—Husbands should love their wives sacrificially—as Christ loved the church.
—Husbands are to love their wives as they love themselves.
—Children are to obey their parents.
—Parents should not exasperate their children.

CHILDREN
Children Topic: Love Is the Way
Key Verse: 1 John 3:23
Print Passage: 1 John 3:18-24

—Active love that is grounded in truth is better than love expressed only in words.
—God commands us to love one another as Christ has loved us.
—We know that Jesus lives in us by the Spirit of God that lives in us.
—Keeping God's commandments proves that Christ's Spirit dwells in us.

I. INTRODUCTION

A. It Is about Family

One of the most important outcomes of the ministry of Jesus Christ was the creation of a new community of faith. Community in this context is defined as "a group of people who share a set of common identities, values, beliefs, and purposes." That new community of faith was called the Christian church. One of the overarching foundations of Christianity is its deep roots in the biblical concept of collective personality, which teaches that the people of God are not individuals, but a community drawn together by common beliefs and practices. Community finds its greatest expression in people living together in harmony and fellowship. Christianity is not a private matter, but a community event.

Every believer has to raise these questions from time to time: "What does it take for me to live together, believe together, worship together, serve together, and be together with other believers? What does God expect from me as a born-again believer? How do I close the gap between what I say and what I do?" The capacity of people to live together in harmony (a community) is one of the most precious gifts given to us by God. Yet, it can be quite difficult to achieve and even harder to maintain once it is achieved. In the lesson today, we are taught that the foundation for the creation of community is within the context of the family. Often families can face enormous tensions because of the demands that many congregations place upon the members. The apostle Paul reminded us that family members should love and care for one another, just as Christ cares for the church.

B. Biblical Background

The Bible presents a positive view of the family and marriage. Marriage and the family were both established by God (see Genesis 1:26-27; 2:18-25). The institution of family and marriage was much different than it is now. Polygamy was practiced and was an accepted social standard. There was nothing wrong with a man having several wives—with each bearing him several children (see Genesis 16:1-16; 29:1–30:24; 1 Samuel 1:1-3). Even King David had multiple wives and children by all of them. His son, Solomon, had seven hundred wives, yet the Law condemned infidelity and disloyalty to the family (see Exodus 20:14). In the Deuteronomic Code, there were certain conditions that would permit divorce (see Deuteronomy 24:1-4). However, in the teachings of Jesus, divorce was never an option for the dissolution of a marriage (see Mark 10:1-12).

In the family, the male was considered to be the head of the household (see Genesis 3:16; Joshua 24:14). As such, he was the provider and protector of the family. When the husband died, a family was usually plunged into deep poverty (see 1 Kings 17:8-16). The father was a provider of love and compassion for his wife and children (see Matthew 17:15; Luke 15). The man was expected to rear and teach his children the traditions of Israel (see Deuteronomy 6:6-8; Joshua 4:1-8; Proverbs 22:6). Within the church, a man could be disqualified from office if he demonstrated an inability to manage his own family life (see 1 Timothy 3:4-5). Any man who would not provide for the needs of his own family was considered to be worse than an infidel—one who had denied the faith (see 1 Timothy 5:8). It was the influence of the church that helped to change the practice of polygamy in many of the ancient civilizations (see 1 Timothy 3:2). A man could not be a leader in the church and have multiple wives. In the Jewish mind, a good Father corresponded in character and disposition to the character of God, whom Jesus addressed as Father (see Mark 14:36).

In Jewish society, women were not accorded the same rights and privileges as men. There were many rights that women did not possess, particularly those that related to divorce (see Deuteronomy 24:1ff); however, the Bible does not take a negative view of women and their role within the family. Eve was created by God to be the help mate of Adam (see Genesis 2:18). Jesus transformed the traditional view of women by including a number of them in His ministry and work (see Matthew 19:9; Luke 10:38-42). Women did not have the right to be educated to study the Law—thus, the prohibition by Paul that women not speak in church but ask their husbands at home came about (see 1 Corinthians 14:34-35). Clearly, much of Paul's thinking was heavily influenced by his Jewish rabbinical training and background. However, we must remember that the Bible does not take a totally negative view of women and wives.

II. EXPOSITION AND APPLICATION OF THE SCRIPTURE

A. Submit to One Another
(Ephesians 5:21-24)

Submitting yourselves one to another in the fear of God. Wives, submit yourselves unto your own husbands, as unto the Lord. For the husband is the head of the wife, even as Christ is the head of the church: and he is the saviour of the body. Therefore as the church is subject unto Christ, so let the wives be to their own husbands in every thing.

Paul urged the Ephesians to act and live like the spiritual community of faith, which had been redeemed by the blood of Jesus Christ. In Ephesians 5:21, the unity of the body galvanizes and comes together under the principle of mutual submission and respect. The word *submission* is from a Greek word that means "obedience." Gene A. Getz remarked (concerning submission), "In its most general use, it means to yield to another's admonition and advice. In Scripture, it appears in contexts describing servant-hood, humility, respect, reverence, honor, teachable-ness, and openness. All of these for one basic purpose—obedience to Jesus Christ."[1]

In our lesson passage, the word *submission* is used, as in other places, to describe our relationship to one another. We are to submit to each other. The question is—what does this mean? What does it mean to be submissive in an age when people like to throw their weight around and intimidate others? What does it mean to be submissive in an age when defiance is the general rule, when people will tell you quickly, "You can't tell me what to do!"? Even among many believers there can emerge this spirit of outright defiance and disobedience, which is really destructive to the life of the community. The word *submission* has in it the idea of deference, respect, honor, preferential treatment of others, and putting others ahead of oneself. In the New Testament, this idea of submission is taught in many places. In Luke 22:24-27 and John 13:1-15, Jesus taught it when He washed the disciples' feet to teach them a lesson about servant-hood. In Philippians 2:3-4, we are told to esteem others more highly than ourselves, and look not just to our needs, but to the needs of others. Hebrews 13:7, 17 reminds us to remember those who are the leaders of the church and to respect their position. The New Testament exhorts us to obey our leaders because they keep watch over our souls. Likewise, 1 Peter 5:3 reminds the leaders that they are not to be tyrants over the flock of God. First Peter 5:5 reads, "Likewise, ye younger, submit yourselves unto the elder. Yea, all of you be subject one to another, and be clothed with humility: for God resisteth the proud, and giveth grace to the humble." The New Testament stresses the importance of mutual submission as the means for building and strengthening the Christian community. Community is the framework by which the people of God learn to live together in harmony and peace.

Verses 22-24 spell out how the command to practice mutual submission is to be lived out among believers. Paul began by exhorting wives to be subordinate to their own husbands, just as they would be to the Lord. Many people, including some Christians, find this command to be repressive and supportive of male dominance over women. Yet, we must remember that God has established creation in an orderly manner, and there is a ladder of hierarchy and authority. The husband is the head of the household and as such, he is the leader of the family. The wife is to submit to her husband just as she would submit to the Lord Jesus Christ. Just as Christ is the Head of the church, the husband is the head of his family and his wife. The wife is to submit to her husband in everything. If there are to be loving relationships in the church, there must be loving relationships at home. Submission in the church begins with submission at home. In 1 Peter 3:1-7, there is a parallel passage that describes some ways in which wives should live in submission to their own husbands.

There is a question that the text implicitly raises: Is there a time when wives are not obligated to obey their husbands or to submit to them? The answer is yes! The Bible does not teach that a wife is to submit herself for abuse, either physically, verbally, or sexually. Wives are *not* commanded to obey their husbands under all circumstances and at all costs. This can be viewed as a moral or ethical test. The command is to do so as unto the Lord. Some husbands may ask, is this right?

B. Guidelines for Husbands and Wives
(Ephesians 5:25-33)

Husbands, love your wives, even as Christ also loved the church, and gave himself for it; That he might sanctify and cleanse it with the washing of water by the word, That he might present it to himself a glorious church, not having spot, or wrinkle, or any such thing; but that it should be holy and without blemish. So ought men to love their wives as their own bodies. He that loveth his wife loveth himself. For no man ever yet hated his own flesh; but nourisheth and cherisheth it, even as the Lord the church: For we are members of his body, of his flesh, and of his bones. For this cause shall a man leave his father and mother, and shall be joined unto his wife, and they two shall be one flesh. This is a great mystery: but I speak concerning Christ and the church. Nevertheless let every one of you in particular so love his wife even as himself; and the wife see that she reverence her husband.

In this section, the apostle Paul drew a comparison between the love that Christ has for the church and the love that a husband should have for his wife. Just as Christ has made sacrifices and safeguards the church, likewise husbands are commanded to do the same thing. The relationship between the church and Jesus Christ cannot be broken or tarnished. Those who see the burden of the marital relationship as placed on the backs of women have failed to read and understand verses 25-33. Husbands bear an enormous responsibility for the well-being of the family, especially in regard to their wives. Husbands are to love their own wives in the very same way that Jesus Christ loved the church. Here, the emphasis is on imitating what God in Christ has done to bring about our salvation. Christ gave Himself up for one purpose—to make the church holy and to present her as blameless. According to verse 28, a husband is to love his wife in the same way that Christ loved the church. He is to love his wife just as he would

love himself. In loving his wife, the husband in effect proves and shows just how much he loves himself. The two are one flesh, so one's loving his wife equates to his loving himself.

C. Guidelines for Children
(Ephesians 6:1-4)

CHILDREN, OBEY your parents in the Lord: for this is right. Honour thy father and mother; which is the first commandment with promise; That it may be well with thee, and thou mayest live long on the earth. And, ye fathers, provoke not your children to wrath: but bring them up in the nurture and admonition of the Lord.

In Roman culture, the father was the absolute ruler of the lives of his children—from birth until his death. William Barclay remarked that "So long as his father lived, a Roman son never came of age, and could not legally own one pennyworth of property."[2] Throughout the ancient world, in Judaism, African, Greek, and Roman cultures it was an absolute given that children were to obey and honor their parents. However, it must be remembered that children were to be taught obedience and respect.

Paul began this section of the household codes with the exhortation to the children in Ephesus. Children were commanded to obey their parents. The implication is that during the normal worship period when the letter was read, the children would hear the words calling them to obedience. Much has been written in the Bible regarding this exhortation (see Exodus 20:12; 21:15-17; Leviticus 20:9; Deuteronomy 5:16; Proverbs 1:8; 6:20; 30:17.)

Children are to obey their parents in the Lord. Their relationship to Jesus became the motivation for their obedience and respect for their parents. Further, they are called to obey because "This is right." Godly parents have the experience necessary to make their children wiser. Verse 2 is a quote from the Torah or Law, which is found in Exodus 20:12, the fifth commandment of the Lord. Paul used the Greek word *Timao* for honor, which means "to accord value and esteem for." It is used in the New Testament concerning the duty of children to parents (see Matthew 15:4; 19:19; Mark 7:10; 10:19; Luke 18:20). Paul pointed out that this is the first commandment with promise. By calling it the first commandment, he did not mean that it was the first commandment listed in the Torah. Rather, the word has in it the idea of significance and importance. It is a commandment with great importance. The promise that is attached is that of a dual blessing—first, the blessing of prosperity, and, second, the blessing of a long life.

In verse 4, fathers are reminded to train up their sons and daughters in the proper way (see Proverbs 22:6). These words are reminders of the Colossians passage which reminded fathers of the same duty (see Colossians 3:21). Parents can become the very reason why their children turn away from them and the church. Often, our parenting skills are not very good and we destroy our children before they get fully started with life.

Listed below are several ways for one to turn his or her children in the wrong direction: (1) *Overprotection*. We can be so protective that the kid never gets a chance to grow up and make mistakes. (2) *Favoritism*. The thing that tore apart the family of Isaac was the favoritism of the parents—Isaac to Esau, and Rebekah to Jacob (see Genesis 25:28). In Jacob's own family, he favored Joseph over his other sons. (3) *Neglect*. King David completely ignored Absalom, which led to his rebellion (see 2 Samuel 14:13, 28). (4) *Bitter and harsh words*. The very words we use can be a source of discouragement to our children.

III. CONCLUDING REFLECTION

America has one of the highest divorce rates in the world. One would think that the divorce rate among believers would not mirror that of the general society, but unfortunately, that is exactly the case. There are just as many Christian families breaking up as there are with those of nonbelievers. Think for a moment about how many families or marriages you know that have failed. What is the solution? It begins with having a true assessment and estimate of what it means to be Christian in every phase of our lives, including marriage or just dating. Marriages become stronger when couples work toward developing attitudes that mirror the attitude of Jesus Christ—who submitted to the will of the Father.

PRAYER

Lord, teach us to love what You love and respect what You respect. Grant that Your servants may be free to live in mutual submission in our relationships and within the body of Christ. In Jesus' name we pray. Amen.

WORD POWER

Submit (Greek: *hupotassos* [hoop-ot-as-so])—to subordinate, place under, or, as in the current lesson, to submit. *Submission* is a word that does not appeal to either the church or the world. It is often misunderstood as denoting a spirit of weakness and inferiority. In the marital relationship, it really speaks of both husband and wife having mutual respect for each other. The wife glorifies God by respecting and submitting to her husband, because this is the order that God wanted. The husband, in turn, honors God by respecting his wife and submitting to Jesus Christ. Submission (when properly understood and followed) resolves a number of relational issues and reflects that we understand the place of order in the kingdom of God (see 1 Chronicles 29:24; Romans 13:1-3; 1 Corinthians 16:16; Hebrews 13:17; 1 Peter 2:13; 5:5).

HOME DAILY BIBLE READINGS
(December 24-30, 2012)

Christ's Love for the Church

MONDAY, December 24: "God Is Love" (1 John 4:7-12)

TUESDAY, December 25: "God's Gift of Love" (John 3:16-21)

WEDNESDAY, December 26: "The Proof of God's Love" (Romans 5:6-11)

THURSDAY, December 27: "The Example of Jesus' Love" (John 13:1-9)

FRIDAY, December 28: "Abiding in Christ's Love" (John 15:9-17)

SATURDAY, December 29: "Following the Commands of Christ" (1 John 3:18-24)

SUNDAY, December 30: "Following the Example of Christ" (Ephesians 5:21–6:4)

End Notes

[1]Gene A. Getz, *Building Up One Another* (Wheaton: Victor Books, 1976), pp. 99-100.
[2]William Barclay, *The Ten Commandments for Today* (Harper and Row: New York, 1973), p. 52.

LESSON 6   January 6, 2013

PROCLAIMING CHRIST

FAITH PATHWAY/FAITH JOURNEY TOPIC: **Motives and Messages**

DEVOTIONAL READING: **Psalm 119:169-176**
PRINT PASSAGE: **Philippians 1:15-26**

BACKGROUND SCRIPTURE: **Philippians 1:12-30**
KEY VERSE: **Philippians 1:18**

Philippians 1:15-26—KJV

15 Some indeed preach Christ even of envy and strife; and some also of good will:

16 The one preach Christ of contention, not sincerely, supposing to add affliction to my bonds:

17 But the other of love, knowing that I am set for the defence of the gospel.

18 What then? notwithstanding, every way, whether in pretence, or in truth, Christ is preached; and I therein do rejoice, yea, and will rejoice.

19 For I know that this shall turn to my salvation through your prayer, and the supply of the Spirit of Jesus Christ,

20 According to my earnest expectation and my hope, that in nothing I shall be ashamed, but that with all boldness, as always, so now also Christ shall be magnified in my body, whether it be by life, or by death.

21 For to me to live is Christ, and to die is gain.

22 But if I live in the flesh, this is the fruit of my labour: yet what I shall choose I wot not.

23 For I am in a strait betwixt two, having a desire to depart, and to be with Christ; which is far better:

24 Nevertheless to abide in the flesh is more needful for you.

25 And having this confidence, I know that I shall abide and continue with you all for your furtherance and joy of faith;

26 That your rejoicing may be more abundant in Jesus Christ for me by my coming to you again.

Philippians 1:15-26—NIV

15 It is true that some preach Christ out of envy and rivalry, but others out of goodwill.

16 The latter do so in love, knowing that I am put here for the defense of the gospel.

17 The former preach Christ out of selfish ambition, not sincerely, supposing that they can stir up trouble for me while I am in chains.

18 But what does it matter? The important thing is that in every way, whether from false motives or true, Christ is preached. And because of this I rejoice. Yes, and I will continue to rejoice,

19 for I know that through your prayers and the help given by the Spirit of Jesus Christ, what has happened to me will turn out for my deliverance.

20 I eagerly expect and hope that I will in no way be ashamed, but will have sufficient courage so that now as always Christ will be exalted in my body, whether by life or by death.

21 For to me, to live is Christ and to die is gain.

22 If I am to go on living in the body, this will mean fruitful labor for me. Yet what shall I choose? I do not know!

23 I am torn between the two: I desire to depart and be with Christ, which is better by far;

24 but it is more necessary for you that I remain in the body.

25 Convinced of this, I know that I will remain, and I will continue with all of you for your progress and joy in the faith,

26 so that through my being with you again your joy in Christ Jesus will overflow on account of me.

UNIFYING LESSON PRINCIPLE

In a media-driven world, we hear many messages without fully knowing what motivates the "messenger." In what ways does the messenger's motive affect the message? Paul claimed that regardless of the person's intentions, the result was still that "Christ is proclaimed in every way"; Jesus used parables to teach us how to proclaim His message.

TOPICAL OUTLINE OF THE LESSON

I. Introduction

A. Communicating the Message

B. Biblical Background

II. Exposition and Application of the Scripture

A. Preaching for Different Reasons (Philippians 1:15-18)

B. Christ Will Be Exalted (Philippians 1:19-20)

C. Caught between Two Worlds (Philippians 1:21-26)

III. Concluding Reflection

LESSON OBJECTIVES

Upon the completion of the lesson, the students will be able to do the following:

1. Comprehend Paul's message of joy in the proclamation of the Gospel of Jesus Christ;

2. Reflect on the variety of motives for proclaiming the Gospel of Jesus Christ; and,

3. Present a personal proclamation of the Gospel.

POINTS TO BE EMPHASIZED

ADULT/YOUTH

Adult Topic: **Motives and Messages**

Youth Topic: **Truth Is Truth**

Adult/Youth Key Verse: **Philippians 1:18**

Print Passage: **Philippians 1:15-26**

—Paul's status as a prisoner advanced the Gospel in an unexpected way.

—Paul's credibility was an issue to those who supposed that a suffering apostle was a contradiction in terms.

—Paul affirmed a high view of Christ and Christ's relationship with God.

—Some people preached Christ for a multiplicity of reasons, both good and bad, but Paul rejoiced that Christ was preached.

—Paul preached Christ out of love, and because he was especially called for that purpose.

CHILDREN

Children Topic: **Salt and Light**

Key Verse: **Matthew 5:13-14**

Print Passage: **Matthew 5:13-16**

—Like salt, followers of Jesus bring out the best in others.

—If Christians make no effort to have an effect on the world, then they are of no value to God.

—Followers of Jesus should be like salt and have a positive effect on others.

—Christians are called to light the way to Jesus by their actions.

—Hiding who we are as followers of Jesus is not an option.

—Christians should live in ways that bring glory and honor to God.

I. INTRODUCTION

A. Communicating the Message

The news media is one of the most influential and powerful means of communication in the world. Advances in technology have given the media the ability to flash breaking news around the world almost instantly. Through the media, we can view major events through the lenses of eyewitnesses as though we were physically present there. The media also opens the door to the lives and struggles of people who live in some of the remotest places on the earth. One can virtually read daily any newspaper that is published anywhere in the world by simply visiting the World Wide Web. The revolutions that overthrew many of the most heinous political regimes in North Africa and the Middle East have been followed daily via the media. Advances in global communications raise a very serious question about accountability in reporting and whether or not media outlets are being responsible in their reporting. Can we say that news organizations are not biased? Or do they all have particular political, social, economic, religious, or ideological agendas? The answer is most likely yes. There are very few truly objective news sources because all of them are motivated by something or someone. In a media-driven world, we may hear many messages without fully knowing what motivates the messenger. In what way does the messenger's motive affect the message? Paul claimed that regardless of the person's intentions, the result was still that "Christ is proclaimed in every way."

B. Biblical Background

Today's lesson is a study of the book of Philippians. The letter to the Philippians encouraged believers to follow the pattern laid out for us by Christ, and to oppose enemies of Christ's cross. The church in Philippi was founded during Paul's second missionary journey, sometime between AD 49–51. We are not sure of the exact dates when the church was founded.

The letter to the Philippians is one of the most beloved of the New Testament writings. There is general consensus that Paul wrote the letter as a thank-you note to the church for their support during his days in prison. Additionally, there has been some debate among scholars as to when and where the letter was written. The most likely and best date is between AD 60 and 62, during his imprisonment in Rome. In the opening lesson, Paul answered his critics, who seemed to delight in his imprisonment. He reminded the saints in Philippi that although he was in prison, the fact that Jesus Christ was still being proclaimed was not a contradiction. He took great delight in the knowledge that the Gospel was going forth, even though there were preachers with ulterior motives.

II. EXPOSITION AND APPLICATION OF THE SCRIPTURE

A. Preaching for Different Reasons (Philippians 1:15-18)

Some indeed preach Christ even of envy and strife; and some also of good will: The one preach Christ of contention, not sincerely, supposing to add affliction to my bonds: But the other of love, knowing that I am set for the defence of the gospel. What then? notwithstanding, every way, whether in pretence, or in truth, Christ is preached; and I therein do rejoice, yea, and will rejoice.

No one knows for certain how and when Paul received word from the Philippians about problems in the church. The word may have come to him through any of the visitors who came to see him while he was in prison. One of the reasons he wrote this letter was to let the saints know that although he had been imprisoned for preaching the Gospel, it had not slowed the advance of the kingdom of God. Throughout Rome and even among the palace guards, the Word was spreading. The suggestion that comes from reading the letter hints that even in prison, Paul was preaching and teaching the Word of God (see Philippians 1:13-14).

It was only natural that those who were envious and jealous of Paul's success would seize the opportunity to advance themselves. He acknowledged that there were two groups of preachers at work in Philippi or throughout Asia and beyond. One group preached out of envy and rivalry, while the second group preached out of a spirit of genuine goodwill and love. We are not told why they envied Paul, but it may have been for some of the same reasons that some preachers and congregations are envious of their peers today. Some congregations are led by visionary men and women who are able to galvanize the collective energies

of their people and achieve great things. Then there are congregations that struggle to grow and just maintain. Success can bring out the worst in people—and Paul saw this firsthand. Paul had been quite successful; and among the Philippians, he was highly esteemed and loved. He was a master theologian and a very gifted teacher and preacher; these may have been the reasons that prompted the spirit of envy and competition among Paul's detractors.

In Galatia, there were preachers who came and declared a message that created confusion over the issue of circumcision and other Jewish practices, but this was not the case in Philippi (see Galatians 1:6-9; 3:1-5). The church was contending with a group of preachers who saw Paul's imprisonment as an opportunity to advance themselves. Paul said that they were not preaching for the cause of Christ, but purely out of selfish ambition. They were not sincere; rather, their primary goal was to stir up trouble for Paul. Whether their aim was to embarrass Paul or set themselves up as more noble is not stated. For Paul it did not matter, because whatever their motivation was, their plan had failed. Instead of pulling Paul down or minimizing his accomplishments, they only succeeded in causing the Gospel to advance even more. The unintended consequence was that Christ was preached—and it mattered little to Paul if the motives were true or false. Rather than be downcast about this situation, Paul saw it as a reason to rejoice because he had spent much of his adult life preaching the Gospel.

One of the temptations that churches and their leaders often face today is the need to be better, bigger, and bolder than the next church or preacher. Rather than seeing ourselves as comrades in the cause of Christ, we often view other congregations as competitors. This limits the effectiveness of the church and often leads to congregational and leadership ineffectiveness. Yet, in spite of the church's inability to cooperate, the Gospel continues to advance.

B. Christ Will Be Exalted
(Philippians 1:19-20)

For I know that this shall turn to my salvation through your prayer, and the supply of the Spirit of Jesus Christ, According to my earnest expectation and my hope, that in nothing I shall be ashamed, but that with all boldness, as always, so now also Christ shall be magnified in my body, whether it be by life, or by death.

One would think that given his situation and the uncertainty surrounding his future, Paul would have spent time trying to get out of prison. Further, one would hardly expect a man who had already endured so much for the preaching of the Gospel to have such an upbeat spirit and attitude. Paul knew that the prayers of the saints were very effective and that he could take comfort in their spiritual support. He reminded the Philippians that he drew strength from their prayers and the Spirit of Jesus Christ, which is a reference to the Holy Spirit. The word *help* (Greek: *epichoregia*) has in it the idea of supplying exactly what is needed to meet the challenge. Paul was saying that his help would come directly from the presence of the Holy Spirit, who would be with him to give him everything that he needed at the moment he needed it (see Romans 8:28; 1 Corinthians 4:17; 1 Peter 1:7-9).

The second part of verse 19 has been a source of debate among New Testament scholars as to exactly what Paul meant by, "What has happened to me will turn out for my deliverance." Was he referring to his upcoming trial? Was he thinking about possibly being proven correct in his preaching? Or was he looking ahead to the possibility that he could be executed, and thinking of facing the judgment of Jesus Christ as a Christian martyr? (See 2 Corinthians 5:10.) The most likely answer to the question lies in Paul's belief that he looked forward to the day when he would see Jesus Christ face-to-face (see 2 Timothy 4:4-8).

Paul noted that it was with eager expectation that he looked forward to the day of his trial. It was not with a sense of dread or fear that he strained to see what lay ahead; rather, it was with a deep sense of anticipation. The words *eager expectation* come from the Greek word *apokaradokiai* and have in them the picture of a man or woman who is straining his or her neck to see what is around the corner. There is an eagerness that cannot be fully expressed in words (see Romans 8:19; compare Psalm 62:5). He was waiting for the time when his day in court would come—and his greatest desire was that on that day he would be filled with courage. He in no way wanted to make the Lord Jesus Christ ashamed (see Mark 8:34-38).

There is one important fact about the life of Paul that may not always be mentioned nor written about. There is never an instance in the book of Acts or in Paul's own letters where he felt like giving up or succumbing to the constant pressures that he faced (see 2 Corinthians 12:7-9). Looking ahead, Paul was not sure about the outcome of his trial, but one thing was certain: Jesus Christ would be exalted. It did not matter whether it would be by death or by life—ultimately, men and women would see Jesus Christ in their lives.

How often have we seen believers give in

to the minutest challenges? One of the fallacies that much of the contemporary church scene has given is the impression that life in Christ is a flowery bed of roses. We have been led to believe that the one great benefit of faith in Jesus Christ is the capacity to have it all and to have life on our terms. This in turn has produced a generation of Christians who have neither the stomach for hardship nor the heart to struggle against the satanic forces of wickedness.

C. Caught between Two Worlds (Philippians 1:21-26)

For to me to live is Christ, and to die is gain. But if I live in the flesh, this is the fruit of my labour: yet what I shall choose I wot not. For I am in a strait betwixt two, having a desire to depart, and to be with Christ; which is far better: Nevertheless to abide in the flesh is more needful for you. And having this confidence, I know that I shall abide and continue with you all for your furtherance and joy of faith; That your rejoicing may be more abundant in Jesus Christ for me by my coming to you again.

Verse 21 stands at the apex of Paul's most memorable quotes. Paul recognized that Jesus Christ was everything to him, and it did not matter whether he lived or died—he was the beneficiary of God's amazing love. He had anchored his life to Jesus Christ from the time of his conversion on the road to Damascus to that present moment (see Acts 9:1-9). He had never desired to do anything but preach the Gospel and pay the debt that he believed he owed to the Lord for his salvation (see Romans 1:14-15; 1 Corinthians 9:17-18; 2 Corinthians 4:5; 10:16; Galatians 1:15-16). His life was literally hidden in Christ and he had been buried with Him in death and raised to new life in the resurrection of Jesus Christ (see Romans 6:8; Galatians 2:20).

Frank Thielman, in his commentary on the book of Philippians, notes that Paul's words would sound strange and almost bizarre to the twenty-first-century mind.[1] Paul declared that he was caught between two worlds—and that the decision to stay where he was and preach or to be executed and be in the presence of the Lord Jesus Christ was not an easy one to make. Thielman notes that "We live in a culture that thinks of physical death with such dread that society's highest goal is the postponement of death as long as possible."[2] Paul did not view death with a sense of hopeless dread; rather, it was the doorway into the presence of Christ. What option would Paul choose? He was torn; he knew that the church in Philippi needed his presence and his fatherly leadership. Staying in the body would be a far better thing for him to do, particularly for the church. He was convinced that his time had not yet come. How he came to this realization is not stated. Maybe he had already had a preliminary hearing before a Roman court and knew that he did not face the prospect of death. Or maybe someone in the court of Caesar gave him the assurance that he would not be executed at that moment. He came to the realization that his staying alive would be better for the church. Paul was their spiritual father, and his continuing presence would ensure that they continued to make progress and grow. It is apparent that Paul thought that one day he would return to Philippi, bringing joy to both himself and the church of Philippi, whom he loved and who loved him.

III. CONCLUDING REFLECTION

In today's lesson, Paul gave us a clear example of what it means to be a man who is driven by his love for God and the people of God. He cared very little for his own welfare and security. His greatest concern was first that the Gospel be preached and heard. Additionally, we see the heart of a man who deeply yearned to see the people he had led to Christ grow and continue in the faith. What is astounding is that although it had been more than ten years since he personally visited Philippi, his love for that church abounded even more. He wanted to visit them and have his own and their joy multiplied. At the heart of the lesson is the simple truth that ministry must always be motivated by the love of God and the desire to serve Him, which fuels the desire to preach the Gospel everywhere.

PRAYER

God of grace and mercy, grant that Your servants may more readily give themselves to the purpose for which You have saved us. Grant us the courage to venture into new places and meet new challenges so that Your name may be exalted. In Jesus' name we pray. Amen.

WORD POWER

Gain (Greek: *kerdos* [ker-dos])—this word was originally used in classical Greek as a commercial term. In some instances, it was used to denote profit, advantage, or, as it is translated in this lesson, "gain." Here in the text, Paul did not use the word as a commercial term, but he attached a greater meaning to the word, particularly as it related to the way he viewed eternal life. For the apostle, the rigors of ministry and the stress of preaching were all blessings, but the far greater blessing would come when he departed to be with the Lord Jesus Christ. This was the ultimate gain and the prize worth more than any earthly possession.

HOME DAILY BIBLE READINGS
(December 31, 2012–January 6, 2013)

Proclaiming Christ

> MONDAY, December 31: "Praising God in Word and Life" (Psalm 119:169-176)
> TUESDAY, January 1: "Giving Glory to God" (Matthew 5:13-16)
> WEDNESDAY, January 2: "Making the Word Fully Known" (Colossians 1:21-29)
> THURSDAY, January 3: "Sharing in the Gospel" (Philippians 1:1-7)
> FRIDAY, January 4: "Speaking the Word with Boldness" (Philippians 1:8-14)
> SATURDAY, January 5: "Toiling to Proclaim the Gospel" (1 Thessalonians 2:1-11)
> SUNDAY, January 6: "Proclaiming Christ in Every Way" (Philippians 1:15-26)

End Notes

---

[1]Frank Thielman, *The NIV Application Commentary: Philippians* (Grand Rapids: Zondervan Publishing, 1995), p. 83.
[2]Ibid.

LESSON 7   January 13, 2013

JESUS' HUMILITY AND EXALTATION

FAITH PATHWAY/FAITH JOURNEY TOPIC: **Attitude Counts**

DEVOTIONAL READING: **James 3:13-18**
PRINT PASSAGE: **Philippians 2:5-11**

BACKGROUND SCRIPTURE: **Philippians 2:1-13**
KEY VERSE: **Philippians 2:5**

Philippians 2:5-11—KJV

5 Let this mind be in you, which was also in Christ Jesus:

6 Who, being in the form of God, thought it not robbery to be equal with God:

7 But made himself of no reputation, and took upon him the form of a servant, and was made in the likeness of men:

8 And being found in fashion as a man, he humbled himself, and became obedient unto death, even the death of the cross.

9 Wherefore God also hath highly exalted him, and given him a name which is above every name:

10 That at the name of Jesus every knee should bow, of things in heaven, and things in earth, and things under the earth;

11 And that every tongue should confess that Jesus Christ is Lord, to the glory of God the Father.

Philippians 2:5-11—NIV

5 Your attitude should be the same as that of Christ Jesus:

6 Who, being in very nature God, did not consider equality with God something to be grasped,

7 but made himself nothing, taking the very nature of a servant, being made in human likeness.

8 And being found in appearance as a man, he humbled himself and became obedient to death—even death on a cross!

9 Therefore God exalted him to the highest place and gave him the name that is above every name,

10 that at the name of Jesus every knee should bow, in heaven and on earth and under the earth,

11 and every tongue confess that Jesus Christ is Lord, to the glory of God the Father.

BIBLE FACT

JESUS' EXALTATION

Scholars tell us that Paul emphatically placed our Savior's exaltation right after the words, "He humbled himself, and became obedient unto death, even the death of the cross" (Philippians 2:8). This self-humbling on the part of Jesus was followed by the Father's exaltation involving His resurrection, ascension, and enthronement. It is also accepted that the exaltation of Jesus is not yet complete. The full realization of His exaltation is when every creature and all creation will come and bow before Him and confess that Jesus Christ is Lord—to the glory of the Father.

UNIFYING LESSON PRINCIPLE

Sometimes people who are driven by the need to succeed exploit others and abuse power as they fight their way to the top. What honor is there in success won at the expense of others? God exalted Jesus because of Jesus' selflessness, obedience, servant-hood, and humility; Jesus talked about the importance of finding the best surroundings in which to grow in faith and serve others.

TOPICAL OUTLINE OF THE LESSON

I. Introduction
A. The True Value of Serving
B. Biblical Background

II. Exposition and Application of the Scripture
A. The Mind of Christ (Philippians 2:5)
B. The Humiliation of Christ (Philippians 2:6-8)
C. The Exaltation of Christ (Philippians 2:9-11)

III. Concluding Reflection

LESSON OBJECTIVES

Upon the completion of the lesson, the students will be able to do the following:

1. Analyze Paul's description of God's exaltation of Jesus, based on sacrifice and selflessness rather than power;
2. Value selfless behavior over power; and,
3. Adopt Christ-like humility in their personal lifestyles.

POINTS TO BE EMPHASIZED

ADULT/YOUTH
Adult Topic: **Attitude Counts**
Youth Topic: **Similar Minds**
Adult/Youth Key Verse: **Philippians 2:5**
Print Passage: **Philippians 2:5-11**

—This passage suggests that selflessness and sacrifice open the door to God's exaltation.
—Paul urged the Philippians to adopt the mindset of Christ.
—Christ did not grasp for power or crave equality with God.
—Christ "emptied" (*kenosis*) Himself.
—Christ humbled Himself; He became a man and an obedient servant (even unto death) in order to fulfill God's purpose for His life.
—God exalted Christ so that all others could worship Him.

CHILDREN
Children Topic: **Soil that Bears Good Crops**
Key Verse: **Matthew 13:8**
Print Passage: **Matthew 13:1-9**

—Crowds gathered to hear Jesus teach in parables or stories, which helped them understand spiritual truths through the use of everyday objects and relationships.
—In Jesus' day, farmers sowed seeds by hand because there was no technology available to plant seeds.
—The crowd listened to Jesus' parable with understanding, because they knew that as farmers sowed their seeds by hand, only the seeds that fell on good soil produced abundantly.
—The different kinds of soil represent the listeners and the various ways they respond to the Gospel.
—The sower represents the teacher or preacher who spreads the Gospel, and the seeds represent the Gospel.

I. INTRODUCTION

A. The True Value of Serving

Hermann Hesse (1877–1962) was a German-Swiss poet and novelist who won a Nobel Prize for literature. One of his most famous works was a short novel entitled, *Journey to the East*. In the novel, he tells the story of a writer named H. H. who joined an elite organization known as "The League." The organization was comprised of men who were very prominent writers, thinkers, philosophers, and scientists. One day, a group of them set off on a journey to the east to find the true purpose of life and wisdom. They were served by a man who was simply known as Leo, who attended to their every need and provided the group with a host of services. One day, Leo disappeared and the group was left alone (without him). They then set out to find him, but eventually gave up when their efforts failed. Not long after that, the men began to experience conflicts, disagreements, and confusion among them, causing their little community to fall apart. Consequently, the group was forced to return to their original starting point. Several years later, H. H. set out to find out what had really happened to Leo, and he made the startling discovery that Leo was in fact the true president of the League. The man whom they all considered to be the servant was in fact the leader.

Humility and service are among the treasured traits of a Christian leader. This short story teaches that often the most valued person in the group is the one who serves others. One of the traits of the current culture is the drive of some people to succeed at all costs, even if it means destroying or bringing down others. What honor is there in success if our success is attained at the expense of others? In the lesson today, we see where God exalted Jesus to the highest honor, because of His selfless love and obedience to God.

B. Biblical Background

Paul knew from firsthand experience that nothing was more destructive to the fellowship of the church and ministry of preaching the Gospel than division and discord within the fellowship. Beginning at Philippians 1:27, he exhorted the church to conduct themselves in a manner that was worthy of the name of Jesus Christ. One of the ways that they could live worthy of the Lord was through the maintenance and practice of unity in the body. In the previous lesson, Paul pointed out that there were those who preached out of hearts of selfish ambition. He did not want the Philippians to adopt the partisanship of the preachers.

At the heart of chapter 2 is the question of how a congregation can maintain the spirit of unity and cooperation. Paul shared with them that they must be like-minded, have the same joy, and be one in spirit and purpose. They must do nothing from the standpoint of self-interest, but always look toward the interests of others and the larger body of Christ.

What is the key? It is simply being who we say we are in Jesus Christ. Not only are believers exhorted to put on the Lord Jesus, but more importantly, Paul encouraged the church to have the same attitude that Jesus had, which was one of obedience, servanthood, and humility.

Philippians 2:5-11 has been debated by scholars for nearly one hundred years. Historically, this passage has come to be known as the "Christological Hymn"—because of the belief that it may have circulated among Christians as a confessional statement of faith in the nature and purpose of Jesus Christ. Verse 5 is the introduction to what New Testament scholars regard as one of the loftiest statements about Jesus Christ in the Scriptures. Verses 6-11 contain the words of the Christological Hymn, which depicts the dual nature of Jesus Christ, who was both God and Man at the same time (see John 1:14; 2 Corinthians 8:9). Paul reminded the Philippians that Jesus Christ came into the world as a humble servant, who was exalted by the Father because of His faithfulness and humility. As a result of our study of this passage, we will gain an appreciation for one of the truly great passages in the New Testament.

II. EXPOSITION AND APPLICATION OF THE SCRIPTURE

A. The Mind of Christ
(Philippians 2:5)

Let this mind be in you, which was also in Christ Jesus.

What did Paul mean when he admonished us to have the same attitude as Christ Jesus? The word *attitude* is translated from the Greek word *phroneo*, which can be translated as "mind, attitude, understanding, or thought." First, Paul was not addressing individuals, but the entire congregation of believers in Philippi. All of the members were to seek to cultivate the same mind that characterized the life of Jesus Christ. The church can only become effective in ministry to the extent that each believer is growing in grace and increasing in the knowledge of God (see Colossians 1:9-11). Paul looked back to what he had previously stated in verse 2, where he appealed for them to be "like-minded," or focused on the same goals and purpose.

Second, Paul was not holding himself up as the model of what their lives were to be like; rather, they were to pattern themselves after Jesus Christ. Jesus walked among His generation as a servant, who sought to always do the things that pleased the Father in heaven (see John 4:32; 6:33, 38; compare Isaiah 61:1-3). Third, we may ask ourselves the question, "How do we develop the same attitude that Jesus Christ had?" In Matthew 11:29, Jesus said that we are to take His yoke upon ourselves and learn of Him. He then is the model and pattern for believers' lives of service and humility (see Luke 22:27; John 13:14-15; Acts 20:35; Romans 15:3, 5).

The word *attitude* refers to one's disposition about a place, person, or thing. In many congregations, believers have the attitude that ministry is not important or that relationships among believers should not be a priority. Yet, when we adopt an attitude that reeks of pessimism and despair, we say to the world that our God is not able. When believers are at war with themselves and among themselves, they negate the unifying presence of the Holy Spirit. The Scriptures remind us that when we take on the attitude of Jesus Christ, confusion and disagreement are neither present nor prevalent within the body.

B. The Humiliation of Christ (Philippians 2:6-8)

Who, being in the form of God, thought it not robbery to be equal with God: But made himself of no reputation, and took upon him the form of a servant, and was made in the likeness of men: And being found in fashion as a man, he humbled himself, and became obedient unto death, even the death of the cross.

In verses 6-8, Paul stated what it means to have the attitude of Jesus Christ. In these verses, Paul laid out the details of the pre-existence of Jesus Christ and declared that He was God and always has been God. He further described what has come to be the doctrine of the incarnation of Jesus Christ—that is, the self-humiliation of Jesus to go from deity to becoming human, with all of the limitations. Yet, there are a few questions that we must come to some conclusions about in order to understand the underlying truths of the passage. What did Paul mean when he stated that Jesus was the very "nature" (NIV) of God? The word translated as "nature" comes from the Greek word *morphed,* which has also been translated as "form" in the KJV and NASB. The word literally refers to one's external appearance. However, that is not what Paul meant by his use of the word; in this instance, "nature" is used to depict the spiritual and divine character of Jesus Christ. In His essence and true self, Jesus was God from the very beginning and did

not cease to be God when He came to earth in the form of a baby, born in Bethlehem. The phrase "did not consider equality with God something to be grasped" (verse 6, NIV) has in it the idea that although He was God, Jesus Christ never tried to use His deity as something to use to His advantage in accomplishing the will of the Father. He had to be totally and absolutely submitted to the Father's purpose if human redemption was to be achieved.

In verses 7-8, Paul pointed out how Jesus demonstrated that He was not self-seeking. He became less than deity—by becoming "nothing" (NIV). The Greek word for "nothing" is *keno,* and literally means that Jesus emptied Himself of. The KJV says that He "made himself of no reputation." The question then is, "What did Jesus empty Himself of?" It is clear that Jesus emptied Himself of the form of God and took on the form of a human being. Here, the reference is to physical form and presence, because God is a Spirit and Jesus was not on the earth as a Spirit (see Colossians 1:22; 2:9; compare with John 1:14; 2 Corinthians 8:9). Does this mean that Jesus became so completely man that He was no longer completely God? The answer is no! He was always completely God and completely man at the same time. He was both God and man—human, yet fully divine. He had all of the character traits of God, yet He faced all of the limitations of being human (see Mark 4:38; Luke 19:41; John 4:7-8; 11:35). Jesus lived on the earth as a human, yet He neither committed sin nor gave in to the temptations of life (see Matthew 4:1-10; Hebrews 4:15).

Notice how Paul made it clear what the attitude of Jesus was: *He who was God came to be a servant.* Two words are used to describe what is meant by Jesus' having a servant's attitude when He emptied Himself: *humble* and *obedient*. He reduced Himself to nothing, which is one of the reasons why He was a stumbling block to the Jews and to Greeks; the idea of God becoming a human being and then allowing Himself to be killed at the hands of His creation was utter foolishness (see 1 Corinthians 1:22-23). Paul indirectly pointed out that in becoming a servant and willingly giving His life as a ransom, Jesus fulfilled the words of prophecy. In the Old Testament, one of the images of the Messiah was that of a servant who would appear at the appointed time in humility (see Isaiah 42:1; 49:3, 6; 52:13; 53:2-4,11; Ezekiel 34:23; Zechariah 9:9).

One of the challenges that Christians often face is trying to explain and defend that which can only be appropriated by faith. How does one explain the Incarnation, informing the unspiritual and unwise of how God became a living human being? It is not our assignment to explain what is within the sole sovereign will and plan of God. In the passage, what we see is the example of the Christ that is to be followed and imitated. The question is not how much we can explain, but rather whether we have become obedient to the Word of God by serving the least of the earth, and have walked in humility before the Lord (see Micah 6:8).

C. The Exaltation of Christ (Philippians 2:9-11)

Wherefore God also hath highly exalted him, and given him a name which is above every name: That at the name of Jesus every knee should bow, of things in heaven, and things in earth, and things under the earth; And that every tongue should confess that Jesus Christ is Lord, to the glory of God the Father.

Jesus Christ did for the human race what it could not do for itself. He became sin for us so that we might become the righteousness of God in Him. The self-sacrifice and self-abasing of Jesus Christ marked His life of obedience and sacrifice. Paul told the Philippians that because of what Jesus had done, God bestowed two honors upon Him. First, Jesus Christ has been given the highest possible place of honor. Paul used hyperbole in the words *exalted* and *highest*. This does not mean that Jesus, in His pre-existent state, was less than God the Father. Rather, it has reference to His place of honor and authority with regards to the church and creation (see Colossians 1:14-18). Second, God gave Him a name that is to be honored and one that is above every name given on the earth. Paul did not describe in any detail what either of these two honors was. It appears to be in full recognition by the Father that the Son has done what was planned since the fall of Adam and Eve in the Garden of Eden.

Verse 10 points to the results of the exaltation of Jesus. First, every knee should bow in heaven and on earth. Second, every tongue should confess that Jesus Christ is Lord to the glory of God the Father. Again, Paul's use of this language does not mean that Jesus was never viewed as God nor regarded as less than the Father. It is in full recognition that one day when the ages have come to an end, everyone will one day stand before the judgment throne of Jesus Christ to give an account of his or her deeds and to acknowledge His lordship over the universe (see Matthew 25:31-46; 2 Corinthians 5:10; Revelation 5:6-14).

The passage clearly points out that with God the way up is down. We live among a people who all want to be recognized for their service and to receive some words of commendation. Yet, Jesus showed us that when we serve the interests of the Father, He will reward and recognize our service, humility, and obedience.

III. CONCLUDING REFLECTION

How does a congregation capture the model of unity and cooperation that Paul here urged upon the Philippians? In the twenty-first-century church, the spirit of competition is alive and well. Congregations compete among themselves for the top prize: members. The members compete among themselves for the top prizes: high positions and power. In many congregations, it is almost impossible to enlist persons to serve in positions that require manual labor or in areas that may not be considered prominent. Yet, in the eyes of God, the one who seeks to serve others is considered the greatest in the kingdom of God. The people who really make ministries succeed and run efficiently are often the ones who go unnoticed and unheralded. Which are you—one who needs to be seen or one who seeks to allow his or her service to speak for him or her?

PRAYER

Lord, grant that Your servants may walk in humility and obedience to You. Keep our hearts and minds from the sin of pride, and may we yield to those who are the least of the earth. May we walk as one, just as You and the Son are One. In Jesus' name we pray. Amen.

WORD POWER

Servant (Greek: *doulos* [doo los])—this term is more properly understood as meaning a slave or bond servant, and is the exact same word used in Ephesians 6:5—in which the NIV, NLT, NRSV, and NASB versions all translate the word *doulos* as "slaves." This adds a different dimension to the understanding of Jesus as not just a servant of the Father, but as one who submitted Himself and became like a slave, whose primary interest was to serve the interests of His Father. This concept of "slave" is used metaphorically of someone who gives himself or herself up to another's will, or those whose service is used by Christ in extending and advancing His cause among the people of the world.

HOME DAILY BIBLE READINGS
(January 7-13, 2013)

Jesus' Humility and Exaltation

MONDAY, January 7: "Sower, Seeds, and Soils" (Matthew 13:1-9)

TUESDAY, January 8: "Hear and Understand the Word" (Matthew 13:18-23)

WEDNESDAY, January 9: "Avoid Envy and Selfish Ambition" (James 3:13-18)

THURSDAY, January 10: "Overcome Evil with Good" (Romans 12:14-21)

FRIDAY, January 11: "Become a Servant and a Slave" (Mark 10:35-45)

SATURDAY, January 12: "Look to the Interests of Others" (Philippians 2:1-4)

SUNDAY, January 13: "Seek the Mind of Christ" (Philippians 2:5-11)

LESSON 8   January 20, 2013

GAINING IN JESUS CHRIST

FAITH PATHWAY/FAITH JOURNEY TOPIC: **Gain and Loss**

DEVOTIONAL READING: **Matthew 13:44-46**
PRINT PASSAGE: **Philippians 3:7-11**

BACKGROUND SCRIPTURE: **Philippians 3:1-11**
KEY VERSE: **Philippians 3:7**

Philippians 3:7-11—KJV

7 But what things were gain to me, those I counted loss for Christ.

8 Yea doubtless, and I count all things but loss for the excellency of the knowledge of Christ Jesus my Lord: for whom I have suffered the loss of all things, and do count them but dung, that I may win Christ,

9 And be found in him, not having mine own righteousness, which is of the law, but that which is through the faith of Christ, the righteousness which is of God by faith:

10 That I may know him, and the power of his resurrection, and the fellowship of his sufferings, being made conformable unto his death;

11 If by any means I might attain unto the resurrection of the dead.

Philippians 3:7-11—NIV

7 But whatever was to my profit I now consider loss for the sake of Christ.

8 What is more, I consider everything a loss compared to the surpassing greatness of knowing Christ Jesus my Lord, for whose sake I have lost all things. I consider them rubbish, that I may gain Christ

9 and be found in him, not having a righteousness of my own that comes from the law, but that which is through faith in Christ—the righteousness that comes from God and is by faith.

10 I want to know Christ and the power of his resurrection and the fellowship of sharing in his sufferings, becoming like him in his death,

11 and so, somehow, to attain to the resurrection from the dead.

BIBLE FACT

THE POWER OF JESUS' RESURRECTION

Christian Apologetics emphatically tell us that Christianity cannot exist without the Resurrection. In fact, the main difference between Christianity and other religions is the reality of the Resurrection. When we look at all of the other religions of the world, they have founders who were born, lived, and died; however, Christianity is the only "religion" that worships a living Founder, in the person of Jesus who was not only born, who not only lived and died, but He rose again from the death. The apostle Paul tells us that there is no faith and hope without resurrection. A person cannot be a Christian without believing and without experiencing the Resurrection.

ARTICLE SOURCE: HTTP://EzineArticles.com/527222

UNIFYING LESSON PRINCIPLE

The self-worth of many people resides in the things that they have accomplished in life. But what is the true value of our lives when we are stripped of our achievements? Paul believed that none of the achievements of this life are worth anything—when compared to the surpassing value of knowing Christ Jesus; Jesus stressed, in the parable of the lost sheep, that value resides in everyone, even the littlest and last.

TOPICAL OUTLINE OF THE LESSON

I. Introduction
A. What Is Really Important?
B. Biblical Background

II. Exposition and Application of the Scripture
A. Paul's Evaluation of His Former Life (Philippians 3:7-8)
B. Paul's New Understanding Regarding Righteousness (Philippians 3:9)
C. Paul's Determination to Know Christ (Philippians 3:10-11)

III. Concluding Reflection

LESSON OBJECTIVES

Upon the completion of the lesson, the students will be able to do the following:

1. Discover Paul's attitude about the value of knowing Christ Jesus;
2. Compare feelings of achievement with living life in Christ; and,
3. Establish a lifelong goal of measuring their achievements against the value of knowing Jesus Christ.

POINTS TO BE EMPHASIZED

ADULT/YOUTH
Adult Topic: **Gain and Loss**
Youth Topic: **Win or Lose?**
Adult/Youth Key Verse: **Philippians 3:7**
Print Passage: **Philippians 3:7-11**

—Paul wrestled with the concept of becoming like Christ in death while remaining alive.
—Paul realized that the things he thought mattered paled in comparison to what he found in Christ.
—Paul acknowledged that endeavoring in his own righteousness was useless and self-serving.
—Paul desired to be found in Christ and desired to know the power of Christ's resurrection.
—Paul gave up everything in order to experience the resurrection of Christ.

CHILDREN
Children Topic: **Finding the Lost One**
Key Verse: **Matthew 18:14**
Print Passage: **Matthew 18:10-14**

—Jesus has a great love for the lost, the little, and the least.
—God does not desire for anyone to perish.
—Loving shepherds (like pastors) treat their sheep with tender loving care.
—Jesus expects His disciples to seek and find the lost ones who have wandered away from the Lord.

I. INTRODUCTION

A. What Is Really Important?

Materialism and unhealthy ambition are two of the most significant challenges with which many twenty-first-century Christians struggle. Our fascination with status, standing, and recognition is a serious threat to an unbridled commitment to the kingdom of God. The struggle for the hearts and minds of believers is to resist Satan's attempt to usurp what God wants to do in our lives by planting within our spirits desires and needs for the things of the world. The fallacy that wealth and prosperity are all products of God's gracious blessings can distort our views of the will and plan of God.

What is the true value of our lives when we are stripped of our achievements? Paul believed that none of the achievements of this life are worth anything when compared to the surpassing value of knowing Christ Jesus. The lesson today will lead us into a time of introspection and a reassessment of our own values and priorities.

B. Biblical Background

In Philippians 3:1-3, Paul wrote about dealing with the confusion that had cropped up in the congregation over the issue of keeping Jewish practices, such as circumcision. A group of Jewish believers or evangelists had come to the church in Philippi and taught that only those persons who practiced the Jewish religious customs could really be saved. The problem of keeping the Jewish law posed a major threat for the early church—and circumcision was at the heart of the issue (see Acts 15:1ff). The Judaizers (as they were called) set themselves up as the chief teachers of the "right way." In his letter to the Philippians, Paul said (in essence), "Listen, if these people think that they are such hot shots, they are really nothing. I am really head and shoulders above them, because I have really got something to brag about." In verse 5, Paul detailed all of his credentials and his advantages. He read his resumé to them just to remind the Philippians that he had achieved the highest levels of piety according to Jewish law and tradition. However, in Jesus Christ, Paul found the true meaning of what it meant to live and have value.

II. EXPOSITION AND APPLICATION OF THE SCRIPTURE

A. Paul's Evaluation of His Former Life (Philippians 3:7-8)

But what things were gain to me, those I counted loss for Christ. Yea doubtless, and I count all things but loss for the excellency of the knowledge of Christ Jesus my Lord: for whom I have suffered the loss of all things, and do count them but dung, that I may win Christ.

Paul began by contrasting his previous life with his current life. The language of profit and loss comes from the financial world, and is part of the many ways that Paul used the everyday things of life to make deep spiritual truths come alive. There was absolutely no comparison to his current position as an apostle of Christ with everything he had achieved prior to meeting Jesus Christ on the Damascus Road. One would never embark upon this work of ministry without being willing to pay the price for what it took to honor that commitment to Jesus Christ. In Paul's case, it was the total renunciation and removal from everything that he had previously held dear. The Greek word for "profit" is *kerdos,* and it literally refers to those things that make a profit for the one who holds them. In his prior life, Paul considered his achievements as worthy advantages. However, His status as a Pharisee and being regarded as a highly learned student of the Scriptures were all to be discarded as rubbish. The word *loss* is written in the Greek imperfect tense and it describes an action that took place in the past which continues to have a bearing on the present. Paul had not changed his mind about the decision he made the day that Jesus Christ apprehended him. His life and ministry had not been easy, yet he saw these trials as momentary light afflictions (see 2 Corinthians 4:7-18; 11:22-33). In Christ, he had gained something far greater, which outweighed and exceeded everything that he had lost (see Ephesians 3:19-20; compare 1 Corinthians 2:9; Colossians 1:27; Philippians 4:9).

When Paul thought about the things he had given up and had gained, two things stood out in his mind as being of great value: the first was his *knowing* Jesus Christ, and the second was his *gaining* Christ. Everything revolved around knowing Jesus Christ and being filled with the knowledge of His will.

The word *knowing* is translated from the Greek word *gnosis,* and refers to a form of knowledge that is deep and intimate. It is experiential and personal. Jesus was not just the miracle worker from Galilee; He was Paul's Lord, a term that he used so often that it appears hundreds of times in his letters. Jesus Christ was his Master and it was to Him that he owed complete allegiance.

B. Paul's New Understanding Regarding Righteousness
(Philippians 3:9)

And be found in him, not having mine own righteousness, which is of the law, but that which is through the faith of Christ, the righteousness which is of God by faith.

Verse 9 is a continuation of the thought of verse 8, which details the things that Paul lost and those he gained. Here, Paul made a distinction between righteousness that is self-produced and that which is by grace. *Righteousness* (Greek: *dikasiosune*) is a very important biblical and theological term that has several meanings; however, only two meanings are the most often used in the Bible. On the one hand, it has to do with the relationship one has with others, particularly the poor, the weak, and widows. We are righteous in the sight of God to the extent that we are in right standing with each other. This is largely an Old Testament concept which is a part of the theme of justice and righteousness (see Amos 5:23-26; compare Isaiah 11:4; Micah 6:5-8). The second important meaning of *righteousness* concerns one's standing before God. This means that one stands in a right relationship with God, because of the finished work of Jesus Christ at Calvary (see Ephesians 2:8-10).

The goal of Paul's life was to be found righteous before God at the last judgment (see 2 Corinthians 5:10; compare Matthew

25:31-46; 2 Timothy 4:6-8). There were three things that Paul listed that defined what it meant to be found in Jesus Christ. The first was expressed as a negative statement—the purpose of which was to make a positive statement. Paul wanted a righteousness that was not the product of his own creation.

The second thing that he mentioned is expressed in a statement of contrast. Rather than have a righteousness that comes from the law, he wanted a righteousness that came from God. This is righteousness that comes as the result of having faith in the Lord Jesus Christ.

Third, the righteousness that Paul spoke of came about by faith in the Lord Jesus Christ. Righteousness is always to be viewed as a gift of grace. The bottom line for Paul was that humans could not make themselves righteous in God's eyes—no matter how much they tried.

Many people believe that if they work hard enough in the church, then God will consider them to be righteous and deeply spiritual. Church work can be extremely frustrating and disappointing, because at the end of the day there is nothing in church that leads to strengthening the inner man or woman. What one discovers is that church work, while fine in its place, is no substitute for a personal relationship with the Lord Jesus Christ. Yet, at the same time, we must never dismiss the doing of works of righteousness as unnecessary. It is our faith that leads us to do the work of missions and ministry (see James 1:22; 2:14-26).

C. Paul's Determination to Know Christ (Philippians 3:10-11)

That I may know him, and the power of his resurrection, and the fellowship of his sufferings, being made conformable unto his death; If by any means I might attain unto the resurrection of the dead.

Paul reached the finality of what it meant for him to have been apprehended by Jesus Christ on the Damascus Road. His ultimate ambition was to know Christ—but then he added something specific. Paul wanted a knowledge that transcended knowing the doctrine of Christ and having a head full of facts and a notebook of bullet points. It is the knowledge that comes from having surrendered one's life totally to Jesus and experiencing the newness of life. In Paul's mind, each believer experiences the power of the Resurrection when he or she dies to sin and self (see Romans 6:4-11). Paul expressed his desire to know the same power that raised Jesus Christ from the dead, both literally and spiritually. Here, Paul spoke of the power of the Resurrection as the power to transform the lives of men and women into something radically different from what they were previously. This is the power that revived the hopes of the women who discovered the empty tomb.

What did Paul mean by the "fellowship of his suffering"? Clearly, Paul had in view the fact that every believer who seeks union with Christ must also be prepared to suffer persecution for the cause of the Gospel. In the first century and in some countries today, suffering persecution because of the Gospel is very real. One cannot be Christian and not expect to experience trials and tests because of his or her faith in the Lord Jesus Christ (see Matthew 20:23; Romans 6:3, 17; 8:18; 2 Corinthians 4:16-18; Galatians 2:20; Colossians 1:24).

III. CONCLUDING REFLECTION

When one is born-again, it is nothing less

than transformation from a life of sin to a life of holiness. God transforms our messed up and ragged lives into newly resurrected ones. The Holy Spirit brings changes to us. He sweetens us by taking the bitterness out of our lives. He rebuilds us into spiritual men and women, who know the power of Jesus' resurrection. He changes our habits and desires, and our principles and practices. The Holy Spirit changes our dispositions and attitudes. He changes our standards and lifestyles.

There are tens of millions of people around the world who know what it means to be lost in sin, but who then experience the joy of being born again. Just think for a moment where you used to be and what your life was like before Christ. We did not change ourselves; it was nothing less than the power of the Resurrection to transform our lives.

PRAYER

Heavenly Father, may we learn to look to You for the fulfillment of our deepest needs and desires. Grant that we may know Your Son and the power of His resurrection. In Jesus' name we pray. Amen.

WORD POWER

Righteousness (Greek: dikaiosune *[dik-as-yos-oo-nay]*)—one of the richest words in the Scriptures. In a broad sense, the word describes one who is in a state of rightness or right standing with God. It connotes that one seeks to live a life of integrity and moral uprightness. It is also used to define the doctrine that speaks of one's having come to a state of peace between him- or herself and God. In some instances, it is used to depict the very nature and character of God—as one who is righteous. In the more narrow use, which is the meaning in the Old Testament, *righteousness* is often seen as the practice of justice and equity (see Psalm 71:15-16; Isaiah 45:24-25; 53:11; Jeremiah 23:6; Daniel 9:24; John 16:8-11; Romans 1:16-17; 3:21-22; 4:5-6, 13; 5:21; 9:30; 10:6,10; 1 Corinthians 1:30; Galatians 2:16; compare also Amos 5:23-25).

HOME DAILY BIBLE READINGS
(January 14-20, 2013)

Gaining in Jesus Christ

MONDAY, January 14: "The Value of Each One" (Matthew 18:10-14)

TUESDAY, January 15: "You Are of More Value" (Matthew 10:26-30)

WEDNESDAY, January 16: "The Value of the Spiritual" (Romans 2:17-29)

THURSDAY, January 17: "The Value of the Kingdom" (Matthew 13:44-53)

FRIDAY, January 18: "The True Value in Following Jesus" (Luke 9:23-27)

SATURDAY, January 19: "No Value in Earthly Achievements" (Philippians 3:1-6)

SUNDAY, January 20: "The Surpassing Value of Knowing Christ" (Philippians 3:7-11)

STAND FIRM

FAITH PATHWAY/FAITH JOURNEY TOPIC: **Gaining the Prize**

DEVOTIONAL READING: **Matthew 25:14-29**
PRINT PASSAGE: **Philippians 3:12-16**

BACKGROUND SCRIPTURE: **Philippians 3:12–4:1**
KEY VERSE: **Philippians 3:16**

Philippians 3:12-16—KJV

12 Not as though I had already attained, either were already perfect: but I follow after, if that I may apprehend that for which also I am apprehended of Christ Jesus.

13 Brethren, I count not myself to have apprehended: but this one thing I do, forgetting those things which are behind, and reaching forth unto those things which are before,

14 I press toward the mark for the prize of the high calling of God in Christ Jesus.

15 Let us therefore, as many as be perfect, be thus minded: and if in any thing ye be otherwise minded, God shall reveal even this unto you.

16 Nevertheless, whereto we have already attained, let us walk by the same rule, let us mind the same thing.

Philippians 3:12-16—NIV

12 Not that I have already obtained all this, or have already been made perfect, but I press on to take hold of that for which Christ Jesus took hold of me.

13 Brothers, I do not consider myself yet to have taken hold of it. But one thing I do: Forgetting what is behind and straining toward what is ahead,

14 I press on toward the goal to win the prize for which God has called me heavenward in Christ Jesus.

15 All of us who are mature should take such a view of things. And if on some point you think differently, that too God will make clear to you.

16 Only let us live up to what we have already attained.

BIBLE FACT

CHRISTIAN PERFECTION

The doctrine is chiefly associated with the followers of John Wesley, founder of Methodism. Perfection can either define the journey to perfection or the state of perfection. Christian perfection is commonly referred to as "going on to perfection." Perfection according to this definition is the process of sanctification which is both an instantaneous and a progressive work of God's grace. Christian perfection, according to Wesley, is "purity of intention, dedicating all the life to God" and "the mind which was in Christ, enabling us to walk as Christ walked." It is "loving God with all our heart, and our neighbor as ourselves."

SOURCE: ENOTES.COM

UNIFYING LESSON PRINCIPLE

Sometimes it is difficult to sustain energy to achieve goals that have lasting value. What motivates us to press on toward a goal? Maintaining a strong relationship with Christ now prepares us for the relationship we will have with Christ in eternity; Jesus stressed that planning and being prepared would help people reach important goals.

TOPICAL OUTLINE OF THE LESSON

I. Introduction
A. Discovering a Higher Purpose
B. Biblical Background

II. Exposition and Application of the Scripture
A. Paul's Admission (Philippians 3:12)
B. Paul's Aspiration (Philippians 3:13-14)
C. Paul's Appeal (Philippians 3:15-16)

III. Concluding Reflection

LESSON OBJECTIVES

Upon the completion of the lesson, the students will be able to do the following:

1. Become familiar with what Paul said about living, so as to attain eternity with Jesus Christ;
2. Appreciate that the journey of Christian living is demanding and a quest for something eternal; and,
3. Pledge to stand firm so they do not jeopardize the gift of Jesus Christ which they have received.

POINTS TO BE EMPHASIZED

ADULT/YOUTH

Adult Topic: Gaining the Prize
Youth Topic: Press On!
Adult Key Verse: Philippians 3:16
Youth Key Verse: Philippians 3:14
Print Passage: Philippians 3:12-16

—Paul recognized that the distinction between spiritual maturity and immaturity is the reason why Christians think differently about spiritual issues.
—The Christian life presents a certain tension or paradox—in that our eternal lives in Christ are both attained and, yet, not attained while we are still in the flesh.
—Paul could stress the importance of forgetting the past, even while recalling his own persecution of the church (see Philippians 3:6).
—Paul could talk with personal experience of "straining" to "press on" toward attaining a goal, while realizing that Christ did everything necessary to make reaching that goal a reality for him.

CHILDREN

Children Topic: Be Prepared
Key Verse: Matthew 25:13
Print Passage: Matthew 25:1-13

—When Jesus returns, we need to be prepared to go with Him.
—Spiritual preparation can neither be bought nor borrowed.
—In Jewish culture, on the wedding day the bridegroom went to the bride's home for the ceremony.
—The parable teaches how we must live now in order to be prepared for Jesus' return.
—Christians are responsible for their own spiritual preparedness.
—Humans have no timetable for Jesus' return.

I. INTRODUCTION

A. Discovering a Higher Purpose

William Borden was heir to the Borden Dairy Estate. At age 16, he was already a millionaire and was looking at a brilliant future. In 1904, William's parents gave him a trip around the world as a high school graduation gift. He traveled through Europe, Asia, and the Middle East—and as he traveled, he began to develop a heart for the hurting people of the world. At the end of his trip, he decided that he wanted to become a missionary and in the back of his Bible he wrote the words, "No reserves." In the fall of 1905, he enrolled in Yale University and quickly became a major influence in the university community. During his freshman year at Yale, he started a Bible study group that quickly grew to more than 150 people. By the end of his four years, nearly one thousand of Yale's thirteen thousand students were attending a weekly Bible study group. Upon graduation, he enrolled in seminary at Princeton University in New Jersey to prepare for full-time ministry as a missionary. He wrote two more words in his Bible: "No retreats." At the end of his seminary training, he had decided to do missionary work in China, working with Muslims. He left the United States and sailed for Egypt to study Arabic. Within a month of his arrival in Egypt, he contracted spinal meningitis and died. Prior to his death, he had written two more words in his Bible. Just below the words "No reserves" and "No retreats" he wrote, "No regrets."

William Borden had every reason to pursue a business career and take over the family business, and no one would have faulted him for doing so. Yet, he chose to give his life in service to a larger purpose, whose rewards would follow him into eternity. He was motivated by a passion to see the Gospel penetrate regions where it had never been presented. What motivates us to press toward achieving our life ambitions? Maintaining a strong relationship with Christ now prepares us for the relationship we will have with Christ in eternity. In today's lesson, Paul reminded us that regardless of how long we have been on our earthly journeys, we will never reach total maturity. We are challenged to continue until that day we see Jesus Christ face-to-face.

B. Biblical Background

Today's lesson is the fourth in this series from the book of Philippians. The verses that form today's lesson are a continuation of Paul's teaching regarding what it means to be a follower of the Lord Jesus Christ. One of Paul's primary concerns was helping the Philippians understand what it meant to reach spiritual maturity. He shared from his own life and acknowledged that he had yet to reach it himself. One of the challenges that twenty-first-century believers may struggle with is complacency and a false sense of their own spiritual growth. Paul made it perfectly clear that he had not yet reached the heights of complete spiritual maturity. He recognized that there was a distinct difference between spiritual maturity and immaturity, and that this was the primary reason why Christians thought differently about spiritual issues. Paul recognized that there are paradoxes in the Christian life—where on the one hand, he had already attained salvation through faith, yet at the same time he was far from perfect. The key to growing in grace was to be found in having a short memory and not becoming consumed by what one had already done or achieved. He encouraged the believers to forget the past and press on toward the prize that comes with knowing Jesus Christ.

II. EXPOSITION AND APPLICATION OF THE SCRIPTURE

A. Paul's Admission
(Philippians 3:12)

Not as though I had already attained, either were already perfect: but I follow after, if that I may apprehend that for which also I am apprehended of Christ Jesus.

Paul made two very important statements about his personal walk with Jesus Christ in the first two clauses of verse 12. First, "Not... already obtained" is a backward look to the day that he was converted on the road to Damascus (see Acts 9:1-10). The question is, "What was he referring to in his use of the word *this*"? (NIV). On the one hand, he could have been referring to having obtained the resurrection of the dead, which he mentioned in verse 11. Or he could have been referring to reaching full spiritual maturity, which is the most likely interpretation. Although he had been saved by grace and justified by his faith in Jesus Christ, for Paul that was merely the beginning of his new life (see 2 Corinthians 5:17; Ephesians 2:8-10). Specifically, on that day he had only begun and had not fully attained the absolute pinnacle of spiritual growth that comes from God through faith in Jesus Christ.

The second statement that he made referred to his present condition, which was expressed in the words, "either were already perfect." The word *perfect* is translated from the Greek word *telioo*, which literally means "to bring to completeness." In this context, Paul was expressing a fact that he had not yet arrived at the point of completeness. After all of his years of teaching, preaching, and working out his own soul's salvation, Paul still acknowledged that he had a long way to go in his faith pilgrimage. He had not reached perfection or maturity, yet he had not stopped trying to reach the fullness of the measure of Christ.

The word *but* introduces Paul's true feelings about his faith in Jesus Christ. He saw himself like a runner who sees the prize off in the distance yet refuses to slow down or even stop to rest. Paul stated that Jesus Christ literally seized him and from that very moment he sought to measure up to the calling that was placed upon his life (see Ephesians 4:1). The one important principle in this verse is that there is never a moment in this life when the believer has reached the fullness of the measure of Christ.

B. Paul's Aspiration
(Philippians 3:13-14)

Brethren, I count not myself to have apprehended: but this one thing I do, forgetting those things which are behind, and reaching forth unto those things which are before, I press toward the mark for the prize of the high calling of God in Christ Jesus.

Paul addressed the Philippians as brothers. This was a word that he used to identify with them—not just as their apostolic father and leader, but as one who shared the journey of faith with them. Maybe there were people in the congregation who felt that they had reached full spiritual maturity; hence, they had need of nothing else. This was not the case with Paul; he told them that he had not yet grasped the full significance of the purpose for which Jesus Christ took hold of his life. "It" in verse 13b (NIV) refers to the assignment that Jesus Christ gave Paul when He took hold of him on the Damascus Road (see Galatians 1:11-24). Although he had been an apostle for many years, he still had not fully mastered the work.

What happens in the believer's life when he or she feels as though there is nothing else for which he or she can strive in the Christian life? What happens to the congregation when the leaders feel as though they have become the men or women God intended them to be? (See Luke 18:9-14.) Paul said that with all that he had done and achieved in his apostolic ministry, he had still not taken hold of that for which Christ had arrested him. Christ had taken hold of Paul for the purpose of being the apostle to the Gentiles (see Romans 11:13; compare Acts 9:15; 13:2; 22:21; Galatians 1:16; 2:2, 7; Ephesians 3:8).

Paul was speaking neither for anyone in the congregation nor for any other apostle. He spoke only for himself: "I do not consider... one thing I do..."; "I press on toward the goal" (NIV). Rather than dwell on his past achievements and failures, he said that he would look forward and not backward. The one thing that he did was to forget the past. The apostle stated, "Forgetting those things which are behind, and reaching forth unto those things which are before" (KJV). Paul did not mean that he was going to forget his past life. If he had meant that then he would have been contradicting himself, for he had just rehearsed his life in verses 4-7. What he meant was that he was not going to allow the past to direct, guide, and influence his present attitude and conduct.[1] The word *forgetting* (NIV) means that everything that has gone wrong in the past is over and tomorrow is an opportunity to start with a clean sheet of paper that has nothing written on it.

We must forget all that we have done and remember only what we still have yet to do. "Forgetting" is in a verb tense which implies a continuous action. This means that every time something from his past came up, Paul would remove it so that he could concentrate on the future. Every time he remembered a failure, he would forget it so that he could concentrate on the future. Every time a heartache wanted to intrude, he would forget it. Paul wanted to forget the past conflicts and problems, because his ministry and life had been full of problems and conflicts (see 2 Corinthians 11:23-33). In addition to his personal struggles, Paul wanted to forget his personal achievements in ministry as well. Earlier, Paul expressed that he had a lot that he could take pride in, but all of his personal attainments were nothing because he sought to know Jesus Christ and His resurrection (see Revelation 3:1ff—the church at Sardis).

In verse 14, we have the picture of a runner who sees the finish line and strains with every fiber and muscle to reach it. He had but one goal: to win the prize. Paul did not say what the prize was, but from the context, it appears that the prize was the calling for which he had been apprehended by Jesus Christ. What better way to finish life than to finish it having fulfilled the assignment given by the Lord Jesus Christ? Here, we see the power of concentration on the one thing that was most important to Paul: his work and ministry. There is power in one's concentrating on what he or she does well and not losing track of the purpose of his or her calling. Believers must make an effort to strive toward continuous growth in their individual lives and in the larger congregation as well. Resting on last year's accomplishments is nothing more than a prescription for future failure and inactivity.

C. Paul's Appeal
(Philippians 3:15-16)

Let us therefore, as many as be perfect, be thus minded: and if in any thing ye be otherwise minded, God shall reveal even this unto you. Nevertheless, whereto we have already attained, let us walk by the same rule, let us mind the same thing.

At the outset, Paul appeared to be contradicting everything he had said previously about not having reached full maturity. In verse 15a, he made a reference to "all of us who are mature…" (NIV). What was Paul referring to when he made that statement? More than likely he was referring to the man or woman who had reached a level of spiritual maturity which kept him or her from being duped by the false teachers and preachers who were often found traveling from church to church,

preaching for money. He could also have been referring to those who were mature enough to keep from being swayed by every new fad and doctrine that came along (see Ephesians 4:11-14). The best interpretation begins with keeping this statement within the context of the entire letter. In Philippians 2:5, he exhorted the people to have the mind of Christ, which would help heal any division that may have cropped up among them. Here, he reminded them that those who were mature could in fact think differently about some things. But those who were not babes in Christ should be open to the revelation of the Holy Spirit, who would reveal all things to them. He did not say how this would happen—only that spiritually mature believers could reach agreement. The point of it all is that wherever they are on the journey of faith, they must all live up to the measure of God's grace.

III. CONCLUDING REFLECTION

The Christian life is not a static enterprise. Growth in grace is a continuous process of striving to become what God in Christ calls us to be. The Christian faith is more than a good feeling and active involvement in the life of a local community of faith. While these are clearly very important, they are not the only things that are important. Christianity is about growth in righteousness and being formed into the very image of Jesus Christ. Christianity calls for a radical transformation in our thinking, conduct, and interaction with others (see Romans 12:1-2; Ephesians 4:22-24). "Christianity is not fundamentally about wholeness, but holiness."[2] Holiness is the acknowledgment that we have been set apart for the distinct purpose of achieving the will of God (see 1 Corinthians 6:9-20). Holiness is developed as we bring our lives into subjection to God's Word and will (see Psalm 119). Spiritual growth is not a clearly identifiable thing that we are trying to reach. Rather, it is, as I have stated above, a lifelong pursuit. It is our attempt and desire to be formed in the very image of Jesus Christ. It is our spiritual movement beyond the elementary stages of repentance, baptism, and salvation (see Hebrew 5:11–6:2).

PRAYER

God of grace and mercy, grant that Your servants may find agreement in the work that You have called us to do. May we never grow weary of the journey of faith, but always recognize that all of our help and strength come from You. In Jesus' name we pray. Amen.

WORD POWER

Forgetting (Greek: *Epilanthanomai* [ep-ee-lan-than-om-ahee])—the idea of neglecting or no longer caring about; to putting away from one's mind. The idea of forgetting the past meant that there was nothing in the past that would impose itself upon what Paul was currently doing. He had completely forgotten the life he lived as a Jewish Pharisee. He had become totally focused on his new life in Jesus Christ.

HOME DAILY BIBLE READINGS
(January 21-27, 2013)

Stand Firm

MONDAY, January 21: "Be Watchful" (Matthew 24:36-44)

TUESDAY, January 22: "Be Prepared" (Matthew 25:1-13)

WEDNESDAY, January 23: "Be Trustworthy" (Matthew 25:14-21)

THURSDAY, January 24: "Be Compassionate" (Matthew 25:31-40)

FRIDAY, January 25: "Be Holy" (1 Peter 1:13-21)

SATURDAY, January 26: "Stand Firm" (Philippians 3:17–4:1)

SUNDAY, January 27: "Hold Fast" (Philippians 3:12-16)

End Notes

[1]Howard F. V. S., *Philippians: A Study Guide Commentary* (Grand Rapids: Zondervan Publishing Co., 1975), p. 71.
[2]James C. Fenhagen, *Invitation to Holiness,* (San Francisco: Harper and Row, Publishers, 1985), p. 9.

THE SUPREMACY OF JESUS CHRIST

FAITH PATHWAY/FAITH JOURNEY TOPIC: **Awed by Greatness**

DEVOTIONAL READING: **Ephesians 1:17-23**
PRINT PASSAGE: **Colossians 1:15-20**

BACKGROUND SCRIPTURE: **Colossians 1:15-20**
KEY VERSE: **Colossians 1:19**

Colossians 1:15-20—KJV

15 Who is the image of the invisible God, the firstborn of every creature:

16 For by him were all things created, that are in heaven, and that are in earth, visible and invisible, whether they be thrones, or dominions, or principalities, or powers: all things were created by him, and for him:

17 And he is before all things, and by him all things consist.

18 And he is the head of the body, the church: who is the beginning, the firstborn from the dead; that in all things he might have the preeminence.

19 For it pleased the Father that in him should all fulness dwell;

20 And, having made peace through the blood of his cross, by him to reconcile all things unto himself; by him, I say, whether they be things in earth, or things in heaven.

Colossians 1:15-20—NIV

15 He is the image of the invisible God, the firstborn over all creation.

16 For by him all things were created: things in heaven and on earth, visible and invisible, whether thrones or powers or rulers or authorities; all things were created by him and for him.

17 He is before all things, and in him all things hold together.

18 And he is the head of the body, the church; he is the beginning and the firstborn from among the dead, so that in everything he might have the supremacy.

19 For God was pleased to have all his fullness dwell in him,

20 and through him to reconcile to himself all things, whether things on earth or things in heaven, by making peace through his blood, shed on the cross.

BIBLE FACT

THE SUPREMACY OF JESUS CHRIST

The Bible clearly teaches that Jesus Christ "is the image of the invisible God" (Colossians 1:15). Jesus is supreme because of His unique relationship with God the Father. He is the perfect resemblance and representation of God; in fact, He was God in the flesh. We understand that God is invisible and unknown except by self-revelation. However, in the person of Jesus Christ the unknowable God becomes known. The very nature and being of God have been perfectly revealed in Christ.

UNIFYING LESSON PRINCIPLE

Because of the immediate availability of images of greatness, from athletics, to space, to technology, our grasp of the amazing becomes desensitized. What does it take to inspire true awe that commands reverence? Paul's use of metaphor strongly conveys Christ's supremacy, which helps us realize who Christ is; when Jesus called the first disciples to follow Him, they responded immediately.

TOPICAL OUTLINE OF THE LESSON

I. **Introduction**
   A. The Uniqueness of Christ
   B. Biblical Background

II. **Exposition and Application of the Scripture**
   A. Christ's Relationship to the Father (Colossians 1:15)
   B. Christ's Relationship to the Universe (Colossians 1:16-17)
   C. Christ's Relationship to the Church (Colossians 1:18-19)
   D. Christ's Relationship to Divine Reconciliation (Colossians 1:20)

III. **Concluding Reflection**

LESSON OBJECTIVES

Upon the completion of the lesson, the students will be able to do the following:

1. Understand Paul's description of Jesus Christ's supremacy;
2. Express feelings of amazement at the supremacy of Jesus Christ; and,
3. Describe to others the awe-inspiring preeminence of Christ for bringing reconciliation.

POINTS TO BE EMPHASIZED

ADULT/YOUTH
Adult Topic: Awed by Greatness
Youth Topic: Eternal Ruler
Adult Key Verse: Colossians 1:19
Youth Key Verse: Colossians 1:18
Print Passage: Colossians 1:15-20

—All powers fall within the sphere of Christ's creative work.
—Christ is the visible representation and manifestation of who God is. Note similarities between Colossians 1:15-16, Hebrews 1, and the gospel of John.
—The sacrifice of Christ became a substitute for the sacrifice of animals on the Day of Atonement (verse 20).
—Christ is the definitive revelation of the invisible God.
—All things were created by Him and for Him.
—The "church" in this passage is not a physical structure; it refers to all people who profess Christ as Lord of their lives, making up the bride of Christ as described in Ephesians 5.
—Christ has reconciled all things to God through His sacrifice on the Cross.

CHILDREN
Children Topic: A Hero to Follow
Key Verse: Matthew 4:19-20
Print Passage: Matthew 4:18-22

—Early in Jesus' ministry, He called four men to be His disciples.
—A *disciple* is someone who trusts and learns from another person.
—Jesus told Simon, Andrew, James, and John to leave their fishing trade and help others find God.
—Both sets of brothers were attracted to Jesus' message and gladly followed Him at once.

I. INTRODUCTION

A. The Uniqueness of Christ

Today we begin Unit III, "Imitating Jesus," which is a four-lesson study of the epistle to the Colossians. These lessons have much to say about the importance of the person and work of Christ as Lord of all creation and the author of our peace with God. Why is it important for believers to have a clear and precise understanding of the person and work of Jesus Christ? First, it is important because the person and work of Christ is at the center of the biblical doctrine and teachings of the New Testament. Second, it is important because we believe that God came down to the earth in the person of Jesus and was born as a babe in Bethlehem. Third, the person and work of Jesus Christ is the linchpin upon which hangs the core of Christian preaching and teaching. Fourth, it is important because the very ground of our hope is anchored in the absolute conviction that Jesus of Nazareth is the very Son of God who died for the sins of the world. Fifth, believers must have a precise understanding of the person of Jesus Christ, because throughout the centuries various doctrines and beliefs have risen—seeking to undermine the deity of Christ (i.e., Gnosticism, Arianism, and Ebonism).

Our study today enables believers to understand that the church, whose head is Christ, is the apostolic agent to proclaim the Gospel of reconciliation in the world.

B. Biblical Background

The book of Colossians is one of the most important New Testament writings because of its lofty Christology (doctrinal statements about Christ). Yet, it is also at the center of great debates among biblical scholars regarding whether or not Paul was the author of the epistle. There have been opinions for centuries, with scholars on both sides of the issue failing to establish enough evidence that supports a definite conclusion. It is clear from the history of the Christian church that it was included in the canon of the New Testament—and that, alone, gives it the authority necessary for doctrine, reproof, correction, and instruction in righteousness (see 2 Timothy 3:16).

The introductory lesson comes from Colossians 1:15-20 and has been viewed by some scholars to be a confessional hymn of the early church that speaks to the cosmic and reconciling work of Christ, the Redeemer. According to Paul, all of the powers of the universe fall within the sphere of Christ's creative work. He (Christ) is the visible representation and manifestation of who God is (see Hebrews 1). When Paul mentioned "thrones," "dominions," "rulers," and "powers," he was referring to what some believed to be four classes of angelic powers; however, we are not certain about this interpretation. Paul did make it clear that Jesus Christ is the first in all things; He is the "firstborn from the dead" (Colossians 1:18)—which is the Resurrection. When Christ died for the sins of the world, He became the substitute for the sacrifice of animals on the Day of Atonement.

II. EXPOSITION AND APPLICATION OF THE SCRIPTURE

A. Christ's Relationship to the Father (Colossians 1:15)

Who is the image of the invisible God, the firstborn of every creature.

This portion of Paul's letter to the Colossians was written in response to the presence of a new heresy that was starting to appear in the first-century Christian church. The word *heresy* is "a religious belief that is opposed to the orthodox teachings of the church or of any religious faith." Heresy is a belief that is distorted and twisted. The most prominent heresy that the early Christian church had to deal with was gnosticism. *Gnosticism* was the belief that salvation was the result of what you knew, rather than the finished work of Jesus Christ at Calvary. The Gnostics, as they were called, were known as the intellectual ones. They were people who became dissatisfied with the simple message of the Gospel and wanted to turn it into another new philosophy, like all of the other philosophies of that day. By writing this letter, Paul was correcting these false teachings and affirming for the church the foundational cornerstones of Christian preaching and teaching.

In these verses, Paul affirmed the relationship of Jesus Christ to the Father. It must be pointed out that this verse is not a contradiction of the Scriptures that discuss graven images of God (see Exodus 20:4). The language is figurative and seeks to capture the essence of the nature of God, which cannot easily be defined in human terms. This verse is among the most important Christological statements in the New Testament because it affirms the deity of Jesus Christ. What did Paul mean when he stated that Jesus is the "image of the invisible God?" The word *image* (Greek: *eikon*) has in it the idea of "likeness." The word as used in this passage does not refer to a physical likeness, as though God existed in the likeness of a human being (see John 4:24). God cannot be seen by human eyes; He is invisible. As the living image of God, Jesus is the living manifestation of who God is and what God is like. "Thus *eikon* does not imply a weakening or a feeble copy of something. It implies the illumination of its inner core and essence."[1] Therefore, to see Jesus is to behold the very essence of God in all of His might, majesty, and glory (see Ezekiel 1:26-28; John 1:18; 14:9; 15:24; 2 Corinthians 4:4, 6; Hebrews 1:3). In Jesus Christ, the very nature of God was manifested upon the earth. The words *firstborn of all creation* are not to be understood as physical birth or a reference to the birth of Christ in Bethlehem. *Firstborn* is a translation of the Greek word *prototokos*—from which we get our word *prototype*. A *prototype* means the first of its kind in time and type. Jesus is the firstborn of all creation, begotten of the Father (see Psalm 89:27; John 1:14; 3:16; 2 Corinthians 8:9).

B. Christ's Relationship to the Universe (Colossians 1:16-17)

For by him were all things created, that are in heaven, and that are in earth, visible and invisible, whether they be thrones, or dominions, or principalities, or powers: all things were created by him, and for him: And he is before all things, and by him all things consist.

In verses 16-17, Paul turned from the relationship of Christ to the Father to Christ's relationship to the universe. The break between verses 15 and 16 is an artificial one. "For" continues the thought that He is the firstborn of all creation and introduces the fact that He is in fact the originator of creation. The presence of three phrases (which all begin with prepositions) points to Jesus Christ as the originator of creation—"by him," and "for Him." In Him, all of creation holds together and is the express manifestation of His glory. He is not a created being, nor did He come after God the Father; rather, He was there in the beginning with God. John 1:1-3 reads, "In the beginning was the Word, and the Word was with God, and the Word was God. He was in the beginning with God. All things came into being through Him, and apart from Him nothing came into being that has come into being" (NASB). When Jesus was on the earth He was in time, yet He is beyond and above time (see Revelation 1:8, 11; 21:6; 22:13). He is the creator of time. Creation is the result of His power. He is the glue, the cement, and the bond that holds creation together.

One of the tenets of Gnosticism was its belief that the body and physical world were evil—and because they were evil, the world could not have been the creation of God. Paul made it clear that everything in creation, whether it is in heaven or on the earth, was created by Him and for Him. He includes those things that are both seen and unseen. The mention of thrones, powers, rulers, and authorities points to the supremacy of Jesus Christ over the entire universe. There is not one thing, person, or power that is greater than He. He is before all things and in Him everything that is visible and invisible is under His authority.

Some interpreters have sought to posit that Paul mentioned thrones, powers, rulers, and authorities as a way of describing a hierarchy of angelic beings and that He (Christ) was the first in that order. However, there is nothing anywhere in Paul's other writings that would support such an interpretation or conclusion. Paul's use of these various terms is a way of simply saying that within creation, there is none greater than Jesus Christ.

Since there is none greater, we owe Jesus Christ our absolute loyalty. Why? Because there is no power or authority greater than that of Jesus Christ. He is the One who builds a hedge around those who have trusted Him (see Psalm 27:1-6; Romans 8:34-38).

C. Christ's Relationship to the Church (Colossians 1:18-19)

And he is the head of the body, the church: who is the beginning, the firstborn from the dead; that in all things he might have the preeminence. For it pleased the Father that in him should all fulness dwell.

In these verses, Paul pointed out the relationship of Christ to the church, which is referred to as His body. The personal pronoun "he" is emphatic, which means that Christ alone and no other is the absolute, sovereign Head of the church. In Matthew 16:18, Jesus said, "Upon this rock I will build my church; and the gates of hell shall not prevail against it." The word *Head* is from the Greek word *kephale,* and it refers to "anything that is supreme, chief, or prominent." In this instance, it is used as a metaphor to denote the primacy of Jesus over the church (see Ephesians 1:10, 22-23; 4:16; 5:23; Colossians 1:24; 2:10-14). Jesus stands in relationship to the church as the husband is to the wife (see 1 Corinthians 11:3). Yet, it is not a relationship of tyranny and oppression, but of love and peace. Jesus founded the church, organized the church, and commissioned and empowered the church for His purposes. Jesus is the Head of the church by virtue of His sacrifice for her sins. What is the church? The word *church* does not refer to a physical building. It does not mean a particular denomination or sect. Rather, the word *church* refers to and means the very people of God who have been called out of darkness and into the light (see 1 Peter 2:9-10). The church receives her life and marching orders through the Son. He is the very One through whom the church has received the hope of eternal life. He is the firstborn from the dead, which is a clear reference to the Resurrection.

Verse 19 continues Paul's argument against the Gnostic teachers who taught that Jesus was human and therefore could not have been God. Their position was that Jesus was a man or that He was an eternal spirit that merely looked like a man. Paul countered by stating that in Jesus Christ dwelt the very fullness of the deity of God. He was both God and human at the same time. Jesus was always fully clothed with all of the divine attributes of omnipotence, omniscience, and omnipresence (see John 1:14; 2 Corinthians 8:9; Hebrews 4:14-15).

As the Head of the church, Jesus alone has complete authority over the people of God. The great tragedy that many congregations struggle with is the quest for power and authority over the church. God ordains pastors to be shepherds of the flock (see Acts 20:28; Ephesians 4:11-14; 1 Peter 5:1-4). Yet, the pastor is not the overlord or ruler. Christ is the Head of the church.

D. Christ's Relationship to Divine Reconciliation (Colossians 1:20)

And, having made peace through the blood of his cross, by him to reconcile all things unto himself; by him, I say, whether they be things in earth, or things in heaven.

Verse 20 concludes the ancient hymn proclaiming the deity of Christ. Christ was the one in whom the very essence and presence of God dwelt—and through Him came reconciliation. The death of Jesus Christ upon the cross was the means by which God brought a healing of the breach between heaven and earth. The disobedience of Adam and Eve was healed and peace was achieved through the Cross. To *reconcile* means "to bring back to a state and condition of harmony and peace." In the cross of Christ, men and women see and experience the love and mercy of God. Reconciliation, forgiveness of sins, and peace through the death of Christ are central affirmations of the New Testament (see Matthew 1:21; Mark 2:5; Luke 2:14; Acts 10:30; Romans 5:1-10; 2 Corinthians 5:21; Ephesians 1:7; Hebrews 2:17; 1 John 4:9; compare with Leviticus 6:30; Isaiah 9:6-7; Ezekiel 45:17-20; Micah 5:2, 5; Zechariah 9:9).

III. CONCLUDING REFLECTION

Jesus Christ is the source of all life. He was there with God when creation was finished and God breathed into the nostrils of Adam and He became a living soul. It is in Him that we live, move, and have our being. Jesus is the pre-eminent one in the universe. And because He is first in the universe, He knows everything that is happening in the universe. Jesus knows our situations. There is no place in the universe where we can hide from Him. There is nothing that we can face that He does not know about. He knows all that there is to know about us and our life situations. That is good news! His being first in the universe means that we have all of the resources of heaven at our disposal.

Because He is first in the universe, He is our helper when mountains have to be moved. He is our helper when difficult problems have to be solved. He is our helper when the storms of life come our way. He is our helper when sickness and disease invade our lives. He is our helper when our financial situations look dim and dark. He is our helper when the toils of life are pulling us down.

PRAYER

Lord God of heaven and the earth, grant that we may never grow weary in well-doing, but will always put our trust and confidence in You. In Jesus' name we pray. Amen.

WORD POWER

Supremacy (Greek: *proteus* [prote-yoo-o])—this word was first used in classical Greek to denote or refer to someone who was first in rank or status; it is not a reference to "first" in relation to time. It is the picture of a man who stands with no equal above or below. In Colossians 1:15, Paul made mention of Christ as the "firstborn," which in the current verse is further developed to tell that He is not only the first to be resurrected, but also He stands alone within the sphere of the Father's love. There is none who is His equal—before, now, or ever. The KJV uses the word *preeminence,* which captures something of the sense that Paul wanted to convey when making reference to the place of Christ within the redemptive plan of salvation.

HOME DAILY BIBLE READINGS
(January 28–February 3, 2013)

The Supremacy of Jesus Christ

MONDAY, January 28: "Christ, the Head of the Church" (Ephesians 1:17-23)
TUESDAY, January 29: "Christ, the Firstborn of the Dead" (Revelation 1:1-6)
WEDNESDAY, January 30: "Christ, One with the Father" (John 17:20-26)
THURSDAY, January 31: "Christ, the Reconciler to God" (2 Corinthians 5:16-21)
FRIDAY, February 1: "Christ, the Channel of God's Grace" (Romans 5:15-21)
SATURDAY, February 2: "The Compelling Call of Christ" (Matthew 4:18-25)
SUNDAY, February 3: "The Person and Work of Christ" (Colossians 1:15-20)

End Note

[1] *Theological Dictionary of the New Testament*, Gerhard Kittel, Geoffrey W. Bromiley and Gerhard Friedrich, electronic eds., Vol. 2, p. 389 (Grand Rapids, MI: Eerdmans, 1964).

LESSON 11   February 10, 2013

FULL LIFE IN CHRIST

FAITH PATHWAY/FAITH JOURNEY TOPIC: **It's a Wonderful Life!**

DEVOTIONAL READING: **Romans 8:31-39**   BACKGROUND SCRIPTURE: **Colossians 2:6-15**
PRINT PASSAGE: **Colossians 2:6-15**   KEY VERSE: **Colossians 2:10**

Colossians 2:6-15—KJV

6 As ye have therefore received Christ Jesus the Lord, so walk ye in him:

7 Rooted and built up in him, and stablished in the faith, as ye have been taught, abounding therein with thanksgiving.

8 Beware lest any man spoil you through philosophy and vain deceit, after the tradition of men, after the rudiments of the world, and not after Christ.

9 For in him dwelleth all the fulness of the Godhead bodily.

10 And ye are complete in him, which is the head of all principality and power:

11 In whom also ye are circumcised with the circumcision made without hands, in putting off the body of the sins of the flesh by the circumcision of Christ:

12 Buried with him in baptism, wherein also ye are risen with him through the faith of the operation of God, who hath raised him from the dead.

13 And you, being dead in your sins and the uncircumcision of your flesh, hath he quickened together with him, having forgiven you all trespasses;

14 Blotting out the handwriting of ordinances that was against us, which was contrary to us, and took it out of the way, nailing it to his cross;

15 And having spoiled principalities and powers, he made a shew of them openly, triumphing over them in it.

Colossians 2:6-15—NIV

6 So then, just as you received Christ Jesus as Lord, continue to live in him,

7 rooted and built up in him, strengthened in the faith as you were taught, and overflowing with thankfulness.

8 See to it that no one takes you captive through hollow and deceptive philosophy, which depends on human tradition and the basic principles of this world rather than on Christ.

9 For in Christ all the fullness of the Deity lives in bodily form,

10 and you have been given fullness in Christ, who is the head over every power and authority.

11 In him you were also circumcised, in the putting off of the sinful nature, not with a circumcision done by the hands of men but with the circumcision done by Christ,

12 having been buried with him in baptism and raised with him through your faith in the power of God, who raised him from the dead.

13 When you were dead in your sins and in the uncircumcision of your sinful nature, God made you alive with Christ. He forgave us all our sins,

14 having canceled the written code, with its regulations, that was against us and that stood opposed to us; he took it away, nailing it to the cross.

15 And having disarmed the powers and authorities, he made a public spectacle of them, triumphing over them by the cross.

UNIFYING LESSON PRINCIPLE

We regularly try but fail to live up to human expectations and traditions. How can we overcome our failures and shortcomings? Through Jesus, God forgives all our trespasses and triumphs over all earthly rulers and authorities. The man with leprosy asked Jesus to make him clean, and Jesus chose to do so.

TOPICAL OUTLINE OF THE LESSON

I. Introduction
  A. The Danger of False Teaching
  B. Biblical Background

II. Exposition and Application of the Scripture
  A. Rooted in Christ
    (Colossians 2:6-7)
  B. Be Aware of False Teaching
    (Colossians 2:8-10)
  C. The New Circumcision in Christ
    (Colossians 2:11-12)
  D. Made Alive in Christ Jesus
    (Colossians 2:13-15)

III. Concluding Reflection

LESSON OBJECTIVES

Upon the completion of the lesson, the students will be able to do the following:

1. Discover Paul's message describing a full life in Christ;
2. Express thanksgiving for God's forgiveness through Jesus Christ; and,
3. Remain rooted in faith by continuing to pursue an understanding of life in the fullness of Jesus Christ and to be thankful to Him.

POINTS TO BE EMPHASIZED

ADULT/YOUTH
Adult Topic: **It's a Wonderful Life!**
Youth Topic: **360° of Living**
Adult/Youth Key Verse: **Colossians 2:10**
Print Passage: **Colossians 2:6-15**

—Paul gave advice and warning to the Colossians to keep their initial pledges of faith in Christ by which their community lives as believers were begun.
—Paul's basic exhortation was that they were to carry on in the fashion in which they had started and to become even more steadfast in the faith.
—Christians are cautioned to be on guard, lest they be deceived through empty rhetoric.
—In Christ dwells the fullness of the Godhead.
—Christians are buried with Christ in their baptisms, but they are raised to new life through faith to live and die in His resurrected power.

CHILDREN
Children Topic: **The Divine Healer**
Key Verse: **Matthew 8:3**
Print Passage: **Matthew 8:1-4**

—Leprosy was a terrifying disease because there was no cure; therefore, lepers were quarantined and considered untouchable outcasts.
—When the leper asked Jesus to heal him, Jesus touched the man and healed him.
—Jesus urged the man to tell and show the priest that he was healed so that he could be restored to his community.
—Physical illness or abnormality was widely regarded in biblical times as an indication of sin that had not been forgiven.
—The leper's physical healing was a sign that his sin had been forgiven.

I. INTRODUCTION

A. The Danger of False Teaching

What happens in a congregation or denomination when false teachings begin to take root in the hearts and minds of the members? What happens to the congregation when someone who may be a reputable and highly regarded member begins to espouse a doctrine that is foreign to the congregation's practices and historical beliefs? The results, if left unchecked and unanswered, can be devastating. Even different views about the right interpretation of the Word of God can breed confusion and conflict in congregations. One of the reasons why there may be so much confusion about orthodoxy today is the growing presence of believers who are biblically ignorant. I do not mean this in a negative way, but merely to point out that the lack of understanding has become the playground for the devil and the cause of congregational division, in many cases.

Today's lesson affirms the importance of being rooted and grounded in the Word of God. Unsuspecting and immature believers who are babes in Christ are easy targets for false teachers, whose persuasiveness may lead many astray. Through Jesus Christ, believers are given everything that they need in order to overcome the challenges that they face each day.

B. Biblical Background

Paul's letter to the church of Colossae was written to address a serious threat that was taking root among the congregation in Colossae. This threat has come to be known as the "Colossian Heresy." *Heresy* means "any teaching that goes against accepted doctrinal standards." The exact nature of the problem in Colossae has eluded biblical scholars for centuries. Although we are not quite sure of the exact nature of the problem, it did raise major theological concerns for the leaders of the church. There have been attempts to link the Colossian heresy to a form of Judaic Gnosticism which was a religious belief that sought to combine Greek philosophy and Christian doctrine.

The "Colossian Heresy" was a new form of teaching that denied the humanity of Jesus Christ. In an effort to refute that teaching, Paul had written earlier in Colossians 1:22 that Christ redeemed humans in the body of His flesh. In 2:9, he remarked that the fullness of God dwelled bodily in Jesus. Further, this new form of teaching had elements of asceticism and ritualism—that is to say, there was a tremendous amount of stress placed upon self-denial and bodily humiliation. Paul cautioned the Colossians to keep their initial pledges of faith in Christ, in which their community lives as believers had begun. By cultivating their relationship with Jesus Christ they would have the means to continue steadfastly in the faith. The power of the Christian faith is its unwavering belief in the forgiveness wrought at Calvary and the resurrection of Jesus Christ, which is the ground for our hope in eternal life.

II. EXPOSITION AND APPLICATION OF THE SCRIPTURE

A. Rooted in Christ
(Colossians 2:6-7)

As ye have therefore received Christ Jesus the Lord, so walk ye in him: Rooted and built up in him, and stablished in the faith, as ye have been taught, abounding therein with thanksgiving.

The words *so then* (NIV) point to everything that Paul had previously discussed about Jesus Christ in 1:15-23. There was a specific message that had been preached among them that proclaimed the supremacy of Jesus Christ over all powers in heaven or on the earth. This message proclaimed the absolute lordship of Jesus Christ. They were not receiving the message new from Paul, but had already received it from Epaphras, who was referred to by Paul earlier in the letter (see 1:6-7). The word *received* comes from the Greek word *paralambano,* and refers to "the oral transmission of a tradition from one person to the next or from one generation to the next." The saints in Colossae had received the word about the Lord Jesus (see Matthew 10:40; John 1:12; 13:20).

The second part of verse 6 is an imperative command that they continue to live lives that are pleasing to the Lord Jesus Christ, based upon what they had received. The expression "continue to live in him" (verse 16, NIV) is a translation from a single Greek word *peripateo,* and it has in it the thought of regulating one's life. It was a common word used by Paul to denote how believers were to live in the world as followers of the Lord Jesus Christ (see Isaiah 2:5; Micah 4:2; 6:8; John 14:6; Ephesians 4:1; 5:1; 1 Thessalonians 4:1; 1 John 2:6; compare Colossians 1:9-12; 3:17). Believers must always be aware that the Christian life is not a Sunday worship performance; rather, it is living each day so that our lights are shining and men and women can glorify God because of us.

Robert Wall noted that in verse 7, we see four metaphors that convey the characteristics of what it means to continue living in Christ Jesus.[1] These four characteristics are expressed in the words *rooted, built up, overflowing,* and *thankfulness* (NIV). In the first two metaphors, there is the "of Christian nurture."[2] The word *rooted* is in the past tense and indicates something that happened in previous years or months. The word *rooted* comes from the word *rhizoo* and means "to make strong, establish, or be completely grounded" (see Psalms 1:3; 92:13; Isaiah 61:3; Jeremiah 17:8; Ephesians 2:21-22; 3:17; compare with Colossians 1:23). Something rooted has stability and is not easily moved. It has strength so that it can withstand many strong forces. The term *built up* comes from the Greek word *epoikodomeoi* and has in it the image of "laying a foundation and then building a house upon it" (see Matthew 7:24; 1 Corinthians 3:9-14; Ephesians 2:20; 1 Peter 2:4). The use of the passive present is an indication that what happened in the past continues in the present. Being built up is an ongoing process of growth. The second two metaphors "strengthened and overflowing" (NIV) are metaphors of worship and point to the spiritual results of one's devotion to God.[3]

B. Be Aware of False Teaching
(Colossians 2:8-10)

Beware lest any man spoil you through philosophy and vain deceit, after the tradition of men, after the rudiments of the world, and not after Christ. For in him dwelleth all the fulness of the Godhead bodily. And ye

are complete in him, which is the head of all principality and power.

"See to it" (NIV) is an imperative command to pay close attention to what is about to be said and then follow these instructions (see Deuteronomy 6:12; Matthew 10:17; 16:6; Mark 7:15; 2 Peter 3:17; compare Acts 20:28-30). What is the purpose of being rooted and built up in Christ? It is to be able to avoid the pitfalls of being taken captive by false and shallow teachers. The word *captive* comes from the Greek word *sulagogeo* and is found only in this verse in the entire New Testament. It has in it the idea of someone "being robbed or captured and held as a prisoner of war." Paul used very strong and forceful language to caution the saints against becoming victims of what he referred to as a philosophy that was hollow and deceptive. We must understand that Paul was not speaking against philosophy or the love of learning. *Philosophy* comes from a Greek word that literally means "love of wisdom." The philosophy that Paul referred to depended on human traditions or man-made religion. We are not told exactly what the traditions were to which Paul was referring. It is not likely that Paul was referring to the oral tradition of the Jews that Jesus was often accused of ignoring (see Mark 7:1-10).

Verse 9 is one of the great Christological statements in the New Testament. It is a reference to 1:19 and emphatically declares that in Jesus Christ is the fullness of God. In other words, the Gnostic philosophers believed that God could not have stooped so low as to become a human being and still be God. The Incarnation declares that the eternal God, who created the heavens and the earth, lived in the very human body of Jesus of Nazareth (see 2 Corinthians 8:9; John 1:14). The very fullness of God means that all of "who" God is (His being) is embodied in Jesus Christ.

In verse 10, it becomes clear that believers do not need to find a supplement to what they have received in Jesus Christ. And because the very essence of God's nature is contained within Jesus Christ, the saints of Colossae did not have to look for anything else in which to find spiritual fulfillment. He alone is the Head over all things to the church and the world.

These verses speak to a common trend in the church today. In many congregations, members or individuals come under the hypnotic spell of charismatic teachers and are lured away under the banner of needing to have more in order to be fulfilled. When we grasp the fullness of the love of Christ, we discover that He is all we need and there is nothing else we need in order to be complete as disciples. What completes us are obedience and faithfulness.

C. The New Circumcision in Christ (Colossians 2:11-12)

In whom also ye are circumcised with the circumcision made without hands, in putting off the body of the sins of the flesh by the circumcision of Christ: Buried with him in baptism, wherein also ye are risen with him through the faith of the operation of God, who hath raised him from the dead.

Circumcision was the sign of the covenant relationship between God and Abraham. According to the covenant, every Hebrew male had to be circumcised eight days after being born (see Genesis 17:9-13). Paul drew a contrast between the Jewish rite of circumcision, which was a sign of inclusion with the covenant community of Judaism, and the circumcision wrought by Jesus Christ. The first was done by human hands, which was the sign of something larger, but which produced nothing in the way of salvation or righteousness. God demanded more than the physical act of circumcision (see Deuteronomy 10:16; 30:6; Jeremiah 4:4; Romans 2:29). The second, done by Jesus Christ, is a spiritual circumcision of the heart where the old nature is stripped away. Within the churches of Galatia, there was a similar situation when the Jewish believers demanded that Gentile converts be circumcised in order to be saved (see Galatians 5:1-13). In Colossae, the belief was far different. Circumcision was the rite that propelled the believer into a higher realm of spiritual mysticism, enabling the person to achieve a greater degree of spirituality.

Paul countered the teaching further by pointing out that it was in the act of baptism that believers were incorporated into the faith community—with baptism being a symbolic act of identity with the burial and resurrection of Christ (see Romans 6:3-5; 1 Corinthians 12:13; 15:20; Galatians 3:27; Ephesians 4:5; Titus 3:5-6). Believers are symbolically buried with Christ and raised with Him, which points to the future and looks forward to the day of the final resurrection of the dead. Just as Jesus was raised from the dead by the power of God, even so believers who live by faith will also experience the same resurrecting power of God.

D. Made Alive in Christ Jesus (Colossians 2:13-15)

And you, being dead in your sins and the uncircumcision of your flesh, hath he quickened together with him, having forgiven you all trespasses; Blotting out the handwriting of ordinances that was against us, which was contrary to us, and took it out of the way, nailing it to his cross; And having spoiled principalities and powers, he made a shew of them openly, triumphing over them in it.

In verse 13, Paul used two metaphors to describe what it meant to be made alive in Christ. In the first metaphor, sin caused spiritual death (see Ezekiel 37:1-10; Luke 15:24; 2 Corinthians 5:14; Ephesians 2:1-5). The second is a return to the use of the metaphor of circumcision as a sign of having a nature that was still floundering in sin. In verse 13b, Paul began a list of blessings that believers received by way of the Cross. First, we have been made alive with Christ. Second, believers have been forgiven of all their sins (see Acts 5:31; 13:38; 26:18; Ephesians 1:7; Colossians 1:14). Third, God has cancelled the legalism of the law—with its endless regulations and requirements—which made it difficult for men and women to achieve righteousness and salvation (see Romans 10:2). Fourth, God has deposed the demonic powers and authorities that have ruled the hearts of men and women since the fall of Adam and Eve. At Calvary, the victory over death and Satan was decisive and final (see 1 Corinthians 15:55-58). It is the very blood of Jesus Christ that covers our sins (see Ephesians 2:13; Hebrews 9:14; 1 Peter 1:2, 19; 1 John 1:7; Revelation 1:5).

III. CONCLUDING REFLECTION

The lesson has been instructive for several reasons. First, we are reminded of the importance of affirming the lordship of Jesus Christ and giving our total allegiance to Him. He has conquered all of the powers of the universe and they are all subject to Him. Second, we have learned that there is nothing else that we need to seek in order to know the fullness of the power and presence of Jesus Christ. In Him and Him alone do we find completion. The death, burial, and resurrection of Jesus Christ are the pillars upon which faith is strengthened and upon which believers and congregations are made stronger.

PRAYER

Blessed Father, grant that we may walk in the knowledge of the fullness of the blessings of our redemption in Christ Jesus. We thank You for His sacrifice, which has made forgiveness of sins possible. In Jesus' name we pray. Amen.

WORD POWER

Fullness (Greek: *pleroma* [play-ro-mah])—refers to that which has been filled, or to the contents that fill a container. It is used in this context to refer to completeness of the nature and essence of God, who filled Jesus Christ. The word *pleroma* does not denote a portion of God; rather, in this context, it is all that God is and ever can be that is found in the Person of Jesus Christ. Pleroma is another way of referring to completeness. Thus, there dwells within the believer the very fullness of the nature of Christ. In Him, one is complete and there is no need for anything or anyone else to be added.

HOME DAILY BIBLE READINGS
(February 4-10, 2013)

Full Life in Christ

MONDAY, February 4: "Those Touched by Jesus" (Matthew 8:1-4)

TUESDAY, February 5: "Those Called by God" (Acts 2:37-42)

WEDNESDAY, February 6: "Those Who Are in Christ Jesus" (Romans 8:1-5)

THURSDAY, February 7: "Those Who Live in the Spirit" (Romans 8:6-11)

FRIDAY, February 8: "Those Who Love God" (Romans 8:26-30)

SATURDAY, February 9: "Those Kept in Christ's Love" (Romans 8:31-39)

SUNDAY, February 10: "Those Who Have Received Christ Jesus" (Colossians 2:6-15)

End Notes

[1] Robert W. Wall, *Colossian and Philemon: The IVP New Testament Commentary Series* (Downers Grove: IVP Academic, 1993), p. 104.
[2] Ibid.
[3] Ibid.

CLOTHED WITH CHRIST

FAITH PATHWAY/FAITH JOURNEY TOPIC: **Breaking Bad Habits**

DEVOTIONAL READING: **Psalm 107:1-9**
PRINT PASSAGE: **Colossians 3:5-17**

BACKGROUND SCRIPTURE: **Colossians 3:1-17**
KEY VERSE: **Colossians 3:14**

Colossians 3:5-17—KJV

5 Mortify therefore your members which are upon the earth; fornication, uncleanness, inordinate affection, evil concupiscence, and covetousness, which is idolatry:

6 For which things' sake the wrath of God cometh on the children of disobedience:

7 In the which ye also walked some time, when ye lived in them.

8 But now ye also put off all these; anger, wrath, malice, blasphemy, filthy communication out of your mouth.

9 Lie not one to another, seeing that ye have put off the old man with his deeds;

10 And have put on the new man, which is renewed in knowledge after the image of him that created him:

11 Where there is neither Greek nor Jew, circumcision nor uncircumcision, Barbarian, Scythian, bond nor free: but Christ is all, and in all.

12 Put on therefore, as the elect of God, holy and beloved, bowels of mercies, kindness, humbleness of mind, meekness, longsuffering;

13 Forbearing one another, and forgiving one another, if any man have a quarrel against any: even as Christ forgave you, so also do ye.

14 And above all these things put on charity, which is the bond of perfectness.

15 And let the peace of God rule in your hearts, to the which also ye are called in one body; and be ye thankful.

16 Let the word of Christ dwell in you richly in all wisdom; teaching and admonishing one another in psalms and hymns and spiritual songs, singing with grace in your hearts to the Lord.

Colossians 3:5-17—NIV

5 Put to death, therefore, whatever belongs to your earthly nature: sexual immorality, impurity, lust, evil desires and greed, which is idolatry.

6 Because of these, the wrath of God is coming.

7 You used to walk in these ways, in the life you once lived.

8 But now you must rid yourselves of all such things as these: anger, rage, malice, slander, and filthy language from your lips.

9 Do not lie to each other, since you have taken off your old self with its practices

10 and have put on the new self, which is being renewed in knowledge in the image of its Creator.

11 Here there is no Greek or Jew, circumcised or uncircumcised, barbarian, Scythian, slave or free, but Christ is all, and is in all.

12 Therefore, as God's chosen people, holy and dearly loved, clothe yourselves with compassion, kindness, humility, gentleness and patience.

13 Bear with each other and forgive whatever grievances you may have against one another. Forgive as the Lord forgave you.

14 And over all these virtues put on love, which binds them all together in perfect unity.

15 Let the peace of Christ rule in your hearts, since as members of one body you were called to peace. And be thankful.

16 Let the word of Christ dwell in you richly as you teach and admonish one another with all wisdom, and as you sing psalms, hymns and spiritual songs with gratitude in your hearts to God.

UNIFYING LESSON PRINCIPLE

Our lives are guided by basic principles. How do we decide which principles to follow? Those who believe in Christ are guided by Christ's example; when Jesus walked on water, Peter tried to follow His example.

17 And whatsoever ye do in word or deed, do all in the name of the Lord Jesus, giving thanks to God and the Father by him.

17 And whatever you do, whether in word or deed, do it all in the name of the Lord Jesus, giving thanks to God the Father through him.

TOPICAL OUTLINE OF THE LESSON

I. Introduction
   A. The Struggle to Be Free
   B. Biblical Background

II. Exposition and Application of the Scripture
   A. Leaving the Old Life Behind (Colossians 3:5-11)
   B. Cultivating Christian Virtues (Colossians 3:12-14)
   C. Walking with the Lord (Colossians 3:15-17)

III. Concluding Reflection

LESSON OBJECTIVES

Upon the completion of the lesson, the students will be able to do the following:

1. Gain an understanding of the principles of living in Christ;
2. Imagine how their life principles and behavior are different because they follow Christ; and,
3. Evaluate their treatment of others and make changes where necessary (as demanded by a life lived in Christ).

POINTS TO BE EMPHASIZED
ADULT/YOUTH

Adult Topic: Breaking Bad Habits
Youth Topic: Clothed with Love
Adult/Youth Key Verse: Colossians 3:14
Print Passage: Colossians 3:5-17

—The acts of dying with Christ and being raised with Christ have a close association with baptism. Colossians 3:1 signifies that believers will participate in the new life and order of the age to come.

—All of the sins set out in serial form (verses 8-9) have to do with the human power of speech that is destructive and hurtful.

—In view of lives with Christ, Christians are urged to put aside sinful endeavors.

—God will judge those who continue to indulge in sin and evil activities.

—As God's chosen people, Christians are to forgive one another as God has forgiven them, and to strive to lead holy lifestyles.

—The Christian peaceful environment for mutual edification needs to be one that eliminates acts of strife and practices harmonious compassion.

CHILDREN

Children Topic: A Friend in Our Need
Key Verse: Matthew 14:30-31
Print Passage: Matthew 14:22-33

—After Jesus sent the disciples across the Sea of Galilee ahead of Him, He later appeared, walking on the stormy sea.

—Peter's faith reaction and his impulsive request of Jesus caused him to experience an unusual demonstration of God's power.

—When Peter lost his focus on Jesus and began to sink, Jesus immediately rescued him.

—As a result of this incident, the disciples believed in Jesus as the Son of God and worshipped Him.

I. INTRODUCTION

A. The Struggle to Be Free

The adult topic for today's lesson is entitled "Breaking Bad Habits." In *Webster's New World Dictionary,* you will find four different definitions for the word *habit*: (1) a distinctive costume, as of a nun; (2) a thing done often and easily; (3) a usual way of doing; and, (4) an addiction, especially to narcotics. The second definition fits the focus of our lesson today—things done often, hence with ease.

All of us know how hard it is to break free of old habits, especially habits that are damaging to our health and spiritual well-being. Social scientists have spent years studying human behavior and have concluded that people tend to revert to their old ways when they are under stress or feel pressured by outside forces. Among the more difficult habits to break are addictions, whether it is to food, gambling, sex, drugs, overspending, or alcohol. Even among believers, the pull and lure of the old ways can draw us back into the activities and behaviors that we thought were dead or at least not as prevalent in our lives (see Romans 7:14-22).

In every congregation, there are scores of Christians who are struggling with some habit that continues to exert control over their lives. One of the common mistakes that many believers make is assuming that once they have been saved and filled with the Holy Spirit, every obstacle to sustaining spiritual growth and vitality is broken and these will no longer reign in their bodies. The first time we experience stress, pressure, or a perceived personal attack, we may respond in ways which are normal and automatic in our pre-conversion days. How do we overcome the tendency to revert to old habits? In our study today, we will learn the importance of living in the present reality of our new lives in Christ. We all face the daily grind of overcoming the gravitational pull of the past—and it is the presence of the Holy Spirit living in us that empowers us to defeat the enemies of our desire to live free in Christ.

B. Biblical Background

One of the more common and sometimes overlooked dimensions of the New Testament is its block of material referred to as "paraenesis," a technical term for ethical or moral instruction. In the lesson today, we have lists of vices and virtues which were typical teaching techniques used by Paul (see Romans 1:29-31; Galatians 5:16-25). These lists were often used as a means of providing examples of the kinds of behaviors to be avoided or cast aside, as well as the kinds of virtues that all believers should seek to practice and incorporate into their lives.

One of the more interesting comments from people who are given to repeated bouts of failure in overcoming commonly committed sins is their sense of helplessness. They feel as though they cannot overcome the things that characterized their former lives because the pull of the past is greater than their new lives in Christ. Paul reminded believers that when the very image of Christ is stamped upon our hearts and minds it expresses itself in their behavior and conduct.

In Colossians 3:1, believers are reminded that in the ritual of baptism, we are raised with Christ, which means that we now participate in the new life and order of the ages to come. Using figurative language, Paul said that we are to put to death the old ways and sinful lifestyles that characterized our former lives without Christ. The sins listed are typical sins of Greek people before they converted to Christianity. Believers are called upon to take responsibility for ridding themselves of habits that are detrimental to sound spiritual growth (see Ephesians 4:22-25).

Did the presence of the false teachers have anything to do with the need to mention this list of vices and their destructive results in the life of the believer? There are two broad categories of sins listed in the passage. In verse 5, there are sins of the flesh and appetites, and in verses 8-9, we see a list of sins that deal with speech. Is it possible that the presence of the false teachers promoted a lifestyle that was abhorrent to Christian values? Is it possible that they promoted a form of sexual immorality under the guise of a deeper spiritual quest? The sins of the mouth are common among believers when they fail to learn patience and practice longsuffering. Paul concluded the section by reminding the saints in Colossae what a believer looks like—who has been clothed in the image of Christ.

II. EXPOSITION AND APPLICATION OF THE SCRIPTURE

A. Leaving the Old Life Behind
(Colossians 3:5-11)

Mortify therefore your members which are upon the earth; fornication, uncleanness, inordinate affection, evil concupiscence, and covetousness, which is idolatry: For which things' sake the wrath of God cometh on the children of disobedience: In the which ye also walked some time, when ye lived in them. But now ye also put off all these; anger, wrath, malice, blasphemy, filthy communication out of your mouth. Lie not one to another, seeing that ye have put off the old man with his deeds; And have put on the new man, which is renewed in knowledge after the image of him that created him: Where there is neither Greek nor Jew, circumcision nor uncircumcision, Barbarian, Scythian, bond nor free: but Christ is all, and in all.

The underlying premise of this passage is that Christians are men and women whose lives have been transformed by their faith in Jesus Christ. In verses 1-4, Paul exhorted the saints of Colossae to be completely focused on the things that are above and not those of the earth. In verses 5-17, he expanded that thought by stating that the old life of sin and separation from God has to be completely eradicated or rooted out. In verse 5, he exhorted them to "put to death" everything that belonged to their former lives. This is a very strong statement and was written as an imperative command, which stresses the seriousness of what follows. Curtis Vaughan notes that these words literally mean "to make dead"—an action that stresses the urgency of the hour.[1] Sin has the power to pull a person back into its menacing grip, when left unchecked. The term *earthly nature* describes the old sinful nature of the former life. Sometimes Paul described the old nature as "the flesh" (see Galatians 5:19-21). What are the behaviors of the earthly nature that are to be put to death?

Sexual immorality (Greek: *porneia*) gives us the English word *pornography* and refers to and includes all forms of sexual sins, adultery, fornication, homosexuality, lesbianism, and intercourse with animals, which was practiced in that day (see Matthew 15:19; Romans 1:29; 1 Corinthians 5:1, 10-11; 6:9, 13, 18; Ephesians 5:3; 1 Thessalonians 4:3).

Uncleanness (Greek: *akartharsia*) is impurity from a moral perspective. One can be infested with immoral thoughts, deeds, and words, all of which are evidence of the life of sin.

Lust (Greek: *pathos*) refers to sexual passion that is driven by evil intentions. The word *pathos* is found in this verse and in Romans 1:26 and 1 Thessalonians 4:5.

"Evil desires" comes from two Greek words—evil: *kakos;* and desires: *epithumia.* An evil desire is a craving for something that is forbidden, which is at the same time sinister and wicked (see Romans 7:7-8; 1 Corinthians 10:6-8; Ephesians 4:19; 1 Peter 2:11).

Greed (Greek: *pleonexia*) is the desire to have more and more for one's own self. It is akin to the sin of covetousness, which is one's insatiable desire to just get for the purpose of consuming.

These things are all identified with idolatry because the lust and craving for things means that worship and service to God has been supplanted by something else.

In verses 6-7, we have the reasons why the presence of these vices in the life of a believer is a contradiction. First, it is precisely because of these sins that the wrath of God is to be revealed. God will judge those harshly who subverted the will of God and replaced Him with a love of self. The second reason is that these sins reflect their former lives without Christ. The Colossians used to walk in these ways. The works of the flesh are manifested through immoral and wicked behavior and are clearly visible for all to see.

Use of the words "But now" in verse 8 (NIV) shows the contrast between the past and the present. "You must rid" is the second imperative command in the passage and points to another list of vices that the believer must shed. Here, the metaphor shifts from that of an executioner who puts to death the sins of the past, to the shedding of old clothes for new garments. Paul pointed out that they had taken off the old man or self and put on the new man or new person (see Ephesians 4:22; Hebrews 12:1; James 1:21; 1 Peter 2:1). The vices in this next list are all related to speech.

Anger (Greek: *orge*) refers to violent emotions that lie beneath the surface. Anger is best portrayed using the image of a volcano that explodes when the right conditions are met. *Rage* (Greek: *thumos*) refers to a sudden, uncontrollable outburst of anger. *Malice* (Greek: *kaki*) refers to the act of deliberately inflicting the worst sort of harm upon another person. It is cold, calculating, and calloused and is the worst sort of meanness. *Slander* (Greek: *blasphemia*) is degrading or demeaning speech that intends to belittle the reputation, character, or name of another person. *Filthy language* (Greek: *aischrologia*) literally means "low speech." It has in it the idea of obscene, profane speech.

Verse 9 is the third imperative command which states that they were not to lie to each other. Lying is one of the seven deadly sins and is not representative of the nature of God or Christ. In receiving Christ, the old nature has been removed and the believer has put on the new nature, which is being renewed in the very image of Jesus Christ.

Verses 10-11 form the conclusion of this section with the acceptance of Christ within the Christian community—meaning all of the things that were barriers prior to their being converted are gone. There are no racial barriers between Jews and Gentiles. There are no religious obstacles dividing the circumcised from the uncircumcised. There are no cultural barriers between those who are Scythian and those who are barbarians. Finally, there are no class distinctions, because both slave and free are treated equally in the kingdom.

B. Cultivating Christian Virtues (Colossians 3:12-14)

Put on therefore, as the elect of God, holy and beloved, bowels of mercies, kindness, humbleness of mind, meekness, longsuffering; Forbearing one another, and forgiving one another, if any man have a quarrel against any: even as Christ forgave you, so also do ye. And above all these things put on charity, which is the bond of perfectness.

"Therefore" in verse 12 forms a connective and shows the relationship between the old life

and the new life in Christ. It is not enough to stop doing some things; believers must clothe themselves with the type of character and behavior that represents Christ as their Lord. The world will know that we are Christians by our love and behavior. Curtis Vaughan noted that Paul reminded the Colossians that they were heirs of Israel's spiritual privileges (see Exodus 19:1-7; Deuteronomy 4:37; 7:7-8; compare with Jeremiah 31:3; Ezekiel 16:8; Romans 1:7; 2 Timothy 1:9; Titus 3:4).[2] They were once not a people, but now they were God's chosen (Greek: *eklektos*), holy (Greek: *hagios*), and dearly loved (Greek: *agapao*).

Believers are to clothe themselves with the virtues that are indicative of a changed life. Compassion, kindness, humility, gentleness, and patience are among the most significant of all Christian virtues and form the foundation for healthy relations among believers. *Compassion* (Greek: *oiktirmos*) refers to an expression of pity and mercy upon the most vulnerable of society. *Kindness* (Greek: *chrestotes*) denotes a disposition of moral goodness that seeks to do what is always best for others. *Humility* (Greek: *tapeinophrosune*) is a deep sense of one's littleness whereby one never exalts nor places oneself above others. *Gentleness* (Greek: *prates*) denotes an attitude of being mild-mannered. *Patience* (Greek: *makrothumia*) refers to having a disposition that is slow to anger, particularly when avenging wrongs (see Romans 12:9-10; Galatians 5:6, 22; Ephesians 4:2, 32; Philippians 2:2; 1 Thessalonians 5:15; 1 Peter 3:8-11; 2 Peter 1:5-8).

Verse 13 speaks of the two means by which these virtues manifest themselves in the lives of believers. It begins with bearing with others, which is the outworking of patience. The

Greek word denotes putting up with the most unlovable and unlikeable person, without losing patience. Second, believers are to forgive without limitations, just as Christ has forgiven them. The overarching means by which all of these things are held together and manifested in the life of the community of believers is through love (see Matthew 5:44; 6:14; 18:21-35; compare John 13:34-35; 1 Corinthians 13:4-7). Without genuine expressions of love, a church becomes a sham and neither heals the broken nor helps build the kingdom of God.

C. Walking with the Lord (Colossians 3:15-17)

And let the peace of God rule in your hearts, to the which also ye are called in one body; and be ye thankful. Let the word of Christ dwell in you richly in all wisdom; teaching and admonishing one another in psalms and hymns and spiritual songs, singing with grace in your hearts to the Lord. And whatsoever ye do in word or deed, do all in the name of the Lord Jesus, giving thanks to God and the Father by him.

Verses 15-17 conclude the passage with three main exhortations. The first is a call to be filled with the peace of Christ—that is, the peace which Jesus Christ gives (see John 14:27; compare Psalms 29:11; 100:4; 107:22; Isaiah 26:3; 27:5; 57:15, 19; Romans 5:1; Philippians 4:7). Peace in this context is not the absence of hostility within the body; rather, it is the inner disposition of calm assurance that refuses to whither under pressure. It is not just present in the life of the believer. "It rules" (Greek: *brabeuo*) literally refers to an umpire who rules, directs, and controls the heart of the believer.

Second, believers are to be saturated with the Word of Christ. In fact, they are to be rich (Greek: *plousios*), which refers to abundance

(see John 5:39-40; 2 Timothy 3:15-17; Hebrews 4:12-13; Colossians 1:9; compare with 1 Kings 3:9-12). The word of Christ then serves as the cornerstone for teaching and encouraging the saints to holy living. The reference to singing psalms, hymns, and spiritual songs may have reference to music that is centered in the word of Christ, based upon how the phrase appears in the text. Worship is to be the public expression of gratitude to God for His goodness, grace, and love.

The third exhortation is concerned with the work of the believers, or the work of the congregation. They were not just to talk about what needed to be done; rather, they must actively, aggressively, and persistently pursue the purpose of God in the world. Believers are exhorted not to work for their particular congregations or for their own benefit; instead, all things are to be done to the glory of God and in His name. Giving thanks to God is the expression of gratitude for both salvation from sin and the opportunity to be used in His service.

III. CONCLUDING REFLECTION

It is easier to talk about being Christian than it is for the vast majority of believers to actually live out their beliefs. Why? There may be a variety of reasons. In the lesson today, Paul helps us with some understanding of what needs to happen in our lives in order to be the persons we claim to be in Christ. We have to spiritually disrobe by taking off the old earthly nature with its sinful habits, desires, and things that have been at the center of our old lives. Sinful vices have to be replaced with

Christian virtues that depict our new lives in Christ. The second reason has to do with learning to live in community with other believers. Authentic Christian living transcends what separates people on the grounds of ethnic status, cultural differences, and social condition. When a local church is at peace, numerical and spiritual growth take place, which is what Christ intended for the church.

PRAYER

Father, may we learn to love as You have loved us, and may we learn to be at peace among ourselves so that the world will see You and not our differences. In Jesus' name we pray. Amen.

WORD POWER

Chosen (Greek: *eklektos* [ek-lek-tos])—this word was used in classical Greek to denote the general choice or selection of a thing or person. It was used in connection with the selection of the best soldiers in the army for special purposes. Israel was God's chosen or elect people, whom He picked for His own possession. Having been chosen by God did not mean that they were free of responsibility from serving Him or His interests (see Isaiah 42:1; 45:4; 65:9, 22). In the Gospel, election (or being chosen) has eschatological overtones—that is, it refers to those happenings at the end of time (see Matthew 24:22, 31; Mark 13:20, 22, 27; Luke 18:7; compare Romans 8:29-33; 1 Peter 1:2; Revelation 17:14). To be the elect of God comes not only with privilege, but also the responsibility to serve the interests of the One who chose us in love.

HOME DAILY BIBLE READINGS
(February 11-17, 2013)

Clothed with Christ

MONDAY, February 11: "Setting Aside Doubt" (Matthew 14:22-33)

TUESDAY, February 12: "Getting Rid of the Old Ways" (Romans 6:12-19)

WEDNESDAY, February 13: "Living in Love" (1 John 3:10-17)

THURSDAY, February 14: "Forgiving as You Were Forgiven" (Matthew 18:21-35)

FRIDAY, February 15: "Living in Peace" (John 14:25-29)

SATURDAY, February 16: "Living in Gratitude" (Psalm 107:1-9)

SUNDAY, February 17: "Living as God's Chosen Ones" (Colossians 3:5-17)

End Notes

[1]Curtis Vaughan, *Colossians and Philemon: Bible Study Commentary* (Grand Rapids: Zondervan Publishing House, 1980), p. 93.

[2]Ibid., p. 98.

LESSON 13   February 24, 2013

SPIRITUAL DISCIPLINES FOR NEW LIFE

FAITH PATHWAY/FAITH JOURNEY TOPIC: **Support through Mentoring**

DEVOTIONAL READING: **1 Corinthians 9:19-27**
PRINT PASSAGE: **Colossians 4:2-6**

BACKGROUND SCRIPTURE: **Colossians 4:2-17**
KEY VERSE: **Colossians 4:17**

Colossians 4:2-6—KJV

2 Continue in prayer, and watch in the same with thanksgiving;

3 Withal praying also for us, that God would open unto us a door of utterance, to speak the mystery of Christ, for which I am also in bonds:

4 That I may make it manifest, as I ought to speak.

5 Walk in wisdom toward them that are without, redeeming the time.

6 Let your speech be alway with grace, seasoned with salt, that ye may know how ye ought to answer every man.

Colossians 4:2-6—NIV

2 Devote yourselves to prayer, being watchful and thankful.

3 And pray for us, too, that God may open a door for our message, so that we may proclaim the mystery of Christ, for which I am in chains.

4 Pray that I may proclaim it clearly, as I should.

5 Be wise in the way you act toward outsiders; make the most of every opportunity.

6 Let your conversation be always full of grace, seasoned with salt, so that you may know how to answer everyone.

BIBLE FACT
SPIRITUAL DISCIPLINES

As believers, we have discovered through the years that certain disciplines and practices help us keep the spiritual channels open and our hearts turned toward God. It is true that these disciplines cannot save us. In fact, they cannot even make a believer a holy person. But they can heighten our desire, awareness, and love of God by stripping down the barriers that we put up within ourselves and some that others put up for us. A spiritual discipline is defined as "a habit or regular pattern in your life that repeatedly brings a person back to God and opens him/her up to what God is saying to him/her."

UNIFYING LESSON PRINCIPLE

Once we commit ourselves to a new routine, it is nice to have guides, partners, or mentors around to help strengthen our resolve. Where do we find mentors who will keep us faithful to our commitment? Paul named spiritual disciplines and faithful persons as examples of support for living a new life in Christ; Jesus showed compassion on those who needed help and brought forth their commitment.

TOPICAL OUTLINE OF THE LESSON

I. Introduction
A. Help for the Journey
B. Biblical Background

II. Exposition and Application of the Scripture
A. Be Prayerful
(Colossians 4:2-4)
B. Be Wise
(Colossians 4:5)
C. Be Courteous
(Colossians 4:6)

III. Concluding Reflection

LESSON OBJECTIVES

Upon the completion of the lesson, the students will be able to do the following:

1. Recognize the importance of spiritual disciplines in maintaining a Christian life;
2. Reflect on those people in their lives who mentor them in faith; and,
3. Accept the role of mentor for a newly committed Christian.

POINTS TO BE EMPHASIZED

ADULT/YOUTH
Adult Topic: Support through Mentoring
Youth Topic: Get Spiritually Fit
Adult Key Verse: Colossians 4:17
Youth Key Verse: Colossians 4:2
Print Passage: Colossians 4:2-6

—Paul appealed to his readers to walk in wisdom and to live wisely, concerning outsiders. Wisdom involves living in a right manner to please God.
—Paul also urged his readers to speak graciously, using words "seasoned with salt" (that is, carefully selected) in order to give appropriate and persuasive responses to nonbelievers so as to answer any questions regarding the validity and sufficiency of the Gospel.
—Paul urged Christians to pray earnestly and with thanksgiving.
—Prayer reveals God's will and is a vehicle that empowers one to do God's will.
—God can use our speech for His redeeming purposes.
—Christians should exercise diplomacy in order to build receptivity for the message of Christ.

CHILDREN
Children Topic: A Leader worth Following
Key Verse: Matthew 20:34
Print Passage: Matthew 20:29-34

—Even though the blind men could not physically see, they knew that Jesus was the Messiah, the Son of David.
—When the crowd tried to silence them, they persistently begged Jesus for help until Jesus had compassion on them and touched them. Immediately their vision was restored.
—Although the crowd following Jesus knew of His reputation as a miracle worker, they were still blind to His identity as the Messiah.

—After Jesus healed the men, they set out to follow Him.

—In healing the blind men, Jesus turned their lives in a new direction.

I. INTRODUCTION

A. Help for the Journey

In 1978, I acknowledged my call to full-time ministry. At the time, I was stationed at Fort Stewart in Hinesville, Georgia, which is about forty miles southwest of Savannah. One of the biggest struggles I had in those infant days of ministry was finding someone who would help guide and show me the way to grow and develop. My father, a pastor in Norfolk, Virginia, was too far away to give me the kind of weekly support and guidance I desperately needed. I had tried unsuccessfully to meet with several local pastors to get some insight into how to pursue the call to ministry. One day, a friend invited me to attend her church: St. Paul Baptist Church on Waters Avenue in Savannah. I arranged to meet with the pastor, an elderly gentleman named Reverend A. E. Hagins, who eventually took me under his wing and began to help me understand the call to ministry. Every week, I would meet with him at his home when I was not on duty and he would share insights and tips about the ministry. One lesson that he taught me was the importance of studying the Bible and developing the skill of teaching the Word. He allowed me to teach a weekly class of older women, which helped me sharpen and hone the skill of teaching. I credit Rev. Hagins for being the catalyst that helped me see the importance of the teaching ministry. He was the mentor at the time when I needed him most.

Most of us realize the tremendous benefit of having a mentor who helps shape our understanding and equips us with skills that enable us to succeed in a new position or profession. Nowhere is mentoring more critical than in the Christian faith, when persons are attempting to make a break with their sinful pasts. Once we commit ourselves to a new routine, it is helpful to have guides, partners, or mentors to strengthen our resolve. Where do we find mentors who will keep us faithful to our commitment? Paul named spiritual disciplines and faithful persons as examples of support for living new lives in Christ. Who and how are you willing to help grow spiritually?

B. Biblical Background

Paul brought the letter to the church of Colossae to a fitting conclusion by reminding them of three very important points. First, he called upon them to be prayerful (see verses 2-4). Second, he exhorted the saints to be wise (see verse 5). Third, he said that in all instances they must be courteous (see verse 6). As he had done at the beginning of the letter, he concluded by appealing to the saints to be vigilant in prayer (see Colossians 1:9-12). The Greek text implies that they were filled with a spirit of wakefulness (verse 2).

A life characterized by prayer is recognition of our creaturely dependence on the creator God. Three elements of prayer are featured in the passage: the necessity of alertness, its characterization by thanksgiving, and its participation in the mission and proclamation of the Gospel.

He also called upon the believers in Colossae to walk in wisdom and live wisely concerning outsiders. Wisdom living involves living in such a way that God is pleased (see Colossians 1:9-10). "Outsiders" refers to non-Christians (see Mark 4:11; 1 Corinthians 5:12-13; 1 Thessalonians 4:12). Wise behavior entails having the right attitude to time. The imagery used is the commercial language of the marketplace and indicates that the readers are to buy up time eagerly.

Paul also urged his readers to speak graciously and with courtesy to each other and to nonbelievers. Their words were to be seasoned with salt (that is, carefully selected) so as to give appropriate responses to nonbelievers who may have questions about the Christian faith and the Gospel. The chapter closes with some of the names of persons who made a decisive impact in the first-century Christian church.

II. EXPOSITION AND APPLICATION OF THE SCRIPTURE

A. Be Prayerful
(Colossians 4:2-4)

Continue in prayer, and watch in the same with thanksgiving; Withal praying also for us, that God would open unto us a door of utterance, to speak the mystery of Christ, for which I am also in bonds: That I may make it manifest, as I ought to speak.

Verse 2 begins with an appeal for the congregation to be prayerful. The word *Devote* (NIV—Greek: *proskartereo*) means "to adhere to or be strongly and consistently devoted to a matter." The words *devote yourselves* (NIV) are written in the present active imperative tense, which means that the appeal to pray was not to be considered as an option. The spiritual and communal life of the people of God hinged on their willingness to pray, and to persist in prayer at all times. Implied in this command to pray is the idea that they must pray always. This was not a command for them to spend all of their time on their knees or in their secret closets; rather, it points to an attitude of petition and supplication that looks to God for all things. The appeal to pray continually differentiated the Christian faith from the Jewish faith. Persons of the Jewish faith would gather at the Temple or synagogue to pray three times a day: morning prayer was at 9:00 a.m.; afternoon prayer was at 3:00 p.m.; and evening prayers were offered at sunset or about 6:00 p.m.

This life of prayer is characterized by two things: *watchfulness* (Greek: *gregoreuo*) and *thankfulness* (Greek: *eucharistic*). The word *watching* has in it the idea of absolute vigilance and attentiveness (see Matthew 26:41; Mark 13:33; Luke 21:36; 1 Peter 4:7). Nothing is more critical in the life of a congregation than to pray with spiritual wisdom and understanding (see Ephesians 1:18; Colossians 1:9). Satan is busy seeking to distract and disrupt the lives of the communities of faith, so believers are cautioned to be alert.

The concept of *thanksgiving* has in it the idea of a heart that overflows with gratitude for God's protection and provision (see Colossians 2:7; 3:15, 17). Our walks with God would be richer if we were more thankful to God for His blessings upon the lives of others. The Christian community would be much stronger if we were truly grateful for God's blessings upon other ministries. We should be joyous when shattered lives are put back together, lost children are found, and marriages are saved. We should be joyous when God blesses others with abundance. Christians should rejoice when others receive good news (see Romans 12:15; 1 Corinthians 12:26).

The one important truth that emerges from this imperative to pray is that every great congregational decision, every new venture, and every new mission endeavor in the life of the church must be saturated with prayer (see Acts 13:1-3). Prayer unlocks the will of God as saints pray with the mind of Christ.

In verse 3, Paul wanted the church members to pray for a specific purpose. They must pray for the church and its mission and message. He began with a reference to praying for "us" and moved to specifically praying for himself (see verse 4). He appealed to the saints to pray for us, which more than likely refers to all of the missionaries and evangelists who had been a part of the missionary enterprise (i.e., Barnabas, Titus, Timothy, and Epaphras).

The request was that God would open a door for the message of the Gospel to go forth. The question is this: how are we to understand the "open door"? We can understand this request in two ways. First, Paul wanted the church to pray that the Gospel would go forth into the entire world (see Matthew 28:18-20; Acts 1:8). This interpretation is supported by the appeal to pray that God would open a door for us, which is a reference to all missionaries. Second, Paul appealed for prayer for

himself—that God would open a door for him to preach the mystery of Christ, a reference to the message about Jesus Christ. He interrupted his thoughts by reminding the saints that it was for preaching this very message that he had been imprisoned. He was not asking them to pray for his release from prison, but that even while in prison a door of opportunity would be granted for him to share the message of salvation (see Acts 16:22-34). His desire was that they pray for him to have clarity of thought and boldness in the proclamation of the truth.

The most difficult thing to get the saints of God to come together and do is pray. Churches will meet for a variety of reasons and tarry long and hard over issues that relate to business and other mundane matters. But prayer is often overlooked as a means of growth and the spiritual health of the body. Prayer is our greatest spiritual weapon; yet, it is the least used by the corporate body. Great things begin to happen among God's people when we pray (see Acts 1:14; 4:31; 12:5).

B. Be Wise
(Colossians 4:5)

Walk in wisdom toward them that are without, redeeming the time.

Paul was mindful that if the message of the Gospel was going to prosper and flourish among the Gentiles, then those who had been saved must remember to live saved. The literal translation of verse 5 is "In wisdom walk..." "Wisdom" (Greek: *sophia*) refers to the knowledge and practice of godly and righteous living. Wisdom comes from God, who gives to all freely and without limitations (see James 1:5; 3:13, 17). *Way* (NIV—Greek: *peripateo*) refers to the regulation of one's life or conduct. The phrase "Make the most of every opportunity" (NIV) comes from two Greek words: *exagorazo,* which means "redeem or buy back," and *kairos,* which is one of the most important Greek words for "time" found in the New Testament. It literally refers to time as the opportune moment, or to a specific season that is ripe for an undertaking. It is the same word used by Jesus in Mark 1:15 and by Paul in Galatians 4:4.

Paul said that the believers in Colossae were to live in such a way that those who were the outsiders—the nonbelievers—could not find a reason to criticize the church or Christ. The witness of the saints must always be above reproach, especially among those who are weak, immature, and newly converted to the faith. Our freedom in Christ must never become a stumbling block to the unconverted or the newly converted (see Romans 14:13; 1 Corinthians 1:23; 8:9; Revelation 2:14).

Often a shadow hangs over the church because of the fact that those who profess Christ as Lord live in ways that contradict their witness. How many nonbelievers have been permanently turned away because of the many public scandals that have racked the Christian faith in the last decade? Rather than present a negative image of the Christian faith by false and faulty living, believers are encouraged to treat outsiders in ways that reflect the love of Jesus Christ.

The appeal is that believers will see every opportunity to present the Gospel, whether by example or in word, as a precious gift ordained by God. We must remember that the authenticity of the Gospel is relevant to the extent that we live out its creeds and testimonies.

C. Be Courteous
(Colossians 4:6)

Let your speech be alway with grace, seasoned with salt, that ye may know how ye ought to answer every man.

The final exhortation in this triad of imperatives has to do with speech and the wise use of the tongue (see James 3:1-10; compare also Colossians 3:16; Deuteronomy 11:19; 1 Chronicles 16:24; Psalms 37:30-31; 40:9-10; 45:2; Proverbs 15:4, 7; Ephesians 4:29). In verse 6, the reference looks back to seizing the opportunities that are presented to share and witness to the saving grace of God. Additionally, contained in this final word is the need to be aware of how one appears and speaks to those who are outsiders. This can also refer to insiders as well. Think of the church meeting you may have attended that degenerated into verbal assaults by one believer or group of believers against others in the same congregation over matters that were insignificant and foolish as they pertain to kingdom priorities.

The word *conversation* (Greek: *logos*) refers to speech in general; sometimes, *logos* is translated to refer to a whole range of ideas, such as a word or words. "Full of grace" speaks of being pleasant, approachable, agreeable, and relating to the ideas that are expressed by someone who is not filled with hostility or resentment. "Seasoned with salt" is a metaphorical image of someone seasoning food so that it has the right savory taste when eaten. Often, difficult conversations can be made more palatable when one gives consideration to the right choice of words. Choose the wrong words and the opportunity to witness can be lost forever.

Responding to and knowing how to answer critics and serious seekers after the truth are necessities. Often we can be well-meaning but say the wrong things that reinforce the negative images that some people have of Christians and churches. How should we answer those who would seek to demean and degrade the message of the Gospel? We should try to live lives that are well-pleasing to God before those whom we seek to witness, and then fill our words and attitudes with a seasoned spirit of love and grace.

III. CONCLUDING REFLECTION

One of the most important truths of the lesson today has been the emphasis on our witness as Christians, both within the body and among those who are outsiders. We are called upon to continue the work begun by our Lord Jesus Christ and passed on by the apostles to future generations. Sometimes local congregations are infected with an incestuous and selfish spirit. As we cultivate the disciplines of prayer, wisdom, and courtesy in speech, we take on more and more of the character of Jesus Christ. The more like Christ that individual believers become, the greater is the witness of the local church. It may be that the world cannot hear what we are saying because what they see us *doing* speaks louder than the rhetoric of our witness.

PRAYER

Lord, teach us how to walk in accordance with Your Words. May we be men and women who have learned to love You—not just with our worship and words, but more importantly by walking in Your ways. In Jesus' name we pray. Amen.

WORD POWER

Mystery (Greek: *musterion*)—Within the New Testament, the word *mystery* does not refer to secrets that have been kept, but to the revelation of God's divine will for all of creation. In the New Testament, there are a variety of usages for the word *mystery*. However, the ultimate revelation of God's redemptive plan of salvation came through Jesus Christ. Within the Pauline letters, the word *mystery* appears twenty times. It is used in the New Testament. It describes the plan of God to include both Gentiles and Jews in the kingdom as people of God (see Ephesians 3:3-8).

HOME DAILY BIBLE READINGS
(February 18-24, 2013)

Spiritual Disciplines for New Life

MONDAY, February 18: "Following Jesus" (Matthew 20:29-34)

TUESDAY, February 19: "Devoted to Prayer" (Acts 1:6-14)

WEDNESDAY, February 20: "Living in Harmony" (Romans 15:1-6)

THURSDAY, February 21: "Living to Please God" (1 Thessalonians 4:1-12)

FRIDAY, February 22: "Guarding Your Words" (Ecclesiastes 5:1-6)

SATURDAY, February 23: "Supporting Others in the Faith" (Colossians 4:7-17)

SUNDAY, February 24: "Devotion and Conduct" (Colossians 4:2-6)

Beyond the Present Time

GENERAL INTRODUCTION

This quarter has three units, tracing the theological theme of hope in both the Hebrew and the Christian Scriptures.

Unit I, *The Kingdom of God,* is a three-lesson study. This Old Testament study is a consideration of the more apocalyptic view of hope as it comes to us from the book of Daniel. These lessons move the learners to see the connection between the hope found in Daniel's prophecy and the Christian's resurrection hope.

Unit II, *Resurrection Hope,* is a six-lesson study for the Easter season. The Scriptures under consideration are drawn from the books of Luke, Acts, and 1 and 2 Thessalonians. The study opens with the Last Supper, the final meal that Jesus shared with His disciples in the closing days of His earthly ministry. On Easter Sunday, the lesson from Luke 24 reminds us of the empty tomb and Jesus' appearance to His disciples following His resurrection. For the following week, the lesson moves to the book of Acts and the anointing of the Holy Spirit that came upon the disciples in Jerusalem. The final two lessons of the unit draw on the letters to the church in Thessalonica and are considerations of the resurrection hope of believers who wait for Christ's return.

Unit III, *A Call to Holy Living,* is a four-lesson study of the books of 1 and 2 Peter. These studies focus on the hope that Jesus inspires for those who are suffering: Jesus' life, death, and resurrection for our "new birth into a living hope" (1 Peter 1:3, NIV).

LESSON 1   March 3, 2013

DANIEL'S VISION OF CHANGE

FAITH PATHWAY/FAITH JOURNEY TOPIC: **Better Days Ahead**

DEVOTIONAL READING: **Daniel 6:25-28**
PRINT PASSAGE: **Daniel 7:9-14**

BACKGROUND SCRIPTURE: **Daniel 7**
KEY VERSE: **Daniel 7:14**

Daniel 7:9-14—KJV

9 I beheld till the thrones were cast down, and the Ancient of days did sit, whose garment was white as snow, and the hair of his head like the pure wool: his throne was like the fiery flame, and his wheels as burning fire.

10 A fiery stream issued and came forth from before him: thousand thousands ministered unto him, and ten thousand times ten thousand stood before him: the judgment was set, and the books were opened.

11 I beheld then because of the voice of the great words which the horn spake: I beheld even till the beast was slain, and his body destroyed, and given to the burning flame.

12 As concerning the rest of the beasts, they had their dominion taken away: yet their lives were prolonged for a season and time.

13 I saw in the night visions, and, behold, one like the Son of man came with the clouds of heaven, and came to the Ancient of days, and they brought him near before him.

14 And there was given him dominion, and glory, and a kingdom, that all people, nations, and languages, should serve him: his dominion is an everlasting dominion, which shall not pass away, and his kingdom that which shall not be destroyed.

Daniel 7:9-14—NIV

9 "As I looked, thrones were set in place, and the Ancient of Days took his seat. His clothing was as white as snow; the hair of his head was white like wool. His throne was flaming with fire, and its wheels were all ablaze.

10 A river of fire was flowing, coming out from before him. Thousands upon thousands attended him; ten thousand times ten thousand stood before him. The court was seated, and the books were opened.

11 Then I continued to watch because of the boastful words the horn was speaking. I kept looking until the beast was slain and its body destroyed and thrown into the blazing fire.

12 (The other beasts had been stripped of their authority, but were allowed to live for a period of time.)

13 In my vision at night I looked, and there before me was one like a son of man, coming with the clouds of heaven. He approached the Ancient of Days and was led into his presence.

14 He was given authority, glory and sovereign power; all peoples, nations and men of every language worshiped him. His dominion is an everlasting dominion that will not pass away, and his kingdom is one that will never be destroyed."

BIBLE FACT

VISIONS

Visions are said to both come from and be about God. The understanding of a vision is given by God, and can only be understood and interpreted if a person has the Holy Spirit of God. Visions cannot be humanly interpreted. There is a divine inspiration and interpretation.

UNIFYING LESSON PRINCIPLE

We live in the hope that the future will be better than the past. How can we learn from the past and apply it to the future? Daniel's experiences taught him to trust in God always, despite the danger he faced; and his vision tells of the Ancient of Days seated on a throne, ruling forever, and giving dominion and power to a Messiah.

TOPICAL OUTLINE OF THE LESSON

I. Introduction
    A. What Lies Ahead?
    B. Biblical Background

II. Exposition and Application of the Scripture
    A. The Ancient of Days and God's Reign (Daniel 7:9)
    B. God's Response to Worldly Powers (Daniel 7:10-11)
    C. The Ancient of Days (Daniel 7:12-14)

III. Concluding Reflection

LESSON OBJECTIVES

Upon the completion of the lesson, the students will be able to do the following:

1. Connect Daniel's dream with the historical incidents to which it is related;
2. Share their feelings about the relationship between their dreams and reality; and,
3. Articulate their vision for future change.

POINTS TO BE EMPHASIZED

ADULT/YOUTH
Adult Topic: Better Days Ahead
Youth Topic: The Future Is Sure
Adult/Youth Key Verse: Daniel 7:14
Print Passage: Daniel 7:9-14

—Throughout history, God often revealed the future through dreams and visions.

—Daniel received dreams and visions from God and was known for his God-given wisdom and talent as a dream interpreter.

—Referring to God as the Ancient One shows God's eternal nature and ultimate power and authority.

—Daniel's vision saw the Son of Man (the name *Jesus* applied to Himself) given authority, glory, and power to rule over the earth and in God's kingdom.

—The vision depicted the Son of Man as endowed with God's eternal power and mission.

—The vision showed the ultimate defeat of a beast with a boastful horn.

CHILDREN
Children Topic: Daniel Keeps the Faith
Key Verse: Daniel 6:23b
Print Passage: Daniel 6:11-13, 16, 19-23

—Daniel prayed to God in private, even though doing so was illegal according to the king's command.

—The other leaders in the kingdom became jealous of Daniel and reported his praying to the king.

—Even though he was thrown into the den of lions, Daniel remained faithful to God.

—The king showed concern for Daniel when he checked on him in the morning.

—Daniel expressed loyalty to the king, but stood firm in the knowledge that God saved him from the lions.

—The king had Daniel removed from the lions' den.

I. INTRODUCTION
A. What Lies Ahead?

History has shown the extremes to which empires and nations have gone in order to maintain supremacy over others in the world. The common thread that causes most human bloodshed is the fear of one's losing control over his or her life and future. The enemy to a country's perceived future is what propels a nation to take up weapons against another nation, as well as one community or tribe against another.

When reading the story of Daniel, readers may see this ancient history in a way that leads them to an encounter with themselves as they confront enemies against the future that God intends for the world. Our present history challenges us to see the world as it is and work for the kind of world that honors God's will for all humanity. The book of Daniel raises key questions about the nature and shape of a communal world committed to a political vision of divine justice and transformation. Daniel and his friends were observant Jews in exile, yet they exhibited tough-minded faith and used their political power and religious influence against the imperial edicts of a foreign empire.

In a nutshell, Daniel's apocalyptic dreams of God's ultimate reign call forth the kind of faith as exhibited by Shadrach, Meshach, and Abednego: "The God we serve is able to save us" (Daniel 3:17, NIV). The question this lesson raises for us is this: When loyalty to one's heritage and faith is threatened by worldly powers, what will the people of God do?

B. Biblical Background

Daniel's dreams and dilemmas were relevant within the framework of Nebuchadnezzar's conquest of Jerusalem (see Daniel 1:1-5). The book of Daniel tells a coherent story of heroic figures who defied great odds to keep alive the faith tradition of the Jewish community. During this period, Daniel showed a decisive commitment to a national ethic of allegiance to God only.

Daniel wrestled with the divergent pagan idolatries and ritual practices of an imperial empire that demanded absolute loyalty to its rule. However, Daniel's allegiance was to the God who had delivered Hebrew slaves from bondage. Daniel was challenged to be steadfast to the God of the Hebrews as he struggled to survive within the Babylonian laws and rules. This lesson demonstrates the ultimate role that Daniel's God played in having the most powerful, earthly sovereign rulers acknowledge God's power and reign. We see God favoring Daniel and his companions as they decline royal rations and wine to consume the healthy diets of "legumes and water." Daniel and his Hebrew associates were found to be vastly more capable than those in the king's entourage. When Nebuchadnezzar was forced to turn to Daniel as the only one who could reveal and interpret the king's dream, Daniel announced (in 2:20-21) the purpose behind his faith: "Praise be to the name of God for ever and ever; wisdom and power are his. He changes times and seasons; he sets up kings and deposes them. He gives wisdom to the wise and knowledge to the discerning."

When Daniel and his companions found their lives in grave danger, they were left only with a commitment to God that gave them victory. In a nutshell, this lesson challenges us with the issue of what God's people do when loyalty to one's own heritage is a costly matter. As you study this lesson, think of how the story of Daniel contributes to your own hope of creating a just world governed by the reign of God.

II. EXPOSITION AND APPLICATION OF THE SCRIPTURE

A. The Ancient of Days and God's Reign
(Daniel 7:9)

I beheld till the thrones were cast down, and the Ancient of days did sit, whose garment was white as snow, and the hair of his head like the pure wool: his throne was like the fiery flame, and his wheels as burning fire.

Daniel's vision of the "Ancient of Days" must be understood against the backdrop of the four beasts that represent the rulers of evil empires. The book of Daniel was written shortly after the Seleucid King Antiochus IV Epiphanes ordered swine to be offered on the Temple altar in Jerusalem. Outraged Jews banded together to form an army, willing to go on suicide missions against a foe that greatly outnumbered them and whose equipment dwarfed their own. The revolt succeeded in 164 BC, at which time the Maccabees came to power. Daniel offered a potent view of the exercise of Jewish political power in terms of a prophetic vision and a deep commitment to resist foreign domination. The book of Daniel speaks of the confidence of Jews who had enough faith in the reign of God's righteous kingdom that they believed that they could throw back the danger of imperial assimilation.

Chapters 1–12 in the book of Daniel outline the resistant faith and civil disobedience of Daniel. Daniel was seen as an influential and wise courtier in the courts of Nebuchadnezzar, Darius, and Cyrus—but as one who refused the domain of the empire as the final edict of his life. Daniel managed life as an exile in a way that honored the God of the Jews. The overall thrust of the book of Daniel is summed up at the end of chapter 6, when Darius issued his decree regarding Daniel's God: "I issue a decree that in every part of my kingdom people must fear and reverence the God of Daniel. For he is the living God and he endures forever; his kingdom will not be destroyed, his dominion will never end" (Daniel 6:26, NIV).

Chapter 7 is considered "the veritable center" or heart of the book of Daniel. The dreams and visions that appear in chapter 7 are connected in many ways to the stories in chapters 1–6, where Daniel's faith in the sovereignty of God was shown.

Chapter 7 begins with the dreams, thoughts, and visions of Daniel. In previous chapters, Daniel was the interpreter of the king's dreams. Daniel's first vision is associated with the time of Belshazzar. As he lay in bed, Daniel's thoughts were consumed with the negative political rule that typified the empire of Belshazzar. The empire of Belshazzar arose out of chaos and evil and its power held hostage the hope for change among the Jewish exiles. Daniel's dream of deliverance was associated with the adverse political rule of Belshazzar and the ultimate reversal of his evil rule. Daniel considered the evil empire of Belshazzar as the rise of the beasts that would rise out of the sea. The winds of heaven that brought forth the beasts from the deep were envisioned, by Daniel, as God's initiating a battle against the evil empire. The four beasts that would rise from the sea are world powers, the enemies against the harmony and peace of the reign of God. They are powers with forces of chaos in the world at odds with the reign of God. The beasts arise one by one to do battle. Theologically, the battle would be between good and evil. The images of the beasts are those of struggle and warfare against the heavens—"the holy one." God is at war with the enemies, chaos, and evil. Daniel's dream was a dream of deliverance associated with the adverse political rule of Belshazzar. The imagery in Daniel's dream is tied to the "four winds of heaven" in battle against the sea and that which would arise from the sea.

Daniel's vision of the "Ancient of Days" or "one like a son of man" expresses God's ultimate power and authority against evil empires arrayed against the reign of God. The vision of the "Ancient of Days" and the imagery of the battle against the four beasts resembles the battle described in the New Testament—where Jesus is tempted by Satan, who is assumed to have control of the kingdoms of the earth (see Matthew 4:8-10).

B. God's Response to Worldly Powers (Daniel 7:10-11)

A fiery stream issued and came forth from before him: thousand thousands ministered unto him, and ten thousand times ten thousand stood before him: the judgment was set, and the books were opened. I beheld then because of the voice of the great words which the horn spake: I beheld even till the beast was slain, and his body destroyed, and given to the burning flame.

The four beasts in Daniel's dream convey the image of destruction of human life. The first beast, a *lion*, represents being a disturber of and wild threat to organized civil life. The lion in Daniel's dream suggests that governments or world powers were powerful threats against world peace and justice. Transformation of rulers was the message of Daniel's dream (see Daniel 6:26-27). Daniel's vision demonstrated the ultimate role of his God in the workings of worldly powers, and made the most powerful earthly rulers acknowledge the power and reign of God. The second beast would be a *wild bear*, symbolizing the devouring of many bodies. The third beast would be a *leopard*, symbolizing world dominance. The last beast in Daniel's dream was not clearly identified as an animal from the wild, but was the most ruthless of them, with its "iron teeth" devouring victims and trampling all enemies under its feet. Scholars believe that the horns of the beast—particularly the fourth horn—represent the unmatched power of Epiphanes, which means "manifest of God" in the Greek. Ultimately, Daniel envisioned that these beasts, the evil empires, and the rulers which they represented encountered the power of the reign of God, whose supremacy is able to transform the world.

C. The Ancient of Days
(Daniel 7:12-14)

As concerning the rest of the beasts, they had their dominion taken away: yet their lives were prolonged for a season and time. I saw in the night visions, and, behold, one like the Son of man came with the clouds of heaven, and came to the Ancient of days, and they brought him near before him. And there was given him dominion, and glory, and a kingdom, that all people, nations, and languages, should serve him: his dominion is an everlasting dominion, which shall not pass away, and his kingdom that which shall not be destroyed.

In these verses, Daniel envisioned "the throne room" or "chariot-throne" of "one like a son of man" (Daniel 7:13, NIV). In Daniel's vision, God Himself intervened in the form of an angelic manifestation and elevated "one like the person" or the "Ancient of Days" who changed the course of Israel's history (Daniel 7:22). It is thought by scholars that the angel Michael, who would do battle on Israel's behalf, was the angelic figure spoken of as "one like the person" (Daniel 10:13, 21). The "holy one" for Daniel was the angelic power of God in the life of Israel. When the holy one would be exalted, God's kingdom would be realized on earth. This represents the "end of days" when God's book would be opened, the dead would be raised, and Israel would rule the world (see Daniel 12:1-4).

Jesus often used the imagery of "the Son of Man" or "one like the person" as a reference to Himself as He supplanted the wrathful pseudo-human deities and powers of Herod Antipas. Jesus perhaps was influenced by the apocalyptic imagery of Daniel as he reflected on "the one like the person" to face the wrath of Antipas, who was a beast with fearsome powers like the beasts in Daniel's vision. As Daniel saw the transformation of world powers, so did Jesus, as He lived with the assurance that Rome's dominance and rule was only for a time.

Daniel was greatly distressed by his vision of the sea and the four beasts. Daniel needed help with interpreting his own dream and sought that help from an angelic attendant, Gabriel. The attendant interpreted and summarized the meaning of Daniel's dream— "Worldly powers will arise" ("kingdoms from the earth"), but God will conquer them all and God's kingdom will be everlasting. Daniel's dreams chart a post-imperial political vision, one in which a person of integrity might support foreign rulers when they act justly, but will not shy away from resistance when oppression compromises the human flourishing of the community.

Apocalyptic dreamers bring our world hope. They are visionaries against the world as it is, and reformers of the world as it should be. Dreamers like Martin Luther King Jr., who revitalized hope for a just society, drew their inspiration from the hopes and passions of people who longed for an alternative world.

III. CONCLUDING REFLECTION

It is the nature of visionary religion to look beyond worldly powers and ask not only about the meaning of these powers, but also about the ultimate reality that can change them. Living with such hope makes apocalyptic dreams like those of Daniel a real possibility for transforming the world as it is. This hope, in the book of Daniel, was translated into apocalyptic dreams of transformation of world powers. Dreams are the beginning of liberation and the release from oppression—that is, dreams focus on what *could* be, what *may* be, and most importantly, what *will* be! One can understand the apocalyptic dreams of Daniel, particularly from the perspective of an oppressed people, as they dream and hope that one day God will miraculously, even irrationally, intervene to halt suffering and end the oppression. Oppressed people are always in a posture of faith, looking for a new approach to reality—a new opening of a way forward for the transformation of life. Dreamers of apocalyptic visions live with the conviction that God's order for the human race is the only way to a world of righteousness.

Christians are called to be visionaries of a new order of equality and world peace. Such dreams can lead to hope, which has the potential of giving birth to a new world.

PRAYER

Eternal God, Your kingdom is an everlasting kingdom where love, justice, and compassionate power govern all people. Help us to live with Your dream and the hope of Your kingdom already accomplished, but not yet fully realized in our world. Until Your reign comes, help us live daily with Your dream. In Jesus' name we pray. Amen.

WORD POWER

"The Ancient of Days"—*one like the person of the Son of Man* is seen as a future reference to the life and ministry of Jesus Christ. The power and authority of the "Ancient of Days" continues in the life of Jesus.

HOME DAILY BIBLE READINGS
(February 25–March 3, 2013)

Daniel's Vision of Change
> **MONDAY, February 25:** "The Lord Deals with the Mighty" (Daniel 5:13-21)
> **TUESDAY, February 26:** "The Lord Judges the Powerful" (Daniel 5:22-31)
> **WEDNESDAY, February 27:** "The Plot to Undermine Daniel" (Daniel 6:1-10)
> **THURSDAY, February 28:** "The Plot Fails" (Daniel 6:11-23)
> **FRIDAY, March 1:** "Daniel's God Is Exalted" (Daniel 6:24-28)
> **SATURDAY, March 2:** "Daniel's Vision" (Daniel 7:1-8)
> **SUNDAY, March 3:** "The Exaltation of the Coming One" (Daniel 7:9-14)

References

Pleins, J. David, *The Social Visions of the Hebrew Bible: A Theological Introduction*, pp. 196-204.
The New Interpreter's Bible, Volume VII, pages 100-108.

LESSON 2   March 10, 2013

DANIEL'S PRAYER

Faith Pathway/Faith Journey Topic: **Have Mercy!**

DEVOTIONAL READING: **James 5:13-18**   BACKGROUND SCRIPTURE: **Daniel 9:3-19**
PRINT PASSAGE: **Daniel 9:4b-14**   KEY VERSE: **Daniel 9:9**

Daniel 9:4b-14—KJV

4 O Lord, the great and dreadful God, keeping the covenant and mercy to them that love him, and to them that keep his commandments;

5 We have sinned, and have committed iniquity, and have done wickedly, and have rebelled, even by departing from thy precepts and from thy judgments:

6 Neither have we hearkened unto thy servants the prophets, which spake in thy name to our kings, our princes, and our fathers, and to all the people of the land.

7 O Lord, righteousness belongeth unto thee, but unto us confusion of faces, as at this day; to the men of Judah, and to the inhabitants of Jerusalem, and unto all Israel, that are near, and that are far off, through all the countries whither thou hast driven them, because of their trespass that they have trespassed against thee.

8 O Lord, to us belongeth confusion of face, to our kings, to our princes, and to our fathers, because we have sinned against thee.

9 To the Lord our God belong mercies and forgivenesses, though we have rebelled against him;

10 Neither have we obeyed the voice of the LORD our God, to walk in his laws, which he set before us by his servants the prophets.

11 Yea, all Israel have transgressed thy law, even by departing, that they might not obey thy voice; therefore the curse is poured upon us, and the oath that is written in the law of Moses the servant of God, because we have sinned against him.

12 And he hath confirmed his words, which he spake against us, and against our judges that judged us, by bringing upon us a great evil: for under the whole heaven hath not been done as hath been done upon Jerusalem.

Daniel 9:4b-14—NIV

4 "O Lord, the great and awesome God, who keeps his covenant of love with all who love him and obey his commands,

5 we have sinned and done wrong. We have been wicked and have rebelled; we have turned away from your commands and laws.

6 We have not listened to your servants the prophets, who spoke in your name to our kings, our princes and our fathers, and to all the people of the land.

7 Lord, you are righteous, but this day we are covered with shame—the men of Judah and people of Jerusalem and all Israel, both near and far, in all the countries where you have scattered us because of our unfaithfulness to you.

8 O LORD, we and our kings, our princes and our fathers are covered with shame because we have sinned against you.

9 The Lord our God is merciful and forgiving, even though we have rebelled against him;

10 we have not obeyed the LORD our God or kept the laws he gave us through his servants the prophets.

11 All Israel has transgressed your law and turned away, refusing to obey you. Therefore the curses and sworn judgments written in the Law of Moses, the servant of God, have been poured out on us, because we have sinned against you.

12 You have fulfilled the words spoken against us and against our rulers by bringing upon us great disaster. Under the whole heaven nothing has ever been done like what has been done to Jerusalem.

UNIFYING LESSON PRINCIPLE

Even though our hopes for the future are grounded in God's past actions, we are human and become fearful. What should we do when fear encroaches upon our lives? Daniel went to God in prayer.

13 As it is written in the law of Moses, all this evil is come upon us: yet made we not our prayer before the LORD our God, that we might turn from our iniquities, and understand thy truth.
14 Therefore hath the LORD watched upon the evil, and brought it upon us: for the LORD our God is righteous in all his works which he doeth: for we obeyed not his voice.

13 Just as it is written in the Law of Moses, all this disaster has come upon us, yet we have not sought the favor of the LORD our God by turning from our sins and giving attention to your truth.
14 The LORD did not hesitate to bring the disaster upon us, for the LORD our God is righteous in everything he does; yet we have not obeyed him."

TOPICAL OUTLINE OF THE LESSON

I. **Introduction**
   A. Devotion to God's Kingdom
   B. Biblical Background

II. **Exposition and Application of the Scripture**
   A. Acknowledging the People's Sin against God (Daniel 9:4b-7)
   B. Confession of Corporate Sin (Daniel 9:8-14)

III. **Concluding Reflection**

LESSON OBJECTIVES

Upon the completion of the lesson, the students will be able to do the following:

1. Hear and understand the passionate words of Daniel's prayer to God;
2. Express the passions that earnest prayer evokes in them; and,
3. Study Daniel's prayer to find words and emotions that fit their situations.

POINTS TO BE EMPHASIZED

ADULT/YOUTH

Adult Topic: **Have Mercy!**

Youth Topic: **Prayer of Confession**

Adult Key Verse: **Daniel 9:9**

Youth Key Verse: **Daniel 9:14**

Print Passage: **Daniel 9:4b-14**

—Daniel 9:4-14 is neither a vision nor a dream—but a prayer.

—Note the use of the word "we" instead of "I" in the prayer. Daniel was praying on behalf of all the people of Judah and Israel.

—Daniel believed that the suffering of his fellow Jews was a direct result of their disobeying God's law (the Mosaic covenant).

—Daniel's prayer mirrored the Israelites' prayer of confession and penitence in Nehemiah 9:2-37.

—Daniel's prayer expressed the sins of the people of Israel and their devastating consequences.

—This prayer was directed to a graceful and loving God who would show mercy and forgiveness—if only Israel would turn from sin and obey God's commands.

—Fasting, dressing in sackcloth, and the application of ashes were common practices in Israel, when they confessed sins and asked for forgiveness.

CHILDREN

Children Topic: Daniel Prays to God

Key Verse: Daniel 2:23

Print Passage: Daniel 2:2a, 10-13, 17-19, 23, 27-28, 44

—King Nebuchadnezzar was troubled by his dreams and wanted them interpreted so that he could understand their meaning.

—When the interpreters could not satisfy Nebuchadnezzar's requests, Daniel stepped in and offered to try to help, if given some time.

—Daniel asked his friends to join him in seeking

God's help through prayer, and God responded by revealing to Daniel in a vision the king's dream and its interpretation.

—Daniel responded by giving God thanks and praise for the wisdom and power he had received.

—Included in Daniel's interpretation of the king's dream was the idea that God would establish another kingdom that would never be destroyed.

—Because Daniel trusted God and prayed, Daniel, his three friends, and all the other wise men of Babylon were saved.

I. INTRODUCTION

A. Devotion to God's Kingdom

The exilic life of Daniel is an example of devotion and loyalty to God. Under circumstances of extreme challenges to his faith, Daniel demonstrated a steadfast loyalty to the covenant rituals and practices of the Hebrew religion (Judaism). Daniel's prayer as recorded in chapter 9 conveys a profound sense of the history of the relationship between God and Israel. As a part of this history, there is an acknowledgment that the human community has often failed to uphold its part of the relationship. Daniel's prayer is characteristic of the confessional tradition of Israel, who sought forgiveness and restoration from God when all else failed. The prayer of confession in the book of Daniel is communal in nature and acknowledged the national sin of the people of God. The book of Daniel is an ancient story of a people struggling to sustain their faith and religious heritage during a threatening period of exile and oppression. Clearly, Daniel was one among a company of Jewish exiles who recognized that their exilic suffering was due to the people's disobedience to the laws of God.

A large percentage of Americans claim the tradition of Christianity as their practice of religious faith. The Protestant churches of mainline Christianity often call for national prayer for the well-being of America. The study of this lesson will engage the students to determine the role that prayer should play in the religious life of a nation. What are our national sins that warrant confession and reconciliation to God? The prayer of Daniel is an example of a communal call for divine forgiveness.

B. Biblical Background

Daniel 9:4-14 is neither a vision nor a dream, but a prayer. The prayer is a traditional prayer of confession. Note the use of the word *we* instead of *I* in Daniel's prayer. Daniel's prayer was corporately focused on the sins of the people of Judah. Daniel was praying on behalf of all the people of Judah and Israel. Daniel addressed the Lord directly in the first part of the prayer (verses 4-8), but then he changed his point of view in verse 10 and spoke of the Lord in the third person. Daniel believed that the suffering of his fellow Jews was a direct result of their disobeying God's law (the Mosaic covenant). Daniel's prayer mirrored the Israelites' prayer of confession and penitence in Nehemiah 9:2-37. The disobedience of the people of Judah set the exilic context—which Daniel addressed—and showed rise to Judah's need of God's forgiveness and deliverance. Daniel's prayer was set in the Babylonian period of exile during the first-year reign of King Darius. Daniel (as one among those exiled) struggled to maintain his Jewish faith and identity as one devoted to the covenant of God. Daniel lived with the hope of Jewish restoration from exile.

II. EXPOSITION AND APPLICATION OF THE SCRIPTURE

A. Acknowledging the People's Sin against God (Daniel 9:4b-7)

O Lord, the great and dreadful God, keeping the covenant and mercy to them that love him, and to them that keep his commandments; We have sinned, and have committed iniquity, and have done wickedly, and have rebelled, even by departing from thy precepts and from thy judgments: Neither have we hearkened unto thy servants the prophets, which spake in thy name to our kings, our princes, and our fathers, and to all the people of the land. O Lord, righteousness belongeth unto thee, but unto us confusion of faces, as at this day; to the men of Judah, and to the inhabitants of Jerusalem, and unto all Israel, that are near, and that are far off, through all the countries whither thou hast driven them, because of their trespass that they have trespassed against thee.

Prayers of confession to God are usually prompted when people face pain and suffering, due to their individual sins or that of the community. In the case of Daniel, he lived with the daily awareness that the ruin and collapse of Jerusalem under the foreign rule of Babylon was due to the sins of Judah and Israel against the covenant of God. The people of God had dishonored the Mosaic covenant and broken the laws of God. Daniel's reference to the book of Jeremiah (verse 2) underscores the idea of the "covenant" and Judah's past sin. Daniel turned his attention to God with petitions and fasting, and sackcloth and ashes (verse 3). The experience of exilic shame and the curse overwhelmed Daniel's spirit to the point of expressing humility and sorrow about the condition of Jerusalem and the apparent corruption of the people. Daniel was fully aware of the history of God's involvement in the life of Israel and called to the God known by Moses and Israel for relief and deliverance. Daniel knew of Jeremiah's prophecy that the people of God would endure a seventy-year period of exilic suffering. However, he appealed to God in prayer, in the hopes that God would respond with mercy to end the suffering and renew the people to the ideals of the Mosaic covenant.

Daniel's prayer invoked the God of the Exodus, acknowledging the fact that the restoration of the people required both political liberation and God's forgiveness of the people's sins. Daniel recognized that only the power of God could match the people's need for forgiveness and liberation from the political dominance of the Babylonian empire. Daniel was unwilling to accept the lasting cost of Judah's sins, so he prayed—acknowledging that this was the only means and available option for the renewal and restoration of God's people. Daniel ultimately believed that God's purpose to build a just community of faithfulness to the divine covenant would be fulfilled.

B. Confession of Corporate Sin
(Daniel 9:8-14)

O Lord, to us belongeth confusion of face, to our kings, to our princes, and to our fathers, because we have sinned against thee. To the Lord our God belong mercies and forgivenesses, though we have rebelled against him; Neither have we obeyed the voice of the LORD our God, to walk in his laws, which he set before us by his servants the prophets. Yea, all Israel have transgressed thy law, even by departing, that they might not obey thy voice; therefore the curse is poured upon us, and the oath that is written in the law of Moses the servant of God, because we have sinned against him. And he hath confirmed his words, which he spake against us, and against our judges that judged us, by bringing upon us a great evil: for under the whole heaven hath not been done as hath been done upon Jerusalem. As it is written in the law of Moses, all this evil is come upon us: yet made we not our prayer before the LORD our God, that we might turn from our iniquities, and understand thy truth. Therefore hath the LORD watched upon the evil, and brought it upon us: for the LORD our God is righteous in all his works which he doeth: for we obeyed not his voice.

Daniel's prayers directed toward God were clearly a true expression of his hope for a better day. What is important to note about Daniel's prayer is that it was corporate in character—not private in its appeal. Daniel's prayer had an intentional motif and concern for national forgiveness. Daniel realized that the national sins of Israel were terrible to God, so he prayed on behalf of the people as a whole. Daniel fasted and wore sackcloth, a ritual practice that spoke to the seriousness of the condition to which Daniel's prayer was addressed. Hardly ever do we see leaders confess the sins of a nation. The understanding of sin and forgiveness has been personalized in Western Christianity so that there is only a modicum of attention given to institutional injustice. Several times in Daniel's prayer, he mentioned the corporate injustice of Israel and her leaders.

Daniel's prayer indicated the following burdens—namely, petitioning God to have mercy, grant forgiveness, show abundant compassion, and demonstrate God's ultimate power to restore and liberate His people so that they could go back to Jerusalem. The weight of Judah's corporate sin lay heavy upon Daniel's heart. Public shame had come to the city of Jerusalem and exile and oppression occurred because of the fact that the people had broken the covenant of God. Daniel was clear about the people's sin: "We have sinned against you" (verse 8, NIV). Daniel's prayer was a communal prayer that took the burden of the people's collective sins to the altar of God. Daniel was aware of that fact and acknowledged in his prayer that God's judgment had come upon the people (see verse 14).

Daniel's confession somewhat parallels the history of America—as our country has not listened to voices of justice. The lives of many advocates for justice have been sacrificed on America's altars of injustice. The nation has been slow to learn that the prophetic demand for justice and righteousness is not only for the sake of the weak, but also for the sake of the nation itself. Martin Luther King Jr. once stated, "If physical death is the price that I must pay to free my white brothers and sisters from a permanent death of the spirit, then nothing can be more redemptive." Prayer for justice and transformation of our world is a continual reality in the life of the church. Prayer works! Prayer joins us with God's power and purpose in the world. A willingness to acknowledge our condition of sinfulness before God and our dependence upon God's mercy and forgiveness is the kind of spirituality that is redemptive and can save a nation.

Daniel's prayer is a model prayer for any church or nation that takes seriously institutional and systemic unrighteousness. There can be no hope until our generation prays in the spirit of Daniel's prayer of confession. Only then will we learn what our nation must do to be saved.

To fully appreciate the significance of Daniel's prayer, we must recall the surrender of King Jehoiachin and the destruction of Jerusalem that occurred in 597 BC. Daniel was among the most prominent and accomplished Jews deported to Babylon. In the prolonged crisis of exile, Daniel dedicated himself to a period of fasting and prayer. Daniel's prayer showed concern about the significance of Jeremiah's prophecy concerning Israel (see Jeremiah 29) as it impacted the liberation and restoration of the Jews.

With the words "We have sinned," Daniel included all elements of his society's unrighteousness. Daniel knew that no human action other than prayer and confession could build hope or reconcile the people to a right relationship with God. Daniel appealed to God for deliverance because his faith was undergirded by the history of what God had done for Israel's salvation. God had been abundantly compassionate toward Israel. The history of God's merciful acts provided Daniel with the confidence that God would again act compassionately in Israel's favor.

Daniel's resolve to depend upon divine compassion for deliverance raises this question: when loyalty to one's own faith heritage is at stake, what should God's people do? First, it is important to note that prayer without a commitment or passion for God's purpose in the world is at best an anemic ritual that does not accomplish anything. When Daniel prayed for God's deliverance, he was convinced that nothing should be the ultimate concern of God's people other than that of elevating God above everything in the world that represented power. Daniel relied on the "God of heaven" who delivers. As noted in chapter 2, verse 47, because of Daniel's confidence in God's deliverance, Nebuchadnezzar openly acknowledged the God of Daniel. Nebuchadnezzar said this (in essence): "Truly your God must be the God of gods and Lord of kings and the revealer of mysteries, to have enabled you to reveal this mystery." In chapter 3, when Daniel's companions found their lives in grave danger from a flaming furnace, loyalty to God became the anchor of their faith. When Daniel prayed for deliverance and restoration of "the sanctuary of Jerusalem," he understood the centrality of worship as the most significant and central act of God's people. Because of Daniel's faithfulness and his total dependence upon God for deliverance, he became the agency by which God's purpose was accomplished. In the end, even Nebuchadnezzar confessed God's sovereign power.

III. CONCLUDING REFLECTION

The writing of the exposition of this lesson took place on the tenth anniversary of the 9/11 attacks that toppled the World Trade Center in New York. Daniel's prayer can serve as a model prayer for the global reconciliation that is needed today. In the wake of the post-9/11 attacks on America, it is time for sincere national prayer and acknowledgment of America's role in creating the kind of world where excessive capitalism, greed, hate, fear, and injustice are seen as fueling terrorism. Prayer is needed not only for the healing of our national wounds, but also for a national commitment to justice and the request for forgiveness for capitalistic arrogance and militaristic exploits in the world. Openness to God requires integrity about who we have been, who we are now, and what divine justice and love call for us to be in the future. The 9/11 attacks made the nation vulnerable as it has never been before; they created a sense of powerlessness that stripped away all pretenses about Americans' being in control and independent from the problems of those frustrated with western power. The nation paused on the tenth anniversary of the 9/11 tragedy to pray. Prayer opens us to God for our own healing and the healing of the world. Daniel's prayer under the conditions of exile can help us frame our prayers as we seek national healing and global reconciliation to the purposes of divine justice.

PRAYER

O God, many of us are weak and fearful in these trying times—when fear and hate combine to create a world of violence. We confess that we have been resistant to doing Your will. Divine compassion and mercy can only heal us and the world. Bless us with the courage and power to trust Your divine purpose. In Jesus' name we pray. Amen.

WORD POWER

Divine mercy—**flows from God in response to sincere prayers of confession. When nations pray for mercy, they must acknowledge their collective sins before God.**

HOME DAILY BIBLE READINGS
(March 4-10, 2013)

Daniel's Prayer

MONDAY, March 4: "Daniel's Resolve" (Daniel 1:8-15)
TUESDAY, March 5: "Daniel's Recognition" (Daniel 1:16-21)
WEDNESDAY, March 6: "The King's Challenge" (Daniel 2:1-11)
THURSDAY, March 7: "Daniel's Intervention" (Daniel 2:12-16)
FRIDAY, March 8: "Daniel's Success" (Daniel 2:36-49)
SATURDAY, March 9: "Daniel's Prayer of Supplication" (Daniel 9:15-19)
SUNDAY, March 10: "Daniel's Prayer of Confession" (Daniel 9:4b-14)

Reference

Pleins, J. David, *The Social Visions of the Hebrew Bible: A Theological Introduction*. Westminster John Knox Press, November 2000.

LESSON 3   March 17, 2013

GABRIEL'S INTERPRETATION

FAITH PATHWAY/FAITH JOURNEY TOPIC: **Dreams for a Better Tomorrow**

DEVOTIONAL READING: **Psalm 91:1-12**
PRINT PASSAGE: **Daniel 8:19-26**

BACKGROUND SCRIPTURE: **Daniel 8**
KEY VERSE: **Daniel 8:26**

Daniel 8:19-26—KJV

19 And he said, Behold, I will make thee know what shall be in the last end of the indignation: for at the time appointed the end shall be.

20 The ram which thou sawest having two horns are the kings of Media and Persia.

21 And the rough goat is the king of Grecia: and the great horn that is between his eyes is the first king.

22 Now that being broken, whereas four stood up for it, four kingdoms shall stand up out of the nation, but not in his power.

23 And in the latter time of their kingdom, when the transgressors are come to the full, a king of fierce countenance, and understanding dark sentences, shall stand up.

24 And his power shall be mighty, but not by his own power: and he shall destroy wonderfully, and shall prosper, and practise, and shall destroy the mighty and the holy people.

25 And through his policy also he shall cause craft to prosper in his hand; and he shall magnify himself in his heart, and by peace shall destroy many: he shall also stand up against the Prince of princes; but he shall be broken without hand.

26 And the vision of the evening and the morning which was told is true: wherefore shut thou up the vision; for it shall be for many days.

Daniel 8:19-26—NIV

19 He said: "I am going to tell you what will happen later in the time of wrath, because the vision concerns the appointed time of the end.

20 The two-horned ram that you saw represents the kings of Media and Persia.

21 The shaggy goat is the king of Greece, and the large horn between his eyes is the first king.

22 The four horns that replaced the one that was broken off represent four kingdoms that will emerge from his nation but will not have the same power.

23 In the latter part of their reign, when rebels have become completely wicked, a stern-faced king, a master of intrigue, will arise.

24 He will become very strong, but not by his own power. He will cause astounding devastation and will succeed in whatever he does. He will destroy the mighty men and the holy people.

25 He will cause deceit to prosper, and he will consider himself superior. When they feel secure, he will destroy many and take his stand against the Prince of princes. Yet he will be destroyed, but not by human power.

26 The vision of the evenings and mornings that has been given you is true, but seal up the vision, for it concerns the distant future."

UNIFYING LESSON PRINCIPLE

Hope points us toward the future. Where can we find help as we seek to discern what the future may hold for us? When he did not understand his vision, Daniel received help from Gabriel in order to clarify its meaning—though there were times when Daniel both knew about and interpreted dreams.

TOPICAL OUTLINE OF THE LESSON

I. Introduction
- A. Dreaming God's Dream
- B. Biblical Background

II. Exposition and Application of the Scripture
- A. Burdened with God's Dream (Daniel 8:19-22)
- B. The Rise and Fall of an Arrogant Leader (Daniel 8:23-25)
- C. Living with the Dream of God (Daniel 8:26)

III. Concluding Reflection

LESSON OBJECTIVES

Upon the completion of the lesson, the students will be able to do the following:

1. Analyze Daniel's vision and Gabriel's interpretation of the vision;

2. Express their uncertainties when trying to make decisions that affect their future; and,

3. Develop spiritual friendships with others who are seeking the kingdom of God.

POINTS TO BE EMPHASIZED

ADULT/YOUTH

Adult Topic: Dreams for a Better Tomorrow

Youth Topic: A Curious Dream

Adult Key Verse: Daniel 8:26

Youth Key Verse: Daniel 8:25

Print Passage: Daniel 8:19-26

—The Print Passage (8:19-26) is the explanation of Daniel's vision in 8:2-18.

—Gabriel is the "he" in verse 19, known as a messenger of God who also brought the announcement of the birth of Jesus to Mary.

—The message to Daniel was an interpretation of a vision that was about the end of time in the future.

—The passage has a historical context and is about a king (Antiochus IV Epiphanes) who would exalt himself against the Prince of princes (God) and would bring God's anger, wrath, and destruction.

—In the Bible, it is often stressed that God punishes arrogance and favors humility.

—God knows what the future holds and wants us to be warned and prepared.

—Even though God is in charge, God's people sometimes suffer.

CHILDREN

Children Topic: Daniel Receives Help to Understand His Dream

Key Verse: Daniel 8:15

Print Passage: Daniel 8:19-26

—After Daniel had seen a vision but did not understand it, Gabriel, the messenger of God, explained its meaning.

—Gabriel explained the meaning of the symbols in Daniel's dream.

—Antiochus IV, a powerful and harsh king who even rose up against God, was a major ruler described in Gabriel's interpretation.

—Because the vision related to the future, Daniel was told to keep the interpretation secret.

—Although he continued to do the king's business, Daniel still did not completely understand his vision.

I. INTRODUCTION

A. Dreaming God's Dream

The record of Daniel's apocalyptic dream or vision has become invaluable literature for understanding the ways in which people are drawn to visions that consider how the world as it *is* might become transformed into the world as it *ought* to be. These visions are driven by humanity's hunger for an alternative world and the determined hope for a new world of transformation and justice. Daniel's dream is a part of the persistent hope of God's people for a future where the sovereignty of God reigns and governs human affairs.

Dreaming God's dream fueled Daniel's quest to clarify the meaning of his vision for the future of God's people. Daniel got help from the angelic counsel of Gabriel, as he relied on God for an understanding of how his dream aligned with divine possibilities. As students reflect on this lesson, the questions will be raised, "What are we dreaming about? Are our dreams consistent with the dream of God?" Answers to these questions will only come when we dream the same dream as God.

B. Biblical Background

As we have seen in the book of Daniel, the Babylonian empire attempted to establish its sovereign rule against the sovereignty of God. Chapters 1–3 of the book of Daniel document how a pagan king, Nebuchadnezzar, came to acknowledge the role of God's sovereign power despite his misguided efforts to undermine Daniel's faith in God. In chapter 4, when Nebuchadnezzar could not interpret his dream, Daniel made it clear that the purpose of God would cause Nebuchadnezzar's deranged wanderings for seven years, which would ultimately lead to his acknowledgment of God. Nebuchadnezzar confessed the following: "At the end of that time, I, Nebuchadnezzar, raised my eyes toward heaven, and my sanity was restored. Then I praised the Most High; I honored and glorified him who lives forever. His dominion is an eternal dominion; his kingdom endures from generation to generation" (Daniel 4:34, NIV). This confession offers a political theology not unlike that of Joseph's in the book of Genesis, in which Pharaoh made Joseph head over the entire Egyptian nation—second only to himself.

God was triumphant over the edicts of the Babylonian empire through the deliverance of Daniel and his companions. The total assimilation of Daniel into the imperial rule and pagan life of the empire failed. What the future held was already appointed by God (see Daniel 8:19; 9:26-27; 11:35). Yet, the thing which would impact the future is yet a mystery. Do the deeds of the saints and the decisions of God actually affect the course of history? This question drove Daniel's dream of an alternative future and caused him (in chapter 8) to shift into the larger divine mysteries that would radically change the course and direction of God's people.

In chapter 8, Daniel's dream involved a complexity of symbols where a ram and the goat bearing a horn functioned as signs of other human kingdoms that he found difficult to interpret. Daniel was exhausted while contemplating the meaning of this dream: "It was beyond understanding" (verse 27, NIV). When burdened with dreaming God's dream, there were turning points of understanding that only God could help clarify. Daniel discovered this when the angelic assistance of Gabriel set forth the vision and focus of liberation for God's people.

II. EXPOSITION AND APPLICATION OF THE SCRIPTURE

A. Burdened with God's Dream
(Daniel 8:19-22)

And he said, Behold, I will make thee know what shall be in the last end of the indignation: for at the time appointed the end shall be. The ram which thou sawest having two horns are the kings of Media and Persia. And the rough goat is the king of Grecia: and the great horn that is between his eyes is the first king. Now that being broken, whereas four stood up for it, four kingdoms shall stand up out of the nation, but not in his power.

In Daniel 8, Daniel is seen to be exhausted and burdened with a dream whose mystery he cannot decipher. The symbols of the rams and goats in Daniel's dream point to animal-like creatures that fight by knocking and locking horns together. In other words, human rulers and kingdoms will inevitably and persistently lock horns with God's purpose. The main complexity of Daniel's dream was finding a way for the Exiles to survive the tumultuous time until they could reach God's kingdom. As students may recall in the previous lesson, Daniel's prayer in chapter 9 was predicated on a renewal of the covenant (see Daniel 9:4-19), which underscored Judah's past sin and its experience of exilic shame and curse, and the calling upon God for relief and forgiveness. Through devotion to God, Daniel had stood firm in the Exile experience. Here in chapter 8,

Daniel needed help to understand the meaning of his vision. First among the major frustrations of Daniel was perhaps the question of how long the desolation and dominance of empires would trump the future of God's people. How long would the abomination last which would make desolate God's people (see verse 13 in the Background Scripture)? How long would "truth be trampled underneath"?

The answer to the question of "how long?" is answered in Daniel 8:14. Despite the "evenings and mornings" left of Judah's suffering and oppression, the God of Daniel would prevail. The angel Gabriel came to Daniel's aid with the interpretation of the dream which had left Daniel exhausted and perplexed. Someone "like a person" broke in and gave Gabriel license to interpret the vision for Daniel. Daniel fell to the ground before the vision of Gabriel, and was told that his vision was for "the time of the end" (verse 17). This actually meant that Daniel already was living in the end time. The time of the end had already begun when the reigns of the succeeding kings of the Assyrian, Babylonian, Persian, and Seleucid empires would end. The time of the end then began; God's purpose was on the move.

The "how long?" question did not only rest

with the burden of Daniel's dream, but was the question asked by both oppressed communities in centuries past and impoverished people today who wonder why they bear the uneven load of human suffering. How long will military and political entities usurp vital human resources—pitting humans against humans? As seen in the book of Daniel, imperial designs of power will not outlast the sovereignty of God. Today's conventions and military regimes respect, honor, and memorialize generals and presidents as the chief actors of history. But the burden of God's dream is a burden that rests upon the shoulders of dreamers for a new world, when nations will have no need to study war anymore. The prevailing dream is that ultimately the instruments of war will be turned into "pruning hooks and plowshares" for an everlasting peace.

Even so, with this kind of apocalyptic hope, Daniel and the exiles would have to endure the period of wrath/indignation associated with the wrath of God. This day of divine anger would also be a day of judgment that eventually brings salvation (see Isaiah 30:27). Whatever the nature of the "wrath" turns out to be, it will end the tyranny of empires that are resistant to God's purpose. The exilic conditions of Daniel's community can be understood as a period of the wrath of God. The idea of God's wrath was rooted in Judaism—that "we brought this upon ourselves by rejecting God and God's prophets." Today, we must resist the temptation of seeing the suffering of oppressed people as punishment from God for sin. Yet, in our caution to prevent this serious theological mistake of portraying God as an angry scorekeeper of sins, we must not overlook the fact that contributing to global conditions of suffering and systemic evil is the reality of

humanity's rejection of God's will. We, like Daniel, bear the burden of God's dream, and, in doing so, we must sometimes realize that God may use pagan empires that are alien to suit His divine purpose to bring about divine change in the world.

B. The Rise and Fall of an Arrogant Leader (Daniel 8:23-25)

And in the latter time of their kingdom, when the transgressors are come to the full, a king of fierce countenance, and understanding dark sentences, shall stand up. And his power shall be mighty, but not by his own power: and he shall destroy wonderfully, and shall prosper, and practise, and shall destroy the mighty and the holy people. And through his policy also he shall cause craft to prosper in his hand; and he shall magnify himself in his heart, and by peace shall destroy many: he shall also stand up against the Prince of princes; but he shall be broken without hand.

Around the globe today, we witness tyrants and dictators falling from power. When human kingdoms collide with God's kingdom, the human kingdoms will come to ruin. The rise and fall of Antiochus IV is an example of a benign paternal figure who assumed that his power was superior to God's. But what we have seen in the witness of Hebrew history is that God ultimately deconstructs all "Pharaohs" who position themselves to mimic God. Antiochus IV's career came to the full measure of transgression and arrogance. Antiochus IV emerged from the four kingdoms as the most politically powerful king; he used skilled intrigue to advance his power. He created internal division among the Jews by aligning himself with certain factions of the people. But in the vision of Daniel, although he would become strong, the power of Antiochus IV would fail. Skilled political intrigue is a strategy which many politicians use today to divide vulnerable communities. Politicians show up in black church pulpits during campaign seasons to dump their politically honed sound bytes that at best are superficial and fall flat in addressing the political substance of black people's lives. Yet, the burden of God's dream rests with the aspirations and hopes of the people whom black churches serve, whose dreams are larger than what conservative politics can imagine or possibly deliver. Like the angelic "holy people" in the book of Daniel (see verse 24), many people are social, political, spiritual, and Christian dreamers for a better world. They do more good in the trenches of oppression doing the unglamorous day-to-day work of liberation than do those who reside in palaces of untenable politics.

The arrogance of Antiochus IV was unparalleled in his ancient setting of power. He believed himself to be too powerful to be defeated, and that he was a skilled manager of power who got his way no matter what the impact on and outcome of the lives of others might be. Even the "Prince of princes" (verse 25) would be no match for him—he thought. The lack of civility and the breakdown of respectable decorum in our national government indicate an appalling arrogance that threatens to bring down our nation. Sophisticated and armed with war-making skills and patriotic notions of wealth and power, many of our national politicians are driven by animalistic intentions, like that of Antiochus IV, to achieve their ends by any means necessary—even if it brings down the entire nation. The book of Daniel portrays such leadership as ultimately falling victim to the kind of hubris (pride) that goes before destruction.

C. Living with the Dream of God (Daniel 8:26)

And the vision of the evening and the morning which was told is true: wherefore shut thou up the vision; for it shall be for many days.

Daniel was instructed to seal up or not reveal the vision he had received in his dream. Keeping the integrity of a dream sometimes requires that it be hidden until the time is ripe for its exposure. Joseph learned this lesson the hard way. In Daniel's case, it was a matter of broadening and deepening his understanding of the implications of his vision; so he was instructed to seal the dream in secret. Indeed, this increasingly becomes a burden when the political environment in which one lives continually calls for the active power of God to create a better world. This must have had a great impact upon Daniel as he went about the daily chores of the king's business as a palace servant, knowing that the king's power had already been taken away. Daniel's dream was in the in between time of "already, but not yet." This causes one to wonder about black mothers and fathers who worked as domestic helpers and laborers with secret, vital dreams of liberation hidden in their hearts. They dared not speak of their dreams in a hostile racial climate of second-class citizenship that made dangerous any exposure of their dreams. This caused anxiety and sometimes led to deep despair as those dreams were deferred again and again. But they, like Daniel, pressed on with the burden of a dream larger than oppression and more powerful than the nightmare of injustice in the community. Our ancestors pressed on, and so must we. Daniel's response to his community's exilic crisis was indicative of his being receptive to God's dream. So Daniel kept dreaming. He lived with the assurance that in the end God's dream would ultimately win. Against all the problems of a world that resisted in every way the dream of God, Daniel's faithfulness and loyalty to God should inspire us to live the dream of God every day.

III. CONCLUDING REFLECTION

Our modern political entities pretend that mistakes do not have consequences, whether they are errors in personal choices, misguided national policies, or worldwide environmental negligence. We must remember that the consequences of sin belong to us, not to God. It was the dream of God that enabled and inspired persons like Martin Luther King Jr., Dorothy Height, Dorothy Day, Howard Thurman, Barack Obama, and the many unheralded heroes of justice to burden their lives with a dream that was larger than their personal ambitions for success. As the first person of color to be called the "commander in chief," when Barack Obama was elected president of the United States, he symbolically carried the dreams for God's justice into the executive branch of American government. For sure, the burden of that dream rests with his presidency every day.

PRAYER

O God, our burdens are heavy with dreams of justice for this world. Your divine dream remains in our hearts. Help us live the dream and become manifestations of the dream that You have in Your heart for us. In Jesus' name we pray. Amen.

WORD POWER

Dream [n]—a state of mind characterized by abstraction and release from reality; "he went about his work as if in a dream;" [n] a series of mental images and emotions occurring during sleep; "I had a dream about you last night."
Vision; imagine—the faculty or state of being able to see; the ability to think about or plan the future with imagination or wisdom. A mental image of what the future will or could be like.

HOME DAILY BIBLE READINGS
(March 11-17, 2013)

Gabriel's Interpretation

MONDAY, March 11: "A Guide into the Future" (Exodus 23:20-25)
TUESDAY, March 12: "A Messenger of Rebuke" (Judges 2:1-5)
WEDNESDAY, March 13: "A Messenger with Good News" (Luke 1:8-20)
THURSDAY, March 14: "A Messenger from God" (Luke 1:26-38)
FRIDAY, March 15: "A Helper in Understanding" (Daniel 8:13-18)
SATURDAY, March 16: "A Helper in Response to Prayer" (Daniel 9:20-27)
SUNDAY, March 17: "A Helper in Facing the Future" (Daniel 8:19-26)

Reference
Pleins, J. David, *The Social Visions of the Hebrew Bible: A Theological Introduction.* 2001.

LESSON 4   March 24, 2013 (Palm Sunday)

THE LORD'S SUPPER

FAITH PATHWAY/FAITH JOURNEY TOPIC: The Privilege of Serving

DEVOTIONAL READING: **1 Corinthians 10:14-22**   BACKGROUND SCRIPTURE: **Luke 22:14-30**
PRINT PASSAGE: **Luke 22:14-30**   KEY VERSE: **Luke 22:26**

Luke 22:14-30—KJV

14 And when the hour was come, he sat down, and the twelve apostles with him.

15 And he said unto them, With desire I have desired to eat this passover with you before I suffer:

16 For I say unto you, I will not any more eat thereof, until it be fulfilled in the kingdom of God.

17 And he took the cup, and gave thanks, and said, Take this, and divide it among yourselves:

18 For I say unto you, I will not drink of the fruit of the vine, until the kingdom of God shall come.

19 And he took bread, and gave thanks, and brake it, and gave unto them, saying, This is my body which is given for you: this do in remembrance of me.

20 Likewise also the cup after supper, saying, This cup is the new testament in my blood, which is shed for you.

21 But, behold, the hand of him that betrayeth me is with me on the table.

22 And truly the Son of man goeth, as it was determined: but woe unto that man by whom he is betrayed!

23 And they began to enquire among themselves, which of them it was that should do this thing.

24 And there was also a strife among them, which of them should be accounted the greatest.

25 And he said unto them, The kings of the Gentiles exercise lordship over them; and they that exercise authority upon them are called benefactors.

26 But ye shall not be so: but he that is greatest among you, let him be as the younger; and he that is chief, as he that doth serve.

27 For whether is greater, he that sitteth at meat, or he that serveth? is not he that sitteth at meat? but I am among you as he that serveth.

Luke 22:14-30—NIV

14 When the hour came, Jesus and his apostles reclined at the table.

15 And he said to them, "I have eagerly desired to eat this Passover with you before I suffer.

16 For I tell you, I will not eat it again until it finds fulfillment in the kingdom of God."

17 After taking the cup, he gave thanks and said, "Take this and divide it among you.

18 For I tell you I will not drink again of the fruit of the vine until the kingdom of God comes."

19 And he took bread, gave thanks and broke it, and gave it to them, saying, "This is my body given for you; do this in remembrance of me."

20 In the same way, after the supper he took the cup, saying, "This cup is the new covenant in my blood, which is poured out for you.

21 But the hand of him who is going to betray me is with mine on the table.

22 The Son of Man will go as it has been decreed, but woe to that man who betrays him."

23 They began to question among themselves which of them it might be who would do this.

24 Also a dispute arose among them as to which of them was considered to be greatest.

25 Jesus said to them, "The kings of the Gentiles lord it over them; and those who exercise authority over them call themselves Benefactors.

26 But you are not to be like that. Instead, the greatest among you should be like the youngest, and the one who rules like the one who serves.

27 For who is greater, the one who is at the table or the one who serves? Is it not the one who is at the table? But I am among you as one who serves.

UNIFYING LESSON PRINCIPLE

Humans seek to exaggerate their own importance. How can we overcome the burning desire to serve ourselves first and others later? Jesus says that those who serve others will eat the bread and sip the wine at the table He has set for them in heaven.

28 Ye are they which have continued with me in my temptations.

29 And I appoint unto you a kingdom, as my Father hath appointed unto me;

30 That ye may eat and drink at my table in my kingdom, and sit on thrones judging the twelve tribes of Israel.

28 You are those who have stood by me in my trials.

29 And I confer on you a kingdom, just as my Father conferred one on me,

30 so that you may eat and drink at my table in my kingdom and sit on thrones, judging the twelve tribes of Israel."

TOPICAL OUTLINE OF THE LESSON

I. Introduction

    A. A Model of Service

    B. Biblical Background

II. Exposition and Application of the Scripture

    A. The Sacred Meal (Luke 22:14-16)

    B. Sharing the Sacred Meal (Luke 22:17-30)

III. Concluding Reflection

LESSON OBJECTIVES

Upon the completion of the lesson, the students will understand the following:

1. The connection between the Lord's Supper and Jesus' teaching on service;

2. The ideal value and kingdom principle of serving others in contrast to being served; and,

3. The spiritual role of humility in the life of Christians, as exemplified by Christ.

POINTS TO BE EMPHASIZED

ADULT/YOUTH

Adult Topic: The Privilege of Serving

Youth Topic: A Lesson in Service

Adult/Youth Key Verse: Luke 22:26

Print Passage: Luke 22:14-30

—The account of the Last Supper is also found in Matthew 26; Mark 14; and 1 Corinthians 11. Luke's account alone mentions a cup before the loaf (as well as the one after).

—Jesus yearned to have His last Passover meal with His disciples.

—The "is" in verse 19 signifies a comparison of God's redemption of Israel from Egyptian bondage with the deliverance of believers from the bondage of sin through Christ's atonement.

—Jesus set the example of true servant leadership for us to follow.

—Jesus knew who would betray Him, yet He still fellowshipped with this person.

—Jesus invites us to fellowship with Him in His kingdom.

—Jesus instituted communion as an act of remembrance for His church to follow.

CHILDREN

Children Topic: Serving Others

Key Verse: Luke 22:27c

Print Passage: Luke 22:14-30

—Jesus was eager to have a time of fellowship with His apostles before He suffered.

—Jesus thanked God for the cup and for the bread, and He shared them with the apostles.

—In preparing the apostles for His death, Jesus distributed the bread and compared it to His body—and compared the wine to His blood.

—When Jesus said His betrayer was present, the apostles began to wonder who it was.

—When the apostles began to argue about who would be greatest among them, Jesus taught them that the greatest among them would not be the one who was served, but the one who served.

I. INTRODUCTION

A. A Model of Service

Christian service today, modeled after Jesus' example, calls for the church to be engaged in ministering to the lives of the poor and oppressed around the world. The cries of the marginalized and poor are heard and seen in our global village. The kind of service Jesus modeled for us calls for us to respond not only with charity, but also with justice. Children die by the thousands from diseases related to malnutrition; yet elsewhere, food is wasted and milk and grain are destroyed, while resources are hijacked in order to provide luxuries and to produce weapons of annihilation.

Jesus' model of service mandated more than individual charity—it called for love in the service of justice. The cries of the poor from human subjugation and marginalization are fueled by inhumane economic manipulation and twisted politics. Those cries need the attention of Christian churches everywhere, whose ministries follow Jesus—who came "not to be ministered unto, but to minister" (Matthew 20:28).

Jesus, as we shall discover in the study of this lesson, saw life as an opportunity for God's love to be glorified through service to others. Jesus declared in deed and in word that the purpose of His coming was to give life in abundance and fullness to everyone. The love of God expressed in service was the basis of His life and teachings. The marginalized of Jesus' ancient world—the lame, the blind, the widows, and the poor—were welcomed to sit with Jesus at communal meals. In Jesus' spirituality, everything God created should be in the service of uplifting the unity of life. Jesus saw the laws of the empire and the laws and ritual customs of religion (Judaism) in the light of love in the service of God's kingdom. It was this theological mindset that created tremendous tension by the time Jesus sat down to eat the Passover meal with His disciples.

As the political tensions surrounding Jesus' public ministry mounted, Jesus yearned to have solitude with His disciples. Preparation for the Passover meal provided Jesus with the appropriate setting to once again confirm His communal ties with the disciples and deepen their understanding of His ultimate vision of the kingdom of God. During the Passover meal, Jesus set an example of true servant leadership for the disciples to follow. The political tension surrounding Jesus' ministry was intense, and many debates broke out among the disciples regarding the political implications and impact of Jesus' teachings on their future. Jesus remained focused on the core spiritual quality of service to others. Jesus knew the struggles that the disciples were having with the worldly power as they sought positions of authority in His kingdom. They thought Jesus' vision of the kingdom of God would mimic the authority of the kingdoms of the world. Jesus also knew who would betray and deny Him during this intense time of political uncertainty. Despite these challenges, Jesus still was, as a servant leader, open to all the disciples, teaching them that the kingdom of God was not like the authority and power of the rulers of the Roman Empire. Jesus took on the disposition of a servant to illustrate the humility, love, and communal qualities present in the kingdom of God. Everything Jesus did pointed to the power of love to bring justice, compassion, and liberation. On the Jericho road, in the town of Samaria, in leper colonies, and at meals with sinners and publicans, Jesus' love illuminated possibilities for those who hungered for a new existence.

B. Biblical Background

Scriptural accounts of the Last Supper or Passover meal are found in Matthew 26; Mark 14; and 1 Corinthians 11. From Luke's account, it appears that the Lord's Supper preceded Jesus' prediction of the betrayal by Judas. A reading of the gospels of Matthew and Mark suggest that the prediction came first.

The significance of this is seen in the gospel of John, in which Judas's departure from the group appears to have come immediately after the prediction. While this raises the question of whether Judas partook of the Lord's Supper, Jesus remained focused on the communal love He shared with His disciples and the impact this would have on them as servants in the kingdom of God. Not only was the issue of Jesus' betrayal a topic at the meal, but also the political tension among the disciples regarding positions in Jesus' kingdom distracted the disciples from Jesus' teachings about the nature and character of the kingdom of God. Jesus' response when James and John asked for special positions (see Matthew 20:25-28; Mark 10:42-45) was very similar to the language in Luke 22:25-27. During the course of Jesus' public ministry, Jesus and the disciples had shared many semiprivate meals together, often behind closed doors in rooms lit with oil lamps. The nature of these meals changed over time, as they acquired a revolutionary meaning and became associated with Jesus' prediction of His suffering and death. When Jesus spoke of sharing His "blood" and His "flesh," He was keenly aware that a servant's life committed to God's kingdom called for life's ultimate sacrifice. In His passion to convey the reality of the kingdom of God to His disciples, Jesus used the Passover meal as a prototype of what is now called the Last Supper, Holy Communion, the Lord's Supper, or the Eucharist. During His Last Supper with the disciples, Jesus endowed the meal with a significance that would underlie the fundamental meaning of the kingdom of God—love and justice in the service of God. Jesus willingly gave Himself as a sacrifice in this divine service.

In the study of this lesson, students should pay particular attention to the connection between the sacred offering of food (the Lord's Supper) and Jesus' offering of Himself as a sacrifice, which expressed the meaning of new life and solidarity with God's kingdom.

II. EXPOSITION AND APPLICATION OF THE SCRIPTURE

A. The Sacred Meal
(Luke 22:14-16)

And when the hour was come, he sat down, and the twelve apostles with him. And he said unto them, With desire I have desired to eat this passover with you before I suffer: For I say unto you, I will not any more eat thereof, until it be fulfilled in the kingdom of God.

New Testament biblical commentators agree that no other act of worship has moved the church through the centuries as much as following Jesus' command to "eat the bread and drink the cup" of the new covenant. When the church institutes what is known as the Lord's Last Supper, it stands in the midst of a divine mystery—as it relates to the life and sacrifice of Jesus. Over the course of His three-year ministry, Jesus' commitment to the righteousness and service of love grew to become the signal vision of His preaching and teaching. Jesus became the very essence of that which He taught, which in turn became the full embodiment of His commitment to the kingdom of God. So when Jesus spoke to His disciples about His body and blood, He was emphasizing the significance of His becoming a sacrifice on behalf of God's kingdom, a reality that had not yet come to fruition, but was present in Him. When Jesus shared wine and bread in the celebration and presence of the new kingdom, He believed that God was delighted in His willingness to become a bodily sacrifice, and that His unselfish offering was more significant than the animal sacrifice presented to the priest on the altar of the Temple. Thus, in the offering of His body and blood, Jesus sought to illustrate to His disciples God's approval of His own life as an eternal sacrifice for the kingdom of God.

The gospel of Luke, more than with any other gospel, showed the significant role that the eating of meals played in Jesus' ministry. The gospel highlights the fact that the hour for eating the Passover meal came close to the same hours of crisis that led up to Jesus' arrest and crucifixion. Luke's account of the Passover meal shows Jesus and His disciples reclining as they shared the ceremonial feast of the Passover. On many previous occasions, the act of eating together cemented Jesus' fellowship with the disciples and with many of those considered outcasts in the community. By eating with the outcasts, Jesus demonstrated His solidarity with them; He gave to them a new existence—that is, a life of love and service in the kingdom of God. Many of these meals Jesus had with His disciples and with outcasts were considered to be fellowship meals, when Jesus crossed social barriers and embodied the love of God for the poor and helpless.

During the Passover meal, Jesus reminded the disciples that they were to love and serve one another. Jesus turned the ceremonial Passover meal into a sacred altar upon which He would become a sacrifice for the new life in God's kingdom. Jesus said to the disciples, "I have desired to eat this Passover with you before I suffer" (verse 15). The *New Interpreter's*

Bible points out that when Jesus said "before I suffer," the words were a reference to His death. The Greek verb "to suffer" is nearly the same as the word for "Passover." During the Passover meal, Jesus' willingness to suffer gave Him a distinction of self-giving service to God's kingdom that none of His disciples had anticipated in their relationships with Jesus. Jesus Himself became the Passover (see 1 Corinthians 5:7). Service to others in the life of God's kingdom was seen as a sacred privilege. In later centuries, the Lord's Supper became a rich symbol of privileged service in the new covenant, which brings spiritual renewal in the kingdom of God.

B. Sharing the Sacred Meal
(Luke 22:17-30)

And he took the cup, and gave thanks, and said, Take this, and divide it among yourselves: For I say unto you, I will not drink of the fruit of the vine, until the kingdom of God shall come. And he took bread, and gave thanks, and brake it, and gave unto them, saying, This is my body which is given for you: this do in remembrance of me. Likewise also the cup after supper, saying, This cup is the new testament in my blood, which is shed for you. But, behold, the hand of him that betrayeth me is with me on the table. And truly the Son of man goeth, as it was determined: but woe unto that man by whom he is betrayed! And they began to enquire among themselves, which of them it was that should do this thing. And there was also a strife among them, which of them should be accounted the greatest. And he said unto them, The kings of the Gentiles exercise lordship over them; and they that exercise authority upon them are called benefactors. But ye shall not be so: but he that is greatest among you, let him be as the younger; and he that is chief, as he that doth serve. For whether is greater, he that sitteth at meat, or he that serveth? is not he that sitteth at meat? but I am among you as he that serveth. Ye are they which have continued with me in my temptations. And I appoint unto you a kingdom, as my Father hath appointed unto me;

That ye may eat and drink at my table in my kingdom, and sit on thrones judging the twelve tribes of Israel.

As an act of worship, Christians should recognize that Jesus is the Passover sacrifice who willingly gave His life that we might have life in the kingdom of God. The elements of the Lord's Supper speak of the great sacrifice and ultimate degree of what Jesus did to bring us back into a relationship with the Father. After sharing the Passover meal with His disciples, Jesus found the disciples disputing among themselves about positions of greatness in the kingdom. The disciples had theologically misunderstood both the implications and meaning of the Passover meal—as it related to Jesus' life as a willing sacrifice for God's kingdom. Just as the apostle Paul sought to correct the inappropriate behavior of the Corinthian church in regard to the Lord's Supper (see 1 Corinthians 11:17-22), Jesus made clear to His disciples that eating the Passover meal in remembrance of Him should inspire unity and love among them. Christians should partake of the Lord's Supper, recognizing its significance and what it cost Jesus. The celebration of the Lord's Supper is a celebration of Jesus' presence now, and an affirmation of the hope that we shall eat and drink with Jesus in the kingdom of God.

The experience of the Lord's Supper spans the breadth of God's love, the depth of Jesus' suffering, and the past, present, and future of God's acts of love. The challenge for the Christian church is to open itself to the full extent of Jesus' love to transform us and create spiritual power and intimacy for service and love to others.

The highest privilege of Christian life is

to serve. We learn from Jesus that greatness is achieved through service, not through positions and titles of authority. If someone wants to be great, Martin Luther King Jr. (in following Jesus) said, "Love your enemies and service with a heart of love."

III. CONCLUDING REFLECTION

Service to others is central to the Christian witness in the world. Jesus took a basin of water and a towel and washed His disciples' feet. Jesus' washing of the disciples' feet is an object lesson for the self-giving service of Christian love. The world in which we live has been described as "a world of capitalism without a human face." In such a world, the poor are expendable; they are rendered invisible because they are deemed insignificant liabilities to a system that does not love them. Jesus faced the same reality as He saw how both Roman Empire and the legalism of Judaism had rendered people as loveless cases of uncompassionate politics. Each time the Lord's Supper is shared and celebrated among Christians, it ought to consciously remind us of how the Lord's sacrificial love opened up to us God's transformation and salvation. It ought to be done in the remembrance of Christ's selfless love of service. It ought to renew us in the love of Jesus, who was crucified by the injustice of a powerful empire. Jesus' broken body and shed blood are symbols of how far the love of God is willing to go in order to lift our humanity to the heights of God's love.

PRAYER

Lord, You gave love to us so that we can know Your love for us. Thank You. We pray that the love Your Son sacrificially gave to us will cause us to remain in the service of Your kingdom. In Jesus' name we pray. Amen.

WORD POWER

Resurrection—a rising from the dead, or coming back to life; the state of having risen from the dead.

Serve/Service—to perform duties or services for (another person or an organization).

HOME DAILY BIBLE READINGS
(March 18-24, 2013)

The Lord's Supper

MONDAY, March 18: "Keeping the Passover to the Lord" (Deuteronomy 16:1-8)
TUESDAY, March 19: "What Does This Observance Mean?" (Exodus 12:21-27)
WEDNESDAY, March 20: "Preparations for the Last Supper" (Luke 22:7-13)
THURSDAY, March 21: "Partaking of the Lord's Table" (1 Corinthians 10:14-22)
FRIDAY, March 22: "Showing Contempt for the Church" (1 Corinthians 11:17-22)
SATURDAY, March 23: "Examine Yourselves" (1 Corinthians 11:23-32)
SUNDAY, March 24: "The Last Supper" (Luke 22:14-30)

LESSON 5   March 31, 2013 (Easter)

THE LORD HAS RISEN INDEED!

FAITH PATHWAY/FAITH JOURNEY TOPIC: **Hope Restored**

DEVOTIONAL READING: **Luke 24:22-26**   BACKGROUND SCRIPTURE: **Luke 24:1-35**
PRINT PASSAGE: **Luke 24:13-21, 28-35**   KEY VERSE: **Luke 24:31**

Luke 24:13-21, 28-35—KJV

13 And, behold, two of them went that same day to a village called Emmaus, which was from Jerusalem about threescore furlongs.

14 And they talked together of all these things which had happened.

15 And it came to pass, that, while they communed together and reasoned, Jesus himself drew near, and went with them.

16 But their eyes were holden that they should not know him.

17 And he said unto them, What manner of communications are these that ye have one to another, as ye walk, and are sad?

18 And the one of them, whose name was Cleopas, answering said unto him, Art thou only a stranger in Jerusalem, and hast not known the things which are come to pass there in these days?

19 And he said unto them, What things? And they said unto him, Concerning Jesus of Nazareth, which was a prophet mighty in deed and word before God and all the people:

20 And how the chief priests and our rulers delivered him to be condemned to death, and have crucified him.

21 But we trusted that it had been he which should have redeemed Israel: and beside all this, to day is the third day since these things were done.

.....

28 And they drew nigh unto the village, whither they went: and he made as though he would have gone further.

29 But they constrained him, saying, Abide with us: for it is toward evening, and the day is far spent. And he went in to tarry with them.

Luke 24:13-21, 28-35—NIV

13 Now that same day two of them were going to a village called Emmaus, about seven miles from Jerusalem.

14 They were talking with each other about everything that had happened.

15 As they talked and discussed these things with each other, Jesus himself came up and walked along with them;

16 but they were kept from recognizing him.

17 He asked them, "What are you discussing together as you walk along?" They stood still, their faces downcast.

18 One of them, named Cleopas, asked him, "Are you only a visitor to Jerusalem and do not know the things that have happened there in these days?"

19 "What things?" he asked. "About Jesus of Nazareth," they replied. "He was a prophet, powerful in word and deed before God and all the people.

20 The chief priests and our rulers handed him over to be sentenced to death, and they crucified him;

21 but we had hoped that he was the one who was going to redeem Israel. And what is more, it is the third day since all this took place."

.....

28 As they approached the village to which they were going, Jesus acted as if he were going farther.

29 But they urged him strongly, "Stay with us, for it is nearly evening; the day is almost over." So he went in to stay with them.

UNIFYING LESSON PRINCIPLE

Sometimes humans are/get caught up in their sense of gloom and despair. How can we be encouraged to see and take advantage of the good news surrounding us? Jesus opened the eyes of two followers whom He encountered on the road to Emmaus, and they recognized that Jesus had risen.

30 And it came to pass, as he sat at meat with them, he took bread, and blessed it, and brake, and gave to them.
31 And their eyes were opened, and they knew him; and he vanished out of their sight.
32 And they said one to another, Did not our heart burn within us, while he talked with us by the way, and while he opened to us the scriptures?
33 And they rose up the same hour, and returned to Jerusalem, and found the eleven gathered together, and them that were with them,
34 Saying, The Lord is risen indeed, and hath appeared to Simon.
35 And they told what things were done in the way, and how he was known of them in breaking of bread.

30 When he was at the table with them, he took bread, gave thanks, broke it and began to give it to them.
31 Then their eyes were opened and they recognized him, and he disappeared from their sight.
32 They asked each other, "Were not our hearts burning within us while he talked with us on the road and opened the Scriptures to us?"
33 They got up and returned at once to Jerusalem. There they found the Eleven and those with them, assembled together
34 and saying, "It is true! The Lord has risen and has appeared to Simon."
35 Then the two told what had happened on the way, and how Jesus was recognized by them when he broke the bread.

TOPICAL OUTLINE OF THE LESSON

I. Introduction

   A. A Life-changing Event

   B. Biblical Background

II. Exposition and Application of the Scripture

   A. The Resurrection: Fact or Fiction? (Luke 24:13-18)

   B. A Life-changing Question (Luke 24:19-21)

   C. Sharing a Meal with New Understanding (Luke 24:28-35)

III. Concluding Reflection

LESSON OBJECTIVES

Upon the completion of the lesson, the students will be able to do the following:

1. Review the story of the walk to Emmaus by Cleopas and the other disciple, who had a life-changing meeting with the risen Lord;

2. Identify with the travelers on the Emmaus road in order to raise their awareness of the places Jesus met them in their personal journeys; and,

3. Celebrate the risen Christ in the most jubilant way imaginable.

POINTS TO BE EMPHASIZED

ADULT/YOUTH

Adult Topic: Hope Restored
Youth Topic: A Mystery Guest
Adult Key Verse: Luke 24:31
Youth Key Verse: Luke 24:15
Print Passage: Luke 24:13-21, 28-35

—Two disciples set out for Emmaus; on the way, they discussed the life and crucifixion of their friend, Jesus.

—Jesus appeared and walked with the disciples, but they did not recognize Him.

—The two disciples explained to Jesus all they had seen, experienced, and felt.

—Jesus used the Scriptures to explain to the disciples His mission as the Messiah.

—After Jesus broke bread with the two disciples, they recognized Him, and then He disappeared.

—The two disciples rushed back to Jerusalem and testified that Jesus was alive.

CHILDREN
Children Topic: Jesus Appears!

Key Verse: Luke 24:34

Print Passage: Luke 24:13-21, 28-35

—While two disciples walked to Emmaus talking about the death of Jesus and the stories that He had risen, Jesus appeared and walked with them; however, the disciples did not recognize Jesus.

—When Jesus asked what they were talking about, they told Him the whole story.

—When they arrived at Emmaus, Jesus stayed with the disciples.

—As Jesus broke bread and blessed it, the disciples recognized Him; then suddenly He vanished.

—The apostles returned to Jerusalem immediately and told the others what had happened.

I. INTRODUCTION
A. A Life-changing Event

Many people today are struggling to define the meaning of Christianity as it is associated with the life, death, and resurrection of Jesus Christ. What is life-changing about the life of Jesus? Troubled teenagers are asking how they can believe in God when there is so much evil in the world. What relevance does Jesus have in a culture of consumerism, where Christianity is in decline and considered by many as not to be needed?

One could imagine that the two persons who traveled home to Emmaus after the crucifixion of Jesus had questions about the meaning of the life of Jesus for their future. The two disciples who set out for Emmaus after Jesus' brutal murder were devastated by Jesus' death. They believed that Jesus was the Promised Messiah, the ancient hope for redeeming/restoring the power and political prominence to Israel. They glorified Jesus' life as an earthly political king upon whom depended the hope of Israel's future. The disciples believed that Jesus' action would restore the kingdom to the Jews. One can see why the disciples were completely dismayed by and fled the scene of Jesus' crucifixion, because they had not counted on Jesus' suffering a Roman crucifixion. The complexity of their questions and struggle for meaning opened them up for a life-changing event that they had not anticipated.

Each year at Easter, Christian churches face similar questions as the two disciples of Emmaus: What does the life of Jesus mean for us? How do we approach the meaning of the Easter experience—the hope of resurrection? Luke 24 invites us to share in the stories of the disciples as they travelled to Emmaus.

B. Biblical Background

After the Transfiguration, when Jesus had taken His place alongside Moses and Elijah by the divine Throne, the topic of the Resurrection was prominently a part of His teachings. By the time of the Passover meal, His teaching on the Resurrection had emerged as the core meaning of hope and life in the kingdom of God (see Matthew 22:29-32; Mark 12:24-27; Luke 20:34-38). Jesus identified His resurrection within the promise of God through the enduring lives of the patriarchs and prophets of Israel (Moses and Elijah).

The fear and pressure of the events leading up to Jesus' crucifixion and the grim suffering that Jesus experienced on the Cross intensified the disciples' understanding of Jesus' mystical spirituality and sharpened their vision of the spirit world in which Jesus lived. The horror of the Crucifixion magnified their transformed consciousness and gave them a common point of focus as they met together, meditated, and prayed. As the two disciples in the text journeyed, they were brought face-to-face with the Lord. This encounter followed the experience at the tomb, and the question of what became of Jesus' physical body was never answered for them. They fled from the spot, trembling. The stone had been moved away from the tomb's entrance. When the angelic young man said to the women, "Why do you seek the living among the dead?" (see Luke 24:5), the event we call the Resurrection was born in the faith of the disciples and in the hearts of future believers.

II. EXPOSITION AND APPLICATION OF THE SCRIPTURE

A. The Resurrection: Fact or Fiction?
(Luke 24:13-18)

And, behold, two of them went that same day to a village called Emmaus, which was from Jerusalem about threescore furlongs. And they talked together of all these things which had happened. And it came to pass, that, while they communed together and reasoned, Jesus himself drew near, and went with them. But their eyes were holden that they should not know him. And he said unto them, What manner of communications are these that ye have one to another, as ye walk, and are sad? And the one of them, whose name was Cleopas, answering said unto him, Art thou only a stranger in Jerusalem, and hast not known the things which are come to pass there in these days?

Jesus never allowed the disciples to forget His mortality; His suffering and crucifixion were intimate parts of His teachings. The foreboding possibility of a violent death persisted—with Jesus' platform of a divine kingdom of love and justice looming large as a political threat to the Roman Empire. In the view of His mortality, the Resurrection symbols we find in the gospels became an intrinsic part of Jesus' self-understanding, especially toward the end of His life. The disciples were basically in denial of Jesus' announcement of His crucifixion. Peter vigorously rejected it, saying, "Be it far from you." But Jesus knew the cause for which He was sent into the world, and the meaning of His life could not be fully understood without an understanding of the meaning of His death and resurrection.

The Easter reality is one of hope, but it is hope born through the crucible and in the face of suffering. What we should note from this lesson is that the vision of God's kingdom was instilled in the minds of the disciples, yet its possibilities threatened them as much as it inspired them with divine possibilities of change and transformation.

Much had happened in Jerusalem which caused the two disciples on the road to Emmaus much confusion and anxiety. The central figure and hero of their hope had been brutally murdered. They and all the other disciples fled the scene of crucifixion in fear. They were confused and defeated. Just a few days before the Crucifixion, a grand parade welcomed Jesus to what they believed was to be His seat of power. Then, that promising beginning was taken away by the Roman authorities, and a mob-like crowd of Jewish antagonists spoke against His teachings, shouting, "Crucify Him." There had been a number of disastrous confrontations with the authorities and other Jewish leaders who seemed determined to eliminate Jesus by whatever means necessary. After the arrest of Jesus, the thickness of fear spread. Palace police were anxiously on the lookout for all who were associated with Jesus. So the disciples, including the two disciples from Emmaus, fled. Jesus' death was necessary for the maintenance of the status quo of the Empire. His movement was considered a subversive plot to fuel a revolution that Roman authorities would not tolerate.

But to the surprise of the disciples, the third day after His crucifixion, confusing rumors broke out about Jesus' resurrection from the dead. Some women had gone to the tomb and reported that the body was missing. To some it seemed to be an idle tale, but for the disciples on the Emmaus road and others in hiding, it deepened their fears and prompted questions about what it meant. They began to reflect on the meaning of *resurrection*. The Romans represented a world more organized for death than for life. The hope of resurrection

conveyed to the disciples a reversal of such a world into justice and life-giving peace. "What does this mean?"

The overall framework of the disciples' questions was the suggestion that they were perhaps threatened by resurrection. If Jesus was truly raised from the dead by the power of God, then a reality was present that challenged the disciples to face the largest of their fear; now they must *be* in the world what they *had not been*—they must live with resurrection hope.

In our own time and place, Jesus' resurrection may also threaten us with its possibilities for transformative change.

The Resurrection as fact or fiction connects with the fears of the Emmaus disciples, and it says something about thresholds in life before which we often stand that cause us to flee from the future that God intends for us. When we are threatened by resurrection, we seek places of safety to forget that the world holds nothing sacred—that even the noblest ideas about love and freedom and justice have always been twisted out of shape by selfish powers for selfish ends.

B. A Life-changing Question
(Luke 24:19-21)

And he said unto them, What things? And they said unto him, Concerning Jesus of Nazareth, which was a prophet mighty in deed and word before God and all the people: And how the chief priests and our rulers delivered him to be condemned to death, and have crucified him. But we trusted that it had been he which should have redeemed Israel: and beside all this, to day is the third day since these things were done.

As the two disciples walked on the road, they were "talking with each other about everything that had happened" (Luke 24:14, NIV). They were reflecting on their previous actions and decisions that turned out disastrously. They, along with the other disciples, were now considered fugitives in a rebellion led by Jesus, who had been crucified. The disciples had misread the evidence of their situation. The phrase, "we hoped that he would be the one to redeem Israel" (see verse 20) led to theological questions birthed out of the failures of previous "false messiahs" whose rebellions had been put down.

The men were having a theological discussion among themselves, airing their perplexity, attempting to unpack their fears and recalculate their possibilities, when a stranger appeared and walked along with them. He seemed to be some sort of rabbi or teacher, but one who was out of touch with the recent events in Jerusalem. The two disciples were stunned when they discovered that this stranger seemingly knew nothing about the crucifixion of Jesus.

In effect, the two disciples perhaps were stuck in their fears because they were not anchored deeply in the knowledge of God's salvation history. In other words, to be a solid theologian, one must know the meaning of what God has done before. If you want to understand the present, then you must understand the past. Or, to say it another way, "If you want to know what is going on now, you have to know what went on before." In the context of the religious experience of black people, if we want to know what it means to be Christian today, then we will have to reflect on what it meant to be black and Christian in our ancestors' time.

The question of whether Jesus was the one to "redeem Israel" opened up the possibility for revelation to occur. To *redeem* means "to draw people together, to set them on a new path, to reconcile and heal, and to usher in a new era of compassion and understanding of justice." When we are exposed to and grasp the truth, things change, as they did for the two Emmaus disciples.

C. Sharing a Meal with New Understanding (Luke 24:28-35)

And they drew nigh unto the village, whither they went: and he made as though he would have gone further. But they constrained him, saying, Abide with us: for it is toward evening, and the day is far spent. And he went in to tarry with them. And it came to pass, as he sat at meat with them, he took bread, and blessed it, and brake, and gave to them. And their eyes were opened, and they knew him; and he vanished out of their sight. And they said one to another, Did not our heart burn within us, while he talked with us by the way, and while he opened to us the scriptures? And they rose up the same hour, and returned to Jerusalem, and found the eleven gathered together, and them that were with them, Saying, The Lord is risen indeed, and hath appeared to Simon. And they told what things were done in the way, and how he was known of them in breaking of bread.

The mystical vision of the kingdom of God only intensified after Jesus' death, and to the disciples' astonishment, they saw Him alive again. In the case of the two Emmaus disciples, the risen Lord was made known through the breaking of bread. As they approached the village of Emmaus, it was clear that the day was far spent, so they invited the stranger to dinner. This meal was the turning point from theology to revelation, from theory to practice, and from reflection to action. Instead of continuing to talk about redemption, the act of showing hospitality to a stranger became revelatory. All of a sudden their act of hospitality had changed the foreigner from a stranger to a companion. From the Latin, the word *companion* means "with bread." A companion is one with whom one shares bread. In His life and teachings, Jesus was the bread of life to the disciples, a companion to the poor, the widows, and the lame and blind. Then in His resurrection, He became the bread that never perishes. Only when they broke bread together did clarity come to them, and they recognized Jesus.

This new awareness not only illuminates the past, but it also brings empowerment to the present and takes away fears about the future. Herein is why the Easter event belongs to the church: it makes us aware and keeps us alert to God's truth and purpose. Easter proclaims that God in Christ is an everlasting salvation for the reconciliation and transformation of life for everyone in every place.

III. CONCLUDING REFLECTION

The risen Lord meets us "on the road to Emmaus," in the ordinary places and experiences of our lives, and in the places to which we retreat when life is too much for us. The story of the disciples on the Emmaus road warns that the Lord may come to us in unfamiliar guises, and when we least expect Him.

During the trip to India, Howard and Mrs. Thurman sat down at a meal with Mahatma Gandhi, who, through nonviolence and civil disobedience, empowered the poor to overthrow British colonial rule. Although he was a Muslim, Gandhi asked if Mrs. Thurman would sing for him the Negro Spiritual, "Were You There when They Crucified My Lord?" It was at that moment that Howard Thurman reports that he understood how the power and presence of God crosses the great divide of men and women, color and creed, and east and west.

PRAYER

O Lord of life, show up in our spaces of fear and reveal to us the truth that guides us beyond our fears and undergirds us with hope. Give us Resurrection faith and hope so that we might tell the story of God's love and grace. In Jesus' name we pray. Amen.

WORD POWER

Hope—**1.** to wish for something with expectation of its fulfillment; **2.** *Archaic*—to have confidence; trust. v.tr. n.; **3.** A wish or desire accompanied by confident expectation of its fulfillment; **4.** To look forward to with confidence or expectation; **5.** To expect and desire.

HOME DAILY BIBLE READINGS
(March 25-31, 2013)

The Lord Has Risen Indeed!
MONDAY, March 25: "The Trial before Pilate" (Luke 23:13-25)
TUESDAY, March 26: "The Crucifixion of Jesus" (Luke 23:32-38)
WEDNESDAY, March 27: "The Death of Jesus" (Luke 23:44-49)
THURSDAY, March 28: "The Burial of Jesus" (Luke 23:50-56)
FRIDAY, March 29: "The Messiah's Suffering" (Isaiah 53:3-9)
SATURDAY, March 30: "Discovery of the Empty Tomb" (Luke 24:1-12)
SUNDAY, March 31: "The Lord Has Risen Indeed!" (Luke 24:13-21, 28-35)

LESSON 6   April 7, 2013

THE LORD APPEARS

FAITH PATHWAY/FAITH JOURNEY TOPIC: **Promises Kept**

DEVOTIONAL READING: **1 Corinthians 15:1-8**   BACKGROUND SCRIPTURE: **Luke 24:36-53**
PRINT PASSAGE: **Luke 24:36-53**   KEY VERSE: **Luke 24:44**

Luke 24:36-53—KJV

36 And as they thus spake, Jesus himself stood in the midst of them, and saith unto them, Peace be unto you.

37 But they were terrified and affrighted, and supposed that they had seen a spirit.

38 And he said unto them, Why are ye troubled? and why do thoughts arise in your hearts?

39 Behold my hands and my feet, that it is I myself: handle me, and see; for a spirit hath not flesh and bones, as ye see me have.

40 And when he had thus spoken, he shewed them his hands and his feet.

41 And while they yet believed not for joy, and wondered, he said unto them, Have ye here any meat?

42 And they gave him a piece of a broiled fish, and of an honeycomb.

43 And he took it, and did eat before them.

44 And he said unto them, These are the words which I spake unto you, while I was yet with you, that all things must be fulfilled, which were written in the law of Moses, and in the prophets, and in the psalms, concerning me.

45 Then opened he their understanding, that they might understand the scriptures,

46 And said unto them, Thus it is written, and thus it behoved Christ to suffer, and to rise from the dead the third day:

47 And that repentance and remission of sins should be preached in his name among all nations, beginning at Jerusalem.

48 And ye are witnesses of these things.

49 And, behold, I send the promise of my Father upon you: but tarry ye in the city of Jerusalem, until ye be endued with power from on high.

50 And he led them out as far as to Bethany, and he lifted up his hands, and blessed them.

Luke 24:36-53—NIV

36 While they were still talking about this, Jesus himself stood among them and said to them, "Peace be with you."

37 They were startled and frightened, thinking they saw a ghost.

38 He said to them, "Why are you troubled, and why do doubts rise in your minds?

39 Look at my hands and my feet. It is I myself! Touch me and see; a ghost does not have flesh and bones, as you see I have."

40 When he had said this, he showed them his hands and feet.

41 And while they still did not believe it because of joy and amazement, he asked them, "Do you have anything here to eat?"

42 They gave him a piece of broiled fish,

43 and he took it and ate it in their presence.

44 He said to them, "This is what I told you while I was still with you: Everything must be fulfilled that is written about me in the Law of Moses, the Prophets and the Psalms."

45 Then he opened their minds so they could understand the Scriptures.

46 He told them, "This is what is written: The Christ will suffer and rise from the dead on the third day,

47 and repentance and forgiveness of sins will be preached in his name to all nations, beginning at Jerusalem.

48 You are witnesses of these things.

49 I am going to send you what my Father has promised; but stay in the city until you have been clothed with power from on high."

50 When he had led them out to the vicinity of Bethany, he lifted up his hands and blessed them.

UNIFYING LESSON PRINCIPLE

People find that promises are easy to make but hard to keep. Which promises can we rely on without reservation? Through the Resurrection, Jesus kept His word and fulfilled the words of prophecy about Him.

51 And it came to pass, while he blessed them, he was parted from them, and carried up into heaven.
52 And they worshipped him, and returned to Jerusalem with great joy:
53 And were continually in the temple, praising and blessing God. Amen.

51 While he was blessing them, he left them and was taken up into heaven.
52 Then they worshiped him and returned to Jerusalem with great joy.
53 And they stayed continually at the temple, praising God.

TOPICAL OUTLINE OF THE LESSON

I. Introduction
A. From Fear and Doubt
B. Biblical Background

II. Exposition and Application of the Scripture
A. Shocked by Death, Surprised by Resurrection (Luke 24:36-43)
B. Death Leads to Life and Commissioning the Disciples (Luke 24:44-49)
C. The Departing Blessing of Jesus (Luke 24:50-53)

III. Concluding Reflection

LESSON OBJECTIVES

Upon the completion of the lesson, the students will be able to do the following:

1. Review the story of Jesus' post-Resurrection appearance and ascension;
2. Understand how the disciples must have felt when Jesus made Himself known to them, and how they felt about His presence in their lives; and,
3. Rest in Christ's promise to be with us always and to be able to share this promise with others.

POINTS TO BE EMPHASIZED

ADULT/YOUTH
Adult Topic: Promises Kept
Youth Topic: From Fear to Faith
Adult Key Verse: Luke 24:44
Youth Key Verse: Luke 24:36
Print Passage: Luke 24:36-53

—Jesus miraculously appeared, stood among His disciples, and spoke to them.
—Jesus' disciples had a hard time believing it was really Him, so He showed them His hands and feet and ate in their presence.
—Jesus opened the disciples' minds to the Scriptures and explained what they said about the Messiah.
—Jesus blessed the disciples and ascended into heaven.
—The disciples worshipped Jesus, joyfully returned to Jerusalem, and stayed at the Temple, praising God.

CHILDREN
Children Topic: Jesus Appears Again!
Key Verse: Luke 24:39a
Print Passage: Luke 24:36-50

—As the disciples talked about what happened to Jesus while on the road to Emmaus, Jesus appeared again.

—The disciples were surprised and frightened when Jesus stood among them and spoke to them.

—Jesus showed them His wounds to prove it was really Him.

—Then Jesus asked for something to eat, and He ate some broiled fish in the disciples' presence.

—Jesus then taught the disciples about the fulfillment of prophecy in what had happened to Him.

—Finally, Jesus lifted His hands and blessed the disciples.

I. INTRODUCTION

A. From Fear and Doubt

The theological challenge for us in the study of this lesson is to determine how the disciples were led from fear and doubt to worship and courageous witness. To use the Gospel's Resurrection narratives as proof of the resurrection of Jesus leads us down the wrong theological path. The Resurrection narratives themselves were theological discourses or stories that reported what the Gospel writers believed happened in the disciples' experiences as they encountered the risen Lord.

Every gospel account reports that at the arrest of Jesus, the disciples deserted Him and fled (see Mark 14:50). The promise of resurrection faded in the fear of death. While on the one hand, the disciples had hoped that Jesus' messianic promises would be fulfilled, on the other hand, they were clearly threatened by Jesus' resurrection—meaning they feared that the vision of Jesus' teachings must live on in them. The most immediate threat was that death summoned the disciples to a place where they did not imagine their relationship with Jesus would carry them. They were bewildered; their bodies and minds hurt with the aching awareness they felt in thinking that Jesus and His promises were beyond their reach. Until they encountered the risen Lord, the disciples never fully grasped Jesus' teachings that death and resurrection to life in God's kingdom are inseparable. Our reflecting on the disciples' experiences as they encountered the risen Lord challenges us to affirm not only what we believe about the Resurrection, but also why we believe it. Do we need proof of Jesus' resurrection, or have we discovered life in the Spirit of God that validates the presence of the living Lord? Your response to this question determines how vitally you can live in union with the promises of Christ.

B. Biblical Background

Luke's report of the events in Luke 24 gives the impression that all the events occurred on the same day. His second volume (the book of Acts), however, clarifies that from the Resurrection (see 24:1-3) to the Ascension (see 24:50-51), there was a period of forty days (see Acts 1:3). The appearance of Jesus reported in verses 36-43 is the same one reported in John 20:19-23, when Thomas was absent. The report that Jesus "stood" among the disciples echoes the language of "angelic presence" found throughout the Old Testament (see Genesis 18:2; Daniel 8:15). Jesus' sudden presence among the disciples startled and terrified them. They thought that He was a ghost or a spirit. Then Jesus spoke those immortal words of hope and promise: "Peace be with you." These immortal words have a measure of eternity in them for all who live with the promise of Jesus' resurrection. The words "Peace be with you!" opened the way for the disciples to enter the Spirit world in which the risen Lord dwells. The death of Jesus summoned them to the place of resurrection as Jesus stood among them, alive.

II. EXPOSITION AND APPLICATION OF THE SCRIPTURE

A. Shocked by Death, Surprised by Resurrection (Luke 24:36-43)

And as they thus spake, Jesus himself stood in the midst of them, and saith unto them, Peace be unto you. But they were terrified and affrighted, and supposed that they had seen a spirit. And he said unto them, Why are ye troubled? and why do thoughts arise in your hearts? Behold my hands and my feet, that it is I myself: handle me, and see; for a spirit hath not flesh and bones, as ye see me have. And when he had thus spoken, he shewed them his hands and his feet. And while they yet believed not for joy, and wondered, he said unto them, Have ye here any meat? And they gave him a piece of a broiled fish, and of an honeycomb. And he took it, and did eat before them.

What does it mean to be resurrected? And how, in Jesus' experience, did it happen? What did Jesus' teaching say about resurrection? When the risen Lord appeared at a closed gathering of the disciples, these sorts of questions were perhaps on the disciples' minds. However, Jesus' appearance removed all doubt that He indeed was the risen Lord of life. Proofs of the Resurrection characterize the exchange between Jesus and the disciples as Jesus offered His resurrected body for examination by the disciples. But Jesus' deeper intent went beyond the need for material proofs. Rather, the focus of Jesus' appearance to the disciples was for them to understand the spiritual presence and meaning of His resurrection (see John 20:29). The gospel stories of the resurrection of Jesus did not pertain to fiction or fantasy but to the experience and transformation of the disciples. Ultimately, it was their story that set the stage for the proclamation of the Gospel, and it is the witness of their story that empowers us to experience Jesus' continuing presence and power. The disciples were changed. They went from fear to faith—by seeing the resurrected Lord. What the ancient witness of the disciples means for each Christian today is that we have to do our own believing and realize that belief is a theological act, not a proof of faith.

At the appearance of Jesus, it was incomprehensible to the disciples that the physical presence of Jesus was real. They thought that He was a ghost or a spirit. To dispel the doubt and fears of the disciples, Jesus moved quickly to confirm and demonstrate the reality of His resurrection. Jesus said to the disciples, "Why are you troubled, and why do doubts rise in your minds? Look at my hands and my feet. It is I myself! Touch me and see; a ghost does not have flesh and bones, as you see I have" (Luke 24:38-39, NIV). While "some doubted," the disciples immediately knew that their experience of Jesus' resurrection was different from the resurrection of Lazarus, who would physically die again. Jesus presented Himself "alive forevermore."

B. Death Leads to Life and Commissioning the Disciples
(Luke 24:44-49)

And he said unto them, These are the words which I spake unto you, while I was yet with you, that all things must be fulfilled, which were written in the law of Moses, and in the prophets, and in the psalms, concerning me. Then opened he their understanding, that they might understand the scriptures, And said unto them, Thus it is written, and thus it behoved Christ to suffer, and to rise from the dead the third day: And that repentance and remission of sins should be preached in his name among all nations, beginning at Jerusalem. And ye are witnesses of these things. And, behold, I send the promise of my Father upon you: but tarry ye in the city of Jerusalem, until ye be endued with power from on high.

The vision of life with Jesus in the kingdom of God only intensified after Jesus' death—and to the disciples' astonishment, they saw Him alive again. Jesus insisted that His disciples understand death as a way to life, which involved the conscious acceptance of suffering. Jesus embraced the prophetic sign that God's kingdom was making its way into a world that resisted transformation, and this transformation could be lost for those who sought to save their lives (see Mark 8:35-38; Luke 9:24-26). Life for Jesus was not about pleasure or pain, success or failure; rather, He taught His disciples to seek life beyond this life. In God's presence alone the sum of one's sojourn on earth would be measured.

For Jesus, the struggle to be truly in the image of God was something one must work for in one's life, in the choices that he or she made, the strength of his or her convictions, and the purity that could only come from his or her heart (see Luke 9:23-28). The disciples were agents of Jesus' kingdom vision and were commissioned to preach or proclaim its message of repentance in Jesus' name to all the nations. The preaching of the kingdom as a witness to the life and resurrection of Jesus was the prophetic vocation to which all disciples were called and is the spiritual vocation of every Christian. The disciples were commissioned to become martyrs for the sake of the Gospel. The Spirit world of the kingdom of God from which Jesus received power, strength, and wisdom would also accompany and fill the witness of the disciples. Without divine energy and spiritual power, the disciples would fail. Jesus conferred the divine Spirit upon the disciples as He taught them to trust God in the endeavors of the Gospel. There would be plenty of work for the disciples to do, but without "power from on high," this work would languish in failure associated with fear and faithlessness.

Luke 24:44-49 recaps major themes of the Gospel and sets the stage for the coming of the Spirit and the work of the disciples as witnesses (prophetic martyrs) for the kingdom of God. The fulfillment of the Scripture is tied to the Resurrection in the proclamation of the early church (see 1 Corinthians 15:3-5). The disciples, even in the midst of danger and fear, had come to a place of hope that Jesus' promise to them would be fulfilled (see John 14:1-14). In Jesus' last words to the disciples in the gospel of Luke, Jesus returned to the central theme of the kingdom of God. Again, Jesus opened the mind of the disciples to understand the Scriptures, as He had done with the two disciples on the road to Emmaus (see Luke 24:31, 45). The message of the Scripture is not self-evident;

one's mind must be opened to it, and that message is rightly understood only in the light of Jesus' crucified life and resurrection.

C. The Departing Blessing of Jesus
(Luke 24:50-53)

And he led them out as far as to Bethany, and he lifted up his hands, and blessed them. And it came to pass, while he blessed them, he was parted from them, and carried up into heaven. And they worshipped him, and returned to Jerusalem with great joy: And were continually in the temple, praising and blessing God. Amen.

The end of the gospel of Luke exerts a powerful influence on our understanding of the themes and theology of the Gospel. Jesus' departing blessing upon the disciples would have an enduring effect on their activities as new agents of the kingdom of God. Luke's gospel ends by elevating three of the most characteristic of God's actions. God was experienced by Jesus in a way that the lives of His followers were transformed. The centrality of their faith was that God had raised Jesus from the dead for the salvation of the world. Through this proclamation, they were commissioned to call nations and all people to repentance. The God we meet in Jesus, our redeemer and Savior, would be the sum total of what they would preach. The transformative vision of life in God's kingdom was transferred from Jesus to the disciples to do "greater works" (John 14:17). The promise of Jesus to the disciples gives final confirmation to the Spirit work among them: "I am with you always" (Matthew 28:20). The vital joining of the disciples' lives to God and God's work in the world was awakened in them as Jesus gave His departing blessing.

The disciples would experience suffering, pain, disappointment, and trials as witnesses to the risen Lord. Preaching of a Gospel that calls for justice, love, and an inclusive community without barriers of race and ethnicity would at best be a risk of faith. But Jesus' departing blessing and their being filled with the divine Spirit and energy would sustain them.

As with the ancient disciples, Jesus enables us to realize who we are in God's presence and entices us to meet Him in human fields of labor for the sake of the Gospel. Luke's continuing narrative in the book of Acts describes scenes of danger and sacrifice—wherein the disciples were made aware of their weaknesses and fragility, but experienced the Spirit's power in those situations. This is the gift of God to the Christian community through the life, death, and resurrection of Jesus.

The great goal of the Gospel has yet to be achieved. The Gospel goes forth through our contemporary witness of its power to transform life. In reality, the message of the Gospel strikes at the very center of human evil—national and global sins of injustice, war, greed, racism, sexism, and all forms of oppression. Christians are called to a new age, an age that has to do with God's action in history on behalf of the salvation of humanity. As black theologian James Cone states, "It is an age of liberation, in which the 'blind receive their sight, the lame walk, the lepers are cleansed, the deaf hear, the dead are raised up, the poor have the good news preached to them'" (see Luke 7:22). This message is a witness in God's name against all suffering due to sin and corruption of human life. In Christ, God enters the world—where the suffering of the oppressed becomes His suffering, their despair becomes divine despair. As the disciples were commissioned to the liberating work of the Gospel, so are we. Throughout the centuries, those who have taken up the mantle of the Gospel have found that God keeps the promise Jesus made to the disciples. Both the ancients' and contemporaries' witnesses of the Gospel can testify that God's Spirit in Jesus is a continuing presence in the world that blesses and sustains them through sacrifice and trial.

III. CONCLUDING REFLECTION

It is important for our contemporary witness to the Gospel that we explore the depth of what it means to be Christians in today's world. In the case of those who are members of black churches, they must theologically engage the Gospel in the light of "What does it mean to be black and Christian today?" What does it mean to live in vital union with God's promise of transformation for those who suffer oppression, racism, sexism, and poverty due to systemic injustices? Death and suffering on behalf of truth is our hardest lesson. Jesus taught His disciples that death and suffering were also the gateways to life and truth. There is no one way to die, but there is only one way into the life and Spirit of God's kingdom. Jesus opened up that way by joining our lives to God through His resurrection. Clearly, the risen Lord calls us to a prophetic vocation as witnesses to the Gospel of God.

PRAYER

O God, our world needs the transformation that comes through proclaiming the Good News of Jesus' resurrection to new life. Help us grow in trust of Your promise to be with us always as we proclaim the Gospel. In Jesus' name we pray. Amen.

WORD POWER

Immortality—1. the quality or condition of being immortal; 2. endless life or existence; 3. enduring fame.
Resurrection—1. *rising from the dead:* in some systems of belief, a rising from or raising of somebody from the dead, or the state of having risen from the dead; 2. *revival:* the revival of something old or long disused.

HOME DAILY BIBLE READINGS
(April 1-7, 2013)

The Lord Appears
  MONDAY, April 1: "Appearances of the Risen Lord" (1 Corinthians 15:1-8)
  TUESDAY, April 2: "The Appearance to Mary Magdalene" (John 20:11-18)
  WEDNESDAY, April 3: "The Appearance to Thomas" (John 20:24-29)
  THURSDAY, April 4: "The Appearance to Seven Disciples" (John 21:1-8)
  FRIDAY, April 5: "Breakfast with the Disciples" (John 21:9-14)
  SATURDAY, April 6: "Simon Peter Called to Follow" (John 21:15-19)
  SUNDAY, April 7: "You Are Witnesses of These Things" (Luke 24:36-53)

LESSON 7   **April 14, 2013**

THE HOLY SPIRIT COMES

Faith Pathway/Faith Journey Topic: **Power to Change**

Devotional Reading: **John 15:1-7**   Background Scripture: **Acts 2:1-36**
Print Passage: **Acts 2:1-13**   Key Verse: **Acts 2:4**

Acts 2:1-13—KJV

AND WHEN the day of Pentecost was fully come, they were all with one accord in one place.

2 And suddenly there came a sound from heaven as of a rushing mighty wind, and it filled all the house where they were sitting.

3 And there appeared unto them cloven tongues like as of fire, and it sat upon each of them.

4 And they were all filled with the Holy Ghost, and began to speak with other tongues, as the Spirit gave them utterance.

5 And there were dwelling at Jerusalem Jews, devout men, out of every nation under heaven.

6 Now when this was noised abroad, the multitudes came together, and were confounded, because that every man heard them speak in his own language.

7 And they were all amazed and marvelled, saying one to another, Behold, are not all these which speak Galilaeans?

8 And how hear we every man in our own tongue, wherein we were born?

9 Parthians, and Medes, and Elamites, and the dwellers in Mesopotamia, and in Judaea, and Cappadocia, in Pontus, and Asia,

10 Phrygia, and Pamphylia, in Egypt, and in the parts of Libya about Cyrene, and strangers of Rome, Jews and proselytes,

11 Cretes and Arabians, we do hear them speak in our tongues the wonderful works of God.

12 And they were all amazed, and were in doubt, saying one to another, What meaneth this?

13 Others mocking said, These men are full of new wine.

Acts 2:1-13—NIV

WHEN THE day of Pentecost came, they were all together in one place.

2 Suddenly a sound like the blowing of a violent wind came from heaven and filled the whole house where they were sitting.

3 They saw what seemed to be tongues of fire that separated and came to rest on each of them.

4 All of them were filled with the Holy Spirit and began to speak in other tongues as the Spirit enabled them.

5 Now there were staying in Jerusalem God-fearing Jews from every nation under heaven.

6 When they heard this sound, a crowd came together in bewilderment, because each one heard them speaking in his own language.

7 Utterly amazed, they asked: "Are not all these men who are speaking Galileans?

8 Then how is it that each of us hears them in his own native language?

9 Parthians, Medes and Elamites; residents of Mesopotamia, Judea and Cappadocia, Pontus and Asia,

10 Phrygia and Pamphylia, Egypt and the parts of Libya near Cyrene; visitors from Rome

11 (both Jews and converts to Judaism); Cretans and Arabs—we hear them declaring the wonders of God in our own tongues!"

12 Amazed and perplexed, they asked one another, "What does this mean?"

13 Some, however, made fun of them and said, "They have had too much wine."

UNIFYING LESSON PRINCIPLE

We often face experiences that produce dramatic changes in our lives. How can positive and lasting change be initiated? The Holy Spirit provides life-transforming power.

TOPICAL OUTLINE OF THE LESSON

I. Introduction

A. A Life-changing Spirit

B. Biblical Background

II. Exposition and Application of the Scripture

A. The Outpouring of the Spirit (Acts 2:1-4)

B. Life in the Spirit (Acts 2:5-11)

C. The Meaning of Being Filled with the Spirit (Acts 2:12-13)

III. Concluding Reflection

LESSON OBJECTIVES

Upon the completion of the lesson, the students will be able to do the following:

1. Review the dramatic story of the coming of the Holy Spirit and discover its meaning for their lives;

2. Explore the "feeling words" in the passage (*bewildered, amazed, astonished, perplexed*) and relate them to their experiences when surprising events occur; and,

3. Identify ways that they sense the presence of the Holy Spirit in their lives as they experience change.

POINTS TO BE EMPHASIZED

ADULT/YOUTH

Adult Topic: Power to Change

Youth Topic: Hope for Power

Adult/Youth Key Verse: Acts 2:4

Print Passage: Acts 2:1-13

—The word *Pentecost* is the Hellenistic name for the Hebrew "Feast of Weeks" and is described in Leviticus 23:15-21; it was instituted to show joy and thankfulness for God's blessing of the harvest.

—Our passage deals with the blessing of the coming of the Holy Spirit (mentioned in Acts 1:8) and the wonders of God and the Holy Spirit proclaimed in understandable language.

—Breath or wind is a symbol of the Spirit of God (see Ezekiel 37:9, 14; John 3:8).

—On Pentecost, the apostles were gathered together and waiting as Jesus had instructed them (see 1:4-5).

—The Holy Spirit came as a wind and tongues of fire, enabling the apostles to praise God in languages understood by the multilingual throngs.

—Humans tend to explain away biblical acts of God as natural phenomena.

CHILDREN

Children Topic: The Holy Spirit Comes

Key Verse: Acts 2:4

Print Passage: Acts 2:1-13

—The believers were all gathered together on the Day of Pentecost.

—A sound like the rush of a violent wind filled the place where they were sitting.

—Then tongues like fire appeared and rested on each person.
—The believers were filled with the Holy Spirit and began to speak in various languages about God's deeds of power.
—All the people were surprised and confused; they wondered what all this meant.
—Some people thought the disciples were drunk.

I. INTRODUCTION
A. A Life-changing Spirit

The book of Acts has been designated as part 2 of Luke's two-volume work that illustrates the power of God's Spirit to empower first-century Christians to overcome the bias and prejudice that divided the ancient world. The book of Acts is a treatise on life in the Spirit of God—the telling of the stories of the first-century urban Christians who faced both the threats of the Empire and threats against the internal unity needed to be effective witnesses for God.

The disciples we see in the four Gospel accounts were not referred to as apostles until after the Pentecost event. As disciples before Pentecost, they were basically speculative about their future positions of power in their hope of the kingdom's being restored to Israel. Becoming apostles after the outpouring of the Spirit upon them, they became prophets of a new age. They demonstrated what the power of God can do when it works through the fellowship of those who trust in God's promise.

The study of this lesson will challenge us to reexamine what it means to be filled with and have "life in the Spirit." The church's spiritual renewal is also a vital issue for contemporary Christianity. If we want church renewal in the Spirit, we will have to renew our thinking about the meaning of Christianity as we have come to know and practice it. Spiritual renewal of black churches can only occur when the churches huddled together in similar fashion (as the disciples) ask themselves, "What is the evil in which we participate that is damning ourselves, our neighbors, and the earth itself to destruction?" When times are hard and political adversity and conflict in the world confront us with decisions about justice and injustice, communities with divine energy and spiritual wisdom are needed in order to face critical theological questions and determine how to channel their faith and actions for change. In the light of chronic social problems that plague the "life communities" black churches, this is a critical task to serve. The concentration of poverty, joblessness, the mass incarceration of black males, poor educational systems, gang violence, and drug cartels are theological matters that call for Spirit-filled responses for liberation (see Acts 16:16-22). Jesus instructed the disciples to wait until God filled them with the same Spirit that made Jesus one with God's purpose (see John 17:20-21). Our task, according to Jesus, is to transform the present by being His witnesses and by opening up ourselves to the Spirit to make and shape us into living demonstrations of what the kingdom of God looks like in the world.

B. Biblical Background

Two signature events impacted the lives of first-century Christians. These included Jesus' resurrection and the Pentecost outpouring of the Spirit. The Day of Pentecost was originally a harvest festival, celebrated fifty days after the Passover. By the first century, however, Pentecost had gradually lost its association with agriculture and was associated with the giving of the Law. It was a celebration of God's creation and of God's people and their religious history. The gathering of the disciples in the Upper Room numbered about 120 believers, according to Luke's account (see Acts 1:15). These disciples represented the most intimate group that had been impacted by the life, teachings, and resurrection of Jesus. Prior to the Pentecost event, the disciples seemed to misunderstand the meaning of the "promise" (verse 4). They still connected the future with the expected restoration of a national theocracy to Israel, so they asked whether the Lord would restore the kingdom to Israel at that time. During His earthly ministry as well as in the post-Resurrection period of forty days, Jesus constantly focused on what the disciples must do. God's presence and purpose through the suffering and resurrection of Jesus to bring the whole of creation into fuller communion with God was to be the sum of their witness and discipleship. They had been commissioned by Jesus to proclaim and teach the Gospel to all nations, and baptize all people in God's name. Jesus shifted the disciples' thoughts from an emphasis on restoration of the past to the transformation of the present. They could not fulfill what is known as the "Great Commission" (see Matthew 28:16) without having "power from on high." They were instructed to wait on the energy and wisdom of the divine Spirit to fill them before presenting the Gospel in Jerusalem, Samaria, and all other parts of the world. The text in Acts 1:2 says that while the disciples were assembled, a sound like the rush of a violent wind totally consumed them. The outpouring of spiritual power on the apostles was the fulfillment of Jesus' promise in Acts 1:8.

II. EXPOSITION AND APPLICATION OF THE SCRIPTURE

A. The Outpouring of the Spirit
   (Acts 2:1-4)

AND WHEN the day of Pentecost was fully come, they were all with one accord in one place. And suddenly there came a sound from heaven as of a rushing mighty wind, and it filled all the house where they were sitting. And there appeared unto them cloven tongues like as of fire, and it sat upon each of them. And they were all filled with the Holy Ghost, and began to speak with other tongues, as the Spirit gave them utterance.

The main theme of the book of Acts is the activity of the Holy Spirit. As the *New Interpreter's Bible* notes, "It is important to realize that in the Acts we do not find the mind of man working out an idea or concept of the Spirit, but rather the Spirit working upon the mind and life of man." The traditional celebration of the Jewish festival of Pentecost became the scene for the outpouring of the Spirit. The Pentecost event was a unifying experience which transcended all barriers of nationality and language. The Spirit's outpouring was actually an "inpouring" of God's presence, power, and divine energy into the lives of oppressed, weak, and vulnerable people from many nations and languages. We live in a world in which the forces that divide us threaten to destroy us.

Today, nations are divided by rival systems of politics and economics; groups within nations are divided by class consciousness and conflict; families are increasingly divided by divorces; and individuals are virtually split between private interests and corporate challenges. The forces behind these divisions are not unlike the societal and political forces in the world of Jesus' disciples. It may be difficult for most of us to see that we live within the world as constructs, and we act out of the world's assumptions. We are shaped more by the world's systems and definitions of life than by the Spirit of God. We see the world as profane rather than sacred, as a place to buy and sell, use and discard; and control and possess. The outpouring of the Spirit shows us God's alternative to this way of living through Jesus.

B. Life in the Spirit
(Acts 2:5-11)

And there were dwelling at Jerusalem Jews, devout men, out of every nation under heaven. Now when this was noised abroad, the multitudes came together, and were confounded, because that every man heard them speak in his own language. And they were all amazed and marvelled, saying one to another, Behold, are not all these which speak Galilaeans? And how hear we every man in our own tongue, wherein we were born? Parthians, and Medes, and Elamites, and the dwellers in Mesopotamia, and in Judaea, and Cappadocia, in Pontus, and Asia, Phrygia, and Pamphylia, in Egypt, and in the parts of Libya about Cyrene, and strangers of Rome, Jews and proselytes, Cretes and Arabians, we do hear them speak in our tongues the wonderful works of God.

We are told in this passage that devout men, representing every known nation on earth, were recipients of the outpouring of the Spirit. It was a phenomenon of communal unity in which people of different languages "understood the meaning of God"—as Howard Thurman puts it—"within the grain of their own wood." In that sacred moment of "the rushing mighty wind" and "tongues of fire resting upon them," this diverse human community (representative of different cultures and languages) was hidden in God's Spirit. They celebrated the results of the Spirit's outpouring as well as the manifestation of the Spirit Himself; they emerged a new communal community, a reflection of divine glory. In our human experiences, we may not know what it is to reflect the glory of God. The experience of this community at the ancient scene of Pentecost gives us a glimpse of what it is and what it looks like. As referenced in the third-century phrase of Irenaeus, "The glory of God is every creature fully alive."

Theologically, how should we apply the message of Pentecost to the witness of the church in the world? The life and message of Jesus lie at the heart of the Spirit's outpouring at Pentecost. Jesus is the lens or model of God through which the church sees the world. His life, ministry, death, and resurrection experiences are the way that Christians look God-ward—the reasons they dare to speak boldly to a world attempting to live outside of God's reality. In many ways, "the world as it is" refuses to reflect God or become like God (show love and mercy in action), by imagining that its systems, social constructs of power and governance can exist outside of a relationship with God. Christians must constantly monitor how they interpret the world that seeks to draw us into its ways of acting out its assumptions. If we see ourselves and everything else as having its being and fulfillment in, through, and with God, then we can no longer treat each other with injustice and the earth itself in a utilitarian way. What we must determine is how life in the Spirit changes us daily. There must be a change; we must struggle for justice beyond the private pursuits of personal fulfillment and salvation. As theologian Sallie Macfague explains it, life in the Spirit challenges us to move away from the "conventional model" of individual self-fulfillment—which is based on building up more and more possessions and prestige—to an emphasis on the "universal self." The Christian spiritual ideal (as manifested at Pentecost) pushes us to empty ourselves so that God's Spirit may fill and enable us to shift from cultures of hoarding and a competitive mindset to one based on radical, inclusive interdependence between God and each other.

C. The Meaning of Being Filled with the Spirit (Acts 2:12-13)

And they were all amazed, and were in doubt, saying one to another, What meaneth this? Others mocking said, These men are full of new wine.

The amazement and wonder of the Pentecost experience caused the people to say to one another (in essence), "What could this be?" Theological reflection takes place at the point where questions are raised about God's presence in the world and what should be the appropriate human response to God's love and gifts. Given our world of human divisions, violent wars, racism and sexism, excessive wealth, extreme poverty, global warming, and environmental disasters, our theological questions about life in God's Spirit must address the worldly temptations that hinder the flourishing of God's creation. We live in a world governed by a pervasive network of unfaithfulness and rejection of God's Word that has become worse throughout the centuries. This distorts the image of God in which all life has been created. Being filled with the Spirit means seeing the world as God sees it. To see the world as God sees it means that we see the world and ourselves through the lens of Jesus' life, death, and resurrection. In Jesus, the Spirit helps us see what we are meant to be and what we are not meant to be. Jesus taught His disciples that all of creation is to reflect life in God's kingdom.

Being filled with the Spirit can be a disturbing, disorienting presence in our lives, because when the Spirit changes us to live the cruciform life of Jesus, we become alternatives in a world that resists the newness of God. We want to believe that sin and evil as we know it belong to the world and do not have a foothold on us. But the reality is that we, too, are drawn to embrace a world that seeks to live outside the reality of God. Being filled with the Spirit "opens our eyes" to the reality of God.

III. CONCLUDING REFLECTION

William J. Seymour, a former slave, began to preach the Pentecost message of the book of Acts in Los Angeles at the Azusa Street Revival, which lasted for several months in 1906. The revival was packed with people of every race and walk of life. Night after night, the Azusa Street Mission pulsated with songs, testimonies, and ecstatic utterances. Seymour had prayed that the Holy Spirit would visit the gatherings in a powerful way. He had an earnest and unchanging desire that the miracle of Pentecost would come about on the earth again. He had the sincere expectation that the gift of the Holy Spirit would enable men and women to live holy lives and would foster unity in the church, even breaking down racial and economic barriers. William Seymour welcomed the full participation of all, whether black or white, male or female, rich or poor, young or old. This would be an example of sincere, God-fearing people longing for the restoration of the vibrant life of the first-century church that they read about in the New Testament. The movement of Black Pentecostalism has its roots in William J. Seymour's Azusa Street Revival.

Clearly, such movements like the Azusa Street Revival play an important role in the progression of Christian communities toward the fulfillment of unity in God's Spirit. What is important is that we remain open to the Spirit's change in us and in society. As the Pentecost event teaches, we must, while we wait, live the change we are waiting for every day.

When Barack Obama was elected to the presidency of the United States, I, along with many African Americans, celebrated the change that we never thought would happen in America. Many are convinced that his election was the work of the Spirit of God against a legacy of racism that has stood for decades against the flourishing of black and poor people in America. In reference to that unprecedented moment, the lyrics of the song by Sam Cooke, "A Change Is Gonna Come" spoke to our collective joy.

PRAYER

God, through Your Spirit, bring transformation and change to us and to our world. Be merciful to us and pour out Your Spirit in ways that bring to light Your truth as we might know it in Jesus Christ—to all people. In His name we do pray. Amen.

WORD POWER

Pentecost—(1) the seventh Sunday after Easter, commemorating the descent of the Holy Spirit upon the disciples; (2) in Judaism, a feast held on the sixth and seventh days of Sivan in commemoration of the revelation of the Law on Mount Sinai and the celebration of the wheat festival in ancient times.

Spirit—*n.* 1. (a) the vital principle or animating force within living beings; (b) incorporeal consciousness; 2. the soul, considered as departing from the body of a person at death; 3. Spirit—the Holy Spirit.

HOME DAILY BIBLE READINGS
(April 8-14, 2013)

The Holy Spirit Comes

MONDAY, April 8: "I Will Not Leave You Orphaned" (John 14:18-24)

TUESDAY, April 9: "Abide in Me" (John 15:1-7)

WEDNESDAY, April 10: "The Coming of the Advocate" (John 16:1-11)

THURSDAY, April 11: "Raised Up and Freed from Death" (Acts 2:22-28)

FRIDAY, April 12: "The Promise of the Spirit" (Acts 2:14-21)

SATURDAY, April 13: "The Promise Received" (Acts 2:29-36)

SUNDAY, April 14: "The Day of Pentecost" (Acts 2:1-13)

LESSON 8   April 21, 2013

LIVING WITH HOPE

FAITH PATHWAY/FAITH JOURNEY TOPIC: **Great Expectations**

DEVOTIONAL READING: **Psalm 38:9-15**   BACKGROUND SCRIPTURE: **1 Thessalonians 4:13–5:11**
PRINT PASSAGE: **1 Thessalonians 4:13-18;**   KEY VERSE: **1 Thessalonians 5:9**
5:1-11

1 Thessalonians 4:13-18; 5:1-11—KJV

13 But I would not have you to be ignorant, brethren, concerning them which are asleep, that ye sorrow not, even as others which have no hope.

14 For if we believe that Jesus died and rose again, even so them also which sleep in Jesus will God bring with him.

15 For this we say unto you by the word of the Lord, that we which are alive and remain unto the coming of the Lord shall not prevent them which are asleep.

16 For the Lord himself shall descend from heaven with a shout, with the voice of the archangel, and with the trump of God: and the dead in Christ shall rise first:

17 Then we which are alive and remain shall be caught up together with them in the clouds, to meet the Lord in the air: and so shall we ever be with the Lord.

18 Wherefore comfort one another with these words.

…..

BUT OF the times and the seasons, brethren, ye have no need that I write unto you.

2 For yourselves know perfectly that the day of the Lord so cometh as a thief in the night.

3 For when they shall say, Peace and safety; then sudden destruction cometh upon them, as travail upon a woman with child; and they shall not escape.

4 But ye, brethren, are not in darkness, that that day should overtake you as a thief.

5 Ye are all the children of light, and the children of the day: we are not of the night, nor of darkness.

6 Therefore let us not sleep, as do others; but let us watch and be sober.

1 Thessalonians 4:13-18; 5:1-11—NIV

13 Brothers, we do not want you to be ignorant about those who fall asleep, or to grieve like the rest of men, who have no hope.

14 We believe that Jesus died and rose again and so we believe that God will bring with Jesus those who have fallen asleep in him.

15 According to the Lord's own word, we tell you that we who are still alive, who are left till the coming of the Lord, will certainly not precede those who have fallen asleep.

16 For the Lord himself will come down from heaven, with a loud command, with the voice of the archangel and with the trumpet call of God, and the dead in Christ will rise first.

17 After that, we who are still alive and are left will be caught up together with them in the clouds to meet the Lord in the air. And so we will be with the Lord forever.

18 Therefore encourage each other with these words.

…..

NOW, BROTHERS, about times and dates we do not need to write to you,

2 for you know very well that the day of the Lord will come like a thief in the night.

3 While people are saying, "Peace and safety," destruction will come on them suddenly, as labor pains on a pregnant woman, and they will not escape.

4 But you, brothers, are not in darkness so that this day should surprise you like a thief.

5 You are all sons of the light and sons of the day. We do not belong to the night or to the darkness.

6 So then, let us not be like others, who are asleep, but let us be alert and self-controlled.

UNIFYING LESSON PRINCIPLE

People find themselves in situations that can be destabilizing and disheartening, and in circumstances that cause despair. How do we find stability, courage, and hope? Paul assured us that the promise of Christ's return provides us with comfort and hope.

7 For they that sleep sleep in the night; and they that be drunken are drunken in the night.
8 But let us, who are of the day, be sober, putting on the breastplate of faith and love; and for an helmet, the hope of salvation.
9 For God hath not appointed us to wrath, but to obtain salvation by our Lord Jesus Christ,
10 Who died for us, that, whether we wake or sleep, we should live together with him.
11 Wherefore comfort yourselves together, and edify one another, even as also ye do.

7 For those who sleep, sleep at night, and those who get drunk, get drunk at night.
8 But since we belong to the day, let us be self-controlled, putting on faith and love as a breastplate, and the hope of salvation as a helmet.
9 For God did not appoint us to suffer wrath but to receive salvation through our Lord Jesus Christ.
10 He died for us so that, whether we are awake or asleep, we may live together with him.
11 Therefore encourage one another and build each other up, just as in fact you are doing.

TOPICAL OUTLINE OF THE LESSON

I. Introduction
   A. Waiting with Hope
   B. Biblical Background

II. Exposition and Application of the Scripture
   A. The Apocalyptic Message of Paul
      (1 Thessalonians 4:13-18)
   B. Living with Confidence
      (1 Thessalonians 5:1-3)
   C. The End Goal of Christian Hope
      (1 Thessalonians 5:4-11)

III. Concluding Reflection

LESSON OBJECTIVES

Upon the completion of the lesson, the students will be able to do the following:

1. Articulate signs of hope and encouragement in the promise of Christ's return;
2. Communicate the feelings they experience because of the promise of Christ's return; and,
3. Find ways to encourage one another by identifying signs of hope in the midst of difficulty.

POINTS TO BE EMPHASIZED

ADULT/YOUTH
Adult Topic: Great Expectations
Youth Topic: Hope for Resurrection
Adult/Youth Key Verse: 1 Thessalonians 5:9
Print Passage: 1 Thessalonians 4:13-18; 5:1-11
—Paul assured believers that those who are alive when Jesus returns will not precede those believers who have died trusting in Jesus.
—The hope that believers in Jesus Christ (both those who have died and those still alive) have in His resurrection and return provides encouragement which Christians can share.
—To be with Christ is to have entered into the light of faith, love, and hope, and a relationship that nothing can destroy.
—Christ will return and take His faithful ones to be with Him forever.

—The Day of the Lord will come unexpectedly—but we can still be ready for it.

—Christians do not have to grieve about death, like those who have no hope.

CHILDREN
Children Topic: A Future Filled with Hope
Key Verse: 1 Thessalonians 5:9
Print Passage: 1 Thessalonians 4:13-18; 5:1-3, 6-11

—Paul was writing to the Thessalonians in order to answer some of their questions about the future coming of Christ.

—Paul assured the Thessalonians that those who had already died would be included among those who will be with Christ.

—Paul said that those who are alive will be with Christ forever.

—Paul warned the Thessalonians that Christ will come again without warning.

—Because the believers in Thessalonica were destined for salvation through Christ, they should live in love and hope.

—The believers in Thessalonica were also to encourage and build up one another.

I. INTRODUCTION
A. Waiting with Hope

The church in Thessalonica was birthed during Paul's second missionary journey. After leaving Philippi, Paul traveled some ninety miles southwest to Thessalonica, where (during a period of several weeks) he entered the synagogue and preached about God's action in the life of Jesus and His resurrection to life from the dead. Many persons in Thessalonica, including influential women, converted to Christianity, and many Gentiles turned from idol worship to the living God.

However, there were a large number of zealous Jews who resisted Paul's message and created much hostility and opposition to the Christian movement. Paul narrowly escaped arrest while one of his pupils, Jason, was imprisoned. The occasion for Paul's letters to the Thessalonian Christians was likely a result of this opposition, which was due to the believers' countercultural glorification of Christ. Paul was concerned for the stability of the community of believers in Thessalonica. Given the hostility from unbelievers, the Thessalonian Christians were encouraged to remain steadfast in their faith while they maintained great expectations and their apocalyptic hope for the return of the crucified Christ.

Waiting on Jesus' return became both a sociological and theological dilemma for the Thessalonian Christians. How could the Thessalonians live faithfully and survive as believers in the Messiah, in a world that ridiculed them for their belief in Jesus' return to earth as the Lord of life? How were they to live practically and make practical decisions about living while they invested hope in a reality that they believed was soon to come? Paul wrote to the Thessalonians with a general concern for the community's stability in the face of continuing hostility from their non-Christian neighbors.

B. Biblical Background

In the letters written to the Thessalonians, Paul addressed the theological topic of Christ's second coming and the meaning of life after death. Paul attempted to unpack the theological content of the *parousia* by balancing the expectation of the return of Christ with an understanding of what it means to have life with Christ amid the practical demands of social existence—while living with faith. The Thessalonian Christians anticipated sharing in the blessings which would come with the arrival of the Lord of life from heaven (1:10; 2:12, 19; 3:13). This anticipation (waiting on the return of the Lord) raised theological concerns regarding the relation of the dead in Christ to the expected *parousia* or "second coming of Christ." Paul's answer to this concern represents the earliest Christian theology about life after death. In Paul's theological perspective, those who had passed away would share equally with those who were still alive at the coming of the Lord. Paul's reference to the dead as those who "sleep" (see 1 Thessalonians 4:13-15) is commonly seen in the Christian Scriptures, but does not necessarily mean that the soul is "asleep" or inactive from the time of death until the Resurrection. For Paul, even those who were/are asleep or who died in Christ have hope of being blessed in the world to come.

II. EXPOSITION AND APPLICATION OF THE SCRIPTURE

A. The Apocalyptic Message of Paul (1 Thessalonians 4:13-18)

But I would not have you to be ignorant, brethren, concerning them which are asleep, that ye sorrow not, even as others which have no hope. For if we believe that Jesus died and rose again, even so them also which sleep in Jesus will God bring with him. For this we say unto you by the word of the Lord, that we which are alive and remain unto the coming of the Lord shall not prevent them which are asleep. For the Lord himself shall descend from heaven with a shout, with the voice of the archangel, and with the trump of God: and the dead in Christ shall rise first: Then we which are alive and remain shall be caught up together with them in the clouds, to meet the Lord in the air: and so shall we ever be with the Lord. Wherefore comfort one another with these words.

The word *apocalyptic* comes from the word *apocalypse,* which means (in the Greek) "an unveiling or revealing." Paul's apocalyptic message of 1 Thessalonians 4:13-18 is that God's action in Jesus unveiled or revealed the coming of a new age in which deliverance and salvation is offered to everyone who affirms and accepts God's action in Christ. This is the hope of Christianity to which the Christians in Thessalonica held onto with faith. Living as domestic servants and former slaves, the Thessalonian Christians worshipped Jesus as the Messiah (the Christ) and believed that He would come from heaven to rule in the world where "first shall be last; and the last shall be first" (Matthew 19:30). In their private gatherings and in the public square, the Christians in Thessalonica stood with hands and eyes uplifted, waiting for Jesus to descend with all the splendor of a Greek god or Roman statesman. They became known by and associated with the name *Christian*—coined in the Hellenistic city of Antioch to mock the ridiculous, deluded expectation and hope of Christian congregations. Yet, Paul encouraged the Thessalonians with the "lively hope" that was in Christ. Thus, Paul made a distinction between the Christian Thessalonians and others who had no hope (see verse 13). The basis for the believer's hope is God's action in Christ, the eternal union of believers with the Lord (see verse 17b).

To understand the Thessalonian Christians' approach to their apocalyptic hope, we must take into account the lens through which the Thessalonian Christians saw the ancient world. The dominant worldview of the ancients was that of a heavenly dome and water bound into a three-story universe—the world above, the world below, and the earth just three miles in distance from each other. The Christians in Thessalonica were challenged theologically to determine the meaning of life in the cosmology of the three-story world. Paul taught them that Christ was the bringer of a new age, and the earth and the evil forces of the world below would all be under the power and governance of the new age.

The Thessalonians had known of Paul's teaching about the resurrection of Jesus, but little had been said about the resurrection of believers. The Thessalonians believed that the *parousia* would come before any of their fellow believers died. When Christians suffered death while awaiting the return of Christ, Paul wrote to console them about those who "sleep" (see verse 13). Death is an enemy of God's new age. Thus, Paul encouraged the church of Thessalonica (in the midst of grief) to recognize the hope they had and the hope that distinguished them from others. Their hope lay in an apocalyptic reality that speaks of Jesus' death and resurrection—His "parousia." They were instruments of God's power and purpose. Paul declared that God has power to keep all Christians (both the living and the dead) and bring them into an eternal union with Christ.

B. Living with Confidence
(1 Thessalonians 5:1-3)

BUT OF the times and the seasons, brethren, ye have no need that I write unto you. For yourselves know perfectly that the day of the Lord so cometh as a thief in the night. For when they shall say, Peace and safety; then sudden destruction cometh upon them, as travail upon a woman with child; and they shall not escape.

Having received a report from Timothy (whom he had sent to Thessalonica) that the faith of the Thessalonian Christians was strong despite the strong opposition of Jewish zealots, Paul then made an effort to console and comfort them by praising them for their faith. As for doctrinal instruction, many of the Thessalonians had questions regarding Christians who had died and wondered whether they would miss out on Jesus' return. As one can see in the letter Paul wrote to them, he addressed them with incredible love and theological insight as he walked them through the issues of death, life, and resurrection. The key to understanding Paul's theology as it relates to matters of death and resurrection of Christians is to understand his placing primary emphasis on the importance of "being with the Lord." In life or death, believers' hopes are never separated from the love of God in Christ Jesus (see Romans 8:28-31). The power of Paul's instruction has symbolic and metaphoric power, more so than a literal interpretation of physical life after death. In giving his theological view of the matter concerning death and resurrection, Paul labored to challenge the Christians in Thessalonica to continue walking in the ways of the Gospel message and its ethical imperatives (see 4:1–5:22). Paul's primary concern was to have them know that God's action in Christ has sustainable power to keep them in the midst of social and political opposition to their faith.

The words of Paul in the book of 1 Thessalonians prompt the Christian reader to think about end times or what biblical theologians refer to as *eschatology*, the "last things" or the "ultimate end of the world as we know it." Paul's reference to the "thief in the night" is a description of the unpredictable "day of the Lord" (verse 2). These verses are saturated with apocalyptic imagery that suggests that the Christian community can live with confidence, since their eschatological hope is tied to God's undefeatable purpose. The Christians in Thessalonica were people of "the Day," which is a reference to the unpredictable "Day of the Lord." The Day of the Lord speaks of the future consummation of the new age in Christ. The distinctive perspective of Paul concerning "the Day of the Lord" is the vindication of believers in the new age of Christ. When the Day of Judgment comes as "a thief in the night," Christians already know the outcome—Christ and His church will be victorious.

C. The End Goal of Christian Hope
(1 Thessalonians 5:4-11)

But ye, brethren, are not in darkness, that that day should overtake you as a thief. Ye are all the children of light, and the children of the day: we are not of the night, nor of darkness. Therefore let us not sleep, as do others; but let us watch and be sober. For they that sleep sleep in the night; and they that be drunken are drunken in the night. But let us, who are of the day, be sober, putting on the breastplate of faith and love; and for an helmet, the hope of salvation. For God hath not appointed us to wrath, but to obtain salvation by our Lord Jesus Christ, Who died for us, that, whether we wake or sleep, we should live together with him. Wherefore comfort yourselves together, and edify one another, even as also ye do.

In the contrast of believers with unbelievers (verses 4-5), Paul described the unbelievers as persons who would be surprised by "the thief in the night." The night represents a condition of unawareness or insensitivity. Believers were not in a state of darkness; rather, they were children of the day (see 5:5), which means that they had the light of awareness and understanding. Children of the day versus unbelievers of the night are in an eschatological battle for the reality which shapes life and living. Paul called for the Christians in Thessalonica to be sober and consistent in their behavior, like children who walked and lived daily in the light. The triad of "faith, hope, and love" was the weaponry of the Christian community in this battle. Members of the Christian community must encourage each other to remain vigilant in their vision of the life, death, and resurrection of Jesus. They are to build up one another in the faith and thus overcome the alienation and hostility of nonbelievers.

The history of Christianity indicates that the first century came and went with little evidence that the transformative vision the people expected and for which Jesus died had been fulfilled. The faith of the Thessalonian Christians was trapped between what biblical theologians describe as "the already" and "not yet" of the kingdom of God. Living in the tensions (sociologically and theologically) between "the already" and "the not yet" is the hermeneutical key to understanding Paul's instructions to the Thessalonian Christians.

III. CONCLUDING REFLECTION

Living with expectations, between "the already" and "the not yet" poses great challenges to one's faith. Paul's exhortation and teaching to the Christians in Thessalonica represent the strongest appeal for steadfast hope in the midst of opposition and resistance to the purpose of God. In many ways, Paul's apocalyptic spirit was similar to that spirit found in the experience and struggle of African slaves who were forced to wait for freedom and lived in the tension between the "hope of freedom" and the "absence of freedom" on American plantations. Like the Christian community in Thessalonica, there was little in the environment of oppression to console and comfort them to know that their struggle for freedom was consistent with God's purpose. Yet out of that tension, the Negro spirituals were born. They found comfort by creating another world of hope in the midst of a world of seeming hopelessness. These songs built up the solidarity of spirit and faith necessary for the slaves to "Walk Together Children" until they found consolation in "the great camp meeting in the promised land." Paul's apocalyptic vision of God's new age in Christ serves to help contemporary Christians hold on to the hope of Jesus Christ.

PRAYER

God, thank You for the hope we have in Jesus Christ. Enable us to allow this hope to grow in our faith as we live in a world resistant to the Gospel message. In Jesus' name we pray. Amen.

WORD POWER

Apocalyptic—(1) **predicting disaster: warning about a disastrous future or outcome; "an apocalyptic scenario of global warming"; (2) involving destruction: involving widespread destruction and devastation; (3) Bible relating to Apocalypse: relating to the events in the book of Revelation in the Holy Bible.**
Second Coming—**the anticipated return of Jesus Christ; in Christian belief, the anticipated and prophesied return of Jesus Christ to judge humanity at the end of the world.**

HOME DAILY BIBLE READINGS
(April 15-21, 2013)

Living with Hope

MONDAY, April 15: "The Hopeless Human Situation" (Isaiah 59:9-15a)

TUESDAY, April 16: "The Source of Hope" (Isaiah 59:15b-21)

WEDNESDAY, April 17: "Waiting in Hope" (Psalm 38:9-15)

THURSDAY, April 18: "Hoping against Hope" (Romans 4:16-25)

FRIDAY, April 19: "Seizing the Hope Set before Us" (Hebrews 6:13-20)

SATURDAY, April 20: "The God of Hope" (Romans 15:7-13)

SUNDAY, April 21: "Encourage One Another with Hope" (1 Thessalonians 4:13–5:11)

Reference
The New Interpreter's Bible, Volume XI, pp. 673-728.

LESSON 9　　　　　　　　　　　　　　　　　April 28, 2013

HOPE COMES FROM GOD'S GRACE

FAITH PATHWAY/FAITH JOURNEY TOPIC: **Sure Source of Hope**

DEVOTIONAL READING: **Titus 3:1-7**
PRINT PASSAGE: **2 Thessalonians 2:1-3, 9-17**

BACKGROUND SCRIPTURE: **2 Thessalonians 2**
KEY VERSES: **2 Thessalonians 2:16-17**

2 Thessalonians 2:1-3, 9-17—KJV

NOW WE beseech you, brethren, by the coming of our Lord Jesus Christ, and by our gathering together unto him,

2 That ye be not soon shaken in mind, or be troubled, neither by spirit, nor by word, nor by letter as from us, as that the day of Christ is at hand.

3 Let no man deceive you by any means: for that day shall not come, except there come a falling away first, and that man of sin be revealed, the son of perdition.

.....

9 Even him, whose coming is after the working of Satan with all power and signs and lying wonders,

10 And with all deceivableness of unrighteousness in them that perish; because they received not the love of the truth, that they might be saved.

11 And for this cause God shall send them strong delusion, that they should believe a lie:

12 That they all might be damned who believed not the truth, but had pleasure in unrighteousness.

13 But we are bound to give thanks alway to God for you, brethren beloved of the Lord, because God hath from the beginning chosen you to salvation through sanctification of the Spirit and belief of the truth:

14 Whereunto he called you by our gospel, to the obtaining of the glory of our Lord Jesus Christ.

15 Therefore, brethren, stand fast, and hold the traditions which ye have been taught, whether by word, or our epistle.

16 Now our Lord Jesus Christ himself, and God, even our Father, which hath loved us, and hath given us everlasting consolation and good hope through grace,

17 Comfort your hearts, and stablish you in every good word and work.

2 Thessalonians 2:1-3, 9-17—NIV

CONCERNING THE coming of our Lord Jesus Christ and our being gathered to him, we ask you, brothers, 2 not to become easily unsettled or alarmed by some prophecy, report or letter supposed to have come from us, saying that the day of the Lord has already come.

3 Don't let anyone deceive you in any way, for that day will not come until the rebellion occurs and the man of lawlessness is revealed, the man doomed to destruction.

.....

9 The coming of the lawless one will be in accordance with the work of Satan displayed in all kinds of counterfeit miracles, signs and wonders,

10 and in every sort of evil that deceives those who are perishing. They perish because they refused to love the truth and so be saved.

11 For this reason God sends them a powerful delusion so that they will believe the lie

12 and so that all will be condemned who have not believed the truth but have delighted in wickedness.

13 But we ought always to thank God for you, brothers loved by the Lord, because from the beginning God chose you to be saved through the sanctifying work of the Spirit and through belief in the truth.

14 He called you to this through our gospel, that you might share in the glory of our Lord Jesus Christ.

15 So then, brothers, stand firm and hold to the teachings we passed on to you, whether by word of mouth or by letter.

16 May our Lord Jesus Christ himself and God our Father, who loved us and by his grace gave us eternal encouragement and good hope,

17 encourage your hearts and strengthen you in every good deed and word.

UNIFYING LESSON PRINCIPLE

Information about the future comes to us from a variety of sources. How can we know which sources to trust? Paul warned us about the deception that can come from satanic sources.

TOPICAL OUTLINE OF THE LESSON

I. **Introduction**

    A. Against Scattered Hope

    B. Biblical Background

II. **Exposition and Application of the Scripture**

    A. The Ingredients of Christian Hope
       (2 Thessalonians 2:1-3)

    B. Be Not Deceived
       (2 Thessalonians 2:9-12)

    C. Reasons to Hold On to the Faith
       (2 Thessalonians 2:13-17)

III. **Concluding Reflection**

LESSON OBJECTIVES

Upon the completion of the lesson, the students will be able to do the following:

1. Review the principles of financial accountability put in place by Ezra;

2. Reflect on being generous givers to the church as an act of worship to God; and,

3. Pledge that every time they drop their offerings into the plate they reflect upon it as an act of worship to God and not just a habit or act of social conformity.

POINTS TO BE EMPHASIZED

ADULT/YOUTH

Adult Topic: Sure Source of Hope

Youth Topic: Hope Grounded in God's Grace

Adult Key Verses: 2 Thessalonians 2:16-17

Youth Key Verse: 2 Thessalonians 2:13

Print Passage: 2 Thessalonians 2:1-3, 9-17

—The church in Thessalonica had been misled and shaken about the "day of the Lord," and Paul reminded them of the truth he preached.

—Paul told the Thessalonians that a "man of lawlessness" (possibly the Antichrist in 1 John 2:18) will precede Christ's return, and that there will be widespread rebellion against God.

—In the midst of all the confusion, Paul was thankful for their faith and encouraged them to hold fast to what he preached and what they had been taught.

—Those who do not embrace the truth of Christ will perish, but from the beginning, God willed that Christians be saved and sanctified through the work of the Spirit.

—Paul asked God and Jesus Christ to encourage and strengthen his friends in their faith.

—God will send a delusion to people who refuse to believe the truth—and they will believe what is false and will be condemned (see 2 Thessalonians 2:11).

CHILDREN

Children Topic: Stand Firm with Hope

Key Verse: 2 Thessalonians 2:15

Print Passage: 2 Thessalonians 2:1-3, 9-17

—Paul asserted to the Thessalonians that the day of Christ's return had not yet come.

—Before Christ's return there will be an outbreak of evil, which is the work of Satan.

—Paul cautioned the people not to be deceived in any way.

—Paul charged the Thessalonians with maintaining the Christian beliefs that had been taught to them.

—Paul prayed that they would receive comfort and strength for good work and word.

—Paul told the Thessalonians to be thankful for their salvation.

I. INTRODUCTION

A. Against Scattered Hope

The church in Thessalonica had great enthusiasm for the apocalyptic Gospel that Paul preached to them in the synagogue. However, the "delay" in the return of Christ caused much controversy. Yet, Paul saw the Christians of Thessalonica as "shining jewels" standing firm in their faith. Their faith was "growing abundantly, and the love of everyone of you for one another [was] increasing" (2 Thessalonians 1:3, NRSV). Even though the faith community had been shaken by the controversy regarding the meaning and reality of "the day of the Lord," they grew into the image of God's love in Jesus Christ. Their hope had seemingly been scattered by the social alienation, hostility, and ridicule of nonbelievers, yet the church's growth was determined by the measurements of steadfast faith and love.

When a people's faith has been scattered, they are swayed by promises of something new and better than the traditions that birthed their faith and ways of thinking. This was essentially the challenge of the first-century Christians—to whom the letter of 2 Thessalonians was addressed. How to remain steadfast in the faith was a formidable challenge amid controversy and crisis.

The study of the book of 2 Thessalonians should help students think theologically about the spiritual and religious traditions that produced their faith in Jesus Christ. There is a need for the church to again go back to the old landmarks of the Christian heritage and determine what the witness of the church means in these contemporary times of injustice, economic meltdowns, and the mega-growth of religion. This seemingly dismisses the core faith values once known and practiced by the church. If the church is to maintain the relevance of its faith traditions amid new trends of religious diversity, then Christians must engage in sincere prayer, study, and theological reflection.

B. Biblical Background

Like the letter of 1 Thessalonians, the second letter to the congregation in Thessalonica is a letter of exhortation in which the author reminded the Thessalonians of previous instructions (see 2:5, 15; 3:7b-10) and reemphasized what they already knew. In the midst of all the doctrinal controversy and confusion, Paul, the assumed author of the book of

2 Thessalonians, was thankful for their faith and encouraged them to hold fast to what they had been taught. Many of the Christians in Thessalonica were driven by social and spiritual dispositions of extreme apocalyptic enthusiasm about the "parousia," or imminent return of Christ. In the letter of 2 Thessalonians, the author responded to this enthusiasm by theologically unpacking the meaning of the *parousia* (verses 1-2), and giving encouraging exhortations for disciplined prayer, daily meditation, and industry (verses 13-17). The author of the book of 2 Thessalonians was concerned that the controversy about "the anti-Christ" and the return of Jesus would unsettle the faith of the Christian community of Thessalonica. It is stated in the book of 2 Thessalonians that before the return of Christ, there will first be a "rebellion" (2:3, NIV) against the rule of God. At the height of the rebellion, the "lawless one" or antichrist (the personification of all wickedness) would manifest itself against the Gospel of God. The epistle exhorts the Christian community not to be deceived and shaken up by the false heresy surrounding the return of Christ. They were encouraged to hold on and stand firm in the faith that was preached and taught to them.

II. EXPOSITION AND APPLICATION OF THE SCRIPTURE

A. The Ingredients of Christian Hope
(2 Thessalonians 2:1-3)

NOW WE beseech you, brethren, by the coming of our Lord Jesus Christ, and by our gathering together unto him, That ye be not soon shaken in mind, or be troubled, neither by spirit, nor by word, nor by letter as from us, as that the day of Christ is at hand. Let no man deceive you by any means: for that day shall not come, except there come a falling away first, and that man of sin be revealed, the son of perdition.

It is perhaps difficult for contemporary Christians to imagine or understand the apocalyptic fervor of the second half of the first century. There were several claims and counterclaims about the apocalyptic message concerning "the Day of the Lord." Second Thessalonians 2 addresses the assumptions of the early believers that the arrival of "the Day of the Lord" would follow in close proximity to the suffering of the church. Thus, the focus of these introductory verses in chapter 2 and the larger texts that follow is both on Jesus and the status of believers who will gather with Christ on "the Day of the Lord." Thus, the major ingredients of Christian hope are the life, death, and resurrection of Jesus. Jesus is the revelation of God, in which Christians come to know the truth about life in the here and now and in the future. The theological struggle of the early Christians as well as for contemporary Christians was/is to determine how God is with us and what the revelation of Jesus means for life. The difficulty for the Christians in Thessalonica was to factor in the revelation of Jesus (God with us) and the imminent expectation of the "parousia."

The reference to "the Day of the Lord" speaks to the eschatological gathering of believers—with the Christ glorified in the "parousia." Verse 2 introduces an immediate response to refute the false claim that events associated with the Day of the Lord had already occurred or "appeared." Such a climate of apocalyptic fervor inspired many prophecies about when and how the Day of the Lord would appear.

Authentic faith became a major ingredient of Christian hope. The many false prophecies that surfaced among these early believers precipitated anxiety, which challenged them to reflect on the meaning of their hope and faith. The writer of the book of 2 Thessalonians spoke against the false claims that had the potential to disrupt and upset the church's faith.

One important lesson we can learn from the Christians in Thessalonica is that false claims exert a powerful force over the lives of people. The reason why false claims about God exert such power over people is because often, they come wrapped in the same garb as truth. The theological challenge for Christian communities is how to guard against falling prey to false claims that often appear as the truth. The immediate answer is not to cave in to loveless logic that highlights messianic individualism against the prophetic presence of God's justice, compassion, and mercy in the world for all persons.

B. Be Not Deceived
(2 Thessalonians 2:9-12)

Even him, whose coming is after the working of Satan with all power and signs and lying wonders, And with all deceivableness of unrighteousness in them that perish; because they received not the love of the truth, that they might be saved. And for this cause God shall send them strong delusion, that they should believe a lie: That they all might be damned who believed not the truth, but had pleasure in unrighteousness.

The writer of the book of 2 Thessalonians made the Christian community aware that there were evil powers that stood against the truth of God. These evil or rebellious forces were stark examples of the hostility that Christians should anticipate and are expected to stand firm against as those forces resisted the flourishing of God's love and actions in Jesus. For the writer of the book of 2 Thessalonians, the hostile environment and rebellion against the truth of God would be manifested in a mysterious figure referred to as "the lawless one" (verse 9, NIV). The urgent appeal made to the Christian community not to be deceived by the teaching of "the lawless one" expressed the concern of how difficult it is to discern truth from lies. The revelations which this figure promulgates (verse 9) should be seen in contrast to the revelation of Jesus (verse 8). Since the "lawless one" and the faith which Paul upheld about Jesus both made truth claims, it posed a great challenge to the Christians in Thessalonica to discern or know which claim bears the authentic revelation of God. The writer of the book of 2 Thessalonians based his theology on the instructions given in 1 Thessalonians 1:5-12, which establish Jesus as the agent of God. Jesus came as a servant of God's love—as expressed in Jesus' life, death, and resurrection. It is in Jesus' life, death, and resurrection that God's name is glorified. The picture of "the lawless one," however, is that of a deceiver: "He opposes and exalts himself as an object of worship, so that he takes his seat in the temple of God, declaring himself to be God" (see 2 Thessalonians 2:4). Satanic forces that resist God's revelation in Jesus are behind the activity of the "lawless one." Unlike Jesus (see 2 Thessalonians 1:8), "the lawless one" (verse 9, NIV) does not have a Gospel, but seeks to deceive people who "refused to love the truth" (2:10, NIV). The revelation of Jesus would have the authority of God, whereas the false claims of the "lawless one" would not. By whose love did the Christian community base the authority and power for their faith and lives? The writer of the book of 2 Thessalonians responded to this question by placing the faith of the Christian community in the larger drama of God's actions in Jesus. The text (2 Thessalonians 2) places the experiences of the church's suffering within the larger drama of what God was doing and would do in the world.

C. Reasons to Hold On to the Faith
(2 Thessalonians 2:13-17)

But we are bound to give thanks alway to God for you, brethren beloved of the Lord, because God hath from the beginning chosen you to salvation through sanctification of the Spirit and belief of the truth: Whereunto he called you by our gospel, to the obtaining of the glory of our Lord Jesus Christ. Therefore, brethren, stand fast, and hold the traditions which ye have been taught, whether by word, or our epistle. Now our Lord Jesus Christ himself, and God, even our Father, which hath loved us, and hath given us everlasting consolation and good hope through grace, Comfort your hearts, and stablish you in every good word and work.

In spite of their struggle, the Christians in Thessalonica were holding on to the faith they had received from the preaching of Paul. Moreover, they stood firm in the faith, because the Spirit of God was the source of their strength and growing maturity in the faith (see 1 Thessalonians 4:3-6). The inner convictions of the Christians in Thessalonica about God's actions in Christ gave them power and strength to hold on to the faith. The reasons for their holding on to the faith are outlined in verses 13-19. First, God's activity in their lives through Jesus is the foremost element that the writer of the book of 2 Thessalonians used to comfort and encourage the Christian community (see verses 13-14). What God had done in electing them and bringing salvation to their lives was the basis for their thanksgiving. Second, the disclosure that the Christians in Thessalonica were chosen (or set apart) by God as agents of divine purpose and salvation in the world was cause for them to rejoice and be comforted (see verse 9). Even though satanic forces against the truth of the Gospel they had received continued to challenge them, they could be assured that God's purpose in and through them would not be defeated. With such assurance, the Thessalonians were admonished to "stand firm and hold fast to the traditions" (see verse 15).

The writer of the book of 2 Thessalonians can be considered a "voice of truth" which gave the Christian community clarity about the faith tradition which they were called to serve and charged to fulfill. The voice of truth sometimes rarely appears on the scene of crisis and controversy—when truth hangs in the balance and clarity is needed in order to discern the choices between good and evil. In the case of the Christians in Thessalonica, the satanic forces behind the false claims of the Gospel versus the authenticity of the Gospel challenged them to hold firmly to their faith in God.

During times of crisis and controversy, the voice of truth always draws us to the larger meaning and purpose of life in and with God. Just as the Christians in Thessalonica needed a voice of truth, such a voice is needed in every context where there are challenges to God's love and justice in the world. The spirit of "anti-Christ" or the "lawless one" recycles in cultures resistant to God's action in Jesus. We should thank God for voices of truth (like that of the writer of the book of 2 Thessalonians) against the spirit of "the lawless one."

III. CONCLUDING REFLECTION

The kind of strength that undergirded the

inner convictions possessed by the Christians in Thessalonica should be a source of inspiration for the church today. For such strength is sorely needed in our times of moral decline and religious controversy. For example, the prosperity gospel appeals of mega-religious movements is a far cry from the theology that says a God of "love and justice" mandates an inclusive community of compassion and freedom for everyone. This was the actual faith that birthed black churches on American soil and was the inner conviction to which African slaves held. What drives and fuels the crises of inner-city youth, the breakup of families, and the decline of civility is the lack of "inner conviction" that grounds us in the faith that once was the source of our hope.

The tragedy of Jim Jones of the People's Temple in Jonestown, Guyana, is an example of how the vulnerability of oppressed communities desperate for hope of better lives can easily be drawn to embrace false claims of truth. Some 918 people died in the Jonestown massacre, because they followed false religious claims. In the light of many false religious claims today, the significant challenge of all Christians and the churches they attend is to examine the relevance of their faith, and theologically reflect on how the experiences of God's liberating love in Jesus Christ impact life in the world.

PRAYER

O God, in the midst of life's daily struggles, only Your love can sustain and help us hold on to faith in Jesus. Thank You for salvation in Christ. Help us always to discern the gift of salvation against all who resist the love of Christ in the world. In Jesus' name we pray. Amen.

WORD POWER

The Day of the Lord—(1) also called "Day of Yahweh"; in Old Testament eschatology, it is a day of final judgment (see Amos 5:18-21; Ezekiel 30); (2) also called the "Day of Christ" or "Day of Jesus Christ"; the Day of the Second Advent (see 1 Corinthians 1:14; Philippians 1:10; 2:16; 2 Peter 3:10).

HOME DAILY BIBLE READINGS
(April 22-28, 2013)

Hope Comes from God's Grace
MONDAY, April 22: "An Appointed Time" (Psalm 75)
TUESDAY, April 23: "The Day Is Coming" (Malachi 4)
WEDNESDAY, April 24: "No Good Thing Withheld" (Psalm 84)
THURSDAY, April 25: "My Help Comes from the Lord" (Psalm 121)
FRIDAY, April 26: "The Hope of Eternal Life" (Titus 3:1-7)
SATURDAY, April 27: "Kept Sound and Blameless" (1 Thessalonians 5:23-28)
SUNDAY, April 28: "Eternal Comfort and Good Hope" (2 Thessalonians 2:1-3, 9-17)

Reference
The New Interpreter's Bible, Volume XI, pp. 753-763.

A LIVING HOPE

FAITH PATHWAY/FAITH JOURNEY TOPIC: **Hopeful Living**

DEVOTIONAL READING: **Lamentations 3:19-24**   BACKGROUND SCRIPTURE: **1 Peter 1:1-12**
PRINT PASSAGE: **1 Peter 1:3-12**   KEY VERSE: **1 Peter 1:3**

1 Peter 1:3-12—KJV

3 Blessed be the God and Father of our Lord Jesus Christ, which according to his abundant mercy hath begotten us again unto a lively hope by the resurrection of Jesus Christ from the dead,

4 To an inheritance incorruptible, and undefiled, and that fadeth not away, reserved in heaven for you,

5 Who are kept by the power of God through faith unto salvation ready to be revealed in the last time.

6 Wherein ye greatly rejoice, though now for a season, if need be, ye are in heaviness through manifold temptations:

7 That the trial of your faith, being much more precious than of gold that perisheth, though it be tried with fire, might be found unto praise and honour and glory at the appearing of Jesus Christ:

8 Whom having not seen, ye love; in whom, though now ye see him not, yet believing, ye rejoice with joy unspeakable and full of glory:

9 Receiving the end of your faith, even the salvation of your souls.

10 Of which salvation the prophets have enquired and searched diligently, who prophesied of the grace that should come unto you:

11 Searching what, or what manner of time the Spirit of Christ which was in them did signify, when it testified beforehand the sufferings of Christ, and the glory that should follow.

12 Unto whom it was revealed, that not unto themselves, but unto us they did minister the things, which are now reported unto you by them that have preached the gospel unto you with the Holy Ghost sent down from heaven; which things the angels desire to look into.

1 Peter 1:3-12—NIV

3 Praise be to the God and Father of our Lord Jesus Christ! In his great mercy he has given us new birth into a living hope through the resurrection of Jesus Christ from the dead,

4 and into an inheritance that can never perish, spoil or fade—kept in heaven for you,

5 who through faith are shielded by God's power until the coming of the salvation that is ready to be revealed in the last time.

6 In this you greatly rejoice, though now for a little while you may have had to suffer grief in all kinds of trials.

7 These have come so that your faith—of greater worth than gold, which perishes even though refined by fire—may be proved genuine and may result in praise, glory and honor when Jesus Christ is revealed.

8 Though you have not seen him, you love him; and even though you do not see him now, you believe in him and are filled with an inexpressible and glorious joy,

9 for you are receiving the goal of your faith, the salvation of your souls.

10 Concerning this salvation, the prophets, who spoke of the grace that was to come to you, searched intently and with the greatest care,

11 trying to find out the time and circumstances to which the Spirit of Christ in them was pointing when he predicted the sufferings of Christ and the glories that would follow.

12 It was revealed to them that they were not serving themselves but you, when they spoke of the things that have now been told you by those who have preached the gospel to you by the Holy Spirit sent from heaven. Even angels long to look into these things.

UNIFYING LESSON PRINCIPLE

Life's trials and tribulations can cause us to experience hopelessness. Where can one go in order to find new hope and reassurance for a joyous future? Peter wrote that a new birth into a living hope can be found in the resurrection of Jesus Christ.

TOPICAL OUTLINE OF THE LESSON

I. **Introduction**

  A. Living with a Revolutionary Salvation

  B. Biblical Background

II. **Exposition and Application of the Scripture**

  A. Rebirth to God's Freedom (1 Peter 1:3-5)

  B. Living with God's Inheritance (1 Peter 1:6-7)

  C. The Tests of Christian Faith (1 Peter 1:8-12)

III. **Concluding Reflection**

LESSON OBJECTIVES

Upon the completion of the lesson, the students should be able to do the following:

1. Interpret Peter's message of hope rooted in the death and resurrection of Jesus;

2. Identify Jesus' resurrection from the dead as a source of hope and a reason for living; and,

3. Identify situations to which they could bring hope.

POINTS TO BE EMPHASIZED

ADULT/YOUTH

Adult Topic: Hopeful Living

Youth Topic: A Clean Slate

Adult/Youth Key Verse: 1 Peter 1:3

Print Passage: 1 Peter 1:3-12

—New life and hope can be found in the resurrection of Christ.

—Peter looked forward to a full revelation of God's salvation "in the last time" (verse 5).

—Peter knew that we would suffer trials before the "last time" comes.

—Peter knew that our trials refine our lives and bring glory to God.

—Peter pointed out that the prophets "searched intently" (verse 10) to learn more about this salvation.

—Because of one's faith, suffering should not stop praise.

CHILDREN

Children Topic: Having Hope

Key Verse: 1 Peter 1:3

Print Passage: 1 Peter 1:3-12

—God has given us the hope of a new birth through the resurrection of Jesus Christ.

—God's power protects us through faith.

—Those who believe in Christ will be able to praise and honor Christ, even though they have experienced or are now experiencing difficult times.

—Even though believers have not seen Christ, they love Him and rejoice because of their salvation.

I. INTRODUCTION

A. Living with a Revolutionary Salvation

The biblical text of 1 Peter 1:1-12 has a revolutionary character that connects it to prophetic dreams and words of Israel's Hebrew prophets. The proclamation of Israel's prophets pointed toward restoration of the ancient Jews through the dawning of God's reign of love and justice in the world. For centuries this hope persisted, ultimately being fulfilled through the life, death, and resurrection of Jesus—who is the "cornerstone" of a new existence in the world. The core message of the book of 1 Peter is that although this cornerstone of God's truth has been rejected by the world, it has become the chief cornerstone upon which the foundation of the reign of God is built. In the face of various "trials and sufferings," the first-century Christians to whom the author of the book of 1 Peter wrote were called to live on the basis of this truth and its radical transformation and revolutionary stance for divine justice and love.

It might be difficult for us to imagine the difficulties that first-century Christians faced as they attempted to live out the revolutionary and transformative consciousness of the "new birth," resulting in their salvation in and through Jesus Christ. These early Christian communities did not separate the social and spiritual needs of life. For them, salvation was inclusive of liberation, the lifting of suffering that burdened and oppressed the inner and outer realities of life. To our contemporary mindset, the word *revolution* carries political connotations without concern for the spiritual or holistic transformation of social worlds that impact the mind, body, and soul. To read the book of 1 Peter as a call for individual piety and ethical behavior is to miss its revolutionary mandate for the radical transformation of the self and the systems in the world that condemn the self.

In the study of this lesson, students will see how "God, the self, and the world" are bound together in "the living hope" that Jesus Christ offers to humanity through His life, death, and resurrection.

B. Biblical Background

The book of 1 Peter was likely written to scattered Gentile Christian communities that faced resistance and ostracism for their faith. In the face of various trials imposed upon them, the author of the book of 1 Peter encouraged believers to look toward Jesus' death and resurrection for their hope, and to see their current circumstances as a test for their faith. The book of 1 Peter makes a clear connection between the prophets of the Hebrew Scriptures and the "Spirit of Christ," affirming that the words of the prophets correlate to the meaning and purpose of Jesus' life, death, and resurrection. Theologically, this connection between Christ and the Hebrew prophets indicates that the ancient prophecies comprise both the context and reason for the first Christians to have been steadfast in faith. Even in the midst of oppression that the Empire imposed upon them, their hope and salvation through Christ was indestructible. They had become heirs to "an inheritance" that was "incorruptible, and undefiled, and that fadeth not away" (1:4). Conflict and opposition between that Empire's existence and the dawn of God's reign were inevitable. There was no escape from the resistance of the Empire that declared itself to be the provider of peace and salvation. The Empire persecuted anyone who accepted the alternative reality of God's reign. Yet, this is the basis for the "living hope" of the early Christian communities. For them, the resurrection of Christ was the decisive action of God that believers have received through God's love, mercy, and grace. New life in Christ is the ultimate goal of salvation (the birthing of a new existence) that calls for faith in the reign of God. This radical transformation changes the course of life from "a dead-end existence" to new life in God's righteous kingdom (see 2:5, 24). How this "new birth" or spiritual kinship with God's righteous reign impacts daily existence and social negotiations is the theological interest of the book of 1 Peter, as it lays out a polemic or defense for living effectively in the midst of opposition and resistance to God's reign by nonbelievers.

II. EXPOSITION AND APPLICATION OF THE SCRIPTURE

A. Rebirth to God's Freedom
(1 Peter 1:3-5)

Blessed be the God and Father of our Lord Jesus Christ, which according to his abundant mercy hath begotten us again unto a lively hope by the resurrection of Jesus Christ from the dead, To an inheritance incorruptible, and undefiled, and that fadeth not away, reserved in heaven for you, Who are kept by the power of God through faith unto salvation ready to be revealed in the last time.

First Peter 1:3 begins with a doxology: "Blessed be the God and Father of our Lord Jesus Christ." This doxology is both redemptive and revolutionary in character; it provides the context for new life in Christ (see verses 3-5). This doxology of praise connects with the suffering and trials of believers who have new identities in Jesus Christ. The phrase "new birth" or "cause to be born again" (see 1:23) serves as a dramatic metaphor for the decisive or radical transformation that occurs when one experiences God's liberating love and recognizes God's merciful action in Jesus Christ.

Because of suffering, trials, and persecution (see 1:1-6), first-century Christians were encouraged by the author of the book of 1 Peter to see their struggle in the light of God's plan—as revealed in the Prophets (see 1:8-12). The Gentile communities of Asia Minor, to whom Peter wrote, had gone through "a rebirthing process" that was no less revolutionary than Jesus' call to repentance in Mark 1:15: "The kingdom of God is near. Repent and believe the Good News!" (NIV). Because of the new birth in Christ, Christians see themselves and the world around them differently—they are children of freedom, people of God who have been incorporated into the dawning realities of the reign of God. This is a radical transformation from living outside the reality of God's love to living inside the reality of God. This radical transformation involved entry into a new relationship (kinship) with God, Christ, and others in the world. In the light of the newness of God in their lives, the book of 1 Peter reminded them that they were to live and make life decisions based upon the reality of God's salvation through Jesus Christ. The darkness of their former bondage and slavery was dead, and their new baptism in Jesus brought them to see the light of God's life in them and God's purpose in the world. Such radical transformation involved a total reversal of social and political habits that characterized the Empire's authority and dominance in their lives. This radical transformation in Christ entailed a total separation from the unrighteous social alliances that are associated with injustice.

Contemporary black churches could take the words that Peter wrote to the early Christians as a parallel to the autobiography of black people striving for freedom. Contemporary black churches are centuries removed from the witness of the book of 1 Peter to Gentile Christians; however, the heritage of a chosen people called to radical transformation to serve God's revolutionary purpose in the world remains the basis of what it means to be black and Christian today. Through God's gift of salvation to ebony sons and daughters, God declares that no one was/is created for dehumanization but for freedom—for righteous purposes and new existences in Christ. As a transformed people for divine love, black churches are constantly called to spiritual "rebirth" and to "be prepared to offer a defense for the hope that fills us" (see 3:15).

Thus, Christ is our "living hope" against all forms of resistance. The reality of God's love in the world shapes who we are. In verse 3, "lively hope" refers to confidence in the power of God. The early Christians were encouraged to "set your hope upon the grace that is coming at the revelation of Jesus Christ" (see 1:13). The stress on trust and hope in God's action (see 1:21) can be linked to faithful Hebrew matriarchs and patriarchs whose hope in God came to fruition in the life, death, and resurrection of Jesus Christ. It was the persistence of this hope in the face of social oppression and opposition that distinguished the witness of first-century Christians.

B. Living with God's Inheritance
(1 Peter 1:6-7)

Wherein ye greatly rejoice, though now for a season, if need be, ye are in heaviness through manifold temptations: That the trial of your faith, being much more precious than of gold that perisheth, though it be tried with fire, might be found unto praise and honour and glory at the appearing of Jesus Christ.

We know from the above text of the book of 1 Peter that God does not exempt believers from persecution or suffering. Believers may suffer agonizing pain—both physical and psychological—because of their faith. The life of Martin Luther King Jr. is a contemporary example of one who suffered both psychological and physical pain for his faith in the justice of God for all people. Crucifixions in various forms come as a result of resistance and opposition to the new existence that God offers through Christ. The book of 1 Peter outlines a polemic that God preserves believers so that they will receive the inheritance of their faith and experience the joy of salvation. Jesus' resurrection is the "cornerstone" of God's power to redeem the righteous and sustain them through diverse trials and sufferings.

Peter did not conceive of faith as a single isolated act. The rebirthing process is continuous until the day of final redemption. Believers must exercise faith daily in order to receive the promise of God's final salvation. In the face of new contexts of opposition and resistance, living with God's inheritance of salvation calls for continuous faith and renewal of commitment. God's power protects our inheritance of salvation through faith and prayer.

Peter believed that the end times had come (see 1:20; 4:7), but that the final salvation of Christians lay with God's power. In other words, the revolutionary actions of God in the world are not complete. Peter called for faith that waits on the decisive moment when God will bring to an end the world as it has always been. Living in anticipation of this radical transformation as inheritors of God's salvation will challenge us to deeper faith and hope. In the theological mind of the author of the book of 1 Peter, faith and hope were gifts of God. God fortifies believers so that they persist in faith and hope until the day they obtain the full measure of their salvation in Christ.

C. The Tests of Christian Faith
(1 Peter 1:8-12)

Whom having not seen, ye love; in whom, though now ye see him not, yet believing, ye rejoice with joy unspeakable and full of glory: Receiving the end of your faith, even the salvation of your souls. Of which salvation the prophets have enquired and searched diligently, who prophesied of the grace that should come unto you: Searching what, or what manner of time the Spirit of Christ which was in them did signify, when it testified beforehand the sufferings of Christ, and the glory that should follow. Unto whom it was revealed, that not unto themselves, but unto us they did minister the things, which are now reported unto you by them that have preached the gospel unto you with the Holy Ghost sent down from heaven; which things the angels desire to look into.

In the book of 1 Peter, faith involved maintaining trust, loyalty, and commitment to the God we meet in Jesus Christ (see 1:8, 21; 5:9). Authentic faith comes to expression when it is tested. Through the crucible of suffering, authentic faith is refined and becomes more valuable to the spiritual life of the Christian than pure gold. In other words, faith in God is of greater value than gold refined by fire. The emphasis here is not so much on faith itself as it is on the nature of faith as a gift from God. It is the tested and proven character of faith (which is more precious than gold) that brings approval from God. Christians receive joy as an outcome of their faith. The foundation of their faith is God's action in Jesus Christ. Thus, all trials and suffering that they may experience are temporary, but God's salvation is eternal.

The sustaining grace of God should not be kept in a separate compartment of our faith. While God's power does not shield believers from trials and suffering, it does protect us from things that cause us to fall away. When the home of Dr. Martin Luther King Jr. was bombed, he reported that his faith began to falter. He wanted to find a way to remove himself from the leadership of the movement. The threats to his life and the opposition to a righteous cause forced Dr. King to pray as he had not experienced prayer before. Through prayer at his kitchen table, Dr. King found "cosmic companionship." What is revealing about Dr. King's experience is that suffering for God's righteous cause transformed a potentially demoralizing experience into the positive light of God's power and love.

The message of the book of 1 Peter is that the worst of persecution imposed on Christians cannot diminish or destroy the salvation they inherited through God's actions in Jesus Christ.

Peter declared to the Gentile Christians—exiles scattered throughout Asia Minor—that God had distinguished them with the gift of salvation and with an inheritance that was holy, imperishable, and indestructible (see verse 4). "Once you were not a people, but now you are the people of God; once you had not received mercy, but now you have received mercy" (verse 10, NIV); Peter penned these words with a consciousness of Israel's revolutionary past, and connected that prophetic past with the faith struggles and sufferings of the first-century Christians. The book of 1 Peter referred to the recipients of God's salvation through Jesus Christ as "living stones," a spiritual house, a holy nation, a chosen race, a people belonging to God, and a people for God's possession in the world (see 1 Peter 2:4-10).

III. CONCLUDING REFLECTION

In the book *Covenant with Black America*, Tavis Smiley begins with a quote from Terry Tempest Williams: "The eyes of the future are looking back and they are praying for us to see beyond our own time." What this wise statement implies and teaches us is that a people's history and faith heritage is never finished. Each generation of Christians in the black church has a moral assignment to uphold the spiritual heritage that birthed our hope and faith. Faith in Jesus Christ challenges us to be agents of God's righteous acts and transformations in the world. Who we have been, who we are now, and what we are striving to become must be grounded in our daily association and faithfulness to the living hope of Jesus Christ.

PRAYER

Holy God, thank You for a salvation that is able to sustain us through all of life's suffering and trials. Strengthen our faith so that we may stand against the world's resistance and opposition to Your reign of love and justice in the world. In Jesus' name we pray. Amen.

WORD POWER

"Hopeful Living"—involves faith and commitment to God's salvation for ourselves and the world. To covenant with this "living hope" means to live daily as the people of God.

HOME DAILY BIBLE READINGS
(April 29–May 5, 2013)

A Living Hope
> MONDAY, April 29: "I Have No Help in Me" (Job 6:8-13)
> TUESDAY, April 30: "Days without Hope" (Job 7:1-6)
> WEDNESDAY, May 1: "Will Mortals Live Again?" (Job 14:7-17)
> THURSDAY, May 2: "My Times Are in Your Hands" (Psalm 31:9-16)
> FRIDAY, May 3: "The Lord Preserves the Faithful" (Psalm 31:19-24)
> SATURDAY, May 4: "Hope in God's Faithfulness" (Lamentations 3:19-24)
> SUNDAY, May 5: "New Birth into a Living Hope" (1 Peter 1:3-12)

EQUIPPED WITH HOPE

FAITH PATHWAY/FAITH JOURNEY TOPIC: **Life worth Living**

DEVOTIONAL READING: **Psalm 130**   BACKGROUND SCRIPTURE: **2 Peter 1**
PRINT PASSAGE: **2 Peter 1:4-14**   KEY VERSE: **2 Peter 1:3**

2 Peter 1:4-14—KJV

4 Whereby are given unto us exceeding great and precious promises: that by these ye might be partakers of the divine nature, having escaped the corruption that is in the world through lust.

5 And beside this, giving all diligence, add to your faith virtue; and to virtue knowledge;

6 And to knowledge temperance; and to temperance patience; and to patience godliness;

7 And to godliness brotherly kindness; and to brotherly kindness charity.

8 For if these things be in you, and abound, they make you that ye shall neither be barren nor unfruitful in the knowledge of our Lord Jesus Christ.

9 But he that lacketh these things is blind, and cannot see afar off, and hath forgotten that he was purged from his old sins.

10 Wherefore the rather, brethren, give diligence to make your calling and election sure: for if ye do these things, ye shall never fall:

11 For so an entrance shall be ministered unto you abundantly into the everlasting kingdom of our Lord and Saviour Jesus Christ.

12 Wherefore I will not be negligent to put you always in remembrance of these things, though ye know them, and be established in the present truth.

13 Yea, I think it meet, as long as I am in this tabernacle, to stir you up by putting you in remembrance;

14 Knowing that shortly I must put off this my tabernacle, even as our Lord Jesus Christ hath shewed me.

2 Peter 1:4-14—NIV

4 Through these he has given us his very great and precious promises, so that through them you may participate in the divine nature and escape the corruption in the world caused by evil desires.

5 For this very reason, make every effort to add to your faith goodness; and to goodness, knowledge;

6 and to knowledge, self-control; and to self-control, perseverance; and to perseverance, godliness;

7 and to godliness, brotherly kindness; and to brotherly kindness, love.

8 For if you possess these qualities in increasing measure, they will keep you from being ineffective and unproductive in your knowledge of our Lord Jesus Christ.

9 But if anyone does not have them, he is nearsighted and blind, and has forgotten that he has been cleansed from his past sins.

10 Therefore, my brothers, be all the more eager to make your calling and election sure. For if you do these things, you will never fall,

11 and you will receive a rich welcome into the eternal kingdom of our Lord and Savior Jesus Christ.

12 So I will always remind you of these things, even though you know them and are firmly established in the truth you now have.

13 I think it is right to refresh your memory as long as I live in the tent of this body,

14 because I know that I will soon put it aside, as our Lord Jesus Christ has made clear to me.

UNIFYING LESSON PRINCIPLE

Many people feel as though they are ineffective, unproductive, and unable to make the right choices in life. Where can we find the strength to surmount this sense of despair? Peter said that the inner strength needed to face life with new assurance and hope comes because of our knowledge of and faith in our Savior, Jesus Christ.

TOPICAL OUTLINE OF THE LESSON

I. Introduction
  A. Facing the Difficulties of Godly Living
  B. Biblical Background

II. Exposition and Application of the Scripture
  A. To Be Christ-like (2 Peter 1:4-9)
  B. Living Out Salvation (2 Peter 1:10-11)
  C. Ethical Christian Virtues that Work (2 Peter 1:12-14)

III. Concluding Reflection

LESSON OBJECTIVES

Upon the completion of the lesson, the students will be able to do the following:

1. Realize how Peter tried to help early Christians be effective and fruitful followers of Jesus Christ;
2. Reflect on the ways that faith, goodness, knowledge, self-control, endurance, godliness, mutual affection, and love are present in their lives; and,
3. Identify ways that they can become more effective and fruitful Christians.

POINTS TO BE EMPHASIZED
ADULT/YOUTH
Adult Topic: Life worth Living
Youth Topic: A Sure Escape Route
Adult Key Verse: 2 Peter 1:3
Youth Key Verse: 2 Peter 1:4
Print Passage: 2 Peter 1:4-14
—Peter knew that God called us by His own glory and goodness and not by our own efforts.
—Peter said that God's promises could help us escape the corruption of lust and enter into the divine nature.
—Faith alone is not enough; it must be supported by goodness, knowledge, self-control, endurance, godliness, mutual affection, and love.
—Believers are to respond to God's adoption of them as His own people.
—Peter kept reminding the believers of these things, because he knew that he would soon die for the cause of Christ.

CHILDREN
Children Topic: Getting What We Need
Key Verse: 2 Peter 1:3
Print Passage: 2 Peter 1:4-14
—God, through His divine power, has given us the ability to persevere (withstand) whatever comes in our lives.
—God enables us to escape corruption.
—Believers must support their faith with virtues that include goodness, knowledge, self-control, endurance, godliness, mutual affection, and love.
—Believers who confirm their calls inherit eternal life.

I. INTRODUCTION

A. Facing the Difficulties of Godly Living

For the next two lessons, the students will study the theological meaning of Christian holiness. Christian holiness is perhaps the most misunderstood area of the Christian life. Much of the confusion in this area of the Christian life develops because of the conflict between the flesh and spirit. Not only have Christians inherited from the ancient biblical world an understanding that the flesh and the spirit battle for supremacy, but also, there is a pervasive conception that the flesh or body is the seat of corruption. But as we shall see in the study of these lessons, the Christian life is a stewardship that honors God in mind, body, and spirit. The Christian life should be understood as more than a personal victory over corruptible desires of the flesh. Rather, the Christian life should be understood as a stewardship of Christ's love (within one's life) that impacts the transformation which God intends for the world.

Christians know that God does not exclude difficulties from the Christian life. Clearly the social constructs and systems of the world are in opposition to God's love and purpose in the world. Thus, the difficulty of the Christian life is not solely about personal battles of the flesh, but, as Paul noted, it is a battle against "principalities and powers, rulers of darkness in high places." Therefore, those who seek to live as stewards of Christ's love can expect opposition and oppression. Christians are challenged to be effective and productive witnesses of Jesus Christ as they live and negotiate the tension between the sacred and the secular, holy and profane, prayer and politics, religion and ethics, spiritual and material. The Christian life can only be productive if persons take up Christ's mandate to love God and the things that God loves.

As the students shall see in the study of this lesson, the holiness of Christ makes life worth living. To be a Christian and live a godly life is to live in the awareness of the divine nature within us—which has been made known to us in Christ. Through Christ's power and promises, Christians have everything needed to live godly lives. It is the knowledge of Christ that helps Christians overcome the difficulties of living out the purpose and meaning of God's salvation. The knowledge of Christ frees us to grow spiritually from the corruption of sin, and become effective and productive in our Christian witness.

B. Biblical Background

A reading of the text from the book of 2 Peter will require us to do theological reflection on what "godliness" means as a Christian virtue. We know from the study of previous lessons on Christian holiness that godliness does not mean pious living without a commitment to God's love and justice in the world. What the book of 2 Peter provides is a theological interpretation of how to handle difficulties, false teachings, and illusions that arise when one's commitment to godliness necessarily brings opposition. Godliness means having the proper attitude or piety toward God, expressed in obedience to His will. It is the mark of Christian maturity (see 1:6-7) and confirms what it means to be called to service in Jesus Christ (see 1:3, 10). Godliness is necessary for being productive and facing opposition to holiness.

The focus of the book of 2 Peter is on Christian holiness; it describes what a Christian life grounded in "the divine nature and the promises of Christ" (verse 4) looks like. According to the book of 2 Peter, a Christian life grounded in divine nature looks like the image of God—that is, freedom, love, justice, and forgiveness in the service of God. A Christian life grounded in God's nature produces holiness.

The word Peter used to describe Christian holiness is *godliness*. To plumb the depths of the nature of God, one must affirm, experience, and know that God is love. The theological word *godliness* relates to "spiritual qualities and virtues that come from God," who is love, and the expression of God's love in one's life toward others. Godliness is a demonstration of love and the things which God loves, with an attitude and action consistent with that love. To be godly is to live reverently, loyally, and obediently toward love, which is the very nature of God.

II. EXPOSITION AND APPLICATION OF THE SCRIPTURE

A. To Be Christ-like
(2 Peter 1:4-9)

Whereby are given unto us exceeding great and precious promises: that by these ye might be partakers of the divine nature, having escaped the corruption that is in the world through lust. And beside this, giving all diligence, add to your faith virtue; and to virtue knowledge; And to knowledge temperance; and to temperance patience; and to patience godliness; And to godliness brotherly kindness; and to brotherly kindness charity. For if these things be in you, and abound, they make you that ye shall neither be barren nor unfruitful in the knowledge of our Lord Jesus Christ. But he that lacketh these things is blind, and cannot see afar off, and hath forgotten that he was purged from his old sins.

The first-century Christians to whom Peter wrote faced heresies against God's revelation in Christ and needed spiritual fortification to stand within the strength of their faith. There were false teachings against the promises of Christ. A formidable foe of Christ's promises was the idea that "the body" and "the flesh" were bad things—centers for corruption and evil desires (1:4). In an effort to fortify unsteady believers in the promises of Christ, the book of 2 Peter expounds on the virtues of a godly life. The goal of Christian holiness is to become like Christ, and to use the gift of mind, body, and spirit for Christian holiness.

Apparently, the writer of the book of 2 Peter was facing death (see verse 14) and wrote to remind his fellow believers about the gift of God's glory and goodness. The writer seems to have been preparing his readers for a period when those who were eyewitnesses of Christ's ministry would no longer be with them. The theological import of the book of 2 Peter sought to reassure believers that their participation in "the divine nature" sets them apart in the world. As recipients of "the divine nature," Christians must avoid the corruption that is in the world and take action to cultivate goodness, knowledge, self-control, endurance, and godliness. God's divine power has given Christians everything they need to fulfill the goal of holy living. Living in harmony with God's revelation in Jesus Christ brings opposition into every Christian's life. Cultures that are antagonistic to God's ways of love and salvation resist conversion to holiness.

Knowledge of Christ and the holiness that it mandates is a lifelong process. Contemporary churches must engage in theological and religious education in order to advance an understanding of Christian holiness. Christian holiness is learned through living the godly life in relationship to Christ (see verses 5-7; 3:18). The marketplace of religion is full of distortions and platforms which are not committed to the core values of God's kingdom of justice, love, and reconciliation through Jesus Christ. Thinking theologically and critically about the nature and character of God's love in the world is as necessary to sustain faith as the acceptance of Jesus' life as the pattern for living a godly life. Theological thinking is not about defending a belief system—it is about living with a mind fully exposed and opened to understanding God's actions and love in the world.

B. Living Out Salvation
(2 Peter 1:10-11)

Wherefore the rather, brethren, give diligence to make your calling and election sure: for if ye do these things, ye shall never fall: For so an entrance shall be ministered unto you abundantly into the everlasting kingdom of our Lord and Saviour Jesus Christ.

The early Christians were challenged daily with the difficulties of living out Christ's love in their behavior. The author of the book of 2 Peter encouraged them to face such difficulties with godliness, letting the love and truth of God guide their behavior and decisions. The book of 2 Peter begins with framing the Christian life with godly virtues which characterize God's love in the lives of believers. He began with faith, without which one cannot please God. To the Christian virtue of faith, the early Christians were admonished to add knowledge (knowing the will of God). To knowledge they were to add temperance (self-control); and to temperance, patience (sober and reflective thinking before acting); and to patience, godliness (truth that reveals God). Without these virtues operating in the spirituality of one's spiritual life, he or she is blind concerning things related to the kingdom of God. These virtues of Christian spirituality yield the fruit of having true knowledge of Jesus Christ. The supreme goal of the Christian life is to become like God and to do what God does. Since love is central to God's being (see 1 John 4:16), it is the ground of godly living that honors who God is and what God does in the world.

How does one live holy and responsibly in the light of Christ's Good News? Peter made clear that it is the story of Christ's suffering, death, resurrection, and ascension that provides motive and measure for Christian holiness. The ancient faith community was admonished to arm themselves with the truth of Christ against opposition and false teaching. A major issue early Christians faced was how to respond to cults of fleshly powers (sexuality cults or human desires) that diminished their faith. In other words, how were they to reconcile the needs and fulfillments of the flesh without violating the core values of their faith? In 2 Peter 1:4-12, the flesh is seen either as the realm of God, or the realm of Satan. The flesh is not only the realm of morality, but also the realm of selfish desires that stands in opposition to the will of God. In the realm of the flesh or human desires, Jesus, through His life, suffering, death, and resurrection, made the right choice. God vindicated Christ's choice, whose death and resurrection triumphed over human desires antagonistic to the righteousness of God. Knowledge of Christ is a divine gift that enables one to live a godly life.

The theological perspective of Paul outlined in Romans 12 is that the body is a holy and living sacrifice that should be devoted to God for Christian service. Since godly living requires the presentation of our bodies to holy service, our bodies should be continuously dedicated to the spiritual things that serve God. This is what makes our bodies holy temples.

When troubled teenagers have problems with drugs and raise questions about sexual pleasure, the ethical response of the church has been less than forthcoming, because the church has not sufficiently engaged the dualism between flesh and spirit. Our culture has taught teenagers to have a negative view of sex and a low view of the body as the site for pleasure and sex only. Sex equals sin. Sex is not viewed as a gift from God, as it should be. The body is an object to be used rather than a place for the embodiment of love, faith, and spirituality. What has resulted is the dualistic conflict between flesh and spirit. The teaching of the apostle Paul was that the body is the temple of the Lord and therefore sacred rather than evil.

C. Ethical Christian Virtues that Work (2 Peter 1:12-14)

Wherefore I will not be negligent to put you always in remembrance of these things, though ye know them, and be established in the present truth. Yea, I think it meet, as long as I am in this tabernacle, to stir you up by putting you in remembrance; Knowing that shortly I must put off this my tabernacle, even as our Lord Jesus Christ hath shewed me.

In Christ, Christians have everything needed to live godly lives—the nature of God in Christ, the love of Christ, the example of Christ, and the Spirit of Christ, which empower holy lives. Having the proper attitude of piety toward God, expressed in obedience to the will of God, is a virtue developed by living in the sphere of the culture of God. Christians are called to live in the sphere of God or God's milieu (culture). The virtues derived from living within a culture shaped by God's revelation in Jesus provides believers with the spiritual light and morality needed to live effectively in a world antagonistic to God's reign of justice and love. Obedience, maturity, self-control, love, forgiveness, and patience are virtues possessed only by those who have knowledge of Jesus Christ. While these virtues are cultivated within the personal or inner life of believers, it is important that they impact the outer world. Christian holiness calls for both inner and outer transformation. Living with the knowledge of Christ—that is, living according to God's purpose—is what causes sin to lose its grip. Just as Jesus' faithful suffering in the flesh brought sin to a halt, love is the primary virtue of Christian life that covers sin (see 1 Peter 4:1b, 6).

It is unfortunate that admonishing Christian virtues has been separated from challenging the world to become holy. The focus has been on inner individual holiness or righteousness, rather than on collective holiness of nations and governments. Some have pushed the idea that the church's task is to initiate us into the spiritual kingdom of Christ, where we can find salvation. Politicians and businessmen and the military should run the earthly kingdom, and as long as they do not interfere with the spiritual matters of the church, the church should not interfere with secular things and politics.

III. CONCLUDING REFLECTION

When faced with difficulties and sufferings, persons are often drawn to reflect on questions of identity—who they are and why and how they should invest their lives. When it comes to Christian faith, such reflection is not an easy task, particularly without spiritual mentorship, study, and guidance from sources dedicated to God's life, love, and reign in the world. Faced with ostracism and opposition from a culture that rewarded nonbelievers economically and politically, the early Christians found strength through their relationship in Christ, and so will contemporary Christians.

The book of 2 Peter provides helpful guidance for those who want to be faithful and effective Christians. The scriptural and theological guidance that contemporary believers find in the book of 2 Peter require critical reflection on the virtues of Christian holiness and what these virtues mean for living spiritually productive lives.

PRAYER

Lord of life and Savior of our bodies and souls, thank You for Your example of love and holiness by which we can live lives of godliness. In Jesus' name we pray. Amen.

WORD POWER

Election (Greek: *ekloge* [ek-log-ay'])—means "to pick out, choose, chosen, elect"; it means to choose some people out of many people. (Who does the choosing? God.)
Godliness—(1) conforming to the laws and wishes of God; devout; pious; (2) coming from God; divine.

HOME DAILY BIBLE READINGS
(May 6-12, 2013)

Equipped with Hope
MONDAY, May 6: "Full of Goodness and Knowledge" (Romans 15:14-21)
TUESDAY, May 7: "The Beginning of Knowledge" (Proverbs 1:2-7)
WEDNESDAY, May 8: "An Example in Self-control" (Titus 1:5-9)
THURSDAY, May 9: "Enduring to the End" (Matthew 24:9-14)
FRIDAY, May 10: "A Life of Godliness and Dignity" (1 Timothy 2:1-7)
SATURDAY, May 11: "Love for One Another" (1 Peter 3:8-12)
SUNDAY, May 12: "Standing on God's Precious Promises" (2 Peter 1:4-14)

LESSON 12   May 19, 2013 (Pentecost Sunday)

HOPE THROUGH STEWARDSHIP

FAITH PATHWAY/FAITH JOURNEY TOPIC: Serving One Another

DEVOTIONAL READING: Luke 16:10-13
PRINT PASSAGE: 1 Peter 4:1-11

BACKGROUND SCRIPTURE: 1 Peter 4
KEY VERSE: 1 Peter 4:10

1 Peter 4:1-11—KJV

FORASMUCH THEN as Christ hath suffered for us in the flesh, arm yourselves likewise with the same mind: for he that hath suffered in the flesh hath ceased from sin;

2 That he no longer should live the rest of his time in the flesh to the lusts of men, but to the will of God.

3 For the time past of our life may suffice us to have wrought the will of the Gentiles, when we walked in lasciviousness, lusts, excess of wine, revellings, banquetings, and abominable idolatries:

4 Wherein they think it strange that ye run not with them to the same excess of riot, speaking evil of you:

5 Who shall give account to him that is ready to judge the quick and the dead.

6 For for this cause was the gospel preached also to them that are dead, that they might be judged according to men in the flesh, but live according to God in the spirit.

7 But the end of all things is at hand: be ye therefore sober, and watch unto prayer.

8 And above all things have fervent charity among yourselves: for charity shall cover the multitude of sins.

9 Use hospitality one to another without grudging.

10 As every man hath received the gift, even so minister the same one to another, as good stewards of the manifold grace of God.

11 If any man speak, let him speak as the oracles of God; if any man minister, let him do it as of the ability which God giveth: that God in all things may be glorified through Jesus Christ, to whom be praise and dominion for ever and ever. Amen.

1 Peter 4:1-11—NIV

THEREFORE, SINCE Christ suffered in his body, arm yourselves also with the same attitude, because he who has suffered in his body is done with sin.

2 As a result, he does not live the rest of his earthly life for evil human desires, but rather for the will of God.

3 For you have spent enough time in the past doing what pagans choose to do—living in debauchery, lust, drunkenness, orgies, carousing and detestable idolatry.

4 They think it strange that you do not plunge with them into the same flood of dissipation, and they heap abuse on you.

5 But they will have to give account to him who is ready to judge the living and the dead.

6 For this is the reason the gospel was preached even to those who are now dead, so that they might be judged according to men in regard to the body, but live according to God in regard to the spirit.

7 The end of all things is near. Therefore be clear minded and self-controlled so that you can pray.

8 Above all, love each other deeply, because love covers over a multitude of sins.

9 Offer hospitality to one another without grumbling.

10 Each one should use whatever gift he has received to serve others, faithfully administering God's grace in its various forms.

11 If anyone speaks, he should do it as one speaking the very words of God. If anyone serves, he should do it with the strength God provides, so that in all things God may be praised through Jesus Christ. To him be the glory and the power for ever and ever. Amen.

UNIFYING LESSON PRINCIPLE

The perilous world in which we live sometimes tempts us to accept the lifestyles and values of others in order to be successful. How can we avoid losing sight of our own integrity and yet find hope for a better life? We learn from 1 Peter 4 that God will strengthen us to serve as good stewards of His manifold grace.

TOPICAL OUTLINE OF THE LESSON

I. Introduction
  A. Being Good Stewards of Salvation
  B. Biblical Background

II. Exposition and Application of the Scripture
  A. Following Christ (1 Peter 4:1-2)
  B. The Realm of the Flesh versus the Spirit (1 Peter 4:3-6)
  C. The Love Ethic of the Christian Life (1 Peter 4:7-11)

III. Concluding Reflection

LESSON OBJECTIVES

Upon the completion of the lesson, the students will be able to do the following:

1. Understand the cost and the discipline required of good stewards of the manifold grace of God;

2. Identify the difference between the stewardship that comes from human strength and the stewardship that is energized by the strength which God supplies; and,

3. Define one act of service that they could carry out in order to demonstrate stewardship of a gift received from God.

POINTS TO BE EMPHASIZED

ADULT/YOUTH

Adult Topic: **Serving One Another**
Youth Topic: **A Changed Life**
Adult Key Verse: **1 Peter 4:10**
Youth Key Verse: **1 Peter 4:2**
Print Passage: **1 Peter 4:1-11**

—The author called believers to a higher standard of behavior, even though this would provoke a negative reaction from outsiders.

—The proper Christian response to the imminence of "the end" is discipline, love, hospitality, and good stewardship of all that God has given.

—Spiritual gifts are discussed in greater detail in Romans 12:3-8; 1 Corinthians 12–14; and Ephesians 4:7-13.

—The goal of Christian stewardship is "that God in all things may be glorified through Jesus Christ" (1 Peter 4:11).

—Believers are to adopt the same self-sacrificing attitude as that of Christ.

—Because Christ suffered innocently, Christians should not be surprised if they suffer unjustly.

—Believers are to live lives of love and service, in God's strength and for God's praise.

CHILDREN

Children Topic: **Being a Good Steward**
Key Verse: **1 Peter 4:10**
Print Passage: **1 Peter 4:1-11**

—Christ suffered for us all; therefore, we must subject ourselves to God's will.

—Christ wants us to be good stewards by using the gifts He has given us to serve Him and others.

—While Christ called His followers from lives dedicated to fulfilling human desires, God holds those who continue in such behavior accountable for judgment.

—The writer warned his readers that they needed to discipline themselves in love, hospitality, and service in order to glorify God.

I. INTRODUCTION

A. Being Good Stewards of Salvation

The story of Christ's suffering, death, and resurrection is the theme of the books of 1 and 2 Peter. The foundation of the Christian faith is based upon what God did through the life of Jesus Christ. Christ is God's gift of salvation to all who receive Him. What does it mean to be a good steward of Christ's salvation?

Serving Christ in the world means that Christians are called to engage the world, not withdraw from it. The study of this lesson will challenge students to think critically and theologically about how the whole of life (mind, body, and spirit) is to be governed and used by the will of God. This lesson highlights the truth that without the divine nature of new life in Christ, the idolatry of human passions inevitably seeks to corrupt God's gift of salvation. This lesson also teaches that Christ's love, operating within us, is the bottom line of Christ's salvation.

B. Biblical Background

The early Christians found themselves living in a culture that was dominated by a Greek worldview. In order to survive in a Greek pagan culture, they were heavily influenced to apply a Greek way of thinking to their new faith in Christ. The ancient Greeks understood human life to be trapped in a dualism where body and soul, and flesh and spirit were in conflict. They believed that the body was evil and the soul good; that time was corrupt and eternity pure; that the earth was to be shunned and heaven sought; and that the flesh was the seat of impurity and spirit was the seat of blessedness.

The study of this lesson should help us celebrate the holiness of Christ, as well as the gifts, pleasures, and joys of the body—and to see the flesh and spirit as gifts from God. The bottom line of the Christian life is for believers to be good stewards of Christ's love and to serve Christ by serving others with the same love that transformed their own lives.

II. EXPOSITION AND APPLICATION OF THE SCRIPTURE

A. Following Christ
(1 Peter 4:1-2)

FORASMUCH THEN as Christ hath suffered for us in the flesh, arm yourselves likewise with the same mind: for he that hath suffered in the flesh hath ceased from sin; That he no longer should live the rest of his time in the flesh to the lusts of men, but to the will of God.

The writer of the book of 1 Peter warned that Christians are not exempt from suffering and can expect to do fierce battle against the carnal and sinful forces that corrupt human desires. When the epistle alerted believers to "arm" against fleshly desires, he knew that believers in Christ would do battle against the same fleshly powers that provided the context for Christ's suffering. Human pride, lust for power, corrupt politics tied to greed and selfishness, hate, and prejudice joined to religious zeal were the manifestations of human desires or fleshly corruption that caused Christ to suffer. What corrupts human or fleshly desires is when the needs of the flesh are elevated to the level of idolatrous pursuit, insatiable drives that violate relationships in life. Christians are enlisted to do battle for righteousness against sin in all its forms and variations (see verse 1). Christians depend upon the strength and power of God in the battle for God's righteousness. This battle is not solely a personal or individual victory over private sins, but is a battle to do the will of God in all areas of life as well: the public and private, economic and political, sacred and secular, and spiritual and social—as well as harmonizing religious creeds with deeds and piety with responsible Christian practice. Following the example of Christ is crucial, if victorious Christian living is to occur. Paul noted that Christians who "make their own attitude that of Christ" would find strength to follow in the way to righteousness (see Philippians 2:5-11).

In the further study of this lesson, we will see that Christians, as with others, live daily in the realm of the flesh or human desires. The realm of the flesh or earthly life binds us with all of its challenges and difficulties, but it is the sphere where Christian living takes place. Paul, heavily influenced by Greek dualism, placed the flesh in opposition to the spirit. Paul noted that in the human flesh, which was/is the locus of sin, no good thing resided (see Romans 7:15-19). The text of the book of 1 Peter challenges us to allow the governance of God's will to guide the expression of human desires which involve a lifelong process of spiritual maturity.

B. The Realm of the Flesh versus the Spirit (1 Peter 4:3-6)

For the time past of our life may suffice us to have wrought the will of the Gentiles, when we walked in lasciviousness, lusts, excess of wine, revellings, banquetings, and abominable idolatries: Wherein they think it strange that ye run not with them to the same excess of riot, speaking evil of you: Who shall give account to him that is ready to judge the quick and the dead. For for this cause was the gospel preached also to them that are dead, that they might be judged according to men in the flesh, but live according to God in the spirit.

These verses characterize the realm or nature of the flesh in contrast to the realm of the spirit. These realms (flesh versus spirit) are understood as being formidable foes in constant conflict for supremacy. Just as non-Christians or Gentiles had to live within the earthly constraints of the desires and struggles of the flesh, so it is with Christians who are not exempt from living out their salvation. They, too, must confront the challenges of the flesh. However, 1 Peter 4:3-4 describes the different way in which the realm of the flesh impacted the Gentile world, and how believers triumphed over the flesh due to the "divine nature" they possessed in Christ. The life choices and ethical decisions of believers were governed by a commitment to obey the will of God, whereas the will of the Gentiles was governed by the passions of human desires (the flesh).

As previously mentioned, one problem

which early Christians were forced to confront was that they found themselves living in a culture where the ethical values of ancient Judaism were in conflict with a culture dominated by a Greek worldview. Greek wisdom was heavily influenced by the understanding that the body was evil and the soul good, that the flesh was the seat of impurity and the spirit the seat of blessedness. Thus, to be "saved" in this conflict of "flesh versus spirit," one must disengage from the evil world. One must scorn the body for the sake of the soul, forsake earth for the sake of heaven, and stamp out or suppress human desires of the flesh because the body is a cage for corrupt passions and licentiousness against the spirit (see Romans 13:13-14 and Galatians 5:19-21).

As early believers began their new lives in Christ, which was based on Christ's death and suffering in the flesh (see 1 Peter 2:24-25), one can see the difficulty they had in resisting the temptation to fit "the divine nature" that was within them and Christ's salvation in the cloth of Greek understanding of the flesh versus the spirit. Rather than engage the world, this philosophy encouraged withdrawal and disengagement from the world in order to be saved. Christ calls us to live unified lives in the Spirit, not a fractured existence where the human desires were in conflict with the Spirit.

C. The Love Ethic of the Christian Life
(1 Peter 4:7-11)

But the end of all things is at hand: be ye therefore sober, and watch unto prayer. And above all things have fervent charity among yourselves: for charity shall cover the multitude of sins. Use hospitality one to another without grudging. As every man hath received the gift, even so minister the same one to another, as good stewards of the manifold grace of God. If any man speak, let him speak as the oracles of God; if any man minister, let him do it as of the ability which God giveth: that God in all things may be glorified through Jesus Christ, to whom be praise and dominion for ever and ever. Amen.

First Peter 4:7-11 provides us with the love ethic of the Christian life. Christ's salvation calls us to a spirituality that expresses love both personally and communally. The idea that salvation is only for our personal blessings, benefit, and individual needs is perhaps the greatest barrier to fulfilling the mandate of the love ethic to which Christ's salvation calls us. During the period of southern antebellum revivalism, the emphasis was much on the otherworldliness of salvation, to the neglect of the injustice and inhumanity of slavery. Personal conversion and structural reform were separated. Even in some churches today, Christ's love has been made into a private affair of individualism, wherein prayer and politics are separated and Christian love and justice are not related. However, the core meaning of Christ's salvation as a gift to believers is the activation of love as a liberating and transforming force in the world.

The practice and spirituality of divine love beyond individualism produces the impetus to serve others who suffer in the world. First Peter 4:8 declares that love (or "charity" in the KJV) covers a multitude of sins. This phrase "love covers a multitude of sins" does not mean that sins are excused by love, or that love hides sin. Rather, the point of Christian love is that it is willing to suffer for the salvation and transformation of persons imprisoned by the bondage of sin.

The point of 1 Peter 4:8 is that Christians should live consciously in a divine milieu of love wherein they not only show hospitality to each other, but also demonstrate the hospitality of

Christian love to change structural and systemic problems of injustice and inhospitality that others suffer in the world.

III. CONCLUDING REFLECTION

The gifts of God through Christ to our humanity are manifold in their potential to transform life. Salvation is the supreme gift that Christ's love offers to us. As Christians are stewards of God's gifts, they are responsible for the faithful use of those gifts. The study of this lesson invites us to critically reflect on the meaning of Christ's salvation for us and our world. Christ's salvation includes all of life, including sexuality and spirituality, politics and prayer. Following the mandates of Christ's salvation not only helps keep us from turning human passion into idolatry, but it also frees us to use human passion to serve the cause of Christ's love and liberation in the world. We are reminded that the Christian life, while intensely personal, is always communal. This means that the bottom line of Christ's salvation for us is love as a gift, which we are to receive in order to share with and for others.

PRAYER

O God, thank You for the salvation You have given us in Christ. Keep us by the power of Your Spirit so that we may serve as channels of Christ's love in the world. In Jesus' name we pray. Amen.

WORD POWER

Flesh—biblically, the flesh is viewed as the created and natural humanity. It is not automatically sinful, but it is weak, limited, and temporal. Such qualities make it vulnerable to sin.
Lust—the basic definition of *lust* is "having a self-absorbed desire for an object, person, or experience." One who lusts puts material things above God.

HOME DAILY BIBLE READINGS
(May 13-19, 2013)

Hope through Stewardship

MONDAY, May 13: "Trust God to Provide" (Luke 12:22-28)
TUESDAY, May 14: "The Unfailing Treasure" (Luke 12:29-34)
WEDNESDAY, May 15: "Be Alert and Ready" (Luke 12:35-40)
THURSDAY, May 16: "The Faithful and Prudent Manager" (Luke 12:41-48)
FRIDAY, May 17: "The Perfect Gift from Above" (James 1:12-18)
SATURDAY, May 18: "Faithful in Little and Much" (Luke 16:10-13)
SUNDAY, May 19: "Good Stewards of God's Grace" (1 Peter 4:1-11)

HOPE IN THE DAY OF THE LORD

FAITH PATHWAY/FAITH JOURNEY TOPIC: **Ready and Waiting**

DEVOTIONAL READING: **John 14:1-7**   BACKGROUND SCRIPTURE: **2 Peter 3**
PRINT PASSAGE: **2 Peter 3:1-15a**   KEY VERSE: **2 Peter 3:9**

2 Peter 3:1-15a—KJV

THIS SECOND epistle, beloved, I now write unto you; in both which I stir up your pure minds by way of remembrance:

2 That ye may be mindful of the words which were spoken before by the holy prophets, and of the commandment of us the apostles of the Lord and Saviour:

3 Knowing this first, that there shall come in the last days scoffers, walking after their own lusts,

4 And saying, Where is the promise of his coming? for since the fathers fell asleep, all things continue as they were from the beginning of the creation.

5 For this they willingly are ignorant of, that by the word of God the heavens were of old, and the earth standing out of the water and in the water:

6 Whereby the world that then was, being overflowed with water, perished:

7 But the heavens and the earth, which are now, by the same word are kept in store, reserved unto fire against the day of judgment and perdition of ungodly men.

8 But, beloved, be not ignorant of this one thing, that one day is with the Lord as a thousand years, and a thousand years as one day.

9 The Lord is not slack concerning his promise, as some men count slackness; but is longsuffering to us-ward, not willing that any should perish, but that all should come to repentance.

10 But the day of the Lord will come as a thief in the night; in the which the heavens shall pass away with a great noise, and the elements shall melt with fervent heat, the earth also and the works that are therein shall be burned up.

11 Seeing then that all these things shall be dissolved, what manner of persons ought ye to be in all holy conversation and godliness,

2 Peter 3:1-15a—NIV

DEAR FRIENDS, this is now my second letter to you. I have written both of them as reminders to stimulate you to wholesome thinking.

2 I want you to recall the words spoken in the past by the holy prophets and the command given by our Lord and Savior through your apostles.

3 First of all, you must understand that in the last days scoffers will come, scoffing and following their own evil desires.

4 They will say, "Where is this 'coming' he promised? Ever since our fathers died, everything goes on as it has since the beginning of creation."

5 But they deliberately forget that long ago by God's word the heavens existed and the earth was formed out of water and by water.

6 By these waters also the world of that time was deluged and destroyed.

7 By the same word the present heavens and earth are reserved for fire, being kept for the day of judgment and destruction of ungodly men.

8 But do not forget this one thing, dear friends: With the Lord a day is like a thousand years, and a thousand years are like a day.

9 The Lord is not slow in keeping his promise, as some understand slowness. He is patient with you, not wanting anyone to perish, but everyone to come to repentance.

10 But the day of the Lord will come like a thief. The heavens will disappear with a roar; the elements will be destroyed by fire, and the earth and everything in it will be laid bare.

11 Since everything will be destroyed in this way, what kind of people ought you to be? You ought to live holy and godly lives

UNIFYING LESSON PRINCIPLE

There have always been people who believe that what has been and what is will always be. What will inspire them to look more positively toward the future? The writer of the book of 2 Peter urged his readers to prepare for the day of the Lord by being patient and by living holy, godly lives.

12 Looking for and hasting unto the coming of the day of God, wherein the heavens being on fire shall be dissolved, and the elements shall melt with fervent heat?
13 Nevertheless we, according to his promise, look for new heavens and a new earth, wherein dwelleth righteousness.
14 Wherefore, beloved, seeing that ye look for such things, be diligent that ye may be found of him in peace, without spot, and blameless.
15 And account that the longsuffering of our Lord is salvation.

12 as you look forward to the day of God and speed its coming. That day will bring about the destruction of the heavens by fire, and the elements will melt in the heat.
13 But in keeping with his promise we are looking forward to a new heaven and a new earth, the home of righteousness.
14 So then, dear friends, since you are looking forward to this, make every effort to be found spotless, blameless and at peace with him.
15 Bear in mind that our Lord's patience means salvation.

TOPICAL OUTLINE OF THE LESSON

I. Introduction
   A. A Waiting Attitude of Hope
   B. Biblical Background

II. Exposition and Application of the Scripture
   A. Holding On to Hope (2 Peter 3:1-5)
   B. Dealing with False Teachers (2 Peter 3:6-15a)

III. Concluding Reflection

LESSON OBJECTIVES

Upon the completion of the lesson, the students will be able to do the following:

1. Review the various eschatological views and understand what is unique about their denomination's particular doctrine of Jesus' return;

2. Express their feelings about the many viewpoints on the Second Coming; and,

3. Identify ways that they can prepare for the Day of the Lord.

POINTS TO BE EMPHASIZED

ADULT/YOUTH

Adult Topic: Ready and Waiting

Youth Topic: Hope Motivates Holy Living

Adult/Youth Key Verse: 2 Peter 3:9

Print Passage: 2 Peter 3:1-15a

—Peter spoke of evil people who believed that the Lord would never return.

—Peter pointed out that the Scriptures record the ancient Flood and point to a future destruction by fire.

—Peter emphasized that God is not slow but patient, wanting all to come to salvation.

—Peter pointed out that the Day of the Lord will come suddenly and unexpectedly.

—Peter encouraged the believers to live holy and godly lives, spotless and clean before the Lord.

—Peter said that holy living can hasten the return of Christ and a new earth in which righteousness is at home.

CHILDREN
Children Topic: Living in Hope
Key Verse: 2 Peter 3:9
Print Passage: 2 Peter 3:3-15a
—Peter wanted his readers to recognize that dissenters would arise to express doubt regarding faith in Christ.

—Peter reminded his readers that God had already judged humankind through the Flood, and had promised judgment through fire.

—Peter also reminded his readers that God is patient in keeping His promises, because His time is not human time.

—Peter warned that the Day of the Lord would come suddenly; therefore, Christ calls for believers to live holy lives.

—Peter admonished his readers to be patient as they wait(ed) for these things to take place.

I. INTRODUCTION
A. A Waiting Attitude of Hope

The ancient community of the book of 2 Peter is among many examples in history of people waiting for change. The delays of history are replete with communities waiting for the purposes of God's justice to prevail.

The hope for the imminent return of Christ was the looming inquiry of first-century Christians. How and when would Christ's promise of a new age occur? When will Christ's reign come to end life as it is? When the *parousia* (second coming of Jesus) was delayed, inquiries intensified with theological debate and heresy about the doctrine of the Second Coming. The first century came and went and early Christians had little to show for the transformative vision for which Jesus had died. In fact, the name *Christian* was coined in the Hellenistic city of Antioch to mock what was considered to be the ridiculous faith of those who radically changed their lifestyles in the hope of Christ's return. In the homes and in the public square, early Christians stood with hands and eyes uplifted, waiting for Christ to descend with the power to bring a new age. The book of 2 Peter was written with a twofold purpose: to respond to an environment of ridicule, and to fortify the hopeful anticipation of believers who faithfully looked to the future return of Jesus. The author of the book of 2 Peter was a serious theologian who responded to the inquiries of his time. The character and nature of Christian hope is what readers of the book of 2 Peter find, as believers were encouraged to hold on to the promise of Christ's return. Peter's answer to the delay of Jesus' return helps contemporary Christians understand their opportunity to live on the basis of God's purpose as they wait in readiness for Christ's ultimate victory. In worship and prayers, Christians live with the conviction that God's purpose in Christ will ultimately triumph over human sin and all its expressions of injustice and oppression.

B. Biblical Background

The theological term *eschatology* ("the doctrine of last things") captures the central theme of the book of 2 Peter and the biblical meaning of the return of Christ. Growing out of the eschatology of Judaism (the restoration of the Jewish community to political prominence and prosperity), early Christians, to whom the author of the book of 2 Peter wrote, believed Jesus was the Promised Messiah who would fulfill their ancient hope.

The hope and history of the early Christians were in the background of the Jewish people as they waited for the covenant's fulfillment. Surprisingly, God's action in the life of Jesus was not tied to the acquisition of land but was linked to the coming new age—the reign of God's kingdom of righteousness in the world. Christ's resurrection fueled the faith and religious imagination of the early Christians with the hope that when Christ, who had ascended to heaven, would return, "the righteous dead" would be raised; people would be judged; Satan, sin, and death would be defeated; there would be a renewal of the world, and a new creation would dawn. The book of 2 Peter relies on the view of God's actions in Jesus (life, death, and resurrection) to respond to the inquiries of his time regarding these expectations. In this lesson, students will discover the way that the book of 2 Peter responded to the theological curiosity of early Christians, whose hope needed fortification against the "scoffers" who did not take the promises of Christ seriously.

As students study this lesson, they will be challenged to identify false teachings in the vast array of religious cultures in the world. This lesson will bring attention to the need for Christians to take seriously the challenge to study the Word of God and think theologically about the meaning of the Christian faith. In this sense, all Christians are theologians, whose faith seeks understanding about how to live on behalf of God's kingdom in the world.

II. EXPOSITION AND APPLICATION OF THE SCRIPTURE

A. Holding On to Hope
(2 Peter 3:1-5)

THIS SECOND epistle, beloved, I now write unto you; in both which I stir up your pure minds by way of remembrance: That ye may be mindful of the words which were spoken before by the holy prophets, and of the commandment of us the apostles of the Lord and Saviour: Knowing this first, that there shall come in the last days scoffers, walking after their own lusts, And saying, Where is the promise of his coming? for since the fathers fell asleep, all things continue as they were from the beginning of the creation. For this they willingly are ignorant of, that by the word of God the heavens were of old, and the earth standing out of the water and in the water.

The key message of 2 Peter 3 is a polemic calling for trust in God's purpose in the world. The revelation of Christ's resurrection in the ancient world of first-century Christians provided the foundation for the faith and hope that the purpose of God's righteous kingdom would be fulfilled. After the crucifixion of Jesus, the early disciples first thought that His death brought an end to God's dream for a transformed world. But the resurrection of Jesus changed everything. The truth of God's love and salvation for everyone in every place was alive in Christ forever. The ascension of

Christ opened the door of opportunity for the first-century Christians to be witnesses of God's salvation until the promised return of Christ was fulfilled. When the imminent return of Christ did not occur—or, as it was put in the book of 2 Peter, "the day of the Lord" was delayed—what were the early believers to do in the face of the ridicule of "scoffers" who mocked them for their faith? The ancient social media of the scoffers flooded the public square with ridicule aimed to embarrass and make irrelevant the faith claims of the Christian community.

The author of the book of 2 Peter anchored his theological response to this environment of "belief and disbelief" by lifting up the eternality of God's purpose in creation. God's purpose in creation did not begin with the first-century world. God's purpose is an eternal purpose that manifests itself in time but is not governed by the constraints or limits of time. Second Peter 3:1 reminds the readers about the Hebrew prophets within the history of Israel and their quest for an alternative world. We are reminded that God's purpose was active and on the move. In the birth, teaching ministry, and crucifixion of Jesus, God's righteous kingdom was ripening toward the day of fulfillment. The immortality of God's love for humanity reached its highest zenith in the resurrection of Christ. The "scoffers" or "false teachers" that berated the early saints for their hope did not connect Christ's revelation with the eternity of God's purpose. But 2 Peter 3 reminds believers that God sees time quite differently from the human understanding of time. God's purpose is always at work in time and beyond time, and is sustainable beyond the constraints of history: "A thousand years are as one day with God" (see 2 Peter 3:8).

As did the ancients of Hebrew history, many first-generation Christians died "not having received the promises" (Hebrews 11:13). What the theology of 2 Peter 3 imparts is that the seeds of eternity ripen in God's time. God's purpose bears the fruit of revolution and transformation that we may not see in our own time, but which will be fulfilled in future generations. Holding onto the hope of transformation is not easy for any Christian. The social litanies of our time of hate marked by incivility, crime, greed, and multiform expressions of injustice make it difficult to maintain the integrity of Christian faith. Yet, what the book of 2 Peter teaches us is that the God whom Christians meet in Jesus is at work, bringing about the salvation, liberation, and transformation of the world. Thus, Peter declared that if anyone suffered as a Christian, then he or she should not be ashamed, but should glorify God (see 2 Peter 4:16).

B. Dealing with False Teachers (2 Peter 3:6-15a)

Whereby the world that then was, being overflowed with water, perished: But the heavens and the earth, which are now, by the same word are kept in store, reserved unto fire against the day of judgment and perdition of ungodly men. But, beloved, be not ignorant of this one thing, that one day is with the Lord as a thousand years, and a thousand years as one day. The Lord is not slack concerning his promise, as some men count slackness; but is longsuffering to us-ward, not willing that any should perish, but that all should come to repentance. But the day of the Lord will come as a thief in the night; in the which the heavens shall pass away with a great noise, and the elements shall melt with fervent heat, the earth also and the works that are therein shall be burned up. Seeing then that all these things shall be dissolved, what manner of persons ought ye to be in all holy conversation and godliness, Looking for and hasting unto the coming of the day of God, wherein the heavens being on fire shall

be dissolved, and the elements shall melt with fervent heat? Nevertheless we, according to his promise, look for new heavens and a new earth, wherein dwelleth righteousness. Wherefore, beloved, seeing that ye look for such things, be diligent that ye may be found of him in peace, without spot, and blameless. And account that the longsuffering of our Lord is salvation.

The scoffers or false teachers based their denial of the parousia on the premise that the world as it was had not experienced the cosmic transforming judgment anticipated with the return of Christ. As the familiar phrase goes, "business went on as usual." Second Peter 3:5-7 refutes this argument. God's judgment moves with mercy, not with the exactness of human rejection of its reality. False teachers appeal to the vulnerability of those whose understanding of God's truth, as it is manifest in Jesus, has not deepened in maturity.

There have been many efforts to understand the mysteries of God by those who have not committed themselves to the faith. They are the scoffers to whom Peter referred. The perspective of false teaching is always to deny the faith rather than to affirm its mystery through the love and grace of the God we meet in Jesus Christ. The fact that the return of Christ did not occur immediately, as many had expected, was the catalyst for false teachings to rise. Thus, the book of 2 Peter reminded his audience that God is not lax or slow in keeping divine promises. God is patient with humanity, not wanting anyone to be excluded from salvation. In other words, God is waiting on humanity to move toward repentance so that He can move toward us for transformation.

The way believers are instructed to deal with false teaching is that they are to remain steadfast in the faith that undergirds the salvation which comes through Jesus Christ. The event and experience of salvation (with its power to transform life) is what Christians must hold on to when false teachers rise. Scoffers against Christian hope will require proof or evidence for the faith of believers. For Peter, God's demonstration of power in the life of Jesus by raising Him from the dead was the basis for authentic faith that became the life and hope in the lives of believers.

Contemporary believers must take seriously the task of what it means to think theologically about the call of Christian faith. Understanding the core meaning of Christian faith will help believers guard against false teachings. God has acted in Jesus Christ to bring salvation and to establish the reign of God's love in the world. Christians must be ready to express the meaning of this faith and be steadfast in waiting upon its fulfillment.

False teachers have led many astray. Prosperity appeals associated with the Gospel continue to be a source of false teaching that Christians need to guard against. The promises of Jesus' life and resurrection lead us to participate in the life in God, which is a life of compassion, love, justice, and reconciliation. It is a life in which one loves God and neighbor as he or she loves self; a life that loves mercy, does justice, and humbly does the will of God. The first-century Christians were faced with understanding the meaning of their faith as it related to the expectation of the imminent return of Jesus. The contemporary challenge to authentic Christian faith is to hold firm to the promises of the reign of God, which promises to unite and save all humanity.

Peter wrote in verses 14-15 that believers are to be diligent in their living. In other words, we are to faithfully live out the precepts of Christianity so that we can be found blameless. Jesus Christ's patience has resulted in our salvation. The way God through Jesus Christ has related and continues to relate to sinners demonstrates His longsuffering or patience. God has promised that He will be patient with us—as we repent of the sins we have committed. His patience is connected to our repentance. We are to also dedicate ourselves to the obedient service of God.

III. CONCLUDING REFLECTION

The seeds for the revolution of justice in America were planted in the soil of hope long before Martin Luther King Jr. stood on the steps of the Lincoln Memorial, proclaiming God's justice for all. The present revolutions in the world are the result of long-standing causes which have been active for generations. Keeping "hope alive" in the purpose of God is the task of Christian churches. Black churches are inspired by the immortal words of Martin Luther King Jr: "I may not get there with you, but we as a people, will get to the promised land." These words of hope resonate with hope that the writer of the book of 2 Peter defended against in the fatalism and evil of his day and time. We must live spiritually prepared lives as we wait patiently for the fulfillment of the promise of Christ.

To wait in readiness for the coming of God's kingdom requires Christians to study the Word of God, worship in truth and spirit, and practice the faith by doing justice and loving mercy.

PRAYER

O God, help us know the power of the salvation You have given us in Jesus Christ. May we grow in the grace of God's salvation daily and not be led astray by false teaching. In Jesus' name we pray. Amen.

WORD POWER

Last Days—also known as the end times, a time when there will be physical upheaval. Nation will rise against nation, and kingdom against kingdom. There will be famines and earthquakes in various places. All these are the beginning of birth pains.

HOME DAILY BIBLE READINGS
(May 20-26, 2013)

Hope in the Day of the Lord

MONDAY, May 20: "Distressing Times Will Come" (2 Timothy 3:1-9)

TUESDAY, May 21: "Warnings for False Prophets" (Jeremiah 23:23-32)

WEDNESDAY, May 22: "Warnings for Rich Oppressors" (James 5:1-6)

THURSDAY, May 23: "Return to the Lord" (Hosea 14:1-7)

FRIDAY, May 24: "Teaching the Ways of God" (Micah 4:1-5)

SATURDAY, May 25: "I Will Come Again" (John 14:1-7)

SUNDAY, May 26: "The Promise of the Lord's Coming" (2 Peter 3:3-15a)

God's People Worship

GENERAL INTRODUCTION

This quarter has three units with a theological emphasis on worship. How does Christian worship today mirror both the pious and impious practices of the ancient world? What can we learn from God's relationship with the worshipping community in Israel that can help us honor and worship God in our communities of faith?

Unit I, *The Prophet and Praise,* is a four-lesson study of worship in Jerusalem during the time of Isaiah.

Unit II, *Worshipping in Jerusalem Again (Ezra),* is a five-lesson study of the book of Ezra. These lessons give us a perspective on worship in Jerusalem after a remnant of Israel returned home from exile in Babylon.

Unit III, *Worshipping in Jerusalem Again (Nehemiah),* is a continuation of the study begun in Unit II. The four lessons of Unit III come from the book of Nehemiah.

LESSON 1   June 2, 2013

HOLY, HOLY, HOLY

FAITH PATHWAY/FAITH JOURNEY TOPIC: **Beyond Description**

DEVOTIONAL READING: **Joshua 24:14-24**
PRINT PASSAGE: **Isaiah 6:1-8**

BACKGROUND SCRIPTURE: **Isaiah 6:1-12**
KEY VERSE: **Isaiah 6:3**

Isaiah 6:1-8—KJV

IN THE year that king Uzziah died I saw also the Lord sitting upon a throne, high and lifted up, and his train filled the temple.

2 Above it stood the seraphims: each one had six wings; with twain he covered his face, and with twain he covered his feet, and with twain he did fly.

3 And one cried unto another, and said, Holy, holy, holy, is the LORD of hosts: the whole earth is full of his glory.

4 And the posts of the door moved at the voice of him that cried, and the house was filled with smoke.

5 Then said I, Woe is me! for I am undone; because I am a man of unclean lips, and I dwell in the midst of a people of unclean lips: for mine eyes have seen the King, the LORD of hosts.

6 Then flew one of the seraphims unto me, having a live coal in his hand, which he had taken with the tongs from off the altar:

7 And he laid it upon my mouth, and said, Lo, this hath touched thy lips; and thine iniquity is taken away, and thy sin purged.

8 Also I heard the voice of the Lord, saying, Whom shall I send, and who will go for us? Then said I, Here am I; send me.

Isaiah 6:1-8—NIV

IN THE year that King Uzziah died, I saw the Lord seated on a throne, high and exalted, and the train of his robe filled the temple.

2 Above him were seraphs, each with six wings: With two wings they covered their faces, with two they covered their feet, and with two they were flying.

3 And they were calling to one another: "Holy, holy, holy is the LORD Almighty; the whole earth is full of his glory."

4 At the sound of their voices the doorposts and thresholds shook and the temple was filled with smoke.

5 "Woe to me!" I cried. "I am ruined! For I am a man of unclean lips, and I live among a people of unclean lips, and my eyes have seen the King, the LORD Almighty."

6 Then one of the seraphs flew to me with a live coal in his hand, which he had taken with tongs from the altar.

7 With it he touched my mouth and said, "See, this has touched your lips; your guilt is taken away and your sin atoned for."

8 Then I heard the voice of the Lord saying, "Whom shall I send? And who will go for us?" And I said, "Here am I. Send me!"

BIBLE FACT

Holy (Hebrew: *Qadosh*): literally means "to be set apart for a special purpose." God alone is truly holy; however, we are separated as servants of God.

UNIFYING LESSON PRINCIPLE

People seek a power beyond themselves that is worthy of praise and worship. How do people respond when they find the higher power to praise and worship? Isaiah, hearing the extravagant praises and worship directed toward God, responded by accepting the call to become God's messenger.

TOPICAL OUTLINE OF THE LESSON

I. **Introduction**
   A. The Awesomeness of God
   B. Biblical Background

II. **Exposition and Application of the Scripture**
   A. The Praise of Yahweh (Isaiah 6:1-4)
   B. Isaiah's Confession (Isaiah 6:5)
   C. Isaiah's Consecration (Isaiah 6:6-7)
   D. Isaiah's Commission (Isaiah 6:8)

III. **Concluding Reflection**

LESSON OBJECTIVES

Upon completion of the lesson, the students will be able to do the following:

1. Connect praise and worship of God with Isaiah's call and commitment response;

2. Recall a meaningful worship during which they made some level of commitment; and,

3. Design a worship experience that includes contemporary components of worship similar to those included in Isaiah's vision.

POINTS TO BE EMPHASIZED

ADULT/YOUTH

Adult Topic: Beyond Description
Youth Topic: Awed beyond Words
Adult/Youth Key Verse: Isaiah 6:3
Print Passage: Isaiah 6:1-8

—King Uzziah was a good and respected ruler of Judah, and his death marked a crisis for the people.

—Upon the death of King Uzziah, Isaiah went to the Temple, where he had an overwhelming experience with the awesomeness and holiness of God.

—When the seraph touched Isaiah's mouth with a coal from the altar, it was an act of cleansing.

—Isaiah's experience in the Temple was interactive: the experience of the holiness of God led Isaiah to repent, and his repentance was met with forgiveness that was followed by God's call, to which Isaiah responded with commitment.

—Isaiah's encounter with God moved him to worship.

—Isaiah was called to a seemingly difficult mission, yet God directed him to persist.

CHILDREN

Children Topic: Worthy of Praise
Key Verse: Isaiah 6:3
Print Passage: Isaiah 6:1-8

—While in mourning for King Uzziah, Isaiah went to the Temple.

—Isaiah saw the Lord enthroned in glory in a vision.

—Seraphs attending the Lord spoke of God's holiness.

—Isaiah recognized and confessed his sins and the sins of the nation.

—A seraph touched Isaiah's lips with a coal and pronounced forgiveness from the Lord.

—When the Lord asked for a messenger to go to the people, Isaiah volunteered.

I. INTRODUCTION

A. The Awesomeness of God

There is an old adage that goes, "Familiarity breeds contempt." Could it be that we have become so familiar with the idea of God that we have lost all sense of awe? Is God just another entity to be controlled and manipulated by us? Could it be that as Christians we have become so familiar with God that we have attempted to make God into a kind of servant who exists to serve our needs? Could it be that we have concocted a God who blesses us at our cajoling (for example, "When praises go up, blessings come down")? Rudolph Otto, in his book *Idea of the Holy*, describes the holiness of God as "Mysterium Tremendum." The word *mysterium* denotes that which is beyond human conception or understanding; it is extraordinary and unfamiliar. On the other hand, the word *tremendum* is the idea of awe, fear, or the awful majesty of Yahweh. God is a mystery who creates awe in creation. The Old Testament concept of the mystery of Yahweh is the *holy otherness* which is beyond human expression.

Thus, the effect on mere mortals when confronted by the *holy other* is "quietness, trembling, speechlessness, or humility." This is what Isaiah experienced. Nevertheless, there appears to be an attempt in many religious circles to reduce God to a mundane creature that requires little more of us than vocal praise. But, when Yahweh allowed Isaiah to enter His presence, the result was the sending forth with the message, "Whom shall I send, and who will go for us?" (Isaiah 6:8). The seraphs worshipped Yahweh, but Isaiah was made not only aware of his own fragility, but also the holiness of God, and the heavenly mandate (the call to serve)—"Whom shall I send, and who will go for us?" Worship without service is shallow!

B. Biblical Background

The first five chapters of the book of Isaiah consist of warnings and woes that would befall the kingdom of Israel because of her rejection of Yahweh's will. After warnings of judgment and doom in the first five chapters came the call of Isaiah in chapter 6. It is agreed upon by many biblical scholars that because of the call narrative placement in the book, unlike that of the prophet Jeremiah, the call came after the prophet had already been introduced to the reader and given some divine utterances against the kingdom of Israel.

Many scholars speculate that the death of Uzziah was not as much to mark the date of the call of Isaiah, as it was to mark the rise of the Assyrian threat against Israel (see 2 Kings 15). It was in the year that King Uzziah died that the Assyrian Empire began to rise against the kingdom of Israel. The call of Isaiah was intended to correlate with the beginning of divine judgment against Israel. Isaiah was allowed to enter the throne room of Yahweh in a vision, where he was an eyewitness to the splendor and the unutterable majesty of the ruler of heaven and earth. Walter Brueggemann says of Isaiah's vision, "It is the core of holiness from which is decreed all that happens everywhere in creation; the song of the heavenly choir begins in holiness and ends in glory and acknowledges the overwhelming otherness of God." This experience led the prophet to one conclusion: "The whole earth is full of his glory." Holiness is one of the moral attributes of Yahweh; He is by nature morally clean, as opposed to ceremonially clean. On the other hand, holiness is not a human attribute or trait—for it is God who makes us holy. In this lesson, the holiness of Yahweh was set in contrast to the infidelity of Israel. Israel was unclean and must be cleansed by a divine act. So, Isaiah's ceremonial cleansing (of the hot coal in verse 6) can be understood as a metaphor for Israel's eventual redemption and restoration by Yahweh.

II. EXPOSITION AND APPLICATION OF THE SCRIPTURE

A. The Praise of Yahweh
(Isaiah 6:1-4)

IN THE year that king Uzziah died I saw also the Lord sitting upon a throne, high and lifted up, and his train filled the temple. Above it stood the seraphims: each one had six wings; with twain he covered his face, and with twain he covered his feet, and with twain he did fly. And one cried unto another, and said, Holy, holy, holy, is the LORD of hosts: the whole earth is full of his glory. And the posts of the door moved at the voice of him that cried, and the house was filled with smoke.

It was in the year that King Uzziah died that Isaiah was called to the prophetic ministry. Isaiah's charge was to speak divine utterance against a people who had walked contrary to the precepts and the laws of the Lord. In the vision, the Lord allowed the prophet to see into the heavens and catch a glimpse of the awesome holiness of Yahweh. This vision was comparable to John's vision while he was on the Isle of Patmos (see Revelation 1:10). Isaiah saw the Lord sitting on a throne, high and exalted, and His train filled the Temple. This image of Yahweh is important because in antiquity, most military conflicts were religious in nature, or referred to as "holy wars." Armies would march under the banners of their gods and victory would belong to their gods. Yahweh, however, is not a petty territorial god; rather, He is the God of all creation—high and exalted: "He is high and lifted up"; Yahweh is Lord of all!

Isaiah also saw a heavenly choir of seraphims flying around the throne of Yahweh, singing praises to Yahweh. They were singing an unending doxology, a hymn of praise: "holy, holy, holy is the LORD of hosts; the whole earth is full of his glory" (verse 3). The biblical word for *holy* carries the idea of "the sacred, or of purity." The repeating of the words "holy, holy, holy" was to announce emphatically the *otherness* of Yahweh. The second part of verse 3 reads, "The whole earth is full of his glory." Not only did the creatures in heaven sing of Yahweh's sovereignty and glory, but also the whole earth (see Psalm 24) and everything in it spoke of Yahweh's majesty and splendor.

Years ago, I had the opportunity to visit the Grand Canyon, and as I sat late one evening on the crest of the southern ridge, the sun filtered down behind the northern ridge, and I thought to myself, "The whole earth is full of his glory." His greatness is beyond human comprehension.

If verse 3 contains the song that they were singing, then verse 4 provides the tone and the tenor of what the seraphs were singing. They sang with so much gusto that the doorposts in the Temple trembled and the room was full of smoke. What an awesome scene! Everyone and everything, even the doorposts of the Temple, were affected by the awesome sounds of worship. This visual image of shaking doorposts and a room full of smoke highlights the awesome presence of Yahweh and the pathos of this worship event. This lesson makes it clear that authentic worship is God-centered and is about God, not us. Israel's theology is anchored in its religious practices and Temple worship. The presence of the seraphs makes it clear that worshipping God is not only our duty, but is also our *delight*.

B. Isaiah's Confession
(Isaiah 6:5)

Then said I, Woe is me! for I am undone; because I am a man of unclean lips, and I dwell in the midst of a people of unclean lips: for mine eyes have seen the King, the Lord of hosts.

Isaiah's response to what he saw was his complete confession of his unworthiness. His only words were, "Woe is me!" His mortal frame was undone by the presence of the Lord almighty. This was a kind of taking down of his self-worth. The biblical concept for the word *woe* is "oh." In the Bible, the word *oh* seems to be a simple expression of total surprise. So, in this context, Isaiah had an epiphany and saw himself in the light of divine holiness, exclaiming, "Oh!" The holiness of Yahweh compelled Isaiah to acknowledge his worthlessness, which came as a surprise to Isaiah. John Calvin says of the "Woe is me!" expression: "Isaiah is reduced to nothing. However, 'Woe is me' is not only an indictment and confessional for Isaiah, but also the entire nation of Israel. Israel too is unholy

(unclean). Isaiah lives among a people who are just like him—unworthy."

This expression of worthlessness mirrors the expression in the book of Isaiah: "All of us have become like one who is unclean, and all our righteous acts are like filthy rags; we all shrivel up like a leaf, and like the wind our sins sweep us away" (see Isaiah 64:6). He laid humanity bare before the Lord almighty. He acknowledged that there was nothing righteous about humanity, and at best all of us are filthy rags in the presence of God. So, the best we can do is confess our unworthiness and ask God to "forgive us our sins, and to cleanse us from all unrighteousness" (1 John 1:9).

Likewise, unclean lips are indeed an interesting expression, because the lips are the gateway to the mouth, which is the gateway to the heart.

C. Isaiah's Consecration
(Isaiah 6:6-7)

Then flew one of the seraphims unto me, having a live coal in his hand, which he had taken with the tongs from off the altar: And he laid it upon my mouth, and said, Lo, this hath touched thy lips; and thine iniquity is taken away, and thy sin purged.

The biblical term *forgiveness* has many different meanings; it can mean "to cover, to relieve, to pardon, or to grant favor." Yahweh covered or relieved Isaiah of his sins. One of the seraphs flew to Isaiah with a live coal from the altar. For the coal to be a "live" coal meant that it was very hot and able to purge Isaiah's lips of uncleanness. Even today, fire and heat are used to purify. Most precious or natural metals such as steel, iron, and gold (in their raw states) are incased in impurities that must be purged. Fire is used to melt away the impurities, separating the impurities from the precious metals. The hot coal touching the lip was a kind of baptism that symbolized the purging of Isaiah's sins—thus making him a new creature.

This is the image in Isaiah's vision. The "live coal" melted away the impurities in Isaiah's life and also would symbolically do the same for the people of Israel. In the presence of the Lord, Isaiah was overwhelmed by his own sins and unworthiness. His only option was confession—"I am undone" (Isaiah 6:5). Dietrich Bonhoeffer calls forgiveness without confession "cheap grace," and of course in the kingdom of God there is no such thing as "cheap grace." It is all or nothing! To be forgiven, we must confess all—and when we do, God will take away our sins. "If we confess our sins, [God] is faithful and just to forgive us our sins, and to cleanse us from all unrighteousness" (1 John 1:9). God covers us according to our willingness to confess our sins. In the second part of verse 7, we cannot be sure whose voice is speaking—a seraph's or the Lord's. Nevertheless, it was declared that Isaiah's guilt had been taken away. This is what the Lord offers to all of us. Forgiveness is one of the anchoring doctrines of the Christian faith.

D. Isaiah's Commission
(Isaiah 6:8)

Also I heard the voice of the Lord, saying, Whom shall I send, and who will go for us? Then said I, Here am I; send me.

"Here am I; send me" (verse 8). The immediate results of the atonement and reconciliation (see verses 6-7) events were the call and sending of Isaiah. "Whom shall I send, and who will go for us?" Of course, Isaiah had to respond with either yes or no. The call is never complete without a response.

Just because God calls does not mean that we have to accept. God never takes our free will from us. Isaiah said, "Here am I; send me." Isaiah, who saw himself as undone and unworthy, then offered himself freely in the service of the Lord. The prophetic ministry is the ministry of words. The prophet is like a government ambassador whose primary task is to get the message right. The prophet was God's mouthpiece to the nation of Israel—he must get the message right. Therefore, the cleansing of his lips was the first step in preparing Isaiah for the prophetic ministry. If his lips were contaminated, then his being sent forth would be in vain. This implication of verse 8 is great and continues to reverberate in the kingdom of God today. Like the call of Isaiah, we are God's mouthpiece in the world, and our primary task is to get the Lord's message right. It is a life-and-death matter.

III. CONCLUDING REFLECTION

As this lesson focused on worship, the Scriptures make it clear that worship is a sacred act which must not be taken lightly. God is holy, and those of *us* who worship God must do so in Spirit and in truth. Worship cannot be arbitrary or capricious just because the Spirit of God is present; we are not worthy of divine engagement. Isaiah was present in the Temple and saw the Lord, but the Lord did not use him until he was purged of his unworthiness. God is God, and we are summoned to turn our attention in response to God. Walter Brueggemann says, "God evokes speech of gratitude, and awe, simply because of who God is." Secondarily, the practical application of the lesson emerges out of the question, "Whom shall I send, and who will go for us?" Isaiah was an eighth-century (BC) prophet, yet the question is, who will answer the call today to be God's mouthpiece in the world? Years ago, while attending a minister's licensure service, after the trial sermon had been preached, a preacher began to sing an old hymn: "I'll go! I'll go, I'll go if the Lord needs somebody. Here am I, send me, I'll go!" The question posed to Isaiah was the one that was answered and is the one that we also must answer thusly: "Here am I, Lord. Send me, I'll go!" (6:9). Over the doorpost in Heyn Memorial Chapel—on the campus of Bethune Cookman College—are these words: "Enter to worship, depart to serve." Isaiah experienced perfect worship, but ultimately, the Lord needed him to go forth and serve.

PRAYER

Eternal God our Father, we are grateful that the kingdom of God still needs ambassadors of good-will to bear Your message in the world. Now, O Lord, cleanse us, that we might be Your worthy ambassadors in the world. Enable us to get the message right. In Jesus' name we pray. Amen.

WORD POWER

Holy *(qadash)*—morally clean or undefiled.
Glory *(kabowd)*—glorious or having splendor, as to shine or glow.
Seraph—fiery, spirit-like creatures (only spoken of in the book of Isaiah).
Woe *(owy)*—lamentation or an interjection—"Oh!" An *interjection* is a sound that expresses pain or surprise.

HOME DAILY BIBLE READINGS
(May 27–June 2, 2013)

Holy, Holy, Holy
MONDAY, May 27: "Setting Yourself to Seek God" (2 Chronicles 26:1-5)
TUESDAY, May 28: "From Success to Pride to Destruction" (2 Chronicles 26:16-21)
WEDNESDAY, May 29: "Following a Father's Example" (2 Kings 15:32-38)
THURSDAY, May 30: "People Dulled to God's Presence" (Isaiah 6:9-13)
FRIDAY, May 31: "Choosing to Serve a Holy God" (Joshua 24:14-24)
SATURDAY, June 1: "Seeking the Face of God" (Psalm 24)
SUNDAY, June 2: "Encountering the Holy God" (Isaiah 6:1-8)

References
Brueggemann, Walter, *Isaiah 1–39 Commentary*. Westminster John Knox Press, Louisville, KY, 1998.
Motyer, J. Alec, *The Prophecy of Isaiah an Introduction and Commentary*, InterVarsity Press, Downers Grove, IL, 1993.
Ogilvie, Lloyd J, *Mastering the Old Testament: Ezra, Nehemiah, Esther*, GE, Word publishing, Dallas, TX, 1993.
Strong, James, *The New Strong Expanded Dictionary of Bible Words*, Thomas Nelson Publishers, Nashville, TN, 2001.
Throntveit, Mark, A., *Ezra-Nehemiah*: John Knox Press, Louisville, KY, 1992.

LESSON 2   **June 9, 2013**

GIVE THANKS

FAITH PATHWAY/FAITH JOURNEY TOPIC: **Sing and Shout!**

DEVOTIONAL READING: **Psalm 92:1-8**   BACKGROUND SCRIPTURE: **Isaiah 12**
PRINT PASSAGE: **Isaiah 12:1-6**   KEY VERSE: **Isaiah 12:4**

Isaiah 12:1-6—KJV

AND IN that day thou shalt say, O Lord, I will praise thee: though thou wast angry with me, thine anger is turned away, and thou comfortedst me.

2 Behold, God is my salvation; I will trust, and not be afraid: for the Lord JEHOVAH is my strength and my song; he also is become my salvation.

3 Therefore with joy shall ye draw water out of the wells of salvation.

4 And in that day shall ye say, Praise the Lord, call upon his name, declare his doings among the people, make mention that his name is exalted.

5 Sing unto the Lord; for he hath done excellent things: this is known in all the earth.

6 Cry out and shout, thou inhabitant of Zion: for great is the Holy One of Israel in the midst of thee.

Isaiah 12:1-6—NIV

IN THAT day you will say: "I will praise you, O Lord. Although you were angry with me, your anger has turned away and you have comforted me.

2 Surely God is my salvation; I will trust and not be afraid. The Lord, the Lord, is my strength and my song; he has become my salvation."

3 With joy you will draw water from the wells of salvation.

4 In that day you will say: "Give thanks to the Lord, call on his name; make known among the nations what he has done, and proclaim that his name is exalted.

5 Sing to the Lord, for he has done glorious things; let this be known to all the world.

6 Shout aloud and sing for joy, people of Zion, for great is the Holy One of Israel among you."

BIBLE FACT

The true meaning of "giving thanks" is related to and is a part of the act of giving God praise. We praise God because He is worthy of praise. This is the highest form of praise. We do not have to have anything specific for which to thank God. We can just say, "Thank You, God!"

UNIFYING LESSON PRINCIPLE

People who experience life-saving blessings are grateful and speak words of thanksgiving. To whom do people direct their praise and thanksgiving for life's blessings? Isaiah gave thanks to God for salvation with joyous songs of praise.

TOPICAL OUTLINE OF THE LESSON

I. Introduction
  A. The Biblical View of Giving Thanks
  B. Biblical Background

II. Exposition and Application of the Scripture
  A. In That Day, Give Praise! (Isaiah 12:1-3)
  B. In That Day, Give Thanks! (Isaiah 12:4-5)
  C. In That Day, Shout! (Isaiah 12:6)

III. Concluding Reflection

LESSON OBJECTIVES

Upon completion of the lesson, the students will be able to do the following:

1. List reasons why Isaiah was thankful to God, and the ways he displayed his gratitude;
2. Understand their beliefs about the connection between gratitude and natural, spontaneous praise; and,
3. Proclaim thanksgiving and praise publicly.

POINTS TO BE EMPHASIZED

ADULT/YOUTH

Adult Topic: **Sing and Shout!**
Youth Topic: **Wow! Thanks!**
Adult Key Verse: **Isaiah 12:4**
Youth Key Verse: **Isaiah 12:1**
Print Passage: **Isaiah 12:1-6**

—The passage is a hymn of praise that concludes a major section of the book of Isaiah.
—The passage was directed to the people of Israel, declaring what they should express in a time of fulfillment.
—God restored the relationship that the people had broken; God's anger had turned to comfort.
—The hymn to be offered recognized God as the source of Israel's salvation.
—Isaiah proclaimed that God's deliverance and deeds were so great and mighty that all the earth should know about them.
—Isaiah proclaimed that God is in the midst of those who sing His praises.

CHILDREN

Children Topic: **Give Praise and Thanks**
Key Verse: **Isaiah 12:4**
Print Passage: **Isaiah 12:1-6**

—Confident that God would deliver Israel from exile, Isaiah praised God.
—Isaiah acknowledged God as the one who provided salvation.
—God's mighty deeds are to be proclaimed to the world.
—Isaiah called Israel to join him in praising the Lord.
—Isaiah recognized that although God was angry, God's anger subsided and became comfort.
—Because of God's salvation, Isaiah trusted God and had no fear.

I. INTRODUCTION

A. The Biblical View of Giving Thanks

In America, the concept of giving thanks—as seen in the holiday of "Thanksgiving"—has become commercialized. As a day of celebration sanctioned by the government, the focus for many has become that of "eating, shopping, and football watching." The people of God are encouraged to give thanks, in return for some gracious act of God. For many people, something has gotten lost in the word *thanksgiving* and the concept of "giving thanks." The Bible is replete with expressions of thanksgiving, which, in most instances, is expressed as an act of worship to God. The psalmist put it best: "Give thanks unto the Lord for He is good and His mercies endure forever."

As we study this lesson and its exhortation to sing and shout, worship is not the end but, rather, is the means to the end. God had been good to Israel and He has been good to us, so let us all shout for joy for His goodness and then proclaim to the world that He is the worthy recipient of our thanks.

B. Biblical Background

Chapter 12 brings to a close the first section of the book of Isaiah. It is believed by many scholars that the first twelve chapters constitute Isaiah's vision of judgment and salvation for Judah and Israel. These two great entities would be brought to ruin, but the prophet had a vision of restoration. So, after the prophet spoke of the wrath of Yahweh meted out against His chosen people, Isaiah saw a day of rejoicing when they would have reason to give thanks and shout for joy in their liberation. This chapter is a song of thanksgiving; yet, it is a futuristic (eschatological) song that would be sung by the captives after God had delivered them from their captivity. The key phrase is in verse 1: "In that day." The prophet did not tell the reader when, but merely that after the Exile they, the people of Yahweh, would have sufficient reason to sing and shout for joy. The people of God would be comforted. However, to get a fuller picture and put this song of celebration in its proper perspective, the student might benefit from reading the prior chapters (especially 5–7). Chapter 11 contains a divine promise that "in that day" there will be a new creation and the status quo will be undone. This is the reason and the context of the festive celebration in chapter 12. In this chapter, it would be water that would be their undoing—"the mighty floodwaters of the River"—but then it will be out of water that their liberation would come (see verse 3). The people "give thanks and sing praises to the Lord, for He has done gloriously."

II. EXPOSITION AND APPLICATION OF THE SCRIPTURE

A. In That Day, Give Praise!
(Isaiah 12:1-3)

AND IN that day thou shalt say, O LORD, I will praise thee: though thou wast angry with me, thine anger is turned away, and thou comfortedst me. Behold, God is my salvation; I will trust, and not be afraid: for the LORD JEHOVAH is my strength and my song; he also is become my salvation.

Therefore with joy shall ye draw water out of the wells of salvation.

There are two introductory verses in this chapter: verses 1 and 4; both announce "in that day" a future day that would come, yet was not known, when hope would be fulfilled. The expression "in that day" is full of hope and expectation, especially for the first hearers of this prophecy. Judah and Israel were at that time ruined and their inhabitants were in captivity in a strange land (Assyria and/or Babylon). Perhaps they wondered about the longsuffering love of their God. When would their ordeal pass? The prophet merely said that the day would come when the people who were broken and bruised would praise the Lord and acknowledge that the Lord's anger had passed. This was a tacit acknowledgment that their captivity was a result of their sins. They were in this predicament because they violated God's covenant. But then they received comfort from God: "O LORD,…thine anger is turned away, and thou comfortedst me" (verse 1). The biblical idea of *comfort* is "to have or show pity." This theme of comfort reached its height for the prophet in Isaiah 40:1-2: "Comfort, comfort my people, says your God. Speak tenderly to Jerusalem, and proclaim to her that her hard service has been completed, that her sin has been paid for, that she has received from the LORD's hand double for all her sins" (NIV).

Yahweh showed pity on Israel, much like He showed pity on Isaiah in chapter 6. Therefore, the reason for the Israelites' praise was based on the following: the Lord's anger had passed and instead of anger, they knew the comfort of their God. Her comfort was that "her warfare was over"; she was liberated and allowed to return to her motherland. This must be a reference to the southern kingdom (Judah), because the northern kingdom (Israel) never returned from exile in Assyria. Nevertheless, when the Lord's anger turned away and they knew His comfort, they were prompted to sing His praises. The psalmist (in Psalm 126:1-2) wrote in song, "When the LORD brought back the captives to Zion, we were like men who dreamed. Our mouths were filled with laughter, our tongues with songs of joy. Then it was said among the nations, 'The LORD has done great things for them'" (NIV). The Lord has done great things for us, and we are filled with joy. Although we cannot be sure, this psalm seems to capture the mood of the people in Isaiah 12.

Verse 2 (NIV) acknowledges the obvious: "Surely God is my salvation; I will trust and not be afraid. The LORD, the LORD, is my strength and my song; he has become my salvation." Again, the people proclaimed their liberation and declared their trust and confidence in the Lord. There are four critical components of salvation: trust, confidence, strength, and song. This biblical idea of *strength* is "security, or boldness to express oneself in praise." Second, "song" in this context is the idea of "music accomplished by vocal celebration."

So, it was not just the playing of musical instruments, but the people who were also singing, "The LORD, the LORD, is my strength and my song; he has become my salvation." But then, verse 3 puts the onus on the people: "With joy you will draw water from the wells of salvation" (NIV). It was the floodwaters that swept Israel into captivity. But then the people would be able to draw water—that life-giving substance—from the "wells of salvation." The wells of salvation are now accessible, but the people must put their buckets into the well of water. Liberation and opportunity are always joyous, and something to sing about. They sing a doxology of hope.

B. In That Day, Give Thanks!
(Isaiah 12:4-5)

And in that day shall ye say, Praise the Lord, call upon his name, declare his doings among the people, make mention that his name is exalted. Sing unto the Lord; for he hath done excellent things: this is known in all the earth.

Again, the prophet used the introductory phrase "In that day"; but then, rather than using the first-person singular "I," he spoke for the people, "Give thanks to the Lord, call on his name." The people were to give thanks and exhort others to give thanks to the Lord and call upon His name; they had been liberated, or set free. They were to tell their story of the mighty acts of the Lord. Unlike the Negro Spiritual, they would not "look back and wonder how they got over"; they would know that it was the Lord their God who brought them out. Therefore, they were to "proclaim that His name is exalted." In antiquity, nations would go to war under the banner (for God's people it would be *Jehovah-Nissi*—"the Lord our Banner") of their gods. This practice was very much like America's flying the U.S. flag in battle: *To the victor go the spoils*. The nation that was victorious would ascribe their success to their god (God versus Baal on Mount Carmel—1 Kings 18). Therefore, the people (after being liberated from captivity) were to exhort each other to do two things: call on the Lord's name, and exalt His name on the earth (see verse 4). The Lord's name was exalted (or lofty) above all others.

Also consistent with Old Testament motif, the Israelites were afraid to mention the Lord's name for fear of the violation of the first commandment (see Exodus 20:7); "You shall not take the name of the Lord your God in vain." Consequently, they probably used one of several pronouns for "God," according to ways in which they had experienced God.

A person's name in antiquity was more than just a tag of identification; it represented the person's character. Of course, the Lord's name is who He is: He cannot be separated from His name. To exalt His name is to exalt Him. So, Isaiah's exhortation to call on the name of the Lord is because of who Yahweh is and the things He had/has done. Yahweh's name is not a light matter; to call His name is to speak to Him and of Him.

Finally, the prophet said, "In the day the people of God will not only call on the name of the Lord, but they would sing of his wonderful works." Their singing would be a doxology of thanks for what God had done. Their singing will give universal testimony to the goodness of Yahweh. Giving thanks in the Old Testament was a show of gratitude and was most often expressed in the context of worship. "Give thanks unto the Lord, for He is good: for his mercy endureth for ever" (see Psalm 106:1 and 107:1, KJV). Verse 5 is a continued exhortation to give testimony to the goodness of God: "Sing to the Lord, for he has done glorious things; let this be known to all the world" (NIV). However, we must be mindful that worship in ancient times for these people was radically different from what we know today. The people worshipped in the Temple or synagogue, primarily on special days. So, more than likely this exhortation was not intended just for when the people assembled for worship; rather, they were to acknowledge the goodness of Yahweh in the public square.

Today, worship has become for us so ritualized that it has practically lost its spiritual focus and relevance. We are so preoccupied with the rudiments (length of service, kind of music, length of sermon, and so forth) of worship that the spiritual often gets lost. But Jesus said, "The day will come when you will worship God in spirit and in truth" (see John 4:23). True worship is worship that not only sings to the Lord for what He has done, but also proclaims to the entire world the things He has done. This is worship beyond the walls of the sanctuary (the public square). Indeed, we as a people have much to give thanks for in our history. The cliché goes, "If God doesn't do anything else, He has already done enough." We have enough examples of the mercies of God that even if God does nothing else, our testimony still ought to be sure.

C. In That Day, Shout!
(Isaiah 12:6)

Cry out and shout, thou inhabitant of Zion: for great is the Holy One of Israel in the midst of thee.

The final exaltation invited the entire covenant community to shout for joy for not only what Yahweh had done, but also because the Holy One of Israel was in their midst. This theological idea of divine presence dates back to the days of the Exodus and the liberation of the children of Israel from Egypt and their subsequent journey into Canaan. Yahweh was present with them and went before them, "making ways out of no way." Thus, when Yahweh was present with them, great things happened. So the same divine presence that went before them in the wilderness would now dwell in their midst. For this reason, they would shout and sing for joy. "Cry out and shout" means that they were to cry aloud with so much gusto that they could be heard near and far. This verse builds on verse 5 and the command for the Israelites to share their testimony with the entire world. Of course, they did not have the mass media capability to broadcast their praise, so they were to use their voices to shout loud enough to be heard near and far. Yet, there are those who have said that contemporary worship is too loud and there are others who say that it does take all of that—but the prophet gave us another viewpoint about the loudness of worship. They were to shout with such volume that they could be heard near and far—not with instruments, but with the voices of the people. There is an adage that goes, "To whom much is given, much is required." This is the premise of the prophet's message not only to Israel, but also to all of us. Their song and their exuberance will reflect appropriately their gratitude. Now, we must do likewise.

III. CONCLUDING REFLECTION

Isaiah had a vision of the day when Israel would be restored as a faith community. Their warfare would be over and the day of rejoicing would come. The impetus for praise and worship was not only what the Lord had done, but also what the Lord would do. It was Isaiah's faith in God that gave him hope for his people.

By the time you read this lesson, the Dr. Martin Luther King Jr. National Memorial in the nation's capital will be open to the public.

The theme of the memorial is "Dream," taken from King's famous "I Have a Dream" speech. In this speech, Dr. King borrowed inspiration from the prophet Isaiah's dream for his nation and people: "I have a dream that one day every valley shall be exalted, and every hill and mountain shall be made low, the rough places will be made plain, and the crooked places will be made straight; and the glory of the Lord shall be revealed and all flesh shall see it together." For Dr. King, America as he saw it was not the final state of her existence; he knew that God had something greater for her. Hence, he proclaimed, "One day all of God's children, black men and white men, Jews and Gentiles, Protestants and Catholics, will be able to join hands and sing in the words of the old Negro Spiritual: 'Free at last. Free at last. Thank God almighty, we are free at last.'" Communal transformation and restoration is never easy or timely, but we must remember that with faith in God all things are possible and that God is on the side of justice.

PRAYER

O Lord, our Lord, how gracious You are. We are compelled by Your love toward us to proclaim Your goodness in the world. Indeed, we are blessed by the marvelous things You have done for us. In Jesus' name we pray. Amen.

WORD POWER

Comfort *(parakaleo)*—exhortation, encouragement, and reassuring to aid.
Name—appellation or a decisive characteristic and reputation.
Salvation—in the Old Testament, it takes on the meaning "to keep" or to be "set free."
Strength—ability (with stress on the power to prevail).

HOME DAILY BIBLE READINGS
(June 3-9, 2013)

Give Thanks
   MONDAY, June 3: "Giving Thanks Is Good" (Psalm 92:1-8)
   TUESDAY, June 4: "Coming into God's Presence with Thanksgiving" (Psalm 95:1-7)
   WEDNESDAY, June 5: "Remembering God's Wonderful Works" (1 Chronicles 16:8-13)
   THURSDAY, June 6: "Giving Thanks and Praise to God" (1 Chronicles 29:10-18)
   FRIDAY, June 7: "Receiving God's Goodness with Thanksgiving" (1 Timothy 4:1-5)
   SATURDAY, June 8: "Where Are the Other Nine?" (Luke 17:11-19)
   SUNDAY, June 9: "Giving Thanks to the Lord" (Isaiah 12)

MEANINGLESS WORSHIP

Faith Pathway/Faith Journey Topic: **More than Words**

Devotional Reading: **Luke 8:9-14**
Print Passage: **Isaiah 29:9-16a**

Background Scripture: **Isaiah 29**
Key Verse: **Isaiah 29:13**

Isaiah 29:9-16a—KJV

9 Stay yourselves, and wonder; cry ye out, and cry: they are drunken, but not with wine; they stagger, but not with strong drink.

10 For the Lord hath poured out upon you the spirit of deep sleep, and hath closed your eyes: the prophets and your rulers, the seers hath he covered.

11 And the vision of all is become unto you as the words of a book that is sealed, which men deliver to one that is learned, saying, Read this, I pray thee: and he saith, I cannot; for it is sealed:

12 And the book is delivered to him that is not learned, saying, Read this, I pray thee: and he saith, I am not learned.

13 Wherefore the Lord said, Forasmuch as this people draw near me with their mouth, and with their lips do honour me, but have removed their heart far from me, and their fear toward me is taught by the precept of men:

14 Therefore, behold, I will proceed to do a marvellous work among this people, even a marvellous work and a wonder: for the wisdom of their wise men shall perish, and the understanding of their prudent men shall be hid.

15 Woe unto them that seek deep to hide their counsel from the Lord, and their works are in the dark, and they say, Who seeth us? and who knoweth us?

16 Surely your turning of things upside down shall be esteemed as the potter's clay.

Isaiah 29:9-16a—NIV

9 Be stunned and amazed, blind yourselves and be sightless; be drunk, but not from wine, stagger, but not from beer.

10 The Lord has brought over you a deep sleep: He has sealed your eyes (the prophets); he has covered your heads (the seers).

11 For you this whole vision is nothing but words sealed in a scroll. And if you give the scroll to someone who can read, and say to him, "Read this, please," he will answer, "I can't; it is sealed."

12 Or if you give the scroll to someone who cannot read, and say, "Read this, please," he will answer, "I don't know how to read."

13 The Lord says: "These people come near to me with their mouth and honor me with their lips, but their hearts are far from me. Their worship of me is made up only of rules taught by men.

14 Therefore once more I will astound these people with wonder upon wonder; the wisdom of the wise will perish, the intelligence of the intelligent will vanish."

15 Woe to those who go to great depths to hide their plans from the Lord, who do their work in darkness and think, "Who sees us? Who will know?"

16 You turn things upside down, as if the potter were thought to be like the clay!

UNIFYING LESSON PRINCIPLE

People sometimes ritualistically repeat words or phrases that have little to no meaning for them. What is the danger involved in insincere speaking? Isaiah relayed God's message—that He will judge those who honor Him with their lips but not their hearts.

TOPICAL OUTLINE OF THE LESSON

I. Introduction
   A. Quality Words
   B. Biblical Background

II. Exposition and Application of the Scripture
   A. The People's Condition (Isaiah 29:9-11)
   B. God's Assessment (Isaiah 29:12-14)
   C. God Knows (Isaiah 29:15-16a)

III. Concluding Reflection

LESSON OBJECTIVES

Upon completion of the lesson, the students will be able to do the following:

1. Locate and review what Isaiah said about meaningless, insincere worship;

2. Examine the meanings and emotions associated with the words they use in worship; and,

3. Paraphrase and "freshen" a common component of worship that has come to be "mere words."

POINTS TO BE EMPHASIZED
ADULT/YOUTH

Adult Topic: More than Words
Youth Topic: Are You for Real?
Adult/Youth Key Verse: Isaiah 29:13
Print Passage: Isaiah 29:9-16a

—The context of the passage is a message chiding Jerusalem for its insincerity in worship.
—The lack of real faithfulness was a problem. Religious leaders failed to function as they should.
—The people practiced the rituals of worship, but it was not sincere and centered on God.
—Because of the people's insincerity in worship, they would not be able to understand and discern the ways of God.
—Humanity's attempts to usurp the knowledge and sovereignty of God will be exposed.
—God's redemptive acts will ultimately prevail.

CHILDREN

Children Topic: Out of a Humble Heart
Key Verse: Luke 18:14b
Print Passage: Isaiah 29:9-16a

—Luke indicated God's rejection of words that come from insincere hearts and lives.
—Jesus told a parable about a Pharisee and a tax collector who went to the Temple to pray.
—The Pharisee praised himself to God, but the tax collector asked God for mercy.
—Jesus praised the humility of the tax collector and called him righteous in God's eyes.
—Luke understood that a humble heart pleases God and leads to God's approval.
—Pharisees were highly regarded religious leaders, while tax collectors were both feared and disliked because they taxed the Jews beyond what the Roman government required.

I. INTRODUCTION

A. Quality Words

We have become a "learned" generation with the ability to speak words in volumes. We have become an eloquent people. However, it appears that too many of us have become mesmerized by our own words in worship; therefore, worship has become an exercise in futility.

In the kingdom of God, worship is more than just words (praise). The words must be substantiated by a positive lifestyle of being a good neighbor. In this chapter, Israel stood under the indictment of Yahweh, because of Israel's wanton disobedience of covenant law. Yahweh would suffer them to be taken into captivity, but the day would come when Yahweh would reverse their fortunes—from doom to blessings. This divine reversal would be evident in their worship. God would judge their worship not by the volume of the music, the loudness of the P/A system, the exhortation of the psalmist, or the contrived energy of the people—but by the sincerity of their hearts. This is why the Bible teaches that men and women look at the outward appearance, but God looks at the heart.

B. Biblical Background

This chapter begins with a "woe (trouble yet to come) to you Ariel, Ariel…" Most scholars agree that *Ariel* was an enigmatic term for the City of Jerusalem, but had no prominence at the time of this prophecy. Just as Jerusalem was the city of God, at one point in Israel's history Ariel was known as the city where David encamped. It was cut off by David and eventually overrun. The prophet used the city as a metaphor for the city of Jerusalem, for just as David encamped to lay siege against Ariel, so would the Lord do likewise against Jerusalem. Therefore, the first half of chapter 29 consists of a series of divine threats against the people of God. God would lay siege against His people, and they would be in distress and begin moaning and lamenting. Acting in judgment, the Lord would reduce the City of Jerusalem to dust (see verses 1-4), and the prosperity of a great people would be no more (verse 4).

Yahweh judged Israel and turned her "to dust" because of her disobedience. Perhaps this is the relevant question before every believer: "How will we use our faith, not as an expression in worship but in the public square?"

II. EXPOSITION AND APPLICATION OF THE SCRIPTURE

A. The People's Condition
(Isaiah 29:9-11)

Stay yourselves, and wonder; cry ye out, and cry: they are drunken, but not with wine; they stagger, but not with strong drink. For the Lord hath poured out upon you the spirit of deep sleep, and hath closed your eyes: the prophets and your rulers, the seers hath he covered. And the vision of all is become unto you as the words of a book that is sealed, which men deliver to one that is learned, saying, Read this, I pray thee: and he saith, I cannot; for it is sealed.

Isaiah was very poetic in these verses; the people of God had been hesitant, indecisive, blind, and deaf in their response to Yahweh. So, Isaiah used images of a person who was in a drunken stupor, but this stupor would not be the result of having consumed too much beer or wine, but would come about because the Lord would cause spiritual blindness and deafness to come upon the person. But, in his language (blind yourselves...be drunk), Isaiah wanted the people to be certain that this calamity was self-inflicted. They had been willful in their disobedience. They had refused to see and to hear the prophets. The covenant laws of Israel date back to the time of Exodus, when God promised both blessings and curses to the people: "You will be blessed if you obey the commands of the LORD your God that I am giving you today. But you will be cursed if you disobey the commands of the LORD your God" (Deuteronomy 11:27-28a, NCV). It is indeed interesting that the Hebrew term for *disobedience* means "to hear incorrectly." Thus, those who disobeyed the Law did not hear correctly what the Lord had said.

Hence, the Lord brought judgment and calamity against Israel because of her disobedience. The key verse is verse 10 (NIV): "The LORD has brought over you a deep sleep"—meaning a deep stupor or coma. The sealing of their eyes indicated the inability to open their eyes (even when they were ready to do so). Their ability to see was now in the Lord's hands. When one is asleep, one's sense of hearing and seeing are impaired and are not as keen. The Lord impaired the spiritual capacity to discern what He said.

It does not matter how intelligent or unintelligent we are or we think we are in the kingdom of God; obedience must be supreme, because God is Lord of all. God is able to confound both the wise and the foolish. Those who could read could either not open the seal or they could open the seal but could not read. The future path of Jerusalem could not be understood; Yahweh was keeping it from them.

B. God's Assessment
(Isaiah 29:12-14)

And the book is delivered to him that is not learned, saying, Read this, I pray thee: and he saith, I am not learned. Wherefore the Lord said, Forasmuch as this people draw near me with their mouth, and with their lips do honour me, but have removed their heart far from me, and their fear toward me is taught by the precept of men: Therefore, behold, I will proceed to do a marvellous work among this people, even a marvellous work and a wonder: for the wisdom of their wise men shall perish, and the understanding of their prudent men shall be hid.

For the first time, the prophet quoted the Lord. Previously, the prophet spoke by revelation, which means that Yahweh spoke to the prophet and the prophet spoke the revelation in his own words. Isaiah attributed these words directly to the Lord: "These people come near to me with their mouth and honor me with their lips, but their hearts are far from me" (verse 13, NIV). The people of Israel had turned the rituals of worship into mere lip service. In the book of Leviticus, the Lord gave Moses concrete rules of worship that the people were supposed to observe when they came before Yahweh in worship. The people knew the laws of worship and could recite them, but they began to modify the law out of convenience. Likewise, certain offenses required certain sacrifices to be made before they could worship—but they were taking shortcuts.

Our first lesson in this series, from chapter

6, tells how unworthy we are in worship before our God. Just as Isaiah was deemed a man of unclean lips, so were his people. What was on their lips was not consistent with what was in their hearts, apart from their practices in the public square.

These verses give us the reason why the Lord caused this spirit of stupor or coma to befall the people. The Lord said in verse 13 that there was a discrepancy between what was on the lips of the people, and what was in their hearts. One of the consistent expectations (theme) for the people of God in the Bible is integrity. God expects us to be men and women of integrity. The word for *integrity* merely means "to be whole or non-fractured." At the time of this prophecy, Israel was fractured in both their theology and sociology. They were committed to the Lord in word only; their religious and social practices were not consistent with the Law of Moses.

The book of Malachi gives an indication of what Israel's religious practices had dissolved to: "But you ask, 'How have we shown contempt for your name?' You place defiled food on my altar. But you ask, 'How have we defiled you?'... When you bring blind animals, is that not wrong?"... "And now this admonition is for you, O priests. If you do not listen, and if you do not set your heart to honor my name," says the LORD almighty, "I will send a curse upon you, and I will curse your blessings. ... because you have not set your heart to honor me" (Malachi 1:6b-7b, 8a; 2:1-2, NIV).

Finally, verse 14 gives the consequences for their lack of true devotion. They were merely going through the motions. Yahweh would punish Israel for her phoniness; He would then work against this people.

C. God Knows
(Isaiah 29:15-16a)

Woe unto them that seek deep to hide their counsel from the LORD, and their works are in the dark, and they say, Who seeth us? and who knoweth us? Surely your turning of things upside down shall be esteemed as the potter's clay.

This section of the text closes as chapter 29 opens—with "woe." This time, the warning or danger sign spoke specifically to those who were both diligent and intentional about hiding their transgressions from the Lord (see verse 15). Yet, they did so with great ignorance of the awareness of Yahweh. These people did not have a well-defined theology of the nature of God. They thought they could venture beyond the seeing eye of Yahweh. In many instances, the thought was that God was localized in the mountains around Jerusalem because many of their patriarchs had divine encounters in the mountains.

It was not until later in Israel's history that they developed a theology that ascribed physical attributes (omniscience, omnipotence, and omnipresence) to Yahweh. They, like many of us, felt that they could hide their plans from the Lord. But not only is Yahweh sovereign, but also He "created the ends of the earth and all in it." Yahweh knew them just as He knows us. The psalmist said that He searches us and knows us—that there is nowhere we can go from His presence (see Psalm 139). Yahweh is omnipresent and omniscient. He sees all and He knows all. Nothing can be hidden from Him. In verse 16, Isaiah spoke what was obvious and practical to him, but not to the people. The created do not dictate to the Creator: Yahweh is the potter and we are the clay.

III. CONCLUDING REFLECTION

There is a popular song entitled "Praise Is What I Do" which contains the following words: "Praise is who I am, I will praise while I can." The song projects praise as an abstract concept that we can routinely control. But is praise arbitrary and capricious? This lesson makes it clear that praise cannot be arbitrary or capricious. There is an ethical quality to authentic praise that has to meet Yahweh's standard. It is not enough for one to praise God if his or her heart is absent of integrity and loyalty; it is possible for praise to come from the lips only, and not from the heart. In this country, the Christian church has had a strong presence for centuries, yet some of the greatest atrocities have been done under the sign of the Cross. It is not our duty to make ourselves feel good about ourselves; rather, our duty is to honor God. The people of the text believed that as long as they went through the motions of worship that this was acceptable to Yahweh—but not so. Yahweh wants more than our praise: Yahweh wants all of us, because when He gets us, He gets our praise. However, the problem connecting worship to life in the public square is a recurring one for the people of Yahweh. Praise is not what we do or who we are, because authentic praise flows out of the depth of a sincere heart; it is the consequence of having a much deeper relationship with God.

PRAYER

Father God, it is our prayer that our praise and worship will meet Your standard of integrity. It is our desire that our lives will be pleasing to You, for You are our strength and Redeemer. In Jesus' name we pray. Amen.

WORD POWER

Praise—recognition that the righteous give in thanksgiving after deliverance. It describes how God has brought restoration.

Prophet—one who spoke on behalf of God by inspiration. The prophet spoke to God on behalf of the people and to the people on behalf of God (for example: "thus said the Lord").

Seer—the forerunner of the prophets in Israel. Samuel was a seer (see 1 Samuel 9:9).

Worship *(proskyneo)*—to bow down or to kiss—the act of venerating God.

HOME DAILY BIBLE READINGS
(June 10-16, 2013)

Meaningless Worship

MONDAY, June 10: "Fruitless Worship" (Isaiah 1:10-17)

TUESDAY, June 11: "Worshipping Our Own Achievements" (Isaiah 2:5-17)

WEDNESDAY, June 12: "Lives Untouched by Religious Observances" (Isaiah 58:1-7)

THURSDAY, June 13: "Refusing to Listen" (Jeremiah 13:1-11)

FRIDAY, June 14: "Tuning Out God" (Zechariah 7:8-14)

SATURDAY, June 15: "Receiving the Word" (Luke 8:9-15)

SUNDAY, June 16: "Hearts Far from God" (Isaiah 29:9-16a)

LESSON 4   June 23, 2013

THE GLORIOUS NEW CREATION

FAITH PATHWAY/FAITH JOURNEY TOPIC: Nothing Is Going to Be the Same

DEVOTIONAL READING: **Isaiah 42:1-9**
PRINT PASSAGE: **Isaiah 65:17-21, 23-25**

BACKGROUND SCRIPTURE: **Isaiah 65**
KEY VERSES: **Isaiah 65:17-18**

Isaiah 65:17-21, 23-25—KJV

17 For, behold, I create new heavens and a new earth: and the former shall not be remembered, nor come into mind.

18 But be ye glad and rejoice for ever in that which I create: for, behold, I create Jerusalem a rejoicing, and her people a joy.

19 And I will rejoice in Jerusalem, and joy in my people: and the voice of weeping shall be no more heard in her, nor the voice of crying.

20 There shall be no more thence an infant of days, nor an old man that hath not filled his days: for the child shall die an hundred years old; but the sinner being an hundred years old shall be accursed.

21 And they shall build houses, and inhabit them; and they shall plant vineyards, and eat the fruit of them.

....

23 They shall not labour in vain, nor bring forth for trouble; for they are the seed of the blessed of the LORD, and their offspring with them.

24 And it shall come to pass, that before they call, I will answer; and while they are yet speaking, I will hear.

25 The wolf and the lamb shall feed together, and the lion shall eat straw like the bullock: and dust shall be the serpent's meat. They shall not hurt nor destroy in all my holy mountain, saith the LORD.

Isaiah 65:17-21, 23-25—NIV

17 "Behold, I will create new heavens and a new earth. The former things will not be remembered, nor will they come to mind.

18 But be glad and rejoice forever in what I will create, for I will create Jerusalem to be a delight and its people a joy.

19 I will rejoice over Jerusalem and take delight in my people; the sound of weeping and of crying will be heard in it no more.

20 Never again will there be in it an infant who lives but a few days, or an old man who does not live out his years; he who dies at a hundred will be thought a mere youth; he who fails to reach a hundred will be considered accursed.

21 They will build houses and dwell in them; they will plant vineyards and eat their fruit."

....

23 "They will not toil in vain or bear children doomed to misfortune; for they will be a people blessed by the LORD, they and their descendants with them.

24 Before they call I will answer; while they are still speaking I will hear.

25 The wolf and the lamb will feed together, and the lion will eat straw like the ox, but dust will be the serpent's food. They will neither harm nor destroy on all my holy mountain," says the LORD.

People desperately long for a time when there will be no more weeping and crying and the earth will be a place of happiness and peace. Will that time ever come? The God of truth and Creator of the earth promised through Isaiah that someday God's children would be so blessed.

TOPICAL OUTLINE OF THE LESSON

I. Introduction
   A. The Answer to "Why?" May Not Satisfy
   B. Biblical Background

II. Exposition and Application of the Scripture
   A. It Is All New
      (Isaiah 65:17-19)
   B. Long Life Promised
      (Isaiah 65:20-21)
   C. Total Harmony
      (Isaiah 65:23-25)

III. Concluding Reflection

LESSON OBJECTIVES

Upon completion of this lesson, the students will be able to do the following:

1. Identify the changes Isaiah claimed God would make in the new creation;
2. Describe their own personal visions of the "new creation" that God has promised; and,
3. Discover (and reinforce) worship experiences as rehearsals for what lies ahead in eternity.

POINTS TO BE EMPHASIZED

ADULT/YOUTH

Adult Topic: **Nothing Is Going to Be the Same**
Youth Topic: **In with the New!**
Adult Key Verses: **Isaiah 65:17-18**
Youth Key Verse: **Isaiah 65:17**
Print Passage: **Isaiah 65:17-21, 23-25**

—The present heavens and earth are temporary.
—God's people should be glad and rejoice over the expectation of God's new creation.
—There will be no suffering in God's new creation.
—God's people and their children will be blessed in the new heaven and new earth that God will create.
—In the new heavens and earth, the loss of homes and harvests brought on by the Exile will be reversed.
—In God's new creation, there will be harmony among all living creatures.

CHILDREN

Children Topic: **Everything Will Be New**
Key Verse: **Isaiah 65:18a**
Print Passage: **Isaiah 65:17-21, 23-25**

—God gave Isaiah a vision of an amazing new creation that He will bring into existence.
—In the new creation, life will reach its full potential.
—People will benefit from their own labors and enjoy the Lord's bounty.
—If it is within God's will, then human desires will be granted before they are asked.
—In the new creation, the natural world will be at peace.
—The fate of the Serpent represents God's banishment of evil, making the new creation secure.

I. INTRODUCTION

A. The Answer to "Why?" May Not Satisfy

In our times of crisis and trouble, we are prone to ponder about where God is in the crisis. "Does God care? Why did God allow this (event or crisis) to happen to us?" Rabbi Harold Kushner raises this question in his famed book, *When Bad Things Happen to Good People*. If God is in control, then why does He allow bad things to happen to good people? However, in such questions, the implicit question is about the existence of God. Does God really exist—and if He does, then why would He allow these things to happen? These are profoundly theological questions that reach all the way back to antiquity and to the eighth-century prophets. Israel's whole reality was defined by their understanding of who God is, so perhaps for them the question would be, "If God is all-powerful, all-loving, and good, and we are the people of God, then why would God allow these terrible things to happen to us?" Also, such questions about God imply that they saw themselves as the victims of their circumstances and did not consider their own culpability. In time, Israel would come to know that Yahweh is not only a God of love and power, but also of judgment. The prophets would help the people come to the realization of their guilt and complicity in their plight: "Surely the arm of the Lord is not too short to save, nor his ear too dull to hear. But your iniquities have separated you from your God; your sins have hidden his face from you, so that he will not hear" (Isaiah 59:1-2, NIV). Isaiah taught that there was a human element to their predicament. "I will destine you for the sword, and you will all bend down for the slaughter; for I called but you did not answer, I spoke but you did not listen. You did evil in my sight and chose what displeases me" (Isaiah 65:12). Israel, like many today, wrongly accused God for their suffering.

There were a father and two children who died in a fatal car accident on a rain-slick roadway when the father lost control of his vehicle and plunged into a ditch, killing him and his two children. The question was asked by their young pastor, "Why did God allow this tragedy to befall this family?" Sometime later the medical autopsy revealed that the father had been under the influence of alcohol. Sometimes, there are painful realities that we must face; we are responsible for some of the hurt, pain, and suffering that befalls us. Finally, chapter 65 contains only the response to the questions raised earlier in chapters 56–64. The prophet assured us that when the people of God did right by God, in time He would make all things new. Likewise, the word *new* did not mean that there would be no loss; rather, God would restore us to a place of wellness and wholeness. This is our hope for the "beloved community" that will become a reality on earth.

B. Biblical Background

Chapter 65 is part of the book called, "Second Isaiah." It was written during and after the Babylonian captivity by the school of prophets of Isaiah. Israel was at this time finished with their exile in Babylon and looking with great anticipation to a fresh start. However, they were still in a quandary about the fidelity of Yahweh: why did their God allow this calamity to befall them? Nevertheless, Isaiah saw the day when their warfare would be over (see Isaiah 40) and all things would be made new. Yet, it would not just be Yahweh's chosen people, Israel, who would participate in this radical reformation and transformation—all the people of the earth would experience a new heaven and new earth. Things would be returned to the idyllic state of the Garden of Eden. The balance of nature would be altered, and that which by nature seemed adversarial and contentious would find peaceful co-existence (see Isaiah 65:25). There would be peace and harmony in all of the earth. The Israelites had longed for the day when they could return home to Jerusalem after all those seventy years in captivity. Israel's hopes and dreams were that Yahweh would defeat their enemy and allow them to return to their homeland and rebuild the city of God, Jerusalem. Their hopes and dreams, however, were limited and parochial at best, for the dream of God was a new cosmic order. In this new order, nothing will be the same—the wolf and the lamb, and the lion and the oxen will co-exist in harmony. In his letter to the Christians in Rome, the apostle Paul said, "Creation is groaning as in child birth, waiting for its redemption" (see Romans 8:22). This is the picture the prophet gave us—a radical new day when creation will no longer groan. The Adamic effects of sin will be eradicated from all of creation and "all things will become new."

Chapter 65 is part of a larger body of work (see chapters 56–66) in which it is made clear that Israel had been blatant in her rejection of the ways of Yahweh. "Yahweh called but they did not answer" (see 64:1-4). Therefore, captivity in Babylon was the consequence of their behavior. Yahweh called and they did not answer in righteousness. So then the promises God made to Abraham—"All nations of the earth will be blessed because of you"—would come to fruition. The people of the world would share in this new vision of peace and prosperity. Yet, Isaiah was clear that this newness would demand something new from all of us who would participate in this newness of life. When Yahweh calls, we must answer; we cannot afford to be insensitive and unresponsive to the calling of Yahweh.

II. EXPOSITION AND APPLICATION OF THE SCRIPTURE

A. It Is All New

(Isaiah 65:17-19)

For, behold, I create new heavens and a new earth: and the former shall not be remembered, nor come into mind. But be ye glad and rejoice for ever in that which I create: for, behold, I create Jerusalem a rejoicing, and her people a joy. And I will rejoice in Jerusalem, and joy in my people: and the voice of weeping shall be no more heard in her, nor the voice of crying.

The prophet brought good news of a new world order to the captives. "Behold" is a verb that immediately called the people to action. The people were invited to see or observe this new thing that Yahweh was about to do. Verses 11-16 constitute an accusation and an indictment of the people of Israel, the chosen ones, because of their rejection of the ways of

Yahweh. "But as for you who forsake the LORD and forget my holy mountain, …I called but you did not answer" (verses 11 and 12). Then in verse 13, the Lord spoke the consequences of their rebellion: "My servants will eat, but *you* will go hungry; my servants will drink, but *you* will go thirsty." We cannot understand the promise without first reviewing the antecedents of these verses, which speak of the judgment before the liberation.

Two groups of people were being discussed in these antecedent verses. "My servants" is spoken of as a single being, and "you" refers to a different person or group. Two peoples are being spoken about: "my servants," and the one who was spoken to—"you." For the prophet, an Israelite would no longer be determined by biological lineage (the seed of Abraham); rather, those who did the will of God would have the same standing before God as the sons and daughters of Abraham (Israelites). Yahweh said that He would create a new heaven and a new earth comprised of people of different ethnicities who will be "my servants." The new creation would be antithetical to the old order. A New Jerusalem would be the hub of this new creation; however, we must be clear and keep in mind that in this case, Jerusalem is a metaphor for the place where the people of Yahweh would gather in obedience to Yahweh. This description of a new heaven and a new earth language is consistent with the New Jerusalem that John the Revelator saw in Revelation 21, coming down out of heaven. Likewise, we must understand these verses in the context in which these exilic Jews heard them. Their ambition and hope was to return to Jerusalem and rebuild the "City of David." The people in exile envisioned the restoration of the old order

of a socio-political society—when Jerusalem would be the center of world dominance. But, Yahweh had something else in mind. Jerusalem will become the spiritual center for all peoples who will be faithful and responsive to the ways and purposes Yahweh has for creation. This newness is expressed in verse 19b. Rather than lamenting over Jerusalem as in times past, Yahweh will rejoice over her and her people will be a delightful people (see Malachi 3:12-17). The day of mourning will be no more—for the sound of weeping and crying would be heard no more (see Isaiah 25:7-8). In light of the many injustices and inequities that blanket the landscape of our world, this must be good news to all peoples who know the pain and disappointment of living in a world not dominated by compassion, but greed. Yahweh, sovereign God, will have the final word and blessing over creation.

B. Long Life Promised (Isaiah 65:20-21)

There shall be no more thence an infant of days, nor an old man that hath not filled his days: for the child shall die an hundred years old; but the sinner being an hundred years old shall be accursed. And they shall build houses, and inhabit them; and they shall plant vineyards, and eat the fruit of them.

One of the signs of this new creation will be long life for all persons (see verse 20). Infant mortality will be no more, which will be a glorious thing. Infant mortality is a major problem in many parts of the world, although they die from curable diseases. Some of the leading causes of infant and child death worldwide are the following: dehydration from diarrhea, pneumonia, malnutrition, malaria, congenital malformation, infection, and SIDS (according to Wikipedia). We, as Americans with access to modern medicine and advancements in technology, have taken for granted that many of the diseases are curable, while millions of children and infants continue to die from them. According to the World Health Organization (WHO), in some parts of underdeveloped countries such as Angola, Sierra Leone, and Afghanistan, the infant mortality rate is as high as 180 infants per 1000 births, many of them who will die before the age of one year. In America, the infant mortality rate is approximately 8 per 1000 births and in countries such as Sweden with nationalized health care, the infant mortality rate is as low as 2.75 per 1000 infant births. However small the mortality rate is in Sweden, the prophet saw a new creation in which the infant mortality rate would be zero. Long life will be a marvelous indication of this new creation, "Never again will there be in it an infant who lives but a few days" (verse 20, NIV). There will be a new ordering of creation. Old standards and norms of mortality will pass away.

Concomitantly, life will be enriched economically for the dwellers in this New Jerusalem. Indeed, this is refreshing news in light of many of the economic hardships that many good marginalized people are suffering in the first half of the twenty-first century. We hear stories of persons who, during this current economic crisis (2008–present), have labored long and for many years to acquire that dream home, only to be evicted through home foreclosure. In other places, farmers are losing their land of many generations because of a prolonged recession. While this text is futuristic and may not benefit many who are in the throes of economic hardship today, it is good news to know that Yahweh will one day make all things new and the "haves" will not get more, and the "have nots" will not have less.

C. Total Harmony
(Isaiah 65:23-25)

They shall not labour in vain, nor bring forth for trouble; for they are the seed of the blessed of the Lord, and their offspring with them. And it shall come to pass, that before they call, I will answer; and while they are yet speaking, I will hear. The wolf and the lamb shall feed together, and the lion shall eat straw like the bullock: and dust shall be the serpent's meat. They shall not hurt nor destroy in all my holy mountain, saith the Lord.

These closing verses speak of the ultimate harmony of Yahweh, people, and creation. All things will be set right again and there will be no dissonance in creation. Of course, the first promise (see verse 24) reflects negatively on the problem before the Exile between Yahweh and people, so this promise is held in tension between what was and what will be. In the old order, Yahweh spoke and the people did not hear—but in this new order, Yahweh and the people will be so in sync that while they are still speaking, Yahweh will "hear" and "answer." What an awesome day this will be when the "old" will be replaced with the "new" and the people of God will know and experience a "pre-Adamic fall" tranquility which has been foreign to a people and world that defines success by greed and peace by the absence of conflict. But Isaiah saw a new world order in which old standards will be turned upside down, and we will know that it is the Lord's doing.

III. CONCLUDING REFLECTION

Years ago in political arenas across the world, leaders talked about a new world order, by which they meant the globalization of government ruled by an elite group. The new world order was to bring an end to war and provide peace on earth. However, since H. G. Wells first published his work on the New World Order in 1940, the world has known five major wars in which millions of innocent people have perished. But, the new world that the prophet saw was not a political order; rather, it was a spiritual one and not one ruled by humankind, but by Yahweh. It has been said that "politics is what politics does." Yet, the prophet Isaiah saw a day that will be radically different than any the world has ever known, regardless of who is in the seat of political power. Likewise, Dr. Martin Luther King Jr., the twentieth-century prophet, envisioned a day of radical transformation. He believed that in time, God would make all things new,

even the mountains and the valleys. King believed, and it must be our hopes also, that our sovereign God will not allow the George Wallaces, Lester Maddoxes, and Ross Barnetts of the world—"whose lips were dripping with interposition and nullification"—to have the final word. God's dream for His people and the world will be fulfilled.

PRAYER

O Lord our God, You are sovereign and rule over all. We trust that You know best for our lives— and even though there may be disappointments and setbacks for us, we believe that in time You will make all things new for those who love You and honor You in Spirit and in truth. In Jesus' name we pray. Amen.

WORD POWER

Create (Hebrew: *bara*)—occurs about fifty times in the Old Testament. Deity is always either the subject or the implied subject of the verb. We therefore conclude that the activity of *bara* is inherently a divine activity and not one that humans can perform or participate in.

HOME DAILY BIBLE READINGS
(June 17-23, 2013)

The Glorious New Creation

MONDAY, June 17: "The Handiwork of God" (Psalm 19:1-6)

TUESDAY, June 18: "The Guidance of God" (Psalm 19:7-14)

WEDNESDAY, June 19: "No One Is Righteous" (Romans 3:9-20)

THURSDAY, June 20: "Sin, Death, Sacrifice, and Salvation" (Romans 5:6-14)

FRIDAY, June 21: "New Things Springing Forth" (Isaiah 42:1-9)

SATURDAY, June 22: "God Makes All Things New" (Revelation 21:1-7)

SUNDAY, June 23: "New Heavens and a New Earth" (Isaiah 65:17-21, 23-25)

LESSON 5
June 30, 2013

JOYFUL WORSHIP RESTORED

FAITH PATHWAY/FAITH JOURNEY TOPIC: **Celebrating What Is Meaningful**

DEVOTIONAL READING: **Matthew 23:29-39**
PRINT PASSAGE: **Ezra 3:1-7**

BACKGROUND SCRIPTURE: **Ezra 1:1–3:7**
KEY VERSE: **Ezra 3:4**

Ezra 3:1-7—KJV

AND WHEN the seventh month was come, and the children of Israel were in the cities, the people gathered themselves together as one man to Jerusalem.
2 Then stood up Jeshua the son of Jozadak, and his brethren the priests, and Zerubbabel the son of Shealtiel, and his brethren, and builded the altar of the God of Israel, to offer burnt offerings thereon, as it is written in the law of Moses the man of God.
3 And they set the altar upon his bases; for fear was upon them because of the people of those countries: and they offered burnt offerings thereon unto the LORD, even burnt offerings morning and evening.
4 They kept also the feast of tabernacles, as it is written, and offered the daily burnt offerings by number, according to the custom, as the duty of every day required;
5 And afterward offered the continual burnt offering, both of the new moons, and of all the set feasts of the LORD that were consecrated, and of every one that willingly offered a freewill offering unto the LORD.
6 From the first day of the seventh month began they to offer burnt offerings unto the LORD. But the foundation of the temple of the LORD was not yet laid.
7 They gave money also unto the masons, and to the carpenters; and meat, and drink, and oil, unto them of Zidon, and to them of Tyre, to bring cedar trees from Lebanon to the sea of Joppa, according to the grant that they had of Cyrus king of Persia.

Ezra 3:1-7—NIV

WHEN THE seventh month came and the Israelites had settled in their towns, the people assembled as one man in Jerusalem.
2 Then Jeshua son of Jozadak and his fellow priests and Zerubbabel son of Shealtiel and his associates began to build the altar of the God of Israel to sacrifice burnt offerings on it, in accordance with what is written in the Law of Moses the man of God.
3 Despite their fear of the peoples around them, they built the altar on its foundation and sacrificed burnt offerings on it to the LORD, both the morning and evening sacrifices.
4 Then in accordance with what is written, they celebrated the Feast of Tabernacles with the required number of burnt offerings prescribed for each day.
5 After that, they presented the regular burnt offerings, the New Moon sacrifices and the sacrifices for all the appointed sacred feasts of the LORD, as well as those brought as freewill offerings to the LORD.
6 On the first day of the seventh month they began to offer burnt offerings to the LORD, though the foundation of the LORD's temple had not yet been laid.
7 Then they gave money to the masons and carpenters, and gave food and drink and oil to the people of Sidon and Tyre, so that they would bring cedar logs by sea from Lebanon to Joppa, as authorized by Cyrus king of Persia.

UNIFYING LESSON PRINCIPLE

People gratefully celebrate the happy turns of events in their lives. What are the marks of celebration for joyous changes of circumstances? The writer of the book of Ezra told of the time when God's scattered and exiled people celebrated their return with sacred festivals and worship.

TOPICAL OUTLINE OF THE LESSON

I. Introduction
A. How Is Your "CQ" (Celebration Quotient)?
B. Biblical Background

II. Exposition and Application of the Scripture
A. Constructing the Altar (Ezra 3:1-3)
B. Celebrating the Feast (Ezra 3:4-5)
C. Offering the Sacrifices (Ezra 3:6-7)

III. Concluding Reflection

LESSON OBJECTIVES

Upon completion of the lesson, the students will be able to do the following:

1. Identify the worship components described in the text and the reasons for the various actions;
2. Recall and describe a meaningful worship experience or celebration; and,
3. Plan (and carry out) a worship festival for the class or the congregation.

POINTS TO BE EMPHASIZED

ADULT/YOUTH
Adult Topic: Celebrating What Is Meaningful
Youth Topic: Let's Get Ready to Celebrate!
Adult/Youth Key Verse: Ezra 3:4
Print Passage: Ezra 3:1-7

—The returning Jews faced opposition from the inhabitants of the land.
—The returning Jews were unified in their mission in Jerusalem.
—The returning Jews built an altar and started sacrificing after returning to Jerusalem.
—This celebration was a renewal of faithfulness to the Law of Moses.
—The return from exile called for appropriate celebration and renewal of commitment.
—The Feast of Tabernacles added to the joy of the celebration of good times by reminding the Jews of their past hard times.

CHILDREN
Children Topic: A Joyous Return
Key Verse: Ezra 3:3
Print Passage: Ezra 3:1-7

—The Persian king Cyrus gave the Israelites an opportunity to return to Jerusalem, as well as the money and resources needed to rebuild the Temple.
—The priests rebuilt the altar and led the people in offering sacrifices and other acts of worship.
—The people returned to their hometowns, but they gathered again in Jerusalem on set days to worship.
—The people celebrated the Festival of Booths, a festival of thanksgiving to God, in the way they had been instructed in the Law (see Leviticus 23).
—The people gave money so that the Temple could be rebuilt.

I. INTRODUCTION

A. How Is Your "CQ" (Celebration Quotient)?

Celebrating what is truly meaningful is a challenge in a society that is self-absorbed and preoccupied with the mundane (self). This is obvious by our priorities and the things we celebrate. We celebrate the mundane: baseball, basketball, football, and hockey championship victories. We celebrate the deaths of our enemies as equally as we celebrate sporting victories. Many grown men will clown up to represent their favorite football teams and do the "wave" in stadiums to celebrate a team with a losing record. It is not uncommon for riots to break out and (in some instances) lives and property are lost and destroyed as people celebrate national championships. Likewise, we celebrate the ravages and tragedies of war and call it "collateral damage" when innocent children and women are killed.

On the other hand, in the worship of our God, we sit in worship services, non-expressive and sedate with little to no enthusiasm and excitement. Are we moving toward a moral vacuum in our society in which the prophecy of Isaiah is being fulfilled? "Woe unto them that call evil good, and good evil; that put darkness for light, and light for darkness; that put bitter for sweet, and sweet for bitter!" (Isaiah 5:20). The direction in which the world has seemed to move is toward self-absorption. We value the things of self and the things that affirm our superiority in the world. But the prophet Isaiah called us to an awareness of the importance of celebrating the right things (the eternal and not the temporal). After all, Jesus did say, "My kingdom is not of this world" (John 18:36).

B. Biblical Background

After seventy years in captivity, the people in Ezra's day had learned to celebrate what was important. They put Yahweh first. After years of disobedience and lewd behavior, Israel suffered divine chastisement under the Babylonian Empire; however, when their "warfare is accomplished" (Isaiah 40:2), Yahweh allowed His people to return to their homeland under an edict by Cyrus, the then-king of Persia. The book of Nehemiah chronicles the second remigration of the people of God from Babylon to Jerusalem. At one point in biblical history, the books of Ezra and Nehemiah were considered to be one book. It appears that the initial group returned with Ezra (the priest) under the original edict of Cyrus; however, they did not fare well during the resettlement of Palestine. So, when the word came to Nehemiah, cupbearer to Artaxerxes (the then-king of Persia), that his people were suffering in Jerusalem, he was saddened. The people who had moved back to Palestine were living under poor conditions: "Those who survived the exile and are back in the province are in great trouble and disgrace" (Nehemiah 1:3, NIV).

King Artaxerxes made Nehemiah governor of the province of Jerusalem and gave him a letter of permission to give to the governors of the Trans-Euphrates area. He also requested other land barons in the region to provide timber for the rebuilding of Jerusalem's wall and the Temple of God. But according to Ezra, before they would rebuild the city and the Temple, they would rebuild the altar of the God of Israel (see Ezra 3:2). The restoration of the community and the Temple was a sign that the prophetic word of Yahweh remained true and reliable. Isaiah 40:8 states that "the word of our God" would stand forever. Therefore, Ezra asserted that Yahweh had indeed kept His promise and brought about the return of the exiles to Judah and Jerusalem and enabled them to rebuild the Temple of God (see Ezra 1:1). Also, the people established Yahweh as their single priority when they rebuilt the altar of God first. This pattern of behavior was consistent with the lore of their ancestral history; Jewish communities were established around the altar of God. The altar represented the centrality of worship in community life. When Jacob had a divine encounter in Bethel, he erected an altar and called on the name of the Lord. The worship of God is central to the flourishing of the people of God—and even though the Israelites had been in captivity for seventy years, they finally returned home. They regained their perspective. They rebuilt the altar of the Lord and offered sacrifices first, before they rebuilt the city walls and the Temple. Worship (at the altar) was foundational to the reality that Yahweh was with them.

II. EXPOSITION AND APPLICATION OF THE SCRIPTURE

A. Constructing the Altar
(Ezra 3:1-3)

AND WHEN the seventh month was come, and the children of Israel were in the cities, the people gathered themselves together as one man to Jerusalem. Then stood up Jeshua the son of Jozadak, and his brethren the priests, and Zerubbabel the son of Shealtiel, and his brethren, and builded the altar of the God of Israel, to offer burnt offerings thereon, as it is written in the law of Moses the man of God. And they set the altar upon his bases; for fear was upon them because of the people of those countries: and they offered burnt offerings thereon unto the LORD, even burnt offerings morning and evening.

The operative phrase in verse 1 is that "the people [of God] gathered themselves together as one man to Jerusalem." They had one common purpose. This is the starting point of any community—to worship God in spirit and in truth. Yahweh is not divided; He calls us to unity of priority and purpose. Of course, one of the threads of truth that runs through the Bible is oneness of focus and purpose. It was with this singleness of purpose that the Israelites gathered at the old site of the Temple and rebuilt the altar of the Lord (see Ezra 3:1).

Every community has visible symbols of divine presence within it. For the Christian community, it is the cross of Calvary. A young lady was feeling destitute (with no place to turn) as she sat in the parking lot of Kroger, crying. Then she saw the exterior crosses of a nearby church lifting up to the skies. She said that she drove to the parking lot of that nearby church and sat in the parking lot, praying, as she focused on the crosses. For her, this was a healing and transformative moment. This is just one story of many accounts of persons who, in their times of great difficulty and struggle, have looked to the skies for the Christian cross. This is the power of religious symbols when they are central to the psyche of a people.

The altar was such a symbol in the recovery and restoration of the Israelite community. The altar was central to communal worship dating back to the Mosaic Law and constituted them as the people of Yahweh, so they rebuilt the altar of the Lord before they rebuilt anything else.

Verse 1 reads, "And when the seventh month was come…the people gathered themselves together as one man to Jerusalem." It was at this time that the people reconstructed the altar. According to Mark Roberts, in his commentary, "The seventh month for Jews signifies a season of intense piety since it contains such major holidays as the Day of Atonement and the Feast of Tabernacles." However, we must be clear that the people of antiquity did not have a well-defined theology around numerology, as we do today; they just happened to do what they did in the seventh month of their calendar year that happened to coincide with some other religious festivals. What they did would be consistent with what many families do today in scheduling family reunions around a national holiday. For many families, this is a practical matter. They were intentional about why they rebuilt the altar first—to offer burnt offerings to Yahweh according to the Law of Moses.

"Sacrifice a bull each day as a sin offering to make atonement. Purify the altar by making atonement for it, and anoint it to consecrate it. For seven days make atonement for the altar and consecrate it. Then the altar will be most holy, and whatever touches it will be holy. This is what you are to offer on the altar regularly each day: two lambs a year old. Offer one in the morning and the other at twilight. With the first lamb offer a tenth of an ephah of fine flour mixed with a quarter of a hin of oil from pressed olives, and a quarter of a hin of wine as a drink offering. Sacrifice the other lamb at twilight with the same grain offering and its drink offering as in the morning—a pleasing aroma, an offering made to the Lord by fire" (Exodus 29:36-41, NIV).

Jeshua was the Aaronic high priest and Zerubbabel was the governor of Judah. Verses 2 and 3 build on verse 1, which speaks of the unity of the people. The religious and civic leaders rose up together to rebuild the altar on the base of the original temple altar. They did this in obedience to the Law of Moses and to atone for their sins. A new beginning required of them to acknowledge and confess their past sins and display a new attitude toward God and others. Likewise, the frequency of sacrifice, morning and evening, was done according to the Mosaic Laws of burnt offering for the atonement of sins. Verse 3 also gives us something of the mindset of the people—they feared other people in the region. They were vulnerable to attacks from the people of other countries because the wall around the city was still in ruins. The book of Nehemiah states that Nehemiah had to station armed guards around the construction site because of threats from their enemies. Nevertheless, they went forward and built the altar of their God in spite of their fears. Doing right by Yahweh was more important than "national security."

Israel put God first, because their ancestors had tried political compromise rather than trusting in Yahweh—leading to their captivity in Babylon (see 2 Kings 16–17).

But perhaps a lesson within the lesson is that there is no restoration and renewal for the people of God without their first showing authentic repentance of sin. The burnt offering was a sin offering of the people.

B. Celebrating the Feast
(Ezra 3:4-5)

They kept also the feast of tabernacles, as it is written, and offered the daily burnt offerings by number, according to the custom, as the duty of every day required; And afterward offered the continual burnt offering, both of the new moons, and of all the set feasts of the Lord that were consecrated, and of every one that willingly offered a freewill offering unto the LORD.

Likewise, they celebrated the Feast of Booths, which is also known as the Feast of Tabernacles. Today, throughout Israel, the people still celebrate the Feast of Booths (*Sukkoth*) (see Leviticus 23:42-43). This festival is a combination of the harvest festival in the fall of the year (similar to our Thanksgiving), as well as a reminder of the Exodus experience when the people had to live in booths (tents) in the wilderness. Again, they offered these sacrifices according to the standards established in the Law of Moses (see Exodus 29). After they had completed rebuilding the altar, "They offered the [regular] burnt offering" and "[appointed] feasts of the Lord that were consecrated." There was a strict process of purification or consecration in order for the sacrifice to be pleasing to Yahweh.

There is a tendency to believe that anything will do and that we can worship God with our mundane selves—but that is not so. God holds His people to higher standards. Although we do not offer burnt offerings in Christendom, the apostle Paul put in perspective God's standards for the believer. We are to offer ourselves as living sacrifices, "holy, acceptable unto God, which is [our] reasonable service" (Romans 12:1). Just as the Israelites worshipped Yahweh according to Yahweh's regulation, so must we worship our God "in spirit and in truth" (John 4:23). The litmus test of their commitment is in the second part of verse 5; they brought freewill offerings to the Lord. I will call this a gratitude offering. This offering then (as well as today) was/is an offering given freely by the people; it was not required, but the people offered it as an expression of gratitude and thankfulness for God's continued blessings to us.

C. Offering the Sacrifices
(Ezra 3:6-7)

From the first day of the seventh month began they to offer burnt offerings unto the LORD. But the foundation of the temple of the LORD was not yet laid. They gave money also unto the masons, and to the carpenters; and meat, and drink, and oil, unto them of Zidon, and to them of Tyre, to bring cedar trees from Lebanon to the sea of Joppa, according to the grant that they had of Cyrus king of Persia.

Finally, verses 6 and 7 are a recap of the process of dedication and sacrifice in verses 2-5; they built the altar first and then made sacrifices to the Lord according to the required ordinances of the Lord. They did this first on the first day of the seventh month; however, these were not one-time offerings. The people routinely offered them according to the criteria of frequency of the burnt offering. This showed their resolve to put Yahweh first as they rebuilt their lives.

This is in stark contrast to how we build and rebuild our lives today. Few of us place God first, but we seek something and someone more tangible to affirm ourselves. This lesson teaches us that the foundation of a successful life is not more money and the material substances which the world seeks after—but God.

III. CONCLUDING REFLECTION

The theme of remigration by the Israelites from Babylon was carried out with reference to worship. Worship was institutionalized in the life and the community of the Jews. The Temple and worship were not just sacred relics from the past; rather, they informed and gave shape to their lives. The author of the book of Ezra named both the high priest (Jeshua) and the governor (Zerubbabel) by the name which served to proclaim the solidarity of the people united in the praise and worship of Yahweh. Solidarity of focus and purpose was essential for the rebuilding of Israel's future. However, one of the most important political principles held by many Americans is the separation of church and state. But for Ezra, it was important that these two entities—the sacred and the secular—not be separated but be in solidarity. The founding father thought this was an important principle for the nation, but should there be a divide between personal faith and public life? The reestablishment of life, community, and worship, according to the Mosaic Law, allowed the Jews to establish a continuity of life and community around the things that Yahweh valued. This lesson teaches that when God is first in our lives, we will learn to put first things first and celebrate the things that are meaningful and important to God as well. When we do this, our faith will inform our lives in the "public square." As with Israel before the Exile, when we put other things ahead of our relationship with Yahweh, the consequences are catastrophic.

PRAYER

Eternal God, we confess that we have strayed away from You and have not done the things You have asked us to do. Yet, You have given us another chance to do the right things. Lord, we praise You and honor You for Your grace and mercy toward Your people. In Jesus' name we pray. Amen.

WORD POWER

Burnt Offerings—the burnt offering was the most common sacrifice for the Old Testament Israelites. The entire animal would be burned completely. The offering of the entire animal symbolized the completeness of their devotion.

HOME DAILY BIBLE READINGS
(June 24-30, 2013)

Joyful Worship Restored

MONDAY, June 24: "Jesus' Lament over Jerusalem" (Matthew 23:29-39)
TUESDAY, June 25: "The Coming Judgment" (Jeremiah 7:30–8:3)
WEDNESDAY, June 26: "Jerusalem Falls to the Babylonians" (2 Kings 24:1-12)
THURSDAY, June 27: "The Destruction of Jerusalem" (2 Chronicles 36:15-21)
FRIDAY, June 28: "Rebuild a House for God" (Ezra 1:1-8)
SATURDAY, June 29: "The People Respond" (Ezra 2:64-70)
SUNDAY, June 30: "Restoring the Worship of God" (Ezra 3:1-7)

LESSON 6　　　　　　　　　　　　　　　　　　　　**July 7, 2013**

TEMPLE RESTORED

FAITH PATHWAY/FAITH JOURNEY TOPIC: **Finding Joy in Restoration**

DEVOTIONAL READING: **Psalm 66:1-12**　　　　BACKGROUND SCRIPTURE: **Ezra 3:8-13**
PRINT PASSAGE: **Ezra 3:8-13**　　　　　　　　　KEY VERSE: **Ezra 3:11**

Ezra 3:8-13—KJV

8 Now in the second year of their coming unto the house of God at Jerusalem, in the second month, began Zerubbabel the son of Shealtiel, and Jeshua the son of Jozadak, and the remnant of their brethren the priests and the Levites, and all they that were come out of the captivity unto Jerusalem; and appointed the Levites, from twenty years old and upward, to set forward the work of the house of the LORD.

9 Then stood Jeshua with his sons and his brethren, Kadmiel and his sons, the sons of Judah, together, to set forward the workmen in the house of God: the sons of Henadad, with their sons and their brethren the Levites.

10 And when the builders laid the foundation of the temple of the LORD, they set the priests in their apparel with trumpets, and the Levites the sons of Asaph with cymbals, to praise the LORD, after the ordinance of David king of Israel.

11 And they sang together by course in praising and giving thanks unto the LORD; because he is good, for his mercy endureth for ever toward Israel. And all the people shouted with a great shout, when they praised the LORD, because the foundation of the house of the LORD was laid.

12 But many of the priests and Levites and chief of the fathers, who were ancient men, that had seen the first house, when the foundation of this house was laid before their eyes, wept with a loud voice; and many shouted aloud for joy:

13 So that the people could not discern the noise of the shout of joy from the noise of the weeping of the people: for the people shouted with a loud shout, and the noise was heard afar off.

Ezra 3:8-13—NIV

8 In the second month of the second year after their arrival at the house of God in Jerusalem, Zerubbabel son of Shealtiel, Jeshua son of Jozadak and the rest of their brothers (the priests and the Levites and all who had returned from the captivity to Jerusalem) began the work, appointing Levites twenty years of age and older to supervise the building of the house of the LORD.

9 Jeshua and his sons and brothers and Kadmiel and his sons (descendants of Hodaviah) and the sons of Henadad and their sons and brothers—all Levites—joined together in supervising those working on the house of God.

10 When the builders laid the foundation of the temple of the LORD, the priests in their vestments and with trumpets, and the Levites (the sons of Asaph) with cymbals, took their places to praise the LORD, as prescribed by David king of Israel.

11 With praise and thanksgiving they sang to the LORD: "He is good; his love to Israel endures forever." And all the people gave a great shout of praise to the LORD, because the foundation of the house of the LORD was laid.

12 But many of the older priests and Levites and family heads, who had seen the former temple, wept aloud when they saw the foundation of this temple being laid, while many others shouted for joy.

13 No one could distinguish the sound of the shouts of joy from the sound of weeping, because the people made so much noise. And the sound was heard far away.

UNIFYING LESSON PRINCIPLE

When people are separated from something they hold dear, restoration is usually a greatly anticipated goal. How do people respond to an accomplished goal? When the returned Israelite exiles laid the foundation stones to restore the Temple, they rejoiced and gave thanks to God with weeping, shouting, and playing of trumpets and cymbals.

TOPICAL OUTLINE OF THE LESSON

I. Introduction
   A. Hope Restored
   B. Biblical Background

II. Exposition and Application of the Scripture
   A. Work on the Temple Begins (Ezra 3:8-9)
   B. The Foundation Is Laid (Ezra 3:10-11)
   C. Shouts of Joy and Sounds of Weeping (Ezra 3:12-13)

III. Concluding Reflection

LESSON OBJECTIVES

Upon completion of the lesson, the students will be able to do the following:

1. Review the Israelites' story of obeying God's instructions for restoring the Temple;
2. Recall their common responses when they reached long-anticipated goals; and,
3. Hold a historical event, recalling an act or acts of restoration in the life of the church.

POINTS TO BE EMPHASIZED

ADULT/YOUTH
Adult Topic: **Finding Joy in Restoration**
Youth Topic: **Let the Good Times Roll!**
Adult/Youth Key Verse: **Ezra 3:11**
Print Passage: **Ezra 3:8-13**

—In the second year, the returning Jews organized to complete the work of the Temple, in order to restore their lives as a faithful community.
—They also appointed a music ministry in accordance with what King David had done.
—The Jews had a massive celebration when the foundation was completed.
—Some Jews wept at the remembrance of the former Temple that Solomon had built.
—After retrieving the ark of the covenant when the tabernacle was placed in a permanent place, David established the priests' roles in music and worship.
—The completion of the new Temple was a landmark event, after years of exile in Babylon.

CHILDREN
Children Topic: **Celebrating a New Beginning**
Key Verse: **Ezra 3:11b**
Print Passage: **Ezra 3:8-13**

—In the second year, the returning Jews organized to complete the work of the Temple, in order to restore their lives as a faithful community.
—After retrieving the ark of the covenant when the tabernacle was established in a permanent place, King David established the priests' role in music and worship. So musicians were appointed to serve in the second Temple in accordance with what King David had done.

—With the foundations of the Temple laid, the people were closer to seeing the reestablishment of a key element in their restoration as a nation.

—When the people saw the foundation, some remembered the former Temple built by Solomon and wept, while others broke out in shouts of joy.

—The people celebrated their accomplishment with praise and thanksgiving to God.

I. INTRODUCTION

A. Hope Restored

In January 2009, the spirit of accomplishment and joy was felt everywhere throughout our nation's capital. The weather was frigid, but the enthusiasm and excitement of witnessing the inauguration of the first African-American president, Barack Obama, was indeed an unbelievable experience and exciting moment in world history. The prayers of many ancestors had been answered in this one event and millions of African Americans wanted a piece of this history. The joy of this historic moment was only slightly dampened by the discomfort associated with standing in line for hours, waiting to get into the Washington Mall for the swearing in of the forty-fourth president of the United States. Because of the massive crowd and the officials' inability to accommodate the millions of people who converged on the nation's capital to celebrate history, tens of thousands of us never made it into the secured area in the Washington Mall. Nonetheless, our disappointments were outweighed by the joy of what that moment represented to the millions of us who were there.

Although the inauguration was not a restoration project as such, it restored the hopes and aspirations of the American dream of many people of color that "all people (we) are created equal and endowed with certain unalienable rights of life, liberty, and the pursuit of happiness." African Americans and other people of hope for what that moment in history could represent came to Washington to celebrate the restoration of an American dream. One newspaper headline by Sandy Banks of the *Los Angeles Times* characterized the moment as the place "Where hope has wrestled with fear." Indeed, her headline captured not only the pathos of millions of African Americans, but that of the book of Ezra as well. The people in hope had wrestled with their fears of the reaction and opposition of others in the region. The people of Yahweh returned to claim what was rightfully theirs; however, the worship of their God was not celebrated by all peoples. But, history assured them and us that no one can stop God's will from being accomplished. Likewise, if a people are to rebuild their lives and their community from a place of brokenness, then God must be at the center of their actions!

B. Biblical Background

This lesson is the continuation of lesson 5, in which we see the bittersweet experience of some of the Israelites returning from captivity after seventy years. They had to wrestle with three of humanity's most powerful emotions—joy, sadness, and fear. The joy of being home again and participating in the restoration of those symbols of their sacred community was an awesome experience for the older Israelites. Can you imagine what it must have felt like to return home after seventy years of captivity and to see the work of rebuilding their lives unfold before their very eyes? Connie Smith captures the joy of being set free in the lyrics of her song, "He Touched Me": "Shackled by a heavy burden, 'neath a load of guilt and shame, the hand of Jesus touched me and now I am no longer the same. O the joy that floods my soul...." It was not Jesus who touched them, but there was joy in knowing that Yahweh had fulfilled His promise of the restoration of the Temple.

Verses 8-13 chronicle the joys of the moment and the sadness of reflection by those who had known the past and what life once was before the Exile. The moment of laying the foundation brought both shouts of joy and tears. On the other hand, the angst of being confronted by a people who opposed the work of rebuilding their community (verse 3) brought fear! Nevertheless, the people trusted in their God to see this project to completion, in spite of the opposition. This happened in the second month of the second year of their return to Jerusalem. This fact gives us more of a chronological perspective of life for the people who were returning home. In the seventh month of the first year, they rebuilt the altar—and in the second month of the second year, they began the reconstruction of the foundation of the Temple.

II. EXPOSITION AND APPLICATION OF THE SCRIPTURE

A. Work on the Temple Begins
(Ezra 3:8-9)

Now in the second year of their coming unto the house of God at Jerusalem, in the second month, began Zerubbabel the son of Shealtiel, and Jeshua the son of Jozadak, and the remnant of their brethren the priests and the Levites, and all they that were come out of the captivity unto Jerusalem; and appointed the Levites, from twenty years old and upward, to set forward the work of the house of the Lord. Then stood Jeshua with his sons and his brethren, Kadmiel and his sons, the sons of Judah, together, to set forward the workmen in the house of God: the sons of Henadad, with their sons and their brethren the Levites.

Verse 8 describes the beginning of the physical restoration of the Temple. Zerubbabel, (governor), Jeshua, (high priest), and the other religious leaders, priests, and Levites led the nation in this rebuilding project; they all joined their efforts together. The intent of this brief genealogy is to highlight the diversity and inclusivity of the effort to rebuild the Temple. Unity or oneness of effort and purpose is a recurring theme in the books of Ezra and Nehemiah. Ezra 3:1b reads, "The people gathered themselves together as one man to Jerusalem." Nehemiah said that they completed the wall because they all "had a mind to work" (Nehemiah 4:6). It is also noteworthy that the author used inclusive language throughout chapter 3—"they" and "all the people"—in order to describe the unity and the people's emotional reaction to rebuilding the foundation: they all worked and they all rejoiced. The work of building or rebuilding a community involves the entire community. How could they have done otherwise?

It must be noted that this unity included age diversity among the men—"appointing Levites twenty years of age and older to supervise" (verse 8, NIV). We must know that more is accomplished when we have a mind to work together and not discriminate according to age, gender, or race. God is no respecter of persons; rather, God looks at the heart of the person. God looks for willing workers. Thus, how much more could we accomplish if the spirit of oneness guided us all? We must be inclined not to discriminate against persons in the church because of age, gender, or race.

B. The Foundation Is Laid
(Ezra 3:10-11)

And when the builders laid the foundation of the temple of the Lord, they set the priests in their apparel with trumpets, and the Levites the sons of Asaph with cymbals, to praise the Lord, after the ordinance of David king of Israel. And they sang together by course in praising and giving thanks unto the Lord; because he is good, for his mercy endureth for ever toward Israel. And all the people shouted with a great shout, when they praised the Lord, because the foundation of the house of the Lord was laid.

These verses focus on the laying of the Temple's foundation and the emotional and spiritual reaction to the moment of seeing the Temple's foundation completed. This was a sign and symbol for the people of the fidelity of Yahweh. They had not completed the rebuilding of the Temple, only the laying of the foundation where the old Temple once stood. It is indeed interesting how sometimes, after a long period of anticipation and waiting, that it is not the completion of the project that brings the greater emotion—it is the first indication that the dream is being fulfilled. It is not the loan closing for the new home, but the news

that the loan was approved or the completion of the new home or even the clearing of the land and the laying of the foundation that engenders the greatest emotional reaction. We cannot be sure what was in their minds as they laid the foundation, but human nature is human nature, so we can imagine what they were celebrating in these verses.

Verse 10 gives us the lineage of those who were responsible for the work of laying the foundation. In Judaism, genealogy was important for connecting the present generation to their ancestral line back to Abraham, Isaac, and Jacob. For the Jews, their present reality was informed by their ancestral history. The promises of Yahweh for them were linked to their forefathers. Perhaps there is much that we can learn from this practice of those faith communities that want to cut themselves off from our past (orthodoxy). In some faith communities, there seems to be an open disdain for tradition, as if tradition were a curse. But, as it has been said, we ought not to "throw the baby out with the bath water." Simply because we do not agree with the past does not mean that all that was done in the past was wrong, or that God was not involved in that past. God comes to each generation in its season; therefore, the purpose of the Bible is to enable biblical history to inform our future.

Likewise, chapter 3 makes two references to the past in verses 3 and 10. As the people rebuilt their lives and their rituals, they were required to do so according to the laws and regulations given to their ancestors. There is immeasurable value to this as the people maintain continuity between the past and the present. The people in today's text were intentional about bridging their past and their present. Just as soon as the foundation of the Temple was completed, the people stopped working to celebrate. The priests put on their religious apparel and grabbed their trumpets; the Levites took their cymbals and praised Yahweh—according to the ordinances of David. This was congregational responsive singing, praising, and giving of thanks to the Lord. They celebrated God's goodness and His covenant faithfulness toward Israel: "His mercy endures forever" (Psalm 106:1, NKJV). His mercy never came to an end, despite their circumstances of captivity. Therefore, in joyous song they gave credit to God for their progress in restoration. There was no place for the timid of heart as they worshipped Yahweh with loud shouts.

C. Shouts of Joy and Sounds of Weeping
(Ezra 3:12-13)

But many of the priests and Levites and chief of the fathers, who were ancient men, that had seen the first house, when the foundation of this house was laid before their eyes, wept with a loud voice; and many shouted aloud for joy: So that the people could not discern the noise of the shout of joy from the noise of the weeping of the people: for the people shouted with a loud shout, and the noise was heard afar off.

Many of the old priests, Levites, and family members "wept with a loud voice" (verse 12) when the foundation of the Temple was laid. Why did many of the older people cry and the others shout for joy? Perhaps for the older people, it was a bittersweet experience as they reflected on what once was and all of those who were not present to celebrate with them on that day. When President Barack Obama was elected as president in 2008, there was a black woman over one hundred years old who was interviewed by the news media. She said that she wept for those from her past who did not live long enough to see this day.

The Hebrew word for "weep" indicates sadness. Clearly, this was a deeply emotional moment for the elders, as they celebrated not just the laying of the foundation, but also the remembrance of the way things used to be in Jerusalem before the Exile. This was a nostalgic moment for the older people, even though the Temple had not yet been completed; they remembered the grand old Temple that once stood in all of her magnificence and splendor to Yahweh. These were the people who were around before the Exile and remembered the Temple in its former glory. We must keep in mind that many who returned to Jerusalem were born in captivity and saw the Temple for the first time in rubble. There seemed to be a different intensity for older people who knew and had lived the whole story of the people. For them, the celebration of the moment was more than just the reality of rebuilding. Their tears represented their hopes and dreams of all the years being fulfilled. Those of us who have lived the story have a different awareness and concept of life from our children and grandchildren who know nothing about the "last hired" and the "first fired," about segregated schools and public facilities, and about the indignities that people of color had to endure in America. Experience gives all of us a different appreciation of the moment than of those who never had to live through it. We cannot know the minds of the Israelites, but we can speculate based on human nature. The older people reflected on what once was a glorious past, and were saddened by how far they had fallen. Likewise, being able to return and rebuild the broken places in our lives is clearly an act of grace and mercy and we, too, must praise God for the pieces that are left for us to rebuild upon. Do you know what this kind of bittersweet experience feels like?—the joy and the sadness of success after the long struggle to get there. Perhaps if we, the people of God, would spend more time reflecting on where God has brought us from and what God has done for us and has enabled us to become, then our worship would be filled with more passion and gratitude.

III. CONCLUDING REFLECTION

Can you recall a moment or an experience long anticipated that finally came to fruition, and the joy that it gave you? Invariably, the more meaningful the thing we have been waiting for, the greater the joy. This was the situation with the children of Israel, especially those who were a part of the exile to Babylon seventy years prior: the emotions of finally returning home and participating in the laying of the foundation of the Temple was too much to bear. They rejoiced to the point of tears and wept with such intensity that those who heard them from afar could not tell the difference between the sound of those crying and those shouting. What a day of rejoicing this was!

There were many Israelites who had lived their histories from freedom to exile and back to freedom. They knew the meaning of restoration. God has restored all of us who believe from a place of brokenness and estrangement to a meaningful relationship with Him; therefore, just as the Israelites rejoiced, we, too, have much to rejoice about. His mercy endures forever!

PRAYER

"God of our weary years, God of our silent tears, Thou who has brought us thus far along the way, Thou who has by Thy might led us into the light…" We are grateful and honored to call You our God. Thank You for Your grace and mercy toward us. In Jesus' name we pray. Amen.

WORD POWER

Remnant—something that is left over, especially the righteous people of God after divine judgment. Several Hebrew words express the idea of the remnant: *yether,* "that which is left over"; *she'ar,* "that which remains"; *she'rith,* "residue"; *pelitah,* "one who escapes"; *sarid,* "a survivor"; and *sheruth,* "one loosed from bonds."

HOME DAILY BIBLE READINGS
(July 1-7, 2013)

Temple Restored

MONDAY, July 1: "A Great and Wonderful House" (2 Chronicles 2:1-9)

TUESDAY, July 2: "Building a House for God's Name" (1 Kings 8:14-21)

WEDNESDAY, July 3: "My Name Shall Be There" (1 Kings 8:22-30)

THURSDAY, July 4: "A House of Prayer" (Matthew 21:10-16)

FRIDAY, July 5: "Make a Joyful Noise to God" (Psalm 66:1-12)

SATURDAY, July 6: "Lead Me in Your Righteousness" (Psalm 5)

SUNDAY, July 7: "Tears of Joy" (Ezra 3:8-13)

LESSON 7   July 14, 2013

DEDICATION OF THE TEMPLE

FAITH PATHWAY/FAITH JOURNEY TOPIC: **Celebrating with Joy**

DEVOTIONAL READING: **Ezra 5:1-5**
PRINT PASSAGE: **Ezra 6:13-22**

BACKGROUND SCRIPTURE: **Ezra 6**
KEY VERSE: **Ezra 6:16**

Ezra 6:13-22—KJV

13 Then Tatnai, governor on this side the river, Shethar-boznai, and their companions, according to that which Darius the king had sent, so they did speedily.
14 And the elders of the Jews builded, and they prospered through the prophesying of Haggai the prophet and Zechariah the son of Iddo. And they builded, and finished it, according to the commandment of the God of Israel, and according to the commandment of Cyrus, and Darius, and Artaxerxes king of Persia.
15 And this house was finished on the third day of the month Adar, which was in the sixth year of the reign of Darius the king.
16 And the children of Israel, the priests, and the Levites, and the rest of the children of the captivity, kept the dedication of this house of God with joy,
17 And offered at the dedication of this house of God an hundred bullocks, two hundred rams, four hundred lambs; and for a sin offering for all Israel, twelve he goats, according to the number of the tribes of Israel.
18 And they set the priests in their divisions, and the Levites in their courses, for the service of God, which is at Jerusalem; as it is written in the book of Moses.
19 And the children of the captivity kept the passover upon the fourteenth day of the first month.
20 For the priests and the Levites were purified together, all of them were pure, and killed the passover for all the children of the captivity, and for their brethren the priests, and for themselves.

Ezra 6:13-22—NIV

13 Then, because of the decree King Darius had sent, Tattenai, governor of Trans-Euphrates, and Shethar-Bozenai and their associates carried it out with diligence.
14 So the elders of the Jews continued to build and prosper under the preaching of Haggai the prophet and Zechariah, a descendant of Iddo. They finished building the temple according to the command of the God of Israel and the decrees of Cyrus, Darius and Artaxerxes, kings of Persia.
15 The temple was completed on the third day of the month Adar, in the sixth year of the reign of King Darius.
16 Then the people of Israel—the priests, the Levites and the rest of the exiles—celebrated the dedication of the house of God with joy.
17 For the dedication of this house of God they offered a hundred bulls, two hundred rams, four hundred male lambs and, as a sin offering for all Israel, twelve male goats, one for each of the tribes of Israel.
18 And they installed the priests in their divisions and the Levites in their groups for the service of God at Jerusalem, according to what is written in the Book of Moses.
19 On the fourteenth day of the first month, the exiles celebrated the Passover.
20 The priests and Levites had purified themselves and were all ceremonially clean. The Levites slaughtered the Passover lamb for all the exiles, for their brothers the priests and for themselves.

UNIFYING LESSON PRINCIPLE

People often assign great importance to specific locations. What makes a particular place so special? The Temple was special to the Israelites because God commanded them to rebuild it, and because it gave them a place to commemorate with worship their original freedom from Egyptian bondage and, more recently, their Babylonian exile.

21 And the children of Israel, which were come again out of captivity, and all such as had separated themselves unto them from the filthiness of the heathen of the land, to seek the LORD God of Israel, did eat, 22 And kept the feast of unleavened bread seven days with joy: for the LORD had made them joyful, and turned the heart of the king of Assyria unto them, to strengthen their hands in the work of the house of God, the God of Israel.

21 So the Israelites who had returned from the exile ate it, together with all who had separated themselves from the unclean practices of their Gentile neighbors in order to seek the LORD, the God of Israel. 22 For seven days they celebrated with joy the Feast of Unleavened Bread, because the LORD had filled them with joy by changing the attitude of the king of Assyria, so that he assisted them in the work on the house of God, the God of Israel.

TOPICAL OUTLINE OF THE LESSON

I. **Introduction**
   A. A "For Real" Celebration!
   B. Biblical Background

II. **Exposition and Application of the Scripture**
   A. The Temple Completed (Ezra 6:13-15)
   B. A Dedicatory Celebration (Ezra 6:16-18)
   C. Celebrating in the New Temple (Ezra 6:19-22)

III. **Concluding Reflection**

LESSON OBJECTIVES

Upon completion of the lesson, the students will be able to do the following:

1. Retell the story of the completion and dedication of the Temple and the observance of Passover, using the format of a news story;

2. Discuss what makes specific places of worship significant to them; and,

3. Work with the youth in their churches to research (as needed) and talk about the story of the dedication of their place(s) of worship.

POINTS TO BE EMPHASIZED

ADULT/YOUTH
Adult Topic: Celebrating with Joy
Youth Topic: Praise in the House
Adult/Youth Key Verse: Ezra 6:16
Print Passage: Ezra 6:13-22

—God ensured, through the power and means of secular government, that Israel would have all of the necessary resources to be successful as they rebuilt the Temple.

—God was actively involved in the process of rebuilding the Temple.

—The sovereignty of God is illustrated in the rebuilding of the Temple.

—This account shows how non-Israelites, who also seek God's protection and benefit, revere God.

—As the Jews labored to rebuild the Temple, they listened to the words of the prophets Haggai and Zechariah.

—After rebuilding, all the people celebrated as they dedicated the Temple and reinstituted the Levitical priesthood, as instructed by Moses.

CHILDREN

Children Topic: A New Worship Place

Key Verse: Ezra 6:16

Print Passage: Ezra 6:13-22

—Foreign rulers over the Israelites gave orders and support that helped complete the building of the Temple in Jerusalem.

—The Israelites held a joyous dedication of the Temple as the house of God, offering sacrifices for it and for the people.

—After this, the priests and Levites were set in place for administering in the Temple.

—At the appointed time, the people kept the Passover and Feast of Unleavened Bread, remembering not only freedom from Egypt but also freedom to return from exile and to rebuild the Temple.

I. INTRODUCTION

A. A "For Real" Celebration!

What does it mean to celebrate with joy in an age in which we celebrate everything from a football touchdown to the birth of a child? We even celebrate the deaths of our enemies! We have built and put in place systems, organs, loud music, and strobe lights, in order to promote and simulate the appearance of celebration. Indeed, creating these moments has become big business and a marketable product. Therefore, celebration has become a mundane event for a culture that celebrates everything with joy. This marketing model of celebration is contrived and leaves little room for spontaneity; consequently, celebration is celebration is celebration. It all looks the same. However, in this lesson, we will revisit our priorities and come to a different understanding of what it really means to celebrate with joy and exuberance, because the joy of the birth of a first child or grandchild ought not be the same joy associated with the American Women's Soccer Team playing in the championship match of the FIFA World Cup. Likewise, the joy of the Lord ought not be the same as the joy we say we have when fulfilling our mundane pursuits.

In this lesson, the Israelites celebrated their return from exile in Babylon and their success of reestablishing their community and their relationship with Yahweh. As they succeeded in each step of rebuilding their faith community, they celebrated by reinstituting past religious rituals and worshipping Yahweh. In each accomplishment, they celebrated and reminded themselves of those ancient days when Yahweh delivered their forefathers from bondage. They reenacted the rituals of remembrance according to the dictates in the Law of Moses. Their celebration of joy was inextricably connected to their ancient story of the fidelity and promises of Yahweh—not of their own mundane achievements. Over the course of this lesson, we want to wrestle with the idea of distinguishing how we celebrate the things of God and how we celebrate other things in our lives.

B. Biblical Background

The book of Ezra (chapter 6) gives us some world history beyond the reconstruction that was going on in Jerusalem. During the reign of Cyrus, king of Persia, he had put in writing the details of his edicts to allow the Jews to return home and rebuild the Temple and Jerusalem. In chapter 4, there arose a question about the full authorization of the edict to rebuild and assist in the reconstruction of the Temple—so Darius, current king of Persia, instructed Tattenai (one of the governors in the region of the Persian Empire) to search the archives in Babylon for the original edict by Cyrus.

The original edict was not found in Babylon, but in Achmetha, a province of Media. Verses 1-12 of this chapter contain the contents of this edict. It appears that Darius followed the lead of his predecessor, Cyrus, and supported the work of rebuilding and restoring the Temple. After finding the original edict, Darius ordered his subjects to "Let the governor of the Jews and the elders of the Jews build this house of God on its site" (verse 7, NKJV). So, as we study this lesson for background information, read Ezra 5 and the books of Haggai and Zechariah, who were the prophets of Yahweh during this time of restoration. They called the people to obedience and inspired the leaders of Judah, Zerubbabel, and Jeshua to oversee the reconstruction project. However, according to some Old Testament scholars, there was a time lag of sixteen years between the laying of the foundation in chapter 3 and the completion of the Temple in chapter 6.

This lesson also makes it clear that true spiritual inspiration and restoration begin with God, who is sovereign over all the earth—and it is God who inspires the desire for new beginnings. Yahweh did not rebuild the Temple Himself; rather, He built up a people who were willing to respond to His initiatives in the world and do the work. The Jews in Ezra 5:5 attributed success in rebuilding to the fact that "the eye of their God was watching over the elders of the Jews" (NIV). What a marvelous idea this is that "the eye of the LORD is on those who fear Him, On those who hope in His mercy, To deliver their soul from death, And to keep them alive in famine" (Psalm 33:18-19, NKJV). As Yahweh moved on the heart of Cyrus, He also moved on the heart of Darius, who reaffirmed the edict and gave orders to Tattenai and his companions to assist the Jews in rebuilding the "Lord's house."

II. EXPOSITION AND APPLICATION OF THE SCRIPTURE

A. The Temple Completed
(Ezra 6:13-15)

Then Tatnai, governor on this side the river, Shethar-boznai, and their companions, according to that which Darius the king had sent, so they did speedily. And the elders of the Jews builded, and they prospered through the prophesying of Haggai the prophet and Zechariah the son of Iddo. And they builded, and finished it, according to the commandment of the God of Israel, and according to the commandment of Cyrus, and Darius, and Artaxerxes king of Persia. And this house was finished on the third day of the month Adar, which was in the sixth year of the reign of Darius the king.

In verses 10-12, we see that Darius issued a similar decree to what was found in the archive written by his predecessor, Cyrus: "So that they may offer sacrifices pleasing to the God of heaven and pray for the well-being of the king and his sons. Furthermore, I decree that if anyone changes this edict, a beam is to be pulled from his house and he is to be lifted up and impaled on it. And for this crime his house is to be made a pile of rubble. May God, who has caused his Name to dwell there, overthrow any king or people who lifts a hand to change this decree or to destroy this temple in Jerusalem. I Darius have decreed it. Let it be carried out with diligence" (NIV).

The language in these verses is interesting for a couple of reasons. It affirms the sovereignty of Yahweh and how He works through all peoples to accomplish His purpose in the world. Indeed, Psalm 8 is correct in declaring that Yahweh rules heaven and earth and all that live on it. Therefore, one of the recurring themes in the Old Testament is the sovereignty of Yahweh and how He, in "various and sundry ways," works and inspires nonbelievers to work on behalf of His purpose in the world. Second, a Gentile king who served the gods of the Medes and the Persian Empire verbally acknowledged Yahweh's sovereignty over Jerusalem and of heaven and that He was at work in the world. King Darius also believed that he had sovereign power over his empire—and in his decree he used threatening language to defend the vision of Yahweh for the Jews. Indeed, it was Yahweh who worked through him to fulfill His promise to the Jews. "May God, who has caused his Name to dwell there (Jerusalem), overthrow any king or people who lifts a hand to change this decree or to destroy this temple in Jerusalem" (verse 12).

Finally, verses 13 and 14 show the enactment of Darius's decree. The governors and all of the ruling officials of the region obeyed the commands of the king. So all the Jews built and prospered through the prophesying of Haggai and Zechariah. In Haggai 1, the Word of the Lord came through the prophet Haggai: "These people say, 'The time has not yet come for the Lord's house to be built'" (verse 2, NIV). Then the Word of the Lord came through the prophet Haggai: "Is it a time for you yourselves to be living in your paneled houses, while this house remains a ruin?" (verse 3). (It is suggested that one should at least read the book of Haggai, which consists of two chapters.) The Lord also spoke to the prophet Zechariah: "'I will return to Jerusalem with mercy, and there my house will be rebuilt. And the measuring line will be stretched out over Jerusalem,' declares the Lord Almighty" (Zechariah 1:16, NIV). After a long period of apathy and complacency, the people finally rebuilt the Temple, but it took three of the Medes Persian administrations (Cyrus, Darius, and Artaxerxes) approximately sixteen years for them to do so. Artaxerxes was a king who came much later, and we cannot be certain why his name appears with the other two in Nehemiah 5:14. King Darius paid for the reconstruction from his royal treasury and provided the animals for the sacrificial offering to the Lord. Finally, he instructed the people to do so with all diligence.

Perhaps the lesson we are to learn is that it takes more than raw enthusiasm to sustain the work of ministry; it takes both faith and passion to "run and not be weary"; and "walk, and not faint." We can never be sure whom the Lord will use to do His bidding in the world.

B. A Dedicatory Celebration
(Ezra 6:16-18)

And the children of Israel, the priests, and the Levites, and the rest of the children of the captivity, kept the dedication of this house of God with joy, And offered at the dedication of this house of God an hundred bullocks, two hundred rams, four hundred lambs; and for a sin offering for all Israel, twelve he goats, according to the number of the tribes of Israel. And they set the priests in their divisions, and the Levites in their courses, for the service of God, which is at Jerusalem; as it is written in the book of Moses.

These verses, like much of the book of Ezra, are a history lesson on how the Israelites celebrated the completion of the Temple. The timeline of Darius's decree until the completion of the Temple was about four years. The longer the wait, the more glorious and joyous the moment of celebration is. This project perhaps took much longer than anyone had imagined. The joy of chapter 3 had dissolved into complacency and contentment with the status quo. According to the prophet Haggai, they were living quite well and said that the time had not yet come to rebuild the Lord's house (see Haggai 1:2). What happened to the enthusiasm and joy when they rebuilt the altar and laid the foundation of the Temple? We must be careful of how we understand ministry, because ministry is not a sprint; it is a marathon race, and if we are not careful, we, too, will be guilty of putting other priorities ahead of the things of God. How many good ministry ideas got started with great hoopla and excitement, only to fizzle out because the people did not understand that ministry has no tenure?

So after years, the Temple project was finally completed and they dedicated it with great joy and made a sin offering to Yahweh.

King Darius provided the animals for the sin offering that was sacrificed on the altar of the Lord (verse 17). However, read 2 Chronicles 5–7 and contrast the dedication of the first Temple by King Solomon to the second dedication in this chapter. Second Chronicles 5:4 says that the number of sheep and oxen sacrificed were so great that the people could not count them. O, how far the mighty had fallen, because of their disobedience to God! When King Solomon built the first Temple and dedicated it, he provided the animals for the sacrifices from his own wealth; yet, centuries later, Israel as a people were like the land—broken and barren—and at the mercy of another country. A Gentile king provided the resources for them to sacrifice to their God, but the sacrifice paled in comparison to those given in the former days of Israel in her glory. This moment of celebration must have been bittersweet; after the Exile was over, only two tribes of the twelve tribes of Israel were left—Judah and Benjamin. Nevertheless, they offered a goat for each tribe—as had been done when the first Temple was built by Solomon. Perhaps, this offering was in memory of the ten tribes which were not there. Sometimes in life, the absence of those who are not there is just as important as those who are present for a celebration. This celebration of joy was both nostalgic and forward-looking, as they offered sin offerings and assigned the priests and the Levites to serve the Temple according to the Law of Moses.

C. Celebrating in the New Temple
(Ezra 6:19-22)

And the children of the captivity kept the passover upon the fourteenth day of the first month. For the priests and

the Levites were purified together, all of them were pure, and killed the passover for all the children of the captivity, and for their brethren the priests, and for themselves. And the children of Israel, which were come again out of captivity, and all such as had separated themselves unto them from the filthiness of the heathen of the land, to seek the LORD God of Israel, did eat, And kept the feast of unleavened bread seven days with joy: for the LORD had made them joyful, and turned the heart of the king of Assyria unto them, to strengthen their hands in the work of the house of God, the God of Israel.

The completion of the Temple and its rededication occurred in the month of Adar—the last month in the Jewish calendar. The first month of the year, Nisan, was also the month of the great festivals of Passover, Unleavened Bread, and first fruits. The chapter concludes with the people keeping these sacred festivals. How appropriate it is that after all of these years in captivity (when the Temple was in ruins), they could finally celebrate with joy for their new beginning. They celebrated these sacred holidays in the new Temple. The Passover was a celebration held to remember God's deliverance of their ancestors from Egypt. The Feast of Unleavened Bread was to remind them of their ancestors' quick departure from Egypt.

However, verse 21 gives some additional insights into the social and religious contexts in Jerusalem at this time. Obviously, some of the Jews had begun socializing and adopting some of the practices of the other inhabitants in the region, which made them unworthy to participate in the rituals of the Temple. Verse 21 reads, "The children of Israel, which were come again out of captivity, and all such as had separated themselves unto them from the filthiness of the heathen of the land...." If deemed unclean under the law, this group had to be consecrated according to the law

before they could participate with those who were not defiled. Finally, verse 22 says that they celebrated with joy and that the Lord made them joyful. This is indeed an interesting phrase: "the LORD had made them joyful." Is there a difference between their celebration of joy and the joy that the Lord gave them? Ezra was being emphatic that their joy came from the Lord. Yahweh was gracious in not only returning them from captivity, but also by providing the resources to complete the rebuilding of the Temple. This was the Lord's doing. He had, indeed, kept His promise!

III. CONCLUDING REFLECTION

According to Haggai, the people got weary and let the Lord's house lie in ruins for several years before they finally returned to work and completed it. It took the preaching of Haggai and Zechariah to encourage and inspire people to complete what they knew was the Lord's doing. This historic fact points out the awesome tendency of human nature to become totally self-absorbed with accommodating self at the expense of a more meaningful relationship with God. But there is a joy in the work of the Lord that cannot be replicated in anything else we might find to do and whose end goal is self-gratification and fulfillment. How dare we think to compare the joy that the Lord gives us to those joyful moments we experience in the pursuit of the mundane—the serving of our little idol gods (i.e., sports, politics, personal achievements)! The psalmist said, "You will show me the path of life; In Your presence is fullness of joy; At Your right hand are pleasures forevermore" (Psalm 16:11).

Before the Exile to Babylon, in order

to be considered a Jew one had to be in the ancestral line of Abraham, Isaac, and Jacob. After the Exile, inclusion depended upon the intention of one's heart (see verse 21) to seek Yahweh. It is a marvelous thing to know that we are accepted by God not through pedigree, but because of our love and desire to be His children. Being in exile has only historical reference for most of us, but without a doubt, God has set us free from something in our lives. What do you have to celebrate in your life that you have only because the Lord made it happen for your good? Pause now for a moment; reflect on your life and offer a joyful praise to God, for indeed He is good and His mercy lasts a lifetime!

PRAYER

O Lord our God, how excellent is Your name in all the earth. Your deeds are remarkable and we are grateful. Bless us now that we might feast on Your Word so that we might not sin against You. In Jesus' name we pray. Amen.

WORD POWER

Feast of Unleavened Bread—this event began two days after the beginning of the Passover feast. This lasted for the duration of the Passover and was marked by the eating of unleavened bread (see Exodus 13:3).

Passover—the celebration that commemorated the Jewish exodus from Egypt (see Exodus 12:14).

HOME DAILY BIBLE READINGS
(July 8-14, 2013)

Dedication of the Temple

MONDAY, July 8: "Resistance to Rebuilding the Temple" (Ezra 4:1-5)

TUESDAY, July 9: "Accusations of Sedition" (Ezra 4:11-16)

WEDNESDAY, July 10: "Temple Construction Halted" (Ezra 4:17-24)

THURSDAY, July 11: "The Eye of God upon Them" (Ezra 5:1-5)

FRIDAY, July 12: "Who Gave You a Decree?" (Ezra 5:6-17)

SATURDAY, July 13: "The Temple's Official Endorsement" (Ezra 6:1-12)

SUNDAY, July 14: "The Temple's Dedication" (Ezra 6:13-22)

LESSON 8 — July 21, 2013

FASTING AND PRAYING

FAITH PATHWAY/FAITH JOURNEY TOPIC: Preparing for a Journey

DEVOTIONAL READING: **2 Chronicles 7:12-18**
PRINT PASSAGE: **Ezra 8:21-23**

BACKGROUND SCRIPTURE: **Ezra 8:21-23**
KEY VERSE: **Ezra 8:23**

Ezra 8:21-23—KJV

21 Then I proclaimed a fast there, at the river of Ahava, that we might afflict ourselves before our God, to seek of him a right way for us, and for our little ones, and for all our substance.

22 For I was ashamed to require of the king a band of soldiers and horsemen to help us against the enemy in the way: because we had spoken unto the king, saying, The hand of our God is upon all them for good that seek him; but his power and his wrath is against all them that forsake him.

23 So we fasted and besought our God for this: and he was intreated of us.

Ezra 8:21-23—NIV

21 There, by the Ahava Canal, I proclaimed a fast, so that we might humble ourselves before our God and ask him for a safe journey for us and our children, with all our possessions.

22 I was ashamed to ask the king for soldiers and horsemen to protect us from enemies on the road, because we had told the king, "The gracious hand of our God is on everyone who looks to him, but his great anger is against all who forsake him."

23 So we fasted and petitioned our God about this, and he answered our prayer.

BIBLE FACT

Praying while fasting adds an element of depth to the spirituality and amazing power that fasting promotes. According to the Bible, Christians have long prayed while fasting. From Old Testament readings where Moses fasted to New Testament readings where Jesus Himself fasted for forty days in the desert; it has long been a Christian practice to abstain from food and devote time to deep prayer. (From: www.ehow.com)

The scriptural definition of *fasting* suggests that it was an act that people did to show humility. Fasting should never be for an outward show to the world.

UNIFYING LESSON PRINCIPLE

As people journey through life, they pause to assess their strengths and weaknesses for reaching their destinations. How can people prepare themselves to make this assessment? Ezra and his entourage stopped on their way to Jerusalem to prepare themselves by fasting and praying for God's protection on their journey.

TOPICAL OUTLINE OF THE LESSON

I. **Introduction**
   A. The Spirituality of Physicality
   B. Biblical Background

II. **Exposition and Application of the Scripture**
   A. Fasting for a Purpose (Ezra 8:21)
   B. The Assurance of Divine Protection (Ezra 8:22)
   C. A Prayer-answering God! (Ezra 8:23)

III. **Concluding Reflection**

LESSON OBJECTIVES

Upon completion of the lesson, the students will be able to do the following:

1. Research the meanings and purposes of prayer and fasting;
2. Reflect on times when prayer made their journeys easier; and,
3. Design their own discipline of prayer and fasting to use along their life journeys.

POINTS TO BE EMPHASIZED

ADULT/YOUTH

Adult Topic: **Preparing for a Journey**
Youth Topic: **Preparing for the Journey**
Adult Key Verse: **Ezra 8:23**
Youth Key Verse: **Ezra 8:21**
Print Passage: **Ezra 8:21-23**

—Ezra knew that the people's journey was uncertain, and that they needed the assurance of God's presence and protection.
—Ezra did not want to diminish his witness to the king about God's graciousness to them and God's wrath against their enemies.
—Dependence on God may mean denying our natural inclinations.
—God's people should be confident in seeking His protection and safety for themselves and their possessions through prayer.
—Ezra was specific about why they were fasting and praying.
—God answered their prayers and protected them.

CHILDREN

Children Topic: **Preparing for the Journey**
Key Verse: **Ezra 8:23**
Print Passage: **Ezra 8:21-23; Matthew 6:16-18**

—Ezra and the families that went with him to Jerusalem prepared for the journey with prayer and fasting.
—The people relied on God rather than the king's armed forces for safe passage.
—This community fast was intended to help the people be attuned to God's leadership.
—Jesus gave instructions in His Sermon on the Mount about the proper practice of fasting.

I. INTRODUCTION

A. The Spirituality of Physicality

In this lesson, we must begin with a disclaimer. There is an old hermeneutical adage that goes, "A text without a context is a pretext." To attempt to interpret these verses without consideration of the full context would only result in the misinterpretation of the text, as well as some misleading and erroneous conclusions. It would be impossible to interpret these three verses without looking at the context from which they emerge. So, before you embark on this lesson, go back and read all of chapters 7 and 8.

Prayer and fasting are staples in Judeo-Christian piety. We cannot be sure when fasting was institutionalized in Hebrew religious piety, but the prophet Isaiah, in Isaiah 58 spoke of an acceptable fast to the Lord. However, long before the second part of the book of Isaiah was written, King David fasted before the Lord that his child, who was stricken with illness, would not die (see 2 Samuel 12:20-22). King Jehoshaphat called the entire nation of Judah and Jerusalem to fast before going to war against the Ammonites and Moabites (see 2 Chronicles 20:3). But, by the time of Ezra, prayer and fasting were a part of the religious tradition of Israel.

So, as Ezra planned for the journey homeward to Jerusalem to begin the process of rebuilding the lives of the people, he came to the realization that the trip would be filled with danger, and that the people could not rebuild their lives and reach their destination without Yahweh. Ezra proclaimed a fast to humble the people before the Lord and seek divine protection for their journey ahead. The lesson in this study is that every physical journey has a spiritual component to it. The Israelites were returning to their homeland, yet they were in fear of the danger from their enemies. So although the trip itself was physical, they needed the Lord's hand to guide and protect them. Can any of us get to where we are going without the Lord's hand leading, guiding, and protecting us? No, we cannot reach our physical or spiritual destinations without the Lord's hand upon us (see verse 18).

B. Biblical Background

The book of Ezra covers several decades and administrations in Persia. After the initial reading of chapter 1, it would be easy to get the impression that all of the Jews returned to Jerusalem at one time. This was not the case. The first group of Israelites returned under King Cyrus; the second group returned to build the foundation (chapter 6) under King Darius, and in chapter 8 another group returned under Artaxerxes. So, in this lesson, Ezra gave us the genealogy of the men (only) who took part in this remigration, not including women and children. It is estimated by some Old Testament scholars that over five thousand men, women, and children participated in this remigration.

Ezra 7:13 says that it was a voluntary trip, which gives an interesting perspective on the return of the exiles. Although these Israelites had been enslaved in Babylon for many years, when freedom finally came, not all of the Israelites returned to Jerusalem from Babylon. This might seem strange, but the human personality can adapt and make the worst of situations seem normal. This was true for the children of Israel—as we read in the book of Exodus—and it was true for the African slaves in America. In 1865, when the Emancipation Proclamation became the law of the land and slaves were free to start life afresh outside of plantation life, many former slaves chose plantation life over the risk of freedom in a world that they did not know. Perhaps this was the case with many of the Israelites who were born in Babylon, or who were taken there when they were too young to remember freedom.

On this trip, Ezra collected the freewill offering of gold, silver, and temple artifacts for the Temple in Jerusalem. However, according to the Levitical Law, only the priests and the Levites were to handle the sacred things of God. So, in verse 15, when they began making preparations for the journey back to Jerusalem, Ezra discovered that there were not enough priests and Levites in the caravan to handle the sacred things. Ezra recruited from "Iddo the chief man at the place Casiphia,…and his brethren the Nethinim at the place Casiphia— that they should bring us servants for the house of our God" (Ezra 8:17, NKJV). These men obviously had to be of Levite pedigree to fulfill the task of service in the house of God. After these men had been appointed to transport the things for the Temple, Ezra called the people to a time of prayer and fasting (verse 21). The journey would be risky, because the precious cargo that they were carrying left them susceptible to roadside bandits who would rob caravans and sell their captives into slavery. The easy thing to have done would have been to ask the king for an armed escort, but this would have undermined Ezra's faith in God. He had already declared that the Lord's hand was upon him (see 7:28). The people fasted and prayed for a safe passage for their journey to Jerusalem. God protected them from the enemy and four months later, they arrived in Jerusalem and offered sacrifices to the Lord (verses 31-36).

II. EXPOSITION AND APPLICATION OF THE SCRIPTURE

A. Fasting for a Purpose
(Ezra 8:21)

Then I proclaimed a fast there, at the river of Ahava, that we might afflict ourselves before our God, to seek of him a right way for us, and for our little ones, and for all our substance.

This section begins with the adverb *then*. After Ezra had assembled the necessary people for the journey, he gathered the people at a river near Ahava, an ancient city near present-day Iran. God had orchestrated matters thus far by allowing Ezra to assemble the right people—the priests and Levites for the journey homeward. Then he called the people to a period of prayer and fasting. This was not some arbitrary fast; rather, it had a twofold purpose, that God might humble them. The Bible is clear that

God does not despise a humble and contrite spirit. Ezra sensed that these five thousand folk who wanted to return to Jerusalem were not quite ready for the journey. Perhaps this group was more of the elite crowd of Israelites who had established themselves in Babylon in spite of captivity. In ancient slavery, unlike modern-day slavery, slaves could own land and wealth, and could buy their freedom. Perhaps this was the crowd that had begun making a name for themselves.

According to Ezra 7:15-19, the people also had financial wherewithal to help finance their journey to Jerusalem. They were the ones who were entrusted with the King's ransom. So they prayed and fasted for humility. *To be humble* means "to humiliate or to bring low." Humility is the opposite of the kind of haughty spirit that God despises. The four-mouth journey to the city of God needed a humble people, because their return was the Lord's doing. They would need protection from the roadside bandits who lay in wait to ambush and rob them. This image of God's going before His people to ward off the enemies (verse 21b) is consistent with other depictions of divine protection in the Old Testament (see images from the book of Judges, when God fought the battle for the people). God gave them a route around the danger. No wonder our slave ancestors believed that God was a Way Maker. Likewise, the people demonstrated their sincerity and reliance on God through prayer and fasting. Jesus said to His disciples, "This kind does not go out except by prayer and fasting" (Matthew 17:21, NKJV). This was a journey that the people could not pull off by themselves; they needed the Lord's hand to guide and protect them. It is also interesting to note that God gave them a way around the enemies, rather than the power to destroy them.

B. The Assurance of Divine Protection (Ezra 8:22)

For I was ashamed to require of the king a band of soldiers and horsemen to help us against the enemy in the way: because we had spoken unto the king, saying, The hand of our God is upon all them for good that seek him; but his power and his wrath is against all them that forsake him.

Ezra became transparent in acknowledging that he was ashamed to ask King Artaxerxes for a military escort, because he had boasted that the hand of the Lord was on them. Ezra said this no less than four times in chapters 7–8—that the gracious hand of the Lord was on them. To ask for the king's help would be a contradiction to his confession and faith in God. Therefore, he called the people to prayer and fasting. One of the few things that we, as leaders, have to offer the people is consistency of testimony and witness. Many would-be great leaders have undermined their witness because their "walk did not match their talk." Let us applaud Ezra for making the right decision when he was caught in the tension between his fears and his fidelity to his faith. This passage also shows us just how typically "human" were the people of old. They were just as vulnerable to human emotions as we are today. The word *ashamed* in the Hebrew (*buwsh*) language carries the idea of "disappointment or worthlessness." Ezra did not want to disappoint the people or prove his faith in God to be worthless by asking for military help from the earthly heathen ruler.

Such a request would have somehow suggested that the people had abandoned Yahweh (God) and did not believe that

He could do what they said He would do. After boasting of the Lord's gracious hand upon them, it would have called into serious theological question the veracity of Yahweh (God) (see verse 22). Could God be trusted and, if so, did He have the power to deliver them? The Exodus theme was that Yahweh was able to deliver and protect Yahweh's people and condemn their enemies. Thus, the second part of verse 22 reflects the promise God made to their ancestor Abram (Abraham) that God would bless those who blessed Him and curse those who cursed Him (see Genesis 12:3). So, the implicit question was whether Ezra and his people would be less trusting than their forefather Abram, who left Ur and settled in Canaan in spite of his enemies. Ezra resolved that he and the people had to trust in God to guide and protect them on their journey. The Lord delivered them in spite of their fears and the uncertainty of the journey. This ought to be the resolve of every believer—we must put our trust in God, not in people and things that we think can provide the protection we believe would/will make us secure.

C. A Prayer-answering God!
(Ezra 8:23)
So we fasted and besought our God for this: and he was intreated of us.

Finally, they fasted and prayed and God answered their prayers. We have to read the rest of this chapter to discover the outcome of their journey, because this verse merely says that God heard and answered their prayers. God delivered the people safely to Jerusalem without incident from the bandits. Once in Jerusalem, Ezra consecrated twelve leading priests and twelve leading Levites and the

artifacts which belonged to the house of God (the Temple)—and the people offered burnt offerings to the Lord (verses 25-36).

III. CONCLUDING REFLECTION

How do you prepare for a journey? It is helpful to know the who, what, when, how, and why of the journey before one can adequately prepare for the journey. The nature of the journey would inform the preparation. Howard Thurman writes of the "Inward Journey" (personal spirituality), Walter Brueggemann writes of the "Journey to the Common Good" (moral obligation to peace and justice for all peoples), and Dr. David Cook (sports psychologist) writes of "Golf's Sacred Journey" (the spiritual and moral lessons to be learned from golf, and the value of living a balanced life). Is *Journey* literal, or is it a metaphor? What kind of journey is it? Who is going with you? When will you be leaving? How long will you stay? One would not prepare for an overnight trip to a nearby city in the same way that one would prepare for a two-week camping trip to the Grand Canyon. The Israelites who were returning from captivity discovered that their physical and spiritual journeys toward wholeness were inseparable from each other, and that they would need the Lord's hand in order to guide and protect themselves adequately.

So, in spite of the offer of safe passage from the royal throne of Artaxerxes, Ezra and the people humbled themselves, prayed, and fasted. They trusted in the Lord and Him only to guide and protect them. How easy would it have been for them, as it is for us, to rely on the powers that be—economic and political—to see them through? Likewise, if we are going to reach our destination of peace and well-being in life, then we need the Lord's hand to guide and protect us. The past few years have taught us that the perceived entities of power (economic and political) are not trustworthy. In 2008, the stock market tumbled to all-time lows and some major investment banks were forced into bankruptcy because of the manipulation of the housing market by greedy people. Billions of investors' dollars were lost, and banks had to be bailed out by an act of Congress. In 2010, there was a tidal shift in the political climate in America, only two years after the election of its first black president. This is why the wise writer from the ancient Wisdom Literature said, "Some trust in chariots and some in horses, but we trust in the name of the LORD our God" (Psalm 20:7, NIV).

The people of God must know whom to trust: "The Lord, the maker of heaven and earth"! As the people of God, we must strive to live more consistently within our confessions of faith. If we believe that God is able to deliver, then we must not just "talk the talk"; we also must "walk the walk." This is the challenge of this lesson—that we learn to trust God in all things!

PRAYER

Loving and faithful God, as sovereign Ruler of the universe, we acknowledge that You care for us. Thank You for the provisions, seen and unseen, that You have made in our lives. All that we are and all that we have is because of who You are. We pray that we will live our lives so that our lifestyles will be consistent with our confessions of faith in You. In Jesus' name we pray. Amen.

WORD POWER

Ashamed *(buwsh)*—**disappointed or worthless.**
Fast—**abstinence; to abstain from food.**
Humble *(daka)*—**to crumble or to break into pieces.**

HOME DAILY BIBLE READINGS
(July 15-21, 2013)

Fasting and Praying

MONDAY, **July 15: "Humbly Calling on God" (2 Chronicles 7:12-18)**

TUESDAY, **July 16: "Beseeching God's Answer to Prayer" (Psalm 69:9-18)**

WEDNESDAY, **July 17: "Humble and Contrite in Spirit" (Isaiah 66:1-4)**

THURSDAY, **July 18: "Fasting Directed to God" (Matthew 6:16-18)**

FRIDAY, **July 19: "Studying and Keeping the Law" (Ezra 7:1-10)**

SATURDAY, **July 20: "Securing Servants for the Temple" (Ezra 8:15-20)**

SUNDAY, **July 21: "Praying for God's Protection" (Ezra 8:21-23)**

LESSON 9   July 28, 2013

GIFTS FOR THE TEMPLE

FAITH PATHWAY/FAITH JOURNEY TOPIC: **Generous Gifts**

DEVOTIONAL READING: **Mark 12:38-44**
PRINT PASSAGE: **Ezra 8:24-30**

BACKGROUND SCRIPTURE: **Ezra 8:24-30**
KEY VERSE: **Ezra 8:28**

Ezra 8:24-30—KJV

24 Then I separated twelve of the chief of the priests, Sherebiah, Hashabiah, and ten of their brethren with them,

25 And weighed unto them the silver, and the gold, and the vessels, even the offering of the house of our God, which the king, and his counsellors, and his lords, and all Israel there present, had offered:

26 I even weighed unto their hand six hundred and fifty talents of silver, and silver vessels an hundred talents, and of gold an hundred talents;

27 Also twenty basons of gold, of a thousand drams; and two vessels of fine copper, precious as gold.

28 And I said unto them, Ye are holy unto the LORD; the vessels are holy also; and the silver and the gold are a freewill offering unto the LORD God of your fathers.

29 Watch ye, and keep them, until ye weigh them before the chief of the priests and the Levites, and chief of the fathers of Israel, at Jerusalem, in the chambers of the house of the LORD.

30 So took the priests and the Levites the weight of the silver, and the gold, and the vessels, to bring them to Jerusalem unto the house of our God.

Ezra 8:24-30—NIV

24 Then I set apart twelve of the leading priests, together with Sherebiah, Hashabiah and ten of their brothers,

25 and I weighed out to them the offering of silver and gold and the articles that the king, his advisers, his officials and all Israel present there had donated for the house of our God.

26 I weighed out to them 650 talents of silver, silver articles weighing 100 talents, 100 talents of gold,

27 20 bowls of gold valued at 1,000 darics, and two fine articles of polished bronze, as precious as gold.

28 I said to them, "You as well as these articles are consecrated to the LORD. The silver and gold are a freewill offering to the LORD, the God of your fathers.

29 Guard them carefully until you weigh them out in the chambers of the house of the LORD in Jerusalem before the leading priests and the Levites and the family heads of Israel."

30 Then the priests and Levites received the silver and gold and sacred articles that had been weighed out to be taken to the house of our God in Jerusalem.

BIBLE FACT

Freewill giving in the Bible—**Giving an offering to the Lord in Old Testament days was vital and necessary and was a part of acceptable worship to the Lord. How we use our money is a test of our spirituality and relationship to the Lord.**

UNIFYING LESSON PRINCIPLE

People often give gifts to others whom they revere. What inspires one to give in this manner? As an act of worship, Ezra prepared gifts of precious metals to be carried by the priests and Levites to the house of God in Jerusalem.

TOPICAL OUTLINE OF THE LESSON

I. Introduction
  A. The Spirituality of Giving
  B. Biblical Background

II. Exposition and Application of the Scripture
  A. Set Apart for God's Use (Ezra 8:24-27)
  B. Holy to God! (Ezra 8:28-30)

III. Concluding Reflection

LESSON OBJECTIVES

Upon completion of the lesson, the students will be able to do the following:

1. Review the principles of financial accountability put in place by Ezra;
2. Reflect on being givers to the church as an act of worship to God; and,
3. Pledge that every time they drop their offerings into the plate, they reflect upon it as an act of worship to God—not just a habit or act of social conformity.

POINTS TO BE EMPHASIZED

ADULT/YOUTH

Adult Topic: Generous Gifts
Youth Topic: Give It Up!
Adult/Youth Key Verse: Ezra 8:28
Print Passage: Ezra 8:24-30

—The Temple was a place where the Israelites could meet together and worship God (see 1 Kings 6:1-17).
—The gifts given to God and the people who presented them were deemed holy unto God.
—The old covenant between God and Israel required priests and Levites to offer gifts to God.
—This Scripture account illustrates that God welcomes gifts from people.
—This passage teaches the importance of people having some responsibility to give back to God for His blessings to them.
—Worship of God brings an assurance of blessings of protection and security from enemies.

CHILDREN

Children Topic: Bringing Our Gifts
Key Verse: Psalm 27:6b
Print Passage: Ezra 8:24-30; Psalm 27:4-6

—Ezra divided the gifts for the Temple among twelve of the top leaders, entrusting them with the delivery of these gifts.
—Ezra reminded the leaders of their consecration to the Lord.
—Ezra challenged the leaders with the sacred importance of the task.
—The psalmist spoke of a desire to be in the Temple.
—The psalmist spoke of bringing offerings to the Lord with joy.

I. INTRODUCTION

A. The Spirituality of Giving

It is often said that all preachers or churches do is beg for money. Obviously, the person who makes such a statement does not know that giving is an act of worship in gratitude to the God we serve (for all He has done for us). Giving is what God asks of us. There is no worship without sacrificial giving! However, many churches and pastors are forced to beg or ask for money because of what the people are not doing and not giving. National statistics say that about 20-25 percent of the people give 80 percent of the money to support the church. This means that two out of ten people are forced to bear the load for the entire congregation. Giving to the Lord's church is not only a theological and spiritual matter, but it is also a practical matter. No human organization, except the church, would allow the recipients of its services to freeload as the church does. People want to use all of the amenities and resources of the church (for weddings, funerals, counseling, and so forth), without being supportive of the church—leaving the pastor no other alternative than to beg. In like manner, we want God's blessings, but we sometimes do not want to do as He asks in order to be worthy of those blessings. From the very beginning of creation, sacrificial giving was an essential and necessary part of worship. Each time one of the patriarchal saints (i.e., Abraham, Isaac, or Jacob) encountered the Lord, he built an altar, offered a sacrifice, and worshipped God. The tabernacle and then the Temple were built around sacrificial offering.

When tribes and families visited the Temple, they brought a choice animal as a sacrificial offering according to the Levitical codes of sacrifice. The sacrifice was given to the priest for preparation and offered to God by the high priest on behalf of the people. God responded to the people according to the acceptability of their sacrifice. So the relevant question for us today is, in light of all the rhetoric about praise and worship, can there be authentic worship without giving an acceptable offering to God? Can praise take the place of a sacrificial gift?

It appears that we have attempted to replace sacrificial giving (in recent years) with total praise. Theologically and biblically, however, they are not the same. We cannot offer praise or service in lieu of our financial gifts.

B. Biblical Background

Ezra, priest and scribe, is considered a reformer of Israel by many scholars. Not only was he the leader of the Exodus from Babylon to Jerusalem, but he later called the Israelites to repent and recommit themselves to the covenant of God. We cannot be sure when Ezra returned to Babylon from Jerusalem for this Exodus. However, upon his return, he was commissioned by King Artaxerxes not only to lead a caravan of Israelites back to Jerusalem, but also to carry a freewill offering of gold and silver and the sacred vessels which belonged to the house of God; He would replace them in the Temple. This gesture of goodwill and benevolence showed a remarkable sensitivity to the God of another people by a heathen king who paid homage to (worshipped) many different idol gods. This chapter also reaffirms that God is sovereign and moves on the hearts of whomever He wishes in order to perform His purpose and will on earth.

Artaxerxes was of the royal linage of Darius and Cyrus, who were non-Jews; yet, God spoke to his heart and gave him a heart (empathy) for the plight of the people of God. Ezra prayed and gave thanks to God for moving on the heart of the king (7:26-27) and being so generous toward his people. In respect for the religion of the Jews, Artaxerxes referred to Ezra as a teacher of the "Law of the God of heaven" (7:21). This shows a kind of sensitivity and tolerance that the Persians had for other gods and religious practices. But we must be clear that their religious empathy was not about the Persians; rather, it was about the sovereignty of God. God in His sovereignty has always used whom He would to bring about His divine purpose. Just as God used Rahab, Ruth, Mary Magdalene, and Saul, even today God continues to move and work in mysterious ways and in strange people and in strange places. We can only conclude that simply because a person has a different theological opinion does not mean that God cannot use and work through him or her. After four months, the people arrived in Jerusalem and rested for three days, taking an account of all the artifacts, gold, and silver that they had brought with them for the Temple. Then they offered a sin offering to the Lord.

II. EXPOSITION AND APPLICATION OF THE SCRIPTURE

A. Set Apart for God's Use
(Ezra 8:24-27)

Then I separated twelve of the chief of the priests, Sherebiah, Hashabiah, and ten of their brethren with them, And weighed unto them the silver, and the gold, and the vessels, even the offering of the house of our God, which the king, and his counsellors, and his lords, and all Israel there present, had offered: I even weighed unto their hand six hundred and fifty talents of silver, and silver vessels an hundred talents, and of gold an hundred talents; Also twenty basons of gold, of a thousand drams; and two vessels of fine copper, precious as gold.

These verses leave much to the imagination—they give us some of the ancillary details of what the people did once they returned to Jerusalem. The trip took about four months, and after they arrived, Ezra appointed twelve of the leading priests, together with Sherebiah, Hashabiah, and ten of his brothers (Levites), and weighed out to them offerings of gold and silver for the house of God. Ezra set them apart to the Lord (see verse 24). The concept of setting apart unto the Lord was part of the precepts of covenant law (see the book of Leviticus) in which persons, animals, and things were set apart from human involvement and participation. These men were supposed to protect and guard the treasury until it was safely presented to the priests in the Temple. These designated priests and Levites were the only ones who were permitted to carry out and handle the contributions and freewill offerings that were holy to the Lord. To call something "holy" meant that it had been designated and transferred from secular use to divine service. If not handled properly, then these items would become profane and unacceptable to the Lord (see Malachi 2). These items constituted the donations that the king and his court had given to be used in the Lord's house.

In order to carry out the demands of the Levitical law, Ezra selected twelve priests and Levites. These twelve priests and Levites represented all of Israel, although only two of the twelve tribes remained after the Exile (the tribes of Judah and Benjamin). There is no biblical account of what happened to the other ten tribes of Israel after the Babylonian captivity. Some scholars believe that those who did not return home became the Jewish Diaspora. Nevertheless, those who returned constituted a community built around Temple practices and the Law of Moses. This is why the trip did not commence until Ezra had commissioned enough (38) priests and (220) Nethinim, who were Temple servants appointed and sanctioned by King David (years earlier before the Exile), after prayer and fasting. Clearly, all that happened and their ability to establish a community resulted from the gracious hand of God. Thus, we must ask whether a true community of peace and justice is possible without the gracious hand of God to guide and to protect them. What makes your church a community, and what is your definition of *community*? The Israelites were able to return home and reestablish their community with the blessings of the oppressor, because the gracious hand of God was upon them!

B. Holy to God!
(Ezra 8:28-30)

And I said unto them, Ye are holy unto the Lord; the vessels are holy also; and the silver and the gold are a freewill offering unto the Lord God of your fathers. Watch ye, and keep them, until ye weigh them before the chief of the priests and the Levites, and chief of the fathers of Israel, at Jerusalem, in the chambers of the house of the Lord. So took the priests and the Levites the weight of the silver, and the gold, and the vessels, to bring them to Jerusalem unto the house of our God.

After Ezra had apportioned the Temple treasure of gold and silver and the Temple artifacts to the priests and the Levites, he pronounced them to be consecrated to the Lord. *To be consecrated* meant to be set aside as sacred and used only for sacred purposes. The gold and silver were freewill offerings to the Lord, the God of their fathers (see verse 28). A freewill offering is exactly what it says: free will. This offering was not required under the law as were the tithes—they belonged to the Lord. Usually, when there was a project to be done around the Temple, the Lord through His agents would ask the people for a freewill offering to support the project (see Ezra 7:11-15). The freewill offering was first mentioned in the book of Exodus: "All the people who had a heart to give gave willingly" (see 35:29). It came from the heart and it was not unusual for some not to give; it was only done by those who had hearts to give. Hence, the freewill offering appears to have been a gratitude offering to God by persons who were grateful for what God had done for them. The operative word in Exodus 35:29 is "heart." The heart was considered to be a metaphor for the center of emotion and will. Thus, giving was a *heart* matter. In his letter to the Corinthian church, Paul encouraged the people to give freely and generously: "Each of you should give what you have decided in your heart to give, for God loves a cheerful giver" (see 2 Corinthians 9:7).

The more gracious the heart, the more generous will be the giver. These gifts were handled according to the laws of the Temple and given to priests and the Levites to be placed in the house of God. The gold and the silver were used to purchase animals, grain, and wine for the Temple's sacrificial offerings (see 7:16-17).

What does this message mean to us as believers today, and what are the implications for us? One of the underlying messages is the need to trust in God. The people obviously had their own needs. To leave their established community in Babylon and travel to and settle in a city after seven decades required faith and trust. Jerusalem was still under reconstruction. It was not a thriving metropolis as was Persia. Yet, these people were willing to follow the voice of the Lord through Ezra and return to Jerusalem, giving their financial resources to the Lord. They put trust in God ahead of financial security! We must remember that ancient slavery was not the cruel system that Africans had to endure in the western hemisphere. Slaves worked for pay and were paid according to their skill sets. There are accounts of slaves buying their freedom and subsequently owning slaves. Nevertheless, when it came time to leave Babylon, only five thousand men, women, and children volunteered to relocate to Jerusalem—while other established Jews refused to leave Babylon (the Persian Empire). Neither the resources and money they had collected, nor the dangerous journey from Babylon to Jerusalem, deterred them from trusting in the Lord, as they ventured into the unknown. In his letter to the Romans, the apostle Paul asked, "Hope that is seen is not hope, for who hopes for what is seen?" (see Romans 8:24). It took a measure of trust to embark on a trip as that one (with so many uncertainties); yet, the people did it and gave willingly to the Lord in the process.

These people understood that their lives—who they were and what they had—were because of the Lord's grace and mercy. All that they had came from the Lord; therefore, they were only giving to the work of the Lord what had come to them from the Lord. In the words of their forefather, King David, "Of thine own have we given thee" (see 1 Chronicles 29).

Finally, they were to guard the treasures and artifacts carefully until they could be turned over to the leading priest and Levites in the Temple. Ezra demanded integrity from everyone who transported and handled the sacred things of God. Hence, stewardship is not just the giving of resources—it is also the care of those resources. The church and those of us who are in leadership would do well to imitate and learn from Ezra's example. Financial accountability must be demanded and expected of the church. There must be checks and balances to account for the resources of the church, because there is a correlation between the people's trust and the people's stewardship. It might not be the right thing to do, but when people do not feel comfortable with the integrity of leadership, they express this in the offering tray. Once given to the church, the offering belongs to the Lord, and those who handle it ought to be consecrated (devoted to the Lord) and handle all things that belong to the Lord with jealous care.

III. CONCLUDING REFLECTION

The word *generous* is a rather arbitrary one, because its meaning depends on several factors.

What is generous to the wealthy person may not be generous when compared to the gift of the widow's mite: she gave all she had (see Luke 21:2). The point that Jesus was making in the narrative of the widow's mite and the woman with the alabaster box of oil who anointed His feet (Luke 12:36ff) is, "People who love much give much, and people who give little love little." This is indeed true also in every aspect of our lives. It does not matter what the arena is—the church or charitable causes or one's alma mater—money follows passion as we give to those institutions for which we have passion. The late Dr. George O McCalep Jr. would say to his congregation at Greenforest Community Baptist Church in Decatur, Georgia, "Show me your checkbook and I will show you where your passions are. How you spend your money reflects your priorities. Giving to the church for many is an afterthought." Yes, we invest our monies where our passions lie! In the SEED curriculum, Series Six, session 5, on "Your Heart and Your Treasure," the writer says, "True motive is inspired by what we treasure in our hearts. Our behaviors and attitudes are reflections of what is in our hearts." Therefore, persons who complain that all the church and pastors do is beg for money are the voices of criticism, giving insight into the secrets of their hearts. If their giving records to the church could be made public, then we should not be surprised if they are a part of the 80 percent who give less than 20 percent of their money to the house of the Lord. Jesus said, "Where your treasure is, there will your heart be also" (Matthew 6:21).

PRAYER

God of grace and God of mercy, we offer ourselves to You today and always. It is our prayer that our hearts have reflected our love as we have given to support the work of Your ministry. In Jesus' name we pray. Amen.

WORD POWER

Freewill offering—"given without coercion" or "to volunteer as a soldier for duty."
Sacrificial giving—"sacrificial" in the Old Testament is associated with "to slaughter"; it carries the idea of the tribute being complete and total. Sacrificial giving is giving unto the Lord without reservation—with complete and total commitment.

HOME DAILY BIBLE READINGS
(July 22-28, 2013)

Gifts for the Temple

MONDAY, July 22: "A Single Offering for All Time" (Hebrews 10:1-14)
TUESDAY, July 23: "Stirred Hearts and Willing Spirits" (Exodus 35:20-29)
WEDNESDAY, July 24: "Bring Offerings before the Lord" (Numbers 7:1-6)
THURSDAY, July 25: "Contributing Tithes and Offerings" (2 Chronicles 31:2-10)
FRIDAY, July 26: "More Important than Offerings and Sacrifices" (Mark 12:28-34)
SATURDAY, July 27: "The Gift of a Poor Widow" (Mark 12:38-44)
SUNDAY, July 28: "The Offering for God's House" (Ezra 8:24-30)

LESSON 10

August 4, 2013

FESTIVAL OF BOOTHS

Faith Pathway/Faith Journey Topic: **Great Rejoicing**

Devotional Reading: **Exodus 23:12-17**
Print Passage: **Nehemiah 8:13-18**

Background Scripture: **Nehemiah 7:73b–8:18**
Key Verse: **Nehemiah 8:17**

Nehemiah 8:13-18—KJV

13 And on the second day were gathered together the chief of the fathers of all the people, the priests, and the Levites, unto Ezra the scribe, even to understand the words of the law.

14 And they found written in the law which the Lord had commanded by Moses, that the children of Israel should dwell in booths in the feast of the seventh month:

15 And that they should publish and proclaim in all their cities, and in Jerusalem, saying, Go forth unto the mount, and fetch olive branches, and pine branches, and myrtle branches, and palm branches, and branches of thick trees, to make booths, as it is written.

16 So the people went forth, and brought them, and made themselves booths, every one upon the roof of his house, and in their courts, and in the courts of the house of God, and in the street of the water gate, and in the street of the gate of Ephraim.

17 And all the congregation of them that were come again out of the captivity made booths, and sat under the booths: for since the days of Jeshua the son of Nun unto that day had not the children of Israel done so. And there was very great gladness.

18 Also day by day, from the first day unto the last day, he read in the book of the law of God. And they kept the feast seven days; and on the eighth day was a solemn assembly, according unto the manner.

Nehemiah 8:13-18—NIV

13 On the second day of the month, the heads of all the families, along with the priests and the Levites, gathered around Ezra the scribe to give attention to the words of the Law.

14 They found written in the Law, which the Lord had commanded through Moses, that the Israelites were to live in booths during the feast of the seventh month

15 and that they should proclaim this word and spread it throughout their towns and in Jerusalem: "Go out into the hill country and bring back branches from olive and wild olive trees, and from myrtles, palms and shade trees, to make booths"—as it is written.

16 So the people went out and brought back branches and built themselves booths on their own roofs, in their courtyards, in the courts of the house of God and in the square by the Water Gate and the one by the Gate of Ephraim.

17 The whole company that had returned from exile built booths and lived in them. From the days of Joshua son of Nun until that day, the Israelites had not celebrated it like this. And their joy was very great.

18 Day after day, from the first day to the last, Ezra read from the Book of the Law of God. They celebrated the feast for seven days, and on the eighth day, in accordance with the regulation, there was an assembly.

UNIFYING LESSON PRINCIPLE

People use festivals and celebrations as observances of things that are most important to them in life. What are some times or events that we celebrate? The Festival of Booths and Ezra's reading were observations of the Israelites' wilderness exile and the giving of the Law, which the people celebrated joyously—followed by solemn contemplation.

TOPICAL OUTLINE OF THE LESSON

I. Introduction
    A. Celebrating God
    B. Biblical Background

II. Exposition and Application of the Scripture
    A. A Biblical Mandate to Celebrate
        (Nehemiah 8:13-15)
    B. God's Joy!
        (Nehemiah 8:16-18)

III. Concluding Reflection

LESSON OBJECTIVES

Upon completion of the lesson, the students will be able to do the following:

1. Compare the lesson text with the earlier text concerning the Festival of Booths (see Leviticus 23:33-43);
2. Explore human emotions associated with being given rules for living; and,
3. Commit to bringing all the faith communities to study God's Word, as Ezra modeled.

POINTS TO BE EMPHASIZED

ADULT/YOUTH
Adult Topic: Great Rejoicing
Youth Topic: Remembering to Celebrate
Adult Key Verse: Nehemiah 8:17
Youth Key Verse: Nehemiah 8:14
Print Passage: Nehemiah 8:13-18

—The three main Jewish festivals (see Deuteronomy 16:16) for which all Jewish men gathered in Jerusalem were the Festival of Unleavened Bread (March–April), the Festival of Weeks (May–June), and the Festival of Booths (September–October).

—The Feast of Booths had two emphases: (1) a celebration of the harvest, reflecting on the harvesters' booths in the fields; and (2) a celebration of the deliverance from bondage in Egypt, in which God and the people used temporary dwellings.

—In the context of their recent return from the Babylonian exile, this celebration focused on the joy of God's deliverance more than on thankfulness for the crops.

—The weeklong celebration of God's deliverance included erecting and living in booths, abstaining from work, sacrificing offerings to God, reading and teaching God's Word, and ending with a great assembly of the faith community.

—Ezra taught so that the people understood and were touched by God's Word, not merely engaging in a shallow and purely ritualistic liturgical reading of Scripture.

CHILDREN
Children Topic: A Freedom Celebration
Key Verse: Nehemiah 8:17
Print Passage: Nehemiah 8:13-18

—The Festival of Booths is a fall Jewish holiday, celebrating the end of the wilderness experience.

—This holiday occurs during Tishri (September or October), the seventh month in the Jewish calendar.

—The Festival of Booths is also a weeklong celebration, during which God's law is read to His people every day.

—God commanded the Israelites to live in booths, so they would always remember the time after leaving Egypt, when God's people lived in temporary makeshift housing.

—Specific resources were given for making the booths, which were erected on rooftops, in courtyards of worship centers, and in places throughout the community.

—Ezra revived the Festival of Booths because the Israelites returning from exile needed to celebrate and remember God's intervening hand in their liberation experience.

I. INTRODUCTION

A. Celebrating God

There is a great legacy of celebration in the Jewish culture for what God has done for them, both in the present and in the past. These celebrations are touchstones of remembrance of what the Lord had brought them through (i.e., Passover, Pentecost, Festival of Booths, and so forth). It is indeed a significant contrast when we consider the things that we as Americans celebrate. The greatest joy for many does not seem to be for the Lord or for what the Lord has done, but for things that add absolutely nothing to our lives. The greatest rejoicing heard in America seems to be in athletic venues like football stadiums and basketball arenas. It appears that we are entertainment-driven, and perhaps this has even become our new god. Jesus said, "Where your treasure is there will your heart be also" (see Matthew 6:21). We celebrate, rejoice, and even worship athletes, entertainers, and people of notoriety with great fanfare. But this text is about a people who celebrated God for what He had done in allowing them to return and rebuild their lives and homes. Hence, their celebration was not arbitrary or capricious, but done according to the standards given by God to their ancestors hundreds of years earlier.

Their celebration reflected their new sense of what it meant to be a covenant community. The law of the Lord, around which they were to build their lives and faith practices, solidified them as a covenant community.

B. Biblical Background

At one point in biblical history, the books of Ezra and Nehemiah were combined into one book. It was only centuries later that redactionists divided them into separate books. Much of the historical background that informed the book of Ezra also informed the book of Nehemiah. Ezra was the priest of the remigration to Jerusalem, while Nehemiah was the governor who was granted authority by King Artaxerxes over their return to Jerusalem and the rebuilding of the city wall and the city. However, it was Ezra who oversaw the reconstruction of the Temple and who called the people to rededication and to re-consecrate themselves to the Lord.

Chapter 8 is the continuation of Ezra's story, as the Israelites reconstructed the Temple. At some point in the renovation, they discovered the laws of Moses, believed to be the book of Deuteronomy. These laws were given to regulate life within the covenant community after the exodus from Egypt. However, according to verse 1, the people were not just situated in Jerusalem, but in neighboring communities. After the Israelites had settled in their particular towns, they came together in the square outside of the water gate for the reading of the book of the Law of Moses. The assembly stood and listened as Ezra read from early morning to midday (about six hours). After Ezra had finished reading, the people fell on their faces and worshipped God. The Levites interpreted the Law for the people. They consecrated the first day of the seventh month (Tishri) as "holy unto our Lord." It is speculation by some Old Testament scholars that the people were grieved because they were convicted by the words of the Law and understood that their plight in captivity resulted from violation of the Law. This was a sign of their contrition.

In the Law, the Lord had promised Israel that if they obeyed His laws and precepts then He would bless them, but likewise if they were disobedient then He would curse them (see Deuteronomy 11:27-28). They were grieved by their sins of disobedience. So in the seventh month, they celebrated the Festival of Booths or Tabernacles for seven days. Although they were centuries removed from their ancestors' days in the wilderness, they celebrated the religious traditions of their forefathers and mothers as they had done centuries earlier.

II. EXPOSITION AND APPLICATION OF THE SCRIPTURE

A. A Biblical Mandate to Celebrate
(Nehemiah 8:13-15)

And on the second day were gathered together the chief of the fathers of all the people, the priests, and the Levites, unto Ezra the scribe, even to understand the words of the law. And they found written in the law which the Lord had commanded by Moses, that the children of Israel should dwell in booths in the feast of the seventh month: And that they should publish and proclaim in all their cities, and in Jerusalem, saying, Go forth unto the mount, and fetch olive branches, and pine branches, and myrtle branches, and palm branches, and branches of thick trees, to make booths, as it is written.

On the second day of the Festival of Booths, the heads of the different ancestral lines, along with the priests and Levites, came together with Ezra the scribe (priest) to study the word of the Law. It was in the Law of Moses (see Leviticus 23:33ff) that they learned that the people were to live in booths (dwellings made of palm leaves, tree branches, and sticks). The people were to offer sacrifices of fire, burnt offerings, grain offerings, and drink offerings each day, according to the words of the Law. They were to live in booths for seven days, and on the first and second day they were to rest, not work. This was to commemorate the time when the Lord brought their ancestors out of Egypt and the people lived in booths in the wilderness. The Festival of Booths was a living reminder of God's involvement in who they had become as a people of God. These annual festivals were to be passed from generation to generation, so that the Israelites would never forget who they were, and whose they were. The Festival of Booths is celebrated in October in Israel even to this day.

Although the people had become city dwellers with houses (see Haggai 1), they were to live in these thatched huts or tents made of the unprocessed resources of nature under the canopy of heaven for seven days. Perhaps we would be much more appreciative and grateful to God if, once each year, we had to move out of our palatial dwellings for seven days and live in a slave cabin or some of the shanties our ancestors were forced to live in. This periodic reminder would keep us humble, just as it kept the people humble and reminded them of where they had come from. However, it was the failure of the people to live in booths and celebrate the Festival of Booths that constituted their sin against God. Israel's story, like our stories, had not only informed their present realities but also shaped them. After reading the Law and understanding what the Lord required of them, they celebrated their newfound freedom and renewed their relationship with God. Once back in Palestine and attempting to reconstruct their lives, they put God at the center of personal and communal life.

With the awareness that this was indeed a patriarchal society, Ezra read the Law on the second day to the male heads of households. It then was their responsibility to proclaim the Law in the land to those who perhaps were not present at its reading. This was consistent with the ethos and pathos of ancient Hebrew culture. The father, the head of the house, was the priest of his family and it was his responsibility to teach the Law of the Lord to his family.

As we look around today and analyze the family crisis in America, there are many who would suggest that the beginning of the breakdown of traditional family life in America began with the diminished role of a strong patriarchal figure in the home. Is this just modern-day sociology, or is the "proof in the pudding"? More persons are incarcerated in this country now than at any other time in its history; correspondingly, the number of divorces, absentee fathers, and single mothers are at an all-time high.

The Israelites attempted to rebuild their lives in concert with the laws and principles that God had given Moses; male leadership was most visible and required. The people reasoned that there was a correlation between the demise of family and community and their disobedience to the Law of God that regulated life within the community and the family. Verse 15 concludes with the people gathering different branches for the construction of the booths. So, the question for us is whether looking back and returning to past sacred traditions are all bad things.

B. God's Joy!
(Nehemiah 8:16-18)

So the people went forth, and brought them, and made themselves booths, every one upon the roof of his house, and in their courts, and in the courts of the house of God, and in the street of the water gate, and in the street of the gate of Ephraim. And all the congregation of them that were come again out of the captivity made booths, and sat under the booths: for since the days of Jeshua the son

of Nun unto that day had not the children of Israel done so. And there was very great gladness. Also day by day, from the first day unto the last day, he read in the book of the law of God. And they kept the feast seven days; and on the eighth day was a solemn assembly, according unto the manner.

Verse 16 is a continuation of the gathering of branches for the booths and where they were constructed. Those who had homes built them on rooftops, while others were built in community gathering places and in the Temple. However, verse 17b reads, "there was very great gladness." We can only imagine what their joy was about. This was a sign to the people that they were in the will of God once again! In the introduction to this lesson, we discussed the things we celebrate in America. The greatest expressions of joy in our beloved nation unfortunately are not seen and experienced in the church. Although many local churches and their polity promote a more festive celebration in worship, festive celebrations will vary greatly from church to church. Nevertheless, none can compare to the festive atmosphere of a sporting event or an entertainment venue. If we emulated the Israelites' worship experience when we gathered for worship, then we would require of ourselves the retelling of our collective story of how we have come this far by faith. One of the great historical hymns of our faith says, "We have come this far by faith, leaning on the Lord. Trusting in His holy Word, He never failed me yet." This is our only story! We sing a lot of contemporary praise and worship songs that focus exclusively on our future blessings. Unfortunately, many of these lyrics are completely disconnected from our lived realities and the past.

One scholar interprets verse 17b as "joy in the Lord" rather than "and their joy was very great." This interpretation puts the emphasis on the Lord and not the people. It was the Lord whom they celebrated for what He had done for them. Likewise, this interpretation would be consistent with that of the psalmist, who declared that the "joy of the LORD is your strength" (Nehemiah 8:10). According to the Old Testament (see Deuteronomy 16:13ff), God demands joy from His people. So, the word *joy* carries the idea of festive enthusiasm that reflects the whole person—and God's work of salvation is the primary occasion for joy (see Psalms 5:11; 9:2; and 16:9). Their joy in the Lord reflected their dedication to the Lord for the great things He had done.

The reading of the Law brought about great reform in Israel, and in this they celebrated greatly and with great joy. So, the writer of the book of Nehemiah saw a connection between what the Jews returning from exile were doing and what Joshua and the children of Israel had done many centuries earlier. Both communities had entered foreign lands and established themselves for no other reason than God's kindness. So, when they reflected on this history, they had cause to be greatly joyful in the Lord. They did this for seven days and on the eighth day, they stopped rejoicing and had a solemn assembly, according to the rules of the Law. Of course, as believers we live under a different dispensation of grace in Jesus the Christ. The Bible teaches that we are to draw water from the well of our salvation with joy. The Lord has redeemed us and set us free from the shackles of sin!

III. CONCLUDING REFLECTION

The festivals that were celebrated in ancient Israel were to be passed down from generation to generation. This served as a constant reminder to future generations that there was to be a continual connection between Israel and the Lord. Leviticus 23:33 and subsequent verses help us to understand the laws that governed the particular festival identified in today's lesson. The celebration of the Festival of Booths was to be a constant reminder of God's presence and provision in the Israelites' lives as His people. They were to always remember that they did not become what they became solely through their own efforts. They owed their very existence to the God of Abraham, Isaac, and Jacob.

One of the challenges of contemporary society is to hold on to the sacred things of our past that inform our collective stories. If our story would be incomplete without that history, then it must become a part of our story and what we celebrate. We cannot separate our individual stories from our collective history. So let us celebrate the goodness of the Lord in what He has done for us as His people. Let us rejoice in His goodness for the marvelous things He has done.

PRAYER

Everlasting God, our Father, thank You for the joy that fills our hearts because You have counted us worthy of salvation. We are because You are, and You thought enough of us to share Your Son so that we might be set free from the penalty and bondage of sin. We celebrate Your goodness in the land of the living. In Jesus' name we pray. Amen.

WORD POWER

Booths—the word *Sukkah* means either "booth" or "hut" in Hebrew. The plural form of *Sukkah* is "Sukkot," meaning "booths" or "huts."

Scribe—the Hebrew term for "scribe" is *sofer,* a participle form of the root *spr,* meaning "to count."

HOME DAILY BIBLE READINGS
(July 28–August 4, 2013)

Festival of Booths

MONDAY, July 29: "Rhythms of Work and Worship" (Exodus 23:12-17)

TUESDAY, July 30: "First Bring Your Offering" (Leviticus 23:9-14)

WEDNESDAY, July 31: "Celebrating God's Bounty to Us" (Deuteronomy 26:1-11)

THURSDAY, August 1: "Fostering the Memory of God's Deliverance" (Leviticus 23:33-44)

FRIDAY, August 2: "Gathering to Hear God's Word" (Nehemiah 7:73b–8:6)

SATURDAY, August 3: "Responding to God's Word" (Nehemiah 8:7b-12 [the Levites])

SUNDAY, August 4: "Discovering a Neglected Festival" (Nehemiah 8:13-18)

LESSON 11   August 11, 2013

COMMUNITY OF CONFESSION

FAITH PATHWAY/FAITH JOURNEY TOPIC: **Admitting Shortcomings**

DEVOTIONAL READING: **Luke 15:1-10**
PRINT PASSAGE: **Nehemiah 9:2, 6-7, 9-10, 30-36**

BACKGROUND SCRIPTURE: **Nehemiah 9:1-37**
KEY VERSE: **Nehemiah 9:2**

Nehemiah 9:2, 6-7, 9-10, 30-36—KJV

2 And the seed of Israel separated themselves from all strangers, and stood and confessed their sins, and the iniquities of their fathers.

…..

6 Thou, even thou, art LORD alone; thou hast made heaven, the heaven of heavens, with all their host, the earth, and all things that are therein, the seas, and all that is therein, and thou preservest them all; and the host of heaven worshippeth thee.
7 Thou art the LORD the God, who didst choose Abram, and broughtest him forth out of Ur of the Chaldees, and gavest him the name of Abraham.

…..

9 And didst see the affliction of our fathers in Egypt, and heardest their cry by the Red sea;
10 And shewedst signs and wonders upon Pharaoh, and on all his servants, and on all the people of his land: for thou knewest that they dealt proudly against them. So didst thou get thee a name, as it is this day.

…..

30 Yet many years didst thou forbear them, and testifiedst against them by thy spirit in thy prophets: yet would they not give ear: therefore gavest thou them into the hand of the people of the lands.
31 Nevertheless for thy great mercies' sake thou didst not utterly consume them, nor forsake them; for thou art a gracious and merciful God.

Nehemiah 9:2, 6-7, 9-10, 30-36—NIV

2 Those of Israelite descent had separated themselves from all foreigners. They stood in their places and confessed their sins and the wickedness of their fathers.

…..

6 "You alone are the LORD. You made the heavens, even the highest heavens, and all their starry host, the earth and all that is on it, the seas and all that is in them. You give life to everything, and the multitudes of heaven worship you.
7 You are the LORD God, who chose Abram and brought him out of Ur of the Chaldeans and named him Abraham."

…..

9 "You saw the suffering of our forefathers in Egypt; you heard their cry at the Red Sea.
10 You sent miraculous signs and wonders against Pharaoh, against all his officials and all the people of his land, for you knew how arrogantly the Egyptians treated them. You made a name for yourself, which remains to this day."

…..

30 "For many years you were patient with them. By your Spirit you admonished them through your prophets. Yet they paid no attention, so you handed them over to the neighboring peoples.
31 But in your great mercy you did not put an end to them or abandon them, for you are a gracious and merciful God.

UNIFYING LESSON PRINCIPLE

It is often hard to tell the truth about ourselves, especially our wrongdoing. What brings us to be honest about our shortcomings? The writer showed us that confession and repentance are necessary acts of worship, because God is merciful in every generation and gives people multiple chances to get it right.

32 Now therefore, our God, the great, the mighty, and the terrible God, who keepest covenant and mercy, let not all the trouble seem little before thee, that hath come upon us, on our kings, on our princes, and on our priests, and on our prophets, and on our fathers, and on all thy people, since the time of the kings of Assyria unto this day.

33 Howbeit thou art just in all that is brought upon us; for thou hast done right, but we have done wickedly:

34 Neither have our kings, our princes, our priests, nor our fathers, kept thy law, nor hearkened unto thy commandments and thy testimonies, wherewith thou didst testify against them.

35 For they have not served thee in their kingdom, and in thy great goodness that thou gavest them, and in the large and fat land which thou gavest before them, neither turned they from their wicked works.

36 Behold, we are servants this day, and for the land that thou gavest unto our fathers to eat the fruit thereof and the good thereof, behold, we are servants in it.

32 Now therefore, O our God, the great, mighty and awesome God, who keeps his covenant of love, do not let all this hardship seem trifling in your eyes—the hardship that has come upon us, upon our kings and leaders, upon our priests and prophets, upon our fathers and all your people, from the days of the kings of Assyria until today.

33 In all that has happened to us, you have been just; you have acted faithfully, while we did wrong.

34 Our kings, our leaders, our priests and our fathers did not follow your law; they did not pay attention to your commands or the warnings you gave them.

35 Even while they were in their kingdom, enjoying your great goodness to them in the spacious and fertile land you gave them, they did not serve you or turn from their evil ways.

36 But see, we are slaves today, slaves in the land you gave our forefathers so they could eat its fruit and the other good things it produces."

TOPICAL OUTLINE OF THE LESSON

I. Introduction
   A. The Importance of True Confession
   B. Biblical Background

II. Exposition and Application of the Scripture
   A. Confession and Acknowledgment (Nehemiah 9:2, 6-7)
   B. A God of Greatness and Faithfulness (Nehemiah 9:9-10)
   C. A God of Righteousness and Mercy (Nehemiah 9:30-36)

III. Concluding Reflection

LESSON OBJECTIVES

Upon completion of the lesson, the students will be able to do the following:

1. Link the public reading of God's Word to personal acts of confession and repentance;

2. Hear God's Word corporately and confess their shortcomings individually; and,
3. Write personal covenants with God because of their experience with hearing God's Word and confessing their shortcomings.

POINTS TO BE EMPHASIZED
ADULT/YOUTH
Adult Topic: Admitting Shortcomings
Youth Topic: Fess Up!
Adult/Youth Key Verse: Nehemiah 9:2
Print Passage: Nehemiah 9:2, 6-7, 9-10, 30-36

—The restored remnant of the Jews confessed their sins and requested God's gracious deliverance from the present oppression.
—The remnant community accepted the corporate guilt of their ancestors' rebellion and disobedience toward God.
—Although much of the fault for the history of disobedience of the Jews was due to ungodly leadership, this did not allow individual persons to disclaim their personal responsibility and involvement in the corporate guilt.
—The confession sincerely accepted full guilt, lacking any attempt at justification through offering excuses.

—This prayer of confession sought forgiveness and deliverance by appealing to the merciful God and God's unchanging purposes.

CHILDREN
Children Topic: Saying We Are Sorry
Key Verse: Psalm 51:10
Print Passage: Nehemiah 9:1-3, 6-8, 26-28

—The Israelites used physical symbols, such as putting on sackcloth and dirt on their heads, along with fasting, to demonstrate their remorse for sins they had committed.
—Public worship for corporate sin included both the reading of the Scriptures and confession of sins.
—God is always merciful and just in forgiving the sins of His covenant people and in cleansing them from all unrighteousness.
—Sinfulness is built into human nature.
—No punishment has proven harsh enough to deter humans from sinning.
—Despite the grace, mercy, faithfulness, and goodness of God, humans have continued to sin.

I. INTRODUCTION
A. The Importance of True Confession

We are living in an age when confession appears to be a lost virtue in the church and in society, unless the facts facing the accused are irrefutable and can no longer be denied. Have we watered down confession to be a last resort to save public face and humiliation? In June of 2011, Congressman Anthony Weiner from New York was accused of sending lewd pictures of himself to a woman over the Internet. When it came to light, he denied it and claimed a conspiracy to besmirch his name and reputation. He denied knowing anything about those pictures and assured Wolf Blitzer on CNN that he would have the matter investigated. After weeks of heated debate and media investigation, Congressman Weiner came clean after the sender of the pictures was traced back to his e-mail. He confessed his shortcomings and asked the public to forgive him. "I am here today to again apologize for the personal mistakes I have made and the embarrassment I have caused" (*The New York Times*). This lesson does not serve to indict Congressman Weiner; he is only one of several public figures who have had to resign in shame after denying corruption or impropriety. Congressman Weiner's story highlights a disturbing trend in the public eye—leaders confessing their faults *only* after getting caught.

The same can be said about religious figures. Ted Haggard, founder and former pastor of New Life Church in Colorado Springs, Colorado—who is also a founder of the Association of Life-Giving Churches, and president of the National Association of Evangelicals (NAE)—was accused by a man of using drugs and engaging in an illicit sexual relationship for three years. Ted Haggard's immediate response was denial. Haggard claimed he had never met his accuser. He also told a Denver television station, "I am steady with my wife. I'm faithful to my wife and I have never done drugs—ever. Not even in high school." It was only after the man produced a voicemail with Haggard's voice on it that Haggard confessed his fault. Must we get caught before we confess our faults? There is virtue in confessing our faults, even if we do not get caught. Rather, we are to confess when we become aware that we have fallen short of God's standards for our lives. This lesson ought to teach us the importance of true confession that comes when we realize that we have fallen short of what God expects of us.

B. Biblical Background

The book of Ezra focuses on the rebuilding of the Temple, while the book of Nehemiah is an account of the rebuilding of the city wall around Jerusalem. It appears that many of the Jews who had gone back to Jerusalem with Ezra were not doing well. After Nehemiah received word about the plight of the people and the city (Jerusalem), he asked his master, King Artaxerxes, for permission to return home to see about his people. In Nehemiah 1:4-6, Nehemiah fasted and prayed and confessed the sins of the people before returning: "I confess the sins we Israelites, including myself and my father's house, have committed against you" (verse 6, NIV). It could be said that two of the watchwords of the book are *confession* and *prayer*.

So, after the Festival of Booths (see chapter 8), the Israelites gathered for another religious ceremony on the twenty-fourth day of the seventh month. The people stood where they were in the public square and read from the Book of the Law of the Lord for the first six hours; then they spent the next six hours in prayer, in confession, and in worship (verse 3). The people were led in this liturgy by the Levites who encouraged the people to stand up and call upon the Lord their God. Therefore, their prayer began and ended with petition and confession (verses 33-35). Also, it is noteworthy that Nehemiah's prayer included some "historical retrospective" of the things that the Lord had done for Israel throughout history.

The graciousness of God could not be overlooked or ignored by Nehemiah, nor can it be overlooked by us. Our present realities must be informed by our history, just as the Exodus event informed the Israelites and constantly called them to remember. Since these verses represent only a portion of a liturgical prayer that covers thirty-three verses, it is suggested that you read the entire prayer in your study of this lesson.

II. EXPOSITION AND APPLICATION OF THE SCRIPTURE

A. Confession and Acknowledgment (Nehemiah 9:2, 6-7)

And the seed of Israel separated themselves from all strangers, and stood and confessed their sins, and the iniquities of their fathers. ...Thou, even thou, art LORD alone; thou hast made heaven, the heaven of heavens, with all their host, the earth, and all things that are therein, the seas, and all that is therein, and thou preservest them all; and the host of heaven worshippeth thee. Thou art the LORD the God, who didst choose Abram, and broughtest him forth out of Ur of the Chaldees, and gavest him the name of Abraham.

On the twenty-fourth day of the seventh month, the Israelites assembled in the public square, wearing sackcloth and ashes on their heads, a sign of contrition and humility. Those who could trace their pedigree back to Abraham, Isaac, and Jacob separated themselves from all non-Israelites (foreigners who had not embraced Judaism) and confessed their sins and the wickedness of their forefathers. They read the Law of Moses and then came to a place where they understood their lives in the light of God's law. The Law was the measuring stick by which the covenant community of Israel was to live and they confessed their sins when their actions did not line up with the words of the Law. However, confession for ancient Israel was more than just acknowledging one's shortcomings. It carried the idea of invoking divine mercy, with a promise and a vow to live according to divine expectation. Verse 2b is especially interesting, in that they confessed the wickedness of their fathers. This correlated their present reality of sinfulness to the sins of their fathers, which had caused the captivity in the first place. For them, this was an issue of "first cause" or "cause and effect." Clearly,

it was the sins of their fathers and mothers that had caused their displacement. The word *wickedness* in this verse takes on the idea of moral judgment against God's people. Refer to Amos 2:6-16 to read some of the wicked actions that brought divine wrath against their fathers and mothers.

Mark A. Throntveit, in his *Interpretation Commentary on Ezra–Nehemiah*, characterizes their confession as "historical retrospect." They confessed not only their sins, but also the pathological patterns of sins that reached all the way back to their ancestors. This is not saying that sin is passed from generation to generation, but it is saying that sinful behavior in many instances is learned and taught, resulting in the consequences of sin lasting for many generations. According to social scientists, certain family and individual dysfunctions (i.e., smoking, drinking, abusive relationships, lying, and so forth), are learned and observed behaviors. Indeed, "We are because of who they were." The willful ignorance of our history cannot serve us well.

B. A God of Greatness and Faithfulness (Nehemiah 9:9-10)

And didst see the affliction of our fathers in Egypt, and heardest their cry by the Red sea; And shewedst signs and wonders upon Pharaoh, and on all his servants, and on all the people of his land: for thou knewest that they dealt proudly against them. So didst thou get thee a name, as it is this day.

This section of the prayer focuses on the grace and mercies of God in the life and history of Israel. The people pointed to the cries of their ancestors in Egypt centuries earlier, and how God had compassion on them. Verses

6-10 constitute a liturgical prayer of confession that focuses on the attributes of God and some of the positive actions God took to liberate their ancestors from bondage. But was this a prayer to God or a confessional prayer for the edification and inspiration of the people? It does not appear that they were talking to God; rather, they were reminding themselves of the great acts and the faithfulness of God throughout their history! Verse 9 is a case in point: "You saw the suffering of our forefathers in Egypt; you heard their cry at the Red Sea" (NIV). So, must they remind God of His past acts? No; this was to remind themselves of their history with God. Likewise, we must be reminded, even in prayer, of the goodness of God, which can be a great source of inspiration and encouragement, especially in times of trouble.

Verse 10 further proclaims the great acts of God in their history. However, for them the Exodus experience was the ultimate in not only defining them as a people of covenant community, but also in distinguishing God. Their God had made a reputation for Himself. The second part of verse 10 (NIV) reads, "You made a name for yourself, which remains to this day." How did God do this? In the days of Moses, Pharaoh defied the only true and living God and refused to let the children of Israel go free. God brought down Pharaoh's mighty empire and consequently the reputation of the God of Israel spread abroad. Rahab said to the spies whom Joshua sent to spy out the land, "I know that the LORD has given this land to you and that a great fear of you has fallen on us, so that all who live in this country are melting in fear because of you. We have heard how the LORD dried up the water of the Red Sea for you when you came out of Egypt, …When we heard of it, our hearts melted and everyone's courage failed because of you, for the LORD your God is God in heaven above and on the earth below" (Joshua 2:8-10, 11, NIV). Before this, God had been just the God of Abraham, Isaac, and Jacob, but after the contest between the powers of Pharaoh and God, He made a "name for himself." The Egyptian, Canaanite, and Babylonian empires worshipped idol gods and ascribed their authority and dominance to their gods. However, God made a name for Himself.

C. A God of Righteousness and Mercy (Nehemiah 9:30-36)

Yet many years didst thou forbear them, and testifiedst against them by thy spirit in thy prophets: yet would they not give ear: therefore gavest thou them into the hand of the people of the lands. Nevertheless for thy great mercies' sake thou didst not utterly consume them, nor forsake them; for thou art a gracious and merciful God. Now therefore, our God, the great, the mighty, and the terrible God, who keepest covenant and mercy, let not all the trouble seem little before thee, that hath come upon us, on our kings, on our princes, and on our priests, and on our prophets, and on our fathers, and on all thy people, since the time of the kings of Assyria unto this day. Howbeit thou art just in all that is brought upon us; for thou hast done right, but we have done wickedly: Neither have our kings, our princes, our priests, nor our fathers, kept thy law, nor hearkened unto thy commandments and thy testimonies, wherewith thou didst testify against them. For they have not served thee in their kingdom, and in thy great goodness that thou gavest them, and in the large and fat land which thou gavest before them, neither turned they from their wicked works. Behold, we are servants this day, and for the land that thou gavest unto our fathers to eat the fruit thereof and the good thereof, behold, we are servants in it.

While the earlier verses focus on the greatness and faithfulness of God, these seven verses focus on the righteousness and mercy of God. The Israelites were sure that God was just in allowing them to be taken into captivity. The life of Israel had come full circle—the land that God had given their ancestors which flowed with milk and honey had become a place of servitude because of their disobedience—so then they were occupying the land again. Although verse 37 is not a part of this lesson, it nonetheless reflects the degree to which the people had fallen. The land that the Lord had given to them as an inheritance had thus fallen to "the kings that the Lord had placed over them."

In verse 33, they confessed their faults: "You have been just; you have acted faithfully, while we did wrong" (NIV). This generation of Israelites took responsibility for what had happened to them. Although they were sure that their culture of disobedience had begun with their forefathers/mothers, they did not try to escape their own responsibility. At some point in life a person has to take personal responsibility for his or her faults. A person cannot continue to blame others for his or her own personal inadequacies.

So, in their prayer there was a pronoun shift in the language: "they or them" (see verses 25-29) to "us and we" (see verses 36-39). The people realized that the persons they had become were inseparable from who their forefathers/mothers had been. So in verse 33, they confessed what they had done: "We did wrong" (NIV). They admitted (see verse 37) that their distress was the result of "our sins." Ralph W. Klein, in his commentary on the books of Ezra and Nehemiah, says, "God's mercy is repeated in each generation and many times in one's own life. God's mercy is boundless and, paradoxically, has its limits." In other words, we must not take God's boundless mercy for granted, because sin does have its consequences.

III. CONCLUDING REFLECTION

Israel's "historical retrospective" of the faithfulness of God also invites us to confess our sins. But there is a difference in Israel's confessions and today's confessions—they confessed to God in the light of who He was, while we sometimes confess to save face or our public reputations. Confession is still a virtue and a good thing and must not be trivialized by admitting guilt only after getting caught— and then only as much as we have to admit. This lesson reminds us not only of the value of admitting our faults, but also of the importance of our heritage in giving shape to both the good and bad in our lives. James Weldon Johnson, in his poem "Lift Every Voice and Sing," captures the meaning of "historical retrospective":

Stony the road we trod,
bitter the chastening rod
felt in the days when hope unborn had died
yet with a steady beat, have not our
weary feet
come to the place for which our
fathers sighed?
We have come, over a way that which tears
has been watered
We have come, treading our path through
the blood of the slaughtered.
Out of the gloomy past,
till now we stand at last,
Where the white gleam of our
bright star is cast.

God of our weary years,
God of our silent tears
Thou Who has brought us
thus far on the way
Thou Who hast by Thy might,
led us into the light
Keep us for-e-ver in the path we pray
Lest our feet, stray from the places our God
where we met thee
Lest our hearts, drunk with the wine of the
world, we forget Thee
Shadowed beneath thy hand,
may we forever stand
True to our God, true to our native land.

Inherent in these lyrics is the acknowledgment that without the aid of God almighty, liberation would not have come to any of us. Likewise, our responsibility to God is transgenerational: "God of the weary years and silent tears. Lest our hearts drunk with the wine of this world forget thee...." Indeed, every subsequent generation of the heritage of this song has a responsibility to God and community to give Him honor, and to honor the vows and the prayers of their ancestors, while admitting their own sins.

PRAYER

O Lord, our Lord, how majestic You are in the world! Thank You for the blessings of knowing You and what You have been through many generations. We love You and confess that we have fallen short of Your glory. Forgive us now and restore us to our rightful place with You. In Jesus' name we pray. Amen.

WORD POWER

Confession *(yada)*—gives "the idea of praise to Yahweh while confessing sins."
Iniquities—the "concrete" meaning in the Hebrew word for "iniquity" *(ayin)* that lies behind the English word *iniquity;* it is something crooked or twisted.

HOME DAILY BIBLE READINGS
(August 5-11, 2013)

Community of Confession

MONDAY, August 5: "Repent and Turn to God" (Acts 3:17-26)

TUESDAY, August 6: "A Changed Mind" (Matthew 21:28-32)

WEDNESDAY, August 7: "I Repent in Dust and Ashes" (Job 42:1-6)

THURSDAY, August 8: "First Be Reconciled" (Matthew 5:21-26)

FRIDAY, August 9: "God, Be Merciful to Me" (Luke 18:9-14)

SATURDAY, August 10: "Joy in Heaven" (Luke 15:1-10)

SUNDAY, August 11: "The Community Confesses Together" (Nehemiah 9:2, 6-7, 9-10, 30-36)

LESSON 12   August 18, 2013

DEDICATION OF THE WALL

FAITH PATHWAY/FAITH JOURNEY TOPIC: **Taking Pride in Accomplishment**

DEVOTIONAL READING: **Psalm 96**
PRINT PASSAGE: **Nehemiah 12:27-36, 38, 43**

BACKGROUND SCRIPTURE: **Nehemiah 12:27-43**
KEY VERSE: **Nehemiah 12:43**

Nehemiah 12:27-36, 38, 43—KJV

27 And at the dedication of the wall of Jerusalem they sought the Levites out of all their places, to bring them to Jerusalem, to keep the dedication with gladness, both with thanksgivings, and with singing, with cymbals, psalteries, and with harps.

28 And the sons of the singers gathered themselves together, both out of the plain country round about Jerusalem, and from the villages of Netophathi;

29 Also from the house of Gilgal, and out of the fields of Geba and Azmaveth: for the singers had builded them villages round about Jerusalem.

30 And the priests and the Levites purified themselves, and purified the people, and the gates, and the wall.

31 Then I brought up the princes of Judah upon the wall, and appointed two great companies of them that gave thanks, whereof one went on the right hand upon the wall toward the dung gate:

32 And after them went Hoshaiah, and half of the princes of Judah,

33 And Azariah, Ezra, and Meshullam,

34 Judah, and Benjamin, and Shemaiah, and Jeremiah,

35 And certain of the priests' sons with trumpets; namely, Zechariah the son of Jonathan, the son of Shemaiah, the son of Mattaniah, the son of Michaiah, the son of Zaccur, the son of Asaph:

36 And his brethren, Shemaiah, and Azarael, Milalai, Gilalai, Maai, Nethaneel, and Judah, Hanani, with the musical instruments of David the man of God, and Ezra the scribe before them.

Nehemiah 12:27-36, 38, 43—NIV

27 At the dedication of the wall of Jerusalem, the Levites were sought out from where they lived and were brought to Jerusalem to celebrate joyfully the dedication with songs of thanksgiving and with the music of cymbals, harps and lyres.

28 The singers also were brought together from the region around Jerusalem—from the villages of the Netophathites,

29 from Beth Gilgal, and from the area of Geba and Azmaveth, for the singers had built villages for themselves around Jerusalem.

30 When the priests and Levites had purified themselves ceremonially, they purified the people, the gates and the wall.

31 I had the leaders of Judah go up on top of the wall. I also assigned two large choirs to give thanks. One was to proceed on top of the wall to the right, toward the Dung Gate.

32 Hoshaiah and half the leaders of Judah followed them,

33 along with Azariah, Ezra, Meshullam,

34 Judah, Benjamin, Shemaiah, Jeremiah,

35 as well as some priests with trumpets, and also Zechariah son of Jonathan, the son of Shemaiah, the son of Mattaniah, the son of Micaiah, the son of Zaccur, the son of Asaph,

36 and his associates—Shemaiah, Azarel, Milalai, Gilalai, Maai, Nethanel, Judah and Hanani—with musical instruments [prescribed by] David the man of God. Ezra the scribe led the procession.

UNIFYING LESSON PRINCIPLE

A sense of pride, joy, and thankfulness accompanies the accomplishment of tasks. What triggers a desire in people to celebrate specific accomplishments? Nehemiah's portrayal of the dedication of the wall was an act of worship, thanking God and celebrating a community's restoration.

.....

38 And the other company of them that gave thanks went over against them, and I after them, and the half of the people upon the wall, from beyond the tower of the furnaces even unto the broad wall.

.....

43 Also that day they offered great sacrifices, and rejoiced: for God had made them rejoice with great joy: the wives also and the children rejoiced: so that the joy of Jerusalem was heard even afar off.

.....

38 The second choir proceeded in the opposite direction. I followed them on top of the wall, together with half the people—past the Tower of the Ovens to the Broad Wall,

.....

43 And on that day they offered great sacrifices, rejoicing because God had given them great joy. The women and children also rejoiced. The sound of rejoicing in Jerusalem could be heard far away.

TOPICAL OUTLINE OF THE LESSON

I. Introduction
A. A Cause for Celebration
B. Biblical Background

II. Exposition and Application of the Scripture
A. Organized for Worship (Nehemiah 12:27-29)
B. Worshipping on the Wall (Nehemiah 12:30-36)
C. The Reason for Worship: God! (Nehemiah 12:38, 43)

III. Concluding Reflection

LESSON OBJECTIVES

Upon completion of the lesson, the students will be able to do the following:

1. Unpack the narrative of the dedication of the wall as a joyous but formal praise service;

2. Identify their feelings upon completing significant tasks; and,

3. Develop worship that celebrates specific accomplishments of the community.

POINTS TO BE EMPHASIZED

ADULT/YOUTH

Adult Topic: **Taking Pride in Accomplishment**
Youth Topic: **Celebration by Dedication**
Adult Key Verse: **Nehemiah 12:43**
Youth Key Verse: **Nehemiah 12:27**
Print Passage: **Nehemiah 12:27-36, 38, 43**

—David had organized the Levites and had given them the responsibility of leading the worship music (see 1 Chronicles 23).

—The worship on the wall may have included antiphonal praise; the leaders' forming "two great companies" (see verse 31) would have been ideal for such worship.

—While the procession and organization speak of formality in the worship, the volume speaks of great exuberance. Formality and joy can abide together in a worship service.

—The public celebration of the dedication was not restricted by age or gender (verse 43).

—In this dedication of the wall of Jerusalem, two large choirs started in the southwest segment of the wall, singing antiphonally—one going clockwise and the other going counterclockwise on the top of the wall, meeting in the northeast sector of the wall to descend and worship in the Temple area.

—The emphasis of the joy of the celebration in this dedication of the rebuilt Jerusalem wall is apparent, the word appearing in some form five times in the closing verse (verse 43).

CHILDREN

Children Topic: Mission Complete!

Key Verse: Nehemiah 12:31

Print Passage: Nehemiah 12:27-36, 38, 40, 42b-43

—The Levite priests were brought to Jerusalem to celebrate the dedication of the wall, which was repaired under Nehemiah's leadership.

—Musicians from throughout the region around Jerusalem gathered to sing, dance, and praise God.

—The priests purified the people, the city gate, and the wall around Jerusalem.

—After the two leaders selected persons for their companies, they all thanked God and then marched to the wall.

—Both companies stood in the Temple, while trumpeters played their instruments, singers sang joyous songs, and dancers danced with thanksgiving.

—The Israelites took great pleasure in offering sacrifices and praises and thanking God for supporting and protecting them during the rebuilding of the wall.

I. INTRODUCTION

A. A Cause for Celebration

The things that really bring joy into our lives can cover a broad spectrum, from the birth of a child to our favorite sports team. There are a number of things that we celebrate with great joy, but there is nothing like a plan finally coming together and seeing the final product of dedication and sacrifice come to fruition. Perhaps it was a church construction project, mortgage burning, or the refinancing of an existing loan or a ministry that the church finally got off the ground. Many congregations have even developed rituals of celebration to mark these occasions as important. At the personal level, it may be the birth of a long-awaited child or grandchild, or the family's first home purchase. These are indeed occasions of pride that represent the untold story of challenge and struggle before ultimate success. The Israelites had the arduous task of rebuilding the wall around Jerusalem that had lain in ruins for over seventy years. Walled communities were essential for security against the enemy in ancient times. The gates were open during the day and closed at night in order to secure the city against marauders who would come under the cloak of darkness and raid and plunder the city.

In this lesson, Sanballat and Tobiah opposed the project from the start with fierce words and rallied the others in the region, who did not want the Israelites returning from exile to complete the project. Perhaps it would be beneficial to read chapters 4–6 in order to understand the degree of ridicule and opposition they encountered as they attempted to rebuild the wall. The accomplishment of completing the wall was a team effort and something that the entire community worked to bring to fruition. Chapter 4 gives insight into the minds and attitudes of the people: "So we rebuilt the wall till all of it reached half its height, for the people worked with all their heart" (verse 6, NIV). The celebration was even sweeter because it was a community-wide effort for which all the people took responsibility. Finally, the people had reason to celebrate their accomplishment, because it affirmed that it was because of their God that they were able to accomplish the rebuilding of the wall. The people testified, "The God of heaven will make us prosper, and we his servants will arise and build" (see 2:20). In chapter 6, we read, "They realized that the task had been accomplished by our God" (see verse 16). When God is in it, it makes the accomplishment even more celebratory and sweeter. This was a major accomplishment for the people, because it secured the city and affirmed that this mission was indeed of God.

B. Biblical Background

In this lesson, the Israelites finally finished the project of rebuilding the wall around Jerusalem; they completed it in fifty-two days. However, chapter 12 is a part of a larger block of material that is about renewal and reform, which begins in chapter 7. As the people attempted to reestablish their lives, two things are noteworthy: the genealogy of those who returned, and their reoccupation of Jerusalem. Genealogy was important to Nehemiah, seeing as though the Israelites were able to trace their lineage back to the original twelve tribes of Israel. Unfortunately, the only family heads who returned to the City of Jerusalem were of the tribes of Benjamin and Judah (see verses 4-10). The other ten tribes did not return to Jerusalem after the Exile. James Burton Coffman, in his commentary on the books of Ezra, Nehemiah, and Esther, says, "Nehemiah accomplished his purpose by listing these names." Perhaps he is correct, because there appears to have been no theological purpose in naming these male heads of families; rather, it was part of their Jewish history to take census by the naming of male heads of households.

Jerusalem was not repopulated until after the wall of the city had been completed. Until then, most of the people lived in the neighboring villages. Verse 2 says that once the wall was completed, the Jewish leaders asked for volunteers to repopulate the city (see verses 1-2). Of course, once the people had completed the project of rebuilding the city wall, it was time to dedicate it and start the religious reforms necessary for the people to bring their lives in line with the covenant laws of God. These were the covenant people of God who needed to rededicate themselves to the Lord if they were going to be in covenant relationship with God again. So, they did not just dedicate the wall—they did so according to the laws of dedication and consecration in the Law of Moses. According to some biblical historians, the wall was nine feet wide, which was ample space for a processional on top of it. A wall this size would have been consistent with some city walls in antiquity. Massive walls were important for the defense of the city. In some ancient ruins, homes have been discovered on top of city walls and served as watchtowers for the security of the city. This was the case in the book of Joshua when Rahab let the spies down through her window on top of the wall of Jericho (see Joshua 2:15).

Nehemiah's wall was such a wall. The Levites, musicians, priests, and singers processed on top of the wall as they dedicated it to the Lord. They were proud of this accomplishment and celebrated with great joy.

II. EXPOSITION AND APPLICATION OF THE SCRIPTURE

A. Organized for Worship
(Nehemiah 12:27-29)

And at the dedication of the wall of Jerusalem they sought the Levites out of all their places, to bring them to Jerusalem, to keep the dedication with gladness, both with thanksgivings, and with singing, with cymbals, psalteries, and with harps. And the sons of the singers gathered themselves together, both out of the plain country round about Jerusalem, and from the villages of Netophathi; Also from the house of Gilgal, and out of the fields of Geba and Azmaveth: for the singers had builded them villages round about Jerusalem.

It is indeed interesting that this was not a simple dedication of a city wall; rather, this dedication was done according to the covenant laws of God and reflected the rededication of the Temple in Ezra 6:17. Nehemiah orchestrated this celebration to impress upon the people the significance of their accomplishment—by starting at the Valley Gate that sat opposite the Temple. This must have been reason for added joy, as Nehemiah and others reflected on where they had come from. This was indeed a major victory for all who had labored with courage on the project, especially in light of the ridicule of Sanballat and Tobiah, who mocked the workers by calling the wall "heaps of the rubbish," and who taunted the people by saying that they did not know what they were doing and that any fox going up on the wall would break it down (see Nehemiah 4:2b-3).

Verses 27-29 tell us that the wall which could not support a fox was now supporting two groups of celebrants. Additionally, this celebration took on a ritualistic nature as they purified themselves and the gates and walls around the city. The celebration was threefold: it included gladness, thanksgiving, and singing.

But before the celebration began, the leaders of the festivities purified themselves, which was a form of ritual consecration. Their purification marked the completion of the wall, not as an end in and of itself, but as a signal that God was indeed with them. It affirmed that it was God who gave them success, so the people celebrated the renewal of their covenant relationship with their God, who keeps His promises to a thousand generations. Perhaps this made their accomplishment even more joyful.

They highlighted their celebration by giving a thanksgiving offering to their God. Thanks offerings were not unusual, according to Levitical laws. The word for *thanksgiving* has the same root word in the Septuagint (LXX) as "grace" (*charis*), which means "to be graceful" or "to demonstrate favor by giving thanks." The Jews held the giving of thanks in high esteem and used sacred occasions or religious festivals to give thanks, but thanksgiving also connoted joy before the Lord (Deuteronomy 16:13ff).

Finally, in verse 29 the people came from neighboring villages to sing and to celebrate their accomplishment. Perhaps the walled city was limited in space and all who lived in the region could not occupy the city. Nevertheless, the spirit of the people reflected the attitude of unity and solidarity among the people. The wall and the city were the center of the entire Jewish community and symbolized divine presence. Today, the City of Jerusalem (Mecca) is revered by Jews worldwide. Imagine what it must have meant to the Jews in the region during Nehemiah's day! They did not have to be the ones living inside the city walls to celebrate the completion of the wall. Therefore, this text ought to inform of what it means to be a true covenant community. If we put God at the center of our efforts to rebuild our communities, then the work will be much easier, and the accomplishments will be sweeter.

B. Worshipping on the Wall
(Nehemiah 12:30-36)

And the priests and the Levites purified themselves, and purified the people, and the gates, and the wall. Then I brought up the princes of Judah upon the wall, and appointed two great companies of them that gave thanks, whereof one went on the right hand upon the wall toward the dung gate: And after them went Hoshaiah, and half of the princes of Judah, And Azariah, Ezra, and Meshullam, Judah, and Benjamin, and Shemaiah, and Jeremiah, And certain of the priests' sons with trumpets; namely, Zechariah the son of Jonathan, the son of Shemaiah, the son of Mattaniah, the son of Michaiah, the son of Zaccur, the son of Asaph: And his brethren, Shemaiah, and Azareel, Milalai, Gilalai, Maai, Nethaneel, and Judah, Hanani, with the musical instruments of David the man of God, and Ezra the scribe before them.

The priests and the Levites purified themselves and then purified the laypeople, the gates, and the walls. The act of purification was done according to the covenant laws of Israel. This signaled how they felt about themselves and their God. God is holy. Before offering anything to God, those who had the responsibility of handling it and presenting it to God had to consecrate themselves to make certain they were not profane and would not profane the offering (see Numbers 19).

After the purification ritual, two choirs were appointed: one went to the south on the wall, and the other group went north. Ezra was the priest who led a group of Israelites in the reconstruction of the Temple, and he led the group of singers that went south. Obviously, this was not a simple matter for the people. We can see that the celebration was well-planned and carried out with all intentionality—as Nehemiah named not only the priests and Levites who led the processional, but he also included the instruments that provided the music for the singers. Similarly, our worship ought to be something that is planned with great deliberation and intentionality. Spontaneity in worship that is under the unction of the Holy Spirit is often desirable, but we cannot leave our gathering and the worship of our God to happenstance. Just as Nehemiah's planning took nothing from the worship, it does not have to take anything from our worship, because it is what is in our hearts for God that will ultimately make our worship acceptable to God.

C. The Reason for Worship: God!
(Nehemiah 12:38, 43)

And the other company of them that gave thanks went over against them, and I after them, and the half of the people upon the wall, from beyond the tower of the furnaces even unto the broad wall. ...Also that day they offered great sacrifices, and rejoiced: for God had made them rejoice with great joy: the wives also and

the children rejoiced: so that the joy of Jerusalem was heard even afar off.

The focus on joy in these verses affirms the intensity and gaiety of the dedication. The people were clear that it was God who gave them reason for joy as they read the Law and the dedication at the wall. The text does not say how long the celebration lasted, but it must have lasted most of the day, based upon the preparation and what they were asked to do. There are some scholars who have called what they did "worship"—and if, in fact, it was worship, then it says a lot to us today about authentic worship. Of course, worship has evolved over the years and has become a production in which everything is orchestrated around the length of the worship service. Conversely, the Jews of Nehemiah's time prepared themselves through purification, of which the length of time appeared to be of no consequence to them.

How many prepare for worship by purifying their hearts? How much more alive and excellent our corporate worship would be if each congregant purified his or her heart before coming to worship. To purify the heart is to remove those thoughts and things that distract us (i.e., workday worries, unresolved problems, after-worship agendas, and so forth) and hinder us from giving our full attention to the worship of God. Authentic worship focuses on God and God alone. He is at the center and is the only one to whom we are to give our full attention. But, as we can attest, too many times God is not the focus of our attention—and when this is the case, we cannot help but find worship to be boring! This lesson ought to teach us the value of the preparation for worship. What if we did as our parents made us do many years ago when life was simpler? We started preparing for Sunday worship on Saturday night by selecting our clothes, shining our shoes, adorning ourselves, and so forth, so that on Sunday morning, we would be ready for worship. Perhaps one thing that we all can do in our hearts to prepare for worship is to feed our hearts and minds with sacred music. Then, once in the sanctuary before the call to worship, sit quietly reflecting on the words of "the goodness of God in the land of the living," and pray that the Holy Spirit will come into our hearts so that we can worship "in spirit and in truth."

III. CONCLUDING REFLECTION

Obviously, this was more than just the dedication of the wall. The dedication of the wall signaled the completion of the rebuilding of the community. God had promised that He would give them success, and this dedicatory celebration affirmed the faithfulness of God. The completion and the dedication of the wall said that the people did not see a separation of the secular and the sacred in their lives. The altar, the Temple, and the wall were all a part of a larger story of what God had done in restoring the people. These achievements were inseparable from the spiritual faith of Israel.

Mark A. Throntveit captures the true significance of this text when he writes, "Ezra-Nehemiah will not allow us to separate the material aspects of our faith from the spiritual formation that allows us to see the holy purpose for which they have been a part." We live in a material world, as does even the church, and everything we do has spiritual implications. This is why Jesus said, "Seek ye first the kingdom of God and all these things shall be added" (see Matthew 6). Jesus is saying that the material things of our lives are connected to our spiritual pursuits and are inseparable entities. We take pride in our accomplishments, but must not lose sight of the fact that our material successes are not ends in and of themselves. There was no individual success or personal piety aside from the communal. As the community flourished, so did the individual. God blessed the community and the people prospered together as one people (read Nehemiah 6:16). God has a greater purpose in personal accomplishments other than merely elevating us to personal aggrandizement. Thus, we must be prone to celebrate individual accomplishments only inasmuch as these accomplishments advance the cause of community. The bottom line is that this dedication signaled a new beginning for those Jews who returned after the Exile. Thus, it was through the reestablishment of the community that God's purpose and restoration were complete. What are some things that you celebrate that bring joy to you?

PRAYER

Eternal God, our Father, we are grateful that You have blessed us and allowed us to see new mercies. As we embark upon this new day and study the lesson, we celebrate You and all that You have allowed us to become—and now, O Lord, it is our prayer that we will be better stewards of our communities. In Jesus' name we pray. Amen.

WORD POWER

Dedication (Hebrew: *Hanukkah/Chanukah*)—**to proclaim; to announce; to immerse oneself with sincerity into a certain subject, or properly the setting apart of anything by solemn proclamation.**
Thanksgiving *(eucharistia)*—**"to be graceful or to demonstrate favor by giving thanks."**

HOME DAILY BIBLE READINGS
(August 12-18, 2013)

Dedication of the Wall

MONDAY, August 12: "Celebrating God's Greatness" (Psalm 96:1-9)
TUESDAY, August 13: "Celebrating the Lord's Coming" (Psalm 96:10-13)
WEDNESDAY, August 14: "Celebrating God's Blessings" (Deuteronomy 12:2-7)
THURSDAY, August 15: "Celebrating Freedom from Oppression" (Nahum 1:6-15)
FRIDAY, August 16: "Celebrating the Restored Nation" (Jeremiah 30:18-22)
SATURDAY, August 17: "Celebrating the Restored Jerusalem" (Isaiah 66:10-14)
SUNDAY, August 18: "Celebrating a Completed Task" (Nehemiah 12:27-36, 38, 43)

LESSON 13   August 25, 2013

SABBATH REFORMS

FAITH PATHWAY/FAITH JOURNEY TOPIC: **Getting It Right**

DEVOTIONAL READING: **Mark 2:23-27**
PRINT PASSAGE: **Nehemiah 13:15-22**

BACKGROUND SCRIPTURE: **Nehemiah 13:4-31**
KEY VERSE: **Nehemiah 13:22**

Nehemiah 13:15-22—KJV

15 In those days saw I in Judah some treading wine presses on the sabbath, and bringing in sheaves, and lading asses; as also wine, grapes, and figs, and all manner of burdens, which they brought into Jerusalem on the sabbath day: and I testified against them in the day wherein they sold victuals.

16 There dwelt men of Tyre also therein, which brought fish, and all manner of ware, and sold on the sabbath unto the children of Judah, and in Jerusalem.

17 Then I contended with the nobles of Judah, and said unto them, What evil thing is this that ye do, and profane the sabbath day?

18 Did not your fathers thus, and did not our God bring all this evil upon us, and upon this city? yet ye bring more wrath upon Israel by profaning the sabbath.

19 And it came to pass, that when the gates of Jerusalem began to be dark before the sabbath, I commanded that the gates should be shut, and charged that they should not be opened till after the sabbath: and some of my servants set I at the gates, that there should no burden be brought in on the sabbath day.

20 So the merchants and sellers of all kind of ware lodged without Jerusalem once or twice.

21 Then I testified against them, and said unto them, Why lodge ye about the wall? if ye do so again, I will lay hands on you. From that time forth came they no more on the sabbath.

Nehemiah 13:15-22—NIV

15 In those days I saw men in Judah treading wine-presses on the Sabbath and bringing in grain and loading it on donkeys, together with wine, grapes, figs and all other kinds of loads. And they were bringing all this into Jerusalem on the Sabbath. Therefore I warned them against selling food on that day.

16 Men from Tyre who lived in Jerusalem were bringing in fish and all kinds of merchandise and selling them in Jerusalem on the Sabbath to the people of Judah.

17 I rebuked the nobles of Judah and said to them, "What is this wicked thing you are doing—desecrating the Sabbath day?

18 Didn't your forefathers do the same things, so that our God brought all this calamity upon us and upon this city? Now you are stirring up more wrath against Israel by desecrating the Sabbath."

19 When evening shadows fell on the gates of Jerusalem before the Sabbath, I ordered the doors to be shut and not opened until the Sabbath was over. I stationed some of my own men at the gates so that no load could be brought in on the Sabbath day.

20 Once or twice the merchants and sellers of all kinds of goods spent the night outside Jerusalem.

21 But I warned them and said, "Why do you spend the night by the wall? If you do this again, I will lay hands on you." From that time on they no longer came on the Sabbath.

UNIFYING LESSON PRINCIPLE

People sometimes make demands of those who break community rules. Which community rules are important enough for everyone to follow consistently? Keeping the Sabbath was so important to the welfare of God's community that Nehemiah ordered the gates shut in order to prevent the Israelites from breaking this law.

22 And I commanded the Levites that they should cleanse themselves, and that they should come and keep the gates, to sanctify the sabbath day. Remember me, O my God, concerning this also, and spare me according to the greatness of thy mercy.

22 Then I commanded the Levites to purify themselves and go and guard the gates in order to keep the Sabbath day holy. Remember me for this also, O my God, and show mercy to me according to your great love.

TOPICAL OUTLINE OF THE LESSON

I. **Introduction**
   A. Line Up with God's Demands
   B. Biblical Background

II. **Exposition and Application of the Scripture**
   A. Doing Wrong: Desecrating the Sabbath (Nehemiah 13:15-18)
   B. Taking Corrective Actions (Nehemiah 13:19-22)

III. **Concluding Reflection**

LESSON OBJECTIVES

Upon completion of the lesson, the students will be able to do the following:

1. Explore what Nehemiah did about the inviolability of the Sabbath;
2. Examine their feelings about the importance of the Sabbath and the ways they may violate it; and,
3. Compare and contrast the Sabbath practices in Nehemiah's day with ours today.

POINTS TO BE EMPHASIZED

ADULT/YOUTH

Adult Topic: Getting It Right
Youth Topic: Profane…No Gain!
Adult Key Verse: Nehemiah 13:22
Youth Key Verse: Nehemiah 13:17
Print Passage: Nehemiah 13:15-22

—Leviticus 26 warns that the people would be removed from the land if they violated the Sabbath. Nehemiah alluded to this occurrence in verses 17-18.

—The "work" of guarding the gates was apparently an allowable exception to the prohibition of working on the Sabbath (verse 22).

—Nehemiah stressed the prohibition against working or doing commercial trading on the Sabbath; he made no mention of worship or other practices that were to characterize Sabbath observance.

—As stated in Nehemiah 13:30-31, Nehemiah's insistence that the restored Jerusalem faith community keep the Sabbath is one of several efforts to prevent the Jews from repeating the errors of their ancestors.

—Nehemiah's concern that the restored Jews not repeat the profaning of the Sabbath and again bring the wrath of God on the faith community echoes in Jeremiah 17:19-27; Ezekiel 20:13; 23:38.

—The keeping of the observance of the Sabbath distinguished the Jews from non-Jews, very important after the collapse of the theocratic state, multiplying the dangers of assimilation into the larger pagan culture.

—Monetary gain proves a poor, inadequate basis for moral values and decisions.

CHILDREN
Children Topic: Shut the Doors!
Key Verse: Nehemiah 13:19a
Print Passage: Nehemiah 13:15-22

—The physical wall around Judah was successfully rebuilt, but not the spiritual walls around the hearts and minds of the people.

—Merchants ignored the fourth commandment requirement to use the Sabbath as a day for worshipping and honoring God and sold their wares in the marketplace.

—When one commandment is broken without penalty, it becomes easier to ignore other commandments.

—Bold, confident, and faithful leaders will devise strategies through which God's people can be reformed.

—If reform is to take place, leaders must be consistent and persistent in enforcing God's standards and values within their communities.

—Leaders must be held accountable for the health and vitality of their communities.

I. INTRODUCTION
A. Line Up with God's Demands

Once the Jews had returned from Babylon and Nehemiah learned that they had violated the laws and precepts of their God by profaning the Sabbath, withholding the tithe, and intermarrying, he said their behavior was evil. He ordered all of the persons who had non-Jewish marriage partners to put their spouses away with a bill of divorcement. Is this a biblical case of ethnic cleansing? "Ethnic cleansing is the purposeful political policy designed by one ethnic or religious group to remove by violent and terror-inspiring means, if necessary, the population of another ethnic or religious group from a certain geographic area" (The Commission of Experts Established Pursuant to United Nations Security Council Resolution 780) (see Nehemiah 13:23-27). Perhaps—perhaps not! There is another obvious conversation that we could have about the practice of ethnic separatism, but this lesson is about "getting it right"! God gave the Jews another opportunity to get the practices of their faith right, according to covenant law. The worship of their God had become so profane and corrupt that it had led to their ultimate exile seventy years earlier. So, without debating the merits and morality of ethnic separatism, we must wrestle with the idea of what it means for the (Christian) believer to assimilate into a pluralistic culture while simultaneously maintaining the appropriate expectation of the believer's covenant relationship with God.

If God was displeased with the Jews in Nehemiah's day because of their willingness to assimilate into other cultures, then can we reasonably expect God to accept anything from us under the guise of pluralism? In order to bring their lifestyles in line with the divine expectations of the Jews, some tough decisions had to be made. It will also require us to make some painful, tough, and politically incorrect decisions. This text is clear that getting ready for the worship of our God is not an easy thing. It might demand that we put away some things or even persons that we care about dearly. Jesus is clear in the Gospels that His followers might have to choose to separate from others, even family members, in order to follow Him: "If anyone will come after me let him deny himself, take up his cross and follow me" (see Luke 9:23); "Anyone who loves his father or mother more than me is not worthy of me; anyone who loves his son or daughter more than me is not worthy of me" (Matthew 10:37, NIV). In the kingdom of God, we cannot get our faith practice right without getting our priorities right; God expects to be the center of our lives in words and in deeds.

B. Biblical Background

Chapter 13, the last chapter in the book of Nehemiah, closes with a bang with the call for absolute reform and revival in Jerusalem. However, this reform and revival are not evangelical in tone and tenor; rather, they are sociological/theological. There is no handing out of religious tracts on street corners, or knocking on neighbors' doors. To the contrary—it began with the call to personal examination and purification. In the words of several biblical passages, reform and revival begin with self-examination, and then dedication of oneself to the new spiritual direction.

Once the altar was completed, the Temple built, and the walls around the city completed and dedicated, Nehemiah returned to Babylon for twelve years before returning to Jerusalem and calling for reforms. It was during his absence that these violations of covenant laws of God (Sabbath, intermarriage, and tithes) were committed. However, reform and revival, if they were to be complete, had to move beyond the cosmetic to substantial changes in the people's lifestyles. The people had stopped tithing and were engaging in commerce on the Sabbath, which was in violation of the Ten Commandments (see Exodus 20:8).

Yet, the prominent and more radical issue facing this people and community was ethnic intermarriage (mixed marriage). However, these mixed marriages were only the symptoms of a deeper spiritual problem in the covenant community; they were living in abject violation of covenant law. The problem was their infidelity to Yahweh. Therefore, this text called for the Jews to divorce the men and women who were not Jews in order to bring their lives back in line with the Torah (Laws of God). One of the sons of the high priest had married one of the daughters of Sanballat, who had mocked the Jews as they rebuilt the city wall. Verse 24 said that the offspring of these marriages could not speak Hebrew, the Jewish tongue. The Jewish tradition of living according to the Torah was a vital part of Jewish community life and required the fathers to teach the precepts and laws of Yahweh to their sons and daughters.

Therefore, the Jewish leaders, including Ezra the priest, summarily concluded that the people had lived in violation of the covenant laws of God. This lesson, then, is about getting a second chance—God gave the Jews an opportunity to get it right. It is important that God's people get it right when it comes to serving the Lord. Living for the Lord cannot be happenstance and capricious; it must be approached with great intentionality. God expects all of His children to represent Him in the world in such ways that our lifestyles do not profane and make a mockery of His name. So sometimes, as this text teaches, radical surgery is required of us in getting rid of those things in our lives which are not in the will of God. The Jews had to get rid of practices that had become stumbling blocks and were clearly outside of the will of God for them: withholding the tithe, working on the Sabbath, and mixed marriages with non-Jews. What will we have to purge from our life practices so that our lives can be more pleasing to God? What do you have to change in your life in order to bring your life in line with the will of God?

II. EXPOSITION AND APPLICATION OF THE SCRIPTURE

A. Doing Wrong: Desecrating the Sabbath (Nehemiah 13:15-18)

In those days saw I in Judah some treading wine presses on the sabbath, and bringing in sheaves, and lading asses; as also wine, grapes, and figs, and all manner of burdens, which they brought into Jerusalem on the sabbath day: and I testified against them in the day wherein they sold victuals. There dwelt men of Tyre also therein, which brought fish, and all manner of ware, and sold on the sabbath unto the children of Judah, and in Jerusalem. Then I contended with the nobles of Judah, and said unto them, What evil thing is this that ye do, and profane the sabbath day? Did not your fathers thus, and did not our God bring all this evil upon us, and upon this city? yet ye bring more wrath upon Israel by profaning the sabbath.

This section begins with an indicator of time: "In those days." Perhaps this phrase marked the second term of office for Nehemiah, who returned to Babylon for about twelve years before returning to Jerusalem a second time (see verse 6). In his absence, the people took upon themselves certain liberties that Nehemiah found objectionable. Eliashib, the priest in charge of the storehouse in the Temple, allowed Tobiah to set up house and live inside the storehouse (see verses 4-5). In verse 6, the author called the actions of Eliashib evil. It appears that the reason this space was available was because the people had stopped tithing with grain, wine, and other items that were supposed to be given for the support of the Temple's operation.

According to the covenant laws of the Torah, the tithe was given to support the Levites, who had no inheritance of land, as well as the Temple singers. In verse 11, Nehemiah equated their behavior with forsaking the house of God. Thus, it is this phrase that points to the activities or sins of the people that prompted Nehemiah to react in such a radical way. In the days after his return to Jerusalem, he observed additionally that the people were in violation of the fourth commandment: "Remember the Sabbath day, to keep it holy" (Exodus 20:8). The people were also making wine, transporting produce, and selling their goods on the Sabbath; "Men of Tyre, Gentiles who lived in the region, sold their goods on the Sabbath and their goods were purchased by the Jews in Jerusalem" (see verse 16). Nehemiah contended with "the nobles of Judah" who were profaning the Sabbath by either working and selling goods and merchandise on the Sabbath or allowing those activities to occur. Nehemiah further reminded the people that this was the sin of their ancestors which had brought divine judgment on the people. The people had put themselves in the same position to be judged by the Lord by "profaning the sabbath" (verse 18).

The consequences of sins are a lost conversation in the church today. How are we to understand the clear language of verse 18—that the reason disaster befell the people and the city was due to the violation of the covenant law of the Sabbath? In the Old Testament, the faithfulness of God was not just rewarding the people for their obedience, but also punishing them for their disobedience (see Deuteronomy 10:19-20; 11:26-28). So the relevant question before us today is this: can God be faithful in rewarding us for our goodness and not punishing us according to our sins? The easy answer is that we are living under grace. But does grace immunize us against the rules of divine law? No, it does not; there are consequences for living in abject disobedience to our God. So if Israel was a type of the Christian church established by the work of Jesus the Christ, then we, too, are a covenant community that must live under the rules of the kingdom of God. So when the apostle Paul was asked whether people could continue to sin so that grace could abound, he said, "God forbid!" (see Romans 6:1-2). God does expect us to live for Him once we have given our lives to Him. We call it "new life" or in the terms of the evangelical, being "born again." God gives us a second chance to get our lives right, so that we might live for Him in ways that bring glory and honor to His name.

B. Taking Corrective Actions
(Nehemiah 13:19-22)

And it came to pass, that when the gates of Jerusalem began to be dark before the sabbath, I commanded that the gates should be shut, and charged that they should not be opened till after the sabbath: and some of my servants set I at the gates, that there should no burden be brought in on the sabbath day. So the merchants and sellers of all kind of ware lodged without Jerusalem once or twice. Then I testified against them, and said unto them, Why lodge ye about the wall? if ye do so again, I will lay hands on you. From that time forth came they no more on the sabbath. And I commanded the Levites that they should cleanse themselves, and that they should come and keep the gates, to sanctify the sabbath day. Remember me, O my God, concerning this also, and spare me according to the greatness of thy mercy.

As the result of the violations of the Sabbath by Jews and non-Jews, Nehemiah commanded that the city gates be closed at sundown before the start of the Sabbath (6:00 p.m. on Friday) and reopened after the Sabbath (6:00 p.m. on Saturday). He also posted guards at the gates to keep the merchants out of the city on the Sabbath. However, as it is with most of us, the people were creatures of habit and ventured outside of the gates and walls in hopes of purchasing the goods. Nehemiah had to threaten the merchants with bodily harm if they continued to sell merchandise on the Sabbath.

Since the days of Moses, Israel was to observe a theocratic form of government. The people were to follow Yahweh absolutely; therefore, the Law of Moses was given to regulate their lives within the Hebrew community. Their lifestyles were not to be as other people and nations who lived around them. As a matter of fact, the children of Israel were warned on several occasions not to assimilate into the cultures around them once they had entered the Promised Land (see Deuteronomy 7:1-16). This divine strategy was to make the Israelites a peculiar people in the world. Yet, the people began to fall under the political and social influences in the region.